Feminist Methods
in Social Research

Feminist Methods in Social Research

SHULAMIT REINHARZ

with the assistance of
LYNN DAVIDMAN

New York   Oxford
OXFORD UNIVERSITY PRESS
1992

Oxford University Press

Oxford   New York   Toronto
Delhi   Bombay   Calcutta   Madras   Karachi
Petaling Jaya   Singapore   Hong Kong   Tokyo
Nairobi   Dar es Salaam   Cape Town
Melbourne   Auckland

and associated companies in
Berlin   Ibadan

Library of Congress Cataloging-in-Publication Data
Reinharz, Shulamit.
Feminist methods in social research / Shulamit Reinharz.
p. cm.   Includes bibliographical references and index.
ISBN 0-19-507385-1
ISBN 0-19-507386-X (paper)
1. Women's studies—Methodology.
2. Feminism—Research—Methodology.
3. Social sciences—Research—Methodology.   I. Title.
HQ1180.R448   1992   301'.072—dc20   91-27838

19 18 17 16 15 14 13 12 11 10

Printed in the United States of America
on acid-free paper

For Yali and Naomi

Preface

The origin of this book lies in a conversation I had in Ann Arbor, Michigan in 1980 with Marti Bombyk, now on the faculty of Fordham University, about forming a "feminist research methods" study group. Nicki Beisel, Sue Contratto, Susan Harding, Carol Hollenshead, Toby Jayaratne, Linda Kaboolian, Phyllis Lassner, Eleanor McLaughlin, Cindy Palmer, Paula Rabinowitz, Betsy Taylor, and Martha Vicinus joined us during the first and/or second year the group existed. At the same time Beth Reed, organizer of the Great Lakes College Association summer workshops on Feminism and the Academy, gave me an opportunity to present a workshop on feminist methodology. Using material from that workshop, Marti Bombyk and Jan Wright helped me compile and later publish a bibliography on feminist methodology. At that early date, Renate Klein encouraged me to publish on feminist methodology and later gave me a detailed reading of a draft of this book. Loraine Obler, Stephanie Riger, Arnie Kahn, Sue Contratto, Linda Kaboolian, and Brinton Lykes also encouraged me by asking me to give papers on the topic. To all of these people, I am grateful.

Since moving to Boston in 1982, I have been a member of a feminist research group that has been meeting regularly. Its members have included Rita Arditti, Tracy Paget, Anne Mulvey, Barbara Gruber, Oliva Espin, Loraine Obler, Margaret Fearey, Hortensia Amaro, Estelle Disch, Althea Smith, Lena Sorensen, and Brinton Lykes, all of whom contributed to my work. During a recent sabbatical in Jerusalem, I was fortunate to join yet another women's writing group. For their multilingual virtuosity and warmth I thank Ruth Gruschka, Aya Meir, Rahel Wasserfall, and Caroline Van Royen. The latest feminist research group I have joined, consisting of sociologists Wini Breines, Lenore Weitzman, Rose Coser, Diane Vaughan, Jeanne Guilleman, Susan Ostrander, and Andrea Walsh, continues these stimulating discussions. The faculty of the Women's Studies Programs at the University of Michigan and at Brandeis University have encouraged me consistently, especially its two former directors, Libby Douvan at Michigan and Joyce Antler at Brandeis. Mary Roth Walsh, Mary Jo Deegan, and Michael Hill inspired me to try my hand at including historical materials and endorsed my efforts.

I have always learned a great deal from graduate students engaged in feminist research such as Linda Andrist, Denise Connors, Todd Crosset, Connie Cutter, Rose DeLuca, Uli Dettling, Paula Doress, Mindy Fried, Mary Gilfus, Robin Gregg, Betsy Hayes, Janice Kahn, Sara Karon, Kathy Kautzer, Kathy MacPherson, Ana Macedo, P. J. McGann, Aluma Motenko, Robbie Kahn, Jim Ptacek, Rachel Rabinowitz, Claire Reinelt, Ingrid Shockey, Ellen Stone, Becky Thompson, Mary Ann Wilner, and Karen Wolf, among others. My colleagues in the sociology department at Brandeis University have provided an atmosphere in which feminist research is respected. My colleagues in the Women's Studies Program, which I now direct at Brandeis, are exemplary.

The fine work of Lynn Davidman is also present in this book. I would like to express to Lynn my gratitude for her commitment, thoroughness, wisdom, and willingness to disagree as we worked together. Lynn, in turn, acknowledges with gratitude the assistance of Steven Freedman, Shelly Tenenbaum, and Becky Thompson. Other people who assisted me by cheerfully providing detailed, frank, encouraging criticism are identified at the start of each chapter. Undergraduates Michael Stein, Staci Silberman, and Stacy Shore provided clerical assistance.

I am indebted to my family for their faith that I would finish this book and their smiles when I did. My husband, Jehuda, helped me stay on track and made it possible for me to write by relieving me of many household chores while carrying out all of his responsibilities. Our daughters, Yali and Naomi, inspired me to work on a book that might make the world a more respectful place for women's intellectual work. This book is dedicated to them.

Newton, Mass.   S. R.
July 1991

Contents

Feminist Methods
in Social Research

1

Introduction [1]

> The question of *difference* is one with the question of *identity*. It is becoming the critical question for feminist theorizing in all the disciplines including social science research methods as feminists begin to question and challenge the implicit male perspective of the dominant paradigms, methodological strictures, and theoretical assumptions of the various disciplines. [2]

In the opening quotation Roslyn Bologh, a U.S. sociologist,[3] writes that feminist theory about research methods involves questions of *identity* (what are feminist research methods?) and of *difference* (what is the difference between feminist research methods and other research methods; how do feminist research methods differ from one another?). This book is devoted to these questions. To answer them, I analyze instances of feminist research to discover which methods feminist researchers actually use and why they say they use them. This grounded approach supplements existing philosophical discussions about the relation between feminism and research.

Many people have asserted what feminist research is. For example, U.S. psychologist Bernice Lott wrote that:

> Feminist scholarship and empirical research . . . have particular qualities that distinguish it from other research . . . in its choice of problems and ultimate objectives. [4]

On the other hand, U.S. natural scientist Cindy Cowden defined it as stemming from two "personal beliefs: that reductionist science is inadequate to understand organisms, whether they are spiders, starfish or women; that we can only understand organisms by seeing with a loving eye." [5] British sociologist Liz Stanley wrote that " 'feminist research' is absolutely and centrally 'research *by* women' because I see a direct relationship between 'feminist consciousness' and feminism." [6] Canadian political scientist Naomi Black wrote that feminist research "insists on the value of subjectivity and personal experience." [7] U.S. sociologist Marjorie DeVault wrote that "the dilemma for the feminist scholar, always, is to find ways of working within some disciplinary tradition while aiming at an intellectual revolution that will transform the tradition." [8] And U.S. literary scholar Carolyn Burke claims the strength of the women's movement lies in its ability to acknowledge "serious disagreement" [9] on topics including feminist methods.

In my view, despite this variety, such definitions mask diversity and downplay

3

the fact that feminist researchers deal with dilemmas that have no absolute solutions.[10] My alternative to saying what feminist research *is*, is to illustrate what feminist research *includes*, i.e., to collect, categorize and examine the multitude of feminist research voices. As Patricia Sexton wrote about her study of female hospital workers:

> generalizations can be misleading, inadequate, and lacking in any flesh and blood reality, they can also fail to take account of the astonishing variations among women and the work they do. Women have not one but many voices. . . . Both the themes and the variations, the individual and the collective voices need to be heard.[11]

The same is true for feminist research. Thus this book is entitled *Feminist Methods in Social Research* with an emphasis on the plural. It demonstrates the fact that feminists have used all existing methods and have invented some new ones as well. Instead of orthodoxy, feminist research practices must be recognized as a plurality.[12] Rather than there being a "woman's way of knowing," or a "feminist way of doing research," there are women's *ways* of knowing.[13]

This book can be read as part of two ongoing discussions about the nature of knowledge: the first is *between* feminist and antifeminist or nonfeminist scholars;[14] the second is a discussion *among* feminist scholars.[15] In the concluding chapter I return to some of these discussions, focusing on the dilemmas of subjectivity, diversity, rapport, and science.

Experiential Origins of My Approach to the Feminist Research Methods Debate

In 1980 a group of feminist students and faculty from several different departments at the University of Michigan invited me to help form a "feminist research methodology group."[16] In its first year, the group met weekly to discuss important publications about feminism and research methods. Our procedure included one of us presenting a talk about the assumptions in a particular article, while another took notes and another tape-recorded the session. Incorporating a transcript of the tape recording, the note-taker wrote a report that we discussed at the start of our next session. This group developed an intensive, transdisciplinary,[17] self-motivated, nonhierarchical form of mutual education. As the amount of material we covered expanded, I decided to publish a bibliography on feminist research methods and wrote to feminist scholars asking for suggestions and materials.[18] Even though people had warned that it is "impossible to synthesize all the feminist research even within one subfield,"[19] it seemed worthwhile to find some sort of organizing framework.

I found that the feminist methodological literature centered on four central questions: (1) is there a feminist research method; (2) if so, what does it actually consist of; (3) should there be a feminist research method; and (4) what is the relation between feminist research methods and other methods?[20] Although interesting answers were given to these questions, the answers typically were not tied to specific research practices an individual could try. Locating unabashedly misogynist research and gynopic mainstream texts was a liberating experience,[21] but defining alternative practices was more difficult. Attempts to outline new "feminist" ways of doing research were often vague or unsuccessful. For example, in a review of one collection, Marjorie DeVault noted:

> [T]he editors say they intend to provide information about a broad range of research approaches, so that researchers can bring "fresh perspectives" to their work. . . . Despite many contributors' attention to feminist critiques of social science [however], they present few solutions for researchers except more faithful adherence to traditional methods.[22]

Canadian nurse/sociologist/political theorist Mary O'Brien wrote that "we must not only develop a theory, but develop a feminist perspective and a method of enquiry from which such a theory can emerge."[23] She speculated that we could apply a dialectical, Marxist method to questions of birth, but what would it be? Feminists were writing that we need something different from what existed, but it was not quite clear what that was.

Even after the bibliography appeared in print, feminist scholars and students continued to send me work-in-progress. At the same time, I began to be invited to conduct workshops and deliver papers on the significance of feminism for issues of methodology.[24] At various meetings I was able to meet feminist researchers, obtain copies of their work, and become part of an invisible college of feminists interested in methodology. The themes in the growing literature were the errors and biases feminists perceive in scientific research,[25] the impact of feminism on the disciplines,[26] the philosophy or epistemology of feminist research,[27] and whether feminist research constitutes a new[28] or impossible[29] paradigm. More recently, collections of classic statements about the relation between feminism and methodology,[30] criticism or praise about specific instances of feminist research,[31] warnings about pitfalls in feminist research,[32] and arguments against the very idea of feminist research[33] have been published, as have discussions about the relation between gender and methods.[34] There has been enough reiteration of some of these points that Charlotte O'Kelly opened the second edition of her book, *Women & Men in Society,* by stating she had eliminated discussion of "sexism in social scientific views . . . [because of her] belief that the gender biases characteristic of much research on gender relations are . . . widely known and condemned."[35]

This book tries to contribute to these discussions without reiterating previous ideas.[36] I will not argue a particular definition of feminism, derive principles from that definition, and then operationalize them as research practices.[37] I am not interested in telling feminists what methods to use.[38] Instead, I believe a fresh approach is needed that begins with the question: What is the *range* of methods feminist researchers use? I accept Mary Daly and C. Wright Mills' idea that we think of method not as "the codification of procedures" but rather as "information about . . . actual ways of working."[39] I therefore treat the question "What is feminist research?" as an empirical problem. My approach requires listening to the voices of feminist researchers at work[40] and accepting their diversity.

Defining "Feminist"

To use this approach means that I have to define feminism. A conversation among members of the Mud Flower Collective, a group of U.S. Christian feminist theologians, illustrates the difficulty of this task.

MARY: I think it's simply the struggle against sexism.

CARTER: I agree, but I'd have to add that this involves a stubborn insistence, a refusal to compromise the well-being of women.

KATE: For me it doesn't have anything to do with women; it's the commitment to end white supremacy, male domination, and economic exploitation.

ADA: For me feminism and feminist are different. Only the person can say if she's feminist; but feminism has to do with understanding sexism as the paradigm of all oppression. And I agree with the refusal to compromise women's welfare—both women's rights and women's well-being.

BEV: I'd have to say that it begins in a woman's assertion of her power. It's not, in the first instance, a theory, but a very personal act.

BESS: For me it always has to be preceded by the word Black, and it means the creation of inclusivity and mutuality, which involves struggle against what I call the trinity of sexism, racism, and classism. . . .

NANCY: I believe it begins with the "experiencing of your experience" and that it means insisting on the well-being of women, all women, which is why racism must be examined in any feminist analysis.[41]

In addition to these differences, there are also traditional distinctions among liberal, radical, and socialist/Marxist feminism, each with its distinctive explanation of the origins of sexism and suggestions to overcome it. Differences in the definition of feminism exist among people of different classes, races, generations,[42] and sexual orientations. Differences among feminists exist around specific issues such as sadomasochism and pornography.[43] Differences exist between academic and activist feminists as well. Sometimes people who do not want to be labeled "feminist" are given the label anyhow. Conversely, some people who want to be acknowledged as feminist are not.[44] That these differences exist is fortunate because the lack of orthodoxy allows for freedom of thought and action.[45]

My solution to the practical problem of a working definition is to use people's self-definition. Thus, this book is guided by three straightforward definitions of feminist research methods:

1. Feminist research methods are methods used in research projects by people who identify themselves as feminist or as part of the women's movement.
2. Feminist research methods are methods used in research published in journals that publish only feminist research, or in books[46] that identify themselves as such.
3. Feminist research methods are methods used in research that has received awards from organizations that give awards to people who do feminist research.

As I gathered material, any piece of work qualified if it was identified in this way. A person did not have to identify her research methods as "feminist research methods" but rather had to identify herself as a feminist doing research. This latter criterion, I believe, is more appropriate since researchers defining their methods as feminist are likely to do so only when the method is unusual.[47]

As it happens, many people identify themselves as feminists in their research publications. For example, in the opening of their study of competent women, U.S. psychologists Rosalind Barnett and Grace Baruch wrote:

> we consider ourselves to be "feminists" in that we believe fully in the goals of the women's movement: to reject old constraints, to make women aware of the conditions that limit their life choices, and to ensure that women are no longer barred from access to high-level position in any social institutions.[48]

Similarly, sociologist Barrie Thorne and psychologist Nancy Henley explicitly acknowledge their feminist orientation:

> [It was] the women's liberation movement that pushed this field of study into prominence and created the atmosphere for its acceptance and legitimation. We cannot begin to thank all the women whose unknown acts of courage, in direct and indirect ways, have made this book possible; but as the women's liberation movement forwarded the book, we hope that the book in turn may forward the movement.[49]

In addition, some journals announce that they publish only feminist research (e.g., *Feminist Studies, Women's Studies International Forum*). The statement of purpose of *Gender & Society* claims that it "aims to advance both the study of gender and feminist scholarship [and] welcomes studies . . . that are framed by a social analysis and a feminist perspective." With such statements as criteria for identifying feminist research,[50] I sought descriptions of the *methods* used in feminist research projects.

The simple criterion of self-identification deliberately bypasses the danger of applying a one-sided definition to *all* feminist researchers. It allows me to go directly to the work of people who take the label for themselves and to avoid deducing what feminist research is from the standpoint of my personal definition. This approach rejects the notion of a transcendent authority that decides what constitutes "feminist," consistent with the antihierarchical nature of many feminist organizations and much feminist spirit. It also seems unfair to apply a current definition to people's work two decades ago. Australian scholar Dale Spender put it this way:

> at the core of feminist ideas is the crucial insight that there is no one truth, no one authority, no one objective method which leads to the production of pure knowledge. This insight is as applicable to feminist knowledge as it is to patriarchal knowledge, but there is a significant difference between the two: feminist knowledge is based on the premise that the experience of all human beings is valid and must not be excluded from our understandings, whereas patriarchal knowledge is based on the premise that the experience of only half the human population needs to be taken into account and the resulting version can be imposed on the other hand. This is why patriarchal knowledge and the methods of

producing it are a fundamental part of women's oppression, and why patriarchal knowledge must be challenged—and overruled.[51]

I also prefer to use self-identification because feminism has been changing so rapidly.

While I believe the approach used in this study is consistent with a feminist valuing of people's self-identification, it has also been frustrating in preventing me from discussing research in which the author does not identify herself as feminist.[52] For example, five nurses studied the "Ethnography of the Menopause-Related Hot Flash" in a Mexican-American and Anglo-American population, using interesting methods relevant to women.[53] From the tenor of their work, I suspect they would label themselves feminist but my criterion prevents me from including their work. I also did not use other pieces recommended to me as "fine examples of feminist research" unless the author stated that she or her research methods are feminist.[54]

Sadly, my definition prevents me from discussing the work of feminists who were somehow prevented from using the term "feminist." It is likely that some feminists studying major social policies deliberately do not mention their feminism to circumvent the prejudiced response many people have to the word. If authors are prevented from labeling themselves feminist because of editorial policies, my not using their work adds insult to their injury. Psychologist Barbara Wallston expressed concern that feminist research find publication outlets. She asked: "Will such work be published in our journals? Have we made sufficient changes in editorial policies to begin to accept these newer methodologies?"[55] Since announcing that one is using "feminist methods" may obstruct publication, I included unpublished work in this book.

Another problem stems from the word "feminist." It is likely that the way a woman labels herself reflects cultural differences, a phenomenon bell hooks mentioned when she wrote that many Black women "do not know or use the term"[56] feminist. Yet bell hooks herself wrote about these women as feminists. Several Black feminists prefer the term "womanist," Alice Walker's term. bell hooks also raised the opposite problem—inappropriate use of the label. She expressed concern that "women who were not opposed to patriarchy, capitalism, classism, or racism labelled themselves 'feminist.' "[57] Black American Barbara Smith angrily voiced the same protest against what she calls "women's studies or academic feminists":

> Women who teach, research, and publish about women, but who are not involved in any way in making radical social and political change, women who are not involved in making the lives of living, breathing women more viable. . . . If lifting oppression is not a priority to you then it's problematic whether you are part of the actual feminist movement. . . . To me racist white women cannot be said to be actually feminist.[58]

While recognizing these controversies, I realized that I had to choose between using researchers' self-labels or using my label in order to identify feminist researchers. I chose the former.[59]

Defining "Method"

My working definition of method was "written passages that the author called 'method.' " In materials that contained no clearly designated sections, I looked for descriptions of the researcher's activity or work. I particularly sought those places in a publication where the author describes having done something because of a decision she made about what needed to be done.[60]

To avoid producing a book swamped by lengthy citations, I focused less on discussions of finding samples and recruiting people to be studied and more on later steps. Typically, I did not focus on how researchers seized the idea for study in the first place, nor how the data were analyzed or the analysis written. Occasionally I mention these when the author stresses them. I also decided (at Lynn Davidman's urging) to paraphrase the author's ideas about method and to include only a short representative segment to convey her "voice."

After I formulated a definition of research as the "production of a publicly scrutinizable analysis of a phenomenon with the intent of clarification," I was able to use a broad range of materials. Unlike some quantitative evaluations of feminist research, I did not focus exclusively on journal articles, but also included monographs, anthologies, and other types of books and reports. A piece of work did not have to be published, but had to be publicly scrutinizable in some form. Dale Spender stressed this point in her book *For the Record*. She was concerned that

> the ideas of women who are not in print are not included; their contributions are non-data from the outset. And in this book, where a lot of space is devoted to the way women are defined out of existence and classified as non-data in men's terms, it is as well to have reservations about a feminist framework which defines some women out of existence.[61]

Sometimes when requesting unpublished papers from authors, I received an attached note about the prejudiced views of certain journal policies. Citing these papers gives me particular pleasure.[62]

As the book progressed, I broadened my approach of weaving analytic comments around the excerpts to include the task of addressing specific questions that feminists have raised about particular methods. Examples are Ann Oakley's question about the possible contradiction in the term "feminist interviewing," and Judith Stacey's question of why there are so few feminist ethnographies. My use of an inductive method obligated me to continue to incorporate new material as I wrote and occasionally to reorganize a completed section.[63]

Reading and Listening to Feminist Voices

Out of respect for women's words and to reduce potential errors in communicating the thoughts of others, I have used quotes in addition to paraphrasing. These brief excerpts enable readers to form their own analyses[64] while also considering mine. Where possible I have tried to provide at least two excerpts for each point so that the reader can see how feminist researchers vary in their approaches. Since I wanted to illustrate the range of perspectives, when either of two selections might do, I opted for the one of an author not yet included in the book. In the process I found that many researchers use a variety of methods rather than a single one.

I have tried to listen to the voices of a wide variety of feminist researchers. I also tried to have a broad range of disciplines—anthropology, biology, economics, history, literature, nursing, political science, psychiatry, psychology, sociology, women's studies, and theology.[65] Although emphasis is on sociology because of my own background, and more broadly on the social sciences, many of the ideas in feminist social science apply to other types of inquiry.

Some chapters focus on a particular discipline because of the linkage between disciplines and certain methods. For example, in the chapter on feminist experimental research, material from feminist psychologists predominates. Yet material from many disciplines appears in every chapter because feminist research is done in every discipline and in various combinations of disciplines. My discussion should also contribute to diminishing the importance of the concept of "disciplines," since feminist researchers draw on so many perspectives to do their work. This discipline-free approach to feminist research was endorsed by Carolyn Sherif, a major figure in U.S. feminist psychology:

> the study of sex and gender has to be cross-disciplinary if it is also to be relevant to the goals of feminism . . . cross-disciplinary study is an essential antidote for the compartmentalized and de-humanizing definitions of contemporary disciplines.[66]

I nevertheless identified people by discipline to give the reader a sense of the person's framework.

I drew on work of graduate students (occasionally undergraduates) and of established scholars and tried to keep the range of subject matter wide. I asked people for suggestions, roamed through library stacks, and browsed through bookstores. I searched both mainstream and nonconventional journals. Nevertheless, despite my interest in a broad scope, there are also emphases that reflect my choices. Like psychologist Bernice Lott, I understand that even a book attempting to be comprehensive, is, in the end, "a personal book that reflects . . . the values and assumptions of its author."[67]

To deal with each method briefly, I had to limit my discussion of recent popular methods such as deconstruction.[68] I tried to include the work of feminists working in various countries, but have drawn primarily on work written in English or on work translated into English. I have tried not to label countries from a United States–centered perspective and have used people's ways of labeling countries when it is important to them, such as the case of Liz Kelly who refers to "first world liberal democracies."[69] In every case, my general principle was to find writing in which people say what they actually do as feminist researchers.[70]

Historical Roots

I believe the materials examined in this book represent a significant step in women's history. During the so-called first wave[71] of the women's movement in the

United States,[72] for example, women struggled for *the right to be educated.*[73] In the so-called second wave, women strove for additional goals related to education: *the right to criticize* the accepted body of knowledge, *the right to create* knowledge, and *the right to be educators* and educational administrators. Regarding these hard-earned rights, Canadian sociologist Dorothy Smith says, "The women's movement has given us a sense of our right to have women's interests represented in sociology, rather than just receiving as authoritative the interests traditionally represented in a sociology put together by men."[74]

At first, the very act of discovering sexism in scholarship was revolutionary. That discovery clarified the mission of feminist scholarship and made it possible to demonstrate to suspicious nonfeminists that there was a problem to be addressed. Elizabeth Minnich, a leader in curricular reform in the United States, expressed this well in 1977:

> To a stunning extent, the interests of one half of the human race have not been thought about through history: men have not thought about them, and women have been kept ignorant. . . . If we adopt uncritically the framework, the tools, the scholarship created overwhelmingly by and for men, we have already excluded ourselves. . . . We are being forced to try to discover new intellectual constructs because many of those we have don't fit our experience and were never intended to.[75]

Discussion of "solutions" to these problems occurred first in small workshops, lectures, study groups, and articles in newsletters—a kind of underground,[76] as Canadian researcher Jill Vickers pointed out, noting that feminists were both "conducting 'proper' research for disciplinary consumption . . . and have created an underground in which the norms of feminist research have emerged." The underground came into existence "Since most have endured a rigorous disciplinary 'education' in orthodox method," making "the sort of open discussions of the newly emerging principles of feminist method" that are necessary "for logical and normative reconstruction" rare. Only in passing or in meetings of the underground was there explicit "convergence of individual feminists' ideas about method."[77]

Many people innovated on their own, trying to find ways of doing research that did not imitate the problems they had discovered. At the same time they hoped to avoid rejecting their disciplinary canon altogether. As in revolutionary struggles, feminist critics of the dominant culture fused their criticism and downplayed their differences. The title of an early (1975), famous anthology by U.S. feminist sociologists Marcia Millman and Rosabeth Kanter, *Another Voice,* for example, implies that its numerous contributors spoke in a single voice. Today, a book about the same topic would necessarily refer to voices.

When the "second" feminist wave began to surge through academia and new rights were beginning to be asserted, it was radical simply to study women. For example, in the early 1970s when Jessie Bernard wrote that "practically all sociology to date has been a sociology of the male world,"[78] a person might call her method "feminist" merely by virtue of the fact that she was studying women. Later in 1978, however, when Mary Daly argued that the very concern with methodology was a reflection of patriarchy,[79] the definition of feminist research became more complicated. Was our very concern with methods reactionary?

When Jeanne Gross and bell hooks claimed in 1984 that academic feminism is part of white culture, feminist research became defined for some as part of *the problem,* rather than *the solution.*[80] bell hooks' harsh critique of white women's research efforts proclaimed that "even though they may be sincerely concerned about racism, their methodology suggests they are not yet free of the type of paternalism endemic to white supremacist ideology."[81] This accusation continues to this day, as Cheryl Townsend Gilkes explains in a recent article showing how white feminist scholarship ignores the church, "the most important social settings that Black people control."[82] Does our concern with feminist methods make us blind to issues of racism? As a white woman, I feel it is my responsibility to learn as much as possible about racial diversity and interracial attempts at mutual understanding[83] to avoid feeding into the type of research that bell hooks and Cheryl Gilkes reject.

One course I teach at Brandeis University, "Women and Intellectual Work," is devoted to locating and studying the work of neglected, historical female sociologists in order to challenge the male-hegemonic history of this field.[84] In this context, I have uncovered examples of early feminist scholars' interest in questions of methodology.[85] The relation between feminism and methodology has been a long-standing feature of women's attempts to change the status quo. It is not a new concern.

From the start feminists have recognized the need to reform research practices. A case in point is nineteenth-century British sociologist Harriet Martineau,[86] who believed that observers typically misunderstood the societies they studied. The problem, as she saw it, was that observers compared other societies with their own.[87] That point was echoed in the writing of feminist critics of the late 1970s who pointed out that male researchers misunderstood women because they compared women to men.

Similarly, Ida B. Wells, a Black nineteenth-century U.S. woman who published analyses of lynchings and led the fight against them, had strong convictions about methods. She believed that the most "reputable" sources must be used so that the conclusions could not be contested by those in power. She wrote:

> For a number of years the *Chicago Tribune,* admittedly one of the leading journals of America, has made a specialty of the compilation of statistics touching upon lynching. The data compiled by that journal and published to the world January 1st, 1894, up to the present time has not been disputed. In order to be safe from the charge of exaggeration, the incidents hereinafter reported have been confined to those vouched for by the *Tribune.*[88]

Drawing on such material, illustrating how a particular method was used by nineteenth- or early twentieth-century feminist researchers,[89] I include a section on "historical roots" at the outset of most chapters of this book. This inclusion also reflects the significance of historical figures in raising the consciousness of contemporary women. The following comment by Celia Eckhardt concerning Frances Wright (1795–1852) is not uncommon: "It was Fanny Wright, in fact, who turned me in middle age into a feminist—both by way of the positions she argued so forcefully and because of the way she was treated in the United States of America.''[90] Just as historical feminist figures permeate the consciousness of contemporary feminists, historic methodological ideas underpin current debates on feminist methodology.

Ongoing Questions and Quests

Just as there was a diverse set of views about educating women during the "first" wave of the women's movement, there are diverse views today about the knowledge feminists wish to produce. Starting in the underground and now above-ground, feminists are engaged in an ongoing discussion about feminist methodology. Does it exist? Should it exist? What is it? Are there different types? Is there a female or feminist cognitive style that could inform an alternative method? Is feminist disciplinary research a contradiction in terms given that for the most part the disciplines still reject the politics of feminism and still deny that they themselves are political? Does academia depoliticize feminism? Is feminist methodology more methodology and less feminism? British psychologist Celia Kitzinger answers this way:

> For me, being both a feminist and a psychologist means to be responsible to other feminists for my psychology, and, equally to be responsible to other psychologists for my feminism. To remain identified with each group, I need to be able to offer something positive to each. To feminism I offer my analysis of the dangers of psychobabble invading the women's movement, and my "insider" knowledge of a patriarchal discipline. . . . To psychology I offer my analyses of the role of rhetoric within the social sciences, a radical and social constructionist perspective as an alternative to positivist–empiricist approaches, and my "insider" knowledge of lesbianism and feminism. . . . While rejecting the label "feminist psychologist" as a contradiction in terms, I am passionate in my commitment both to feminism and to psychology. The intellectual excitement and the practical impact of my research and teaching are lodged in the space created by this contradiction—and the challenge of contradiction seems infinitely more creative than the comfort of compromise![91]

Clearly, she is engaged passionately in the contradictions of her identity rather than being debilitated by them.

Judith Lorber, former editor of *Gender & Society,* a major U.S. feminist sociological journal, answers the ongoing questions in a strikingly different way. Although acknowledging that women's realities are different from men's, she doubts that "a special way of doing research—feminist methodology—is the only way women's realities can be tapped and understood" and she questions "whether feminist methodologies are unique to feminists." She does not accept the claim that

> feminist methods were different from masculinist methods. . . . While I do not think that feminist methodology is unique, I think feminists do uniquely contribute to social science by seeing patterns and interrelationships and causes and effects and implications of questions that nonfeminists have not seen and still do not see.[92]

Some feminists argue that there is no special affinity between feminism and a particular research method. Others support interpretive, qualitative research methods; advocate positivist, "objective" methods; or value combining the two. Some imply "use what works," others "use what you know," and others "use what will convince." How can we do research without perpetuating the very problems we have identified? Is it enough to make women visible? Are certain techniques more appropriate than others for feminist research?

A Note about Men

Some men (and some women) are hostile to the idea of feminist research,[93] while other men label themselves feminist and their research "feminist research." The feminist community is divided about men's roles as feminists. Psychologist Nancy Henley argues against antimale feelings, writing that "being pro-woman and anti-male supremacy does not necessary mean being anti-man."[94] Others such as Mary Daly claim that men can support feminism but cannot *be* feminists because they lack women's experience:

> Male authors who are now claiming that they can write accurately "about women" give away the level of their comprehension by the use of this expression. The new consciousness of women is not mere "knowledge about," but an emotional-intellectual-volitional rebirth.[95]

Men, on the other hand, have pointed out the oppressive nature of being excluded by women. For example, U.S. male sociologist Terry Kandal wrote:

> Feminist critical discourse has raised the epistemological question of whether one must be a woman in order to contribute to an authentic sociology of or for women. Obviously, having written this book, my answer is: not necessarily. Although a man cannot experience what it means to be a woman, this does not preclude making a contribution to the sociology of women. William James' distinction between "knowing" and "knowing about" is apropos. Oppression seems to me to have transgender aspects, which those who have experienced it can communicate.[96]

Those feminists who disagree with the exclusion of men point to the excellence of some feminist research conducted by men.[97] In Del Martin's view, for example, Detroit Police Department Commander James Bannon's sociological study of domestic social conflict "shows a high degree of feminist consciousness and a keen awareness of the victim's predicament that is generally lacking in police attitudes."[98] She suggests that feminists differentiate among men.

Men who study problems faced by women sometimes present themselves as closely aligned with the victims. For example, Edward Donnerstein, Daniel Linz, and Steven Penrod concluded their study of pornography by explaining that they

> attempted to approach the topic of violence against women in the media as objectively as possible. But as men, husbands, significant others, and fathers . . . we are personally and morally deeply offended by many of the media depictions of

women we have described in this book. We have undertaken our investigations both because we are intellectually curious about the effects of exposure to pornography and other images of women in the media, and because we are concerned about the negative impact of these materials on the members of our society—particularly our fellow male members. Our . . . hope is that in the end the truth revealed through good science will prevail and the public will be convinced that these images not only demean those portrayed but also those who view them.[99]

Some feminists distrust the intentions of people who are "intellectually curious" rather than passionately angry about the idea of pornography. But pornography, to continue this example, is a topic on which there are also differences within the feminist community itself!

Men who conduct what they call "feminist research" are a minority in a minority and thus report being under special scrutiny. Richard Evans described

historians and archivists . . . in East and West Germany [who] were unable to conceal their surprise that [he] had chosen to study feminism, and some of them clearly thought [he] would have done better to have picked a subject that was more central to the concerns of the historical profession in general and to have left feminism to women. At the same time, [his] research aroused a good deal of interest in supporters of the Women's Liberation movement, and it naturally brought [him] into contact with many of them. These two influences forced [him] to embark on a more general consideration of women's history, the reason for its neglect, and the problems involved in researching and writing it.[100]

Men might not be aware that women conducting feminist research or research about feminism are likely to receive the same ambivalent reaction from nonfeminists.

Another reaction from the wider public is an assumption that male researchers who study topics such as masculinity and the sociology of gender are homosexual. Clive Pearson wrote:

The point of course, is not whether I am or even what the categorisation means for gay people in sociology, but that it was automatically assumed that a heterosexual man would not have a research interest in male practice. My research is concentrated on the responses to the Women's Movement of men in "men's groups" and the impact of the Women's Movement on left political groupings, but my position within sociology, as defined by many of my male colleagues has led me to attempt to open up the positions and practices of men in sociology.[101]

In an opposite vein, U.S. psychologist Michelle Fine points out that men are not victimized when they study feminists or women. Rather they are viewed as *greater* authorities than the people about whom they speak:

those who study injustice are often ascribed more objectivity, credibility, and respect. When men discuss feminist scholarship, it is taken more seriously than when women do. When whites study the Black family the work may be viewed as less "biased" than when Black scholars pursue the same areas. . . . But if a Black social scientist studies white people, one might expect the resulting analyses to be considered the "Black perspective."[102]

My use of the criterion of self-definition provided me with a straightforward approach to these conundra. I include the work of men who call themselves feminist in a research publication. Since I have found so few instances, I suspect the closer men come to understanding feminism, the more reluctant they are to take the label. Nevertheless, it seems important to examine the specific instances where it occurs.

My Voice and Hope

Many feminists have written that "finding one's voice" is a crucial process of their research and writing.[103] During this phase the researcher understands a phenomenon *and* finds a way of communicating that understanding. U.S. political theorist Jean Bethke Elshtain describes going through this process of starting her book many times, experimenting with different ways of writing, and trying out alternative voices.[104] That certainly was the case for me in writing this book.

Renate Klein suggests that we cannot speak for others, but that we can, and must, speak *out* for others. In this book, I try not to speak *for* feminist researchers. Rather, I present their voices and include my own whenever I have personal experience using the method discussed. My voice also frames the argument.[105] Each chapter begins with what I consider to be a defining quotation, followed by an introduction in which I specify the method, a section that deals with historical roots, the body of the chapter containing numerous examples, and a set of conclusions consisting of my reflections on methodological controversies.

Stylistic choices also express my feminist stance. For example, I use the spelling "women" rather than "womyn," "her" as the generic pronoun rather than "him," nonmasculinist terms such as "distribution" rather than "dissemination," women's full names such as "Nancy Chodorow" rather than vague, impersonal, masculinist surnames such as "Chodorow,"[106] nonmilitary language and female metaphors when referring to action, and the pronoun "we" rather than "they" when referring to feminist researchers.

I assume that the reader has some basic knowledge about research methods and is interested in learning how feminists have used them or created modifications and alternatives. If this book is part of a research methods course, I hope comparisons between feminist methods and conventional methods in the social sciences are discussed. Such comparisons enable us to ask if feminist methodology is a form of separatism contributing to a women's studies "ghetto" without affecting mainstream research.[107] A comparative framework might also illuminate how feminist research is sometimes, but not always, different from nonfeminist research.

I would be pleased if this book encouraged development of and support for feminist research, and if readers followed through to read the book or article from which the excerpts are drawn. I would be pleased if this book were read as part of feminist or women's history, as part of the history of social science, as part of women's studies courses, as a teaching tool for those who want to learn/teach about research methods, and as a contribution to feminist theory. I would also be pleased if other researchers and methodologists continue this work by publishing whole volumes on one or a cluster of methods.

This book demystifies feminist research by examining what practitioners actually do, it offers models to emulate or to modify. In this sense it takes us beyond "fighting patriarchy" and shows us what we can do.[108] It illustrates how some people have struggled for "the right to be producers of knowledge without being trapped into the reproduction of patriarchal ways of knowing."[109] I hope this book is read as a call for the production of more feminist knowledge.

2

Feminist Interview Research[1]

The use of semi-structured interviews has become the *principal means* by which feminists have sought to achieve the active involvement of their respondents in the construction of data about their lives.[2]

Why Is Interviewing Appealing to Feminist Researchers?

Semistructured or unstructured interviewing,[3] the method given prominence in the opening quote, is a qualitative data-gathering technique. It differs from ethnography in not including long periods of researcher participation in the life of the interviewee[4] and differs from survey research or structured interviewing by including free interaction between the researcher and interviewee. Survey research typically excludes, and interview research typically includes, opportunities for clarification and discussion. Open-ended[5] interview research explores people's views of reality and allows the researcher to generate theory. In this way it complements quantitatively oriented, close-ended interview research that tries to test hypotheses. Patricia Sexton, a feminist researcher, stressed this difference in her study of female hospital workers:

> Unfortunately, the abundance of statistics and generalizations about "work and its discontents" gives us little real understanding of how women lead their daily work lives, experience their jobs, or perceive work-related issues. Personal documents are needed, individual and group portraits of workers, slices of real working life, statements by the women themselves—the handwoven fabric of their daily work lives. To this end, I have tried to make the mountainous statistics and theories about work life more intimate and familial by asking hospital workers: Who are you? What do you do? What issues trouble you? What do you want from your union or from the women's movement?[6]

Similarly, feminist ethicist Janice Raymond favors "the 'unstructured research interview' employing open-ended questions," because it "maximizes discovery and description."[7] Open-ended interview studies frequently rely on the grounded theory perspective to data analysis[8] developed by sociologists Barney Glaser and Anselm Strauss.[9] The discovery of grounded theory uses an inductive approach to analyzing data.

Open-ended interview research produces nonstandardized information that allows researchers to make full use of differences among people. For example, psychologist Rae Andre reports that in her study of the attitudes of 29 female and 1 male homemakers, the number of responses for specific questions varies from 12 to 30 because of variations in respondents' knowledge and because of the reluctance of her paid interviewers to probe questions that seemed painful to the respondents:

> On one occasion an interviewer reported getting so involved with the homemaker's story that she forgot to ask the questions. On other occasions, interviewers decided that one or another question would be intrusive. Yet another problem was that of constant unavoidable interruptions and time pressures: one interview had to be carried out with interviewer and homemaker propped up on the bed in the homemaker's bedroom (and they were still interrupted).

Rae Andre did not not interpret this variation as poor-quality data but rather as a valuable reflection of reality:

> If the purpose of this project had been to make inferences about a whole population based on our sample, or to compare ideas from one interviewee to another, these interview irregularities would have presented more of a methodological problem. As it is, our goal in this project is simply to record a range of possible ideas—to tap as many homemaker values as possible—and in designing our project we felt that diversity of interviewees, of interview styles, and of settings would be facilitative.[10]

Fortunately, her assistants reported on the process of the interviews rather than hiding their variability.[11]

Feminist researchers have also used open-ended interviewing to study people whose behavior is abhorrent to them. An example is Diana Scully's examination of the attitudes toward sexual behavior and women, among 114 convicted rapists of female adults and teenagers. These men were incarcerated in seven maximum- or medium-security prisons in the Commonwealth of Virginia and all had volunteered to participate in the study. "Respondents were given an 89-page interview that included . . . 30 pages of open-ended questions intended to explore their perceptions of their crime, their victim, and themselves."[12]

Feminist researchers find interviewing appealing for reasons over and above the assets noted by social scientists who defend qualitative methods against positivist criticism. For one thing, interviewing offers researchers access to people's ideas, thoughts, and memories in their own words rather than in the words of the researcher. This asset is particularly important for the study of women because in this way learning from women is an antidote to centuries of ignoring women's ideas altogether or having men speak for women. Some feminist researchers have gone to great lengths in this regard by carefully recording and analyzing women's speech.[13] For example, Mary Belenky and her colleagues studied women's ways of knowing with an "intensive interview/case study approach." Although they included certain questions so as to test previous research, the rest of the questions were open-ended

> because we wanted to hear what the women had to say in their own terms rather than test our own preconceived hypotheses, particularly since we included a num-

ber of disadvantaged and forgotten women whose ways of knowing and learning, identity transformations, and moral outlook have seldom been examined by academic researchers. We proceeded inductively, opening our ears to the voices and perspectives of women so that we might begin to hear the unheard and unimagined.

Given this goal, the researchers used the following format:

> Each interview began with the question, "Looking back, what stands out for you over the past few years?" and proceeded gradually at the woman's own pace to questions concerning self-image, relationships of importance, education and learning, real-life decision-making and moral dilemmas, accounts of personal changes and growth, perceived catalysts for change and impediments to growth, and visions of the future. We tried to pose questions that were broad but understandable on many levels, hoping that all—even the less articulate and reflective women— would respond in their own terms without feeling inadequate to the task.[14]

New Zealand sociologist Bev James, on the other hand, suggested that interviewing for language is not enough. Instead, we should supplement "verbal communication in interviews, with attention to nonverbal communication, since 'often members of a subordinate group cannot clearly articulate their frustrations and discontents [which] may be expressed in inchoate ways such as laughter.' "[15]

Other feminist thinkers focus on the importance of interviewing to the interviewer, arguing that open-ended interviewing is particularly suited to female researchers. Asking people what they think and feel is an activity females are socialized to perform, at least in contemporary Western society. According to U.S. gerontologist Kathy Charmaz, interviewing draws on skills in the traditional "feminine role"—"a passive, receptive, open, understanding approach . . . recognizing and responding to the other's feelings and being able to talk about sensitive issues without threatening the participant."[16] But sociologist Rosanna Hertz expressed concern about the impact of this cultural pattern on the research process.[17] At the end of her interview project on dual-career marriages, she wrote:

> When I asked them how they felt about something, women were more likely to launch into lengthy discussions of their feelings, whereas men were more likely to keep their answers short or to tell me they never thought about how they felt. . . . I wonder if my own concern as a woman with people's feelings about what they do may have made me somewhat more sensitive to the greater ability of women to express those feelings.[18]

Interviewing is also consistent with many women's interest in avoiding control over others and developing a sense of connectedness with people. This idea of abdicating control comes through in Hilary Graham's opening quotation about respondents being "actively involved" and "constructing data about their lives," and in Robin Gregg's decision to allow her interviewees to choose their own pseudonyms.[19] Bev James, mentioned above, applied feminist ideas to in-depth interviews, group discussions, and participant observation. She tried to interview in a way that built connections and avoided "alienation of the researcher from the researched." Similarly, group discussions afforded participants a greater role in formulating the research project, consistent with her feminist aim of "developing more egalitarian research methods."

Some feminists who engage in intensive interviewing label their method "phenomenological interviewing," an interview*ee*-guided investigation of a lived experience[20] that asks almost no prepared questions. Margarete Sandelowski and Christine Pollock carried out a phenomenological study of the experience of infertility "in an attempt to understand what being infertile is like to women who perceived themselves as being or having been unable to conceive or carry a child to term." In their study "nothing about the initial interviews was planned in advance beyond asking the participants to 'tell me about what it's like not to be able to have a baby when you want to.' " In a second stage of the project, they discussed their interpretation of the first interview with the interviewee. The purpose of the second interviews was

> to clarify and validate data from the initial interviews . . . based on the themes found in the initial analysis of data. The investigators summarized these themes for the women and asked them to comment on how well they fit their own infertility experiences. Their comments were then analyzed and incorporated into the final study report.[21]

Christine Webb's interview study of women recovering from hysterectomies was also inspired by the feminist and phenomenological goals of "starting with women's experiences,"[22] to which she added an action component. She hoped "to describe women's experiences and perceptions on having the operation and focus[ed], among other aspects, on the information they would have liked to have received to help them cope with the process."[23] Feminist phenomenological interviewing requires interviewer skills of restraint and listening as well as interviewees who are verbal and reflective.

Sociologists Pauline Bart and Patricia O'Brien explain that careful listening allows the interviewer to introduce new questions as the interview proceeds. Thus, the interviewer, the interview, and the study become interviewee oriented. They studied 94 women 18 years or older who in the previous two years either had been attacked and avoided rape ($N = 51$) or had been raped ($N = 43$), using an interview that combined demographic variables and unstructured and semistructured questions. Most important to these researchers was the decision to incorporate questions as new topics arose:

> Because of the exploratory nature of the research, questions were added when unanticipated patterns emerged; e.g. on incest and child sexual assault and other violence in the woman's life, and on whether the women were primarily concerned with being killed or mutilated or primarily concerned with not being raped.[24]

The more carefully they listened to the women, the more their project honed in on the reality of rape or its avoidance.

Versatility and Variations in Feminist Interviewing

The versatility of feminist interviewing is evident in the vast array of topics studied, including housework, mothering,[25] and religious experience;[26] experiences of violence, sexual abuse, and harassment;[27] feelings about being incarcerated; and decisions about abortion and childcare.[28] The particulars of interviewing vary widely as well. In each study, the researcher must consider the duration of and desirability of repeat interviews,[29] the number and sequencing of questions, if questions will be closed-ended, open-ended, or both, if interviewees will have an opportunity to question the interviewer, if interviews will be standardized, and the ethical dimensions of interviewing about particular topics.

Other practical details also vary widely—where will the interview take place, and who will decide? How will information be recorded (notes, check-marks, audiotape, videotape)? Should the principal investigator or hired individuals do the interviews? Should hired interviewers or interviewees analyze the data? Should the interview be face-to-face or conducted over the telephone?[30] Who should be present during the interview? Should individuals or groups be interviewed? Is it appropriate for the interviewer and interviewee to know each other in advance? Can the interviewees read the research results and modify the interpretation of the study?

Feminists' answers to these questions vary. Agreement does not even exist about how to refer to an interview and an interviewee. Is an interview a conversation? Is the interviewee a participant? A subject? An informant? This variety reflects the fact that feminist research methods are both rooted in the mainstream disciplines and represent a protest against them. Using unconventional terms such as "participant" instead of "subject" is a signal that the researcher is operating in a feminist framework that includes the power to name or rename.[31] Eschewing standardization in format allows the research question, not the method, to drive the project forward. It has also encouraged creativity.

Historical Roots

Historically, feminist researchers used interviews for social reform purposes.[32] For example, Helen Stuart Campbell (1839–1918) observed female sweatshop workers and their male employers, conducted interviews, and incorporated statistical data in *Prisoner of Poverty,*[33] *Prisoners of Poverty Abroad,* and *Women Wage-earners.*[34] Directing her books to a wide public, she sometimes wrote her findings as a story or tale.[35] Contemporary historian Alice Kessler-Harris claims that these tales "captured the public conscience."[36] The following excerpt based on an interview with a male factory owner illustrates Helen Campbell's style of combining general principles with specific quotations:

> "It's pretty bad, yes, I know it's pretty bad," said one large employer of women, and his word was the word of many others. "But we're not to blame. I don't want to grind 'em down. It's the system that's wrong, and we are its victims.[37] Competition gets worse and worse. Machinery is too much for humanity. I've been certain of that for a good while, and so, of course, these hands have to take the consequences."[38]

Helen Campbell's studies revealed that managers valued women's "docility," which she reinterpreted as their "vulnerability."

U.S. sociologist Mirra Komarovsky has been a long-time champion of interview research for feminist purposes, from her early studies of unemployment's effect on family life during the Depression to her recent studies of the social–psychological development of women in college.[39] Margaret Hagood was also a pioneer in interviewing women. Her study, *Mothers of the South,* focused on women tenant farmers in the U.S. southeast in the 1930s and includes a methodology chapter. Calling herself "the visitor," she explained how she selected tenant women for study and how she conducted exploratory interviews. She stressed the importance of rapport and found that it "was more easily established if the visitor knew the woman's name in advance." For 16 months "the visitor" repeatedly visited tenant farm mothers:

> the visitor . . . introduced herself as Mrs. Hagood from Chapel Hill, stated that she was interested in women who live in the country and their problems of bringing up children, and asked if she might visit for a little while. The pattern of cordial hospitality . . . usually brought an invitation to come in and have a seat before even this much explanation was given.
>
> Conversation began most frequently on some aspect of the immediate situation—children or work. During the visits certain questions were asked directly, such as "How many children do you have?" or "How is your health?" but, in general, questioning was avoided. Topics on which an expression of attitudes was desired were approached obliquely and the interview was kept as much as possible to a friendly, conversational, "just visiting" tone.
>
> No notes were taken during the first visits to the North Carolina group, but the visit was written up as quickly as possible after the interview and much of the conversation was recorded practically verbatim. . . . The visits varied in length from a half hour to four hours with a modal length of about an hour and a half. . . . There was an opportunity to talk privately with over half of the mothers; with the rest, children, husbands, relatives, or neighbors were never absent.[40]

Contemporary feminist interviewers are apt to report, just as Margaret Hagood did, whether others were present, if material was recorded as it was obtained, how long the interview lasted, and how the researcher strove to establish rapport.

Women Interviewing Women

For a woman to be understood in a social research project, it may be necessary for her to be interviewed by a woman.[41] Such a situation represents woman-to-woman talk, which Dale Spender and others have shown is different from talk in mixed-sex groups.[42] U.S. sociologist Marjorie DeVault bases her interviewing style on this self-revealing and consciousness-raising potential of woman-to-woman talk.[43] She explains the importance of using categories that represent what women do (e.g., feed their families) rather than categories that reflect men's activities or terms derived from social science. Feminist researchers who interview women frequently discuss topics that are not part of typical public or academic discourse and therefore "have no name." This makes it all the more important to avoid naming the interviewee's experience. A woman listening with care and caution enables another woman to develop ideas, construct meaning, and use words that say what she means. U.S. psychologist Stephanie Riger has argued this perspective:

> Traditional research methods, as indeed American culture, emphasize objectivity, efficiency, separateness and distance. . . . Let us consider as well connection and empathy as modes of knowing, and embrace them in our criteria and in our work.[44]

Rosemary Barrington and Alison Gray used this approach in their interviews of 100 New Zealand women for the purpose of investigating the impact of social class, cohort, and life cycle stage on their lives. Because they used "intensive, semi-structured interviews [and] 'listened carefully to attitudes and feelings, those non-quantifiable things that are not usually covered in social surveys,' "[45] their interviews got at "subtleties" imbedded in women's speech itself, such as hesitancies. In their view, nonfeminist researchers consider such "subtleties" to be marginal.

One of the ways to get at these subtleties is to be interviewee-guided, which means focusing less on getting one's questions answered and more on understanding the interviewee. Mona Harrington and Nadya Aisenberg explain their approach to interviewing 37 "off-track" academic women in these terms:

> Because we did not know at the outset what the particularities of each woman's relevant experience would be, we did not conduct the interviews through preset questions. Rather, we identified general areas we wanted to cover, but let the interviewees' responses determine the order of subjects, the time spent on each, and the introduction of additional issues.[46]

Interviewee-guided research requires great attentiveness on the part of the interviewer during an interview and a kind of trust that the interviewee will lead the interviewer in fruitful directions.

Feminists who interview women, such as British social scientist Susan Yeandle, get a sense of people as "rounded individuals rather than as numbers in boxes." Susan Yeandle also reported that her 64 interviewees needed to tell stories in order to communicate meaning. Feeling that interviews enabled her to recognize the women's humanity, she tried to write in a way that would create the same impression in readers. Her technique was to include a "coda" of stories that conveyed the reality of "workers' wives," illustrated points made in the chapter, and served "as a reminder that each of the women in the study had her individual characteristics."

In her reflexive methodological discussion—a component of much feminist research—Susan Yeandle explained how a feminist approach affected her choice of questions and ways of relating to the interviewee. Designing "a specifically feminist sociological contribution to the existing literature on women's labour," meant that she looked for differences among the women, which in turn led her "not to use highly structured interviews or (except in a few specific cases) fixed-response questions." She also thought of ways to put each woman at ease while being interviewed, just as Margaret Hagood did. She began each interview with a standard form that asked for demographic information such as the woman's age, marital status, and the composition of her household. Following this, the interviewer began to tape-record their conversation, beginning with questions about the woman's current jobs. This section of the interview also contained a few fixed response questions concerning attitudes toward pay and working conditions. Susan Yeandle considered this first phase of the interview important both for the data collected and for its function

> as an "ice-breaker," enabling women to relax and talk about themselves. All the questions asked invited respondents to disclose information which was very well known to them, thus putting them at their ease, and convincing them that the interview had relevance to them as individuals.

Having created an atmosphere in which the women felt knowledgeable, she urged them to tell her their life stories "in their own way (rather than to restrict them with close and rigid questioning which might have been inhibiting or confusing.)."

> Women were always . . . encouraged to "digress" into details of their personal histories and to recount anecdotes about their working lives. Much important information was gathered in this way; the opportunity was given for women to discuss the progress and decisions of their employment careers in all their complexity, and this helped to eliminate the danger that the framework of my questions might impose external meanings and interpretations on the events which constituted a respondent's individual history. . . . When the employment history was complete (in the respondent's eyes), I asked any supplementary questions, and checked any points which were unclear.

Clearly, Susan Yeandle valued the "digression" as much as the core information and allowed interviewees to define the end of the story. After asking the women for opinions about legislation, she included what she called a "reliability check" that consisted of asking women to review the chronology of key events in their employment history. Confirming (or disconfirming) the women's stories was as important to her as hearing them.[47]

Because of the interviewee-guided nature of much feminist interview research, there frequently are large variations in the duration of interviews within a single project. Margaret Gordon and Stephanie Riger, for example, reported that in their project, "most in-person interviews lasted approximately 90 to 100 minutes, but some ran as long as three hours."[48] Similarly, Naomi Gerstel reported a study with Catherine Riessman of relationships following divorce. This project had three interviewers (the two women mentioned above and Larry O'Brien, a graduate student at the time) and studied "52 women and 52 men . . . using a schedule composed of both open- and closed-ended items. The interviews [lasted] from two to seven hours (an average of three hours)."[49]

Notwithstanding this concern for mutual understanding, feminist interview-based research is unable to guarantee that the interviewee will not be misunderstood or rejected in the research process. For example, Catherine Riessman argued that women have to share cultural patterns in order to understand each other.

Putting it succinctly, she claims that "gender is not enough."[50] In a related vein, British social psychologist Susan Condor discovered to her dismay that despite her use of an open-ended questionnaire, she could *not* sympathize with "traditional women who support the existing roles of men and women." Although she tried to reach "an understanding of women in their own terms," she found that "regarding individuals and social events from the perspective of feminism . . . may . . . encourage the very tendency to objectify our 'subjects' which feminism opposes so forcefully."[51] Her project thus raises the question—Are we able to empathize with some women and not with others? I think the answer reflects the more general principle that every aspect of a researcher's identity can impede or enhance empathy. In ethnographic and interview research that requires interaction, this issue may be more significant than in survey or experimentation that does not rely on empathy. Fortunately, some feminist researchers such as Susan Yeandle and Kristin Luker, cited above, wrote candidly about this matter and explained how the research process changed their views about women with whom they previously had little identification.

Friend, Stranger, Neither, Both?

A related controversy in both mainstream and feminist interviewing is the comparative benefit of being a stranger or a friend to the people one is studying.[52] On the basis of her intensive interview study in a Chicano community, Denise Segura wrote about the necessity of having close relations *before* the interview takes place. In the five years prior to her study, she became

> familiar with the local Chicano and Mexicano communities as a junior high school teacher and as a parent with children at the child care center used by many of my future informants' families. In addition, [she] gave numerous employment workshops. . . . All of these activities helped establish [her] credibility in the community. Such credibility is important inasmuch as Chicana and Mexicana women can be reluctant to be interviewed, given their vulnerability to the hostile inquiries of immigration officials and other public agencies. . . . Moreover, Chicanas and Mexicans are likely to feel more comfortable talking to someone who is known within their social network than to an unknown researcher. Finally, the quality of the interview data and their reliability is enhanced when the researcher is knowledgeable and integrated into the community under study.

In addition to giving her access to the women she wanted to study, familiarity enable her to "have shorter, more focused interviews than researchers in unfamiliar terrain."[53]

By contrast, the methodological appendix to U.S. sociologist Mary K. Zimmerman's interview-based study of abortion takes up the question of why a woman would volunteer to be interviewed for her study. Her answer is the lack of a relationship!

> [T]he interviewer was a stranger—not a part of the woman's world and someone she would be likely not to see again. The interviewer was also a professional who

would not discuss the interview with anyone else. For these reasons, the women may have felt they could talk about their most private lives and feelings relatively freely.[54]

In the opening section of her study of the origins of the contemporary women's movement, Sara Evans describes the "knowledgeable stranger" position that falls between Denise Segura's "interviewer as friend" and Mary Zimmerman's "interviewer as stranger." She knew that her background as a southern, white, activist, feminist was valuable for its intimate knowledge. On the other hand, Sara Evans tried to avoid substituting her experience for that of others (i.e., autobiography for history) or failing to ask questions that would challenge her assumptions.

> Fortunately, I had neither met nor heard of most of the people I interviewed before I began this research, nor was I present at the main events described here. . . . Yet the rapport that developed in many interviews resulted in part from my own and my informants' confidence that my prior research and my personal experience together allowed me to comprehend what they had to say in a way that no "outsider" could.[55]

In a sense she was both stranger and friend.

Adding another twist, Michelle Fine raises the ethical question of whether it is appropriate to study people opportunistically. Drawing on her experience as a rape counselor in a hospital emergency room, she asks what we should do with material we "happen to collect."[56] She is neither friend nor stranger, but counselor, and in the act of writing, she becomes retrospective researcher. Michelle Fine resolves her ethical quandry by going ahead with an analysis of the transcript of a conversation while also ensuring the confidentiality of the interviewee.[57] Ethical questions are heightened in feminist interview research because feminists try hard to avoid perpetuating the exploitation of women.

Believing and Being Trusted by the Interviewee

In 1981 British sociologist Ann Oakley posited a contradiction between "scientific" interviewing requiring objectivity, and feminist research requiring openness, engagement, and the development of a potentially long-lasting relationship.[58] She advocated a new model of feminist interviewing that strove for intimacy and included self-disclosure and "believing the interviewee." Guiding this new model was a proposed feminist ethic of commitment and egalitarianism in contrast with the scientific ethic of detachment and role differentiation between researcher and subject. Although some of these ideas already guided the work of interviewers and ethnographers who are not feminist, Ann Oakley argued that a new model of interviewing must be developed as an alternative to the dominant mode.

Using these ideas, Ann Oakley reissued her 1974 study of the sociology of housework in 1985 with a new preface in which she criticized her former methodology. The original "study . . . was done within a specific academic context [that] emphasized the role of social scientists as collectors and analysts of objectively verifiable data.'' In retrospect, the meant ''treating women who are inter-viewed merely as data-providers.'' Although this objectification was required by science, she felt it should be ''disclaimed by feminists . . . [for it] undermines the very importance of subjectivity in the mapping of social experience.''[59] She suggests that feminist interviewing involves commitment on the part of the re-searcher to form a relationship, and on the part of the interviewees to participate with sincerity.[60] In another of her studies, more than a third of her interviewees continued their ties with her after four years: ''four have become close friends, several I visit occasionally, and the rest write or telephone when they have some-thing salient to report such as the birth of another child.''[61] Presumably these women became friends of the researcher because they felt valued as individuals rather than ''data providers.'' Perhaps being listened to and respected led to a kind of ''bonding.''

''Believing the interviewee'' is a controversial idea because social interaction typically involves a certain amount of deception[62] and because science relies on skepticism. Some feminist researchers reinterpret the notion of believing the inter-viewee as a utilitarian and decidedly feminist approach. Specifically, a believed interviewee is likely to trust the interviewer and thus likely to disclose ''the truth.'' Emily Abel notes the importance of this stance in her study of 20 faculty women who

> filed charges of sex discrimination against colleges and universities. . . . I have accepted at face value the accounts of what the women experienced and have not tried to assess whether or not they were ''deserving'' of the jobs and promotions they were seeking. It would have been impossible to assess the qualifications of the women, compared with those of their male colleagues. Moreover, statistics about the position of women in academia suggest that, although individual women may well be unqualified, discrimination is pervasive.[63]

In this case, the interviewer's ability to take the women's words at face value stemmed, in part, from her familiarity with feminist scholarship. Her acceptance of their statements encouraged them to share their ideas extensively with her. This is not to say that all feminists believe the women they interview all the time.

In a contrasting example sociologist Margaret Andersen did *not* believe the women she interviewed: 20 ''corporate wives and members of a newcomers' club in a small southern city . . . generally . . . between [the ages of] 25 and 40 . . . well-educated and politically liberal, most [of whom] do not work'' [outside the home], who say they are happy with their lives as women and who support feminism only as it addresses the issue of employment discrimination. Instead, she wrote that they suffered from ''false consciousness.'' In response to her arti-cle,

> the women organized a collective rebuttal. . . . In their letter, they adamantly defend their place and they strongly argue that women like themselves can, in spite of what sociologists say, find fulfillment in the roles of wife, mother and volunteer . . . they write of the contribution they make to their community and to their family. . . . In another part of the letter they claim the author is jealous of their economic resources, thus underscoring the material basis of their situa-tions.

After reading their rebuttal, Margaret Andersen studied the same women from a new accepting perspective that enabled her to explain their ideas in a way more satisfying both to her and the women:

> [If] researchers assume that the women's claims are insincere, they are put in the untenable position of being unable to believe what their subjects report. A more appropriate research strategy is to look not for the falsehoods of their claims, but to the actual conditions of the women's lives and the way those conditions might generate the contentment the women express.[64]

It seems to me that a feminist researcher should begin a research project intending to believe the interviewee and should question the interviewee if she begins not to believe her. A task for data analysis then becomes a discussion of this conflict between belief and disconfirmation. In a sense, that is what Margaret Andersen produced.

A related issue for feminist interview researchers is trust. Sociologist Jessie Bernard described how participating in a consciousness-raising group forced her to recognize that she had to be trusted if she hoped to obtain information about people's lives:

> Early in 1968 I became exposed to the Women's Liberation Movement in the underground press. . . . When, after considerable effort on my part, I received an invitation to a consciousness-raising session, one of the young women there said that I "threatened" her. Sitting quietly on the floor in their midst, showing, so far as I knew, no disapproval at all, my academic objectivity, my lack of involvement, my impersonality, was giving off bad vibrations. This incident gave me something to think about, including my stance vis-à-vis research and also my discipline.[65]

Pauline Bart explains that she, too, had to disassociate herself from the research role to enable the 32 women who worked in Jane, an illegal abortion service run by feminists, to trust her:

> Originally the women I approached did not wish to be interviewed because they were antiprofessional and antiacademic. However, when it became clear that I had been a feminist activist in Chicago and did not have a "professional demeanor" (a negative word in the Women's Health Movement), they agreed. Since I did not have a grant, they decided I had not been co-opted and could be trusted.[66]

Downplaying one's professional status is an option for feminist researchers who study people distrustful of professionals. Other societal sources of distrust (e.g., racism) are not so easily manipulated or overcome. To encourage the development of trust, some feminist researchers define themselves as learners and listeners rather than "researchers." For example, Audrey Bronstein downplayed the academic aspect of her research in her own eyes in order to have a more egalitarian orientation to the women she was studying:

> I wanted to learn from the Latin American peasant women about how they felt their "development" experiences had affected them. . . . I didn't want to "study" them or development in Latin America. I hoped to speak with women, who, within a peasant, "macho" society, rarely speak, or give their opinions publicly

on anything, much less on their own living conditions and the changes introduced by both foreign and indigenous development agencies.[67]

When feminist interviewing is planned as a component of ethnography, the researcher may defer the interviewing of people until they trust her. Australian sociologist Judy Wajcman had this intention in her study of a group of formerly employed women running a recently closed factory. For five months she "kept a comprehensive diary of events and conversations, which [she] diligently wrote up every evening" after working full-time in the factory, but she also "needed to collect more systematic information about the women and their husbands through interviews." When she felt confident of her ability to ask useful questions and had created a trusting relation, she used a semistructured questionnaire. At that point the factory closed for the summer vacation, and Judy Wajcman visited each woman in her home.[68] Reflecting back on those interviews, she believes that trusting relations led the women to raise additional topics over and above those she had prepared.

For Hilary Graham this feminist ethic of interviewing leads to "informant-structured interviews" (which she also calls narratives and self-surveys) in which the researcher communicates to the interviewee that she cares about her as a human being. Under these circumstances, it is improper for "interpretation and analysis to remain the prerogative of the investigator." To avoid this, she encourages her "informants" to tell stories.

> In stories, data and interpretation are fused, the story-line providing the interpretive framework through which the data are constructed. The story, moreover, marks the boundaries of what the individual is prepared to tell. . . . It is a method, too, consistent with a feminist research programme which seeks to involve women in the faithful recording of their experiences.[69]

Several feminist interviewers have attempted to foster trust by downplaying status differences between themselves and people of lower social status. For these feminist researchers interviewing requires personal commitment between themselves and the research participant. When "interviewing up," on the other hand, feminists must find ways to increase their status and credibility.[70] In the concluding chapter, I will reevaluate the ethic of commitment focusing on several conflicts it can create in the researcher.

Helping the Interviewee

One conflict frequently arises when feminist researchers study relatively powerless groups in a hierarchy. In her study of hysterectomy described earlier, for example, Christine Webb explains that if the feminist researcher formulates a study of use and interest to women, she is likely to be asked politically charged questions during the interviews. At the same time, access to women is frequently monitored by people who do not want the researcher to upset the status quo. If relatively powerless, the feminist researcher may feel constrained not to become fully engaged with the women so as to "protect" her project. Christine Webb found that from the start, the women in her study "took the opportunity to ask . . . direct questions and to seek information and advice." Despite Webb's feminist consciousness, when the interviewee requested information or solicited support in her criticism of others, Webb felt unable to violate the definition of interviewer as "neutral." Her article gives interview excerpts to show the contradictions between being beholden to the doctors as a nurse and researcher on the one hand, and her "feminist consciousness" on the other:

> INT: Did he explain the operation to you?
> SUB: To tell the truth, this man was very arrogant and off-hand. I was petrified and the next time I went I was really petrified because I hadn't lost all the weight he told me to. When I sat on the bed I was trembling and having a cold sweat while I was waiting. Then it was a different doctor. He told me there was only one way to go after you are 40 and that's downhill. The second doctor was very nice. He just said he would leave the ovaries because I would need them for the menopause. And I did not really know anything about that. Then he just buzzed off. So nobody has said anything.
>
> To respond to these women with "uh huh" or "that's interesting" . . . would have been somewhat awkward to say the least and would not have contributed to encouraging them to speak openly about their experiences. . . . But neither did I feel it appropriate to collude in criticizing the hospital or doctors in the context of a research interview.
>
> As a nurse and experienced researcher I had knowledge which could be useful to the women, but I felt highly constrained in my research role because a nurse formally works under the control of doctors and may not initiate treatments of her own accord. . . . [I]f I diverged from the approved research protocol by giving information to women, permission to continue the study might be withdrawn. . . . I had received permission only to collect data and not to give information or advice, and women might thereby not have access to a potentially useful resource for coping with their hysterectomy and recovery.

Christine Webb decided to confront the dilemma directly by adopting the role of patient advocate:

> I decided to tell women at the beginning that I saw the interview as an exchange of information. I had some questions to put to them but they should ask me anything they wanted at any stage and I would answer as fully as I could, based on my experience as a nurse and what I had learned from my previous study. But although this would mean that I was not exploiting or "ripping off" the women, it did not go far enough. I as an "expert" had access to wider information than they did, and I could not justify keeping this to myself. Therefore I would give information and advice wherever I detected a need or opportunity during the interview. The effect of this has been that at times I talked more than the women but this seems an inevitable consequence of my decision.

Christine Webb's resolution of the "what side am I on?" dilemma meant self-disclosing about her own life. In response, the interviewees took on the role of the researcher's advocate!

> Once these decisions were made, it was clear that I should share my own experiences as a gynaecology patient with the women when this would help to

show that I understood their feelings or when it would validate what I and they were saying. . . . Great sympathy was shown to me, I was given advice about how to cope with my condition, and when I met women again they asked me how I was feeling.

As I continued to do more interviews after making these decisions I was convinced even more strongly that in fact there had been no choice. Either I could have adopted this kind of methodology, developed intimacy with the women, and invested my subjectivity in the research and in return learned in great depth and richness about their feelings and experiences. Or the project would not have been feasible and would have ground rapidly to a halt. My consciousness had been raised in relation both to feminist research and to the women's sense of isolation and lack of knowledge and resources when facing a hysterectomy, and this had an immediate effect on my research practice and a more long-term influence on my nursing practice. I felt that my responsibilities to the women justified the risk that the doctors might disapprove of what I was doing.

Resolving the dilemma enabled Christine Webb to see the great potential of feminist interviewing research for nursing:

By adopting a sharing, non-hierarchical approach with patients, nurses could give better care because they would have greater understanding of patients' feelings, problems and needs. By working together with patients, nurses' own consciousness would be raised in relation to medical dominance over all patients, but especially women patients, and all nurses.[71]

Another perspective on the "whose side are you on?" question is available when one studies the group of people who comprise a social system rather than a set of individuals who share a characteristic. Janice Raymond did such a study of the sex-transformation social system by talking to 15 transsexuals, 13 of whom were male-to-constructed females, and to professionals involved in the study and treatment of transsexualism. She also "interviewed many of the active figures in the field of transsexual research and therapy, . . . persons involved in gender identity clinics, . . . [studied a particular organization] which has funded much transsexual research and activity, [and] . . . interviewed several doctors and counselors who are active in the area of transsexual treatment and counseling on a private basis."[72] Interviewing people in interconnected roles allowed her to uncover the "transsexual empire" as a whole and to take a more complex stance on advocacy.

Researcher Self-Disclosure

Several studies, including those I have discussed earlier such as Christine Webb's work with gynecology patients, argue that researcher self-disclosure during interviews is good feminist practice. For example, Elissa Melamed writes that when she studied aging, women denied they were fearful until she told them she was afraid.[73] Researchers Ann Bristow and Jody Esper told potential interviewees that one of them had been raped. They found that this disclosure put the women at ease:

[S]he [the volunteer interviewee] prefaces a description of her fears by saying that, "you're going to think I'm crazy, but . . ." She is answered by a woman [the researcher] who shares her own fears as a rape survivor and reveals that many of the women interviewed have expressed similar fears. She seems relieved.

In this project the researchers modeled interviews on what they call "a true dialogue" rather than "an interrogation." Self-disclosure initiates "true dialogue" by allowing participants to become "co-researchers." [74]

A paper co-authored by social work researchers Marti Bombyk, Mary Bricker-Jenkins, and Marilyn Wedenoja, however, challenges this idea. Their project consisted of "exploratory, semi-structured interviews conducted by telephone with a group of 29 social and human service workers" who were feminist practitioners. Marilyn Wedenoja, an interviewee, writes that she felt constricted by the interviewer's self-disclosure:

> personal sharing on her part (where she was from, what she has done, some of her own views) was triggering off in me a self-censoring process. I began to notice myself stereotyping her and second guessing what she would want to hear and not want to hear based on my perception of the information about herself. . . . She was giving me . . . personal information as a way of equalizing the relationship and revealing herself as I had been revealing myself, yet it seemed more out of her need to self-disclose rather than my need at that point to know about her. At that early stage of the interview, I felt like I first needed time to establish myself within the role of participant before moving towards more of an interactive sharing.

Fortunately, the interviewee notified the interviewer:

> Once I voiced my concerns . . . I was able to influence the process and it contributed to my sense of safety and trust. The fact that [she] was responsive to my concerns and took time within the interview process for ongoing feedback made a big difference in creating an atmosphere that facilitated self-exploration and self-disclosure. As the interview progressed, I was delighted to learn more about Mary and to have a dialogue about some of the topics. . . . I began to see how it was unrealistic to think that such a relationship within a brand new situation like this would be able to be "instantly" created—as some of the guidelines of feminist research seem to suggest—without some form of a developmental process and adaptation to the unique needs and concerns of the individuals involved.

Mary Bricker-Jenkins, one of the interviewers, wrote, "Thanks to feedback from respondents . . . I have learned to 'pace' my interactions and look for cues from the participant as to readiness to know more about me." [75] She concurs with Marilyn Wedenoja's view that the timing of researcher self-disclosure is the key to its value.

U.S. sociologist James Ptacek used transcripts of batterers' talk about their violence, along with researcher self-disclosure and reflexivity to report his interview-based study of 18 abusive men, "one of only a few successful attempts to gather evidence systematically of batterers' perspectives on wife beating." Publishing in a feminist anthology, he stressed the value of a feminist perspective, including self-disclosure to interviewees. I interpret his writing in the first-person singular, in contrast to the conventional third-person or passive voice as continuing his practice of informing interviewees of his values:

> I came to study wife beating as a way of contributing to social action against men's domination of women. Prior to entering graduate school, I became involved with Emerge in Boston. I have continued my affiliation with Emerge while in school, working as a group counselor, public speaker, trainer and researcher for the organization. As Emerge defines wife beating in political terms and draws its analysis from the women's movement, I am both an activist and a researcher on the issue of violence against wives.[76]

Researchers who self-disclose are reformulating the researcher's role in a way that maximizes engagement of the self but also increases the researcher's vulnerability to criticism, both for what is revealed and for the very act of self-disclosure. Receiving feedback from the interviewees, on the other hand, enables the self-disclosing researcher to continuously correct the interview procedure. For example, U.S. sociologist Terry Arendell studied mothers during the aftermath of divorce while a divorced mother herself.[77] Referring to her interviews as "partially structured personal conversations," she saw herself as similar to the women she studied, and this, in turn, promoted meaningful conversations between them.

Hearing other people's stories also provides the researcher with an alternative case that *prevents* her from generalizing exclusively from her own experience. Ann Bristow and Jody Esper encountered this situation in their study of rape:

> we began the process by contacting a group of rape survivors to meet and discuss, informally, our mutual rape experiences. As we sat and listened to one another we became aware of ways of experiencing rape that were both like and unlike our own experiences. The information which accrued from these and subsequent dialogues was germane in the construction of the first draft and further revisions of our interview schedule. If we had been unwilling or unable to listen to the voices of these women telling their stories, the final form of the interview schedule and the associated data would have been incomplete, at best, and an extremely biased piece of academic rhetoric, at worst.[78]

Clearly, there is no single feminist perspective on researcher–interviewee relations and self-disclosure. Rather there is openness to numerous possible meanings of these phenomena.

Stress from Interviewing

The ethic of commitment exposes feminist interviewers to stress, particularly in studies of traumatized women. In her study of women with "eating problems," sociologist Becky Thompson writes that stress can occur in numerous phases of the research process including the interview process itself:

> I sometimes found myself trying to escape from the pain of their stories as they spoke. Many of the women have been multiply victimized including enduring poverty, sexual abuse, exposure to high levels of violence, and emotional and

physical torture. One way I tried to escape the pain of their stories was by interrupting them with comments such as: "I know what you mean" or "I went
through a similar thing." . . . . Recognizing psychological consequences of interviewing on the researcher elucidates dilemmas involved in using feminist interviewing techniques . . . [I had to sort out] when making a comment during an
interview is actual support and when it is dysfunctional rescuing. . . . sitting
with the pain may be the only response that doesn't cheapen the power of its
recounting. But sitting with the intimacy of such silence is intense and often left
me completely drained after the interviews. I also noticed that my immediate
desire to comfort them was my wanting to escape the pain myself and wanting
someone to comfort me. . . . I sometimes had to remind myself that the woman's ability to retell a traumatic story meant she had already survived the worst
of the pain.

Stress also occurred in later phases of this research project:

While I was transcribing each woman's words, I felt as if I were doing the interview again: I could see the woman's face and hear her exclamations and pain.
. . . While analyzing the interviews, I experienced some of the same types of
protective responses that survivors experience following trauma. For example,
while immediately following the interviews, I could retell the woman's story
almost verbatim, within two or three days I had a hard time remembering basic
aspects of the women's experience . . . . sometimes I found myself changing
their stories in my memory and in doing so, was minimizing the abuse they had
suffered. . . . while I was transcribing interviews, I would typically fall asleep
soon after beginning to transcribe each interview. This had nothing to do with
whether I needed sleep or not. Rather, [it] was another way of coping with the
extreme stress and pain of painstakingly chronicling [what] many of the women
experienced.[79]

Sociologist Margaret Gordon and psychologist Stephanie Riger described similar
problems in coping with painful rape interviews. They "found it difficult at times
to separate ourselves from the topic. Constantly reading about and discussing rape
and other forms of violence against women often left us anxious and depressed.
Staff working with us also found themselves disturbed."[80] Similarly, sociologist
Barbara Katz Rothman's study of amniocentesis for prenatal diagnosis led her to
write:

It was like lifting the proverbial rock and having it all crawl out—ugliness, pain,
grief, horror, anger, anguish, fear, sadness. Women in their fifth month of pregnancy afraid to feel their babies move—because they may not be babies at all,
but genetic mistakes, eventual abortuses. . . . It was a nightmare.[81]

Sociologists Janet Kahn and Patricia Gozemba studied working-class lesbian bar
culture focusing on women who had frequented a bar in Lynn, Massachusetts, in
the 1950s and 1960s.

[We] . . . have had our own experiences of marginality stemming from our
sexual identities. . . . We . . . found that our conversations with these older
lesbians caused us to reflect upon our own lives. . . . For instance there was a
period of about 14 months during which we did almost no work on the paper.

> When we finally found the courage to discuss this with each other, we realized
> that we were shaken and depressed by the number of stories we had heard of
> alcoholism, suicide, and other forms of violence. Our avoidance of the project
> became data that we used to help us look at these women's lives from another
> angle.[82]

Renate Klein reports that she was in tears during about ⅓ of her interviews on
infertility, tears mostly of anger.[83] All of these stressful reactions occur, I believe,
because feminist researchers discover there is more pain in the interviewees' lives
than they suspected. The interview process gives the researcher an intimate view
of this pain and the shock of discovery may eventually force her to confront her
own vulnerability. Sometimes stress can be mitigated by the social support made
available by co-researchers. For example, sociologist Lenore Weitzman concludes
her book on "no-fault" divorce with a detailed explanation of how hired interviewers developed an esprit de corps with positive implications for their relations
with interviewees.[84] Thus feminism frequently adds coping with stress to the other
challenges of interview research.

Multiple In-Depth Interviewing

Multiple interviews characterize much feminist research perhaps because multiple-
interview research helps form the strong interviewer–interviewee bonds some people define as characteristic of feminist research. Whereas I think feminist research
should not be bound to a format requiring such ties with interviewees, feminist
interest in them is apparent. In addition to the potential for developing trust, the
asset of this method is the opportunity to share interview transcripts or notes with
the interviewee and then invite the interviewee's analysis.

Feminist researchers who do multiple interviews of each individual may engage their interviewees in designing the interview format as they proceed. Sociologist Denise Connors used this approach "in a series of informal, unstructured,
conversational interviews with women" over the age of 90. Her description reveals sensitivity to how relationships develop and how relationships, in turn, affect the quality of the information exchanged. She described learning that her first
interviews had to be informal, and that only in the second interview could she
introduce the tape recorder and "get down to business."

> During later interviews we would sometimes listen to a previous tape and further
> discuss and elaborate on certain themes. As we became more comfortable with
> one another, we shared more of ourselves in the process. The desire to please
> and to give socially acceptable answers changed over time. For example, it was
> months before Norah expressed any anger or revealed how she felt about living
> in elderly housing. Later interviews allowed the women time to clarify earlier
> statements and to share more of the context of their experiences.

Since each relationship was unique, later interviews were far more diverse than
initial ones. As Denise Connors' relationships with the women developed, the
uniqueness of each woman's personality began to stand out.

Phone calls and cards were used to maintain contact between interviews. One of the women seemed able to be more at ease on the phone. During one of our calls the conversation was interspersed with the details of the Red Sox baseball game she was watching. Even though much of it was lost on me, she seemed to enjoy sharing it with someone. I later discovered that due to her transportation problems she maintained close connections with many of her friends over the telephone.

Tape recordings and notes from her series of interviews enabled Denise Connors to improve her skills: "What stands out from listening to the tapes over time are the increasing periods of unselfconscious silences. Initially I asked too many questions in an almost desperate attempt to mine some gems." [85] Her comment suggests that there may be some truth in interviewers' unwitting use of the phrase "talking with" or "talking to" rather than "listening to" even when the goal is to "listen to women's voices."

Claire Reinelt had a more sympathetic view of talking in her study of activities in the battered women's shelter movement:

I was uncertain about how to establish the "anthropologist–informant" relationship. For lack of any well-developed plan, I followed my intuition. I began asking questions and listening, the cornerstones of all inquiry but I also found myself talking—talking about my ideas and thoughts about what I observed and heard. We engaged in conversation about strategy, politics, social change, and communication. It was these dialogues in which we were mutually engaged that gave meaning to my fieldwork. It was not meaning that I imposed, but meaning that we created. Meaning emerges through interaction. . . . The anthropologist interprets what the informant says, articulates that interpretation to the informant, to which the informant again responds. This process of interpretation and clarification creates meaning and understanding between those engaged that leaves neither of them unchanged. [86]

Multiple interviews are likely to be more accurate than single interviews because of the opportunity to ask additional questions and to get corrective feedback on previously obtained information. As times passes, the researcher also can see how thoughts are situated in particular circumstances.

When explaining what exactly was feminist about her research practice on sexual violence, British sociologist Liz Kelly pointed to "the style of interviewing, the return of the transcripts, and the content of the follow-up interviews." She explained the last two items as the opportunity for each woman to read her transcript, and correct, qualify, or add anything she wanted. During the follow-up interviews, Liz Kelly asked the women to talk about participation in the project, to give their reactions to reading the transcript, and to tell her about additional memories they might have had (75% had additional memories). By returning the transcripts, the women exerted control over the researcher's interpretations. The interviewees usually asked her if their experiences were typical and requested an explanation of

the most important things emerging from the research. This enabled discussion of the themes and analysis I was developing. I did not assume that women would want to take part in this process, but the interest in it suggests that there may be ways of making this a more formal part of research methodology. One possibility I would now consider is a third meeting in which the researcher discusses with small groups of participants preliminary findings and analysis.[87]

Similarly in her study of pregnant women's decision making about prenatal diagnosis, Robin Gregg used two interviews to learn about the "women's thoughts, feelings, and decisions . . . as the process(es) unfolded. . . . [and to] hear women at different moments during the processes of their pregnancies and their lives." She then added a third interview for "coanalysis" or "participatory analysis."[88] Multiple open-ended interviews are well suited to understanding how a woman develops her ideas. They can be done, however, only among interviewees who have time to invest in the process. Paying participants for their time is sometimes advisable as compensation.

Instrument-Based Interviewing

In a format I call "instrument-oriented interviews," as contrasted with "interviewee-oriented interviews," feminist researchers try to collect the same types of data from many different people. Sarah Fenstermaker Berk used this approach in her study of "the gender factory," i.e., the household. Her study required that various household members understand and faithfully complete a number of carefully designed instruments. Her careful attention to the development of instruments and close monitoring of people's participation allowed her to fulfill her goals of producing "non-polemical feminist research of service to women."[89]

In her instrument-oriented study of "judicial paternalism," Kathleen Daly "interviewed [23] judges to determine if their sentencing differs for men and women defendants, and if so, why." She combined carefully designed instruments with some open-ended components but did not self-disclose. The open-ended component

> elicited information on the judges' professional backgrounds, their perceptions of changes, if any, in men's and women's criminality, and their reliance on other court officials in deciding sentences. Most of the 1- to 2-hour interview time was devoted . . . to determining what factors judges took into account in sentencing and whether these varied for women defendants. . . . The judges were first asked, "What specifically do you want to know about the defendant in sentencing?" Almost all replied by assuming that the defendant was a man. This question was followed up by asking them what their considerations were for women defendants.

The instrument-based component of the study was as follows:

> The judges were . . . asked to react to a hypothetical case to see whether a defendant's gender, familial situation, or both were salient in sentencing. . . . [the case is as follows:] A defendant is appearing before the court with a . . . [grand larceny], and the defendant is found guilty. . . . This latest larceny represents a violation of probation. How would you sentence if the defendant was . . . a woman with two young children? a woman who was single and living

alone? a man with a job who was supporting his wife and child? a man who was single and living alone? . . .

After obtaining their responses . . . , I asked the judges if the following statement in the research literature applied to them: Judges treat female defendants more kindly or protectively than they do male defendants because the female defendants remind them of their daughters, or their wives, or sisters—women close to them. Or . . . judges find it hard to be as tough on a woman as a man. . .

My research assistant and I independently evaluated the interview transcripts by coding the judges' replies to the questions; then we compared our interpretations of what the judges said.[90]

In Kathleen Daly's view, this combination of methods enhanced her credibility, produced comparable data, and avoided influencing her respondents.

Instrument-based research does not require the intimacy of open-ended interviewing, and yet is used for feminist purposes. Feminist interview research includes the entire gamut of interview approaches ranging from the phenomenological to positivist. For each approach, a particular feminist rationale has been developed. Just as every type of research method is used for feminist goals, so too is every variation of that method.

Displaying the Interview

Interviewing allows interviewers to envision the person's experience and hear the multiple voices in a person's speech. In many studies, feminist researchers attempt to convey some of these phenomena in the report itself. Transcripts of the interviews, for example, familiarize readers with the people who were studied and enable the reader to ''hear'' what the researcher heard. Some feminist researchers take great pains to reproduce interviews as speech spoken by the interviewee rather than as answers to questions designed exclusively by the researcher. In sociologist Marianne Paget's transcripts, the speaker's meaning and multiple voices come through. The following excerpt from an interview with a female artist displays ''the inner turmoil of the self in solitary discordant discourse with its own voices'':

''I decided it was tiime that I ghot into the real worldn art ws the fake one,'' or ''its not productive n it n n I'm hh ah parasite to: society becuz I'm not contributing anything that can be uti*l*ized.'' Of course, these are not just her own voices. They are the voices of her family and friends, the voices of her peers, other women's voices, the voices of her countrymen and her man. She didn't just do this to herself. Though she says, ''*I* put myself thru that,'' she was trained.[91]

Psychologist Michelle Fine reproduced both her own speech and that of Altamese Thomas, the woman with whom she was talking, revealing great differences between them. These differences help us understand her growing awareness that she understood little about Altamese Thomas's ways of coping successfully with stress. Her answers were written as spoken, rather than rephrased as ''correct'' English.

At 2:00 a.m. one October morning, Altamese Thomas was led out of a police car, entered the hospital in pain, smelling of alcohol. Altamese had been drinking with some women friends in a poor, high crime, largely Black neighborhood in Philadelphia. . . . I was awakened, in the small office for volunteer rape counselors. . . . I spent the remainder of the evening and some of the morning with Altamese. . . . we held hands as she smarted through two painful injections to ward off infection; traveled through the hospital in search of X-rays for a leg that felt (but wasn't) broken; waited for the Sex Offender Officers to arrive; watched Altamese refuse to speak with them; and returned to the X-ray room for a repeat performance—and we talked. I introduced myself and explained my role. . . . Altamese did not want to . . . talk with . . . counselors.[92]

MICHELLE FINE: 3:00 Altamese, the police will be here to speak with you. Are you interested in prosecuting? Do you want to take these guys to court?

ALTAMESE THOMAS: No, I don't want to do nothin' but get over this. . . . When I'm pickin' the guy out of some line, who knows who's messin' around with my momma, or my baby. Anyway nobody would believe me.

According to Michelle Fine, this interview taught her "how persons of relatively low social power do assert control, and how easily a psychologist can misread these as efforts to give up."[93] Altamese asserts control by trying to return to her family as quickly as possible. The reader can better understand both the interviewer and the interviewee because of the way the interview is reproduced. In addition, Michelle Fine's inclusion of her own speech presents her as a human being, not a disembodied data-gatherer.

Marjorie DeVault has a similar attitude toward communicating honestly with interviewees and then reproducing their speech. She suggests we respect the intention behind women's words and learn to listen to phrases such as "you know" as a request for understanding.[94] If we do not understand, we must say so; if we do understand, we must say *what* we understand. She also suggests that we allow phenomena to have many different labels. Rather than giving phenomena conventional pigeonholes, we should pay attention to the particular descriptions women use. We should hear the richness of speech, and allow our writing to be similarly complex.

British psychologist Liz Kelly made it possible for the reader to "hear" the speech of the women she interviewed by using the following method:

Whilst transcribing the taped interviews on which this book is based I became aware of problems involved in transposing the spoken to the written word. Meaning in the spoken word is often conveyed through gesture, tone of voice and emotional expression. . . . In order to retain some of the meaning that is lost in transcription, I developed a method for coding tone of voice and emotional expression. . . . A dash (–) indicates a jump; the spoken word is seldom as coherent as the written. Three dots (. . .) indicate a passage of speech has been deleted. Six dots (. . . . . .) indicate a long pause. Italics indicate that the word or words were stressed. Emotional expression is recorded in brackets after the passage of speech it refers to: for example (angry), (ironic), (upset).[95]

Catherine Riessman believes it is important to identify interviewers in studies with multiple interviewers.

> In the identification codes, the letters N, C, and L indicate which interviewer conducted the interview. I decided not to ignore the context of production of each quotation . . . (N and C are women; L is a man); in a study of gender and divorce, it seemed inappropriate to act as if the gender of the interviewer were not important. This form of representation is not typical (it may even make some social scientist readers uncomfortable by implying that interviewers are not interchangeable). But . . . I [believe] it is more "objective" to take into account the dialectic between speaker and listener in analyzing speech.[96]

Clearly, feminist researchers interested in women's voices and the way people express themselves are experimenting with formats for putting those voices on paper, including their own.

Interviewing Husbands

Feminist researchers have also given methodological attention to marital couples. For example, sociologist Lillian Rubin wrote that involvement in the women's movement showed her the need to interview husbands and wives separately and privately because "women tend to discuss their feelings about their lives, their roles, and their marriages more freely when men are not present."[97] Judy Wajcman (discussed above) stressed the significance of interviewing husbands because of their importance to the women

> and to elucidate aspects of working-class experience common to both sexes. In exploring the dynamics of family life it is essential to hear "both sides of the story." It is customary for the woman's version to be neglected, but in redressing this imbalance I did not want to leave out of the account what the men had to say.[98]

She concurs with Lillian Rubin that separate interviews are preferable, although fruitful discussions can occur if both spouses are present. Interviewing husbands and wives separately has the disadvantage of obscuring how interaction occurs in the couple. The views the researcher hears expressed separately may rarely be expressed when the couple is together.

Sarah Fenstermaker Berk also conducted interviews separately for wives and husbands. Not expecting extensive cooperation from husbands, she gave them a single interview rather than two as in the case of wives:

> Because a larger proportion of husbands than wives were employed during the day, we sought an instrument that would accurately reflect the household activities of husbands without incurring the costs of administering a diary to a large sample of (perhaps uncooperative) husbands. The result was a card-sorting operation unique to the husbands' interview, requiring a retrospective accounting of domestic activities for two time periods in the previous 24 hours. . . . For each of the two time periods, husbands sorted a list of 81 household activities and indicated those activities that they had undertaken. . . . [R]espondents were [then]

> . . . asked to sort . . . cards in their order of accomplishment. . . . As a final
> task, husbands answered a set of questions on the back of each of the sorted
> cards: (1) how long each activity took; (2) whether TV, radio, or the like was
> "on" during the activity; and (3) what adjectives husbands would use to describe
> the activity (e.g., boring, pleasant, satisfying, or frustrating)—the same adjec-
> tives offered to wives for their diary activities.[99]

In my view, the reticence of Sarah Berk to make demands on husbands reflects a
general reluctance to study people of greater social status or power than the interviewer, a phenomenon known as "studying up."[100] When feminists engage in
research on men, upper-class people, and institutions with considerable power,
they are likely to demand less and self-disclose less because self-disclosure dimin-
ishes one's power.

Linking Feminist and
Mainstream Interview Research

Mary Belenky's study mentioned earlier, had the double purpose of putting women
on existing maps of intellectual and ethical development (e.g., as developed by
William Perry and Lawrence Kohlberg) while also assessing "the adequacy of the
maps themselves."[101] Linking feminist and mainstream ends in this way requires
complex interviewing. An example is psychologist Carol Gilligan's studies of
women's approaches to moral dilemmas reported in her book *In a Different Voice*
and widely applied to many fields.[102] I am aware of the fact that this study has
been criticized by other feminists for its small sample size and for its inconsistent
interpretation of the relation between gender and moral orientation.[103] My focus
here, however, is on how the interviews were conducted:

> The women were interviewed twice, first at the time they were making the deci-
> sion [about abortion], in the first trimester of a confirmed pregnancy, and then at
> the end of the following year. . . . In the initial part of the interview, the women
> were asked to discuss the decision they faced, how they were dealing with it, the
> alternatives they were considering, their reasons both for and against each option,
> the people involved, the conflicts entailed, and the ways in which making this
> decision affected their views of themselves and their relationships with others. In
> the second part of the interview, the women were asked to resolve three hypo-
> thetical moral dilemmas, including the Heinz dilemma from Kohlberg's research.

Despite her inclusion of *both* types of questions, Carol Gilligan emphasized the
questions that tapped women's experiences. She "asked how people defined moral
problems and what experiences they construed as moral conflicts in their lives,
rather than . . . focusing on their thinking about problems presented to them for
resolution." She saw no contradiction between asking preset questions and having
the interviewee take the lead: "The method of interviewing was to follow the
language and the logic of the person's thought, with the interviewer asking further
questions in order to clarify the meaning of a particular response." Her interview
snippets illustrate how she (or other interviewers) asked preset questions (how

would you describe yourself to yourself?), how she followed the language of the interviewee, and how the interviewee, in turn, followed the questions of the interviewer. In her text, she set off the interviewer's question with italics and brackets, as in the following example:

> *[Is there really some correct solution to moral problems, or is everybody's opinion equally right?]* No, I don't think . . . it is possible to choose in certain cases among different courses of action that obviously promote or harm that goal. *[Is there a time in the past when you would have thought about these things differently?]* Oh, yeah, I think that I went through a time when. . . . *[When was that?]* When I was in high school. . . . *[What led you to change, do you think?]* In a lot of ways this pregnancy has helped me because I have stopped getting high and stopped drinking, and this is the first time in three years that I stopped. And now that I have, I know that I can do it, and I am just going to completely stop. *[How did your pregnancy help you to do that?]* [104]

In the second part of the interview, she asked the women to respond to the standard hypothetical scenarios that had been used to study the moral development of males.[105] Thus, unlike some feminist researchers who initiate the interviews with standardized questions, Carol Gilligan concluded hers with such questions. Ultimately, these feminist researchers support the idea of combining both approaches in their work.

Large-Scale Feminist Interview Studies

When it is extremely important to the feminist researcher that her results be accepted as generalizable to a larger population, she is likely to construct a large-scale study with a carefully chosen sample[106] and to hire and train carefully chosen interviewers. Diana Russell's study of marital rape includes a highly informative methodology chapter that makes a strong case for using the most conventionally rigorous procedures possible when studying topics of concern to women, in order to maximize opportunities for creating change on women's behalf.

> I began my study with the hypothesis that the percentage of women in the population at large who have been raped is much higher than the percentages obtained in previous [unrepresentative] studies . . . and higher also than is commonly believed. . . . Assuming that my research would confirm this hypothesis, my primary objective was to establish the magnitude of the problem, both in terms of the number of occurrences of rape as well as the effects, in order to stimulate concern and provide a basis for demanding that the problem receive greater attention and that more efforts to resolve it be made. I also wanted to find out the relative frequencies of rape by strangers, acquaintances, friends, lovers, husbands, other relatives, and authority figures.

To obtain this sensitive information, she matched the demographic characteristics of interviewees and interviewers:

> After careful screening, thirty-three female interviewers were hired: seventeen white, six Asian, five Black and five Latina. They were carefully selected not

only for their interviewing skills, but also for their empathetic attitudes to rape victims. A serious attempt was made to hire interviewers from all class backgrounds, as well as all age groups. All were given approximately sixty-five hours of intensive, paid training, an amount extremely rare in survey research. Since a key hypothesis of our study was that with high quality interviewing by women who had been sensitized to the issue of sexual assault, we would find that rape and other kinds of sexual assault are prevalent, developing the best possible training therefore became a primary commitment. This training included at least ten hours of "consciousness raising" about rape and incestuous abuse, as well as a half day of defining and desensitizing sexual words so that interviewers would be as relaxed as possible with whatever vocabulary respondents might choose to use . . . An interviewer followed up the [initial] letter with a visit to the address.

In addition, Diana Russell carried out extensive verifications of the interview data and interviewer performance:

Twenty-two percent of the interviews were verified, which is an unusually high verification rate (about 10 percent is average). This means that the interviewer supervisors checked that the interviews had indeed happened in 22 percent of the 930 cases, and that they also checked the accuracy of two sample questions. All 22 percent of the respondents recalled the interview and said the interviewer had been polite. And there were very high correlations between the answers to both questions reported by the interviewer and then reported to the interviewer supervisor (these correlations were 0.91 and 0.99). All but twenty-two of these verifications were done by telephone, the remainder being done by postcard. At least half of the verified interviews were drawn at random. . . . Interviewers were . . . paid by the hour, not by the number of completed interviews. It was believed that the latter policy might motivate some interviewers to keep interviews as short as possible by discouraging disclosure, or worse, to fabricate interviews entirely.[107]

Similarly, Margaret Gordon and Stephanie Riger's study of the fear of rape interviewed 299 women and 68 men in Chicago, Philadelphia, and San Francisco "in respondents' homes by interviewers matched with them by race and language."[108] The interest among feminist researchers in studying diversified populations empathically has produced a methodological principle of training interviewers from a variety of ethnic and racial backgrounds. The matching of interviewers and interviewees is thought to maximize trust and candor. In the concluding chapter, I will discuss at greater length this emerging feminist "ethic of diversity."

Revising Concepts and Practices

Feminists researchers who have done interview studies have modified social science concepts and created important new ways of seeing the world. By listening to women speak, understanding women's membership in particular social systems, and establishing the distribution of phenomena accessible only through sensitive interviewing, feminist interview researchers have uncovered previously neglected or misunderstood worlds of experience. Rae Andre's interview study of the quality of homemakers' working lives, for example, uncovered the fact that previous surveys about "worker satisfaction" were extremely limited. Pauline Bart and Patricia O'Brien's interview study of women who avoided being raped challenged the view that rape is a clear-cut phenomenon.[109]

Given the versatility of interviewing and its compatibility with feminist concerns, we are likely to continue refining and elaborating this multiform method. As we proceed, we undoubtedly will discover further distinctions in feminist interview research disguised by the use of the generic word "interview." If feminist interview researchers carefully describe exactly what occurs during interviews and during the analysis process we are likely to discover additional methodological and ethical dilemmas that can be clarified and perhaps resolved. In my view, the emerging norm of self-reflexive reporting of the interview process and the experiments in exact reproduction of people's speech are steps in this direction.

3

Feminist Ethnography[1]

> Feminist fieldwork is predicated upon the active involvement of the researcher in the production of social knowledge through direct participation in and experience of the social realities she is seeking to understand. . . . however, feminist field researchers add [another dimension] which is not included as a part of conventional field methods . . . *the necessity of continuously and reflexively attending to the significance of gender* as a basic feature of all social life and . . . *understanding the social realities of women as actors* whom previous sociological research has rendered invisible.[2]

Introduction and Definitions

Contemporary ethnography or fieldwork is multimethod research. It usually includes observation, participation, archival analysis, and interviewing, thus combining the assets and weaknesses of each method.[3] It does not typically include testing or large-scale surveys, methods identified with a positivist perspective in the social sciences. In the early stages of feminism's recent entrance into the academy, feminist critics demonstrated that positivist methods skewed knowledge in an androcentric or male-oriented way. For this reason, they argued that "alternative"[4] or nonpositivist methods—particularly open-ended interviewing and ethnography[5]—must have a prominent place in feminist social science. These "alternative" methods focus on interpretation, rely on the researcher's immersion in social settings, and aim for intersubjective understanding between researchers and the person(s) studied.

Some feminist researchers continue to reject positivism as an aspect of patriarchal thinking that separates the scientist from the phenomenon under study.[6] They repudiate the idea of a social reality "out there" independent of the observer. Rather, they think that social research should be guided by a constructivist framework in which researchers acknowledge that they interpret and define reality.[7] In this context, feminist fieldwork has a special role in upholding a nonpositivist perspective, rebuilding the social sciences and producing new concepts concerning women.

Feminist fieldwork and "institutional ethnographies" can generate grounded concepts that will lead to new theories.[8] For example, Kristen Yount did fieldwork with women and men underground coal miners guided by the following framework and procedures:

46

My interest . . . was generated by my commitment to feminism, the pressing need to facilitate the entry of blue-collar women into higher-paying jobs numerically dominated by men, and the relative paucity of data in the literature on these women. . . . To conduct the study, I lived in mining communities in two western states for a total of 5 months. . . . I first contacted district union officials and mine managers. . . . I then dissociated myself from this strata and [contacted] miners at . . . bars, private parties, baseball games and company picnics. [I became] a temporary member of the miners' social worlds. . . . [In addition to] in-depth interviews with mine employees . . . I spent some 44 hours observing work procedures and interactions in mines. . . . [taped] six group discussions with miners [and] . . . persons associated with mining . . . and taped workshops . . . at four national conferences sponsored by . . . a national advocacy organization for women miners. I transcribed and coded all of these recordings throughout the data collection process and then used theoretical sampling procedures to formulate propositions.

Using this method, she discovered a culture of sexual harassment in the mines to which each woman adapted by taking one of three different roles (Lady, Flirt, and Tomboy). By observing the development of interaction *in situ,* she was able to take her analysis beyond the formulation of these specific roles. Instead, she demonstrated that sexual harassment is an effective "means by which men are able to . . . preserve more prestigious jobs as male domains."[9]

Judith DiIorio explained the importance of feminist fieldwork in reforming such subfields as the sociology of sport. She argued that most research "on gender-socialization in sport or gender differences in the social psychological effects of sports participation has employed an [inappropriate] positivistic methodology." By employing ethnography, on the other hand, we could " 'deconstruct' some of the patriarchal assumptions . . . and perhaps eliminate once and for all the term "role-conflict" from our research agenda." Most important to her, ethnographic research could enable us to "ascertain which girls and women engaging in what forms of physical activity under what conditions develop and affirm what identities through what processes."[10] Thus, for some feminists, fieldwork represents a struggle against positivism and androcentric concepts.

Others believe that it is misguided to link feminist critiques and ethnographic methods, or to put feminist research squarely in the qualitative, as opposed to the quantitative, "camp."[11] Psychologist Virginia O'Leary, for example, urges us *not* to link feminist research exclusively with qualitative methods. After endorsing the need for "alternative approaches," she writes:

[T]he current tendency to equate traditional modes of psychological inquiry with an exclusively masculine perspective and to replace it with the ethnological[12] approach as a feminine alternative . . . does little more than reify dichotomies that have proven inadequate.[13]

While arguing that fieldwork is important for correcting the patriarchal bias of social science, feminists generally have not claimed that fieldwork is *inherently feminist* or that qualitative methods such as fieldwork are the *only* research method that feminists should utilize. If this were so, disciplines such as cultural anthropology would have been successful in avoiding male bias.

One feminist who demonstrated that fieldwork in and of itself does not rectify the problem of male bias is Annette Weiner, an anthropologist who studied Trobriand Islanders. Male anthropologists who preceded her, such as Bronislaw Malinowski,[14] concluded that Trobriand women had little power. After studying these women's perceptions of their role, however, Annette Weiner concluded that Trobriand women *do* have power and that they "enact roles which are symbolically, structurally and functionally significant to the ordering" of their society. She then tried to understand why she and her male colleagues diverged and concluded that the source of the problem is male bias in cultural anthropology:

> We have accepted almost without question the nineteenth-century Western legacy that had effectively segregated women from positions of power. . . . We unquestioningly accept male statements about women as factual evidence for the way a society is structured. . . . From this view . . . we should not be surprised that we arrive at the almost universal notion that women's status is secondary to that of men. . . . Any study that does not include the role of women—as seen by women—as part of the way the society is structured remains only a partial study of that society.[15]

By virtue of their sex and ideological orientation, male ethnographers had been unable to understand women. The challenge for feminist ethnographers is to use the potential of fieldwork to get closer to women's realities. Ethnography is an important feminist method of it makes women's[16] *lives* visible, just as interviewing is an important feminist method if it makes women's *voices* audible.[17] Thus, it is not ethnography per se, as Annette Weiner showed, but ethnography in the hands of feminists that renders it feminist.

Historical Roots

Harriet Martineau

Harriet Martineau's *Society in America,* published in 1837, is an example of an early feminist ethnography. The introduction to her book explains that the researcher's duty is to give detailed observational data so that readers may judge her interpretations. Heeding her own rules, Martineau gave a full report including dates and the principal means she used to "obtain knowledge of the country":

> In the course of this tour, I visited almost every kind of institution. The prisons of Auburn, Philadelphia, and Nashville; the insane and other hospitals of almost every considerable place; the literary and scientific institutions; the factories of the north; the plantations of the south; the farms of the west. . . . I was present at orations, at land sales, and in the slave market. . . . It would be nearly impossible to relate whom I knew, during my travels. Nearly every eminent man in politics, science and literature, and almost every distinguished woman, would grace my list. . . . I travelled among several tribes of Indians; and spent months in the southern States, with negroes ever at my heels.

Martineau reports being told frequently that as a woman she was at a disadvantage in doing her study. To this she replied how helpful being a woman actually was, because

> she saw much more of domestic life than could possibly have been exhibited to
> any gentleman travelling through the country. The nursery, the boudoir, the kitchen,
> are all excellent schools in which to learn the morals and manners of a people;
> and, as for public and professional affairs,—those may always gain full infor-
> mation upon such matters, who really feel an interest in them,—be they men or
> women. . . . I doubt whether a single fact that I wished to learn, or any doctrine
> that I desired to comprehend, was ever kept from me because I was a woman.

Whether being a man or a woman is more advantageous in fieldwork is a question still debated today.

Because of her thoroughness, self-confidence, and sensitivity to women's lives, Harriet Martineau was able to produce a devastating appraisal of the role of women in American society:

> The Americans have, in the treatment of women, fallen below, not only their
> own democratic principles, but the practice of some parts of the Old World. . . .
> While woman's intellect is confined, her morals crushed, her health ruined, her
> weaknesses encouraged, and her strength punished, she is told that her lot is cast
> in the paradise of women: and there is no country in the world where there is so
> much boasting of the "chivalrous" treatment she enjoys.[18]

In my view, *Society in America* deserves to be studied as one of the earliest feminist ethnographies and as a profound contribution to the understanding of U.S. women's lives. Sixteen years earlier (1821) Frances (Fanny) Wright, another radical young British woman, published her ethnographic study of the United States, *View of Society and Manners in America, in a Series of Letters from That Country to a Friend in England, during the Years 1818, 1819, 1820,*[19] similarly criticizing the institutions of slavery and womanhood. These two books suggest that contemporary feminist ethnography is rooted in the travel literature of nineteenth-century radical British feminists.

Alice Fletcher

In 1881 Alice Fletcher got word from Susette La Flesche, an Omaha Indian woman, and Thomas Henry Tibbles, a Caucasian Nebraskan journalist, that she could camp with them for several weeks among the Sioux Indians and then continue her travels by herself. Alice Fletcher's biographer Joan Mark wrote that living "with Indians for scientific purposes, in order to study their way of life, was . . . new in the early 1880s" and had never been attempted by a woman. Joan Mark concluded that "to [Alice Fletcher and one or two others] we owe the whole notion of 'doing field-work,' that hallmark of twentieth century anthropology." Apparently, another woman, astronomer Maria Mitchell, worked closely with Alice Fletcher in the Association for the Advancement of Women and inspired her to undertake her scientific journey. Maria Mitchell believed that women should study "observational sciences like astronomy" and Alice Fletcher had the insight that "ethnography could be an observational science" because, like astronomy, ethnography utilized "long periods of looking (and listening) and meticulous recording of what one saw and heard." [20]

The place of women such as Harriet Martineau and Alice Fletcher in the history of ethnography is generally ignored or unknown. Instead, major reference works attribute the founding of ethnography to others such as Franz Boas and Bronislaw Malinowski. The *International Encyclopedia of the Social Sciences* has the following entry:

> The publication of Malinowski's *Argonauts of the Western Pacific* in 1922 revealed the great potentialities of field work. This study of Trobriand Islanders, among whom Malinowski had lived for almost three years, set new standards for fieldworkers which continue to operate. Fieldwork came to mean immersion in a tribal society—learning, as far as possible, to speak, think, see, feel and act as a member of its culture, and at the same time, as a trained anthropologist from a different culture. [21]

In my view, Alice Fletcher developed the dimensions of what has come to be known as anthropological fieldwork, just as Harriet Martineau did for sociological fieldwork.

Helen Merrell Lynd and Faith Williams

Originally, Helen Merrell Lynd was one of four staff members of her husband Robert Lynd's study of Middletown, a midwestern U.S. city. [22] The other three staff members were Faith Williams and Dorothea Davis, both statisticians, and Frances Flourney, a stenographer. When the group of five arrived in Muncie, Indiana, in 1924, they were unsure of their methodology. Helen Lynd later wrote:

> There was a question about how to divide the work. We wanted to do it more or less in the same way one would do an anthropological study of a strange community. So the work was divided into the areas of getting a living, making a home, the things that people do everywhere and how they did them here. Then there was a combination first of interviewing some of the key people, and of going through the press. I did a lot of work on the press and the records of various organizations. Bob went to the Rotary Club and to high school ceremonies. The interviewing of ordinary people came later. Faith Williams insisted, "We're getting generalities. We need to talk to individuals." It was one of the best things we did.

In her view, Faith Williams' idea of combining fieldwork with interviews enabled the study to move from generalities to specifics, from examining the community as a whole to examining the individual in the community. This combination allowed them to see people in contexts, and to understand women (and men) from their own perspectives.

Helen and Robert Lynd spent the years 1926–1929 writing, rewriting, and collating the data they had collected. In her autobiographical essay, Helen recalled:

At first it was his study. Then when it came to writing, it was decided that we were sharing the book. . . . A funny thing was that Bob used *Middletown* as his doctor's dissertation and in order that it be his doctor's dissertation we had to take the volume and go through it and blue pencil everything I had written. This was an absurdity because what we did as we actually wrote it was that we would each write a chapter and then we would exchange and rewrite. The one absolutely unbreakable rule was that no matter how silly either of us felt to be something that the other had written, it couldn't be thrown away. We had to consult. Well, we did go through the manuscript and cross out the things that were obviously mine, but it was a fake process.[23]

Later, Helen Lynd also earned her Ph.D., but her contribution to fieldwork theory may not be recognized.[24]

Contemporary Feminist Ethnography

Feminist ethnography is consistent with three goals mentioned frequently by feminist researchers: (1) to document the lives and activities of women, (2) to understand the experience of women from their own point of view, and (3) to conceptualize women's behavior as an expression of social contexts.[25] The next section illustrates each briefly.

Documenting Women's Lives and Activities

Sociologist Lyn Lofland voiced the importance of documenting women's activities in her critique of the androcentric tradition of community studies.[26] She claimed that, at best, women were simply "there" for participant observers because ethnographers had not seen how women played significant roles in the social settings of which they were part. A feminist orientation lifts these androcentric blinders, as Annette Weiner argued, and allows the participant observer to see women as full members of their social, economic, and political worlds. This vision was also the objective of Carol Stack[27] in her study of poor black women and of Denise Connors in her study of Irish, working-class women over the age of 90. To make these old women "real" to her, Connors supplemented interviews with involvement in their daily lives:

Whenever possible I spent time with them as they went about their daily routines. . . . In the process, I met and interacted with the families, friends, neighbors and acquaintances. We went shopping and out to eat together, we went on walks, to the bank, the library, the welfare department, drove by their old workplaces, visited their friends in their own homes and in nursing homes, and went on tours of local attractions.[28]

Similarly, in a study of a small, rural town with a population size of approximately 2700, Susan Stall examined the world of its women by doing interviews in the context of a larger ethnographic approach:

The town has Scandanavian cultural ties, Lutheran religious beliefs, and conservative Republican politics. . . . I have interviewed a diverse cross section of women: Women who serve on local volunteer boards, who are active in business clubs, who are involved in local political organizations, who work in local service organizations, who are members or officers of local women's clubs, who belong to church groups, or who participate in cultural activities in the town. One purpose of my study is to uncover the power of women within the volunteer structure of this small town.[29]

Similar to people who do interviews of various members of a social system, feminist ethnographers participate in the social system, put diverse groups of women on the social map, and then sometimes use interviews to understand the perspective of individual women.

Understanding Women from Their Perspective

Understanding the experience of women from their own point of view corrects a major bias of nonfeminist participant observation that trivializes females' activities and thoughts, or interprets them from the standpoint of the men in the society or of the male researcher. Georg Simmel (1858–1918) was one of the few early social scientists to recognize this problem.[30] As he put it, "Almost all discussions of women deal only with what they are in relation to men in terms of real, ideal or value criteria. Nobody asks what they are for themselves."[31] This problem is endemic in Western civilization and in the social sciences. The misogyny and gynopia[32] of a culture are mirrored in its social science.

By contrast, Canadian sociologist Dorothy Smith refers to research that asks "what women are for themselves" as research from "the standpoint of women." U.S. sociologist Irene Dabrowski's study of women workers is an example:

Working-class women appear to hold static jobs with little prestige, minimal pay, and no advancement potential. . . . I propose that women employed as clerks, waitresses, operatives, and the like, may experience paid work as positive and even growth-enhancing. A developmental framework for understanding their work combines an objective assessment of job movement with a subjective assessment of career path.[33]

In a related ethnography, Roberta Goldberg studied the process through which women workers come to experience and name their dissatisfaction as workers.[34] Her study challenges conventional discussion of "class consciousness" and suggests that it must be reformulated when referring to women. Her conclusion supports other feminist critiques of the concept of class, such as that of Christine Delphy,[35] who argues that assigning women the class of their husbands is demeaning, unreliable, and inaccurate. Women's class consciousness may in fact be a general "gendered consciousness" that transcends class, or may be a precarious class consciousness. Other feminist sociologists, such as those cited below, routinely refer to working-class, middle-class, or upper-class women without considering class assignment to be problematic.

One of the ways feminist ethnographers attempt to understand women's experience is to have women serve as key informants. Sociologist Judith Stacey's three-year study of two nonethnic Caucasian kinship networks in Silicon Valley during the period of postindustrialization is an example. Her "key informant in each network is a white woman now in her late forties who married in the 1950s and became a homemaker for a white man who was to benefit from the unusual electronics industry opportunities of the 1960s."[36] The relationships she developed with these women allowed her to observe the changes they experienced over time. In particular she explored the link between the woman's ideology and the quality of her marital relations, and the link between her daughter's and her own ideologies.

In another example, sociologist Carolyn Ellis's study of a mid-Atlantic fishing community relied on an 80-year-old primary informant and landlady with an unusual ability to discern social relations in the community.[37] Marjorie Shostak worked with a female key informant, Nisa, in her study of !Kung society.[38] Similarly, Carol Stack came "to know a young woman who had grown up on welfare in The Flats," had entered the university where Carol Stack taught, and who introduced her to two families. These people, in turn, led Carol Stack to two women and a man who became her "part-time and casual assistants"[39] and enabled her to understand the socioeconomic system that these women managed.

Understanding Women in Context

Feminist ethnographers try to interpret women's behavior as shaped by social context rather than as context free or rooted in anatomy, personality, or social class. Another excerpt from Irene Dabrowski's study of working-class women illustrates the importance of context. Specifically, she uncovered types of female working-class workers, each with its own marital relation:

> The cooperative attitude of the "continuous workers' " husbands became obvious to me during the interviews. These men were polite and seemed to understand and respect their wives' need for privacy with me. In fact, as I was speaking with their wives, these men nonchalantly diverted themselves to household and child care responsibilities . . . washing dishes and helping children with their homework.
>
> In contrast, the husbands of the "housewives" were less open to my presence and even hostile in some instances. After interviewing a few of the housewives, I could expect to be snubbed by their husbands. Husbands insisted their wives hurry to finish, and even demanded meals. To avoid such encounters, I made an effort to schedule interviews when the husbands were absent from the home. Some housewives themselves made such a suggestion. For instance, "I really can't talk when my husband is here. It would be best to come Wednesday night. He is out bowling."[40]

Faye Ginsburg's ethnography of pro-life and pro-choice activities surrounding an abortion clinic in Fargo, North Dakota, also revealed the importance of social context.[41] Participant observation enabled her to see the commonality of the two groups beneath their polarized ideologies. She understood that their common purpose was to support other women in the context of values that permeate the city. As an ethnographer, she experienced the sense of community she observed.[42]

Although feminist fieldworkers seem to prefer studying women, they sometimes interview and observe both sexes for the purposes of examining how behavior is patterned by gender. For example, in their studies of families and food, sociologists Nickie Charles and Marion Kerr reported that men in two-parent families consumed larger portions of meat and ate meat more often than did women and children. The researchers interpreted this behavior as a reflection of the men's breadwinner status.[43] In an observational study of women and men in TV panel discussions, sociologist Jessie Bernard found that "males out-talked females by a considerable margin . . . [and that] women have a harder time getting the floor in groups and are more often interrupted than men."[44] Her study is an example of feminist observational research in a mixed-gender setting.

A Typology of Settings

Lois Easterday and her colleagues developed a typology to conceptualize the range of field settings. She used the variables traditional/nontraditional (in terms of culture) and heterogeneous/homogeneous (in terms of demography). This typology allows us to see that canonized sociological ethnographies such as William Foote Whyte's *Street Corner Society,*[45] Elliot Liebow's *Tally's Corner,*[46] and Laud Humphrey's *Tearoom Trade*[47] represent only three types of settings: primarily male, traditional male–female, and nontraditional male–female.[48] Moreover, these studies are male oriented in three ways: they were carried out by male researchers in male-dominated settings and focused on male behavior.[49] John Van Maanen commented on this male orientation as well. After pointing out some exceptions, he concluded that "most ethnographic writing was created by male fieldworkers concerned mostly with the comings and goings of male natives. . . . One result of the growth of feminist scholarship is the realization that there are many tales of the field to be told."[50] Arlene Kaplan Daniels is one of the few ethnographers who discussed the effect of studying settings with different gender compositions, specifically a male-dominated military group and the exclusively female Junior League.[51]

Ironically, although the classic ethnographies were done in a limited range of settings, their methods are considered generic for all types of settings. Sociologist Joan Gurney wrote an important critique of these guidelines for feminists who conduct studies in gender-heterogeneous settings:

> a frequent suggestion is that the beginning fieldworker adopt a passive, submissive, nonexpert, incompetent, nonthreatening or nonassertive role vis à vis settings members. . . . Once accepted and trusted by setting members, the researcher is advised to discard the naive incompetent role in favor of the competent, somewhat knowledgeable, professional role. . . . Failure to accomplish this transition can preclude observation of anything setting members consider too complex for the naive observer to understand, even with their expert assistance.
>
> While stereotypical attitudes toward females generally assure their acceptance in the naive incompetent role in a male-dominated setting . . . , those same attitudes hamper females' efforts to make the transition to the professional role. Female researchers must work especially hard to achieve an impression combin-

ing the attribute of being nonthreatening with that of being a credible, competent professional. By failing to acknowledge this problem, the fieldwork instructional literature does not offer realistic guidance to novice female researchers.[52]

Realistic guidance can come, instead, from accounts written by feminist ethnographers in the whole gamut of settings.

Building on Lois Easterday's typology and Joan Gurney's example, we can now extend Judith DiIorio's definition of feminist fieldwork with which this chapter started. Feminist ethnography is research carried out by feminists who focus on gender issues in female-homogeneous traditional or nontraditional settings, and in heterogeneous traditional and nontraditional settings. In feminist ethnography, the researchers are women, the field sites are sometimes women's settings, and the key informants are typically women.

An example of a feminist ethnography is sociologist Sheryl Ruzek's study of workplaces in the women's health movement. This project compares 19 feminist settings with 5 nonfeminist settings. To understand the women's health movement, Sheryl Ruzek did more than study these settings, however. Rather, she attended many public events such as

> university lectures on women's health issues, abortion rallies, self-help gynecology demonstrations, women's health films, health fairs, and conferences. At these events, [she] learned of health projects, chatted informally with health activists, and made contacts for interviews and additional fieldwork. [She] also participated in, obtained printed material from, and/or interviewed members of major feminist organizations involved in health work. . . . Similar information was gathered from non-feminist organizations . . . that provided obstetrical and gynecological services.

In her view of feminist ethnography, the boundary between her life and her field site disappeared. Feminist ethnography meant going to bookstores in the course of her regular travels, enlisting her friends to send her materials they found, and subscribing to a wide range of periodicals.[53] Because every field setting can be thought of as immersed in a larger social context, which itself is imbedded in a larger social system, field settings can be amorphous. It is easy to understand how a feminist ethnographer can take information in from everywhere, at all times, for her project. Although this attitude may be true of all ethnographers, it is significant for feminists who seek an understanding of the links between the micro- and macrosystems of gender politics.

Women-Only Field Sites

Certain field sites are particularly accessible to female ethnographers that are either inaccessible or uninteresting to male ethnographers. By virtue of being a woman, for example, Laurie McDade had access to women's everyday experiences in college residences. She defined these places as "female households" and noted the abundance of "symbolic markers that the female students" use to signify "physical and social maturities." These markers were consumer products such as sanitary napkins, bras, deodorants, make-up, and other "hygiene and beauty aides."[54]

Feminist ethnography includes the study of women's private domains, work-places, and organizations. Indian scholar Ursula Sharma, for example, conducted

> a theoretically rich ethnography of women's work and urban life in Shimla, North India. Her objective . . . was to explore the nature of women's household work in a modern Indian city and show how it contributes to the maintenance, and sometimes mobility, of the household. To accomplish this, she combined partic-ipant observation with interviews of 72 women in different income groups . . . between the ages of 20 and 55, who had one or more children, and who had at least one child still living at home.[55]

Although the household itself was sex-integrated, Ursula Sharma studied it as a women's work setting. It would be very useful for further development of the methodology of feminist ethnography to have additional studies of female-only settings. One promising development is the ethnography of lesbian life.[56]

Mixed-Gender Field Sites

Cathleen Burnett and Mona Danner's examination of 300 deviance and criminol-ogy field research studies published between 1960 and 1985 found that female researchers study mixed groups (56%) much more than they do female-only (25%) or male-only (19%) settings, while male researchers tend to study male-only groups (56.6%) rather than mixed (36.6%) or female-only groups (6.6%).[57] Feminist eth-nographies of mixed-gender settings are similarly plentiful. An early example is Gloria Steinem's covert participant observation study of a Playboy Club.[58] Al-though a very brief investigation, her study succeeded in exposing women's com-plicity, underpayment, and harassment in this line of employment.

A prize-winning large-scale feminist ethnography of female workers in a mixed-gender setting is Rosabeth Moss Kanter's study of the role of women and men in corporations. She chose her method because of a debate within feminism concern-ing women's relative lack of success in corporations. Macroscopic explanations relied on "global variables such as general rates of work force participation by time period and social class," while microscopic explanations referred to "the psychology of women." Her participant observation study, by contrast, tapped a "third, intermediate level" of "forms of work organization and conceptions of roles and distributions of people within them."

Rosabeth Kanter designed her study to demonstrate how organizations affect women. At the same time, she was interested in finding ways to promote equal opportunities for women in organizations. Her methodological "Appendix" lists 10 different "sources of information" she used, including open-ended interview-ing of people in sales, a mail survey, individual and group interviews with the first 20 women to enter the sales force, analysis of preexisting survey data, a content analysis of performance appraisal forms, interviews with secretaries and bosses, group discussions recorded verbatim, participant observation in meetings, training programs, official events, and informal interaction at social events. In addition, over the years she developed close working relationships with a small group of people. In the classic style of participant observers, she writes that

I tended to record everything I could that occurred in my presence. . . . I found even time waiting outside of people's offices valuable. Time designated as "social" in which I engaged in informal discussions with people was perhaps the most valuable of all.[59]

The detail and range of these methods enabled her to demonstrate the corporation's unacknowledged dependence on female labor.

Some have suggested that women have an easier time than men as ethnographers in mixed-gender settings. For example, David Riesman wrote that Laura Bohanan's

Return to Laughter . . . illustrates . . . the advantages women can sometimes have in field work because they have access to all the private worlds of women as a member of their sex, and they are also able to penetrate such male worlds as magic and statecraft by virtue of their occupational role and the kind of assertiveness it allows them.[60]

U.S. anthropologist Hortense Powdermaker wrote that a female anthropologist's advantage over her male colleague stems from the fact that "No one fears her."[61] Anthropologist Laura Nader tentatively agreed, writing "that it is easier for women to achieve good rapport—at least working in Mexico or Lebanon." People living in societies characterized by highly differentiated sex roles may perceive a female anthropologist as a biological female and a cultural male. The cultural male status stems from being educated, living alone, and initiating conversation and questions. In this regard, the "foreign female researcher" is more akin to the native male than to the native female. This was Laura Nader's experience:

I was respected as a woman somehow different from their women. Consequently I had access to both men's and women's culture. No man, even if he was considered different from the local men, would have had access to women's culture equal to mine to the men's culture. Of course it may be said that personality makes for considerable variation; but I would still support the common hypothesis that women anthropologists, if they want it, have access to a wider range within a culture than men.[62]

An example from Laura Bohanan's account, however, shows how complex this androgynous role can be for the female field researcher. As neither a male nor a female, she was dangerously close to being a demon. Her asexual role paradoxically simultaneously distanced her from men and women, while giving her access to both.

There are many sights forbidden to women, but only to protect the women from powers they are not strong enough to withstand. As a European, I was considered probably immune to many of these influences; my continued survival confirmed their opinion. Only some of the women interpreted my hardihood as a sign of more occult powers; they thought I might possibly be a witch. But today even the men looked curiously at me as I stood by the side of the open grave and watched them lower Amara's body into it.[63]

The passage suggests to me that if the female researcher role is asexual, she is considered nonhuman.

Sociologist Barrie Thorne has also written about fieldwork relations in a mixed-sex field site, in this case, the Boston Draft Resisters Group.

> The Resistance had a sexual division of labor which placed women in a subordinate and derivative position. . . . Exempted from conscription, women did not personally confront choices about the draft, and they were, at least initially, exempted from some of the pressures toward risk-taking that were directed at men. If I had been a male participant observer, especially in the N.E.R., I would have been under continual pressure to turn in my draft card and risk jail. As a woman, I entered with relative distance and immunity from risk.[64]

Being a woman enabled her to retain her research role while uncovering gender-based inequality in the organization.

Negotiating Gender in the Fieldwork Setting

Feminists conducting field research in mixed-gender settings are vulnerable to a special set of obstacles. Fortunately, much feminist ethnographic writing includes a frank, reflexive discussion of these problems, particularly sexual harassment, physical danger, and sex stereotyping. In a society that is ageist, sexist, and heterosexist, the researcher who is female and young may be defined as a sex object to be seduced by heterosexual males. For example, in a study of homeless people in Boston, the researcher reports that she converted her project into a team study so as to reduce the possibility of rape.[65] Another researcher reports that "a few male interviewees asked for dates . . . and . . . one threatened me when I refused."[66]

Furthermore, both the men and the women in the field site may conspire unwittingly to put the female observer in the role of a daughter to be protected,[67] a non-sex-object-non-daughter female to be ignored, a nurse/mother who will care for them, a lesbian of limited interest to men, a teacher, or some other conventional stereotype.[68] The fieldworker then must decide if she is willing to "go along" in order to "stay in the field" or if she can find some other way to maintain her study without collaborating in these roles.

Female fieldworkers have handled sexual harassment in two classic ways: forgoing the right to continue their work (i.e., "making the choice" to leave),[69] and/or engaging in "interactional shitwork."[70] I call the latter another form of field"work." Joy Browne described interactional shitwork in her study of used car salesmen:

> [T]hat used car lots have little shacks which can cozily accommodate a salesman (nearly all are men, and all those I encountered were men) and a researcher (who happened to be a woman) created a methodological problem. I had to develop a method of convincing a sometimes overeager informant that I did not want to be *that* kind of participant. (The solution, as is often the case, was to leave the field for a while and let things cool off naturally rather than face a showdown and lose an informant.)[71]

Anthropologist Peggy Golde engaged in interactional shitwork to keep her suitors at bay and to convert their sexual interest into a research asset:

A man or boy might come to my house to ask for medicine or to have a letter typed, and we would chat. When he called a second and third time without an ostensible purpose, I sensed what might eventually happen [i.e. I would receive a marriage proposal], but nonetheless I took advantage of his presence and willingness to talk until the moment when the covert would be made overt and I would have to reject any proposals. . . . I came to have no serious compunctions about playing the innocent or prolonging the game, since there was no deep feeling involved and since they were, in effect, trying to exploit me too.[72]

When she studied auctions, on the other hand, sociologist Mary Jo Deegan could not tolerate the sexism of certain auctioneers. She decided to avoid particular auctions even though it meant altering her sample.[73]

Other feminist ethnographers may decide to not reject the harasser completely to avoid losing him as an informant or provoking him to redouble his effort. At the same time, female researchers usually avoid any expression of their own sexual interest, should it exist. Sometimes feminist researchers are so committed to their "job" that they cannot bear to acknowledge being harassed. Sociologist Joan Neff Gurney provides an example:

During my field research I overlooked incidents which my colleagues regarded as sexist. I explained away my problems and believed they were related to something else, such as my youth. This oversight was not due, I believe, to an inability to recognize sexist statements or treatment. In other settings and contexts I am quick to recognize such biases and discrimination. However, the thought that my work as a researcher had been compromised by my gender was so discomforting that I persisted in denying this fact for many months after leaving the field. It was only after carefully examining the negative treatment accorded other women in the organization that I was able to recognize that I was being treated the same way. . . . Extensive self-reflection and debriefing with colleagues were required before I was able to acknowledge that my informants were not as kind as I had thought.[74]

Reflexive accounts of feminist participant observation research include tales in which the researcher was unable to control her relationships in the field. To me this suggests that general methodological writings about participant observation have an unwarranted (male-oriented?) assumption that the researcher can control his/her stance. It also highlights the common attitude among patriarchal scientists, including natural scientists, that one does not talk about problems or failures and only reports "positive" research results.

Since women are relatively powerless vis-à-vis men and are at greater physical risk if attacked, female researchers are less able than men to control the way others interact with them. Many of the classic ethnographies simply could not have been done by women because of physical danger. Perhaps the unconscious avoidance of danger led some female anthropologists such as Margaret Mead to the study of adolescents and children who are even less powerful than they.[75] Judith A. DiIorio, a sociologist who studied a leisure club called "Vanners,"[76] highlights the fact that since the fieldworker usually works alone, she typically lacks the emotional support necessary to challenge the way she is treated. If she lacks the physical strength to ensure her own safety as well, the female researcher must find ways of adapting that men do not have to learn.

In some settings women fear that a female researcher might "take away their man." In these cases, the researcher finds that as her closeness to men increases, so does her distance from "their women." Under these circumstances, research relationships are fraught with potential intrigue, suspicion, and danger.[77] In projects where the community studied consists of lesbians or gay men, the dynamics of jealousy may be similar.

Female researchers may find that their very presence threatens anyone who believes that the [hetero]sexual balance should not be tipped. These researchers will be confined, or confine themselves, to the world of their own gender. Anthropologist Nancy Scheper-Hughes describes the way Irish peasant men kept her in her place, that is, in the world of women:

> In one rather trying experience, a local shepherd made belligerent by alcohol and losses at the local sheep market announced to all and sundry that he had been told by some Dubliners that "the anthropologist" was only interested in the villagers' sex practices and that I would write a book which could convert "people into numbers," and that I would ultimately degrade the Irish way of life. . . . As it became increasingly apparent that I was concentrating on mothers, children, and adolescents, the village seemed to relax somewhat.[78]

Sociologist Arlene Kaplan Daniels describes how military men demanded extensive deference and "feminine" behavior from her before they would cooperate:

> The military officers resented the introduction of a sociologist, a civilian and a female into their midst. . . . In the view of the liaison chief and his officers, my attitude was overbearing, demanding, and all too aggressive. . . . the behavior these officers found most difficult to tolerate was my assumption that I was the director in the situation. . . . Interpersonal problems with the officers were exacerbated at each contact by my initial obtuseness about and resistance to the demeanor they thought I should exhibit. My manner tended toward the brisk, businesslike, and friendly. I usually entered offices quickly and in an assured manner. I looked each officer directly in the eye, presented my hand for a firm grasp, and proceeded to an agenda for the meeting which I had drawn up and distributed in advance. I never hesitated to interrupt, contradict, or control the conversation, pulling it back to the agenda when necessary. If any jokes or pleasantries were introduced, I initiated them.

Arlene Daniels' behavior reflected her identity as a feminist and professional researcher. The officers, however, wanted her to behave differently.

> Two main lines of opposition in response to my demeanor developed. One line took the form . . . of "passive aggressive" behavior. . . . The other main line of opposition was to respond in frankly seductive fashion. . . . I interpreted both sulky and seductive responses as expressions of hostility and resentment against a woman exhibiting inappropriate behavior to a man.

To gain their cooperation, she did her share of "interactional shitwork":

> I developed mediating and soothing strategies. . . . I learned the necessity for changing my tone. And, once I was in the field, I abandoned my picture of

myself as the director of a research project and returned to the role of student and humble observer. . . . What I began to learn was that certain kinds of deference to the idea of superior male status had to be paid. Certain behavior was considered inappropriate or even insulting from women: a firm hand clasp, a direct eye-to-eye confrontation, a brisk, businesslike air, an assured manner of joking or kidding with equals were all antagonizing. Most galling of all was my naive assumption that, of course, I was equal. It was important to wait until equality was given me. When I learned to smile sweetly, keep my eyes cast down, ask helplessly for favors, and exhibit explicitly feminine mannerisms, my ability to work harmoniously and efficiently increased.[79]

Issues of deference and access are acute when feminist ethnographers study women who are newcomers in a primarily male setting, as in Susan Martin's study of female police. To enter the setting and understand the experience of new female recruits, or "rookie cops," she took on the role of a patrol officer in a Washington, D.C. district in which 30 of the 400 officers were female.[80] Susan Martin's description of her participant observation techniques, including use of material gained in the women's lockerroom, demonstrates a commitment to thoroughness. She was barred by her gender from gaining material in the men's lockerroom, and thus her understanding of male perceptions of female police officers rested on interviewing. Regardless of her research intentions, being a woman made it possible to do certain things and not others.

Sociologist Nancy Shaw wrote that being a woman undercut her desired role as a nonparticipating observer in delivery rooms.

On my first day on the delivery floor, I found myself running errands and giving simple nursing care to patients I was near. I was never able to abandon this role, and was encouraged in it by subtle staff pressure and my own feeling that I had no right to stand by while another suffered in front of me, or to write while someone else was doing a job that needed two people.[81]

Although Nancy Shaw expresses a lot of ambivalence about her helpfulness, the practice of making themselves useful to others is a theme of many feminist ethnographic accounts. Being involved in the setting where work is done leads many such ethnographers to help out. Just as the desire to be helpful appeared in many discussions of feminist interviewing, so too it characterizes much feminist ethnography.

A final example of negotiating gender in fieldwork settings comes from Pamela Dorn, who traveled from the United States to Turkey to study ethnomusicology. She soon learned that there were two significant social classes in the community she was studying (nouveau riche and elite), and that her status as a "nice, middle-aged, unmarried 'girl' " would give her the label "promiscuous" among the nouveau riche if she interviewed men. They would see her research as a pretext covering her immoral intentions. In the excerpt below she refers to herself as "the researcher" or "the anthropologist":

The nouveau riche segment of the society, while being outwardly Western . . . in cultural style, had yet retained very Ottoman . . . ideas about women, e.g., women belong at home and they are held accountable for their activities at all times. Since the nouveau riche segment of the community had decided that the researcher was really in Istanbul to find a husband (unlike the elites who knew better and had some idea about what ethnology entails), the researcher's appointments were viewed as capricious and inappropriate behavior. These nouveau riche families immediately began making arrangements for proper introductions to eligible young men and supplied "cousins," a mixed group of young people (male and female) for the researcher to socialize with. Thus, the first task of the researcher in the field was to better understand perceptions of women's gender role and, in general, constructions of appropriate behavior for her own age and gender designation.[82]

She was compelled to study norms concerning men's and women's behavior, although this had not been her plan.[83] Pamela Dorn converted this communal push into an asset. She decided to do a study of gendered proverbs and the construction of "personhood."

Heterosexual couples who do field research together are likely to divide their roles, or have them divided, in line with the sex-role division in the community studied. Anthropologist Hans Buechler's statement is typical:

> (My wife)[84] was studying child-rearing patterns and market relations. Her position in the community differed from my own because her informants were primarily women and children, while mine were for the most part men. . . . As a man I had not been able to talk to many women; in fact the female view of society was practically closed to me, except for relatives, Aymara men do not interact with women frequently.

He also explains that this community's particular culture also placed obstacles before his wife:

> Women attend community meetings only when the male household head is absent, and it is imperative for the household to be represented at the meeting, or when a complaint is lodged against them; and they do not hold separate meetings. Therefore, it was impossible for my wife to explain the nature of her study to the women as a group.[85]

In other words, women in the field are forced to deal with issues of gender in ways that are not always consistent with their own values. Although it is possible that there is more awareness nowadays of women's rights to engage in nondeferential behavior, feminist ethnographers must always be prepared to deal with the intersection of their behavior and the gender ideology of the setting they are studying.

I draw two conclusions from this material. First, women ethnographers have difficulty escaping the study of gender no matter what their research agenda. Second, generalizations about the relative advantage of women or of men in fieldwork settings are useless. Societies differ in their receptivity to and treatment of female researchers. While in some it may be advantageous to be a female, in others it is clearly problematic, and it can even be both in any society.

Being Consigned to the Role of Daughter

In numerous cases female researchers face problems that male researchers typically do not face. One example is placement in the role of daughter, particularly if they are alone in the field and are young, and if the field consists of families or older people. The daughter role can be as problematic as the sex object role. Ironically, the more successful the feminist researcher is in gaining access to a family-oriented community, the more likely she will be seen as a daughter and the more difficult for her to muster a rationale eschewing this role. Furthermore, the role of daughter may be attractive, comforting, and useful if it is consonant with her emotional needs and research interests.[86] This was the case for Jean Briggs in her study of an Eskimo group[87] as well as for Marjorie Shostak who wrote: "With older women, I went further, presenting myself as a child in need of help in preparing for what life might yet have to offer."[88]

For anthropologist Barbara Myerhoff, perception as a daughter in a setting of elderly Jews meant inculcation with guilt:

> Many of the Center people continued to "make" me feel guilty. After greeting me warmly, Basha would often ask, "Never mind these other things you all the time ask about. Tell me, who's with your children?". . . . When I was away too long, they scolded and snubbed me . . . at times their resentment spilled over. My presence was a continual reminder of many painful facts: that it should have been their own children there listening to their stories; that I had combined family and a career, opportunities that the women had longed for and never been allowed. And too, that I knew so little of their background suggested to them that they had failed to transmit to future generations any but fragments of their cherished past. . . . Diffuse and even irrational guilt plagued me until I had to laugh at myself. I had become a tasteless ethnic joke, paralyzed by Jewish guilt: about my relative youth and strength, about having a future where they did not, about my ability to come and go as I chose while they had to await my visits and my convenience, when I relished food that I knew they could not digest, when I slept soundly through the night warmed by my husband's body, knowing the old people were sleeping alone in cold rooms. . . . I considered quitting.[89]

The role of daughter may threaten the fragile identity the female researcher tries to construct as a competent adult researcher. As a result, her identity may begin to dissolve, as anthropologist Dorinne Kondo described:

> As an American researcher, I had been taught to act: independence, mastery, competence, were deemed key virtues. As a Japanese daughter, independence and mastery of one's own fate were out of the question: rather, being a daughter meant duties, responsibilities and interdependence. The more I adjusted to my Japanese daughter's role, the keener the conflict became. In exchange for the care the family accorded me, I was glad to help around the house in any way I could: cleaning, some laundry, cooking for the head of household when his wife was away at meetings of the many volunteer organizations in which she participated. It was this last task, however, that produced profound conflicts for me as an American woman. The cooking in and of itself did not offend me. . . . But the etiquette surrounding the serving of food—e.g., that the head of the household is always served first and receives the finest delicacies; that men ask for a second helping of rice by merely holding out the bowl to the woman nearest the rice cooker, perhaps uttering a grunt of thanks—was irritating to me. I carried out my duties uncomplainingly, in what I hope was reasonable good humor. But I was none too happy about these things "inside." Moreover, I began to chafe under

certain restrictions on my movement, such as having to come home at a certain hour. These are perfectly understandable, given the responsibility the family had for the welfare of their female guest, and I abided by their regulations. But I was still exquisitely sensitive to the constraints of my position, and I felt keenly the deconstruction of the self into various constituents at war with one another.[90]

As with the sex object role, female researchers sometimes retain people's cooperation by enacting a daughter-like role. The critical issue here is not the particular role the researcher is compelled to adopt, but whether she is able to negotiate the role after she adopts it. Barbara Myerhoff, for example, gradually understood that she was volunteering for guilt. This recognition enabled her to "reenter" the setting with a new role and identity.

Racially Heterogeneous Research

Discussions of feminist methodology must take into account the fact that in many societies, sex role differentiation is supplemented by deep racial divisions. In such societies, the female researcher is likely to have access to men and women of her race and to women of other races, but to be discouraged from solitary interaction with men not of her racial group. Abiding by these norms reinforces these divisions. If she does not cooperate, she may be stigmatized and have access reduced to people of her own race. U.S. sociologist Patricia Remmington acknowledged this issue in her study of a police department:

> Since the researcher is a white female, this study is based more on the white segment of the Atlanta Police Department than on the whole force. . . . the researcher rode with almost every white male, white female or black female. However, few black males were interviewed or observed. The prevailing ethos largely precluded a white female—be she officer or observer—from being a partner of a black male. At the time of the study, the Commissioner of Police was black and according to white officers had followed a course of reverse discrimination in hiring and promoting policies. Deep racial tension in the force was expressed daily in comments made to the researcher and in informal racial segregation at roll calls, dinner stops, encounters between officers, and social activities.[91]

As a black woman, Laura Fishman was careful to develop credibility in her study of white women whose male partners were incarcerated.[92] And Carol Stack, a white woman, discussed at length the special dynamics of her attempt to study a poor black community.[93] In both cases, being a woman seemed to create a bridge with women of a different race. Feminist consciousness typically makes researchers sensitive to gendered behavior, racism, cultural misogyny, and coping behaviors.[94] The ability to understand a setting, however, is linked to the researcher's own ways of dealing with these issues. The most favorable scenario is one in which she can create a role that balances safety, self-respect, and the ability to do her work.

Dilemmas of Feminist Ethnography

Despite its rich historical roots, feminist ethnography is burdened with many controversies and dilemmas. I have labeled these the problem of trust, the closeness/distance dilemma, and the dilemma of the complete observer and complete participant roles.

The Problem of Trust

Even though feminists try to study women from the standpoint of women and generally have access to women's settings, the women they study do not always trust them. Feminists' access to women is potentially as problematic as men's access has been to men,[95] particularly when there are differences of social class, race, ethnicity, or sexual preference. This is a dilemma for these researchers as feminists and as ethnographers. Sociologist Ruth Horowitz's study of Chicano gangs provides an illustration:

> One evening I was sitting with two young women in the bedroom of one of them and asking a series of very pointed questions about school, who was friendly with whom, whether friendship networks in the school and street overlapped, and whether they ever had been friends with any of the more street-oriented youths. They both jumped on me, saying that I was just a researcher and not there because I liked them. One of them ran out of the house crying that she never wanted to see me again. I had a long talk about fieldwork with the other young woman, who was equally hurt but willing to listen. . . . It took me more than two weeks to rebuild an understanding with the second young woman, but she remained wary of our relationship for a long time afterward. I felt uncomfortable and worried also.[96]

This excerpt suggests that a bond of sisterhood must be earned. Differences exist in socioeconomic status, life-style, sexual identity, marital status, and more, and must be overcome to gain access to the views of a diverse range of women.

A relationship between women is not necessarily one of intersubjective agreement or even understanding. If a feminist is unable to earn the trust of the women she is studying, she potentially suffers a sense of failure both as a researcher and as a feminist. Lois Easterday and her colleagues report that in their study of "parent groups composed primarily of poor, divorced women in their twenties and thirties," the researcher was challenged—" 'How can you [single, childless] understand what it's like for us?' "[97]

Feminist researchers are sometimes forthright in questioning the degree to which a female researcher can understand women of a class different from her own. For example, in her study of a high school clerical preparation class, Linda Valli wrote:

> Although I am convinced that the culture of femininity the students produced functioned to bind them to subordinate and inferior societal roles, I am not clear about whether this culture was perceived by them as inferior to masculine culture

or just different from it. Because I so strongly perceived traditional feminine culture as working against women, I . . . failed to systematically explore the consciousness with which the students produced that culture.[98]

She admits not understanding the women because she did not want to deal with the fact that their view of the world was different from her own. This confession brings to mind Margaret Andersen's interview-based study of wealthy women (discussed in the previous chapter), who resented her interpretation of them as suffering from false consciousness.

The problem of "false consciousness" pervades feminist ethnography of non-feminist groups. Sherryl Kleinman encountered this problem studying a counter-cultural setting:

> I was disappointed that the women seemed unaware of their subordinate position in the organization. Could they not see through the veneer of equality that the hugs and friendly relations provided? . . . I felt that because of their identification with the counterculture they should see things the way I did. This reflected my own view of feminism at the time—women could and should achieve like men and they are responsible for advancing themselves.

Recognizing that she had no empathy for the women, she began to look at her own history:

> As a woman who had just left graduate school and who needed to believe in the meritocracy while on the job market, it is understandable that I held this view. What kind of sociological story was I writing, then? The men have the power, the women have false consciousness . . . , and the status quo continues. But, I was also bothered by my lack of empathy, angry at myself for being angry at them. I had the sense that something was wrong, but put those uncomfortable feelings aside. Instead, I kept collecting data.
>
> Only when I did in-depth interviews and also found my own view of feminism changing, did I develop empathy for the women. I began to see that they valued the organization as a community rather than as an instrumental place of work and that they did not join the organization for money. Rather, they wanted to feel they were participating in a good cause while developing loving relationships. This change in my feelings toward the women coincided with changes in feminist theory, spawned in part by Carol Gilligan's work (1982) on differences in moral reasoning between men and women. . . . I began to question the sociologist's taken-for-granted concept of inequality. If the women largely wanted feelings of connection in the organization—and got them—and the men largely wanted a place to practice their trade—and did so—then could one speak of inequality, or was the situation fair?
>
> I tried to live with the "different but equal" story, but my gut reaction told me this was wrong. . . . I think it reflected my role as. . . . feminist sociologist. . . . [Eventually I constructed a new story that] reflects my current feminist perspective, which adopts humanist values and looks at the cost to women (and men) of trying to live out those values in conventionally gendered environments.[99]

Lois Easterday and her colleagues pointed out variations on Sherryl Kleinman's dilemmas:

The researcher may find herself more attracted to "feminist" men and women. Tensions among non-feminists and feminists in such settings are problematic; the researcher may find herself typed as a "female libber" and tested for "where she stands"—as either friend or enemy, but clearly as female.[100]

Feminist ethnography introduces new questions about political rapport or lack of rapport when both the researcher and the setting members are feminist, or when one is feminist and the other is not.

Again, this can apply to teachers as well

Redefining the Closeness/Distance Dilemma: Nurturing as a Field Method

The methodological literature on participant observation is divided among those who advocate closeness and those who advocate respectful distance between the researcher and the person studied.[101] Respectful distance is supposed to avoid the danger that the researcher will "go native" or identify with the people studied; closeness is supposed to enhance understanding. In the "respectful distance" model, overrapport represents the researcher's neurotic failing to maintain objectivity or maintain his/her separate identity.[102] Many feminist researchers, by contrast, take the position that closeness with women is necessary in order to understand them.

The question then arises—would the methodology of participant observation have been defined differently if it had been based on the way women study women in all-female settings? Sociologist Arlie Hochschild has two interesting responses to this question. She suggests that ethnography done by women [not all of whom are feminist] is different from ethnography done by men to the extent that men and women interact in different ways. She notes that when women study the elderly and/or when women study women, they can act on a "nurturing" impulse that is reciprocated.[103] Denise Connors' study of elderly Irish women, mentioned earlier, is a case in point of reciprocated nurturing:

> We shared experiences, stories, letters, cards, photographs, newspaper clippings and poems. After a visit with Hannah she told me that our talk about music motivated her to play her accordion which she had set aside years ago. I was treated to tea, coffee, soup in a bowl preheated in the oven, cheese, crackers, cake, muffins and cookies. One woman saved quarters to make change for me to use at the toll booths. I was sent home with Irish bread, "holy cards," a pot-holder and once with a bottle of non-alcoholic wine that had been a gift from an alcoholic priest.
>
> I often brought something with me when I went to visit . . . I brought dulse (seaweed) to Mary after hearing how she used to collect it along the shore and plants to the women who "loved flowers." I brought D-Zerta to Norah who is diabetic and couldn't find it in her local supermarket. . . . The enduring friend-ships that have evolved are based on a sense of reciprocity and understanding of one another's lives.[104]

Reading these descriptions suggests to me that the friendship between researcher and "subject" Ann Oakley advocates in *interview* research is more likely to be the product of *ethnographic* research. In Australian anthropologist Diane Bell's fieldwork, for example, full reciprocity led to mutual identification.

At Warrabri the first question concerned my marital status. Where was my husband, I was asked. I explained I was divorced. How did I support myself, was the next question. On a pension from the government and a scholarship from the university which had sent me to learn, I explained . . . "In that case," said Nakamarra, my older sister, "you are just like us." In the next eighteen months I came to understand the ramifications of the comment.[105]

According to this feminist view, not only is closeness necessary for understanding, but the case for respectful distance must be understood as a product of males' developmental history that requires distance from their mothers in order to produce the male identity.[106]

In general, feminist participant observation values openness to intimacy and striving for empathy, which should not be confused with superficial friendliness. Rather it means openness to complete transformation. This transformation—or consciousness-raising—lays the groundwork for friendship, shared struggle, and identity change. It is important, however, that the possibility of developing close relationships in the field not become an oppressive mandate.

Another way to think about the dilemma of closeness/distance is to acknowledge that each setting requires the fieldworker to take a different approach. Some settings require anonymous relationships[107] while others require intensely personal relationships.[108] From this perspective, any stance is acceptable as long as research findings are analyzed in terms of the particular types of relationship that occurred. The setting, rather than methodological ideology, defines the appropriate role.

It should also be remembered that fieldwork relationships are fluid over time.[109] In contrast to Raymond Gold's frequently cited idea[110] that a researcher's stance has a particular form in a given project, Sheryl Ruzek's study, mentioned earlier, highlights the fact that the stances change over time and can be multidimensional at any time. The different dimensions of the study of a social movement, in this case the women's health movement, rather than of a particular setting, called for this multifaceted approach. Moreover, researchers inevitably have different types of relationships with different individuals or groups in any particular field setting, and as long as the researcher is self-aware, whatever happens is useful data.[111]

Arlie Hochschild claims that empathy is enhanced in feminist ethnography because empathy emerges easily among the relatively powerless.[112] Judy Wajcman offers an example from her study of a women's cooperative:

> The women were friendly and tried to put me at ease. I think they felt sorry for me. The role I quite consciously adopted, which was not hard in the circumstances, was that of a shy student. . . . As it turned out, my inability to use a sewing-machine was also an advantage. . . . Doing odd jobs gave me the freedom I needed to move around the shopfloor. . . . After they had sewn several items, the women would cut off the loose threads and pack the items in bundles. I often sat by a few machinists and did this job for them, folding the jackets into plastic bags, and stacking them near the fire exit, where work was collected and delivered. . . . Trying to make myself useful, I ran errands, did bits of shopping and sometimes made the tea, which was a great joke, as I myself drank lemon tea and always made a weak brew. More helpfully, I would collect some of the

children from school if their mothers were having to work late to finish a contract on time.[113]

Women are concerned with many things other than nurturance; and women do not always identify with other women. It is important, therefore, not to think about feminist fieldwork only in terms of traditional female stereotypes, but to include these stereotypes as one possibility.

Complete Observer and Complete Participant Roles

In addition to the closeness/distance dichotomy, methodological literature concerning fieldwork suggests that there is a dichotomy or continuum of "complete observer" to "complete participant" roles.[114] The two variables in this continuum are the extent to which those observed know they are studied, and how much the researcher *participates in* the ongoing activities. Feminists conducting participant observation research have adopted stances within this entire range. Some feminists such as Sheryl Ruzek reject as unethical the complete observer role.

> Although many fieldworkers disagree, I object to participant observation without revealing one's role as a researcher in any but public settings, partly because it impedes asking simple questions outright ("normal" behavior for a researcher but not for everyday participants). I also believe that it is important to explain one's role and specify what is to be investigated, as well as why and how. [P]resenting an identity other than one's own violates the ethos of many groups and individuals.[115]

In contrast with Sheryl Ruzek's careful delineation of her researcher role, Karen McCarthy Brown[116] first presented herself as researcher in her study of a Haitian Voudou cult, then adopted the "complete participant" stance, eventually becoming one of the people she was studying. Many feminist researchers have written about the ethical and epistemological importance of integrating their selves into their work, and of eliminating the distinction between the subject and the object. The complete participant approach fits this particular feminist goal, although it is not shared by all researchers who consider themselves to be feminists.

Feminist ethnographers who emphasize closeness rather than distance in fieldwork relations believe that understanding based on participant observation is enhanced by total immersion in the world one is studying.[117] Total immersion comes about when the researcher begins to share the fate of those she is studying. In a brief self-reflexive essay about her study, Karen McCarthy Brown mentioned that her experiences in other cultures sensitized her to the social construction of reality, particularly gender hierarchies. This understanding shaped her distrust of social institutions, including her vocation as an anthropologist. When she became disillusioned with the "objective" stance in which she had been trained, she began to rely more on her "intuitions about people and processes" and to draw on her relationships as "primary resources." The alternative feminist stance was open, receptive, and waiting, an approach she believes reflects her experiences as a woman, "socialized as women are to the skills of empathy, the importance of relationships, and the interconnection of thought and experience."

Increasing her involvement in an "alternative world view," Karen Brown "submitt[ed] her own life to the Voudou systems of interpretation and healing."[118] She came to believe that her deep involvement in this world view was personally fulfilling and the most useful way to accomplish her research goals of understanding Haitian religion. By trying to act "as if" Voudouism were her religion, she engaged "the deepest parts of who she is." Thus her fieldwork took her out of the context of academic compartmentalization and allowed her to fuse her self and her work, a principle she believes underpins feminist methodology and is rejected by mainstream social science.

Many feminist ethnographers have eliminated the distinction between the researcher and the researched and have studied their own experience. Taking this point to the extreme, British sociologist Liz Stanley wrote that the subject matter of feminist research must be the everyday life experiences of feminists,[119] a view many feminists would reject as limiting. In some cases such as that of Karen Brown, the researcher begins as an outsider and then changes profoundly during the course of her study. Sheryl Ruzek's involvement deepened throughout the course of her research on women's health settings, so that by the end of the study she considered herself a member of the women's health movement.

Another way feminist ethnographers address the question of closeness versus distance is their decision concerning working in the setting. In her report on a shelter for battered women, for example, Noelie Rodriguez reports being told by "the administrator that [she] was 'welcome to just hang around,' " which she interpreted as meaning that she did not have to be a "shelter worker" but could adopt the role of "inquisitive researcher":

> Aside from occasionally helping out in the kitchen or with child care, I generally took the role of a nonparticipant observer and identified myself to everyone as "a researcher, interested in understanding how the shelter operates." I attended 47 meetings of the staff and visited the shelter every few days to attend meetings, to conduct interviews, or to observe daily life.[120]

In contrast with Noelie Rodriguez, Kathleen Ferraro conducted an ethnography of a shelter in which she *was* employed.

> As staff researcher, I had access to all aspects of life and decision making in the shelter. I gave particularly close attention to the staffing sessions held weekly to discuss and evaluate the cases of all women in the shelter at that time. I sat in on and tape recorded all such sessions during the 14-month period I worked at the shelter.[121]

In her case, her role as worker became the basis of her ability to do participant observation research.

When studying a hierarchical women's setting, feminist ethnographers face the classic dilemmas of not appearing to align themselves with one group rather than another. In the case below, Judy Wajcman explains how this conflict arose in the workers' cooperative she studied.

> The first thing that struck both Hilary and myself during our initial visits was that we were always greeted by Nancy and Jackie, who would take us into the office

to discuss the firm's problems. The possibility of replacing Jackie [a feminist helping out in the factory] foreshadowed some of the difficulties I was to experience during my stay at Fakenham Enterprises. Jackie had spent most of her time at the factory in the office and was seen by the other women as Nancy's assistant. She often answered the telephone and had access to information simply by virtue of being in the office. I did not want to inherit her position because, in order to carry out my study, I wanted to work on the shopfloor with the women and talk to them. I wanted to avoid being identified with Nancy and restricted to the office. This was the classic problem of a researcher trying to avoid identification with the management, but in the strange context of a workers' cooperative.[122]

She resolved this dilemma by requesting permission to work in the factory.

By contrast, Sheryl Ruzek avoided working in the settings she was studying, for precisely the reasons that led Judy Wajcman in the opposite direction.

My decision not to actively work with or for any particular group was also influenced by concern that "joining" would force me to take sides in schisms and squabbles. By maintaining some distance, I could learn more about all sides of disputes and could maintain a critical stance—difficult when too closely associated with one group. (I was reminded of the importance of this after observing a clinic a colleague was studying. When reviewing my observations of the clinic's problematic features with her, she bristled; she later told me she was surprised that she felt so defensive over my criticizing "her" health group.) Overall, the advantages of maintaining some distance seemed to outweigh the advantages of being a true "insider."[123]

Finally, Canadian sociologist Patricia Baker took a position as a teller in order to study a bank, a "complex capitalist organization." She found that the differential power and gender inequality in the setting, and her membership in one position in the hierarchy, had a major impact on her ability to conduct her research and maintain her critical perspective.[124] The dilemmas I reviewed above are true dilemmas—there seems to be little consensus as to how they should be resolved. For this reason, feminist ethnographers typically make double contributions when they conduct their research. They contribute to our understanding of feminist ethnography as a method of social research, and they contribute to our understanding of the subject matter they chose to study.

Feminist Analysis of Ethnographic Data

A feminist perspective on data analysis includes many components such as understanding women in their social contexts and using women's language and behavior to understand the relation between self and context. It includes the problem of finding a way not to omit any person's voice while still having a manuscript of manageable length. It includes the use of feminist theory to analyze data[125] as well as flexibility and creativity in format. Susan Krieger, for example, argued that feminist ethnography must be redefined to include autobiography and fiction[126] and Marianne (Tracy) Paget argued that feminist research should be performed as theater.[127]

Much feminist ethnography hopes to contribute to feminist theory. As participant observation research is done on a growing spectrum of settings relevant to women's lives, researchers are using their data to evaluate, not only to apply, feminist theory. For example, in a review of Carole Joffe's participant observation study of a family planning clinic, Marian Sandmaier points to the significance of Carole Joffe's discovery that " 'front-line' birth control and abortion counselors play a pivotal and largely unacknowledged role in the regulation of sexual behavior.'' This role reflects the fact that the Federal Government, the feminist movement, and the New Right "fail to adequately address the often wrenching conflicts faced daily by birth control and abortion workers.'' [128] These unaddressed conflicts suggest that feminist theory must find a way to help these counsellors. It is not simply a question of feminism's developing a "pro-choice" position.

When doing data analysis, feminist ethnographers point out the important difference between *drawing on* feminist theory and *imposing* feminist theory. Susan Stall, for example, believes that feminists will be able to see the changes women are making in their lives only if they do not measure everyone against their own standards. She writes:

> If we utilize liberal . . . feminist arguments that emphasize abstract and universal (simple) conceptions of equality as the basis for meaningful political activity for women, we may be oversimplifying our understanding of the roots of social resistance and innovation in the everyday experience of women. A politics of community promises to avoid the dangers of abstraction and simplicity by starting from the diverse forms of social change women already make to subvert the inequality of discrimination and exploitation—forms that emphasize a different political agenda than the popular feminist arguments allow for.

Feminists should obviously be vigilant lest "research from the standpoint of women" be a slogan masking the feminist researcher's application of her own ideas onto the women she studies. As Susan Stall put it,

> Current *feminist arguments* about political action are limiting and inadequate because they do not take into account the complexity of women's lived experience within community, and thus reinforce and call for political activities which are similarly limiting. [129]

The challenge for feminism is to both develop feminist theory and find ways of understanding the way it is rejected by some of the very people whose lives it tries to explain.

The analysis of feminist ethnographic materials and the manner in which they are reported also leads feminist researchers to questions posed by scholars who are interested in problems of writing. To what extent should the ethnographer utilize her own voice, to what extent should the members of the setting have control over the product, and to what extent should materials be interpreted in ways that diverge from members of the setting? These are some of the current dilemmas.

Feminist Ambivalence toward Ethnography

In a provocative article, U.S. sociologists Judith Stacey and Barrie Thorne wrote in 1985 that if there *were* a theoretical link between feminism and interpretive methods, there would be more feminist ethnographies.[130] I have two approaches to this complaint about the paucity of feminist ethnography. First, there seem actually to be quite a few. In addition to those I have discussed in this chapter, I would include Sue Webb's study of a department store,[131] Kathleen McCourt's study of Chicago working-class neighborhoods,[132] Arlene Kaplan Daniels' study of upper-class women's volunteering activity,[133] Michelle Fine's ethnography of a New York public high school,[134] Rahel Wasserfall's study of Moroccan Jewish marital relations in an Israeli moshav,[135] Eleanor M. Miller's study of female criminals,[136] Marcia Millman's study of obese people,[137] Arlie Hochschild's studies of old women and of stewardesses,[138] Jeanne Guillemin and Lynda Holmstrom's study of intensive neonatal care units,[139] Lynn Davidman's study of Jewish women who become orthodox,[140] Laura Fishman's study of wives of prisoners,[141] Kathleen Kautzer's study of the Older Women's League,[142] and Mary Eaton's study of a courtroom,[143] among many others.

Second, if it *is* the case that ethnography is underrepresented in feminist research, it may be for the same reasons that limit the production of participant observation studies generally—the difficulty of gaining access to the study site, their time-consuming nature, the inadequacy of training, the difficulty of obtaining funding, and the derogatory attitude of some powerful groups within social science toward nonquantitative research.[144] To do intensive ethnography frequently requires the ability to suspend personal and work obligations, to travel, and to expose oneself to risk.

Although the practical demands of fieldwork may inhibit some women from undertaking it, I also believe that participant observation research has provided some nontraditional intellectual women a legitimate avenue for freedom and adventure.[145] One reason for studying other cultures and groups is to circumvent one's discomfort as a woman in one's own culture. In the field, the woman may intensify her search for freedom, finding herself increasingly distanced from conventions such as marriage. In her frank account of fieldwork experiences, Manda Cesara discussed that

> something was happening to me and I needed solitude. I know that if I could have wiped away our marriage with a magic wand I would have done so. It was not Bob who bothered me. Rather, in the Maloba environment, free among my equals who were all preoccupied with similar worries, the oppression of marriage hit me "like a ton of bricks." Even when "happy" couples passed through our research quarters I pitied them. I would find myself observing their every demeanor, nonverbal signs and signals used to keep the other in line, and I felt repulsed. The recognition of subtle controls passing back and forth between man and woman made me feel nauseous. In the presence of these couples I felt as if their iron bars were also enclosing me and my fury increased and I wanted to

burst through these bars with the rage of a maniac. It occurred to me then that during times of mental growth and change, one must be alone. . . . It was not Bob but marriage that oppressed me. It is what marriage does to one's brain, anyone's brain, that I dislike. There are simply times in the lives of men and women when marriage is inappropriate. It suffocates the flow of creative thought and personal growth, something that is understood by every living and dead creative mind.[146]

Ironically, women may also undertake participant observation because it is considered consonant with the traditional role of women. In fact, some argue that women have been disproportionately attracted to and successful in anthropology because participant observation is the predominant method of that discipline.

Whether or not women are more likely to do fieldwork than are men, and despite the complexity of a particular feminist's motivation for undertaking fieldwork, it seems to be the case that the written text that emerges from the study is a blend of writing about the self, the group studied, and the methods by which that group was studied, or as I previously put it, "person, problem and method." [147] In her study of Women's Studies practitioners, Women's Studies scholar Renate Klein wrote that this is the mandate of feminist ethnography: "doing feminist research explicitly demands transparency in all stages of our research, making visible why we do what we do—and how we do this." [148] This self-disclosure reveals the extent to which the researcher learned about herself and helps instruct the reader how to engage in similar work. As sociologist Carol Warren put it:

> Entering the field, developing a place within the social order, talking, feeling, and living in the setting, are the terrain of understanding the intersection of gender, self, and others in fieldwork. Writing field notes, writing essays, seeking and incorporating reviews and editing, are the terrain of understanding the web of data, self and discourse.[149]

In an article published in 1988, Judith Stacey goes beyond her original comment on the paucity of feminist ethnographies, and questions if there can actually be a feminist ethnography, implying some agreed-on definition of feminism.[150] She claims that fieldwork relations are inherently deceptive and instrumental, and that feminists should not relate to women in this way.[151] Her criticism echoes that of Ann Oakley who called interviewing a contradiction in terms. Unlike Ann Oakley, who suggested that we reform interviewing by introducing more commitment, Judith Stacey implies that to do so would add even more hypocrisy to an inherently manipulative relationship. My view on this matter is that there is no agreed on definition of feminism, but that there are many people who call themselves feminists and whose ethnographic research follows their own definition of feminism. Moreover, fieldwork relations that may seem manipulative might, in fact, be reciprocal. The possibility of manipulating someone can easily be reduced by reminding them of your research intentions. There is always the chance that the setting member will have expectations of the researcher that cannot be fulfilled, but it seems unreasonable to me to abandon all ethnographic studies because of the impossibility of the researcher being all things to all people at all times. The feminist ethnographer like all ethnographers is simply human and is motivated by concern for women, not for their exploitation.

Feminist fieldworkers are likely to examine how the setting itself affected them as women and how being female affected their ability to study the setting.[152] They are likely to report these findings as part of their formal ethnographic manuscript. Although female fieldworkers' unique difficulties (and a few advantages) in the field have been analyzed for some time, these insights have not yet been incorporated into mainstream methodological writings about participant observation research. Because women have remained on the outside, their challenges to conventional methodological procedures have not been recognized and definitions of ethnographic practices have not yet been modified. A shared conceptual framework has not yet developed and perhaps should not be developed, to embrace all the components and dilemmas of feminist ethnography.[153] Every feminist ethnography seems to generate its own new sets of concerns in addition to touching on familiar ones. I therefore do not share Barrie Thorne and Judith Stacey's assessment that there are substantially fewer feminist ethnographies or that they are inherently contradictory. Rather, I think we have been slow in weaving the connections among all the studies that exist and therefore deficient in reaching a grounded understanding of what feminist ethnography actually is.

4

Feminist Survey Research and Other Statistical Research Formats[1]

In designing my study . . . it was my intention to combine the *most rigorous, scientifically sound* methodology with a *deep knowledge* of, and sensitivity to, the issues of rape.[2]

It is not surprising that Diana Russell, the author of this quote, turned to surveying a carefully drawn sample in her quest for a methodology that was "the most rigorous and scientifically sound." Many people believe survey research possesses these qualities. In the social science community and in the public at large there is widespread acceptance of the objectivity of survey research findings.[3] For this reason governmental bodies frequently solicit survey research to provide answers to pressing social concerns. For example, the 1970 Pornography Commission undertook survey research to determine whether the U.S. public considered pornography to be a significant social problem.[4]

In addition to this widespread acceptance of survey research findings, there is also criticism. My review of feminist research practices suggests that ambivalence characterizes the feminist response to survey research, an ambivalence that can be detected even in the opening quotation. Some feminist researchers have found survey research and other statistically based forms of research to be excellent devices for their purposes,[5] while other have expressed deep distrust.

Historical Roots

Feminist (and nonfeminist) researchers have a history of doing survey research to study social change and social problems. Historian of anthropology Joan Mark points out that in the late nineteenth century "a tolerance for painstaking, tedious work, applied in this case to the gathering of statistics" was even considered to be "peculiarly feminine." One of the people to use this "feminine" trait to women's advantage was the renowned astronomer Maria Mitchell. In her 1875 presidential address to the Association for Advancement of Women established in 1873, she urged members to "collect statistics." Particularly important to her were statistics concerning the effect of study on women, and on the number of female scientists in the United States.

Maria Mitchell's statement and the widely accepted notion at that time that educated women have a propensity to collect statistics, culminated in the Association for the Advancement of Science forming six committees in 1875 "to take practical action in various areas: science, statistics, industrial training, reform, art and education."[6] A similar interest in collecting statistics existed among women in England[7] and in Russia.[8] Despite this rich history, landmarks and key figures in the history of feminist survey research are still relatively unrecognized.[9] To bring some attention to this neglected, yet impressive, history, I will describe several important examples—that of Marion Talbot, Mary Roberts Smith, Jane Addams, Helen L. Sumner, Crystal Eastman, and Mari Sandoz. Many others, such as Edith Abbott, whose 1905 University of Chicago doctoral dissertation was entitled *A Statistical Study of the Wages of Unskilled Labor, 1830–1900*,[10] and Margaret Hagood, whom historian of sociology Mary Jo Deegan calls a pioneer of statistics, made significant contributions.[11]

In 1870 Marion Talbot (1848–1948), a recent college graduate, formed the Association of Collegiate Alumnae (ACA) with the assistance of her mother, Emily Talbot. She then proceeded to canvas the ACA membership and question the women about their health so as to challenge the spurious claim that women's intellectual work damaged their reproductive organs. At that time, the assertion of biological damage had become the chief rationale for opposing higher education for women. Historian Rosalind Rosenberg explains the significance of statistics for Emily and Marion Talbot's battle against the barring of women from higher education:

> The ACA's attempt to examine empirically [Dr. Edward] Clarke's claim of feminine frailty represented the most important development in the discussion of women's nature in ten years. Emily Talbot had been introduced to the reform possibilities of statistics in her work as secretary of the education department of the American Social Science Association (ASSA), and she helped pattern the study of alumnae health on early ASSA surveys. With the help of a group of doctors and teachers, they composed a questionnaire, which they sent to the 1290 graduates belonging to the association in 1882. [They] found that 78 percent of the respondents enjoyed good health, 5 percent were in fair health, and 17 percent suffered from bad health.[12]

Another example of the early link between feminism and questions of methodology is the work of Mary Roberts Smith[13] (1860–1945), associate professor of sociology at Stanford University and first full-time female professor in sociology in the United States. In a recent biographical essay, sociologist Mary Jo Deegan identifies Mary Roberts Smith as a "statistician on women's poverty . . . an authority on social welfare, feminism, Chinese immigration to the U.S.A., Victorian sexuality and Native Americans."[14] In one of her important studies, Mary Roberts Smith showed that the low birth rates of college women reflected their general upbringing, rather than the specific experience of having attended college. One should not compare college women to "average woman of the Census" but rather to their sisters, cousins, and friends who had not gone to college.

Using this comparison group, Mary Roberts Smith found that the average delay of marriage for women who received a college education was only two years

(26 versus 24 years of age at marriage). Of both groups 87% were married by the age of 30. She also examined the likelihood of both groups to bear children, and found that "19% of the college women were childless, compared to 15% for the noncollege women, and that the average number of children per college woman was 1.65 (in 9.6 years of marriage) compared to 1.87 (for 11.6 years of marriage) for the noncollege women."[15]

A "concern with statistics" was "central to the work of female sociologists in the city of Chicago," all of whom were connected to Hull-House.[16] Mary Jo Deegan writes that "collecting quantitative data was considered 'women's work' by the University of Chicago's male sociologists prior to Ogburn's introduction to the staff in 1928."[17] Jane Addams' *Twenty Years at Hull-House*[18] describes several instances of the methodological approach developed at Hull-House that included the following steps: identifying a local problem, investigating it, creating a clear-cut statistical explanation, bringing the study's conclusions to the attention of authorities, agitating until appropriate action is taken, and, in the meantime, assuming responsibility for alleviating the problem to the greatest extent possible.

Historian William L. O'Neill drew attention to a survey done by Helen L. Sumner, a University of Wisconsin Ph.D. She was hired in 1906–1907 by the New York City Collegiate Equal Suffrage League to evaluate the effects of woman suffrage in Colorado, the first state to enfranchise women:

> Her findings were published in 1909 under the title *Equal Suffrage*. She discovered that few women held public office because few woman ran for office, and those who did were "handicapped by the discovery that other women in voting cling much closer to party than to sex lines." There was, in fact, no woman's vote as such in Colorado except on a very few issues, and the party structure had been undisturbed by equal suffrage. Because the caucus and primary system was rigged in favor of "the machine," women had no more incentive than men to attend meetings whose outcome was foreordained. "It is no reflection, then, on equal suffrage to show women's incapacity to cope with the existing machinery of nominations. Equal suffrage, indeed serves to show, in the most striking way, the essential rottenness and degrading character of the existing system."[19]

Another important early U.S. feminist survey researcher is Crystal Eastman (1881–1928) who earned an M.A. in sociology from Columbia University in 1904. Feminist theorist Blanche Wiesen Cook explains:

> In 1907 Crystal graduated from law school second in her class with a particular interest in labor law. At the same time her good friend Paul U. Kellogg, then editor of the social work magazine *Charities and the Commons,* was organizing the celebrated Pittsburgh Survey for the Russell Sage Foundation and invited Crystal to join the staff. Crystal remained in Pittsburgh for over a year to complete the first in-depth sociological investigation of industrial accidents ever undertaken. Her work catapulted her to prominence, and in June 1909 Governor Charles vans Hughes appointed her New York's first woman commissioner, the only woman among fourteen members of the Employer's Liability Commission.[20]

In 1930, sociology student Mari Sandoz noticed that in the city of Lincoln, Nebraska, men were driving close to the curb, trying to pick up women who were walking on the sidewalk. Clergy and social workers condemned these men, but Mari Sandoz felt judgment should be withheld pending her investigation to determine who these "knights of the pavement," as she called them, actually were.

> Why not interview them? I would at least get their "line" that way. I purchased a tiny blue notebook with an inch of pencil attached, pulled on my only dress with any air at all, looked to my lipstick, rehearsed a few questions and a pose or two before my slightly distorting mirror and took to the streets.
>
> I asked the first 385 curbers who stopped me a set list of questions that might or might not be revealing but were undeniably impertinent. Upon each man's scrap of paper I jotted, with the answers I succeeded in extracting, his probable age, the make, type, and antiquity of his car, and the state in which it was licensed.

By the end of the study, Mari Sandoz concluded that pick-ups are a function of

> the growing isolation of the urban individual. Perhaps pick-ups are the modern substitute for the cave man's club. . . . But first he must catch the woman, and therefore he slithers up to the curb and beckons, in defiance of the city fathers, the church, the social workers, and the good women of my acquaintance, who all seem to see only degradation in the practice but haven't done anything much about it except elevate hands and eyebrows.[21]

The Value of Survey Research for Contemporary Feminists

Psychologist Toby Jayaratne has developed an important analysis of the pros and cons of quantified research for the development of feminist theory and political action. In her chapter "The Value of Quantitative Methodology for Feminist Research," she argues that

> there must be appropriate *quantitative* evidence to counter the pervasive and influential quantitative sexist research which has and continues to be generated in the social sciences. Feminist researchers can best accomplish this. If some of the traditional procedures used to produce that needed evidence are contrary to our feminist values, then we must change those procedures accordingly. In the process of change we not only must remember to view our research in a political context . . . but we must support one another against the academic and professional pressures to compromise our standards. The better quality research that we do, the more likely that that research will influence others and ultimately help in achieving their goals.[22]

This section of chapter 4 contains examples of feminist survey and other forms of quantitative research that have been successful in the ways Toby Jayaratne suggests.

Survey research can put a problem on the map by showing that it is more widespread than previously thought. Feminists have used survey research for precisely this purpose, dispelling the common argument that the complaint of a particular woman is idiosyncratic. For example, Betty Friedan's *The Feminine Mys-*

tique cited numerous surveys to demonstrate the malaise of the contemporary white American middle-class housewife.[23] These materials helped her develop an analysis of the "problem that has no name," one of the many problems named by the women's movement. Surveys and other techniques that rely on the gathering and analysis of large quantities of numerical data have proven useful in generating interest in the women's movement and feminist scholarship. Using a pattern that has become normative for some feminist research,[24] Vivian Gornick and Barbara Moran,[25] in one of the earliest books on sexism, begin with income statistics and then discuss the number of women in the labor force.

Since statistical techniques exist for generalizing from a small population to a larger one, survey research is used to provide information about problems that seemingly occur to only a few people. Statistical information about sexual harassment, for example, contributed to its reification in ways that encouraged the establishment of sexual harassment committees in universities and public school systems, and eventually provided legal redress for individuals. Survey-based prevalence data are useful in demonstrating that a problem is distributed in a particular way throughout a population. This distribution may suggest factors that contribute to the problem, and these factors, in turn, provide hints as to how the problem may be prevented or remedied through particular forms of action. For this reason the "action research" chapter of this book contains many examples of survey research. Advocates of surveys and the gathering of statistical data argue that basing our practical efforts on behalf of women on qualitative research will, by contrast, lead to errors. An example of this comparative endorsement of quantitative research can be found in a study by Edward Gondolf and Ellen Fisher concerning battered women.

> The field has . . . [hitherto] relied extensively on clinical observations, qualitative interview studies, and polemical essays in shaping its concepts and interventions. While this basis provides a vivid portrayal of the nature of abuse and confronts us with the harsh reality of real people, it overlooks the scope and differentiation of abuse and women's response to it. The more qualitative approach thus allows undocumented or untested generalizations to develop. The empirical basis of this book [by contrast] serves . . . several important purposes for the practitioners. One, it offers a context by which to weigh and sort one's individual hunches and observations. This is particularly useful given the emotionally charged and crisis-oriented settings in which most practitioners find themselves. Two, the empirical base of statistics enables us to develop generalizations about a category of individuals. These generalizations are vital to formulating meaningful policy and effective programs that, by their very nature, must address large groups of people. Three, many . . . statistics . . . attempt to move beyond descriptive bivariate analysis to a more explanatory multivariate analysis that suggests "why" as well as "what" is going on. In the process, patterns and associations are discovered that are not readily apparent in everday observations. . . .
>
> While statistical descriptions in themselves often blunt the experience and tragedy of wife abuse, they . . . also serve as a harsh reminder of its extent and severity. The statistics from our sample of more than six thousand women . . . portray a group of women severely, extensively, and cruelly assaulted.[26]

Survey research can also help identify differences among groups and changes over time.[27] For example, statistics comparing men and women have been used to document inequality and highlight areas where change is needed. Labor statistics demonstrate a pattern of sex-based employment, with women clustered in a small number of jobs characterized by low status and low pay. Certain gender-based income statistics resulting from this pattern have become widely known such as the facts that in the United States women earn 70 cents to the man's dollar,[28] women with four years of college have lower salaries than men who completed high school, nearly two of every three poor persons are women, and after divorce, women experience a 73% loss in their former standard of living and men experience a 42% rise.[29]

Statistical data are useful to feminists for rhetorical purposes. For example, Barnard College President Ellen Futter, quoted below, used statistics to spur women to keep working toward their goals even if they feel they have made some progress. In a speech to students, faculty, and potential donors, she

> acknowledged the many gains of the women's movement and the great strides women have made in many fields. But she pointed to statistics showing that despite those gains . . . 77% of this nation's poverty is borne by women and children, and . . . 60% of working American mothers have no right of maternity leave.[30]

Statistics are used not only to document differences between the sexes, but also to demonstrate similarities and differences among women. In an early article, Elizabeth Almquist compared U.S. Black women and U.S. white women. Using available statistics, she reviewed the Black women's positive attitudes toward feminism and showed the increasing similarities between Black and white women, which help explain these attitudes.[31] Faye Wattleton, on the other hand, in a fund-raising effort for Planned Parenthood, highlighted the particular problems of Third World women:

> In many of these [less developed] countries, a woman is 10 to 30 times more likely to die in childbirth than a woman in a developed Western nation. And her child is ten times more likely to die before it's one year old. (p. 1). . . . And when it comes to abortion, the legal barriers abound. About one-third of the world's people live in countries where abortion is illegal. But every year—20 million women have illegal, unsafe abortions anyway. As a result, illegal abortion is one of the leading causes of death for women in the poorest nations on our globe.[32]

Statistical information concerning differential rates of cesarian section at various hospitals have led to questioning this obstetric procedure and its relation to hospital policies. Statistical information has even brought the myth of vaginal orgasm and the relation between educational attainment and the experience of orgasm to our attention.[33]

Surveys have been used by feminists to test theory. An example published in the first issue of *Gender & Society* is Barbara Risman's use of questionnaires distributed to single fathers, single mothers, and married couples to differentiate between individualist and microstructural explanations of parenting behavior.[34] Her analysis of the data supported the idea that it is opportunities and situational exigencies, rather than the individual's sex, that determine parenting behavior.

Psychologists Jeanne Plas and Barbara Wallston studied the impact of networking (informal and formal systems of relationships) on women interested in male-oriented careers. They sent three different scales to "43 women enrolled in a workshop designed to encourage the participation of women in science careers" asking them to fill out the scales at their leisure. After the women returned the questionnaires, the two researchers subjected the data to analysis procedures specifically oriented toward single samples. These were standardized stepwise regression methods in the service of feminists questions.[35]

Demographic data are useful in showing that a problem is increasing, is spreading into new sectors of the population, or is distributed unequally in a population. Studies based on these kind of data have been extremely important in generating and legitimizing feminist critiques of society. For example in 1974, Sue Eisenberg and Patricia Micklow, two law students at the University of Michigan, gathered data concerning the prevalence of wife battering in the local area. Among the data they collected are those showing that family assault calls are received *daily* by police chiefs even in small towns in a rural county. Similarly, they obtained data from a judge informing them that wives claim they have been beaten by their husbands in 80% of the 16,000 divorces initiated annually in that county.[36] Their study helped establish wife battering as a widespread "social fact" in the United States, not a problem confined to a particular class or group. Their data contributed to the understanding of battering as a part of a more general social climate of violence against women. As Edith Altbach wrote shortly after their landmark study:

> About 95 percent of the victims of sexual abuse are girls, and rape statistics increase annually. In terms of our most recently discovered crime—spouse abuse—more than 2 million American women are severely beaten in their homes every year, 20 percent of the visits by women for emergency medical services are caused by battering, and one out of every four female murder victims is killed by her husband or boyfriend.[37]

Action concerning wife battering, though limited, soon followed its new definition as a problem of women in general, rather than the problem created by a particular batterer.

The following year (1975), Susan Brownmiller brought the issue of rape to national attention in the United States.[38] Her book *Against Our Will* made the powerful point that *all* women are vulnerable to rape, and that this shared vulnerability is one foundation of sisterhood. She drew attention to the fact that rape is a common, rather than rare, phenomenon: "According to F.B.I statistics, a forcible rape is committed in this country every six minutes."[39] She also made a strong case for statistical methods as she described plans for the initial conference on rape:

> Conferences require objective information, statistics, research and study. . . .
> The conference, which I had proposed out of restlessness and participated in only

marginally, as a sort of senior planning consultant, proved to be my moment of revelation.

Susan Brownmiller also praised Menahem Amir's *Patterns in Forcible Rape* for giving "us charts, tables, diagrams, theories of social relevance, and, above all, hard, cold statistical facts about crime."[40]

Survey researchers have developed strong links with many social institutions such as medicine, politics, the economy, and government. The census is legally mandated. Statistical summaries of surveys have also become conventional aspects of consumer market analyses and political campaigns. As political scientists Sandra Baxter and Marjorie Lansing put it:

> National surveys are common now and most people have a general ideal of how they are conducted. Newspapers and television carry the results of the latest Harris, Roper, and Gallup surveys, and the image comes quickly to mind of an interviewer stopping pedestrians on a busy street corner or interrupting persons in their homes.

People are so used to the idea of surveys, Sandra Baxter and Marjorie Lansing claim, that most do not realize how sophisticated the method actually is:

> The methodology of survey research is precise and complex, and the seeming simplicity of asking a number of people a series of questions in a well-designed survey hides a great deal of hard, systematic work. First, the respondents must be selected carefully so that they represent a much larger group . . . and secondly, the questions they are asked must be phrased so they can be understood by everyone without conveying the suggestion that one answer is better or more correct than another.[41]

Statistics are powerful in part because they are concise. Their brevity makes them easily communicated to reporters and lawmakers who seek information. Statistics have legal force and are important in lawsuits concerning sex bias and other injustices of concern to women. Statistics are also powerful because they are easy to remember and comprehend. Survey results can be presented in pictorial form to people who are illiterate or to those who have little understanding of numbers. The fact that survey research is typically associated with governmental institutions and is costly may also enhance its prestige in the eyes of the public and of researchers, since, nowadays, value often reflects cost.

Secondary Data Analysis

Contemporary feminist scholars utilizing survey research make their contributions both by initiating studies and by analyzing other people's data. For example, feminist sociologists Karen Mason and Yu-Hsia Lu analyzed data derived from

> two national samples of the U.S. population, one interviewed in 1977 and the other in 1985. They were collected by the National Opinion Research Center as part of the General Social Survey (GSS), an ongoing project in which Americans' attitudes in a variety of spheres are measured in successive national probability

cross-sectional samples. In 1977, the GSS for the first time included four questions centrally concerned with the roles of wife and mother, items that were replicated in 1985. Two of these items asked about the desirability of the traditional division of labor and power between husband and wife in which women take a subordinate, domestic role in relation to the husband. The remaining two asked about the consequences for their children of women's employment outside the home, an issue that in the past has provided a major rationale for the traditional division of labor between spouses.[42]

Feminist researchers have been interpreting behavioral statistics produced by government bodies and attitudinal statistics produced by polling organizations and social scientists. They also use such data to forecast imminent conditions relevant to women.

Magazine Surveys

Betty Friedan's *The Feminine Mystique*[43] was cited above for its use of survey results to generate theory about the malaise of housewives. That book is also notable for its extensive use of magazine surveys to convey the opinions of middle-class American women. Magazine surveys are used frequently by feminist academic psychologists and sociologists to explore women's behavior and attitudes. For example, Graham Staines, Carol Tavris, and Toby Epstein Jayaratne report on a questionnaire distributed in February 1971 to the readers of *Psychology Today* that drew 20,000 replies from both sexes:

> Although we cannot say that this sample is representative of the American public, we thought that the diversity of women, of many occupations and philosophies, would give us a preliminary empirical look at the Queen Bee syndrome. . . . The Queen Bees in the *PT* sample—the professionally successful women—were more likely than feminists or nongroup traditional women to be individualists, deny discrimination, and to reject the assumptions and goals of the women's movement. . . . Last year Tavris and Jayaratne conducted a survey, similar to the one that appeared in *PT*, for *Redbook* magazine ("How do you Feel about Being a Woman?"). Over 120,000 women sent in their questionnaires. . . . There are signs that the Queen Bee syndrome is fading.[44]

This study is only one of many that generated concepts about women's lives based on large-scale magazine surveys of people who self-select themselves for study. Because the respondents are not randomly chosen, the results cannot be generalized to a specific population. The great number of responses, however, suggests opinion trends among magazine readers.

Attitudinal Surveys

Feminist survey research reports on attitudes as well as behaviors. A case in point is the information contained in "Women and Men: A Socioeconomic Factbook,"[45] a publication of the feminist research organization Research Group One.

Consisting entirely of tables culled from other sources, this book is divided into two major sections: socioeconomic differentials and supporting attitudes. The authors imply that behavioral statistics tell only half the story. We cannot understand the *meaning* of behavior without knowing the attitudes behind it.[46]

Attitudinal surveys conducted by Black feminist researchers have tapped attitudes among women in Black families. Gloria Joseph provides an example:

> Data from my nationwide survey of Black women conducted 1979–80, reveal that an overwhelming number of mothers (72 percent) gave their daughters negative messages about men. . . . Data from the research also reveal that daughters (age 17 and over) overwhelmingly (94.5 percent) showed great respect for their mothers despite difficulties that exist in the relationships.[47]

Studies such as Gloria Joseph's suggest that in survey research, just as in in-depth interviewing, some feminist researchers are concerned with matching the race of the respondent and the researcher.

Attitudinal studies are important because statistics demonstrating inequality are inconclusive unless discriminatory intention is demonstrated. As reported in a newsletter concerning higher education:

> In order to establish a Title IX violation [sex discrimination in federally assisted education programs and activities], sex discrimination suits must prove schools to be exercising intentional discrimination, and not simply disparate impact, whereby the school's policies affect women differently than they do men.[48]

Since feminism has become a recognized social movement, survey researchers have also been studying public attitudes toward feminism. An example is a study conducted in December 1985 and January 1986 by Israeli sociologists, Dafna Izraeli and Ephraim Tabory based on questionnaires (884 men and 1312 women) distributed in a wide variety of university classrooms on different days and at different hours. Students were requested to complete the questionnaires on the spot and 95.5% complied. One set of questions asked students to rate the

> severity or importance of 15 items commonly defined as social problems in Israel on a scale from 1 (not at all a social problem) to 9 (a very severe social problem).

Eleven of these social problems were gender neutral: unemployment, kidnapping, traffic accidents, political morality, crime, ethnic inequality, emigration, insufficient immigration, racism among Jews, civil rights, and religious coercion; and four related to gender: inequality between the sexes, violence against women, discrimination against women in promotion, and prohibitions against abortion. The four gender items were dispersed throughout the list. Included in the survey were a seven-item dogmatism scale to measure psychological security, a left-to-right political ideology scale and a five-item feminism scale to measure identification with feminist ideology and the feminist movement. The study demonstrated that the attitudes of young educated Israelis are not conducive to the development of radical feminism but rather support a series of gradual changes "without fury or urgency."[49]

Attitudinal surveys that utilize carefully differentiated case vignettes can help

feminist researchers understand the specific reasoning underlying particular attitudes. An example is a project by sociology graduate student Bhavani Sitaraman
who mailed 20 different abortion vignettes to 291 respondents in a Massachusetts
town and asked them to indicate whether they approved of the woman's choice to
have an abortion in each case. Through this method, she found that "three key
situational factors shape abortion attitudes: the reasons individual women provide
for their abortion decisions, the woman's health condition, and the phase of ges-
tation when an abortion is contemplated."[50]

Local Surveys

Perhaps inadvertently following in the tradition of Mari Sandoz who conducted a
local survey to understand a local problem, sociologist Martha Thompson carried
out a local study to resolve a personal problem. After a restaurant employee treated
her rudely in 1986 for breastfeeding in public, she

> wrote to the manager of the restaurant, describing [her] experience and inquiring
> about the policy of the restaurant regarding breastfeeding. The manager re-
> sponded that breastfeeding is a natural function but is inappropriate in the dining
> room. He also said he had spoken to others in the restaurant business and that
> this was a common policy. Since [she] had nursed [her] daughter in various pub-
> lic settings, including restaurants, [she] decided to check out his assertion that
> prohibiting breastfeeding is a common policy in Chicago area restaurants.
>   With the help of Candace Wayne, a Chicago attorney, and three legal interns,
> [she] surveyed a sample of Chicago restaurants about their policies on breastfeed-
> ing. For comparison purposes, managers were also asked about their smoking
> policies. . . . [She] used a systematic random sampling procedure to select 100
> restaurants from the almost 4000 restaurants listed in the Chicago Consumer Yel-
> low Pages (1982). After introductory remarks, the managers of these restaurants
> were asked two questions. "Does your restaurant permit smoking in the dining
> room area?" After noting the answer in detail, the interviewers then said, "I
> have another question. Does your restaurant permit women to breastfeed their
> infants in the dining area?". . . . In sum . . . [she] found that restaurants are
> more likely to permit people to smoke in dining areas than to permit women to
> breastfeed. Given the benefits of breastfeeding for mothers and children and given
> the health costs of smoking for smokers and others, the greater support for smok-
> ing over breastfeeding reflects social values unrelated to concerns for public health.[51]

Feminists create surveys such as this to collect data suitable for confronting sexism in their environment.

Feminist Critiques of Survey and Statistical
Research

Despite the power and ubiquity of surveys and other forms of statistical research,
feminists have also been critical of their use. One root of this criticism is hostility

to statistics that are seen as part of patriarchal culture's monolothic definition of "hard facts." Psychologists Dee Graham and Edna Rawlings, for example, completely reject quantitative research for feminist research purposes. They argue that there are three forms of research—feminist, sexist, and nonsexist. In their view, a "feminist perspective in research is predominately qualitative. If quantitative techniques are used, [the feminist researcher] will apologize for their use." On the other hand, sexist and nonsexist research perspectives are "predominately quantitative. If qualitative techniques are used, [the researcher] apologizes for lack of scientific rigor." [52]

Some feminist criticism draws on criticism of survey methodology in general showing that many factors, including gender, affect the respondents' answers. [53] In addition, feminist critics, just as nonfeminist critics, point out that the results of a survey hinge on the exact form a question takes. Moreover, since we already know that language is linked to gender, the choice of words used in a survey has great significance. Del Martin's discussion of wife-beating statistics mentions many of these problems:

> A survey conducted for the National Commission on the Causes and Prevention of Violence by Louis Harris and Associates . . . in October 1968, consisting of 1176 interviews with a representative national sample of American adults, showed that one-fifth approved of slapping one's spouse on "appropriate" occasions. In this survey, 16 percent of those with eight years of schooling or less approved, and 25 percent of college-educated people approved of a husband slapping his wife. . . . In the Harris poll cited above, if the word had been "hit" instead of "slap" would the result of the poll have been the same? [54]

Del Martin is concerned that the great authority of surveys makes it difficult to eradicate from the public's view erroneous, survey-based information.

Feminists have pointed out several related problems. First, inaccurate statistics may underestimate the extent of a problem and thus work against women. Edith Altbach referred to an essay by Betty Gray that discussed this problem in terms of a "statistical-industrial complex" that colludes to disguise problems.

> The U.S. Women's Bureau in the Department of Labor . . . accentuates the numerical gains women have made in the labor force and interprets these as signs of the growing power and well-being of working women and of the country as a whole. It is in fact, however, a distortion of women's position in the nation's economy to equate the increasing labor force participation with their liberation. Whereas the opening up of the job market to women creates options that women in earlier periods may have had only in restricted numbers, it could be argued from several points of view that women's overall status in the labor force has declined since the beginning of the century. . . . A "statistical-industrial complex" . . . hides the truth of women's position in the labor force by means of contrived definitions and categories. Included in this complex of interest groups are some government agencies and departments, the business and industrial community, independent educational and research foundations, politicians, and portions of the mass media. At issue are critical statistics on levels of poverty, unpaid work, unemployment and underemployment.

The statistics on the female labor force not only fail to report the problem areas but also leave hidden certain groups of working women. The main group of hidden working women is to be found in family businesses. It will probably never be known how many women labor beside their fathers, brothers, and husbands to run the thousands of small businesses that come and go annually. Lack of information, misinformation, and deceptive information combine to obscure the true situation of these and other women in the labor force.[55]

Just as labor statistics exaggerate women's gains in the labor market, so too crime statistics minimize women's victimization in the private sphere. Del Martin described this problem clearly:

> Accurately determining the incidence of wife-beating per se is impossible at this time. Obvious sources of information are police reports, court rosters, and emergency hospital admittance files, but wife-abuse is not an official category on such records. . . . It is worthwhile mentioning here that divorce statistics are not a reliable gauge of the frequency of wife-abuse, since mention of marital violence can be negotiated out of the record before the trial or because the wife was unable to produce medical and police records to prove it occurred.[56]

Since "between 40 and 60 percent of all crimes against women are not reported,"[57] information about crimes against women must always be reinterpreted and revised upward. As U.S. sociologist Margaret Andersen wrote:

> Information on incest is even harder to obtain [than on wife battering] because social taboos against it make it one of the most hidden of social problems. But as victims of incest begin to speak out, it becomes apparent that the incest taboo is a taboo against discussing it, not doing it. . . . It is important to point out that most official statistics on violence are also weighted against the poor because the middle and upper classes are better able to keep it secret.[58]

Ann Oakley and Robin Oakley offer an extensive overview of sexism in statistics.[59] They show that sexism occurs in the areas chosen for statistical analysis, the concepts employed to organize the statistics, the ways data are collected, the ways statistics are processed, and the ways statistics are presented. They offer three case studies of sexism in official statistics: the way data are collected concerning "head of household," "work," and "crime."

The collecting of statistics requires financial and human resources. The U.S. Commission on Civil Rights, an organization charged with collecting sex inequity statistics, has been rendered virtually powerless by recent federal administrations. Statistics on this problem will therefore suffer. If a group has little power, information relevant to its needs is less likely to be gathered than on other groups. Statistics are not always gathered on issues relevant to women, and the way they are gathered frequently keeps women invisible. The following quote illustrates this point with regard to the field of gerontology:

> Although aging is a process in which sex matters, it is only in recent years that the importance of sex differences has been widely reflected in empirical work. Prior to the mid-1970s, some of the major data sets on the aging included males only. For example, the Baltimore Longitudinal Study, started in 1969, included women for the first time in 1976.[60]

As a result of increasing sensitivity to these problems, some gerontologists organized a conference in 1984 simply to bring data sources concerning women to the attention of other gerontologists.[61]

Lisa Brush's research concerning intimate violence is also motivated by an attempt to overturn sexist research methods:

> Survey instruments characteristically used to conduct quantitative research on intimate violence have reproduced a bias toward nonfeminist interpretations of power and violence in relationships. . . . The most important barrier to adequate assessments of the extent and dimensions of intimate violence through surveys is the context of the interaction between interviewer and interviewee.

Her solution to his problem drew on feminist ideas about the importance of context:

> To elicit adequate information about the highly stigmatized, traumatic phenomenon of battering requires an infusion of trust, safety, and intimacy into the interviewing relationships. Methods of empirical inquiry used in battered women's shelters, rape crisis centers, consciousness-raising groups, and explicitly feminist research provide models for the transformation in survey methods that would establish new research practices and relationships, appropriate to studying violence.[62]

Another criticism concerns which data are and are not collected. Anthropology student Nancy Weiner, for example, criticized the fact that "Western economists rarely figure the work done by women in the country's GNP."[63] And economist Barbara Rogers pointed out that

> all of these essential activities performed by women—post-harvest work on the crops, storage, food processing, provision of relishes, care of small livestock, and marketing—tend to be relegated by development researchers to the despised "domestic" sector and therefore disregarded by all except the home economists.[64]

Other feminist criticism of statistical methods focuses on the way statistical information can be used to *obscure* phenomena. Sidney Verba and his associates[65] focus on the ability of surveys to uncover unreported complaints of sexual harassment on a university campus:

> Surveys are useful but limited tools of social investigation. They are particularly useful in relation to the kind of question with which we are dealing: how extensive is a particular social problem in a population? If one focuses only on complaints about some social problem, one may underestimate its extent since many instances of a problem may go unreported.
>
> Some would argue that a problem—a possible incident of sexual harassment, for instance—is not a serious problem if it is not brought forward. However, the absence of a complaint is not evidence of the nonexistence of a problem . . . targets of harassment are often seriously inhibited from complaining. Surveys, by actively seeking respondents rather than waiting for respondents to come forward, can get at these unreported events.

In contrast to this proactive asset, however, Sidney Verba and his associates recognize that surveys lack subtlety:

Surveys are also limited instruments. One limitation is the fact that they oversimplify complex issues by reducing them to the responses to a limited number of questions. The relationships involved in events that are perceived as sexual harassment are often subtle and complex. These cannot be adequately captured in a questionnaire. We tried to deal with this problem by asking many questions that attempt to get at some of the details of events. We sought concrete information rather than abstract statements of opinion. We also presented our respondents with opportunities to comment at length on their experiences, and many did.

To compensate for the lack of subtlety, they employed various techniques, such as the following:

> Appendix A contains verbatim descriptions of harassment incidents. Appendix B contains additional comments by respondents. These comments put the issue in context . . . the subjective response of the victim of sexual harassment is crucial. Only the victim can identify the consequences of harassment events. It is, indeed, the purpose of this survey to bring such subjective reports to the Harvard community.[66]

As most people know, data gathering can be an efficient mechanism to avoid action. And once collected, of course, there is nothing inherent in statistics to require that those in power will abide by their implications. I encountered this very problem in a study commissioned by the U.S. Congress concerning the Washington, D.C., public school system. Shortly *before* the study results were compiled, major policy decisions were enacted for the school system.[67] In the following example concerning the Office of Management and Budget, the crass disparagement of study results illustrates that statistics can lead to action only if there is power and will behind them. As reported in a newletter of the (U.S.) House Committee on Constitutional Revision and Women's Rights, "Ed Dale, an OMB spokesman, called studies showing that 67% of the U.S. poor are women who would be harmed by the budget cuts a 'bunch of junk.' 'If they (women) don't like it,' he said, 'tough luck.' "[68]

It is not only elected officials who dismiss statistics they do not wish to hear. In their review of sexist attitudes and practices, for example, Nijole Benokraitis and Joe Feagin suggest that

> most Americans rarely see or pay attention to statistics that show that sex discrimination abounds. Even when such statistics are provided, the initial reaction is denial or skepticism: "That was last year. What about statistics for this year?" "Even national data aren't accurate." "But anyone can lie with statistics." Or, people point to exceptions: "My neighbor just got a job in construction, and she says she's getting the same salary as the men."[69]

It may be that people consider statistics authoritative when they support a view already held, and dismiss them, when their views are challenged. Psychologists would probably consider this behavior to be a way that people deal with cognitive dissonance. The public seems to accept both that one can lie and say anything at all with statistics, and that statistics are decisive.

Ironically, the more sophisticated the survey and statistical techniques and thus the more likely a study will pressure those in power to act in line with results, the more likely the study will be incomprehensible to potential beneficiaries and will be manipulated by those who wish to retain their power. An example can be found in the work of sociologist Ronnie Steinberg, an expert on comparable worth. In an article about her cumulative research experience, she illustrates how a feminist researcher can utilize the survey method for change purposes and how those threatened by change can impede the study's progress.

> I directed the largest comparable pay study that has ever been undertaken. . . . We used fairly standard social science research methods to ask a large sample of employees what they do on their job. We then related what employees do on their jobs to what they are paid. In following this design, we parted ways with conventional approaches to job evaluation, which had been widely criticized by proponents and opponents alike. Specifically, we designed and pilot tested a 112-item questionnaire and distributed it to over 37,000 employees in over 2,900 different job titles.
>
> Our 73% response rate was a function of almost an obsessive concern with improving the rate of response in the face of New York State experience with extremely low response rates. Once we developed the model describing implicit state policy, we adjusted it in two ways recommended by the National Research Council to remove the effect . . . other . . . than the sex or race of the typical incumbent.

Because Ronnie Steinberg's design was as "rigorous and scientifically sound" as possible, her study posed a danger if it came up with the "wrong" findings. She soon found that this was the case.

> As the study evolved, the State project monitor got increasingly concerned with the financial and political ramifications of the study. To a certain degree to protect himself, he set up an Advisory Committee within management. . . . The fights that had taken place before the study contract was signed continued in this forum. These fights climaxed when the Division of the Budget, in effect, stopped the study completely for three full months, raising concerns with the methodological rigor of the study. What went on for the next three months included a detailed review of our design and pilot results by two consultants retained by the Budget Division, followed by a 110-page rebuttal by the Center's Comparable Worth team. . . .
>
> Budget didn't want the study to proceed at all and thought the research could be discredited. Had our research not followed strict social science guidelines, they may well have succeeded. Yet the fact that the research was carefully designed was only a necessary condition to ensure its continuation.

Ronnie Steinberg's next strategy is reminiscent of Ida B. Wells' comment, mentioned in the introductory chapter, that only the "most reputable" sources should be used when studying topics that threaten the status quo.

> The New York State study was designed so carefully that every facet of it was defensible in a court of law. Moreover, although the Center staff was entirely female, we hired two white male methodologists to assist in the study design and the data analysis—both because of their superb credentials . . . and because they were not regarded as pay equity proponents. We validated every question on the questionnaire. We used sophisticated sampling procedures. We used state-of-the-

art data analytic techniques to sum up with the compensation model and the estimates of wage discrimination. We even used a technique called jackknifing to develop error estimates.

The rigor that Ronnie Steinberg had hoped would give the study credibility had, in fact, toughened its opponents. In addition, this rigor led to other disappointing consequences, in her view:

> having proven to myself and to others that a rigorous and sophisticated study of wage discrimination would be completed, the results of the New York State Study were deeply disturbing to me. First, by using these rigorous methods, the study details remained inaccessible to the very employees that were supposed to benefit from the reform. This also allowed the results to be manipulated in numerous ways by the State without the employees knowing that they were receiving lower wage adjustments than would otherwise have been the case.
>
> Second, even though we used this careful methodology, the New York State study established a major pay equity precedent without cleansing gender and race in the wage system. Thus it opened the way to argue that the New York State approach should become the general policy approach, which would, in essence result in a permanent redefinition of the reform.[70]

Although Ronnie Steinberg faults sophisticated survey research for being inaccessible, her major criticism is that survey research, as other research, is only as powerful as its context allows it to be.

An article by Anne Pugh provides a complementary example on a smaller scale study. In a poignant essay about her statistical research, its feminist qualities and its shortcomings, Anne Pugh wrote that feminists should always take a critical, reflexive position:

> In this paper I want to show how my feminism affects the research process and, indeed, in what ways I regard this particular research process as feminist. I also want to assess the research product, the paper itself, in terms of a feminist perspective. The statistics I did concerned young homeless people's usage of a small youth advice and counselling agency, Shades. Shades, a voluntary organisation, has four paid workers, of which I am the research worker, and is based in Manchester's city centre. . . . As an agency we supported a philosophy of quality not quantity in our youth work and always stated that we did not believe in "playing the numbers game." Yet we did: we did rough and ready headcounts and tabulations in our reports. We were, it seemed, fascinated by numbers and allocated to them a power and legitimacy about which, though, we always felt ambiguous.

The ambivalence of "playing the numbers game," on the one hand, and being "fascinated by numbers," on the other, is a theme that runs through much discussion of feminist survey research. Anne Pugh continues:

> Once on the computer, I developed my data into some statistics. Using these I was able to explore some hypotheses, which had indeed been the aim of the study. I was able to comment on such issues as how many people used Shades, were they increasing or decreasing, whether they were local to Manchester or came from further afield, their age range, their ethnicity, whether young women's experience of homelessness was different from men's, all of which was important to Shades in its policy formation.

Anne Pugh was an insider who was not mystified by statistics because she understood the conditions under which they were created:

> Unfortunately, I was less than happy with the process of producing the statistics. I knew what tricks I had to perform to create them. . . . The statistics . . . do not constitute the "objective facts" of what is going on. . . . As a feminist, I am accustomed to questioning the apparent surface realities, the status quo. . . . This is how I approached my critique of my statistics. . . . with due attention to the research process of producing them. . . . [A] feminist framework considers the researcher as central in the research process.[71]

These concerns and others have led some feminist survey researchers to claim that as feminists, we should not overrely on any single method and should instead use multiple methods [the subject of a separate chapter in this book]. An eloquent voice on behalf of the multiple methods viewpoint is Charlene Depner, who in 1981, while employed at the Survey Research Center at the University of Michigan, delivered a paper at the Association for Women in Psychology, with the following "central thesis":

> Feminist psychology must move outside the limitations of the androcentric research tradition—to recognize what is of value in it and to move beyond this evaluation to the development of *new constructs, new methods and new frameworks*. . . . [We must] revise existing research methods in accord with the feminist critique [and consider] the new and daring concept of a distinctively feminine insight[72] and way of knowing. . . . [We must] examine our assumptions, our methods of systematizing observations and making inferences as well as deficiencies in language and inquiry which make insights difficult . . . there is no perfect design, no perfect methodology . . . the richness of our subject matter demands a full array of methodological tools . . . feminist psychology must implement every tool at its disposal—and create new ones—rather than reject any out of hand.[73]

Charlene Depner's view is to reduce her expectations that survey research will have the power to persuade, while also supplementing this research method with many others.

Dual Vision Rather Than Ambivalence

At the start of this chapter, I mentioned the ambivalence that characterizes feminist survey research. In a psychoanalytic sense, ambivalence has negative connotations. But sociologist Roberta Spalter-Roth and economist Heidi Hartmann suggest a different positive meaning, a feminist way of seeing, or "dual vision," that provides a fitting conclusion for this chapter. They define dual vision in light of one of their feminist survey research projects:

> This study[74] was produced at the Institute for Women's Policy Research (IWPR), a feminist think tank devoted to conducting research on policy issues affecting women's lives and to developing networks between the research, policy and advocacy communities. Given these goals we must, on the one hand, conduct policy

research that meets the standards of the mainstream social sciences of validity, reliability, objectivity and replicability. On the other hand, our work is influenced by the principles of feminist methodology and especially by its challenge to the rigid dichotomies between researcher and researched and between activists and truth seekers. . . .

In addition, like others of our generation we have been schooled in both social sciences and social movements. We believe that the research that results from these two perspectives, provides a useful synthesis in these times, despite some risks. We refer to this synthesis of the political and scientific as the "dual vision of feminist policy research." . . . When we produce policy research, we accept the standpoint of the objective expert using largely quantitative methods (rather than in-depth interviewing or participant observation) to evaluate policy options. And we use the dominant paradigm of cost-benefit analysis when it is appropriate. . . . Unlike mainstream policy analysts, however, we also follow the principles of feminist research[75]. . . . We view our research as political as well as scientific. We use our expert stance to legitimate feminist ideas. . . . We reject that part of the objectivity canon that distances the production of knowledge from its uses and thus we apply a constituency test to see if research that we undertake will be of use to grass-roots and advocacy groups in defining and solving problems. . . .

This dual vision is reflected in the concepts and methodology of our study of family and medical leave. The study, *Unnecessary Losses,* uses both techniques of cost-benefit analysis and a feminist standpoint that centrally locates women's work in order to evaluate a proposed policy. . . . Our credibility as a feminist policy research think tank is based on our embracing the contradictions.[76]

This dual vision feature of feminist survey researchers may also be characteristic of feminist researchers who use *other* methods. Dual vision may, in fact, be a central characteristic of feminists' perspective on social research in general.

5

Feminist Experimental Research[1]

Assumptions about the greater scientific utility of laboratory over field studies may have led to the neglect of sex as an important social variable. . . . Psychologists appear to contribute to the social reality of sex by the way they do their studies. *It is time to reexamine our methodologies.*[2]

Feminist sociology does not reject quantification or experimentation where these are relevant, but it does admit a wider range of methods and techniques which are less rigid, but not less rigorous.[3]

In the first quotation, psychologist Rhoda Unger suggests that laboratory experimentation may have led to a particular blindness in psychology with regard to sex. This suggestion is striking given that laboratory experiments are the normative research method in much of psychology, as well as in the physical sciences and clinical medicine. As psychologists Michelle Fine and Susan Gordon noted: "What academic psychologists do well are experiments in laboratories. In 1980 this method accounted for 71% of studies reported in major social psychological journals. In 1985, it accounted for 78%."[4] Moreover, Sandra Lipsitz Bem, the feminist psychologist of women whose work was most frequently cited, developed her famous concept of "androgyny" on the basis of experimental research.[5]

The large proportion of studies based on experimental methods in the major psychology journals suggests a kind of fusing between psychology as a discipline and laboratory experimentation as a method. In psychology, laboratory experiments are rhetorically referred to as the dominant or distinguishing method; they constitute what is considered to be "mainstream" research.[6] In the eyes of the public as well, a laboratory experiment symbolizes the very essence of the scientific method. Yet for such feminist psychologists as Rhoda Unger, experiments are problematic. As she puts it, the preferred method of psychology is a method that leads to a particular blindness.

For the purposes of this book, experiments pose an additional problem. The standardized procedure for writing experimental research reports discourages the use of the first person singular, eliminates reference to actual people, and attributes actions to concepts. Thus, it is nearly impossible for me to present feminist "voices" doing experimental research. For this reason I have to confine my analysis of this method to feminist experimenters' discussions *about* experimental methods. Even though this methodological material is unusually rich and deals with all aspects of experimental design, it deviates from my general principle of basing this book on feminists' actual research activities as they describe them.

The second quotation, by feminist sociologist Marcia Segal, is also striking to me, but for the opposite reason. Her remark suggests that experimentation is an option for sociologists, even though sociology lacks a tradition of experimental research.[7] Because of this lack of tradition, as a sociologist I have little personal experience with experiments beyond what I have read and what I participated in as an undergraduate "volunteer" in my psychology courses. I rely heavily on feminist experimental psychologists to understand this method.[8]

Social research methods textbooks almost always contain a chapter on experiments,[9] even though it is not a conventional sociological research method. I believe experimentation is included in such books because society bestows prestige and scientific credibility on the results of laboratory experiments. In her influential chapter, "Bias in Psychology," social psychologist Carolyn Sherif explained the stultifying effects on her intellectual development stemming from the hierarchy of prestige in psychology.[10] The source of this prestige may lie in experimenters' manipulation of variables, an image that appeals to people who value control. Literary images of scientists as dramatic discoverers of helpful remedies undoubtedly also contribute to the appeal of experiments. Similarly, the media portray scientific breakthroughs as emanating from carefully controlled experiments.

In this chapter I will discuss feminist experiments from the perspective of such psychologists as Rhoda Unger, who conducts experiments and yet is critical of them; and from the perspective of such sociologists as Marcia Segal, who suggests that feminist sociologists should engage in experimental research. In the conclusion below, I discuss the utility of experimental research for achieving feminist goals.

Historical Roots

Our understanding of the history of women's role in experimental psychology is still rudimentary.[11] Yet, the historical research that has been undertaken suggests that the earliest generation of female psychologists in the United States—women working in the late nineteenth century—overcame nearly insurmountable barriers in the pursuit of opportunities to do psychological research.[12] Not surprisingly, those few early female psychologists who eventually obtained the resources and authorization to conduct psychological experiments chose topics concerning women's lives.[13] For example, psychologist Mary Calkins, who began her work at Wellesley College in 1887, conducted experiments to demonstrate that women are just as intelligent as are men.[14]

Helen Thompson Wooley, another early U.S. female psychologist, completed a doctoral dissertation in 1903 entitled *The Mental Traits of Sex: An Experimental Investigation of the Normal Mind in Men and Women.* Her study foreshadowed contemporary feminist psychologists' critique of the overemphasis on sex differences and the relative disregard of similarities between females and males. She demonstrated that the distribution curves of numerous types of behavior performed by men and women actually overlap.[15] Interestingly, part of her refutation of Havelock Ellis' opposing view rested on careful laboratory research, in contrast to what she saw as his less than scientific methods.[16]

According to historian Rosalind Rosenberg, another early feminist experimental psychologist, Leta Hollingworth, utilized unused data from her husband's experiments to begin to establish important patterns concerning women.

> Henry Hollingworth introduced his wife to experimental psychology by asking her to assist him on an experiment measuring the effects of caffeine on mental and motor abilities. One of the precautions he took in his "zeal to control all of the possible variables," as he later recalled, "was to have the women subjects record the occurrences of the menses, during the six week experimental period." When the results of the experiment were reported, Leta Hollingworth noticed that no mention was made of the influence of menstruation on the work of the women subjects. Out of curiosity she studied the data herself and found no evidence that the women's performances had varied with their menstrual periods as her husband had feared they might.

Leta Hollingworth displayed the typical feminist intellectual characteristic of interest in ignored information about women. Rosalind Rosenberg also mentions Leta Hollingworth's anger about misconceptions concerning women, another source of her motivation to conduct research:

> Though Henry Hollingworth saw no special importance in this nonfinding, Leta Hollingworth found it highly significant. No dogma about women's nature enjoyed wider acceptance among doctors and psychologists, from Edward Clarke to Havelock Ellis, than the idea that women suffered periodic incapacity from menstruation. . . . Incensed by charges of menstrual-related disability, Leta Hollingworth chose to study the effects of women's menstrual cycle on their motor and mental abilities for her doctoral research.[17]

In her resulting study, *Functional Periodicity: An Experimental Study of the Mental and Motor Abilities of Women during Menstruation* (1914), Leta Hollingworth gave 24 women tasks to do when they were menstruating and when they were not. The tasks including tapping a brass plate as many times as possible within a brief time, holding a rod in a hole without letting it touch the sides, naming a series of colors and a series of opposites as quickly as possible, and learning to type. Her data demonstrated that women have no learning or performance deficiency[18] while menstruating, as compared to while not menstruating. Thus, from the perspective of methodology, one of the striking features of early feminist psychologists' work was their use of experimentation to shatter sexist social beliefs,[19] just as sociologists did with surveys. Interestingly, contemporary feminist psychologists are ardently critical of the very method that was so liberating for the earliest generation, just as many contemporary feminist sociologists are of surveys.[20]

Experimental sociology has roots in the United States that reach at least to the work of Frances Kellor (1872–1952), a resident of Hull-House and student of criminology and sociology at the University of Chicago. Frances Kellor challenged then current theories of criminal behavior by attempting to do rigorous, empirical research. In the summer of 1899 she

> traveled to five reformatories and prisons in New York, Ohio, and Illinois to investigate the female prison population. . . . [There she] unpacked her anthropometric gear and set up a . . . laboratory. She took physical measurements, conducted psychological tests, and pursued sociological research drawing on prison records, interviews with female inmates, and field visits to their home towns.

After collecting this information, she gathered analogous information on female college students, which she cleverly defined as her control group. A comparison of the data from these two groups

> challenged the [physiological theory of crime] . . . and suggested that economic factors contributed to crime. . . . Within a year, Kellor had collected enough material on crime to publish a book . . . under the title *Experimental Sociology: Descriptive and Analytical. Delinquents.*[21]

Feminist Critiques of Experiments

Whereas Leta Hollingworth turned to psychology with hope, U.S. psychologist Naomi Weisstein turned against psychology in anger in a 1970 article about psychology's deficiencies with regard to understanding women. Her article was the opening salvo in feminist psychologists' continuing attack on experimental and clinical research.[22] Two years later Rae Carlson[23] criticized the prominence of experimental research in social science, arguing that the rigid control and manipulation of variables demanded by experiments is a male, agentic style of research rather than a feminine, communal mode. And 10 years later, Australian feminist psychologist Beverly Walker reiterated Naomi Weisstein's views.

> Central to the feminist critique is the argument that psychology is not objective, and that it and its practitioners have contributed to the oppression of women by theory and practice. This view is antithetical to the way most psychologists had seen and taught about their discipline.[24]

In addition to a general critique of experimental research, feminists have shown that sexist biases can influence each of the stages that comprise an experiment.[25] These stages proceed sequentially from formulating the problem or asking the question, to reviewing the literature, operationalizing a design, selecting subjects,[26] collecting data, and finally analyzing, interpreting, and writing up the data. Psychologist Barbara Strudler Wallston wrote a powerful critique of the first stage— the asking of questions.[27] Others have focused on remaining stages.

Two feminist criticisms of the fourth stage, "subject selection," concern the use of animals and the introduction of sex/class bias when humans are research subjects. Feminist physician Susan Gordon is an ardent critic of experimentation on animals. She points out that endocrinology focuses primarily on sex hormone research, the vast majority of which is performed on animals by "men in industrialized, western capitalist nations with patriarchal societies'' and then extrapolated to people:

> One can question why so much research is being done in the area of sexual dimorphism with its particular emphasis on gene ''programming'' and male and female behavior as determined by hormones and genes, and the extrapolation of this information on rats, guinea pigs and monkeys to men and women. Is this not sexism and an attempt to continue the concept of genetic determinism and thereby, racism too? . . . [T]his kind of research deters us from focusing on other more important problems such as those having to do with health and well-being, not only of women but of all humankind.[28]

Feminists who are critical of animal experimental research cite a variety of additional reasons for their opposition.[29] As Donna Spring explains,[30] experimenters frequently mistreat animals (through confinement, deprivation of contact with parents, injections of disease, burns, shocks, poisons, mutilation, and killing). The purposes for which animals are used include tests related to chemical warfare and nuclear radiation. Animal experimentation research is a multibillion dollar industry consuming funds that could be diverted to rehabilitation, education, and primary prevention. Most animal research is extremely wasteful because it is repetitive, and because the analogy with human beings is inexact and even misleading. Finally, given the numbers of animals used, if animal research were actually efficacious, we should have achieved lower rates of certain diseases on which animal-based research has focused, i.e., cancer and heart disease.[31]

Nevertheless, some feminists have drawn on experimental research that uses animals, extrapolating the findings to issues important to women. An example is Lenore Walker, whose theory concerning the response of women to battering is modeled on Martin Seligman's experiments with dogs and shock therapy.[32] As Lenore Walker explains, Martin Seligman gave shocks to caged dogs and noted that after a number of shocks, the dogs ''remained passive, refused to leave and did not avoid the shock.''[33] Lenore Walker claims that women stay in battering relationships if they have learned to be helpless.[34] ''Once the women are operating from a belief of helplessness, the perception becomes reality and they become passive, submissive, 'helpless.' ''[35]

In a different critique of the selection of subjects, psychologists Brinton Lykes and Abigail Stewart, among others, have illustrated the preponderance of males as experimental subjects in psychological research.[36] For example, Michelle Fine and Susan Gordon wrote:

> Psychologists typically generate theory and evidence from accessible populations—white, college aged, privileged male undergraduates . . . and write about that evidence as ''human behavior.'' In 1980 75% of reviewed social psychological studies were conducted with students. In 1985 this profile accounted for 83% of studies.[37]

Another area in which feminists have been critical of experimental research is ''experimenter effects.'' Feminist psychologist Rhoda Unger discussed the significance of experimenter effects on experimental outcomes in her 1981 Presidential

Address to the Division on the Psychology of Women, of the American Psychological Association.[38]

Whereas early feminist critiques of experiments focused on the near exclusive use of male subjects, more recent critiques are focusing on what happens when women are *included* in the lab. These critiques discuss the "unnatural" characteristics of laboratory behavior and group composition. In Michelle Fine and Susan Gordon's view:

> Removed from social relationships, interaction in the lab is typically limited to a "subject" and a white [often male] experimenter. There may be some strangers[39] present, who are euphemistically called group members. Defining features of this context include a lack of trust, longevity, and connection.[40] In caricature, this sounds like a scene designed for Clint Eastwood, and a scene which would drive women mad. And given the ambiguity of the circumstances, the absence of relationships, and the anonymity, it is also a scene in which racist behaviors by white "subjects" may be most likely to be enacted. . . . So much for the study of "objective" phenomena in "uncontaminated" spaces.[41]

Their final point is that the experimental setting typically prevents subjects from acting in ways that might please the experimenter. Others say that it encourages people to please the experimenter.[42] There is no reason to conclude, however, as experimenters do, that subjects' behavior during an experiment represents the subjects' "true" feelings. This assumption pervades experimental research, however, as can be seen in the following typical excerpt:

> Two hundred twenty-six male and 264 female college students were randomly assigned to one of six groups. The subjects were blind to our manipulation in order to avoid the possibility that they would respond out of sympathy with the political implications of our hypothesis.[43]

The experimental situation is supposed to maximize the subject's inability to "respond out of sympathy." However, this set of circumstances is itself a special social situation. Experiments are usually conducted in laboratories because a laboratory is thought to be a kind of "neutral social environment" in which the experimenter can maximize control over the subjects, and, thereby, maximize control over the variables. Critics argue that a laboratory is not "neutral" but is rather a specific social environment that exerts its own effects.

Psychologist Reesa M. Vaughter has proposed a way of dealing with many of these criticisms. She argues that experiments should not stand alone when analyzing women's behavior. Instead, experiments should always be combined with descriptions of contexts.

> [W]ithin the context of any single experiment . . . constructing a psychological analysis requires not only the measurement of some pattern of behavior (e.g., academic achievement) and of cognitions (e.g. expectancies of achievement) but also descriptions and analyses of the situational context and the environment (e.g. a college science class in which the male to female student ratio is four to one and the instructor is male).

She calls this contextual description "ethology."

Ethological approaches can enhance our understanding of the development of behavioral patterns of women. Ethological as well as antecedent-consequence analyses of cognitive and behavioral development encourage us to ask questions of "why." Without investigating "why" questions, we have only traditional theoretical models to call upon, which often lead us back to the mysterious, feminine psyche.

While advocating ethology, she also recognizes that some psychologists may be unequipped to carry out this form of research.

Social-political analyses, in conjunction with psychological analyses, may be facilitated by collaborative, interdisciplinary research. Advances through interdisciplinary research are possible as we change the current policy of isolating psychologists from other scientists. The isolation of men and women in departments of psychology may keep our territories of status clearly intact, but it may also be a significant impediment toward an understanding of human behavior, which is influenced by many factors.[44]

Posing another critique in 1978, psychologist Alice Eagly argued that we have to understand the *historical* context that shapes the results of experimental research.

Various sex differences in social influence studies are a product of contextual features of experimental settings. The importance of the cultural context in which research is conducted is suggested by the fact that findings reporting greater influenceability among females were more prevalent in studies published prior to 1970 that in those published in the 1970s.[45]

She suggests that phenomena in the larger social context were influencing the laboratory results.

The next year psychologist Mary Brown Parlee published an essay expressing a view similar to that of Reesa Vaughter and Alice Eagly. She argued that there is an inherent *contradiction* between experiments and feminists psychology because experiments are context-stripping[46] and thus reduce the political to the personal:

[P]sychology's commitment to the experimental method makes our relationship [to this discipline] different from that of feminists in other disciplines. . . . [T]his commitment to method is a problem of more than academic interest as far as women are concerned. . . . The commitment to the experimental method which characterizes mainstream psychology not only functions to exclude feminist research, it also serves to obscure the connections between individual experience and social roles and institutions.[47]

Her suggestion to feminist psychologists is to study roles in the context of particular institutions. She recognizes, however, that this is not what traditional psychology wants. On the other hand, she urges feminists to do precisely what the tradition does not want them to do because then they know they are onto something important!

Social psychologist Susan Condor offers an example of a researcher who seems to have taken this criticism to heart. The research she planned to do involved the use of psychometric tests purporting to measure individual differences in various beliefs. Instead of simply using the tests, however, she explored the validity of the scales by asking

> some women to "talk through" some existing psychometric instruments. It became apparent that many of the women who did not wish for widespread change in sex role definitions were experiencing difficulties answering the sex role attitude scales. . . . Several women became quite aggressive, claiming that the questions were unanswerable. Others who placed their answers toward the "appropriate" poles of the dimensions provided appeared to feel the need to qualify their responses.[48]

[handwritten margin note: I'm thinking about student teacher evaluations.]

She responded to this problem by conducting in-depth interviews with the women.

There has also been a lot of feminist discussion about control groups, an essential component of experimental designs. Psychologist Mary Brown Parlee analyzed the political meaning of control groups,[49] while three sociologists, Laurie Wardell, Dair Gillespie, and Ann Leffler, echoed her point, showing that there is a political bias in sociological research's use of comparison groups parallel to the choice of control groups in experimental psychological research. These feminist sociologists show that research on men's violence against wives, based on a design that compares "beaten" and "unbeaten" wives, insidiously blames the victims. On the other hand, comparisons of "American families to families in other cultures or times, or heterosexual couples to other couples, or the well-being of women alone compared to women with men"[50] would shift attention to the process of male dominance in a particular culture or time period and thus take the blame off the victim.

Summarizing the wide array of ways in which experiments can contain sexist bias, U.S. feminist psychologist Paula Johnson compiled a chart pointing out pitfalls and suggesting remedies.[51] Perhaps these critiques help explain why a smaller portion of articles published in the *Psychology of Women Quarterly* are experiments, in comparison with the portion of experiments published in the more mainstream *Journal of Personality and Social Psychology*.[52]

One subfield of sociology that employs the experimental method is feminist ethnomethodology, as reported by Sarah Kessler and Wendy McKenna who created ethnomethodological "games" to ascertain how people define the essential characteristics of female and male:

> When we first began to think about gender as a social construction, we devised a "game" called the Ten Question Gender Game. The player is told, "I am thinking of a person and I want you to tell me, not who the person is, but whether that person is female or male. Do this by asking me ten questions, all of which must be answerable by 'yes' or 'no'. You may ask any question except, 'Is the person male?' or 'Is the person female?'. After each question, based on the answer I have given you, tell me, at that point in the game, whether you think the person is female or male and why you have decided that. Then ask your next question. You need not stick with your first answer throughout the game, but regardless of whether you stay with your original choice or change your decision you must, at each point, explain your choice. At the end of the game I will ask you to give your final decision on the person's gender."

The game is reasonably simple, fun to play, and is not unlike "Twenty Questions." Our game, however, is not just for fun. Instead of answering the player's questions on the basis of the characteristics of some real person, we responded with a prearranged random series of "yes's" and "no's." The game is a form of the "documentary method,"[53] and we treated it both in order to find out what kinds of questions the players would ask about gender, and, more importantly, to uncover how the players would make sense out of what is, in many cases, seemingly contradictory information.

Wendy McKenna and Sarah Kessler continued their series of experimental ethnomethodological research with another project. In this case the goal of their experiment was to obtain

an "objective" measure of the relative weight of various characteristics in making gender attributions . . . [and to see] how people construct gender from "contradictory" cues [so that we could] gain some understanding of the phenomenological reality of femaleness and maleness.[54]

They used the following method:

A set of plastic overlays was prepared. Drawn on each overlay was one physical characteristic or one piece of clothing. The eleven overlays were: long hair, short hair, wide hips, narrow hips, breasts, flat chest, body hair, penis, vagina, "unisex" shirt, "unisex" pants. When the overlays were placed one on top of the other, the result was a drawing of a figure with various combinations of typically male and female physical gender characteristics. The overlays, in combination, produced ninety-six different figures. . . . Each of the ninety-six figures was shown to ten adults, five males and five females. The 960[55] participants[56] were asked three questions: (1) is this a picture of a female or a male? (2) using a scale of 1 to 7, where 1 means not at all confident and 7 means very confident, how confident are you of your answer?. . . . (3) How would you change the figure to make it into the other gender?

They found that

it is the penis which is conspicuous and apparently impossible to ignore, and it is the male figure which dominates the reality of gender. These findings hold for both male and female viewers of the figures.[57]

Another area in which feminist sociologists have utilized experimental procedures (though not necessarily laboratory experiments) is linguistics. For example, sociologist Mary Glenn Wiley and linguist Dale E. Woolley studied how students differentially perceive identically employed men and women who interrupt others.

To investigate these research questions, we designed a transcript of a putative conversation between two vice presidents of a national corporation. In the one-page script, one speaker interrupts the other three times. . . . The gender of the two speakers was varied to create two versions of this transcript. In one version, the interrupting speaker was a man and the person interrupted was a woman. In the other version, the genders were reversed: the interrupter was a woman and the person interrupted was a man. The respondents were 107 students in introductory-level linguistics courses at a large midwestern university. . . . After reading one version of the conversation, respondents were asked to respond to a questionnaire.[58]

This study produced the surprising results that interrupters were *not* seen as more powerful than those they interrupted; and men were *not* seen as more powerful than women.

Other U.S. sociologists who have used experimental designs in studies concerning gender, perception, and language include Joseph W. Schneider, Sally L. Hacker, Janet Hyde, and Sharlene Hesse-Biber. These researchers used varying techniques but consistently found that people visualize males when hearing or reading language that relies on the generic male pronoun.[59] Their sociological experiments have contributed to changes in textbook and newspaper style policies.[60]

A final area of feminist sociological experimental research is that form of program development or program evaluation that utilizes experimental designs. An example is Joyce McCarl Nielsen and Jeana Abromeit's study of curriculum transformations. They write that the data for their project "were generated according to a pretest–posttest experimental and control group research design, a standard procedure used in evaluation research."[61] Specifically, they compared faculty syllabi before and after training, administered questionnaires, posed two open-ended questions, and asked people to categorize themselves according to a scheme the researchers presented. Their study permitted assessment of the effectiveness of the particular curriculum transformation techniques used on specific campuses, and to test theory about curriculum change more generally.

Utility of Experimental Research for Feminist Goals

Since the public generally accepts experiments as objective, feminists (who are not critical of experimental research) attempt to bring results of experiments to the public's attention in order to create attitudinal and social change. For instance, in her now classic work *Sexual Politics,* Kate Millett demonstrated her ideas by drawing on "a witty experiment by Philip Goldberg[62] [that] proves what everyone knows." She claims everyone knows from experience that women have "internalized the dis-esteem in which they are held [and thus] . . . despise both themselves and each other." She nevertheless buttresses her contention by drawing on Philip Goldberg's experiment:

> This simple test consisted of asking women undergraduates to respond to the scholarship in an essay signed alternately by one John McKay and one Joan McKay. In making their assessments the students generally agreed that John was a remarkable thinker, Joan an unimpressive mind. Yet the articles were identical; the reaction was dependent on the sex of the supposed author.[63]

Her point was to help women recognize their self-hating behavior so they could change it, and to encourage society at large to alter its attitudes toward women.

Related studies have shown that both females and males listen to and remem-

[handwritten margin note: Why I don't object to "their"]

ber information from male public speakers more than they do from female public speakers, regardless of the topic.[64] Brandeis undergraduate Abigail Drexler found that male college students were less able to remember the names of their previous female professors than they were to remember the names of their male professors, even if they thought the women had been excellent teachers.[65] Her goal was to bring this information to the attention of male undergraduates and their professors in an effort to have them acknowledge their selective memory.

In a similar vein, sociologist Dorothy E. Smith discussed a study by L. S. Fidell published in the *American Psychologist,* a journal in which psychologists address issues relevant to the discipline or profession as a whole. Fidell's study concerned sex discrimination in university hiring practices in psychology. She

> used an approach very similar to Goldberg's, constructing two sets of fictional descriptions of academic background and qualifications (including the Ph.D.). Identical descriptions in one set had a woman's name attached and in the other a man's. The sets of descriptions were sent to chairpersons[66] of all colleges and universities in the United States offering graduate degrees in psychology. They were asked to estimate the chance of the individuals described getting an offer of a position and at what level, etc. Her findings supported the hypothesis of discrimination on the basis of sex: "The distributions of level of appointment were higher for men than for women. Further, men received more 'on line' (academic positions leading to tenure) responses than women. Only men were offered full professorships."[67]

Here the obvious point is to illustrate that women do not have a fair chance to be employed in departments of psychology, in comparison to men. Such a revelation could then be used to change public attitudes and to modify laws by bringing cases of sex discrimination to court. The 1954 Supreme Court decision concerning racial segregation in U.S. public schools is only one of many landmark cases that used sociological and psychological experimental research in this way.[68]

Psychologist Matina Horner's studies of women's "motive to avoid success"[69] were also widely publicized. At first, her results were interpreted as reflecting characteristics of the women themselves. Later research helped educate the public that the behavior of women and men may be a reaction to expectations about them rather than an inherent quality of their gender.[70] Matina Horner[71] elicited stories from the people she studied and then analyzed the attitudes embedded in those stories. Her goal was similar to that of the earliest generation of feminist experimental psychologists in stressing that "the intellectual capacities of the sexes were identical." Because of societal arrangements, however,

> their patterns of learning were not. Girls achieved more than boys in elementary school but began to slip behind in high school; by college, women were not only achieving less than men but were even rating men's potential to achieve higher than their own. The key to the puzzle was societal values. As girls matured, they fell victim to cultural judgments that brains and beauty did not mix, that learning was a man's business, that a woman who was too smart would become an old maid. . . . The implication of Horner's research for the women's movement was clear: to promote a new image that made success compatible with womanhood.[72]

Here, too, the point was to alert women that they may be handicapping themselves by believing that success was incompatible with being a woman.

Experiments concerning pornographic materials also shape policies and laws.[73] Experiments have helped demonstrate the gendered power dynamics of nonverbal behavior and interaction.[74] Experiments have shown that sex role assumptions guide the practice of mental health clinicians.[75] And experimenters have shown the impact of being the only member of a group without a characteristic all other group members share, being part of a sizable minority, or being in the majority.[76] These ideas have helped people formulate revised employment practices, affirmative action programs, and socialization practices.

Some Final Words of Concern and Caution

Phenomenologists and critical theorists argue that no matter how close the experimenter gets to "the natural setting," social life cannot adequately be comprehended through the detached "objectivity" demanded by the experimental method. This critique was stated powerfully by Max Weber and Wilhelm Dilthey, who asserted that social life should be comprehended through the method of *verstehen,* or empathic understanding. Putting it personally, Michelle Fine and Susan Gordon wrote:

> If you really want to know either of us, don't put us in a laboratory, or hand us a survey, or even interview us separately alone in our homes. Watch me (MF) with women friends, my son, his father, my niece or my mother and you will see what feels most authentic to me. These very moments, which construct who I am when I am most me, remain remote from psychological studies of individuals or even groups.[77]

Agreeing with this perspective many feminist scholars argue that it has been detrimental to women to have knowledge founded on limited ways of knowing. Instead of orthodoxy, they argue for heterodoxy. Letitia Peplau and Eva Conrad's review of the criticism of experimentation led them to adopt this view:

> We think it is very much in the spirit of feminist scholarship to encourage and legitimate nonexperimental research methods. But we oppose the view that nonexperimental methods are inherently more feminist than experimental ones.[78]

Just as women know in many different ways, we must be known in many different ways. A truly rational approach to knowledge excludes little and is open-minded.

In an American Psychological Association Master Lecture on issues of sex, race, and class in psychotherapy research, Annette Brodsky stressed this point:

> If one accepted only the evidence from well controlled, double blind, large N, statistically significant, empirical studies in refereed journals, there would be no paper on any of the variables discussed in this presentation [i.e. race, ethnicity and class]. The nature of demonstrating bias [however . . .] in psychotherapy, is fraught with restrictions in research design, controls, availability of subjects, objectivity of researchers, funding, etc. A cycle in the history of psychotherapy

research continues as the pendulum swings from the need for getting good experimental data to the need for keeping the data close to the real situation. . . .
Prescriptions to return to single case studies and clinical field studies are now in
vogue. . . . An integration of both paradigm I (experimental control groups,
direct manipulation of experimental variables) with paradigm II (clinical case studies,
in-depth inspection of the total situation in the field) is perhaps the direction of
choice if one wishes to avoid the pitfalls of either single approach.[79]

Although her position may sound logical, it is not the mainstream approach in
psychology, as Michelle Fine and Susan Gordon's data at the start of this chapter
show.

But Annette Brodsky argues an important case. Just as we cannot exclude
from the repertoire of knowledge studies *without* an experimental design, so too
we should not assume that information derived from experiments can be applied
to natural settings. Experiments frequently extract statements from subjects that
only imply behavior. They rely on simple responses to "stand for" reality. Clearly,
there is a big leap between "standing for" reality and "being real."

The fame of many experiments (and thus the ability they have to influence
public opinion) makes it essential that the results of experiments be linked precisely to the exact variables and groups studied. Feminist psychologists have shown
how publication practices and experimental design highlight differences and hide
similarities between groups. Overgeneralization that masks differences in race,
age, education, and other factors is clearly inappropriate and possibly dangerous.
Too often studies done on white populations are generalized to all groups, just as
studies done on men are generalized to all people, thereby producing distorted
results.

Thus, the fact that the public and courts invest experiments and statistics with
so much credibility is a double-edged sword. On the one hand, if feminists can
design experiments that illustrate important feminist insights, then experiments are
a powerful tool for policy formation.

> Recent advances in statistical techniques for meta-analysis have enhanced femin-
> ist research by. . . . showing that males and females do not differ in statistically
> significant ways on standardized measures of performance. . . [Such] quantita-
> tive data have been vital to efforts to end sex discrimination. For instance, the
> U.S. Supreme Court . . . ruled in the case of Watson vs. Forth Worth Bank and
> Trust that plaintiffs in white-collar professional and managerial jobs could use
> statistical analyses to prove sex discrimination at work.[80]

From this perspective, then, the task of feminist researchers is to design experiments that illustrate what needs to be changed. On the other hand, all issues are
not amenable to experimental research and thus certain types of reform become
extremely difficult to achieve if we accord experimental research an exclusive
position in the "truth hierarchy." In the words of one set of pornography researchers:

> social psychologists have not conducted a study whereby one group of persons is
> exposed to sexually violent materials and another is not, then waited to see if
> subjects in the exposed group committed crimes closely resembling the depictions

to which they were exposed. These studies obviously cannot be done for ethical reasons. Consequently, we have no experimental data on specific imitation effects.[81]

And as sociologist Pauline B. Bart put it:

Proof of the harm of pornography that will satisfy those on the other side seems impossible to come by. As MacKinnon points out,[82] the standard of proof they require can only be obtained through controlled experiments.[83]

These controlled experiments cannot be ethically done. Thus, we have a catch-22 situation that impedes regulation of pornographic material harmful to women if we say harm must be demonstrated by experiments.

We should also recognize that society is unlikely to be willing to change *even if* experimental research does provide information suggesting that change is needed. This point arose in the previous chapter on survey research as well. Putting one's eggs in the basket of so-called definitive research is a very risky strategy to use to achieve social change. Such persuasive experiments as those conducted by Eleanor Maccoby on the lack of cultural supports for the full development of female intelligence[84] have been brought to the public's attention repeatedly. In fact, reading about the early history of feminist experimental research shows the extent to which the topics studied by the first generation continue to be of concern to women today. Feminist psychologists have utilized experiments in the service of greater understanding and social change, while also criticizing the many inherent flaws of experimental research. At the same time feminist sociologists seem poised to take advantage of the power that does reside in this method. Combining the strengths of the experimental method with the strengths of other methods is probably the best way to avoid its weakness while utilizing its power. Similarly, combining the strength of research with the power of other forms of persuasion is probably a useful approach for creating change.

6

Feminist Cross-Cultural Research

There must be more empirical and cross-cultural investigations of the life experiences of women. In other words, we cannot speak of a psychology or sociology or anthropology of women, if the frameworks of these perspectives are applicable to White, middle-class, or professional women only.[1]

Although women have been welcomed in anthropology more than in many other disciplines,[2] anthropology's persistent male bias continues to be lamented. In 1985 Linda Mitteness wrote:

> Reading much of traditional social anthropology might lead one to think that cultures other than ours consist entirely of men of indeterminate adult age who have mothers only in order that they might have mothers' brothers. This ethnographic slant can probably be accounted for by a variety of factors, including the relative importance of men in the societies studied, the predispositions of Western anthropologists to think of male institutions first, and the age and sex of the fieldworker. . . . It is time for anthropologists to reflexively analyze their selection of topics for study.[3]

In the opening quotation, Patricia Bell Scott reminds feminists that working to overcome the male orientation of cross-cultural materials requires the study of diverse groups of women within societies. The paucity of cross-cultural studies of women may stem from practical difficulties such as needing to learn languages, obtain funds, and find time for travel. Cross-cultural research requires cooperative local political conditions that may be tenuous if studies concern women. Such research depends on the willingness of governments to reveal information about conditions inside their borders. Robin Morgan specified how these problems affected her ability to include all countries in her encyclopedic review of global feminism:

> Although [there is] a . . . large representation from North Africa and the Arabian Peninsula, Jordan, sadly is absent. China is present, but Taiwan, unfortunately, is not; we tried but failed to gain access to feminist activities, including Lu Hsiu-Lien, the leading Taiwanese feminist writer currently serving a twelve-year prison sentence for "seditious feminist activism." Our best efforts were . . . unsuccessful in obtaining articles from Angola, Bangladesh, Belgium, Bolivia, Cameroon, Chad, Czechoslovakia, Ethiopia, Guinea, Iraq, Mozambique, Paraguay, Syria, Tanzania, Tunisia, Turkey, Uruguay, the Yemens, Zaire and Zanzibar.

. . . [I]n certain . . . countries, despite the existence of an established movement, a woman could not write publicly about that movement in an international forum because of censorship strictures; in still other cases, where a totalitarian government or the rise of religious fundamentalism had placed the women's movement in a totally suppressed or highly endangered state, no feminist activist could risk open communication.[4]

When the problems of access are overcome, feminists have many remaining challenges in doing cross-cultural research.

Just as previous chapters revealed catch-22 problems concerning particular methods, such a problem exists here in the sense that a separate chapter on cross-cultural feminist research may reinforce the very ethnocentrism I wish to avoid. Simply imbedding cross-cultural material in other chapters would have denied such research the special attention it deserves. Thus, I decided to both integrate cross-cultural material throughout the book and to give it a separate chapter.

Historical Roots

Feminist ethnographers Harriet Martineau and Fanny Wright, discussed earlier, conducted cross-cultural research in the early nineteenth century. Fanny Wright studied the United States and compared her observations to British society and to the ideals of the United States. Harriet Martineau did the same, and also studied the Middle East. In 1886 and 1887 social reformer Helen Campbell (see chapter on feminist interview research) did cross-cultural studies concerning women's industrial labor in the Great Britain, as contrasted with the United States. Having learned that "wretchedness and want" transcend national boundaries, she felt driven to inform those who thought otherwise.

> Day by day, the desire has grown stronger to make plain the fact that this is a world-wide question, and one that must be answered. It is not for a city here and there, chiefly those where emigrants pour in, and so often, the mass of unskilled labor, always underpaid, and always near starvation. It is for the cities everywhere in the world of civilization, and because London includes the greatest numbers, these lines are written in London after many months of observation among workers on this side of the sea, [including] . . . one or two representative cities on the continent. London, however, deserves and demands chief consideration, not only because it leads in numbers, but because our own conditions are, in many points, an inheritance which crossed the sea with the pilgrims, and is in every drop of Anglo-Saxon blood. If the glint of the sovereign and its clink in the pocket are the dearest sight and sound to British eyes and ears, America has equal affection for her dollars.[5]

Helen Campbell's multiple rationales for cross-cultural research were to determine if conditions varied in industrial countries, to investigate the roots of U.S. attitudes in Great Britain, and to show that workers' economic problems in both countries were not the product of their work attitudes.

A mid-twentieth-century example of feminist cross-cultural research is a study conducted by Swedish sociologist Alva Myrdal and her British associate, Viola

Klein. Alva Myrdal writes in the foreword to their book[6] that immediately following World War II, the International Federation of University Women conducted
"an international survey of the needs for social reform if women are to be put
into a position to reconcile family and professional life." Originally she had intended to analyze these data, but they did not lend themselves to meaningful
comparison. At the same time, she began to work for the United Nations and was
so overwhelmed by "the problems in the underdeveloped countries that [she] found
it intellectually impossible to proceed with a manuscript which could only concern
a few highly favoured nations." Finally, she felt compelled to study the original
problem and turned to Viola Klein in Great Britain. Their book is the outcome of
"harmonious cooperation" concerning data collected in many different countries.
The fact that they came from two different societies assured that theirs would not
be an analysis of "women and work" from one national perspective.

The Guiding Principles of
Cross-Cultural Feminist Scholars

Four assumptions guide the feminist cross-cultural research I have located: (1) the
importance of cultural specificity, (2) the necessity of intensive study, (3) the
possibility of commonalities among women of different cultures, and (4) the need
for a critical evaluation of study materials. The first point—the importance of
cultural specificity for understanding women—is mentioned frequently. Ann Pescatello, for example, explained the multiple contexts of Iberian women:

> This book is about Iberian females—in Europe, Asia, Africa, and America—and
> about females of those Asian, African, and Amerindian cultures with whom the
> Iberians came in contact and on whom they left their imprint, either in shadow
> or in substance. In order to arrive at an understanding of contemporary female
> life through an examination of females in Iberian cultures, it is necessary to dis-
> cuss the place of women in the world view of all cultures involved.[7]

Similarly, Janet Mancini Billson studied nine distinct cultural groups of women in
Canada: Chinese (Vancouver), Blood Indian (Standoff, Alberta), West Indian (To-
ronto), Mennonite (Elmira, Ontario), Iroquois (Six Nations Reserve, Ontario),
Scottish (Rice Point, Prince Edward Island), Inuit (Pangnirtung, NWT), French-
Canadian (Quebec City), and Ukrainian (Saskatoon, Saskatchewan). Her purpose
was to test

> the subordination hypothesis on a cross-cultural basis: have women in these nine
> cultural communities been subordinate to men traditionally, and are they now?
> . . . I am [also] seeking to uncover cultural factors that might help explain the
> nature and extent of subordination of women, or their dominance and power,
> wherever that might occur. Furthermore, I am exploring the changes in male and
> female roles as changes in the mode of production have occurred in each com-
> munity. . . . In order to achieve these objectives, I have worked closely with
> women (and men) in each community, stimulating discussion of what gender
> relations were like in the times of their greatgrandparents, grandparents, parents,
> and now, for themselves.[8]

In other words, it is senseless to talk about "women's subordination" in general. Even if female subordination is universal, each instance must be understood within its particular cultural context. The insistence on cultural specificity represents a challenge to essentialism, a theory claiming that women have particular qualities or essences, stemming from universal biological factors.

The second assumption—that women must be studied intensively before anything can be said about them—challenges feminists and traditional scholars to explore the relation between women and their context in depth. Concerning her study of Aboriginal women's rituals, white Australian anthropologist Diane Bell wrote:

> [T]he extreme separation of the sexes in desert society represents an analytic challenge which I suggest is best met in the first instance by increasing our ethnographic understanding of women's domain. . . . [W]e know too little of the female half of society to argue for male dominance as an enduring, timeless reality. We need to be clear regarding the nature of woman's contribution to her society, her rights and responsibilities, before we endorse one particular model of male–female relations.[9]

One of the most massive efforts to compile exact information about women is Robin Morgan's *Sisterhood Is Global,*[10] the result of an extensive international feminist network's effort to compile data about the status of women in every country in the world. Preferring "internationalist" rather than "cross-cultural" to describe her perspective, she explains how her project shaped its method.

> As both our knowledge and our curiosity deepened, our standards rose, and the information categories became more sophisticated. The data that came in were simply too vital and fascinating to exclude, especially since much hitherto had been unavailable and/or unpublished. Thus, the Statistical Prefaces came into being. They then necessitated a larger research staff, still more international phone calls and cables, increased office space, and eventually, the use of word processors and computers—all of which in turn required additional fundraising. Every aspect of *Sisterhood is Global* developed in this fashion.[11]

Feminist cross-cultural research explores how women's lives in seemingly disparate societies actually have much in common, the third point mentioned above. For example, Mexican psychologist Sylvia Marcos studied popular medicine in Mexico as a form of cultural resistance similar to self-help groups and consciousness-raising among U.S. feminists. She thus was able to rename these groups as forms of "popular healing."[12]

A fourth characteristic of feminist cross-cultural research is critical evaluation of available materials given the dearth of records about women in numerous societies. Economists Lisa Leghorn and Katherine Parker were characteristically self-conscious about the politics of their choice of materials for their cross-cultural study of women's economies. Their book, *Women's Worth,* tries to envision

> what a female-value-based economy might look like. . . . [T]he range of relevant literature . . . was not adequate—. . . we . . . [were] forced to seek out new sources of data for the work we are doing. Most of the cultures we . . . describe are cultures in which women have published accounts of their experi-

ences, or from which we have known women who could give us an initial picture of what women's lives are like there—pictures which we supplemented with more traditionally-gathered data. We also use studies done by western women in other cultures in those cases where we feel they have a minimum of cultural and male bias in their research. Women as a group have developed an understanding of their place in the economy. And they have tried to communicate it, though their efforts have been neither rewarded nor recognized by the patriarchal cultures they live in. Women have written—so we have explored novels, journals, poems, and unpublished papers. Women have passed on information verbally—so we have spoken with women from different cultures, and women who have visited, lived in or studied in such cultures.[13]

Many feminist cross-cultural research projects discuss the difficulties of obtaining comparable data and of having people in other societies understand their intentions. In her study of "foreign"[14] wives living in the countries in which their husbands were born (Japan and Nigeria), Anne Imamura used questionnaires and interviews. She learned of "the problems and strategies of women who learned to be women in one world, but who had to behave as women in another." Difficulties occurred, however, in identifying "the entire population of foreign wives in either country" from which a sample could be drawn. Since this was impossible, she distributed a questionnaire to members of foreign wives' associations in both countries with a 33⅓% response rate. Unfortunately, the respondents did not provide the detail necessary to examine "social womanhood."[15] If cultural differences make it necessary to use separate data collection techniques in each country, however, the researcher may lose confidence in comparing the data.

Contemporary Purposes of Cross-Cultural Research

The purposes of contemporary feminist cross-cultural research are to compare and evaluate social policy, to illuminate a phenomenon these societies share, and to generate feminist theory. One radical[16] conception of feminist cross-cultural research is to explore the researcher's self or identity as revealed during fieldwork in an unfamiliar society.[17] A more overarching agenda is consciousness-raising concerning feminist ethnocentrism, a subspecies of Western ethnocentrism and racism.

A cross-cultural study by Deanne Bonnar evaluates social policy. She examined

> alternative income support strategies which have either been proposed for consideration or are currently in operation in other countries [and] examined current policies in Hungary, Israel and Sweden. These countries' policies are examined in part because the materials were readily available, but also because they represent different mixes of planned and market economies with extensive official commitment to the political and economic equality of men and women. The findings reveal that women as caregivers are in many ways more adequately protected by policy in those countries than they are in the United States, but in some crucial

ways the positions of women and female based households are surprisingly similar.[18]

Quantitative cross-cultural research also helps develop such policy-relevant correlations as John Court's discovery of a positive correlation between permissive pornographic materials laws and the incidence of rape.[19]

An example of cross-cultural research designed to generate theory is Peggy Reeves Sanday's[20] evaluation of anthropologist Sherry Ortner's theory[21] that women are universally subordinated to males because females represent nature, and males culture. Peggy Sanday uses the Standard Cross-Cultural Sample published by George Murdock and Douglas White in 1969.[22] In her view, that material

> offers to scholars a representative sample of the world's known and well-described societies. The complete sample consists of 186 societies, each "pinpointed" to an identifiable subgroup of the society in question at a specific point in time. The time period for the sample societies ranges from 1750 B.C. (Babylonians) to the late 1960s. The societies included in the standard sample are distributed relatively equally among the six major regions of the world.

Although she was committed to using this particular sample, she was also impressed by ethnographies of males and female power. These studies made her realize that

> symbolism played a key role in channeling secular power roles. . . . Moving into symbolic territory meant moving away from the positivist framework that normally accompanies the cross-cultural, large-sample approach. . . . Only with time was I able to resolve the basic tension between explanation required by the positivist approach and interpretation required by the particular brand of the semiotic approach I adopted.[23]

Political scientist Vicky Randall uses comparative data from numerous countries to develop a feminist theory of women and politics that could "undermine the system of male dominance."[24] Material about voting behavior, membership in political parties, and participation in revolutionary movements enable her to evaluate five stereotypes about women's political acumen: women are conservative, women personalize politics, women are moralistic, women are apolitical, and women are politically superior. Building on this information she then tackles the question of women's underrepresentation in political elites. Her continuous reference to information from studies of numerous countries prevents overgeneralization and helps illuminate reasons for women's success or failure in particular situations.[25] Throughout her book, she faults the sexist bias of political science and finds she must rely on research done by feminist sociologists and anthropologists.

Marian Sawer and Marian Simms reach the same conclusion in their study of women in Australian politics:

> Australian political science has been characterized by a singular lack of curiosity abut the role played by women in the political system. This reflects both the male-dominated nature of the political science profession and its orientation towards the formal process of power. Few political scientists have paid much attention to the underlying structure of power within our society—the sexual division of la-

bour. Hence the profession has been ill-prepared to grapple with questions raised by the increasing visibility of women within politics. We have learned more from historians and sociologists than from political science textbooks about the historical conditions placed upon the entry of women into formal political life.[26]

Fortunately, the transdisciplinary nature of Women's Studies and feminist research prompts women to go outside their discipline when faced with inadequate data and sexist bias.

An example is sociologist Rae Lesser Blumberg's development of feminist gender stratification theory on the basis of anthropological materials.

> My first effort involved a sample of sixty-one preindustrial societies, chosen to provide about ten societies each from Murdock's main world culture regions and about ten societies each from the main productive bases found in technographic data sets (ranging from hunting-gathering to intensive agriculture). Each society chosen was included in the *Human Relations Area Files* (HRAF), the *Ethnographic Atlas* and the *Standard Cross-Cultural Sample*—a "triple overlap" sample. . . . The two most powerful independent variables proved to be economic power and force. . . . Life options, the dependent variable, was measured by an . . . index of how women's degree of freedom compared with men's with respect to (1) marriage, (2) divorce, (3) premarital virginity, and (d) household control.[27]

A major theoretical concern for many feminists doing cross-cultural research is whether, and how, economic development alters the preexisting sexual division of labor. To answer the question of whether development is good for women, comparative cross-cultural studies and feminist theory are necessary. An example is the framework presented by Carmen Diana Deere and Magdalena Leon de Leal who

> demonstrate the importance of . . . material conditions in analyzing the sexual division of labor in productive activities. . . . We analyze the variations in the sexual division of labor in peasant agricultural production and in wage employment as it relates to the uneven development of capitalism among [three Andean] regions . . . [O]ur analysis illustrates the manner in which the sexual division of labor in production tends to build upon women's subordinated position within agrarian societies.[28]

Vandana Shiva moves this concern one step further by questioning the link between women and economic development, and then extending this concern to the impact of development on nature. Her term "maldevelopment" refers to patriarchal modern science, which has depleted the soils and forests of India with particular hardship for women.

> Recovering the feminine principle as respect for life in nature and society appears to be the only way forward, for men as well as women, in the North as well as the South. The metaphors and concepts of minds deprived of the feminine principle have been based on seeing nature and women as worthless and passive, and finally as dispensable. These ethnocentric categorisations have been universalised, and with their universalisation has been associated the destruction of nature and the subjugation of women. But this dominant mode of organising the world is

today being challenged by the very voices it had silenced. These voices, muted through subjugation, are now quietly but firmly suggesting that the western male has produced only one culture, and there are other ways of structuring the world.[29]

My own studies of miscarriage[30] are an attempt to generate theory from cross-cultural research. I examined how women in different societies understood their miscarriage experience. I discovered that miscarriages are deeply intertwined with the efforts of others to control women.

As the foregoing examples show, cross-cultural studies use qualitative or quantitative methods or both. In their review of feminist cross-cultural research, Marcia Texler Segal and Catherine White Berheide argue that both are needed:

> Those who use cross-cultural materials, especially . . . non-Western and nonindustrial societies, are pursuing the question of the specific conditions under which females have more or less power vis-à-vis males. . . . Lipman-Blumen (1976) focuses on how and why male dominance, once established, is maintained. Her homosocial theory might be called exchange theory from a women's perspective. She notes that to the extent that males control all socially valued resources, it is only for the procreation of children that women are needed. There are few factors to motivate men, or even other women, to interact with women. The process is circular: women lack skills and material resources because they are excluded from all male groupings; they are excluded because they are unable to provide anything that a male could not provide as well or better. Empirical studies of the factors affecting women's position in society are needed in addition to such theoretical treatises. Stewart and Winter (1977) report a quantitative analysis of cross-cultural data which suggests that women have higher status in societies with high educational levels and socialist governments.[31]

U.S. Feminist Ethnocentrism

U.S. citizens are frequently criticized for ethnocentric behavior and attitudes such as the inability to learn foreign languages, locate countries on a map, or appreciate phenomena other people value. Cross-cultural awareness is not particularly high among U.S. feminists as well. Many important foreign events escape the attention of U.S. feminist scholars because our focus is local. A case in point is the recent remarkable power shift in Iceland, which received almost no attention or analysis in feminist publications.[32] One would expect feminist theory to devote a great deal of attention to the acquisition of power by feminists in Iceland.

U.S. feminists themselves criticize the ethnocentrism of U.S. feminist scholarship. For example, bell hooks discusses overreliance on the English language and suggests "we can change this by encouraging one another to learn Spanish, English, Japanese, Chinese, etc."[33] U.S. sociologist Elise Boulding criticizes our focus on urban life:

> Social scientists have obfuscated the dynamics of social change in industrial society by overvaluing urbanism and by failing to note the rural sector. This sector I have variously referred to as the fifth world, the underside of history, and the gender-based undergirding of structural dualism in the third world. . . . First

world women, except for a small minority of internationalists, tend in both Europe and North America to be preoccupied with their status problems in the urban enclaves of their own countries even often the status problems of their own class within those enclaves, although in theory they affirm the world rural-urban sisterhood of women. Third world women, rural and urban alike, have few opportunities to enter such a sisterhood, and even the internationalists in the world of women's nongovernmental organizations (NGO's) have done relatively little to foster the further participation of third world women in the world community. Partly this is due to lack of resources, but partly it is due to an incomplete development of world perspective on the part of even the best educated and most idealistic of first world women.[34]

The following excerpt by sociologist Arlene Daniels, written in the style of a Ms. Manners newspaper column, summarizes the problem of U.S. feminist ethnocentrism and offers solutions:

Ms. Manners on the Gaucherie of Ethnocentrism in Feminist Research

[C]reeping ethnocentrism . . . occurs in much feminist writing dominated by concern for the problems of middle-class or even working-class white women. This problem has been especially, and most bitterly, commented on by such Black writers as bell hooks; but it bears repeating and additional emphasis.

Too often, we write about the problems of white women in America (sic) as though they were generic to womankind. Maybe they are, sometimes, but we need the consciousness of examining issues, always and everywhere, with an eye to how widely they apply. Take, for example, such fine studies of working class women's life as Meg Luxton's *More than a Labour of Love* or Lillian Rubin's *Worlds of Pain*. Are they about all working-class women or only white women? What would we learn about commonality and difference from equally fine studies of the women in Black, Hispanic and Asian-American working-class families? We need to undertake such studies—and encourage our students to do likewise, if we are ever to shake free of the ethnocentrism that creeps, insidiously, into our thinking about significant problems for study.

In a similar vein, I have recently been thinking about transnational comparative studies, a subject brought to my attention by Hanna Papanek in her recent presentation at the ASA meeting in Chicago: "The World is not Like Us: Limits of Feminist Imagination." It is not only gauche to ignore the experience of our sisters in other nations when we generalize about such matters as women in the labor market, or women's power in public and private life; it is poor sociology. Papanek notes that much of feminist research in the U.S. is "disturbingly context-free—and therefore implicitly U.S.-centered." In her example of comparisons between the U.S. and India, Papanek shows us what we can learn about the nature of women's movements and women's work in the labor force. Both increased participation (as in the U.S.) and decreased opportunities (as in India) can mobilize women's movements. . . .

She points out that the way materials on U.S. women are ordinarily organized into topics (Women and Work, Women and Religion, Women and the Family) omits a space-time referent connecting the material to the U.S. This code encourages both authors and audience into thinking we deal with universals. The problem is compounded since materials about women from other parts of the world are rarely integrated with U.S. data under these topics. Materials about other societies are tagged separately as "Third World Women" or "Women in Development." It is ironic, as Papanek notes, that this separation of domains of knowledge leaves information about most of the world's women as "other," since it is we[35] who are in the minority. It is also ironic that we who have rallied against a division from the male perspective that leaves women as "other" or "the second sex" should make similar distinction between our own interests and experiences as core and those of the rest of the world's women as periphery.

Papanek offers some strategies for combatting our own limited vision. She tells us "to look for the contradictions and ambiguities in each society's treatment of gender differences, gender relations and gender inequalities." She points out that changes in labor utilization within many societies has sharpened gender difference in distributing the rewarding work. She exhorts us to "a global perspective on the shifting gender fault line.". . . For even the most monolingual of us, as she notes, there are many original works in English as well as English translations of work on women in many different societies. Let us inform our own research and course work with insights from these works. In this way we can avoid both gaucherie and bad sociology in our treatment of women's issues.[36]

This argument covers a lot of ground—white feminist scholarship's lack of attention to Black women's lives, middle class feminist's obliviousness to working class women's lives, and U.S. feminist scholarship's disregard for women in other societies. The problem is exclusion.

Elly Bulkin accuses heterosexual feminists of "ethnocentricism" toward lesbian issues. She claims that lesbians are erased by heterosexual feminists; U.S. lesbians of color even more so; and Third World lesbians even more. Specifically criticizing theologian Mary Daly's *Gyn/Ecology,* she asks:

Will we accept as a veritable sacred text a theoretical book written by a white lesbian feminist that excludes the concerns about racism expressed repeatedly by Third World feminists? Will we consider how the lesbian community—Third World and white—suffers from again finding total acceptance by white lesbians for a book that exludes these concerns? Will we accept without question scholarship as unbiased simply because it is put together by a (white) lesbian-feminist academic whose tone assumes great authority? I am . . . disturbed as I read through the Second Passage chapters on Indian suttee, Chinese footbinding, and African genital mutilation by Daly's almost entirely uncritical use of white Western sources, nearly all male, and by her failure to acknowledge the racism both in passages she quotes in *Gyn/Ecology* and in those she omits from her book.[37]

Strongly supporting Elly Bulkin's general point about lesbian erasure, Sara Karon writes:

In the context of the continuing struggle for recognition of the different experiences and perspectives of people of different genders, races, and ethnicities, Lesbians are conspicuous by their relative absence. Beyond marginalization, Lesbian existence is often denied.[38]

Marilyn Frye[39] writes that primarily heterosexual women's history and literature is taught, when material about women is taught at all. Sara Karon also shows that

Black feminists who write Black history tend to ignore Black lesbian history, contributing to the problem of lesbian erasure. In both examples, women are presumed to be heterosexual unless proven otherwise. Taking a radical stance against erasure, Sarah Hoagland[40] refused to define lesbianism since the very act of definition evokes the heterosexual standpoint in her view. There seem to be unfortunate parallels between feminist ethnocentrism and feminist heterosexism.

Aihwa Ong claims that Western[41] feminism is an oppositional subculture and requires an Other with whom it does not share experience. Creating an Other whom one can oppose is a form of power relations that feminists engage in unwittingly:

> Feminist voices in the social sciences unconsciously echo this masculinist will to power in its relation to non-Western societies. Thus, for feminists looking overseas, the non-feminist Other is not so much patriarchy as the non-Western woman.

She believes that the Otherness of the non-Western woman in the eyes of the Western feminist ethnographer rests on unexamined images concerning their labor and reproductive powers. Thus, "non-Western" is essentially "non-modern" or incapable of participating in positive economic activities.

> By and large, non-Western women are taken as an unproblematic universal category. . . . The status of non-Western women is analyzed and gauged according to a set of legal, political and social benchmarks that Western feminists consider critical in achieving a power balance between men and women.[42]

In her view, Western- and U.S.-originated feminist cross-cultural research sadly has not escaped the colonial history of anthropology.

Feminist critics of feminist cross-cultural research charge that U.S. feminists who study other societies project their own experiences instead of understanding the other society on its own terms.[43] This is particularly the case in cross-cultural feminist research about women's subordination. Critics argue that women who seemingly are subordinated in the researcher's eyes are not necessarily subordinated in their own. For example, the introduction to a collection of life stories by Black Jamaican women, contains the following:

> [T]he white feminists of the 1960s and 1970s . . . spoke about women's oppression when what they meant was their own experience of it. They spoke about women's history when they really meant European women's history. Their approach was often narrowly chauvinistic, confusing demands evolving out of their specific short-term needs with panaceas for women internationally.[44]

Anthropologist Lila Abu-Lughod, author of a two-year study of a Bedouin village in Egypt, struggled with the problem of projecting her experience onto women of another society. She is a U.S.-based anthropologist whose father is Egyptian and whose mother is from the United States. When she went to the Egyptian Bedouin village to begin her study, her father insisted on accompanying her.

> I suspect that few, if any, fathers of anthropologists accompany them to the field to make their initial contacts. But my father insisted that he had something to do in Egypt and might just as well plan his trip to coincide with mine. I had accepted

his offer only reluctantly, glad to have the company but also a bit embarrassed by the idea. Only after living with the Bedouins for a long time did I began to comprehend some of what had underlain my father's quiet but firm insistence. As an Arab, although by no means a Bedouin, he knew his own culture and society well enough to know that a young, unmarried woman traveling alone on uncertain business was an anomaly. She would be suspect and would have a hard time persuading people of her respectability. I of course knew of the negative image of Western women, an image fed by rumor, films, and, to be sure, the frequent insensitivity of Western women to local standards of morality and social communication patterns. But I had assumed I would be able to overcome people's suspicions, first by playing up the Arab half of my identity and not identifying with Westerners, and second by behaving properly. I was confident of my sensitivity to cultural expectations because of my background.[45]

As it turned out, Lila Abu-Lughod would never have been able to conduct her study had it not been for her father's unique way of presenting her to the Bedouin community. His method was so finely tuned that they reversed their long-standing hostility toward Europeans, and she, in the end, overcame her resistance to veiling and gradually felt proud to veil. As she altered her behavior, she also changed her interpretation of the meaning of veiling from ''an expression of male domination'' to

an expression of cultural notions of morality and virtue, modesty and honor. It certainly connotes submission, but is an act in which women voluntarily engage and is not perceived by them to be an exercise of male power.[46]

On the other hand, such feminist researchers as Fatima Mernissi, professor of sociology in Morocco, argue that the veil disguises or cloaks ''Muslim exploitation of the female,'' which is why the ''first gesture of 'liberated' Arab women was to discard the veil for Western dress.''[47]

While it is likely that these two interpretations emanate from the different cultural locations of the two researchers, a larger question cross-cultural ethnographic study raises is ''whether or not behaviors are meaningfully interpreted outside their cultural contexts?''[48] This question is particularly difficult for feminist cross-cultural researchers because it challenges the premise of transcultural interpretation.

Marla N. Powers offers a biting criticism of the tendency of U.S. feminists to project their experience onto women in other societies. She implies that when feminists study women in a society other than their own, they are doing unintentional cross-cultural research because the researcher cannot avoid comparison with her own society. Marla Powers also warns feminist scholars not to delude themselves with the notion of women's universal subordination:

A number of feminist writers view women's productive and reproductive roles as the basis for female subordination. . . . They contend that a woman's biological and reproductive (private, domestic) role is the basis for her inequality because it precludes her active involvement in the powerful, prestigious (public) spheres open to men. . . . For the Oglalas, it is just the opposite.

To see Oglala women as subordinated is to not understand them:

> Specifically, among the Oglala, the traditional roles of a woman—wife and mother—
> are part of a set of Lakota values that have . . . facilitated her movement into
> economic and political roles modeled after Euramerican concepts of propriety,
> albeit in part inadvertently.

The case of the Oglala raises questions about the universality of subordination on
the basis of female sex.

> Oglala society provides a good example of what others have called the myth of
> male dominance. . . . I suggest that Oglala women purposely perpetuate this
> myth by making males and outsiders believe that men are in charge. Cross-cultural
> studies have shown that male dominance, despite its frequent assertion, simply
> does not exist as a social fact. . . . In summary, equating women's productive
> and reproductive roles with subordination, plus an unfounded belief in the uni-
> versality of male dominance, precludes the possibility of seeing more complex
> relationships. . . . But these errors do not apply to women exclusively. Rather,
> they are a function of viewing any non-Western group, and even certain segments
> of Western society, ethnocentrically.[49]

While she forcefully cautions against overgeneralization, she does not consider
ways in which generalization may, in fact, be appropriate. Generalizations, after
all, allow us to see multiple ways in which women in different cultures are actually similar. Some feminist scholars would argue that women's vulnerability to
rape, for example, is not an overgeneralization but an unfortunate universal fact.

The two forms of "limited vision" I have been discussing—projection and
assumptions of subordination—are accusations feminists make of other feminists
who are thought to overlook context. As far as I can tell, this accusation has not
led to the argument that "Third World Women" alone are entitled to study their
society. To develop that view would legitimize Western feminist ethnocentrism
by stating that women should study their own society only rather than learn about
other societies.

Perhaps the answer to these dilemmas is that feminists should support women
from countries other than their own to do research. Feminists with resources should
assist other women to obtain funds and publish their materials. Increased indigenous research activity would make it possible to compare research by native and
foreign women. This long-range view suggests that at the early stage, women
from "Third World" countries should be the ones to study their own societies.

Unfortunately, current feminist cross-cultural research tends not to include much
collaboration between scholars from the host society and from other societies.
Feminist psychologist Rae Andre has argued this point.

> It seems clear that the time is past when one culture can impose its methodology
> on another with impunity, that if we are to have any dialogue at all, participation
> must begin with the creation of methodology itself. The result, of course, will
> not be pure science as we in America (sic) or even in the wider scientific com-
> munity know it. Rather it will be an openness to discussion of new methodolo-
> gies, whatever they are, that spring from the needs and values of the cultures to
> be studied.[50]

And Chandra Mohanty agrees.

> Clearly, the analysis of Third World societies in the context of cross-cultural research has generated considerable divisiveness among feminists. Whereas those who engage in it generally believe they are doing non-ethnocentric work, others consider research done by Western feminists on non-Western societies to be an aspect of colonialism itself. This colonizing effect stems from . . . assumptions of privilege and ethnocentric universality . . . and inadequate self-consciousness about the effect of Western scholarship on the "third world" in the context of a world system dominated by the West.[51]

What we have, then, are more catch-22 situations. Western feminists are criticized for *not* studying "Third World" women (i.e., ethnocentrism) and criticized for *doing so* as outsiders to those cultures (i.e., colonialism). Feminists studying women in cultures other than their own are criticized if they *accept* that culture's way of subordinating women (i.e., misogyny) and are criticized if they *repudiate* the culture's subordination of women (i.e., ethnocentrism). Andrea Dworkin is an example of a researcher who did not get caught in these dilemmas. She examined violence against women in another society and then applied that knowledge to an understanding of violence in her own (the United States). At the end of her study of Chinese footbinding, she drew parallels with the cult of beauty in the United States.[52] In this way she avoided singling out the uniqueness of a particular culture's violence against women.

In addition to the range of criticisms reviewed above, charges of colonialism relate to Western feminist scholars' tendency to think of "Third World Woman" as a monolith. Contributors to Sistren criticize scholars who use the term "development" because of its connotations of Western superiority[53] and its disguising of the fact that imperialist nations and corporations have exploited these areas. To my ears, development is a strange word with connotations of child-rearing. As the countries "develop," will they grow up and become like their putative parents, the developed countries? The metaphors of growth, benevolence, nurturing, and natural change that underlie this term seem inappropriate given the actual relations among countries.

Chandra Mohanty has also disparaged feminist cross-cultural scholarship for its "uncritical use of particular methodologies in providing 'proof' of universality and cross-cultural validity." She argued that it is improper to assume that power and struggle are the necessary analytic categories. Her criticism is meant to steer feminist cross-cultural scholarship away from ethnocentrism and toward cross-cultural feminism.[54]

In contrast to these numerous feminist attempts to avoid ethnocentrism, sociologist Kathleen Barry argues that the very charge of ethnocentrism has been *dangerous* for feminist cross-cultural research. Charges of ethnocentrism have led cross-cultural researchers into the snare of cultural relativism, an even greater danger in Kathleen Barry's eyes. Cultural relativism asserts that

> the practices within any specific culture are unique to the values, systems, and practices within that culture. For the cultural relativist there are no universal standards and the morality and values of one national culture cannot be compared to that of any other. Cultural relativism dominates social, political and academic thought today and it serves as a justification of many inhumane social practices.

If one questions the principles of cultural relativism, one is charged with ethnocentrism. Ethnocentrism assumes that the judgements made about another culture stem from the assumption of the superiority of one's own culture.

Drawing on her study of female sexual slavery in many different countries, she knows the danger of taking a culturally relativistic perspective.

These attempts to respect the cultural integrity of different societies, well intentioned though they may be, serve to separate and isolate women in their common experience of sexual domination. There is nothing unique across cultures in the practices of the enslavement of women except perhaps the diversity in the strategies men employ to carry them out. Female sexual slavery is a global phenomenon. . . . Applying the same standard or value to human life across all national cultures lifts considerations of female sexual slavery above arguments of ethnocentrism.[55]

Mary Daly made the same point in *Gyn/Ecology* when she argued that speaking out for women is more important than expressing respect for different cultures. For such scholars as Mary Daly and Kathleen Barry, charges of ethnocentrism keep feminist researchers from uncovering and condemning injustices perpetrated on women and keep women from developing cross-cultural solidarity. The challenge for feminist scholars, then, is to engage in research that avoids ethnocentrism and cultural relativism and builds cross-cultural solidarity.

Betsy Hartmann, a researcher in the field of population control and reproductive rights, shares the perspective of Mary Daly and Kathleen Barry. She concludes her examination of reproductive policies and practices in various "Third World" nations and in the United States as follows:

I have come to believe more firmly in the inviolability of individual reproductive rights . . . [N]o matter how perilous the population problem is deemed to be, the use of force or coercive incentives/disincentives to promote population control is an unjustifiable intrusion of government power into the lives of its citizenry, amounting in many cases to physical violence against women's bodies . . . I do not believe this stand is culturally specific, simply the product of Western civil libertarian philosophy, as many in the population establishment argue . . . [M]any people from different cultures share this point of view . . . they are not prepared to see human rights sacrificed on the altar of population control.[56]

Feminists doing cross-cultural research seem to be confronting two competing sets of ethics—respect for women and respect for culture. Each person contemplating such research must decide where she stands. The reflexive writing of feminists mentioned above provides useful guideposts for addressing the opening plea for more cross-cultural research.

Final Comments

A shift may be occurring in feminist interest in, and ability to conduct, cross-cultural research. The International Women's Year conference held in Mexico City in 1975 initiating the United Nations Decade for Women (1976–1985), the mid-decade conference in Copenhagen in 1980, and the concluding conference in Nairobi in 1985[57] helped generate contacts among women and opportunities for cross-cultural feminist research.[58] Some feminist theorists and activists have begun to describe their transition from local to global feminism, thereby guiding the way for others.[59] Since 1978 *Women's Studies International Forum* (first titled as *Women's Studies International Quarterly*) has been publishing articles by feminist writers from all over the world and reviewing feminist books with a cross-cultural or internationalist perspective. In winter 1981/82, the First International Interdisciplinary Congress on Women was held at the University of Haifa, in Israel. In the book that emerged from that Congress, there is a listing of numerous international meetings of women that occurred between the Haifa Congress and the publication of the volume.[60] In April 1984 the Second International Interdisciplinary Congress on Women was held in Groningen, the Netherlands. At that conference the Feminist International Network on the New Reproductive Technologies (FINRET) was formed, renamed FINNRAGE in 1985.[61] Since then there have been similar Congresses in Dublin, Ireland, and New York City. The current relaxation of East–West tensions may also portend increased opportunities for feminist cross-cultural research between capitalist and formerly communist societies.

On the other hand, cross-cultural research that focuses on certain countries may blind feminist researchers to the fact that other countries are ignored. Political scientist Jane Jaquette made this point in her introduction to an edited collection of studies comparing the role of women in the transition process from authoritarian to democratic politics in Argentina, Brazil, Uruguay, Peru, and Chile. Such blindness is unfair and contributes to bias in our generalizations.

> Feminists in the United States claim a universal theory of injustice and a global vision of what is to be done, despite the fact that their experience is generally limited to societies that are wealthy, industrialized and democratic, and where women of color are a minority. U.S. feminists are increasingly aware of the work of Canadian and European feminists, particularly French and British writers, but they still tend to view women in the Third World as victims of oppression rather than as creators of feminist theory or as agents of change.[62]

A comment in the fall 1989 issue of the Sex and Gender section newsletter of the American Sociological Association suggests to me that although some diminution in U.S. ethnocentrism may have occurred, there is a very long way to go.

> With increasing numbers of our membership involved in the International Sociological Association and in international research, it is long-past time to hold a session on research on women in other nations. Possible themes for this session could be women and development, Canadian feminist sociology, or new European perspectives on women and work.[63]

Given all the dissensus concerning feminist cross-cultural studies, the topics proposed above do not seem to meet some of the major criticisms. Therefore, a comment by Rayna Reiter in one of the early feminist anthropology collections seems as apt today as it did in 1975:

> Focusing first on women, we must redefine the important questions, reexamine all previous theories, and be critical in our acceptance of what constitutes factual

material. Armed with such a consciousness, we can proceed to new investigations of gender in our own and other cultures.[64]

While I think it is important to acknowledge the paucity of feminist work that has a cross-cultural perspective, the dearth of scholarship that truly escapes ethnocentrism, and the overly uniform theorizing applied to the research that is done, I believe it is also important to not limit a discussion of cross-cultural feminist research to criticisms. Instead we should examine what feminists who do this type of research confront, so that we can build on their experience. This, in turn, can be done only if feminists engaged in cross-cultural research write reflexive analyses of their work.

7

Feminist Oral History [1]

Women's oral history . . . is a feminist encounter, even if the interviewee is not herself a feminist. [2]

Introduction and Terminology

Sociologist Sherna Gluck continues the foregoing quote by explaining that women's oral history is a feminist encounter because it creates new material about women, validates women's experience, enhances communication among women, discovers women's roots, and develops a previously denied sense of continuity. In the same article, she subdivides oral history into types: *topical* (similar to an open-ended interview,) [3] *biographical* (concerns an individual other than the interviewee, or follows a life history format), and autobiographical (the "interviewee's life . . . determines . . . the form and content of the oral history"). [4] This chapter discusses some of these properties and types, while also raising some controversies.

Historical Roots of Feminist Recording of Women's Lives

Biographical work has always been an important part of the women's movement because it draws women out of obscurity, repairs the historical record, and provides an opportunity for the woman reader and writer to identify with the subject. [5] Historian Elisabeth Griffith, biographer of Elizabeth Cady Stanton, described the special connection between biography and the women's movement.

> Initial efforts to record the lives of eminent American women were made in the 1890s, as the first generation of college-educated women sought to identify women of achievement in an earlier era. [These women] established archives for research and wrote biographies of colonial and contemporary women, like Abigail Adams and Susan B. Anthony. Organizations like the Daughters of the American Revolution related their members to a past that provided proud models of accomplishment. The second surge of biographies came with the renaissance of women's history in the late 1960's. [6]

Feminist biographers frequently looked to the women they studied for more than models of accomplishment—they also looked to them for help. Margaret Caffrey describes the poignant plea of anthropologist Ruth Benedict who, as a young woman, lacked a sense of purpose in her life. As a result, she felt a " 'desperate longing' to 'know how other women have saved their souls alive' and accorded 'dignity' to the rich processes of living."[7] To satisfy her longing,

> her "pet scheme" was to steep herself "in the lives of restless and highly en-slaved women" of past generations and write a series of biographical papers from the standpoint of the "new woman." . . . For . . . four years (1914–1918), the heyday of suffrage fervor in America, culminating in the passage of the Nine-teenth Amendment giving women the right to vote, Benedict worked on her manuscript. . . . She was having trouble writing, but by 1916 had refined her "series of biographies" to three: Mary Wollstonecraft (1759–1797), the English author of *A Vindication of the Rights of Woman,* the classic book that sparked the Woman's Rights Movement in England and America; Margaret Fuller (1810–1850), American Transcendentalist, author of *Woman in the Nineteenth Century,* the classic American argument for feminism; and Olive Schreiner (1855–1920), the contemporary author of *Woman and Labor.* . . . Her purpose for writing this book . . . [was] . . . the affirmation their lives gave other women. "I long to speak out the intense inspiration that comes to me from the lives of strong women," she wrote. "They have made of their lives a great adventure." They had proved "that out of much bewilderment of soul," steadfast aims could be accomplished.[8]

Although Ruth Benedict tried to save her life by writing biographies, she ulti-mately realized she could not live through others.

> Women . . . had to learn to re-see life as a chance for "vigorous living". . . . She wanted her book [*Adventures in Womanhood*] to have an impact on society, but its impact on herself was already profound. . . . By writing about them and researching their lives she communed with them and with herself, keeping her creative energy alive in what became more and more a restrictive, isolated marital relationship.[9]

The idea of sisterhood gives feminists a sense of connection with women of the past. When we turn to women of the past for help, we help them as well by restoring them to a place in history. Adding another level to these connections, Australian historian Jill Matthews suggests that by writing about women of the past, "[t]he feminist historian [also] recognizes herself as part of the history she writes."[10]

My own experience using biographical methods includes a study investigating the specifically female type of political action of Manya Wilbushewitz Shohat, a woman instrumental in the creation of a Jewish homeland in Palestine. In the article I claim that feminist research on individual lives is

> a type of scholarship that begins with an insight about women's condition that requires further elaboration so as to solve the puzzle of one's own life. . . . It may begin with a discovery about a hitherto ignored woman or trivialized aspects of women's competence that needs careful examination and then distribution.[11]

Once the project begins, a circular process ensues: the woman doing the study learns about herself as well as about the woman she is studying.

Types of Oral History Products

Many things have been done with completed feminist oral history projects. *Single* oral histories have been published as analyzed or unanalyzed documents;[12] *sets* of oral histories have been published with or without analysis;[13] *collections* of oral histories have been obtained and stored as an archive for future analysis;[14] and groups have been asked to record their life histories for subsequent collection by an editor.[15] Many accounts or collections contain accompanying photographs that give additional "life" to the life histories.[16]

In one instance, Gretchen M. Bataille and Kathleen Mullen Sands reanalyzed a group of previously published oral histories and autobiographies using techniques of literary criticism and ethnography. They gathered the autobiography

> of Maria Chona, a Papago woman whose story was published by Ruth Underhill, an anthropologist, in the 1930s; of Mountain Wolf Woman, a Winnebago who told her story to anthropologist Nancy Lurie in the 1950s; of Anna Shaw Moore, a Pima whose story was published in 1974; of Helen Sekaquaptewa, a Hopi who wrote her autobiography with the help of a non-Indian woman editor during the 1960s; and of Maria Campbell, a Metis woman from Canada whose autobiography, *Halfbreed,* was published in 1973.

The authors stress the shared characteristics of the oral histories of these women despite their differing life-styles and cultures. Clara Sue Kidwell, a reviewer of this book, points out, that in

> these works drawn from oral traditions, . . . the sense of time . . . is not strictly linear. . . . there is emphasis on event, attention to sacredness of language, concern with landscape, and attention to tribal values. . . . these autobiographies stress not the importance of women as individuals within their cultures but as representatives of their cultures, preservers, as it were, of traditions and values and a tribal way of life.[17]

Oral histories are also used to identify empirical patterns. For example, in an oral history study of 25 black U.S. urban women between the ages of 32 and 80 identified by community members as having been activists for at least eight years, sociologist Cheryl Townsend Gilkes found that their activism served as a trajectory into the middle class.[18] This study showed that institutions other than formal education and employment[19] provide opportunities for upward mobility.

Groups of oral histories may be examined quantitatively. An example is social psychologist Brinton Lykes' work drawn from the Black Women's Oral History Project collection at Radcliffe College. The intent of her study was to analyze the

> perceptions of discrimination among American black women 70 years of age or older who have made a significant contribution to the improvement of the lives of black people especially in the 1940s and 1950s. By listening directly to the voices of black women as spoken in their oral histories we may perhaps more effectively resist the temptation to "artificially dissect" . . . them, to think of them sometimes on the basis of sex and other times on the basis of color or race.[20]

The oral histories enabled her (and others) to "hear" individual women and to "see" patterns derived from the study of larger numbers of women. Her work is also an example of the way journalists, historians, and social scientists who did not collect histories can use oral history collections stored in libraries and other archives for secondary analyses.[21]

Oral histories have also been published as what I would call "paired histories." An example is Susan Tucker's collection of southern black female domestic workers and their white female employers.[22] Juxtaposing how each woman spoke about her relation with the other, Susan Tucker illuminates the texture of their relationships. Encountering oral histories in this paired, contextualized way, the reader learns about each woman and about the social distance and myths that sustained their seemingly close relations.

Feminist oral history projects combined with the collection of artifacts and photographs have been developed into full-scale exhibits. Kathryn Anderson and Susan Armitage, for example, worked together on the Washington Women's Heritage Project, which illustrated the everyday lives of women by drawing on photographs and excerpts from oral history interviews.[23] Sociologist Doris Wilkinson created "The Afro-American Presence in Medicine: A Social History Exhibit (1850–1930)," which raises consciousness by displaying history in a tangible way. My own related work is the creation of a set of videotapes of contemporary feminist social scientists speaking about other female social scientists or themselves. I use these tapes for teaching and for comparative analysis of women of different generations.[24]

Terminological Variety

A striking feature of the literature on oral history is the lack of uniformity in terminology, as in the case of interviewing. Because of the variety of terms, people may be doing similar research under different labels. In reviewing this work, I found the following terms used interchangeably with "oral history": case studies, in-depth life history interviews,[25] biographical interviews, life histories, and personal narratives. In addition to the variety of labels for the overall method, anthropologist Faye Ginsburg questions what the *parties* should be called:

> Because the creation of these life stories was so clearly a collaborative effort, I chose to call the people with whom I worked "interpreters" rather than "informants." While the latter connotes betrayal, voyeurism, and infiltration, interpreter suggests that the ethnographer is more of an interlocuter, in dialogue with both the people with whom she or he works and the audience "back home."[26]

Furthermore, she explains the origin of her choice of labels:

> Credit for this term belongs to Melissa, the woman in whose home I lived while in Fargo (ND). During the course of my fieldwork, I had occasion to use the word "informant" in conversations with people in Fargo with whom I was working. Although I had long accepted the term as part of the jargon of anthropology, I had always felt uncomfortable with it. One evening, Melissa asked me what the

term meant. I explained that it referred to the people who, like herself, were helping me to understand what was going on in the community. She paused—a long pause appropriate to the rhythms of Fargo conversations—and then said, "Don't you think we're really more like your interpreters?" I was struck by her comment and felt her choice of that term better expressed my experience of the relationship I had with people there. They were translating a discourse I was struggling to master.[27]

Sociologist Ruth Linden, on the other hand, uses the terms "interlocutor," "respondent," and "subject." Unlike Faye Ginsburg, she believes these terms reflect the intersubjective nature of the interview process.[28]

A third area of terminological disagreement is the distinction between oral history and other related methods. The question is how texts produced by feminist oral history are different from interviews, autobiographies[29] and biographies. Marcia Wright classifies work in terms of

> the degree to which the subject controls and shapes the text. Autobiography entails the telling of a story to convey what was important in a person's development, arranging and restating events to prepare for a climax or denouement. It is retrospective, in effect making a case. The life story, on the other hand, is ambiguously authored, and may be more or less actively composed by a mediator who arranges the testimony and quietly supplies explanatory interventions. Resulting frequently from interrogation, life stories are constructed to serve the ultimate purposes of ethnography, or of a court case, or simply of eliciting the common and uncommon experience of ordinary people, in the mode of new social history. Biography brings to the fore the commentator, whose portrait is usually based on a diversity of sources and whose goal is not only to reveal but also to judge. . . . The line between autobiography and life stories is subtle. . . . People who may begin their recording of experience in response to questions may develop their own agenda and convert the enterprise from life story to autobiography, discover a drama in their own lives, so to speak . . . A life history is the product of sustained conversations between a social scientist and a subject. . . . Biography often derives from a political interest.[30]

Marcia Wright's comment that life histories are "ambiguously authored" is one of their perplexing features. The subtle lines she draws among oral history, interviews, biographies,[31] and autobiographies means that features of each method are shared by others. For example, oral history and autobiography involve a person telling her own life story. The fact that oral histories are typically created through interaction, however, means they draw on another person's questions. That person may inhabit a very different culture.

Interviews and oral histories, too, are similar, but interviews focus typically on a particular experience or phenomenon, while oral histories deal more broadly with a person's past. Oral histories generally range over a wide range of topics, perhaps the person's life from birth to the present. In her study of 21 incarcerated women in Massachusetts, for example, Mary Gilfus used oral histories (which she sometimes called interviews) to understand the chronology of the woman's experiences from her earliest memories to the present. To accomplish this, she used a set of questions that ensured coverage of certain topics such as family composition, childhood development, family patterns of substance abuse, educational history, physical and sexual violence, own substance abuse, and arrest histories. Within this loose structure, "every woman was encouraged to tell her own life story in her own words as much as possible within a chronological and developmental framework."[32] The openness and thoroughness of these oral histories enabled Mary Gilfus to see that being sexually abused as children destroyed these women's ability to distinguish right from wrong, and prepared them, even as very young children, to be exploited by others. When feminist oral histories cover extensive portions or profound experiences in an individual's life, they assist in a fundamental sociological task—illuminating the connections between biography, history, and social structure.[33]

Oral histories differ from biographies in the method of transmission. Some histories *must* be transmitted orally because the individual is incapable of writing. Oral testimony is invaluable for historians who seek information unlikely to be contained in written records. To the extent that men's lives are more likely to produce written documentation, men are more likely to be the subject of analysis by historians who use archival data. Thus oral history, in contrast to written history, is useful for getting information about *people* less likely to be engaged in creating written records[34] and for creating historical accounts of *phenomena* less likely to have produced archival material.[35] Relatively powerless groups are therefore especially good candidates for oral history research.

Despite the variation in terminology and focus, there is also some common ground among these forms of research. Most feminist oral historians share the goal of allowing/encouraging/enabling women to speak for themselves,[36] although there is some disagreement about how much the interviewer should be "present" in the resulting manuscript. The role of the oral historian is to produce the written document, audio- or videotape (or a combination) alone or with the assistance of the person being studied. The role of the "interpreter," "informant," "interviewee," or "subject" is to discuss the development of all or part of her life, as an individual, as a representative of a specific group, or as an eyewitness to specific historic events or periods.[37] The interviewee is assisted by the questions and attentive attitude of the oral historian.[38] The oral historian and interviewee collaborate in a single, retrospective conversation or in a series of conversations[39] in which either may take the lead in defining the most important topics.

The wealth of U.S. oral history projects about women suggests an affinity between the study of women's lives and oral history as a research method. I located one such project in a small New Hampshire newspaper article about Rebecca Courser, a woman who won an award for 15 years of substantial service to her community:

> One of her greatest achievements has been the development of the Warner Women's Oral History Project. In its early stages she was the driving force for the project, personally conducting many interviews and transposing tape recordings for hours on end. Funded by the New Hampshire Council of Humanities, this fine program has been performed more than one hundred times to audiences

throughout New Hampshire over the past five years and this November it will receive national recognition when it will be presented before the National Oral History Association in Cambridge, Mass.[40]

The Summer 1977 issue of *Frontiers: A Journal of Women Studies* contains lengthy appendices with lists of women's oral history projects.[41] Undoubtedly there are many others.

Although feminists have shown that oral history is valuable for the oral historian and the "subject," Marcia Wright insists that women also deserve *more than* oral histories, a "lower order" type of autobiography or biography. She argues that we should not be complacent with oral histories. Women deserve full-fledged biographies and should be encouraged to write their own autobiographies. Thus, oral histories have both value and hidden costs for African women, in her view:

> We must . . . encourage the transition from life history to autobiography, increasing the self-management of the communicators, even though it entails much work to understand what is propelling the story line. As scholars, on our side, we must come away from the ambiguity of authorship and behind-the-scenes arrangement of life histories to become fully responsible biographers. Social and intellectual accountability will follow, if not from our own successful internal debates, then by the vigor of the public exchanges that will become increasingly possible.[42]

The distinctions among autobiography, biography, and life history illustrate the numerous ways the story of a life can be told. When a feminist scholar selects a particular method, she chooses a certain type of control over her subject matter and a certain type of focus. If she chooses oral history, she must contend with the difficulties (and enjoy the delights) of writing about a living person in a way that satisfies both parties. In general, the feminist oral historian must make crucial decisions concerning her own role, her choice of the individual(s) whose oral history she will write, and the analytic framework she will use.

The oral history method has been used by historians, journalists, community groups, anthropologists, women's studies scholars, and sociologists who want to understand individual lives or social phenomena.[43] Oral histories or life histories have been created as a solo project by an individual scholar[44] and have been coordinated by larger organizations devoted to specific oral history projects. The flexibility of the method makes it amenable to scholars working alone or in teams. The conversational quality of the method facilitates collaboration with community members.

Marginality of Oral History
in Mainstream Social Science

One reason for the variety of terms concerning oral history is its marginal place in the social sciences.[45] Typically oral histories are not even discussed in research methods texts. Because mainstream social scientists find little value in studies of individuals that draw on subjectivity, there is little discussion of and training in this method, and little agreement on terms. Sara Evans' experience is an exception to this conventional lack of training. In the introduction to *Personal Politics,* she describes "the anxious, ecstatic summer of my oral research. I prepared for it by attending Lawrence Goodwyn's inspiring seminar on oral history methodology and by extensive research in traditional literary and archival sources."[46] Typically, the only context for oral histories in mainstream social science is in ethnographies or community studies. Although there was some interest in the first quarter of the twentieth century in the United States, the method has long been overshadowed by other approaches to social science research.

Michal McCall and Judith Wittner, on the other hand, claim that "life history research is enjoying a revival" among feminists, because feminists can use the method "to study social life from the vantage point of women."[47] Feminist interest in these methods may reflect an attempt to work outside the mainstream.[48] Elizabeth Higginbotham writes that in the United States,

> in the South, the oral history or personal narrative has emerged as a critical means for sharing with others the details and fabric of women's lives. This tradition has produced many lasting autobiographies, oral histories and personal statements that challenge stereotypical images of southern women.[49]

In doing an oral history, the researcher's purpose is to create a written record of the interview*ee*'s life from his/her perspective in his/her own words. Judy Long, a theorist of sociobiography stressed the value of this perspective for the social sciences:

> The feminist scholarship of the past two decades has made it clear that third-person accounts and "generic" sociology have not, in fact, told us anything about women's experiences. First person accounts are required to understand the subjectivity of a social group that is "muted," excised from history, "invisible" in the official records of their culture (including sociological theory).[50]

One contemporary methodological contribution of feminist scholarship to the social sciences, therefore, is the revival of this dormant method.

On the other hand, many obstacles prevent its acceptance in the mainstream. People whose view of social science is parochial and who fear or discount the debunking results of feminist historical research are likely to marginalize this work.[51] For example, sociologist Mary Jo Deegan had difficulty getting support for her work on Jane Addams and the Chicago School of Sociology:

> Over a decade ago, I wanted to write a popular paper, only eight or ten pages long, on an early woman sociologist. I believed there must have been at least one woman who worked in my discipline, and I wanted to remember and celebrate that work. To my utter amazement, when I examined the early sociology journals, I found not one but dozens of early women sociologists. . . . I haunted archives, read musty organizational records, and pored over correspondence. These were unfamiliar tasks for a sociologist of our era. . . . Financial support for this research was very difficult to obtain. Because Jane Addams has been defined as "not a sociologist" and because I was using historians' techniques instead of "mainstream" sociological methodology, peers who read my funding application did not feel that my project was justifiable as a sociological inquiry.[52]

Mary Jo Deegan's work in feminist biography was threatening because it had the potential to rewrite standard sociological history and question conventional heroes. I encounter the same incredulity from sociologists when I suggest that students read Harriet Martineau's *How to Observe Morals and Manners,* a text that preceded Emile Durkheim's canonical *Rules of Sociological Method* by 60 years, or her *Society in America* in contrast with Alexis de Tocqueville's *Democracy in America.*

Biography and oral history have the potential of bringing women "into" history and making the female experience part of the written record. This form of research thereby revises history, in the sense of forcing us to modify previously published accounts of events that did not take women's experience seriously. Sara Evans found that the oral history method enabled her to uncover completely undocumented material in the U.S. political movements of the 1960s:

> I set out with a growing file of names, most without addresses, and a list of people with whom I might stay. The research grew as I travelled. I had not imagined the subtle complexity, both positive and negative, of women's experiences in various parts of the new left, or the intricacy of a network of relationships that stretched across the country and over nearly a decade. None of the written sources gave more than the barest hint of what I would find.[53]

Feminist oral history's success in increasing awareness of women's lives and in modifying the historical record is responsible for a shift in historical methodology, according to Mary Jo Maynes. The shift reflects, in part, "the distinctive feminist agenda," that "focused on making women central to historical interpretations." Because of this focus,

> the attention of feminist historians . . . has turned to the search for sources permitting glimpses into female perspectives on life in the past . . . [At first] the heavy emphasis on personal testimony so central both to the women's movement and to feminist theory and scholarship was largely eschewed by early social historians, who sought statistical averages and perhaps feared that reliance on such testimony represented a return to past practices that had privileged the point-of-view of the educated and powerful creators of most written records.[54]

But women's oral history has this potential only if it reaches out to study the greatest possible diversity among women.[55]

Contemporary Reasons for Doing
Feminist Oral History

Just as in the past, contemporary feminist researchers are interested in oral histories and biographical work for several reasons: to develop feminist theory, express affinity and admiration for other women, contribute to social justice, facilitate understanding among social classes, and explore the meaning of events in the eyes of women. I will discuss each of these briefly, using the researcher's own words.

Margaret Randall collected oral histories of women involved in the Nicaraguan Revolution against Somoza. She deliberately "talked with women from very different backgrounds . . . whose levels of involvement varied widely'' because she ''wanted to know how they began to articulate their need to join in the political struggle, how they made the decision, a decision that would affect every facet of their lives; and how they overcame the traditional obstacles thrown up by family and social prejudice.''[56] Her purpose was to illuminate the relation between feminism and Marxism, a topic long debated in feminist theory. As Lynda Yantz points out in the preface to this book, *''Sandino's Daughters* situates that debate in an actual practice,''[57] i.e., feminist oral history helps the theoretician test feminist theory, in this case Marxist–feminism. On the other hand, Elizabeth Roberts did an oral history project of working-class women between 1890 and 1940 in three British towns. She deliberately suspended feminist theory even though she had planned to incorporate it:

> [S]ome feminists may be disturbed to find that the book does not seek to investigate patriarchy or male oppression of women. . . . Such a great proportion of women's lives was spent in the private sphere of home, family and neighbourhood . . . [I]t became evident that there was little feeling among the majority of women interviewed that they or their mothers had been particularly exploited by men, at least not by working-class men. . . . In their interviews many women indicated their awareness of the limited horizons and opportunities of their lives, but were just as likely to associate their menfolk with this lack of choice. . . . They tended to blame the poverty. . . . In other words, women who were conscious of their exploitation interpreted it in terms of class conflict. . . . only two [were] involved in the suffragette/suffragist movement, but eleven were active in the Labour Party.[58]

Feminists have used the oral history method to pay tribute to people they admire. For example, Sydelle Kramer wrote

> that this project started on my grandmother's knee, for it was there, when I was a small girl, that I first heard the stories about life and death in Russia, emigration to America, and the struggle to ''make good'' here. Years later, at a small feminist publishing meeting, some women and I discussed the need for some sort of book describing the experiences of our grandmothers and paying tribute, however, indirectly, to their lives. The sharing of his kind of desire, and the same early fascination with our grandmothers, led Jenny Masur and me into the collaboration which produced this book.[59]

Similarly, Pat Taylor uses oral history to express her respect for a faith healer who is a ''model . . . of a strong, individualistic woman coming into her own powers without benefit of the support either husband or community would usually provide.''[60] Feminist oral history acknowledges the value of women's lives. It encourages identification among women through the recognition of common experience.

In some instances a feminist researcher begins with one purpose and finds that her material leads her in new directions. An example comes from the work of sociologist Evelyn Nakano Glenn's oral history project:

> When I started gathering materials for what turned out to be this book, my goals were modest. . . . to collect and assemble a set of oral interviews of Japanese-

American women employed as domestics. In teaching and writing about women and work, I had become acutely aware of the dearth of materials documenting the day-to-day struggles of Asian-American, Latina, and Black women working in low-status occupations, such as domestic service, the most prototypical job for racial-ethnic women. Little was known about the conditions they confronted, what they felt about their situation, or how they responded to menial employment. Accounts in which women spoke in their own words about themselves and their work seemed the best vehicle for illustrating how gender, race, and class intersect to shape the lives of racial-ethnic women. Once started, the project took momentum and drew me along. Questions raised by the initial interviews led to a broadening of the study both empirically and theoretically. My new aim was to uncover the relationship between Japanese-American women's experience as domestic workers during the first seventy years of the twentieth century and larger historical forces: the transformation of the economy and labor market in Northern California and the process of labor migration and settlement in that locale. How did these forces affect women's work, both paid and unpaid, and what were their strategies for dealing with the conditions engendered by these forces?[61]

Some feminist scholars believe that injustices can be righted when "people tell their stories"; others believe that history can be improved. In my view these are two aspects of the same phenomenon. The production of an oral text may "right the injustice" of a particular person's (or group's) voice being unheard. Jean Bethke Elshtain wrote:

> One who bears witness voices the discontents of society's silenced, ignored, abused, or invisible members. The witness proffers reasons for that suffering in order that the silenced may find a voice, cry out for justice, demand to be seen.[62]

At the same time an oral history corrects the biased view of history that had not included her/their voice. A poignant example of "righting the injustice" comes from the work of Daphne Patai, a collector of Brazilian women's life stories:

> On one occasion a young man . . . took me to the house of a nun working in a slum in Recife. He had told her about my project and she had agreed to the interview. . . . Hours later the young man came back to get me, having spent the evening hanging around waiting for me to finish. We walked down the steep paths back to the avenue at the bottom of the hill, where I could catch a bus. When I thanked him for his help, he said, "I don't give a damn about you or your research. I'm helping you because it's important that these people's stories be told."[63]

Reflecting on her own work with the !Kung[64] and on Barbara Myerhoff's[65] work with elderly U.S. Jews, anthropologist Marjorie Shostak believes that we have an *obligation* to collect life histories. She writes that "We should . . . go out and record the memories of people whose ways of life are preserved to some extent in those memories; and . . . we should do it urgently, before these ways of life are destroyed by one force or another."[66] Diana Russell suggests the same, in her study of women antiapartheid activists in South Africa. First she marvels at their willingness to risk their lives and speak to her; then she recognizes how important it is to them that "the real story of their struggle be known in the United States and other countries."[67]

There is a dilemma, however, in publishing life histories of women's suffering and courage. Although oral histories may break the silence, they may also encourage readers to view sociopolitical problems in individualistic terms. While reading a personal story is useful in making a distant society seem less remote, the personalized form of the story may detract from our ability to develop a sociopolitical understanding of events and forces.[68]

Oral histories of lower- and working-class women have the potential of enabling middle-class readers to get to know women of those classes, as Nancy Siefer observed.[69] In her view, this knowledge is useful to the extent that it is authentic and not mediated by "an interpreter." She claims that working-class women usually are not heard and when they are, it is through someone else's voice. She also worries that her middle-class origins might interfere with her understanding of working-class women's lives. Thus she commits herself to letting the subjects of her working-class oral histories speak for themselves. To achieve this, she does not analyze the accounts she collects, but presents them as they were given to her. By not analyzing the accounts, she prevents herself from speaking for, speaking better than, or transforming them. Her politics concerning how she wants to relate to working-class women is the basis of her methodological position of *not analyzing* oral histories.[70] Nancy Siefer believes that the women are capable of analyzing their lives, and that an analysis is contained in what they are saying. Moreover, she believes that if the women are heard directly, without her interference, the reader will be able to identify with them. It is this identification that will produce social change,[71] not the oral historian's analysis of the women's lives. Nancy Siefer is not alone in this view, as the following quotation from Patricia Sexton shows:

> While the book tries to let the women come through, the task has not been easy, for many wise people have urged me to interpret more and include more of myself in the account. I have resisted those urgings but not with total success; yet I have tried to listen carefully to what others say, without imposing my own voice on theirs.[72]

Elizabeth Hampsten[73] disagrees. She urges us to *use our authority* to help bring other voices into print and to use our voices to comment on what we have learned. She encourages us to analyze women's writings and women's words from many different perspectives.[74] She suggests we worry less about imposing our ideas and worry more about taking initiative. She would like us to take women's journals and diaries that were not intended for publication, for example, and "nudge them along" into publication. Not only should we examine the form and content of these materials, we should also question if the documents actually reveal women's experiences or someone else's.

In my view, feminist oral historians need not silence themselves to let other women be heard. The refusal to analyze transcripts does not produce a kind of purity in which women speak for themselves in an unmediated way. After all, the oral historian already had a role in producing the oral history and preparing it for publication. Since any involvement at all by the oral historian is a de facto interpretation, feminist researchers should be interested in providing an analysis so that the reader has a sense of the perspective used. Fran Buss, mentioned above, included analyses in her oral histories of lower income women and shared some of her personal history:

> The stories told by the women in this book did not occur as monologues, but were the product of a developing relationship between each woman and myself. As much as I tried to be objective and encourage each woman to take the lead in what we discussed, by asking certain questions, responding in specific ways, and choosing which material to include in the final editing, I have certainly influenced the final telling of each story. Because of the influence I had, it is important that readers have some knowledge of my background, beliefs, and interests.
>
> I did not enter these women's lives as a total stranger to the life experiences they describe. I am a white woman who grew up in a primarily working-class neighborhood in a small city in the Midwest. Our neighborhood bordered on some of the most impoverished areas in our community, and when I was young, my mother pointed out to me the disturbing inequities between the neighborhoods.
>
> I was married relatively young and divorced when my three children were preschoolers and we were living in the West. Following my divorce, my struggle to support the children became especially difficult. At one point, I worked four part-time jobs and spent more than 50 percent of my income on child care. Food stamps were crucial to our physical and emotional survival, and we went on welfare for a period of time. It was during this time that I came to understand the importance of the strength women can give each other. Despite this valuable resource, I became ill and received several years of extremely poor, indigent medical care. I also personally experienced sexual violence and institutional violence against women and the poor.
>
> Then I married again, and with the assistance of my present husband and those close to us, I became healthier and finished my education. During those years I did community organizing with low-income women, founding a women's crisis and information center, and thus came in contact with many other women experiencing some of the basic struggles of life. I have continued community organizing throughout the years and am presently on leave of absence from the ministry of the United Church of Christ and am teaching women's studies part time at the University of Wisconsin at Whitewater.[75]

Similarly, Diana Russell begins her moving collection of the oral histories of South African women with the story of her own life and her connection to these women.[76]

Whose Voice Is It?

Julia Swindells raised important questions about the "voice" in oral history and in personal documents such as diaries. Her question might be put this way: who is speaking when women speak for themselves? She believes we have been naive in not analyzing the conditions under which voices are speaking. Her skepticism about the "authenticity" of voices hinges on the fact that their very production may be a form of oppression.

The case of Hannah Cullwick suggests this broader point. Hannah Cullwick was a nineteenth-century British maid who was asked to write diaries of her labors by Arthur Munby, an upper-class British man who derived sexual pleasure from reading about women immersed in dirt and hard work. As Julia Swindells dramatically demonstrates, Hannah Cullwick felt compelled to service Arthur Munby with her gender and her class. Recognizing that she was not free in writing her diary means that we cannot use her diary to "give her a voice." If we abandon that project, we begin "to liberate ourselves as socialist feminist subjects" from the myth that we are ending her silence or that women like her led liberated lives.[77] Julia Swindells' analysis of the Hannah Cullwick case leads her to conclude that instead of deluding ourselves that we are "liberating" women, we should take on the responsibility of "analyzing the conditions of their lives":

> There is no "authentic" voice of woman in history, no unity of that sort, transcending history. Neither should we muddle up the business of enabling voices to be heard with finding our sisters suddenly "liberated" in their lives as in the sounds of these texts. Rather, we should be asking questions about specific histories, specific texts. Whose stories do the diaries of Hannah Cullwick tell? Whose subject is being inscribed? . . . [If] we listen carefully to the voices . . . we begin to hear and see, surely, the liberation, not of Hannah Cullwick, but of Arthur J. Munby, finding a voice in text, already a relatively free(d) man in life.[78]

In a related paper, Katherine Goodman[79] suggests that the so-called "authentic voice" may be a form of imitation. In this case, the author imitates fictional genres that are popular at the time.

Anthropologist Marjorie Shostak suggests that in a published oral history there actually are three voices, as in her own book, *Nisa: The Life and Words of a !Kung Woman*:

> First, there was Nisa's. I presented that as a first-person narrative, translated and edited from the tapes, and chronologically ordered (from "Earliest Memories" to "Growing Older"), in 15 chapters. The second voice was the anthropologist's, putting Nisa's story in cultural perspective: the ethnographic background to each topic Nisa touched upon is included as headnotes preceding each chapter of narrative. The third voice was mine, not as anthropologist, but as an American woman experiencing another world. Sandwiching the 15 chapters of narrative and headnotes, a personal introduction gives an overall framework to Nisa's story and to my own, and an epilogue summarizes my second field trip, my final encounter with Nisa, and my closing thoughts.[80]

Thus, feminist oral historians disagree about what kind of voice and whose voice is present in a published oral history—is it the voice of oppression, the voice of imitation, the authentic unsilenced self, or multiple voices?

The Interviewer's Voice

Usually the printed version of an oral history is an edited version of the interviewee's speech excluding signs of the interaction with the interviewer. The feminist oral historian's role in obtaining the transcript is muted. In other cases, the oral history is an amalgam of material obtained through interviews, material written by the interviewee, and observations made by the interviewer. This was the case in Pat Taylor's oral history of Jewell Babb, an example that clearly separates the various voices:

> A great deal of the material in this book was transcribed orally during a three-month period when I stayed with Mrs. Babb. . . . However, Mrs. Babb also wrote long segments of the story in long hand. Her voice is weak, and she is somewhat reticent about speaking directly about herself. Thus, after long talking sessions would wear her out, she would turn to writing. We would then go over the written sections together, so that she could supplement orally in places which seemed to need elucidation. She also continued to send me additional segments whenever she would recall some incident which seemed to her to be of value in the story. I have tried to edit her writing as little as possible, other than to arrange the spoken and written segments in order to preserve the enjoyable way of telling which is Mrs. Babb's unique "voice."[81]

Pat Taylor was explicit about the reasons for including her own voice:

> I have included my own impressions of the time I spent with her and of the environment which, in my opinion, has contributed to the formation of her personality and beliefs. These personal notes have been provided so that historical and descriptive material which would provide a context for her story could be supplied and so that some ideas of the circumstances in which the interviewing was done would be supplied to enable the readers to judge for themselves how these circumstances might have influenced Mrs. Babb in shaping her story. Mrs. Babb and I consider this to be a joint writing project, and we have worked equally hard putting together a manuscript which we hope will be both informative and enjoyable.[82]

Feminist oral histories concerned with clarifying the different voices find ways of *highlighting* the dialogue and sharing that occurred.

In some instances the researcher and the person whose story is being told are one and the same person. Because many feminist researchers self-disclose as a research method in interviewing and oral history, examples exist of researchers who include autobiographical material in analyses of a particular topic. Sociologist Ruth Harriet Jacobs did so in a study of sexism and ageism,[83] as did Lee Zevy and Sahli Cavallaro in their study of lesbian identity:

> This is the story of an odyssey. A story about lesbian invisibility: how lesbians grow into, maintain, and attempt to undo this invisibility so that they may know themselves and love other women; so that the quest for the princess is reconciled, and intimacy with a real woman and a charmed relationship is attained. To explain the complexity of this process, we chose to combine psychological theory with the telling of one of our stories. Although the details . . . are about Lee Zevy's life, the themes of invisibility and fantasy and the subsequent search for intimacy are common threads that run through the lives of women we both know and the lesbians with whom we work professionally.[84]

The self-disclosure in interviewing, and the self-study in some oral histories are examples of some feminists' disdain for the separation of subjectivity and objectivity, self and other, and personal and public.

Contradictions in Listening

Feminists typically advocate oral histories for "getting at the experience" rather than at facts. But, according to Kathryn Anderson, the prestige of "facts" may lead feminist oral historians claiming to seek insights into women's experiences to be drawn to the "facts" instead of listening to the feelings.[85] Too often, an avowed interest in experience masks a deeper interest in activities, networks, and other "hard information."[86] Dana Jack suggests another subtle contradiction: oral historians are likely to give more authority to their own orientations than to the women's stories. To avoid this,

> the first step is to ask the meaning of words in order to understand them in the subject's own terms. . . . When one listens, one hears how women use the language of the culture to deny what, on another level, they value and desire. We must learn to help women tell their own stories, and then learn to listen to those stories without being guided by models that restrict our ability to hear.[87]

In this vein, Michal McCall and Judith Wittner, theorists of feminist oral history, suggest that we not turn to oral histories for history or "eyewitness accounts" of events; rather, we should seek women's interpretations, thus honoring their minds.[88] In their view, oral history compels researchers to confront how individuals and groups create meaning.

Feminist researchers document changes that occur in their own lives as a consequence of doing deeply engaging research. In words reminiscent of Ann Oakley,[89] Fran Buss described the personal changes that resulted from her oral history work:

> I have become personally involved with most of the women, maintaining friendships through letters, the telephone, and visits. I have also tried to help them locate resources when specific needs have arisen, but primarily the total experience has deepened my political conviction that we must all struggle to make our society more just.[90]

Fran Buss' inclusion of this reflexive information enables me to better understand the oral history material she presented.

Who Is Studied by the Oral Historian?

Oral histories are typically, though not exclusively, done with two frequently overlapping types of people: older and relatively powerless people. In many societies older individuals are seen as repositories of historical knowledge. They may have the time and inclination to share what they know, but may lack access to publication and may not choose to express themselves in written form. Many feminist writers and researchers have adopted the oral history method precisely for the purpose of enabling people to publish their views who otherwise would not have done so. For example, in a play on the "speak-out" concept,[91] which she calls a "sing-out," Patricia Sexton presents her study of largely unseen and unrecognized hospital workers. Her book represents a unique amalgam combining analysis of the problems of hospital workers with their own testimony about their lives.

> The form of the book underscores its main substance in that it gives women a voice, an opportunity to discuss matters that affect their work lives, and recognition for what they say. The voices of the workers and the unionists are sometimes separate and sometimes mingled, which is the way it is in real life too. My own voice is also in there, and louder than the sheer quantity indicates, since I also edited all the other voices. . . . The book does not examine the views of doctors, administrators, or the public with respect to hospital care or the experience of work. It is perhaps more than enough that it breaks the silence of workers and unionists on these subjects. Nor does the book focus on the registered nurse, the "professional" hospital worker, although her presence is often noted. Rather, the book is about "hospital workers," those non-professionals who assist in patient care and in typing, cleaning, cooking, and keeping the hospital going. References to literature on hospital workers are very slim since little is written about them.[92]

Although feminist oral historians generally study the relatively powerless, Fran Buss makes the point that this is not usually the *most* vulnerable populations. Commenting on her own work, she wrote:

> On the whole, the women whose stories appear in this book are survivors, and they are often not the desperately poor. For each of these women who have somehow made it through all the barriers of class, racial, and sexual discrimination, there are those who did not survive. Those women's stories tend not to be told, because they are not very visible, because they are so vulnerable that publicity would be dangerous, or because they have died or have been too "beaten down" to discuss their lives.[93]

Whom do we exclude because of our fears? Do we study only "captive" populations? People with whom we can create rapport?

The Study of Men

Feminist research is not restricted to the study of women and Marcia Wright argues the value of feminist oral histories of men, using an example from her African research.

> A feminist approach to male subjects must be ventured, in part because men who are "public" affect women and in part because they must also be rendered as private persons influenced by women and involved in the social reproduction of gender relations in the intimate as well as the extradomestic arenas. In a bio-

graphical sketch of a British magistrate, who shaped the early colonial political economy in Meli's neighborhood, I moved from an appreciation of the special way in which he had allied with African women in his jurisdiction at the turn of the century, to a focus on the way in which his career was a dramatization of upward mobility in British class terms. In the course of this transition, it was his marriage to a solidly middle class woman which sealed the success of the trans- formation . . . I am committed to the scrutiny of male lives for the sake of showing the play of power in its fullest sense, inclusive of women.[94]

This example illustrates what may be a more general pattern of the focus in fem- inist oral history of men. These studies examine the role women played in their lives, or the impact these men had on women.

Writing One's Own Story

Aside from oral history studies of relatively powerless people, and of men who affect women's lives, some feminist autobiographical/life history work is done among people who are literate and highly educated but who have experiences that have remained hidden. In these cases, a feminist research method may consist of soliciting written statements about a particular topic, without prior interviewing or subsequent analysis. These products do not "give voice to the voiceless," but rather allow a different voice within some person to emerge. When a set is gath- ered, the result is a collection of personal statements such as the following by Stephanie Dowrick and Sibyl Grundberg about voluntary childlessness.

We set out to sample the effect of the Second Wave of women's liberation on women's choices about motherhood, wanting to explore further the knotty problem of "choice" . . . In seeking contributors to *Why Children?* our aim was to convey the complexity, the deep personal significance of the decision whether or not to have children, the most irrevocable and important one that most of us will make. We sought women with a wide range of backgrounds and experience. Inevitably the end result does not put forward as many different views or life situations as we would have liked. All the women writing in this book have something strongly felt to say. We opted to go with their urgency rather than attempt the impossible: a truly representative cross-section of women. Sadly, there were women whose perspectives we cherished who found the subject too painful to write about, or who felt that the honesty crucial to the project would have been too hurtful to others involved in the consequences of their "choice."

Our contributors do include mothers in traditional "nuclear" families, single mothers, women bringing up children to whom they did not give birth, women involved in raising children collectively; heterosexual, bisexual and lesbian women, mothers of teenagers, mothers of infants; women who have made the decision not to have children with reluctance and pain, women who have made that decision conscious of the benefits for them of a childless life; women who still hope to exercise their choice in the future . . . It is an intense and many-sided dialogue among women who speak in many different voices. Except to ask for clarification or explanation, we did not intervene in the expression of those voices.[95]

The point they make about some women being unable to write is reminiscent of Fran Buss' point that oral histories do not include the stories of the most distressed.[96]

Oral Histories Are Trans- or Interdisciplinary Endeavors

Historian Susan Armitage writes that oral history is not a unique method but draws on the methodologies of history, psychology, and sociology. At the same time, oral history criticizes these disciplines. For this reason, she believes it is important to recognize the interdisciplinary nature of feminist oral history. She explains that feminist oral histories should be done by teams of researchers with different skills:

> We propose a definite structuring of oral history methods to achieve the goals of feminist research . . . we will not find out about women's consciousness unless we ask. We will need to incorporate considerable psychological awareness and listening skills into our interviews in order to succeed. The stance we adopt toward our completed interviews is equally crucial. The desire of feminist researchers to make sure that women are the subjects and not the objects of study is laudable but difficult to accomplish. Here we need the sophisticated sociological awareness of the reciprocal relationships between individual and institution developed by interactionist sociologists. . . . This range of skills makes it virtually mandatory that future women's oral history projects be conducted by interdisciplinary teams. Why bother? Why not just continue our present uncritical interview methods? The answer, of course, is that they do not reflect the insights of the new feminist scholarship. The old methods will not tell us what we now know we can learn about women if we ask the right questions.[97]

Women's Studies programs seem ideally suited to the creation of such inter- or transdisciplinary teams.

Concluding Thoughts

It is difficult to summarize this chapter—there is little agreement on terminology, the product, whose voices are being expressed, whether an individual can even do an oral history, whether the oral historian should analyze the material, and even if oral history exists as a separate entity or overlaps with the various disciplines. Despite these disagreements, I also detect an esprit de corps among feminists who do oral histories and biographical work. I believe this enthusiasm stems from the blending of purposes that feminist oral history affords—the writing of history, the encounter with other women, and the development of new concepts. The enthusiasm is probably also related to the disagreements. Feminist oral historians may feel particularly free to work in ways that reflect their personal resolutions of these methodological dilemmas precisely because there is no orthodoxy, and because feminist oral history remains outside the mainstream.

8

Feminist Content Analysis[1]

> To arrive at the facts of the condition of a people through the discourse of individuals, is a hopeless enterprise. . . . The grand secret of wise inquiry into Morals and Manners is to begin with the study of THINGS, using the DISCOURSE OF PERSONS as a commentary upon them.[2] (1838)

> The cultural products of any given society at any given time reverberate with the themes of that society and that era.[3] (1977)

In the opening quotations nineteenth-century Harriet Martineau and twentieth-century Rose Weitz extol the value of studying "things" or "cultural products." On board ship preparing to study the United States in 1834 Harriet Martineau wrote:

> The eloquence of Institutions and Records, in which the action of the nation is embodied . . . , is more comprehensive and more faithful than that of any variety of individual voices. The voice of a whole people goes up in the silent workings of an institution; the condition of the masses is reflected from the surface of a record. . . . The records of any society . . . whether architectural remains, epitaphs, civic registers, national music, or any other of the thousand manifestations of the common mind which may be found among every people, afford more information on Morals in a day than converse with individuals in a year.[4]

In current parlance, Harriet Martineau was stressing the value of nonreactive data or "unobtrusive measures."[5] Although the value of unobtrusive measures is still recognized today, her idea of "reflection" is challenged. Some texts may, in fact, "reflect" conditions, but others (e.g., television and movies) are thought to "mediate" experience, i.e., to reflect those who produced it, such as culture industries.[6] Contemporary feminist scholars of cultural texts are likely to see meaning as mediated, and therefore to examine both the text and the processes of its production. They are also likely to examine the processes that prevent texts from being produced.[7]

Historical Roots

Harriet Martineau's enthusiastic endorsement of the examination of documents for sociological research has echoes in the work of teacher, journalist, lecturer, researcher, and activist, Ida B. Wells (1862–1929),[8] a daughter of freed slaves. In 1891 Ida Wells investigated the circumstances surrounding the lynching of blacks in the South, particularly questioning if black men were lynched for raping white women, as was commonly believed, or for some other reason. To conduct her study, she culled newspaper reports for accounts of lynchings, went to the scene of the crime, and interviewed eyewitnesses. Women's studies scholar Paula Giddings described Ida B. Wells' work as follows:

> All in all, she researched the circumstances of 728 lynchings that had taken place during the last decade. . . . Only a third of the murdered Blacks were even *accused* of rape, much less guilty of it. . . . Most were killed for crimes like "incendiarism," "race prejudice," "quarreling with whites," and "making threats." Furthermore, not only men but women and even children were lynched. . . . In the course of her investigations, Wells uncovered a significant number of interracial liaisons. She dared to print not only that such relationships existed, but that in many cases white women had actually taken the initiative. Black men were being killed for being "weak enough," in Wells's words, to "accept" white women's favors.

Ida Wells concluded that black men were lynched because of whites' racial hatred and sense of threat, rather than for a particular wrongdoing. On June 5, 1892, she published the landmark results of her study in newspaper article form. In response, a large group of New York black women held an unprecedented, successful fund-raiser to support the publication of her findings as a pamphlet, seeing in her research a defense of their own moral integrity as well as that of black men. This reaction "opened the way for the next stage of political development" of black women.[9] Ida Wells stressed that her research relied on the collection and analysis of documents written by whites. She knew that such data alone would make her findings credible in white society. As she predicted, her methods forced whites to confront ugly truths and challenged them to alter their stereotypes, a process most resisted.

Types of Materials in Contemporary Feminist Content Analyses

People who do content analyses study a set of objects (i.e., cultural artifacts) or events systematically by counting them or interpreting the themes contained in them. Sociologists, historians, literary analysts, anthropologists, and archaeologists—whether feminist or not—are interested in cultural artifacts as something produced by people. These products stem from every aspect of human life including relatively private worlds, "high" culture, popular culture,[10] and organizational life. The only limit to what can be considered a cultural artifact—and thus used as a "text" for research—is the researcher's imagination. Feminists' studies of "texts" include children's books,[11] fairy tales,[12] billboards,[13] feminist nonfiction and fiction,[14] children's art work,[15] fashion,[16] "fat-letter postcards,"[17] Girl Scout Handbooks,[18] works of fine art,[19] newspaper rhetoric,[20] clinical records,[21] research publications,[22] introductory sociology textbooks,[23] and citations,[24] to mention only a few. One way to categorize these in terms of gender is to consider artifacts produced *by* women, *about* women or *for* women, artifacts produced *by* men, *about* men or *for* men, or any combination of these. Sometimes an artifact falls into more than one category, as when a woman studies a text written by women for women about women. Joan Pennell, for example, studied the ideology in the "statement of purpose" of a shelter she helped establish for battered women in St. John's, Newfoundland.[25]

Cultural artifacts are the products of individual activity, social organization, technology, and cultural patterns. Of course, the interpretations of these materials, such as this very book, are cultural artifacts too. In this wide array, four types of materials predominate as objects of feminist study. They are *written records* (e.g., diaries,[26] scientific journals, science fiction,[27] and graffiti), *narratives and visual texts* (e.g., movies,[28] television shows,[29] advertisements, and greeting cards);[30] *material culture* (e.g., music,[31] technology,[32] contents of children's rooms,[33] and ownership of books);[34] and *behavioral residues* (e.g., patterns of wear in pavement).

Typically, studying cultural products through the lens of feminist theory exposes a pervasive patriarchal and even misogynist culture.[35] Sometimes these cultural themes are found even when feminist literature is the object, as was the case in Nancy Chodorow and Susan Contratto's study of feminist treatments of the topic of mothering.[36] Similarly, Judith DiIorio's content analysis of scholarly articles about gender role research concluded that the methods used reify social facts and are a conservative force.[37] On the other hand, some cultural artifacts *oppose* the dominant culture. Popular culture created or chosen by women may express resistance to male domination. Feminist scholars are likely to interpret these in terms of the resilience of "women's culture."

The Key Characteristics of Cultural Artifacts

Cultural artifacts have two distinctive properties. First, they possess a naturalistic, "found" quality because they are not created for the purpose of study. Second, they are noninteractive, i.e., they do not require asking questions of respondents or observing people's behavior. Cultural artifacts are not affected by the process of studying them as people typically are. Instead, scholars can examine a written record or some other type of "text" without interacting with the people who produced it. An example is Emile Durkheim's use of suicide rates to analyze the cohesiveness of society,[38] an approach that was to become the paradigmatic research model for many sociologists.[39]

Contemporary applications of this model include the work of then undergraduate Bonita Iritani, and her teacher, Candace West, who did a quantitative content analysis of marriage licenses to study the "male older norm" in heterosexual mate selection.[40] In addition to marriage licenses, feminist scholars have used birth certificates, wills and testaments, and divorce settlements to examine the status of women as a social group without interacting with the particular women mentioned in these records.[41]

Many feminist research projects combine analysis of data that are "found" with data that are "produced" for the specific study. One example is U.S. sociologist Kristin Luker's study of activist groups on various sides of the abortion debate. Her work used "written records that were not created for the purposes of this research and intensive, verbatim interviews that were."[42] Examples of the first category are content analyses of newspapers (e.g., articles in the *San Francisco Chronicle, Los Angeles Times,* and *San Diego Union* on the topic of abortion, including letters to the editor), "persuasive literature" (e.g., newsletters, pamphlets, hand-outs, flyers, and other items designed to sway public opinion), and organizational records (e.g., minutes of meetings, constitutions and by-laws, lists of funders and donations). This material gave her

> a picture of the social perception of abortion in California from the nineteenth century, through the tumultuous days of abortion reform in the 1960s, and up to the present day [and] . . . a list of names of people involved in or identified with one side or the other of the abortion debate. . . . Examining those [organizational] documents enabled us to cross-check with documentary evidence some of the assertions made in interviews about the early history of pro-life and pro-choice organizations and, in particular, the social composition of the early movements.[43]

Kristin Luker integrated these written materials with "long, semistructured interviews with 212 people who had been identified as activists in the abortion debate." Comparison of researcher-produced interview material with researcher-located archives and organizational literature enabled her to understand the relation between individual belief and organizational ideology and history. Her insights clearly would have been limited had she relied on only one of these data sources.[44] Checking back and forth in this way is also a rationale for doing multimethod research.

Feminist Content Analysis or Deconstruction

As has been true in chapters devoted to other methods, there is no terminological consensus for the method discussed here. Sociologists tend to use the term "content analysis," historians the term "archival research," and philosophers and students of literature the term "text analysis" or "literary criticism."[45] Different disciplines also apply different interpretive frameworks to the analysis of cultural artifacts. Discourse analysis, rhetoric analysis, and deconstruction are additional terms that refer to the examination of texts.

An example of feminist deconstruction[46] is Laurel Graham's comparative analysis of four "texts" that deal with the same phenomenon—a year in the life of Dr. Lillian Moller Gilbreth, a pioneer in the field of scientific management. Laurel Graham's four texts are Lillian Gilbreth's personal diaries, her biography written by colleague Edna Yost, a book written by two of Lillian Gilbreth's 11 children about their parents, and a film rendition of that book. Laurel Graham advocates "feminist intertextual deconstruction" or "feminist multi-text analysis" by which she means looking for contradictions within or between texts that illustrate the pervasive effects of patriarchy and capitalism. Her method relies on "an oppositional or subversive feminist reading of this year using all four texts." The diary allows us to hear Lillian Gilbreth's voice. This voice is then distorted by social forces as her life takes new shapes in the biography, book, and film. Although these subsequent texts encourage a "dominant reading," feminists can read them in "subversive ways" by constant rereading and looking for particular clues:

> Dominant readings need to be deconstructed in order to make sense of the specific ways texts teach their audiences to structure personal systems of meaning. Through deconstruction, readers can find in each text the information to construct oppositional readings. . . . As I read and reread each of these, I found myself repeatedly tempted to compare each to the one that came before. . . . Instead of succumbing to this realist temptation to identify a "true" version, my idea is to be reflective about this nasty tendency and to put it to use methodologically. . . . By finding the points of discontinuity between the texts, one can illuminate the mythologizing strategies and tools unique to that text.[47]

The "nasty tendency" by which a culture teaches us to privilege some types of information and invalidate others becomes apparent in feminist subversive intertextual reading. Similarly, Linda Blum examined the transformation of Marilyn French's novel, *The Women's Room*,[48] into a television production. Her sociopolitical study demonstrates the "tendency of the mass media to present feminism and feminist themes, critical of the existing male dominated sex/gender system, in a liberal frame."[49] The feminist themes contained in Marilyn French's book were softened in the rendition produced for television.

Organizational scientist Joanne Martin deconstructed a story told at a conference by "the president and Chief Executive Officer of a very large, multi-national corporation." The transcript of the story as spoken is as follows:

> We have a young woman who is extraordinarily important to the launching of a major new (product). We will be talking about it next Tuesday in its first worldwide introduction. She has arranged to have her Caesarean yesterday in order to be prepared for this event, so you—we have insisted that she stay home and this is going to be televised in a closed circuit television, so we're having this done by TV for her, and she is staying home three months and we are finding ways of filling in to create this void for us because we think it's an important thing for her to do.

After presenting the story, Joanne Martin explains her deconstructionist analytic method:

> I deconstruct and reconstruct this story from a feminist viewpoint, examining what it says, what it does not say, and what it might have said. This analysis highlights suppressed gender conflicts implicit in this story and shows how apparently well-intentioned organizational practices can reify, rather than alleviate, gender inequalities.[50]

Anecdotes of daily work are texts for feminist deconstruction.

Scholars in many fields use the term "literature review" to refer to an interpretation of relevant literature on a given subject matter.[51] Feminist literature reviews both summarize the salient findings of pertinent studies and question the assumptions of the paradigm underlying the studies. For example, British psychologist Celia Kitzinger's analysis of "scientific literature about homosexuality" examines how it attempts to convey an aura of "science."[52] She looks at texts not for their findings but for the rhetoric used to appear to have found something. This rhetoric is "positivist empiricism." She cautions us to avoid the "condition of entrapment" posed by positivist–empiricism that deflects us "into arguments about scientific evidence and methodological technique":

> We need to take an imaginative leap beyond the boundary walls of the positivist paradigm. Only if we can rise to the challenges of post-positivism can we begin to deconstruct social psychology's oppressive structure and create practical alternatives which offer real opportunities for radical social and political change.[53]

A final example of deconstruction is organizational scientist Barbara Gray's analysis of the hidden problematic assumptions in her earlier book, *Collaborating*.[54] This wide-ranging set of examples demonstrates that extent to which rhetorical analysis of texts has become a significant enterprise in feminist scholarship.[55]

Examples of Materials Used in Feminist Content Analysis

Many feminist scholars are troubled by the cultural expression, production, and perpetuation of patriarchy, ageism, and racism, and intrigued by the resistance of subgroups to these forces. These topics can be explored by analyzing cultural artifacts and documents. Magazine articles are a popular document for this type of analysis. Betty Friedan's early study of women's magazine fiction was devoted to this purpose. In chapter two, "The Happy Housewife Heroine," of her classic *The Feminine Mystique*, Betty Friedan explains the childish themes that dominate women's magazine fiction, and then plaintively expresses her guilt:

> I helped create this image. I have watched American women for fifteen years try to conform to it. But I can no longer deny my own knowledge of its terrible implications. It is not a harmless image. There may be no psychological terms for the harm it is doing. But what happens when women try to live according to an image that makes them deny their minds? What happens when women grow up in an image that makes then deny the reality of the changing world?[56]

In another study Francesca Cancian, past president of SWS (Sociologists for Women in Society), and her colleague, Steven Gordon, discovered that women's magazines contain "emotion norms." These norms focus on the appropriate emotions in marriage.

> [P]opular magazines socialize women to emotional culture by using particular vocabularies, advocating norms of emotional expression, and other mechanisms. . . . Our primary data are a random sample of nonfiction articles in U.S. popular magazines about how to have a happy marriage. This advice literature provides a

rich and easily available source of data on emotion norms over a long period of time, as other researchers have realized. . . .

The articles on marriage that we examined are from women's magazines like the *Ladies' Home Journal* and *McCall's,* as well as general magazines like *Reader's Digest* . . . from 1900 to 1979. For each five-year period, we selected eight articles listed in the *Reader's Guide to Periodicals* under the topic "Marriage." Because of the ease of obtaining articles from *Reader's Digest,* we randomly selected four articles in the *Reader's Guide* from *Reader's Digest* after it began publication in the early 1920s, and four from other high-circulation magazines. . . . In addition to the content analysis, a subsample of articles from each decade was selected for a qualitative analysis of the mechanisms of emotional socialization and the content of major normative changes.

Having selected their articles, they analyzed the material qualitatively and quantitatively, using the following methods:

Using . . . six categories, we coded the dominant messages that we believed the articles would communicate to a reader for 128 articles; 16 randomly selected articles for every decade. The coding system for the content analysis was refined until we reached a criterion of two coders agreeing on 85 percent of the categories assigned to a particular article.[57]

The quantitative content analysis of emotion norms supported the qualitative analysis and clarified the timing and magnitude of changes in norms about love and anger.

Sociologist Wendy Simonds used a method similar to that of Francesca Cancian and Steven Gordon but also included letters to the editor. Instead of focusing on emotion norms concerning "happy marriages," however, she sought magazine articles concerning maternal grief: "I found a total of 71 items in *True Story* from 1920 to 1937, and from 1950 to 1985, including 21 letters to the editor, which dealt on some level with maternal grief concerning infant death, miscarriage, stillbirth, abortion, or loss due to kidnapping or adoption."[58] The procedure she used was qualitative or interpretive content analysis. Her purpose was to understand how these articles instruct women to feel and define their experiences.

Newspaper columns, advice books, homilies, and other material have been written for women (sometimes by women) instructing them how to perform their roles. An example of research using this type of material for content analysis is Barbara Ehrenreich and Deirdre English's study showing that " 'experts'—from domestic scientists to child-rearing experts to psychologists—have all presumed to tell women what their true nature is, the proper method of rearing children, etc.," and frequently "'the advice they prefer is in direct contradiction to the experts' opinions ten years earlier."[59] By using such documents, feminist researchers identify social norms without using interactive methods that may affect the norms they are trying to study.

Cultural documents also shape norms; they do not just reflect them. Because of this, various feminist academic researchers and advocacy groups have been vigilant monitors of the way women, minorities, and elderly people are stereotyped in newspaper articles (with accompanying photographs) and advertisements.[60] They then examine these materials using statistical and/or interpretive procedures to illuminate underlying patterns.[61] Feminist research is also done on artistic and documentary photographs and popular movies.[62] For example, Denise Farran did

> a feminist sociological analysis into how a photograph of Marilyn [Monroe] works. . . . in this case, how is the "sexuality" of this photograph achieved or not achieved? At the heart of my paper is the idea that what this or any other photograph is about is not an object of fact, but rather meaning and understanding of it is socially constructed. That is, people invest meaning into photographs by bringing to them their current social ways of perceiving. In this photograph of Marilyn Monroe, I shall argue that people bring to it various ideas concerning what are the signifiers of sexuality and in this way what is "sexual" is actually a socially achieved phenomenon.

Her article begins with a large photograph physically attached to the page and ends with a discussion of how feminists studying such phenomena must confront basic epistemological questions. These include the problem of false consciousness, the meaning of individual experience, and the relation between theory and experience.

> The concept of false consciousness is often used to "understand" such women as Marilyn Monroe. It implies there is only one way of understanding the social world, there is just one truth. I much prefer an analytic approach which examines different versions of "the truth" and "reality" from different perspectives. I would argue that Marilyn Monroe, from her own experience of the modelling and film world, knew exactly what a male dominated world she lived in and decided that she wasn't going to beat the system, so she'd get what she could out of it. That is, she was all too conscious of the kind of world she lived in and chose what she thought to be the best strategy for herself.[63]

Modifying sociologist Erving Goffman's frame analysis techniques,[64] Mary Jo Deegan did a "feminist frame analysis" of the stills comprising the filmed episodes of "Star Trek." She defines feminist frame analysis as the "study of the rules of society and experience that limit the opportunities, experience and autonomy of women in everyday life." This type of research is a form of "praxis . . . [because] the knowledge of rules previously hidden provides a method to change consciousness." Concepts used in "feminist frame analysis" concern "sex classes and their role in the oppression of women." Finally, "feminist frame analysis draws on the insights of Freudian thought" because of its power in defining "the underlying structure for rules of behavior in society."[65]

Jean Kilbourne's films, "Killing Us Softly: The Image of Women in Advertising" and "Still Killing Us Softly,"[66] offer analyses of sexist and violent messages in advertisements. She points out that these explicit and subtle messages help form the environment in which we live. Dolores Hayden analyzed the environmental impact of these advertisements. She says that

> the public domain is misused for spatial displays of gender stereotypes. These appear in outdoor advertising, . . . commercial displays, architectural decoration, and public sculpture. . . . Most Americans are accustomed to seeing giant females in various states of undress smiling and caressing products such as whiskey, food, and records. Male models also sell goods, but they are usually active

and clothed—recent ad campaigns aimed at gay men seem to be the first major exception. Several geographers have established that men are most often shown doing active things, posed in the great outdoors; women are shown in reflective postures responding to male demands in interior spaces. As the nineteenth-century sexual double standard is preserved by the urban advertising, many twentieth-century urban men behave as if good women are at home while bad ones adorn the billboards and travel on their own in urban space. . . . By presenting gender stereotypes in the form of nonverbal body language, fifty feet long and thirty feet high, billboards turn the public space of the city into a stage set for drama starring enticing women and stern men.[67]

Cultural documents (e.g., Western philosophical texts,[68] scientific works, and theories)[69] are reread through feminist lenses. For example, historical and contemporary feminist scholars have examined the Bible to evaluate and modify its messages about females.[70] A famous historical instance is Elizabeth Cady Stanton's publication in 1895 of *The Woman's Bible*[71] two weeks after her 80th birthday.

Published in two parts, the work dealt only with those sections of the Old and New Testaments that mentioned women or that Stanton felt ought to have included them. The Biblical texts were printed at the top of each page with Stanton's commentaries below. For example, Stanton printed both versions of the creation of man from the Book of Genesis. She pointed out that in the one most frequently quoted, Eve was an outgrowth of Adam's rib. In the less well known passage, man and woman were created at the same instant in the image of God. Stanton used that example to argue the existence of an androgynous God and to illustrate how male ministers employed the Bible for their own advantage—to support the socially conservative position favoring subordinate womanhood—rather than an interpretation indicating equality of the sexes.

Elizabeth Cady Stanton understood that a feminist rewriting of the Bible would threaten people, but she turned her critics' attacks against them. When *"The Woman's Bible* was condemned at The National-American Women's Suffrage Association's annual meeting for being too radical . . . she appended the censure resolution to [its] next edition. . . . Two years later, ignoring [Susan B.] Anthony's objections, she published the second volume."[72] An example of a current feminist Biblical textual analysis is the work of J. Cheryl Exum whose "methods . . . draw on sociological and anthropological studies of women's status in biblical times, [and] literary approaches. . . . of close reading, which pays careful attention to the portrayal of women in selected texts."[73] Similarly, Biblical scholar and archaeologist, Carol Meyers, credits "developments in feminist scholarship and in sociohistorical analysis of ancient Israel" for constituting "the methodological potential through which . . . to discern the outlines of Eve, the Israelite Everywoman."[74]

Others who have conducted critical analyses of prestigious texts, such as sociologist Jennifer Pierce, comment on the courage required to be "nasty" after having been socialized to be "nice."[75] I felt this need when I reinterpreted scientific and philosophical texts as "symptoms" of a physiological disorder I called L.T.M.D.T. (low threshold for male dominance theorizing),[76] a term that "explains" why many male philosophers and scientists attributed physiological disorders to women. Political scientist Jean Bethke Elshtain also commented on the need to be brave when toppling heroes through feminist textual analysis. Courage was required and then allowed her "to be more provocative and less abstracted from the wellsprings of [her] own thought."[77]

Feminist Analysis of Fiction

Feminists have actively pursued literary criticism.[78] An early influential feminist study of fiction by Kate Millett[79] carefully examined male writers' language in describing heterosexual sex and women. Katherine Pope discovered a pattern of "discrepancy between the self and the female role" in many well-known novels written by women and men. She argued that fictional portraits of women have psychological value for teaching literature and as a tool for therapy because they "provide a source of identity and validity for the woman who is struggling with debilitating and alien cultural assumptions about herself. Fictional portraits are a form of realistic fantasy, a therapeutic vehicle through which women recognize their own situations and validate their own perceptions. . . . The reader sees herself as not alone in her experiences."[80] Fiction, here, is understood as a political text in both the social and personal domains.

Feminist literary criticism has also provided a model for the social sciences. Recently, social psychologist Margaret Wetherell adopted such methods to analyze the discourse of interviews. Her term "linguistic repertoire analysis" refers to an approach to the study of underlying themes, stereotypes, and Jungian dichotomies in people's speech. If a researcher applies this method, "the unit of study is not the person but the linguistic repertoire . . . and its ideological implications." Since variability and inconsistency are aspects of speech, she argues that giving people questions with yes/no options requires them to repress their thoughts and feelings. In her view, "linguistic repertoire analysis" respects speech's variability and inconsistency. "Strictly applied content analysis," on the other hand, does not examine "the recurrent stylistic, grammatical and lexical features (of speech)" which are a window into the social psychology of gender. They convey "the richness and subtlety of everyday conceptions of femininity and masculinity." She argues that the researchers must display the speech and the analysis, so that readers can uncover disagreements and keep discourse analysis political and "engaged with feminism."[81]

Quantitative Content Analyses

Researchers who collect cultural artifacts for analysis can interpret them using quantitative or qualitative methods. Computer programs that count word frequencies, for example, can reveal hidden meanings embedded in large sets of documents.[82] Similarly, quantative content analyses of the authorship and substance of academic journal articles can evaluate the impact of feminist critiques. Canadian psychologist Paula Caplan used this method to demonstrate psychology's continuing antagonism to mothers:

> The practice of mother-blaming in major clinical journals was investigated in nine mental health journals using 63 categories for classifying each of 125 articles. Articles were taken from the years 1972, 1976, and 1982 to see whether the common practice of blaming mothers for their children's problems might have changed during the time that the recent women's movement became particularly visible. Results revealed very few changes in mother-blaming . . . mother-blaming was not affected much by the type of journal or the author's sex. Recommendations for journal authors and editors in regard to avoidance of unwarranted mother-blaming are suggested.[83]

Similarly, Diana Scully and Pauline Bart's quantitative content analysis of gynecology textbooks[84] led to the conclusion that obstetricians and gynecologists portrayed women as mentally ill by virtue of the normal functioning of the female body. Sociologists and social psychologists who do quantitative analyses may carry out interrater reliability tests to demonstrate that they are not categorizing artifacts idiosyncratically.[85]

Quantitative content analyses are done to assess the percentage of professional articles authored by women[86] and the percentage in which women are the object of research.[87] U.S. psychologists Brinton Lykes and Abigail Stewart used this method to explore the impact of feminist thinking on the fields of personality and social psychology. They

> coded for types of methods employed in the research, use of female subjects, use of college students as subjects, inclusion of gender as an aspect of the research question, and use of other-than-traditional experimental research techniques; and a few substantive concerns (. . . whether discovered gender differences were interpreted in any way, whether the research included any references to issues of sex-role, and whether the basic research question reflected stereotypically masculine, feminine, or neutral content.)[88]

In sum, feminist researchers use quantitative content analysis to identify patterns in authorship, subject matter, methods, and interpretation. Findings from such studies are then used to generate or test hypotheses relevant to feminist theory and concerns, or to press for social change.

Qualitative or Interpretive Content Analysis

Historical research relies on cultural artifacts to learn about the lives of people in former times.[89] Historians classify artifacts either as primary sources that are the "raw" materials of history or secondary sources that may be considered the "cooked" analyses of those materials.[90] Feminist historians use cultural artifacts to study individual women or groups of women, the relation between women and men, relations among women, the intersection of race, gender, class, and age identities, and the institutions, persons, and ideas that have shaped women's lives. In line with these goals, feminist historians are expanding the range of cultural artifacts to include items related to private life, and are using feminist theory as an interpretive framework.

Records produced by public organizations (e.g., churches, courts, governments), the conventional source for historians, are appropriate for the study of public events, a domain in which men have predominated. The study of women, particularly "ordinary women," must draw on other types of materials as historian Gerda Lerner suggests:

> The voices of anonymous women were present as a steady undercurrent in the oral tradition, in folksong and nursery rhymes, tales of powerful witches and good fairies. In stitchery, embroidery, and quilting women's artistic creativity expressed an alternate vision. In letters, diaries, prayers, and song, the symbol-making force of women's creativity pulsed and persisted.[91]

Autobiographies, oral histories, clinical records, letters to the editor, fiction, poetry, folk art, worksongs, recipes, and cookbooks[92] are also appropriate for studying the world of women. Feminist social historians,[93] and sociologists[94] use this type of artifact for the study of individuals and groups. Professor of English Elizabeth Hampsten concurs:

> The literature of working class women is the literature of a class of women who have been silent, and it bears few resemblances either to public literature of the period or to the private writing of men or of upper class women. To reach it, one must read letters and diaries, for the thoughts of working women are recorded nowhere else.[95]

Historically ignored women are made visible when relevant artifacts are located and studied,[96] and conversely, analysis of this type of material illuminates the forces that shape the lives of the vast majority, in contrast to the elite minority.[97]

Historians looking through a feminist lens at the material women have produced often challenge conventional knowledge. Educator and philosopher Elizabeth Minnich, for example, highlighted the way Gerda Lerner's reading of women's diaries challenged the gender-neutral definition of adolescence. She wrote: "As young men pass through adolescence on the way to responsible adulthood, young women have passed through on the way to dependency, giving up the freedom experienced as children for the restrictions placed on women."[98] Thus, new methods produce new concepts and theories.

Generally, historians are not self-conscious about method nor do they discuss methods used in their publications. By contrast, feminist historians seem to have great interest in method. They are likely to modify and discuss conventional definitions of data.[99] For example, Elizabeth Hampsten contrasted her approach with that of others:

> Studies using private writing typically have been organized around the life of a notable person, . . . a group (women who corresponded with George Bernard Shaw . . .) or . . . important event . . . , these studies have sought out from historical archives only those parts of private writings that apply to the topic, omitting the rest. My own effort is the reverse. I . . . read entire collections and . . . stay in one place, reading whatever I come across no matter what its sub-

ject. . . . Staying in one spot . . . and reading all that was available by any given writer, I sought to learn what women were saying about their lives at the turn of the twentieth century.[100]

Another example of methodological self-consciousness is historian Nancy Cott's "Introduction" to her study of U.S. women, offering her view of primary sources. To understand "women's sphere" she

> turned to women's personal documents (such as diaries and letters) in preference to published, prescriptive works, in order to broaden my inquiry into the relation between change in the material circumstances of women's lives and their outlook on their place as women. . . . In order to pursue questions about women's experience, consciousness, and outlook in the decades leading to the 1830s, I have relied on their own private writings, and have also drawn on words spoken to and published about women by ministers, educators, and other authors.

Even though these materials allowed her to examine women's experience, she knew they represented a certain class, not the

> whole female sex but . . . the literate (and, perhaps, writing-prone) portion of it, particularly those whose lives conformed to the ruling norms of American life. . . . While this study must exclude the poor and illiterate, it covers a broad middle-to-upper range of the population.

She found that these materials were also disproportionately written by women of a particular age and marital status:

> slightly more than half of the women—53—were single. . . . young women in their late teens and early twenties who had not yet married, rather than confirmed middle-aged spinsters. . . . Why do more private writings from women's youth rather than from their maturity survive? The simplest answer is that they had more time when unmarried, or thought they had more time, to ponder and record their thoughts. . . . Unmarried women were "unsettled," in the language of the day, and had stronger motives for self-scrutiny—for the examination of their prospects—than did married women who already had made their most significant life-choice.

Her most important methodological point is the value of personal documents for the feminist historian. Instead of thinking of them as biased, historically peripheral materials, they are central to understanding women's consciousness:

> Such documents have a unique combination of assets, because they were unintended for strangers' eyes, yet attempted to communicate something of the authors' selves. No other historical source is more likely to disclose women's consciousness.

Despite the value of such documents, they lack completeness and are not strictly comparable one with the other: "One [woman] may record every task accomplished, while another may do more but disdain to write about it." For this reason, she recommends that personal documents be triangulated with public documents *about* women, including advice books:

> Without some corollary information a present-day reader cannot tell what was left
> out of a diary, letter, or memoir, and whether items were left out because they
> were unimportant or the very most important to the writer. (In an ironic sense,
> the writers thus protect their "unknownness" from historians' prying.)

Alone, public documents "establish the cultural milieu in which women found themselves" but cannot tell us about their actual behavior. Used together, public and private materials enabled Nancy Cott to define the concept of "womanhood" "rooted in the experience of Yankee middle-class mothers but applied to the female sex as a whole."[101] Commenting on such statements, Jane Lewis wrote: "Perhaps because they have always been conscious both of their close relationship to social historians and yet of their separate status, women's historians have constantly reviewed the methodology they employ."[102] In my view, being "close . . . and yet separate" is a variation of the "dual vision," "ambivalence," and "dilemmas" discussed in previous chapters; an emerging hallmark of feminist methodology.

Just as feminist historians have rescued shards of evidence from the lives of *anonymous* women, they have also resuscitated the record of *literate* or *powerful* women. An example is Marina Warner's study of Joan of Arc:

> I wanted to learn about her because she has an almost unique standing: she is a
> universal figure who is female, but is neither a queen, nor a courtesan, nor a
> beauty, nor a mother, nor an artist of one kind or another, nor—until the ex-
> tremely recent date of 1920 when she was canonised—a saint. She eludes the
> categories in which women have normally achieved a higher status that gives
> them immortality, and yet she gained it.[103]

It is important to remember that some women were not powerless or voiceless. Some women did have access to education, some were inspired, and some were able to produce important work. In certain cases their work was recognized during their lifetime only to be overlooked later.[104] Uncovering this work might be called "feminist intellectual archeology," in Gerda Lerner's words.

> [H]istorians buried the activities of women. The effort to resurrect this meaning
> and to re-evaluate women's literary and artistic work is recent. Feminist literary
> criticism and poetics have introduced us to a reading of women's literature, which
> finds a hidden, deliberately "slant," yet powerful world-view.[105]

An attempt to pay attention to both the anonymous majority and the later ignored minority has produced an important methodological perspective in feminist historical research. I would call this the search for an interwoven interpretation that understands women whose voices were heard in the context of women whose voices were muted or silenced. The "extraordinary" woman and the "ordinary" woman may not be as different from one another as they seem at first glance. In order to fully understand each, we need to understand both. Literary scholar Elaine Showalter wrote about such interwoven interpretation, contrasting it with a "great person" focus:

> In the past, investigations have been distorted by the emphasis on an elite group,
> not only because it has excluded from our attention great stretches of literary

activity between, for example, George Eliot and Virginia Woolf, but also because it has rendered invisible the daily lives, the physical experiences, the personal strategies and conflicts of ordinary women. . . . we need to see the woman novelist against the backdrop of the women of her time, as well as in relation to other writers in history.[106]

In a mode of analysis similar to historians, qualitative sociologists apply an inductive, interpretive framework to cultural artifacts. What differentiates sociologists from historians is simply the use of sociological theory as an aid in the explanation, and the tendency to use documents of a more recent period. Examples are Joan Pennell's study of the statements of purpose written by organizers of shelters for battered women,[107] Judith Sabronsky's study of documents of the women's movement,[108] and Lynda Glennon's qualitative content analysis of "RAT, an underground newspaper taken over in 1970 by a feminist coup."[109] Feminist content analyses can treat a document as a whole or analyze its parts. An example of a qualitative content analysis of documents that examines parts is my study of phrases, examples, and metaphors concerning women in classic sociological texts. An example is an image at the start of Peter Berger's widely read *Invitation to Sociology* (1963) that reappears in numerous forms throughout the book: "Perhaps some little boys consumed with curiosity to watch their maiden aunts in the bathroom later became inveterate sociologists." By examining such classic texts, it became obvious to me that what had been defined as "sociology" was actually "male sociology."[110]

My discussion of feminist sociologists' and historians' content analysis highlights the fluid disciplinary boundaries between them. Many feminist scholars have pointed to the need to *ignore* disciplinary boundaries in the name of altering the production of knowledge. Feminist scholars trained in one discipline move into others, in line with the need of their projects. Many feminist sociologists venture into the field of history to learn about the lives of ordinary and extraordinary women and to reconstruct the relation between gender, work, class[111] in different historic periods. In her introduction to the edited diaries of the British servant, Hannah Cullwick (1833–1909), discussed in Chapter 7, sociologist Liz Stanley explains that feminism justifies her historical work:

Although not a historian by trade, I suppose that in this book I'm entering into what is customarily seen as "historian's territory" (and probably treading on historians' toes too). It has been written because I am a feminist and believe that its contents are important for feminism. . . . Feminism is concerned with reclaiming the past lives of past women because in understanding our past we can better know and act upon our present. And of course within this feminist work "the personal," the realm of everyday life and of relationships and experience, is included to a large degree as well as what is conventionally seen as "the political", those activities which men have defined as more important and significant for too long. Feminism rejects any sharp distinction between "the personal" and "the political", among other reasons because it insists that "the personal" is what all of us (even men) spend most of our lives engaged in; and what people spend most of their lives being engaged in should be seen as both important and political.

In an argument similar to Nancy Cott's, she explains the need to analyze diaries when studying women:

> According to conventional thinking, Hannah Cullwick's diaries are all "personal" and in political terms hardly deserve reclamation at all. Yet, like "the personal" more generally, they are actually deeply political in nature. In their description upon description we can find, have we but the eyes to see, sex, class, race, power, labour, diet, housing, sanitation, employment, poverty, theft, fun, commitment, friendship, tears, love, joy, trust and betrayal. In this one woman's life we see ample evidence of oppression, exploitation and dominance—and all the complexities that scatter such vast and one-dimensional categorisations of the human condition to the four winds.[112]

Similarly, Israeli sociologist Deborah Bernstein writes:

> Some eight years ago I came across a book in a second-hand bookshop. Written by Ada Maimon, *Fifty Years of the Women Workers' Movement (1904–1954)* told the story of the Jewish Women Workers' Movement in Palestine. I read it through the night. The picture it revealed was new—and unexpected. I had accepted uncritically the prevailing notion that in the Yishuv, the new Jewish settlement in Palestine, women had been equal to men. And yet the story I was reading, written by one of the leading women activists of the period, was quite different. . . . Having made contact with the pioneering women workers, I wanted to share the experience with other women in Israel. History is an ever-present dimension of the Israeli existence. . . . Women, however, have been absent from this history. They are neither the focus of historical study, nor are they referred to in passing. The outcome is inevitable: a combination of no history, on the one hand, and mythified pseudo-history on the other. *I wanted not only to show women that they did have a share in history, but also to point out that women in the recent past had faced problems that were similar to those confronting contemporary women, and that they had evolved interesting, if not always successful, solutions.*[113]

Feminism brings scholars from one field to another and creates hybrids. It exposes the artificiality of disciplinary boundaries and the need for transdisciplinary fields such as women's studies.[114]

As mentioned earlier, feminist sociological content analysis frequently addresses questions of theory, such as identifying the processes through which gender is socially constructed. An example is the work of Australian historian Jill Matthews, who presents case records of women institutionalized in a mental hospital to shed light on the social construction of femininity in her society. Psychiatric case notes enabled her to do a kind of "deviant case analysis in reverse," with the assumption that if she could understand which behaviors and attitudes earned a woman the label "mad," she could construct the cultural definitions of "normal" femininity to which all good and sane women strive.[115]

While attempting to construct a feminist history of what it means to be a woman in twentieth-century Australia, she also developed a "theory of feminist history," arguing that feminist history must not simply "add women and stir" or be what she calls "women and . . ." histories. Nor should we simply slap standard sociological concepts onto women's experiences recorded in artifacts. Rather, feminist historians must "locate the independent patterns of women's historical experiences." In her first chapter Jill Matthews offers a reflexive account of the decisions she made in defining her research topic and methods and in analyzing the data. She reveals the way questions emerged from her data and led to continuous redefinitions of her project:

> At this point in my research, as well as losing my justification for using the data, I had also lost sight of my original project which, since it had never been precisely defined, was not surprising. . . . All I could do was the magician's trick of pulling arbitrary sociological and historiographic concepts out of a hat, and attempt to work the casenotes into some sort of shape. But the concepts didn't work. I tried production, reproduction, ideology. . . . Then I realized I was back with the old problem. These were concepts derived from male experience of history and society.[116]

In essence, she realized the necessity of breaking down "apparently universal categories into their masculine specificity" in order to bring to the surface "submerged female experience."

Cultural artifacts invite grounded research if the researcher allows the analytic categories to emerge from the artifacts themselves. British sociologist Mary Louise Ho followed this process in her work to uncover the ideology in "agony columns" found in three women's magazines: *Woman, Woman's Own,*[117] and *Cosmopolitan* in 1959, 1964, 1969, 1974, and 1976–1981. She examined "these columns' presuppositions about marriage, sexuality (including homosexuality), and the experts—[Mary Grant, Evelyn Home, Virginia Ironside, and Irma Kurtz]— looking at how each differs from the other and changes over time." Her approach was to combine inductive and deductive methods to explore how these columns communicated patriarchal ideology:

> The way in which I discuss this subject may suggest that I presume to know all about patriarchy and patriarchal ideology. I do not wish to appear so presumptuous! What I have tried to do is to construct a picture of how patriarchal ideology may work with particular reference to the agony column. Consequently I have had to presume a prior knowledge which is not yet fully worked-out. Even so, we do have an informed intuitive sense (based on consciousness-raising sessions and previous research) about patriarchy.[118]

In one of my qualitative sociological studies of miscarriage, I collected women's accounts[119] as recorded in diaries, essays, and other personal documents. Attempting to avoid class bias, I tried to identify both differing and invariant meanings of miscarriage for women of different eras, social classes, and geographic locations. I discovered that women vary widely in the degree to which they understand they are miscarrying, their view of the cause of their miscarriage, whether or not they want to miscarry, the consequences of their miscarriage, and the extent to which they feel they can help themselves and expect help from others.[120] Deliberately seeking and locating miscarriage accounts of women in a wide variety of times and places produced these categories. Dual attention to women as a single category and as differentiated is, I believe, a hallmark of feminist research.

The Study of What Is Missing

An early impetus of feminist scholarship was recognizing that information was missing about particular women and about women in general. Identifying such exclusions, erasures,[121] and missing information[122] is characteristic of much feminist scholarship. The following quote by sociologist Cynthia Epstein expresses this recognition of something not studied:

> It is unusual to see popular fiction which has its central character the happy career woman, married or single by choice, whether artist or opera star, much less lawyer or surgeon. Here clearly truth is stranger or more accurate than fiction, for real cases of fulfilled productive women can be found though they are conspicuous by their absence in storyland. There have been a few novels about women in the professions which have been based on the lives of real women but they have not been widely read. I do not know of any major author who has written about women of this type.[123]

Feminist literature reviews similarly have noted the absence in scientific literature of any discussion of violence against wives until the 1970s.[124] This interest in pointing out what is missing is different from mainstream scholarship's practice of delineating "lacunae" to stake out a research turf that can be "filled in." Rather, of interest to feminist researchers are the ways certain topics came to be missing and the implications of these gaps.

Nancy Datan (who "considered herself a psychologist, a sociologist, an anthropologist, an evolutionary biologist, and, always, an essayist"[125]) asked the kind of question feminist scholars typically ask. In her case, why "a number of significant characters in Greek tragedy have failed to make the grade in psychological literature despite the fact that evidence for eternal tensions, which they might reasonably be considered to represent, abounds." Specifically why have the Bacchae been excluded "from the group of tragedies and tragic heroes which are part of popular consciousness"?[126] The answer is that the Bacchae represent androgyny, a concept many find frightening for its sexual ambiguity and connection to greatness. Nancy Datan's study of "the missing" led directly to a study in the sociology of knowledge—she connected the disappearance of the androgyny theme with the role of androgyny in contemporary psychology.

Similarly Jane Haggis has written a paper explaining the importance of recognizing processes by which certain topics or materials are made to disappear, in her case "women's experiences within colonial social transformations." This topic "encapsulates a set of exclusions . . . expressed in the following research hypotheses":

> 1. that women's experiences have not, as yet, been described, identified or included within the study of colonialism; 2. that this omission is the result of a series of exclusionary practices operating at various levels within Western academic knowledge; 3. that the task is not simply a matter of inclusion but of major analytical and methodological reconceptualisation of the tools at hand; 4. that this task is of considerable contemporary relevance.

Viewing documents in this way contributes to an understanding both of the subject matter and of the sociology of knowledge, or as I call it, "the sociology of the lack of knowledge." Jane Haggis wrote: "The identification of such exclusionary practices raises questions about how research methods contribute directly to exclusions; about what is recognized as 'knowledge'; the kind of knowledge research produces; and, finally, where the researcher herself fits into these various ways of producing 'knowledge.' "[127]

Thus feminist content analysis is a study both of texts that exist and texts that do not. A feminist sociologist can link the existing and missing documents with the social conditions of the time, as Angela John's work on Victorian women coal industry workers suggests. She connects efforts to exclude these women from employment with exclusion of these women from the historical record. Ironically, she recovers "from obscurity a group of nineteenth-century women workers who have been virtually ignored by historians yet who, in their lifetime, became the center of a spirited and protracted debate about their right to continue working."[128] By discovering patterns between existing and missing documents, and with power/gender relations in the society of the time, and by bringing this material to the attention of people today, new ties are made that help explain the current relation between gender and power and give some groups a greater sense of their own history. To make this connection vivid, some feminists reprint texts and photographs so others can formulate their own interpretations and ties.

Concluding Thoughts

In this chapter, the inter- or transdisciplinary nature of feminist research is apparent. So too is the fact that feminist researchers utilize both qualitative and quantitative methods. Feminist researchers recognize the significance of studying unobtrusive documents as well as data they create. Moreover, those who study texts point to the significance of certain types of texts for understanding women, and for recognizing the relation between "extraordinary" and "ordinary" women. Finally, feminist researchers focus not only on texts that exist, but on the fact that many types of texts are missing. These characteristics of the feminist study of texts are as much in evidence today as they were in the nineteenth century when Harriet Martineau strenuously advocated the study of "things."

9

Feminist Case Studies

Theory must remain at best hypothetical, at worst unreal and barren [unless we have detailed] case studies and surveys dealing with the experience of selected groups of women in diverse cultures and time periods.[1]

Importance and Definition of Case Studies

Case studies have an ambiguous place in social science although professional schools of nursing, business, public administration, social work, medicine, and psychoanalysis[2] use them extensively, particularly for teaching purposes.[3] Case studies are integrated into feminist explications of women's legal and clinical problems (e.g., Jean Baker Miller's *Toward a New Psychology of Women*)[4] to explain and illustrate concepts. A dictionary of sociological terms defines case studies as

> a method of studying social phenomena through the thorough analysis of an individual case. The case may be a person, a group, an episode, a process, a community, a society, or any other unit of social life. All data relevant to the case are gathered, and all available data are organized in terms of the case. The case study method gives a unitary character to the data being studied by interrelating a variety of facts to a single case. It also provides an opportunity for the intensive analysis of many specific details that are often overlooked with other methods. This approach rests on the assumption that the case being studied is typical of cases of a certain type, so that through intensive analysis generalizations may be made which will be applicable to other cases of the same type.[5]

In its broadest application, ''case study'' refers to research that focuses on a single case or single issue, in contrast with studies that seek generalizations through comparative analysis or compilation of a large number of instances.[6]

The opening quotation by historian Berenice Carroll warns that feminist theory is impoverished without case studies. The three major purposes for feminist case studies—in addition to generating and testing theory—are to analyze the change in a phenomenon over time, to analyze the significance of a phenomenon for future events,[7] and to analyze the relation among parts of a phenomenon.[8] Feminist case studies usually consist of a fully developed description of a single event, person, group, organization, or community. Given this definition, many studies I discuss in other chapters could also be included here. I limit this chapter, however, to research that feminist scholars label case studies or cases.

The research methods in feminist case studies span the spectrum of literary analysis, surveys, archival research, interviewing, and others. For example, Rebecca Shuster used

> interviews, survey results, observation and a review of . . . psychological research . . . to consider the nature and implications of bisexual-identified women's experience. [She then] presents as particular examples the case histories of two bisexual women, Allison and Barbara.[9]

An example of a feminist case study that deals with a political contest's development over time is Jane Mansbridge's *Why We Lost the ERA* (Equal Rights Amendment). Her book explains what happened between March 1972 when the Senate of the United States voted 84 to 8 in favor of the ERA, and June 30, 1982 when only 35 of the required 38 states had ratified the amendment, thus ending the effort to pass the ERA. Although she did not include a methodology section in her study, she writes that she was a participant in the struggle to ratify the ERA. Her method seems to have been to collect every piece of information she could, and then sift it through her double commitments to ratification and to political science. As she put it, she tried "to combine both scholarly disengagement and political advocacy," and to work as "a political being as well as a scholar."[10]

Feminist researchers select the case they will study to illustrate a particular point of theory that may be posed as a question. One example is Jacklyn Cock's research project that examines the interrelations of race, gender, and class through the specific relation of the white "madam" and black "maid" in South Africa.[11] Her question of whether or not sisterhood is possible between women who diverge extensively is ideally addressed through a case study of this particular relationship.

Another example is Eva Gamarnikow's exploration of "the structural determinants of the sexual division of labour," a very broad question. She achieves specificity by examining her question through a "particular reference to the occupational structure of nineteenth- and early twentieth-century nursing" in England and concludes that

> the sexual division of labour is a patriarchal ideological structure in that it reproduces patriarchal relations in extra-familial labour processes. . . . Any analysis seeking an explanation for the fact that women's work under capitalism is different from men's—both within marriage or the domestic mode of production and in wage labour in the capitalist mode of production—must unquestionably address itself to the pervasiveness of patriarchal relations. The forms of these relations cannot be assumed to be self-evident, but must be analysed in their specificity.[12]

Her implication is that we must do case study after case study to build a complex theory of the sexual division of labor within the household and the market.

As mentioned above, feminist case studies in political science deal with the historical development of a particular political struggle. These research projects follow a tradition of mainstream political science case studies concerned with particular political struggles. In the field of sociology, by contrast, case studies are a research format with a marginal status, albeit a long-standing tradition.[13] Sociologists have produced case studies of groups (e.g., a street corner in Washington,

D.C.),[14] events (e.g., the aftermath of a flood or an industrial pollution crisis),[15] institutions (e.g., a mental hospital, mines),[16] and communities (e.g., *Middletown, Yankee City,* Boston's West End, an ethnic subculture).[17] These studies have been praised for their lively description and generation of interesting theory; they have been criticized for being unconducive to theory testing.

Female sociologists in Chicago connected with Jane Addams and Hull-House carried out many case studies at the turn of the century.[18] These researchers studied the problems of a particular group of women employed in the labor market. New York-based industrial sociologist Mary Abby van Kleek (1883–1972) conducted analogous studies for the Russell Sage Foundation. *Women in the Bookbinding Trade* (1913), *Artificial Flower Makers* (1913), and *A Seasonal Industry* (1917) focused on particular trades. After completing these in-depth case studies, she went on to do comparative analyses of women in different trades, of men and women in a single trade, and of management and workers.[19]

Male academic sociologists rarely undertook case studies of women's organizations or communities. And it was rarer still for social researchers to notice this omission. At least three things were lost because sociologists did not do case studies of women's settings. First, sociology itself contributed to the invisibility of women and the disappearance of women's accomplishments from the historical record. Second, a distorted sociological understanding of women was reinforced because women's groups were not studied and the social forces responsible for women's status were overlooked. And third, sociology invited additional errors because generalizations were grounded in a single sex perspective.

The first point—that sociology contributed to the invisibility of women and the disappearance of women's's accomplishments—has been voiced with regard to nearly every discipline. Many feminists have complained that we do not have adequate historical records of the organizations in which women have been involved. Case studies of effective organizations and women's experience in them are necessary both as models for future generations and as the raw data of future secondary analyses, comparative research, and cross-cultural studies.[20]

The paucity of case studies of women's experiences hampers our ability to engage in cross-cultural or comparative analyses of women's lives and organizations. Yet cross-cultural research is a necessary design if generalizations are to be produced that are not ethnocentric.[21] Because of her concern with this problem, Cathy Rakowski did a case study of "the incorporation of women into heavy industry during the Ciudad Guayana, Venezuela employment boom of 1974–1979 and the reduction in female employment during the post-boom period." She used feminist organizational theory to explore the particular situation in Venezuela and found that

> male discriminatory behavior and female coping mechanisms result from the interaction of gender roles and stereotypes on the one hand, and institutional/structural factors on the other. Discriminatory practices and women's responses to them are mediated by class and age differences. These are shaped by the individuals' prior experiences and the historical context in which discrimination evolved.[22]

In other words, her case study of women in Venezuelan heavy industry lent further credibility to particular feminist sociological interpretations of the relation between gender and work. The case of Venezuelan heavy industry emphasized the extent to which class and age must be integral components of feminist organizational theory that focuses on gender issues.

In support of the second point—that a distorted sociological understanding of women is reinforced by the paucity of case studies of women's settings—Jessie Bernard explains that case histories of women's organizations allow us to reevaluate images of women. As an example of an effective feminist case study, she praised Kathleen McCourt's research on working-class women in the Southwest Side of Chicago. Kathleen McCourt found that "ethnic women of working-class backgrounds found they had to leave their homes in order to protect their neighborhoods against pollution, racism, bad housing, and also in order to deal with old agencies that were no longer serving them adequately."[23] The women she studied did not fit the patterns uncovered by previous researchers, reinforcing the need for case studies of specific populations.

In his discussion of case studies, U.S. sociologist Howard Becker elaborated on my third point—that sociology itself is distorted if generalizations are based on single-sex studies

> because . . . early studies [of prisons] were all of men's prisons, they could not discover what a later study of a women's prison revealed: that the informal organization of the prison varied according to the kind of people recruited, because deprivations differ according to what it is one values and, therefore, misses when deprived of it. Women apparently set far less store by autonomy than men, do not miss it, and do not develop a sub rosa government; they are, however, very dependent on intimate affectional ties, miss their families intensely, and develop homosexual liaisons as their form of informal organization.[24]

To take another example, if sociologists document only mainstream organizations (e.g., medical schools), rather than the organizations of those who are attempting to change society (e.g., members of a feminist illegal abortion collective), then we have a skewed image of medical services.[25] If, as Melinda Bart Schlesinger and Pauline Bart wrote, "there is no current sociological literature on lay abortions,"[26] then it is impossible to develop a sociologically accurate and comprehensive model of medical services. Feminist engagement in the production of woman-centered case studies is thus a greatly needed corrective device in such disciplines as sociology.

Feminist Interest in Case Studies

Feminists write case studies for the same reasons that nonfeminist scholars write them—to illustrate an idea, to explain the process of development over time, to show the limits of generalizations, to explore uncharted issues by starting with a limited case, and to pose provocative questions. For example, a carefully chosen case can illustrate that a generalization is invalid. For this reason studies of the exceptional case have great heuristic value. Although they cannot establish a generalization, they can invalidate one and suggest new research directions.

The exceptional case is valuable for feminist action, as a positive model to emulate or as a negative model to avoid. An example of the first type is a study by Belgian women's studies scholar Paige Cousineau who wrote about the Women's Organisation for Equality (WOE), a Belgian, English-language feminist organization. She explains that WOE

> is a rare bird among feminist groups—it is over twelve years old and still going strong. This paper attempts to look at its history and the personal experience of being a member for several years to see what wisdom WOE can offer to all of us in the business of social change.[27]

Feminist interest in case studies (as in other research formats) stems from a desire to rectify research tainted by gynopia, misogyny, and male-dominant theorizing. Gynopia is the inability to perceive the very existence of women or to perceive women in undistorted ways;[28] misogyny is the hatred of women;[29] and male-dominant theorizing is the creation of theories that assert the superiority of males.[30] With few exceptions gynopia has made it difficult or impossible for androcentric researchers of factories, mines, unions, and other male-dominated settings to "see" the women in these settings. Traditionally, the presence of women was limited to their being mentioned as "there."[31] Women's "being," when noted at all, was defined in terms of men's needs.[32]

In response to these distortions, feminist social scientists have produced case studies of previously unstudied individual women, women's activities, and women's organizations.[33] An early example is the work of Sophonisba Breckenridge who in 1933, toward the end of her long experience of being discriminated against by the University of Chicago, published *Women in the Twentieth Century*. This book documents the achievement of women in their organizations, employment, and status as citizens, while also carefully describing "the reality of sex discrimination in the academy."[34] An illustration of how gynopia sparked a contemporary case study, in this instance a study of secretaries' working conditions, is the following incident: "One afternoon a young male student came into our office. Standing in front of Karen and looking directly at her, he asked, 'Isn't anyone here?' "[35] Realizing that secretaries had become invisible to large groups of people, Ellen Cassedy and Karen Nussbaum went on to study them.

Feminist social scientists have been very active in producing case studies that compensate for, or address, the deficiencies noted above. For example, psychologist and historian Mary Roth Walsh opened her social history of female physicians in the United States with the following comment:

> Even social scientists who specialize in the study of the medical profession seem oblivious to the fact that women physicians are a part of that profession and have a past of their own. In Eliot Freidson's *Profession of Medicine*, voted the prestigious Sorokin award in 1972 by the American Sociological Association, women in medicine are discussed only under the category of nursing and paramedical work. Similarly, in *Boys in White*, a participant observation study of a medical school class over several years, the four to five women in each class are entirely ignored. . . . It is almost as if the social scientists had decided to complete the work of the medical establishment and excise women physicians from the record.[36]

For the same reason, feminist anthropologists have restudied cultures previously studied by male anthropologists. In the words of anthropologist Annette Weiner:

> [U]nlike the earlier Trobriand ethnographers, this ethnographer is a woman. A critical difference between myself and my male predecessors is that I took seemingly insignificant bundles of banana leaves as seriously as any kind of male wealth. I saw Kiriwina women as active participants in the exchange system, and thus I accord them an equal place beside Kiriwina men. In my return to the beginning, I move the role of women into the foreground. . . . My assumption in this book is that, regardless of the variation between the economic and political roles of men and women, the part that women play in society must be accorded equal time in any study concerned with the basic components of social organization.[37]

These "restudies" shift attention to women's roles. They help social researchers see the relation between gender and power in all social settings.

Feminist Case Studies of Groups and of Individual Women

Although it had been an essential component of the University of Chicago's research program in sociology in the first quarter of this century, the case study of an individual is very infrequently undertaken nowadays by nonfeminist sociologists.[38] Some feminist social scientists, on the other hand, have defined case studies of individual lives as an important heuristic.[39] These feminist-produced case studies are typically collected in anthologies of oral histories or become full-scale biographical studies. As described in the chapter on oral history, this increasingly popular form of feminist research allows the researcher to reflect on processes of identification and separation between the researcher and her subject,[40] while at the same time it allows her to generate inductive theory.

Sometimes individual cases are combined in order to examine the relation between cases and particular social structures or processes. For example, Ann Jones studied prominent cases of female murderers. She recognized that female and male murderers differ: men "are apt to stab a total stranger in a drunken brawl or run amok with a high-powered rifle, [while] we women usually kill our intimates; we kill our children, our husbands, our lovers."[41] After examining individual case histories, she concluded that the cultural problem underlying this pattern (i.e., the relation between gender and homicide victims and perpetrators) would become the object of her study. Another study of this phenomenon is Seattle attorney Cynthia K. Gillespie's study of women who kill their batterers.[42]

U.S. jurist Catharine MacKinnon produced a study of the sexual harassment of women at work based on case studies and case law. She opened her book with a preface that contained the following methodological comments:

> I hope to bring to the law something of the reality of women's lives. The method and evidence chosen for this task deserve comment. To date, there are no "systematic" studies of sexual harassment in the social-scientific sense. So how do I

know it exists? Chapter 3 presents evidence from women's observations on their own lives. Something worth knowing, uniquely appropriate to this investigation, and not adequately revealed in other ways can be found in such statements. . . . Personal statements direct from daily life, in which we say more than we know, may be the primary form in which such experiences exist in social space; at this point they may be their only accessible form. I therefore take immediate reflections on lived-through experience as data. How valid and generalizable are such data? This issue is particularly important in the sex discrimination context. . . . Individual experiences of sexual harassment are here seen to derive from a social context: the shared material experience of women as a group, with focus upon the world of work. The testimony of individual women, in this context, represents and substantiates a dimension of the social reality of women as a sex.[43]

An innovative format for writing feminist case studies of individuals is the novel. This format is useful if there is a possibility that the researcher or the individual being studied would be endangered by publication. Nawal El Saadawi's study of Firdaus, an imprisoned woman, is a case in point:

I wrote this novel after an encounter between me and a woman in Qanatir Prison. . . . At the end of 1972 the Minister of Health had removed from me my functions as Director of Health Education and Editor-in-Chief of the magazine *Health*. This was one more consequence of the path I had chosen as a feminist author and novelist whose views were viewed unfavourably by the authorities. . . . The idea for my research in fact arose as a result of the women who sought my advice and help to deal with situations which had led to a greater or lesser degree of "mental affliction." I decided to choose a limited number of cases from amongst women suffering from neurosis, and this entailed regular visits to a number of hospitals and outpatient clinics. . . . [S]lowly the idea of visiting the prison to see the women there grew on me. . . . I was enabled to obtain a special permit to visit Qanatir Prison as a psychiatrist and to examine the women. . . . Firdaus at first refused to receive me in her cell, but later she agreed to meet me. Little by little she was brought to tell me her story, the whole story of her life. . . . [I collected] 20 in-depth case studies for my research, the results of which were published in 1976, under the title *Women and Neurosis* in Egypt. At the end of 1974, Firdaus was executed, and I never saw her again. . . . When in 1981, it was my turn to be confined behind bars, I would watch the other women prisoners as they moved through the inner courtyard, as though looking for her. . . . This is the story of a real woman. . . . The prison doctor told me that this woman had been sentenced to death for killing a man.[44]

The few full-length individual case studies written by feminist researchers are extremely instructive in demonstrating the relation between individual lives and societal arrangements. One example is U.S. philosopher Janice Raymond's article about Mary Daly's struggle against academic discrimination. In that study, Janice Raymond portrays the development of Mary Daly's intellectual work in the context of her struggle with employers:

What I wish to do in this article is to tell the story of this decade of harassment [of feminist academics by Boston College.] In order to do this, I have woven a tapestry of quotes from old and recent newspaper clippings, from official letters and documents, and from Mary Daly's own writings. This collage of information is more than a chronology, or orderly arrangement of events. Rather, it is meant to be what Mary Daly has called a Crone-ology.[45]

"Telling the story of" is a way the writer indicates that the format is a case study.

Feminist case studies of groups are more common than those of individual women. An example of a feminist case study of a group is reported by Judith Stacey and Susan Gerard in their paper, "We Are Not Doormats." Their study examines the question of whether feminist and postfeminist consciousness exists among contemporary Christian evangelicals.[46] They use the study of this particular group to examine its ideology and relation to feminism, leading to the suggestion that there is a form of "evangelical feminism."

An example of an organizational case study is Kathleen Kautzer's examination of the structure of the Older Women's League. She explains that

> my historical case study of the Older Women's League was designed to examine the relationship between OWL's internal structure and strategic choices, and its external effectiveness in achieving its self-stated goals. My research design is based on the case study method. . . . Consequently I have chosen three basic research methodologies including interviews, participant observation and review of organizational literature.[47]

Feminist scholars produce case studies of feminist movement organizations in order to document the very existence of these settings and sometimes to challenge feminists' blindness about particular settings. Canadian political scientist Naomi Black wrote poignantly about the selective vision of feminists in the self-reflexive opening chapter of her book on "social feminism":

> One motivation for this book is my strong feeling that the accepted categories of feminism have no place for my beliefs or the beliefs of those I worked with on projects we were convinced had the potential to transform the world. . . . In this book, my specific subjects are the Women's Co-operative Guild (WCG) of England, the Union Feminine Civique et Social (UFCS) of France, and the National League of Women Voters (LWV) in the United States. I draw also on my own experience as an early member of the Ontario Committee on the Status of Women, a small Canadian pressure group founded in 1971. . . . This book presents detailed studies of three feminist organizations, at least one of which would often have rejected that designation.[48]

As this type of literature accumulates, organizations developed for and by girls and women (e.g., Girl Scouts troops, community action groups,[49] women's social movements,[50] abortion clinics) may have a chance of becoming the building blocks for a new sociology of organizational structure and social life.

As mentioned above, feminist interest in case studies stems from the desire to document aspects of women's lives and achievements for future secondary analysis and future action on behalf of women.[51] Internationally oriented scholars such as Robin Morgan argue forcefully that documenting women's status and accomplishments (or lack thereof) in different countries must be a top research priority, so we can clarify the way women's lives are similar and vary globally and so we can engage in effective action on women's behalf.[52]

Sometimes feminist scholars embed case studies in a theoretical perspective to "permit analysis as well as description."[53] This is the goal of Mary Jo Deegan and Nancy Brooks in their collection concerning women with disabilities. In discussing her theoretical framework for her case study of physically disabled women, Mary Jo Deegan wrote:

> This chapter is addressed specifically to defining the . . . [multiple minority] group and analyzing their effect on majority and minority relations. This is done first by examining the theoretical concepts of "minority status," "minority group," "the single minority group," "multiple minority statuses," "multiple minority group," and the "interaction effects of the multiple minority group."

Having defined her framework, she then explains the selection of a case to illustrate and then refine her points:

> These concepts are then extended to an analysis of one specific multiple minority group: physically disabled women. For this case study, physically disabled women must be seen as separate from, but related to, their "single minority groups" of women and the physically disabled. After defining these relationships theoretically, a brief review of the literature concerning physically disabled women is presented and the relationships of disabled women to the single minority groups are examined. From this completed analysis, the conclusion summarizes why this multiple minority group concept is central to our understanding of minority rights. This concept clarifies the number of people who are oppressed in this society, the process of continuing such massive discrimination, and the participation in this process of disenfranchisement by all members of this society. Therefore, we link theory and practice as interconnected units for action.[54]

This book utilizes feminist scholarship's ability to reveal populations hidden conceptually even from those who could be expected to see them clearly. In the foreword, Rose Lynn Sherr and Beatrice A. Wright make this achievement clear. They state that "despite [their] long professional involvement in the field of rehabilitation psychology and [their] appreciation of a feminist viewpoint, [they] had been remarkably unaware of the unique issues of women with disabilities."[55]

There have been numerous examples of feminist case studies of organizations. Case studies of feminist movement organizations, for example, allow us to see if classical organizational theory has been limited because it stems from the study of male-dominated settings. Kathleen Weston and Lisa Rofel studied a strike by workers in a lesbian auto repair shop. They wrote:

> We undertook a case study of a recent strike at a lesbian auto-repair shop [Amazon Auto Repair] in a metropolitan area with a sizable lesbian community. The study was based on in-depth interviews with eight of the ten women who worked in the shop at the time of the strike, including the two owners. Although this is just one example of the conflicts that have emerged in lesbian institutions in recent years, its dynamics clarify cultural constructs and material relations that operate in larger social processes. . . . we want to be able to explore the theoretical issues it raises without reducing those issues to the sum of the personalities involved.[56]

They found that the women's behavior reflected both features of the organization and their class membership.

Case studies of particular initiatives on behalf of women can illuminate why certain strategies succeed and others fail,[57] or why certain movements "catch on" more than others. Some of these accounts are written from a journalistic perspective, others from a sociological perspective,[58] and yet others experiment with fictional forms. Together these case studies provide the experiential, analytic, and historical information feminist researchers and activists need to understand women's lives and themselves.[59] Erin Pizzey's *Scream Quietly or the Neighbours Will Hear*,[60] for example, documents the founding and development of the first shelter for battered women, and describes the women who came for help, provided help, or tried to impede the process. This book was instrumental not only in bringing wife battering to the public's attention but also in mobilizing women throughout the world to create shelters to help their battered sisters.

In a related example, Patricia Searles and Ronald Berger uncovered dilemmas in particular organizations whose purpose was to prevent vicitmization. The subject of their study was WSDC (Women's Self-Defense Council), an early attempt to move beyond the limitations of traditional martial arts and create a practical form of self-defense for women based on a feminist model:

> In an effort to understand the mobilization and organizational dilemmas of the self-defense movement, we have compiled a case history of WSDC. This case history is derived from unpublished teaching materials and organizational correspondence of WSDC and from participant observation in WSDC classes and meetings by Searles from 1980 to 1984. The history of WSDC illustrates a number of problems and processes common to organizations within the feminist movement as a whole, as well as some significant differences between the feminist self-defense movement and other branches of the feminist antiviolence campaign. Feminist self-defense organizations have been much less successful than antibattering and antirape organizations at attracting external funding, and have had to develop independent means of survival. Consequently, the self-defense movement has not experienced the co-optation of feminist principles and the service orientation that has characterized the battered women and antirape movements.[61]

The women's movement itself, as an historical phenomenon and as a social movement, has been the subject of numerous sociological case studies by feminist scholars.[62] Perhaps the first of these was Jessie Taft's doctoral dissertation, *The Woman Movement from the Point of View of Social Consciousness*, written in 1913 for the University of Chicago.[63] In addition, since feminist research is a dynamic, heterogeneous process, some researchers are beginning to address the conflict among feminist theories (e.g., radical, socialist, and cultural feminisms, among others)[64] by undertaking comparative case studies of different feminist organizations.

Relatively wealthy organizations can fund self-studies while financially strapped organizations typically lack resources for this purpose. This imbalance in funds curtails the publication of case studies of poorer settings.[65] On the other hand, the plight of certain organizations or groups may be the very factor that attracts humanistically oriented researchers. For example, as discussed in the chapter on feminist ethnography, sociologist Judy Wajcman, a member of the women's movement in Cambridge, England, joined the "Fakenham support group" in response to publicity at a National Women's Liberation Conference she attended. The Fakenham women had formed a cooperative to salvage a failed shoe factory where they were formerly employed. When the cooperative faced financial crisis, Judy Wajcman offered herself as "unpaid help" and undertook a case study of the group. As she put it:

> A the time my research interest was in the political consciousness of working-class women in employment. Fakenham Enterprises seemed an ideal setting for a case study. Here was a group of women in a work situation which could be expected to have a dramatic effect on their political consciousness. Orthodox industrial sociology would find it hard to explain how working-class women in the heart of the Norfolk countryside succeeded in establishing a manufacturing co-operative. If, as is generally assumed, working in a co-operative requires a higher level of commitment to work than a conventional job, this would be expected to entail a change in women's domestic responsibilities. Otherwise, a women's cooperative would appear rather puzzling. In this book I try to explain the puzzle by exploring the interconnections between women's paid labour and sexual divisions within the family and tracing the significance of these factors for the political consciousness of working-class women.[66]

In general, feminist activists and researchers have played a role in publishing case studies of financially marginal women's events, organizations, and activities.

Some Concluding Thoughts

The case study is a tool of feminist research that is used to document history and generate theory. It defies the social science convention of seeking generalizations by looking instead for specificity, exceptions, and completeness. Some feminist researchers have found that social science's emphasis on generalizations has obscured phenomena important to particular groups, including women. Thus case studies are essential for putting women on the map of social life.

The power of the case study to convey vividly the dimensions of a social phenomenon or individual life is power that feminist researchers want to utilize. Defying the contemporary social science norm that puts little value in case studies, feminist researchers continue to create them to suit their own purposes. As each case study is produced, however, it becomes important to recognize all the cases that have yet to be written, particularly cases that reflect the variety of experiences of diverse groups of women. The more case studies we have, the more we should recognize we need.

10

Feminist Action Research[1]

The integration of activism and scholarship is essential to the emerging feminist consciousness of the last decade.[2]

analysis . . . must always accompany action for fundamental social change.[3]

this will be a value-oriented inquiry, based on the premise that it is good to better the condition of all individuals in society. The best should be models for the rest.[4]

Possibly the one characteristic that most feminist scholars would agree upon is the need for social change.[5]

In the quotes above, psychologists Rhoda Kesler Unger and Carla Golden, anthropologist Rayna Reiter, and sociologist Cynthia Fuchs Epstein argue that feminist scholarship is inherently linked to action. The purpose of feminist research must be to create new relationships, better laws, and improved institutions. They concur with philosopher Sandra Harding who wrote that "the benefits of the new feminist learning are to be used. . . . [F]eminism . . . sees inquiry as comprising not just the mechanical observation of nature and others but the intervention of political and moral illumination."[6]

Feminism's mandate for change is as broad as saving life itself. It does this by working to prevent "lovers" from battering heterosexual,[7] lesbian, and bisexual women;[8] to prevent abortion restrictions from butchering women;[9] to prevent individuals and organizations from sexually enslaving girls and women;[10] to prevent families from committing infanticide;[11] physicians and pharmaceutical companies from physically endangering women;[12] and men from raping women,[13] to name only a few examples. Because of the need for such changes, methodologists such as Patti Lather believe research is feminist *only* if it is linked to action:

I [engage in] feminist efforts to empower through empirical research designs which maximize a dialogic, dialectically educative encounter between researcher and researched. . . . What I suggest is that our intent more consciously be to use our research to help participants understand and change their situations.[14]

In her view, feminist action research must be oriented to social and individual change because feminism represents a repudiation of the status quo.

Historical Roots

Two early practitioners of feminist action research are Marion Talbot and Crystal Eastman. To counter the late nineteenth-century accusation that women had no talent for mathematics, Marion Talbot undertook an action-oriented study of gender and mathematical ability. She found that

> At the University of Chicago 24% of the men graduates and 16% of the women graduates chose Mathematics after having completed their required Mathematics, but of the Bachelors of Sciences, 47% of the women as against 39% of the men, chose Mathematics—a fact which is in startling contrast to the current statement that women have no aptitude for Mathematics.[15]

These data were part of her successful argument to prevent the University of Chicago from becoming sex-segregated.

In 1907, having completed an M.A. in sociology and receiving a law degree, Crystal Eastman joined the Pittsburgh Survey staff to study industrial accidents. In the following excerpt describing her view of action research, she questions the ethics of "investigation into social and industrial conditions . . . which involves going into people's homes and asking questions about personal affairs."

Danger of self-fulfilling prophecy?

> Investigation just for the sake of investigation does not appeal to me. Social investigators should know what they are driving at. They should have not only evidence that there is an evil but a rough plan for remedying it in mind before they commence an investigation.

According to her standards her role as a work-accident researcher was ethical because it was linked to examining whether compensation laws adequately protected injured workmen and their widows and children. She discovered that states did not have public records of industrial accidents, although coroners did keep data on fatal accidents.

> We got permission to use these and made a record of every industrial fatality reported to the coroner during the twelve months from July 1906 to July 1907, taking down on a separate card for each case, the name and address of the man killed, his age, occupation and conjugal condition, the name of his employer, the circumstances of the accident, the names of important witnesses, and the verdict. The plan was to learn from the evidence in the coroner's record, how each accident happened, and to learn from visiting the family what happened after the accident, i.e., how great a financial loss was suffered by the family of the workman killed, how much of this was made up by compensation received from the employer, and how the family was affected in its economic life by the accident. When we had done this with the fatalities, we followed the same course with the records of three months' industrial injuries which we secured from the hospitals. We found that in one year 526 men were killed by accidents of employment in Allegheny county; 195 steel workers, 125 railroaders, 71 miners, and 135 miscellaneous workers, including house-smiths, carpenters, electric linemen, elevator men, teamsters and quarrymen. Of these, nearly half were American born, 70 percent were workmen of skill and training and 80 percent were under forty years of age.

Having computed deaths, roles, age, and ethnicity, she then investigated responsibility. In 30% of the cases no one was responsible, in 30% the worker was responsible, in 30% the employer was responsible, and in 10% responsibility was shared. She then pressed for a law that would change fiscal and legal responsibility for work accidents.

> If [industry] were carried on slowly and carefully with safety as the first concern of all, there would be few accidents, but carried on as it is today in America, there are many accidents. . . . Every work-accident leaves a problem of poverty behind. . . . I am an enthusiastic advocate of this compensation law [because] it established the principle that the risks of trade, borne through all these years by the workmen alone, should in all wisdom and justice be shared by the employer.[16]

Clearly, Crystal Eastman's research model was designed to change the conditions under investigation.

Applied and Basic Research

In contrast to the legacy of Marion Talbot and Crystal Eastman, contemporary mainstream social science frequently differentiates, rather than integrates, knowledge and action. Sociologist Mary Jo Deegan has located the roots of this differentiation in many male members of the Chicago School of Sociology who

> considered themselves "abstract," "theoretical" or "scientific" versus the complementary branch of "applied." In general, the males were associated with the first branch and the females with the second. . . . This [female] devotion to society and its liberation has been generally interpreted as an embarrassing mistake by its successors, particularly the Chicago sociologists who followed in the 1920s. The founders were fervent advocates of a sound community based on social justice and they were generally replaced by "disinterested" statisticians, bureaucrats, and people who "studied" but did not "make" policy.[17]

In her view, contemporary feminist social scientists' blending of knowledge and action has its roots in the first generation of Chicago sociology and in the work of female sociologists of the turn of the century.[18] Psychologist Mary Brown Parlee explains that the same disparaging distinction between basic and applied research, and the same correlation with gender, exists in mainstream psychology.

> By and large, feminist research does not appear in the "major" journals, feminist psychologists do not survive at the "major" universities, and when feminist research receives federal funding, after stringent peer review, this external evidence of scientific excellence is disregarded on the grounds that the work is "faddish" or "applied."[19]

From the mainstream perspective applied research is political, polemic, and derivative. Many feminist researchers, by contrast, believe this differentiation is mere rhetoric because "basic" research has political consequences and "action" has theoretical implications.

Some feminists complain that research may be a way to avoid action. They advocate taking steps to "stop doing research and start doing something about the problem." An example is a statement following an international meeting to combat traffic in women:

> We called our meeting a workshop because we saw it as a working session, not a paper-producing conference. Research and background papers are of course valuable and we had such papers. However, our focus was on action and strategy. What we hoped to produce from the 10 days in Rotterdam was more knowledgeable action in the world, not just more knowledge of the problem.[20]

Clearly for feminists, research that has action goals is at least as, if not more, valuable than "basic research."

Even though many feminists claim that feminist research must be oriented toward feminist goals, the exact set of goals is rarely specified. Vagueness is warranted because our vision and imagination are limited by current experience.[21] For this reason, sociologist Roslyn Bologh advocates open-ended goals:

> the objective is not some end state, external changes in law or socialization, . . . changes in parenting, nor changes in institutions, including political economy. . . . these changes are the consequences of the struggle, they are not its end because there can be no new identity or institutional arrangement that does not constrain or limit or repress possibilities. The objective is not the product but the process, not a new final identity or institutional arrangement but the movement beyond a given identity or institution.[22]

For Roslyn Bologh, the goal of feminist action research is not a particular set of arrangements but the process of continuous change. She argues that our "limited vision" is freed by loosening theoretical frameworks and methods, allowing them to be antipositivist, antipatriarchal, and open-ended.

Criticizing the idea that feminist research can be converted to action in this open-ended way, Ann Bristow and Jody Esper urge that research must be tied to *specific* implementation practices. They outline exact procedures to convert research into action in their project on rape:

> We believe that we must utilize our privilege as researchers to go beyond the vacuum of professional dissemination qua professional advancement and bring the voices of raped women into public awareness. This means deliberate attempts to introduce our research findings into arenas where access to professional literature is least likely to be available (e.g., lower class women). This can be done through popular media and community presentations. Furthermore, we introduce our research to people in social policy areas . . . by educating judges and attorneys, as well as jurors, through expert testimony regarding rape myths. . . . In addition, we hope to raise the consciousness of mental health workers to both the prevalence and long-term effects of rape.

They show that raising mental health workers' consciousness about rape helps women by affirming their experience:

> Women's "irrational" fears, sexual dysfunctions, sense of vulnerability and low self-esteem may be due to prior sexual assault(s), even ones which occurred many years ago. A woman experiencing these effects will find little or no affirmation

from others that these effects are part of her rape(s). She is tempted or persuaded to create other reasons to explain her actions: for example, she may doubt her sanity. Failure to develop intervention, research and public policy that devolve from women's experiences is a failure of consciousness. In contrast, we believe that research embodying consciousness-raising in its process, as articulated by feminists, is research that empowers oppressed people.[23]

Although feminist research findings frequently "find their way" into the clinical practice of feminist therapists,[24] Ann Bristow and Jody Esper insist that a feminist research ethic requires researchers to educate clinicians. Feminist researchers are responsible to plan for the distribution of information in optimally helpful ways.

Ann Bristow and Jody Esper exemplify feminists who do change-oriented research in the hope of empowering,[25] liberating, and otherwise assisting specific groups of people. These changes can be sought through the distribution of research findings *after* the research has been concluded and/or *during* the research process itself.[26] An example of change efforts following research is a study by Joseph Schneider and Sally Hacker who discovered in 1972 that students of introductory sociology associate the term "man" with males and "people" with mixed gender groups. The researchers then tried to change the policy by sending a letter to over 100 major publishers of sociology texts by informing them of the research findings and urging them to adopt a policy avoiding the use of generic "man." A report on this implementation effort, with its less than 20% response rate, became part of their publication.[27]

In a similar vein, some feminists urge mainstream social scientists to integrate specific change recommendations into research papers. Cynthia Chertos, an advocate of "usable research," writes:

> I suggest that sociologists and other social scientists . . . write more reports, write more articles, and deliver more papers which not only present findings, or even make broad policy recommendations . . . , but which . . . lead the way in explaining how to make things happen, how to change our social reality, how to make the society more equitable.[28]

Heeding this suggestion, many feminist researchers publish in both the academic and popular presses. But feminists are also quick to note that research alone cannot change the conditions under which women live. As noted in the chapter on survey research, Christine Bose and Glenna Spitze remind us that "research may uncover the needs of women, and policy may address them, but without political action there is no reason to expect those policies to be implemented."[29] Feminist researchers are also careful to note that research may be *harmful* to women, particularly medical and pharmaceutical research. In the case of DES studies, researchers' unbridled quest to demonstrate its effectiveness led them to "steadily increase the size of the dosages until they were giving single doses that far exceeded a woman's lifetime production of estrogen.[30] On the other hand, our caution should not blind us from potentially useful opportunities. As Linda Wastila showed, although women sorely need new, improved methods of birth control, there has been a sharp decline in the number of U.S. pharmaceutical companies involved in the research and development of new contraceptives, in part because feminists' distrust of pharmaceutical companies' practices diminished our lobbying for increased contraceptive research.[31]

Just as in medicine, social science research occasionally can *undermine* women's interests. At the outset of her study on the ERA campaign, for example, political scientist Jane Mansbridge states that social research almost always undermines "the organization or cause we love" by showing that appearances are deceptive.[32] In addition, some women believe that social research is harmful because it distorts or obscures women's lives. An example is the way researchers of work invalidate women's unpaid labor by using the criterion of paid employment. For this reason the November 1984 "Sisterhood Is Global Strategy Meeting" in New York City issued a

> call for women in both private and professional capacities to refuse to participate in censuses or household surveys or registration systems—or to fill them in by listing all the jobs they do—until the invisibility of women's unpaid work as producers *and* reproducers is recognized in the national accounts.[33]

Despite the commitment to change, feminist researchers differ as to the value they give to research and the ways they believe research is linked to social change.

Forms of Feminist Change-Oriented Research

My search for feminist research with an explicit action connection revealed five types, each of which draws on *all* the techniques in the social sciences. The types are action research, participatory/collaborative research, prevalence and needs assessment, evaluation research, and demystification.

Action Research

Barbara Smail, Judith Whyte, and Alison Kelly define action research as research in which action and evaluation proceed simultaneously. They carried out an action study to "initiate and support school-based efforts to improve girls' attitudes to physical science and craft subjects, and to encourage more girls to study these subjects." They achieved this goal by a fluid approach that they constantly evaluated, rather than by a "traditional research project where the design is thought out at the beginning by the research team, implemented in a carefully controlled way in the schools, and finally evaluated." Their goal was to create changes that would stem from teacher preferences.

> [M]any of the interventions . . . arise from teachers' ideas developed during the course of the project. . . . If something does not seem to be working, it is dropped. Conversely we are prepared to capitalize on any fortuitously presented opportunity. Many variables are changing at once. This is not a neat experimental situation, but it does approximate to everyday life in a school. We hope to show that, under normal school conditions, teachers can bring about changes in girls' attitudes and achievements. Our main outcome measure is the proportion of girls choosing to study physical science and technology in fourth year in the action

schools; if this proportion increases, relative to the control schools, we shall have succeeded.[34]

Feminist action research can be applied to a wide range of issues including pupil preferences and abuse of women in the family. German feminist scholar Maria Mies[35] presents an example of action research on the latter problem that simultaneously attempted to implement seven "principles of feminist methodology." Her project was based on a group formed to create change while studying itself doing so.

> A high visibility street action [in Cologne] drew people who were then interviewed regarding their experiences with and views on wife beating.[36] The resulting publicity led to the creation of a Women's House to aid victims of domestic abuse. A desire for transformative action and egalitarian participation guided consciousness-raising around the sociological and historical roots of male violence in the home through the development of life histories of the women who had been battered. The purpose was to empower the oppressed to come to understand and change their own oppressive realities.[37]

Patti Lather discussed a project by Jlana Hanmer and Sheila Saunders[38] in which forms of violence against women were studied through

> community-based, at-home interviewing with the purpose of feeding the information gained back to the community in order to "develop new forms of self-help and mutual aid among women." Research involvement led to an attempt to form a support group for survivors of violence and make referrals to women's crisis and safety services.[39]

These projects attempt directly to change people's behavior while gathering data in traditional or innovative ways. They intervene and study in a continuous series of feedback loops.

Participatory or Collaborative Research

In participatory or collaborative research the people studied *make decisions* about the study format and data analysis.[40] This model is designed to create social and individual change by altering the role relations of people involved in the project. The model can be limited to a slight modification of roles or expanded so that all participants have the combined researcher/subject role. In feminist participatory research, the distinction between the researcher(s) and those on whom the research is done disappears. To achieve an egalitarian relation, the researcher abandons control and adopts an approach of openness, reciprocity, mutual disclosure, and shared risk.[41] Differences in social status and background give way as shared decision-making and self-disclosure develop.

Feminist researchers who do this type of research use many different labels. Social psychologist Brinton Lykes, for example, calls feminist participatory research "passionate" or "engaged scholarship."[42] For the last several years she has been talking with Guatemalan Indian women refugees in Mexico. Her interest is in learning how they develop their revolutionary consciousness (part of her ongoing research in "self theory"), and assisting them in the development of that consciousness. She has found that engaged research requires changing numerous aspects of conventional research, including the selection of a sample, the design of instruments, and the use of informed consent. In the excerpt below, she discusses the selection of the sample:

> Together the [two] North American "researchers" have had ongoing involvement in and engagement with Guatemalans in the United States, Mexico and Guatemala for over 10 years. The identification of Guatemalans who might have been interested in collaborating in this project came out of this previous work and without this work the project would not have been possible. . . . "Subject selection" involved a process of articulating our interests to a number of different groups of Guatemalan women and continuing dialogue with those individuals or groups who expressed interest in the work and wanted to know more.

Brinton Lykes puts "subject selection" in quotes because the project actually relied on community decision making:

> The decisions about which particular women would be interviewed emerged out of continuing conversations among ourselves as researchers, our contact people (who work with or are members of the communities described above) and individual women in these communities. Participation in the project reflects therefore both an individual's decision to tell her story and a decision about how her participation contributes to and is shaped by her own and her community's current experiences. Hence, although the decisions were made by individual researchers and participants, they also quite clearly reflect the individual's and her community's and/or organization's interests.[43]

For Brinton Lykes, passionate research is communal rather than hierarchical. It develops egalitarian relations among the "researchers," the "subjects," and between the two groups.[44]

U.S. sociologist Francesca Cancian defines participatory research as

[handwritten margin note: Research question chosen by the subjects?]

> an approach to producing knowledge through democratic, interactive relationships. Researchers work with community members to resolve problems identified by the community, and the process of research is intended to empower participants . . . the three core features of participatory research are: (1) political action and individual consciousness-raising . . ., (2) relationships are democratic and participants share in making decisions and acquiring skills, (3) the everyday life experience and feelings of participants are a major source of knowledge.

To illustrate this integration of action, sharing, and experiential knowledge, she described some participatory research projects in which she was engaged:

> My first experience . . . was to organize a group of ten academic women with children, to discuss the problems of combining career and family, and consider possible solutions. Our group met for two months and was only moderately successful in raising our consciousness and changing our situation. But we were very successful in producing rich, qualitative data on conflicts between home and work, sexism at the university, and ideological barriers to feminist political action. . . . Partly because of our emphasis on individual responsibility, the group did not move towards any collective action to resolve our problems, although I repeatedly

urged the group to consider taking action and several proposals were discussed, including establishing a program for mentoring female graduate students, and getting the school to allocate a room for baby care. . . . While we did not engage in collective action, the group seemed to produce change on an individual level.

She then described an instance of "individual level" change in which a graduate student

raised the issue of male faculty interrupting female graduate students. . . . Her dramatic statement broke the official silence on sexism in our program and produced an immediate (if temporary) reduction in male faculty interrupting others. Nora told me later that the group had helped to give her the courage to speak out.

This participatory research project had a similar effect on the researcher: "I noticed that I was less fearful of senior male colleagues after discussing my fears with the group; I became less ingratiating and more comradely towards them, and they seemed to treat me with more respect." A sense of personal change pervaded the members of the group:

In the questionnaire that I gave to all members after the group ended, half the members said that the group had changed their behavior. . . . Turning to the results of the group from the perspective of producing knowledge for social science, the discussions produced rich data on the daily lives and conflicts of women graduate students and faculty with children. . . . New findings also emerged because of the discussion format and/or the possibility of action. In particular, discussions of whether to take action revealed how internalized oppression works, i.e., how fear, self-blame, and an ideology of individual achievement maintain the status quo.

Her "second experiment in participatory research" had a similar goal of empowering women. In this project, she worked with her secretary, Linda Clelland, and organized

a group of women at the university—primarily secretaries—to discuss problems at home and at work. Linda and I co-led the group. . . . After four meetings during which we discussed pressures at home and irritations in working with faculty, we began to take some action to resolve problems at work.[45]

Like Francesca Cancian, psychologist Reesa Vaughter advocates "a participatory model in which the constituents of science (the public) and research subjects become part of the scientific enterprise."[46] But some feminist scholars believe that nonprofessionals have a role only in the *initial* stages. For example, psychologist Barbara Wallston wrote that nonprofessionals can formulate hypotheses but they should have little further responsibility. An example of this approach is a project of sociologist Laurel Richardson concerning female sales clerks. Marcia Segal describes this project as follows:

To begin her research she approached a clerk she regarded as especially competent in a clothing store in which she (L.R.) is a regular customer. She sought the clerk's reaction to the proposed study and solicited from her ideas on what would be important to know if one were really to understand the occupation and also on what she (the clerk) thought a sociologist might investigate that *would be useful to her and other clerks*. Eventually, this study of sales clerking as an occupation [included] the collection of quantifiable data with a structured questionnaire, but the initial steps involved allowing the research subject to help formulate the research.[47]

In participatory projects, the researcher invites members of the setting to join her in creating the study. Nancy Avery and Estelle Disch circulated a flier for BASTA! (Boston Associates to Stop Therapy Abuse) asking therapy clients who have been abused to suggest topics of study:

> We are working on our research design and would like input from clients as to what you think we ought to study. If you have been sexually involved with a therapist or human service provider, and would like to talk with a member of the research team about your experience and about what you think the study should focus on, please call . . . who will match you with an interviewer you don't know. . . . If you would like to make input into the research design in writing, please send ideas to BASTA! Anonymous input is welcome. Input from professionals is also welcome.

Marcia Segal organized a feminist collaborative project that adds a layer of complexity. Her project based on Jewish women in Louisville, Kentucky, was

> part of a long-term multi-study effort to specify some aspects of the relationship between gender and ethnicity. . . . The organization [that sponsored it] was interested in knowing the demographic and social characteristics of the population it served and wished to assess programmatic needs. [She] was careful to maintain control over the technical aspects of data collection and analysis, but in other senses the project was a collective effort. [She] was an insider in the population [she] studied.

The description of her methods explains this collaboration:

> The mailed questionnaire used to gather the bulk of the data was developed in stages. First a group of sociologists and social service personnel, all part of the community being studied, met and composed a list of general areas of life to be investigated. An open meeting was called to which any woman wishing to serve on the committee under whose auspices the study was conducted was invited. Those who attended discussed the topic areas, questioned their utility, eliminated some and added others.
>
> The professionals met several times to draft questions. During these sessions I also presented blocks of questions from previous studies which I thought might serve our purposes and provide a means to compare our data with that of others. When a complete draft questionnaire was prepared, a large number of copies was made and a second open meeting held. This time efforts were made to include women who were not initially interested in the project. These women completed the draft questionnaire as if they were research respondents, but also provided verbal and written criticism of it.
>
> A second draft was prepared. This draft was distributed to a small random sample of the target population for the standard pretest of an instrument and its instructions. After a final set of revisions, actual data collection was undertaken.[48]

In other cases, collaboration is more extensive than the shared piloting of questionnaires. Patti Lather offers the example of a study sponsored by the "Women's Economic Development Project, part of the Institute for Community Education and Training in Hilton Head, South Carolina":

> Low-income women were trained to research their own economic circumstances in order to understand and change them. The participatory research design involved eleven low-income and underemployed women working as community researchers on a one-year study of the economic circumstances of 3000 low-income women in thirteen South Carolina counties. Information was gathered to do the following: 1. raise the consciousness of women regarding the sources of their economic circumstances; 2. promote community-based leadership within the state; 3. set up an active network of rural low-income women in South Carolina; 4. support new and pending state legislation centering on women and work, and on educational issues.

She also describes a complex, long-term project of her own in which students interviewed each other about an introductory women's studies course, then developed a survey and group interviews about the readings, and interviewed previous students. Among other results, she found that *studying* the course changed students' attitudes *toward* the course.[49]

In some instances, a project does not begin as an exercise in collaboration, but in the midst of the work, the researcher discovers the necessity of reducing the distance between herself and those studied.

> Tetreault [. . .] began her evaluation study of a four-week N.E.H. funded faculty development seminar on integrating perspectives and materials on women into general studies courses using a traditional research design. She found herself experimenting with a "new paradigm of research methodologies and procedures" [. . .] as she realized the need for the participation of the researched in cross-checking the coding of syllabi and interviews. An unexpected reciprocity developed which helped place confidence in the usefulness of the Feminist Phase Theory Evaluation Model to analyze pre- and post-seminar interviews and syllabi.

According to Patti Lather, research can emancipate participants when certain research approaches are taken. The most effective emancipatory approaches are interactive interviews in which researchers self-disclose; multiple, sequential interviews; group interviews; negotiation of the interpretations; and dealing with false-consciousness in ways that go beyond dismissing resistance. In her words,

> the research process is a powerful place to go for praxis to the extent we can formulate research designs that change people by encouraging self-reflection and a deeper understanding of their situations in the world.[50]

In participatory research, participants make decisions rather than function as passive subjects. Liz Stanley and Sue Wise cite the "interaction methodology"[51] of Nancy Kleiber and Linda Light as an example of this approach. The purpose of that study was to do research on the basis of feminist principles, particularly breaking down power differences between "researched" and "researcher":

> Their research was carried out on, within, and for, the Vancouver Women's Health Collective and not from the traditional research vantage point outside the group

studied. What they describe as their "interactive methodology" is, as it stands, not more nor less than a traditional battery of research techniques. However, they attempt to use these techniques and methods in a new way, so that "the researched" becomes much more a part of the research process. In attempting to do this the people who were the "objects" of the research helped to choose methods, to decide what should be focused on within the research, and were involved in the interpretation of results and the use of these in changing the operation of the Health Collective. . . . this research was truly "interactive," because the Collective was always in a state of change, to a large extent because of the ongoing application of the research findings.

This approach [involved] . . . the sharing out of power, the ownership of information by everyone rather than just the researchers, and the rejection of traditional interpretations of "objectivity." However . . . this rejection of objectivity, so-defined, doesn't mean that "basic standards" of research aren't conformed to. The *type* of research methods used in Kleiber and Light's work are very traditional, so for us what is particularly interesting about it is the part played by "the researched" rather than its "methodology" as such. A consequence of this new role of the researched was that the research results became interpreted as for them. This research insists that the primary recipients and users of feminist research should be the people who are its subjects rather than the researchers.[52]

This is an example of research methods defined as feminist by virtue of the roles of and benefits to the participants rather than the techniques used.

Prevalence and Needs Assessment

"Needs assessment" or "prevalence assessment" research seeks to determine the absolute or relative number of people with a particular experience or need. Needs assessment research usually relies on surveys to ascertain how widespread the problem or need is.[53] Catharine MacKinnon's groundbreaking legal work on sexual harassment builds on prevalence studies conducted with a variety of methods. She credits the "pioneering survey by Working Women United Institute" and draws on numerous other surveys that have documented the existence and pervasiveness of men's harassment of women at work. The initial survey she cites found that

out of a sample of 55 food service workers and 100 women who attended a meeting on sexual harassment, from five to seven of every ten women reported experiencing sexual harassment in some form at some time in their work lives. Ninety-two percent of the total sample thought it a serious problem. In a [similar] study of all women employed at the United Nations, 49 percent said that sexual pressure currently existed on their jobs. During the first eight months of 1976, the Division of Human Rights of the State of New York received approximately 45 complaints from women alleging sexual harassment on the job. Of 9000 women who responded voluntarily to a questionnaire in *Redbook* Magazine, "How do you handle sex on the job?" nine out of ten reported experiences of sexual harassment. . . . Using the *Redbook* questionnaire, a naval officer found 81 percent of a sample of women on a navy base and in a nearby town reported employment-related sexual harassment in some form.

In her words, the pervasiveness of harassment, as indicated by these figures, reveals that the problem is structural:

> Even extrapolating conservatively, given that nine out of ten American women work outside the home some time in their lives and that in April 1974, 45 percent of American women sixteen and over, or 35 million women, were employed in the labor force, it is clear that a lot of women are potentially affected. As the problem begins to appear structural rather than individual, *Redbook*'s conclusion that "the problem is not epidemic; it is pandemic—an everyday, everywhere occurrence" does not seem incredible.[54]

Julie Campbell, Irma Levine, and Jane Page describe an attempt at needs assessment research that dealt with menopausal women. They argue that needs assessment research can have a change-outcome simply by disrupting the status quo. To achieve this effect, however, researchers must overcome the reluctance of study participants to question powerful norms.

> In 1972 several of the middle-aged women serving on the University of Washington (Seattle) YWCA's board of directors suggested that the organization consider investigating health problems related to older women. . . . It was agreed that the central health question for women in middle age was menopause, so the Ad Hoc Committee on Menopause was formed. The committee decided first to gather information from women who had already experienced menopause. They compiled a questionnaire to be answered anonymously, and proceeded to distribute it to elderly women. The committee members approached groups of women in retirement homes and various senior citizen clubs, but these women were reluctant to answer such personal questions; most refused altogether. Questionnaires were also sent at random to a number of women's groups. The response to this effort was meager; 70 out of 1000 were returned.

Some groups of women were more amenable to discussing menopause than others, a fact that researchers did not realize until they advertised their project broadly:

> The project received some unexpected newspaper publicity. A syndicated column, "Women Alone," appearing in newspapers across the country included a report about the Ad Hoc Committee's efforts to gather information on menopause. With that, the YWCA was inundated with requests for the questionnaire. . . . Many of the requests . . . were accompanied by personal letters describing the physical and emotional difficulties women were experiencing. Two themes were repeated time after time: These women had felt patronized, if not ignored, by their doctors, and they felt isolated and embarrassed about discussing their difficulties. The Ad Hoc Committee realized that it had hit a nerve, that hundreds of women throughout the country needed information about menopause. Of the 1,200 questionnaires sent out, over 700 were returned.

As women answer inquiries about their experience, researchers frequently have to redefine the issue. In this case, the project was redefined from the physical or medical dimensions of menopause, to a broader complex of social, emotional, and economic changes concurrent with menopause.

> Two of the committee members interviewed doctors in the Seattle area. They found wide differences of opinion among them about both menopausal symptoms

and their treatment. By this time the Ad Hoc Committee on Menopause had decided to become a permanent group. It broadened its name to Women in Midstream, or WIM (combining the ideas of "mid-life" and "mainstream") because it had learned during the physical transition of menopause, women often confront other problems as well, with emotional, social and economic causes. WIM's programs encompass two major functions: dissemination of information and counseling/support for women.[55]

In some instances, needs assessment research mobilizes people to set up organizations to respond to the needs that have been identified, measured, and redefined. In this case, the Ad Hoc Committee on Menopause became Women in Midstream.

Needs assessments also provide information that can be used later to prevent certain problems. A dramatic example is the set of public forums organized in 1980 and 1981 by the Michigan Department of Mental Health to define the mental health problems and needs of Michigan women and their prevention. Instead of relying on a conventional survey approach or interviewing experts, the Women's Task Force of the Department of Mental Health conducted a series of ten widely advertised speak-outs[56] throughout the state. Anyone wishing to make a presentation was invited to do so. In these well-attended forums, speakers, audience, and Task Force members were all able to listen to the testimony.[57] In the words of one organizer, psychologist Carol Mowbray:

> Among the topics which the forums address are: life stages and stressful life events, including single parenting, abortion, divorce and widowhood; sexist bias in treatment and diagnosis, inappropriate practices in admission and discharge; use of psychotropic medications; health problems mislabeled as psychiatric; victims of violence; rural women; minority women; ex-offenders, etc. . . . The format uses a key-informant approach: presentations by several individuals who have recognized expertise or experience with the issue. Presentations are followed by discussion with WTF members and audience comments. . . . To our knowledge, this is the first time in the nation that such an extensive examination of women's mental health treatment and problems has been carried out in this manner.[58]

In 1982 the Women's Task Force published its report of recommendations drawn from these public forums, concluding that women experienced support groups as more helpful than psychotherapy. It therefore urged that the state mental health office adopt a policy of assisting women in establishing such groups rather than encouraging them to undergo psychotherapy[59] or institutionalization. By diverting state resources away from ineffective, potentially harmful treatment, this needs assessment project played an important prevention role.

In speak-outs and tribunals,[60] large groups of women join to give public testimony about a particular issue.[61] In the process, those present learn about experiences of women similar to themselves and are likely to deepen their self-understandings and be moved to action. Frequently, the proceedings of a speak-out are published, so that the voices of the typically unheard can be heard. In many instances, organizers of speak-outs notify the press and inform policy makers about problems of concern to women. Susan Brownmiller states that her desire to write about rape was sparked by a speak-out[62] in which women revealed their rape experiences.

> personal testimony . . . opened up the subject of rape from a woman's point of view for the first time in history. . . . at The New York Radical Feminist Speak-Out on Rape, January 24, 1971; The New York Radical Feminist Conference on Rape, April 17, 1971; and the joint New York Radical Feminist-National Black Feminist Organization Speak-Out on Rape and Sexual Abuse, August 25, 1974.[63]

Because the speakers hear one another, they can readily join one another for action. The new knowledge created on the spot can be used rapidly to work for prevention.

Speak-outs and consciousness-raising are more likely to be considered techniques of activism than ways of gathering or presenting data. But in my view, they clearly are research devices if their results are made available for public scrutiny. The following excerpt from a conference about the concerns of older women used a speak-out to inform women and gather information. Immediately following the conference, a successful activist organization was founded:

> "Growing Numbers, Growing Force" opened with the participants giving the opening address in the form of a Speakout. Laurie Shields, who chaired the session, had asked many of the women to come to the conference and explain what they wanted it to accomplish. One by one, they told of the problems in their communities and the issues that concerned them.
>
> Jane Molson, Los Angeles, California: I came prepared with a seven minute speech. That's how long it took to outline all the hassles I have had with Social Security and with employment. I had to go back to the job market at 63. I had to take reduced Social Security benefits because it was absolutely necessary in order to eat. I am a spokeswoman for Older Women for Economic Independence which is part of the Wages for Housework campaign. We are launching a national Social Security Wage for Housework campaign."[64]

The transcript of a speak-out in Boston in 1986 on the topic of middle-aged female caregivers conveys this same potential for assessing needs. In the transcript, three themes are evident: women discovering their own experience as they speak, women identifying with each other as they listen, and the potentially politicizing impact of both processes.[65]

Evaluation Research

The purpose of "evaluation research" is to evaluate the effectiveness of different types of actions in meeting needs or solving problems. It is used to evaluate individual and organizational behavior, and to evaluate evaluation research itself.[66] For example, Pauline Bart and Patricia O'Brien evaluated the effectiveness of different forms of individual behavior to determine which strategies enabled women to stop a rape in progress. Their intention was to generate

> data-based advice . . . that could be given to schools, hospitals, police, courts, or individuals, stating how rape could be avoided. This lack of data left unanswered the question of "What do I do if someone tries to rape me?" This book

was written to help women answer that question. . . . This book is based on an analysis of 94 interviews with women 18 or older who had been attacked and avoided being raped ($n = 51$) or had been raped ($n = 43$) in the two years prior to the interview.[67]

Mainstream and feminist organizations or settings frequently solicit evaluation to improve their own practice and create an action blueprint other women can follow.[68] For example, Linda Valli assessed a high school internship program that teaches girls how to become clerical workers. She demonstrated that contradictions inherent in the curriculum mystified the teacher and her students:

> Many of the jobs the students filled were so routinized and specialized that they were already overqualified for them before they completed high school. That lack of correspondence between skill level and job requirements created a feeling of dissatisfaction that resulted in low-quality work, requests for changes, and/or a marginalization of wage labor identity.[69]

She also demonstrated that the curriculum could be modified to eliminate these contradictions and provide a more coherent education for the students.

Another form of evaluation research is self-study. Guides such as *The Institutional Self-Study Guide* offered by the Washington-based Project on the Status and Education of Women enable groups to assess problems in their own institutions. In this case, the focus is the degree of sex equity in a particular university.[70] In her study, sociologist Pamela Roby evaluated the effectiveness of a *role*. Structured interviews with 35 union stewards showed her that

> stewards significantly influence women's employment conditions by enforcing and extending the contracts. In addition, stewards' recruiting new members, communicating with members, and organizing members for strike action strengthens unions in collective bargaining for wages, benefits, and working conditions. Finally, service as a steward affects the employment of many of those who so serve by providing training in leadership skills and being a step toward higher level positions in unions, companies and government agencies.[71]

For this reason, women should be encouraged to take the steward role.

Sociologist Lenore Weitzman's study of the impact of a groundbreaking public *policy*—the California no-fault divorce law[72]—and Susan Estrich's study of the effectiveness of judicial policy concerning rape,[73] both of which evaluated specific policies, behaviors, and organizations did a great deal for the feminist movement.[74] For example, because Weitzman found that "the major economic result of the divorce law revolution is the systematic impoverishment of divorced women and their children," she proposed "reforms based on fairness, equity, and equality-of-results"[75] in the final chapter of her book. These reforms are currently being examined, and in some cases adopted, on a state-by-state basis.

Feminist evaluation research is sensitive to the danger of sexist bias creeping into the very process of evaluation, particularly in the form of sexist concepts and inappropriate comparisons. In her paper on this topic, Linda Kamens argues that "the present program evaluation philosophy is inadequate from a feminist perspective" because "evaluation, as it is typically done, involves utilizing the stated goals or purposes of the program as the criteria for the evaluation. . . . The evaluation generally does not question the program goals or procedures'' or define their side-effects.[76] In her view, feminist program evaluation requires that the evaluator and program recipient articulate their values. She urges the evaluator to introduce the concept of justice, and to attend to the process, not only the content, of the evaluated program. Joan Poliner Shapiro and Beth Reed created a model of evaluation to meet these requirements. Using the term ''Illuminative Evaluation,'' they described their work as evaluators of the first and second national Summer Institutes in Women's Studies.[77] Their evaluation focused on the *process* of working in the Institute, not only on the *results* of participation.

Demystification

In the *demystification* framework, researchers believe that the very act of obtaining knowledge creates the potential for change because the paucity of research about certain groups accentuates and perpetuates their powerlessness. Researchers on women's employment note that ''there is little data . . . on Hispanic or Native American women, or on the employment situation of other groups such as disabled or lesbian women.'' Because the needs and opinions of these groups are not known, their views have less influence on the conditions under which they live. Thus, the study of certain groups is political because it demystifies. Feminist research ''raises consciousness'' when those in power are taken aback by the audacity of a feminist research project, especially if the very questions asked challenge vested interests. As Christine Bose and Glenna Spitze put it: ''The development of a research and policy agenda to meet women's employment-related needs is a political act in and of itself.''[78]

Another vivid example of demystifying research threatening vested interests is the addendum to Mary Louise Ho's study of the patriarchal ideology underpinning ''agony columns'' in three popular women's magazines in Britain. Shortly after she presented her research at a conference, the following incident occurred:

> I was happily enjoying my beer and the company of a friend, when one of the conference organizers approached me with the warning that the *Daily Mail* wanted to speak with me. I had barely got out the question ''What do they want?'' when I was set upon by two unpleasant and very aggressive men. One of them was shoving copies of *Woman* and *Woman's Own* at me and demanding that I answer the letters on the problem pages! The other was insisting he should take my photograph and wanted to know what I was so afraid of. They then showed me a list of quotations which, I was very surprised to discover, were identical to the paper I had just given. I couldn't remember any journalists at my talk, no doubt they simply got hold of a spare copy (all papers were publically available) . . .
>
> [A] couple of people . . . helped to divert attention from me which gave me time to piece together enough of the situation to realize that I should tell these idiots to piss off. I refused to make any comments or have my photograph taken. They kept on persisting until they felt sure I wouldn't comply, then they had a drink at the bar and mixed with other delegates who probably thought they were British Sociological Association members (they wore no identification).
>
> The next day there was a smear job of my paper on page 3 of the *Daily Mail*.

This set off a cascade of media researchers from radio and press to Granada TV who tried to contact me for comment. The urge to do something about the ridiculous article really plagued me. But being completely inexperienced with the media and having heard enough horror about what they can do to women (never mind feminists and sociologists!), I decided that it wouldn't be doing myself or the women's movement any good to take them up. The media pursuit followed me back to York where it eventually died out.

As I never had a chance to "set the record straight," I thought I could make a very brief reply to the *Daily Mail* article here (to make it any longer would be taking them too seriously). As I explained in a latter to the agony columnists, I am not attacking them as people or accusing them of giving the "wrong" advice. What I am doing is looking at how the ideas and presumptions (ideologies) communicated by these agony columns manifest and attempt to reinforce patriarchy. Any two people could argue until eternity about whether an answer was "right" or "wrong"—but that is a completely different issue. All things considered, I am glad to have had the experience for what it has taught me. My deepest sympathies to all women who have been exploited by the media; no doubt many have suffered much worse.[79]

Clearly, the interests of the newspapers were threatened by the success of her research in demystifying the underlying ideology.

Kathy Ferguson's study of bureaucracy similarly discusses knowledge-creation-as-praxis:

By exposing the contradictions and manipulations contained within a bureaucratic society, one can demystify the theory and practice of that society. Since the organizational society is maintained in part by creating and perpetuating the appropriate ideology, one that both reflects and distorts the reality it describes, a different form of understanding is in some ways also a form of action. . . . I do believe that political theory can be transformative, can help us to live well, if it is used to rethink our lives, reshape our possibilities, and resist the official definition of reality.[80]

She uses the word "demystification" to mean the change in consciousness that occurs among the relatively powerless when they consider their situation in a new light.

The Boston Women's Health Book Collective has demystified women's health issues and has had an empowering impact on a wide variety of women. In the following excerpt from *Our Bodies, Ourselves,* collective members describe their process of action research:

It began (1969) in a small discussion group on "women and their bodies" which was part of a women's conference held in Boston in the spring of 1969, one of the first gatherings of women meeting specifically to talk with other women. For many of us it was the very first time we had joined together with other women to talk and think about our lives and what we could do about them. Before the conference was over, some of us decided to keep on meeting as a group to continue the discussion, and so we did.

The lack of information about their bodies prompted them to try to create change.

We decided on a summer project—to research those topics which we felt were particularly pertinent to learning about our bodies, to discuss in the group what we had learned, then to write papers individually or in groups of two or three, and finally to present the results in the fall as a course for women on women and their bodies.

The process of demystification started with self-education.

> As we developed the course, we realized more and more that we really were capable of collecting, understanding, and evaluating medical information. Together we evaluated our reading of books and journals, our talks with doctors and friends who were medical students. We found we could discuss, question and argue with each other in a new spirit of cooperation rather than competition. We were equally struck by how important it was for us to be able to open up with one another and share our feelings about our bodies. The process of talking was as crucial as the facts themselves . . . .
>
> When we gave the course we met in any available free space we could get— in day schools, in nursery schools, in churches, in our homes. We wanted the course to stimulate the same kind of talking and sharing that we who had prepared the course had experienced. We had something to say, but we had a lot to learn as well; we did not want a traditional teacher-student relationship. At the end of ten to twelve sessions—which roughly covered the material in the current book— we found that many women felt both eager and competent to get together in small groups and share what they had learned with other women. We saw it as a never-ending process always involving more and more women.

The initial efforts to share their information with other women was part of a process of demystifying an ever-widening audience of women.

> Our first publication of *Our Bodies, Ourselves* helped spark many women to explore the health issues more important to them. Since then, women throughout this country and the world have generated such a wealth of information and resources—research papers, books, health groups and centers, newsletters and journals—that this time around we turned to them for help in rewriting the book. . . . The thousands of women who contact us in person, in letters and by phone have opened up whole new subjects and issues for revisions: "I looked in your book for a discussion of in vitro fertilization and couldn't find it." "You've got to include the experiences of differently-abled [disabled] women next time." "This is what happened to me when I got PID; tell other women about it so they will be forewarned and know how to get the right kind of treatment." "Could you please say more about lesbians and medical care?"[81]

A measure of their success was the demands they received from other women to incorporate material into their book about which they had not been aware.[82]

Egyptian feminist Nawal El Saadawi gives a parallel example of the cry for help elicited by social research. After her book *Woman and Sex* appeared, there was an "avalanche of letters, telephone calls and visits from young and old, men and women . . . most of them asking for a way out of problems, most of them friendly or desperate, and a few, very few, menacing."[83] All of these people were reacting to her making public problems they had suffered in private. The desire to create social change through research is also evident in a study by U.S. sociologist

Alice Rossi[84] who surveyed 2000 people at the first national women's conference in Houston, Texas in November 1977. Her purposes were to collect data about the current feminist movement for future historians, to study the impact of the conference on participants, and to recruit women into mainstream politics. In addition, her study addressed basic research questions in social psychology and political sociology.

Finally, some people cooperate as research "subjects" because they believe that information about their experience will demystify the problem for others. Israeli sociologist Lea Shamgar-Handelman described this common hope of people who choose to participate in research, in her case war-widows. Widows she interviewed wanted to avoid wasting their painful experiences, mistakes, successes, and knowledge. "'I am telling you my story,' said one, 'with the hope that others will be able to learn from it.'"[85] Feminist researchers who hear such statements assume the responsibility of trying to fulfill people's expectations.

Changing the Researcher

Although changing the researcher is not a common intention in feminist research, it is a common consequence. In *On Becoming a Social Scientist*[86] I suggested that learning should occur on three levels in any research project: the levels of person, problem, and method. By this I meant that the researcher would learn about herself, about the subject matter under study, and about how to conduct research. Many feminist researchers report being profoundly changed by what they learn about themselves. Changes may involve completely reconceptualizing a phenomenon and completely revising one's worldview. As Del Martin wrote:

> A year ago I knew that wife-beating was a problem in some marriages. But I had no idea of the prevalence of marital violence, nor of its tacit acceptance as a part of life in so many families. Information on the subject was not readily accessible. When I spoke to people about my projected book on battered wives, they swiftly changed the subject or twisted it around to a safer, more socially acceptable topic—child abuse. Men put up their guard at the mention of battered wives, though a few feigned mild curiosity to cover their embarrassment. Women, too, were reticent about discussing the issue. Many, however, when they were later able to talk to me privately, revealed that they were or had been battered wives. To my amazement I learned that "some of my best friends" are among those who had experienced violence at one time or another in their intimate relationships with men. They spilled out their stories as if they had waited for years to find someone who would listen and take them seriously.

Recognizing the prevalence and secrecy of wife-beating and people's inability to even listen to her study, she carefully specifies actions that can reduce this form of torture.

> Working on this book was a consciousness-raising experience for me. . . . I have been swamped with letters and phone calls from people who are concerned about family violence and want to know what to do, how to start a refuge for battered

wives, and where to obtain funding. I have no magic answer or blueprint. My advice is to start at the local level; form coalitions and task forces; research applicable state laws and city ordinances; investigate policies and procedures of law enforcement (police, district attorney, and the courts); gather statistics from every conceivable source; canvass emergency housing and note admission policies; determine what services are already available and which need to be established; draw up proposals based on that information; make funding agencies aware of the need; lobby for remedial legislation at every level of government; demand a re-ordering of priorities in government and foundation spending; and don't stop until all necessary programs are realized.[87]

The changes researchers undergo can lead to harsh recognition of their own shortcomings. Billie Dziech and Linda Weiner poignantly conclude their book, *The Lecherous Professor,* with this description of their personal change:

> To write a book about harassment is to discover with shock how easily individuals and institutions delude themselves. The process brought us face to face with our own irresponsibility and the irresolution of our colleagues. We began to wonder why we had ignored so much and taken so long to speak out about what we had seen and heard. To write a book about harassment is to realize that the morality of an entire profession can be tested by its response to a single issue. Most of all, it is to hope that the test proves successful and that our words, however belated, will somehow make a difference.[88]

Not all research projects end with self-criticism. Some feminist researchers discover, instead, that their research has sustained their lives. Judith Fetterley writes:

> My book is for me more than an academic matter, more than an act of literary criticism, more than a possible text for courses on women in American literature, more even than the source of dialogue; it is an act of survival. . . . I see my book as a self-defense survival manual for the woman reader lost in "the masculine wilderness of the American novel." At its best, feminist criticism is a political act, whose aim is not simply to interpret the world but to change it by changing the consciousness of those who read and their relation to what they read.[89]

Perhaps the expectation that our research will provoke self-criticism or provide a means for survival is too demanding, a topic I return to in the conclusion where I discuss "the great demands" of feminist research. Perhaps we can only hope that our research will clarify our vision and improve our decisions. Lydia O'Donnell is a case in point of a researcher who began her project thinking of women as oppressed "victims and captives of their domestic work" and then changed her mind while listening to the way women experienced motherhood, homemaking, and community involvement, and giving birth to her own first child.

> The women . . . forced me to reassess many of my original biases and rethink what it means to be a woman in modern times. They made me realize the deep satisfactions of mothering as well as the stresses, and they helped me appreciate that children are young only for a short time and that the years women spend child rearing can provide pleasures and rewards which are difficult to incorporate

in any formal cost-benefit analysis of the tradeoffs between employment and family life.[90]

The voices of feminist scholars engaged in different forms of action research thus include the individual who honestly assesses what she has learned about herself. By including this perspective, I find a strong connection between the activism of feminist action research, and the self-reflexive nature of much feminist research that does not label itself as activist. For this reason, although a chapter on action research is useful in stressing change-oriented forms, it would be misleading if it suggested that other forms of feminist research are static. To the extent that feminism is change-oriented by definition, all feminist research has action components.

11

Feminist Multiple Methods Research[1]

An emerging postulate for feminist research—is using a variety of methods in order to generate multifaceted information.[2]

Just as feminist research often draws on multiple disciplines, so too it often draws on multiple, rather than a single, method in a particular project. By contrast, many studies in the social sciences do not use multiple methods but rely on one data type or method of analysis. The use of multiple methods in a single study has earned its own name—triangulation.[3] Although like mainstream research, feminist research is frequently unimethodological, there are many instances where it is triangulated. There may be a greater proportion of triangulated feminist research than mainstream research because of the special relation triangulation has with feminist concerns.

Feminists choose multiple methods for technical reasons, similar to mainstream researchers, and for particular feminist concerns that reflect intellectual, emotional, and political commitments. Feminist descriptions of multimethod research express the commitment to thoroughness, the desire to be open-ended, and to take risks. Multiple methods enable feminist researchers to link past and present, "data gathering" and action, and individual behavior with social frameworks. In addition, feminist researchers use multiple methods because of changes that occur to them and others in a project of long duration. Feminists describe such long projects as "journeys." Sometimes multiple methods reflect the desire to be responsive to the people studied. By combining methods, feminist researchers are particularly able to illuminate previously unexamined or misunderstood experiences. Multiple methods increase the likelihood of obtaining scientific credibility and research utility.

Historical Roots

Agnes Riedmann argues that Margaret Loyd Jarman Hagood (1907–1963), a pioneer in statistics and demography, should be recognized as an early advocate of combining qualitative and quantitative methods in sociological research.[4] After earning an M.A. in mathematics, Margaret Hagood earned a Ph.D. in sociology.

Her 1936 doctoral dissertation consisted of a statistical analysis of the fertility patterns of white women in the rural southeast of the United States, then the region of highest population growth in the country.

In her first position as a research associate in the Institute for Research in Social Science at the University of North Carolina, Chapel Hill, Margaret Hagood reexamined the same population she had studied in her dissertation. This time she also traveled throughout the south and interviewed farm tenant wives at length. Her resulting book, *Mothers of the South,* was a well-received qualitative study. She wrote:

> It is already well established that rural women in the South have a high level of fertility and a low level of living, but little is known of what these quantitative measures mean in the lives of the mothers and their children. Therefore, the effort was made to be both more realistic and comprehensive in a sort of attempt to get away from restricted statistical treatment and stereotyped "case studies," and yet to combine as far as possible some features of the statistical, case and survey methods.
>
> Preliminary work included first a statistical analysis of the regional and subregional variations in fertility, which served to locate and define certain groups of high fertility levels, and to examine the implications of fertility differentials with particular reference to the Southeast. . . . The actual first-hand gathering of data consisted of repeated visits made by the writer to the tenant farm mothers during a sixteen months' period of field work.[5]

At the same time, she maintained her interest in statistics and demography and published the very popular text *Statistics for Sociologists* in 1941.[6]

Margaret Hagood expertly combined quantitative and qualitative methods in her studies of the life experiences of women and families in the rural south. She personally interviewed members of 254 homes at least once, choosing the households on the basis of indices of mobility, education, age, age at marriage, number of years exposed to pregnancy, fertility, and occupation. The farmers were able to speak freely with her because they saw her as only slightly removed from their life-style, having been raised in the same area. One of her interesting findings is that seven of eight of the women she interviewed preferred to work in the field rather than in their homes. They were prouder of their accomplishments outside the home than inside.

At the same time she found that the women and their families had inadequate diet, housing, medical treatment, education, social life, and recreation. The major culprit was "the burden of involuntary and frequent childbearing," which in turn was aggravated by lack of regional planning, inadequate state contraception programs, overreliance on a single crop system, and disregard for this region by the federal government. Margaret Hagood subsequently made use of another method— photography—which I will discuss in the next chapter on "feminist originals."

For more than 50 years, sociologist Mirra Komarovsky has identified herself as a feminist and has conducted multiple method research.[7] In her latest major study, funded by the National Institute of Education and various private foundations, she offers a model of multiple methods research that integrates methods within sociology, and combines these with psychological instruments. Her study documents how women change when educated in an elite women's college in the United States:

> The study began in the fall of 1979 when 630 freshmen entered college. A random sample, stratified by race and religion, was selected out of the total. It consisted of 241 students who each received a set of questionnaires, scales, and tests. By my and my assistant's deadline, two weeks later, the rate of return was 96 percent of the original number approached, giving us a sample of 232 students, including both residents and commuters.

Following the distribution of self-administered questionnaires and scales, Mirra Komarovsky used interviews and diaries:

> 201 students were interviewed for about an hour, to clarify and supplement their completed forms. . . . In the spring semester, nine freshmen kept diaries, following an outline I prepared, and were interviewed every two weeks. (They received a modest honorarium for this work.) The purpose of the diaries was to generate hypotheses regarding the impact of college on the study's dependent variables for the interviews in the fall of 1980.

In keeping with this longitudinal design, in the fall of their sophomore year "students received replications of all the research instruments measuring dependent variables." In addition, "a subsample of 70 students agreed to two two-hour interviews." The students were not studied during their junior year, but as seniors, materials replicating those sent them in their sophomore year were collected. Sixty-five seniors consented to two-hour interviews. As Mirra Komarovsky summarized,

> Our methods . . . combined quantitative measures (questionnaires and scales) and qualitative data (interviews and diaries). Although the interview was the major research tool, the interplay of both methods was a distinct feature of the study.

Mirra Komarovsky does not draw on feminism to explain her use of multiple methods. In fact, in other publications she rejects the idea that there is a particular feminist methodology. At the same time she advocates strongly that data be interpreted in feminist ways. Mirra Komarovsky regards interviews as providing internal validity for the statistical patterns uncovered by surveys. At the same time interviews convey additional information about experience unobtainable in surveys. She explains her inclusion of excerpts from the interviews throughout the book as a "kind of fusion of scientific and 'literary' functions, to convey the immediacy of an experience even as it seeks to communicate some of the major theoretical concerns of this study."[8] Finally, she expresses the hope that this combination of data will make her book even more useful to students, professors, college personnel, parents, and policy makers than it would be if based on one type of data alone. Thus, in addition to providing a model of personal continuity in multimethod research, Mirra Komarovsky illustrates two rationales for doing this type of research: to enhance its scientific status and increase its potential utility to readers.

Rationales for Contemporary
Feminist Multimethod Research

Triangulation of Quantitative and Qualitative Methods

An article concerning sexual harassment, by psychologist Bernice Lott and her colleagues Mary Ellen Reilly and Dale Howard, is an example of a straightforward triangulation of quantitative and qualitative materials. In the following excerpt they explain the items in their questionnaire, the nature of their interviews, and the fact that they provided counseling services on request:

> The questions in our nine-page survey . . . were applicable to the experiences of both women and men and covered the following areas: demographic information (age, university status, etc.); knowledge of other persons on the campus who had been sexually assaulted; personal experience of assault on campus; personal experience of sexual assault anywhere; actual and potential experience as sexual assaulter; knowledge of sexual intimidation experienced by others on campus; personal experience of intimidation on campus; experience of having been offered sexual contact in exchange for job- or school-related benefits; opinions about the frequency of sexual insults on and off campus; personal experience of sexual insult; and finally, attitudes toward and acceptance of specific sexually harassing behaviors . . . .
>
> A separate sheet of paper was included with each survey on which a respondent could volunteer to be interviewed. We also supplied the names and phone numbers of campus counselors available to anyone who wished "to talk confidentially with someone about any of the issues raised" in the survey. Persons who indicated a willingness to be interviewed were contacted individually by one of five interviewers familiar with the objectives of the investigation and the contents of the questionnaire. Each interview was conducted by a same-sex interviewer. . . . Each interview was open-ended and began with the simple question "What would you like to tell me about the issues dealt with in the survey?"[9]

In sum, their study consisted of distributing surveys following by open-ended interviews with a subgroup of volunteers, each method fleshing out the other.

Sociologist Pauline Bart and her colleagues Linda Freeman and Peter Kimball studied attitudes toward pornography in a multimethod manner. Their first step was to obtain preliminary data in a natural setting. They did this by handing out

> stamped, addressed, pre-folded questionnaires to patrons exiting a theater showing the film *(Not a Love Story)*. This questionnaire asked only for the gender of the respondent. After telling them the importance of the issue, they were asked to cooperate by writing their reactions to the film including any changes it had made in their attitudes about pornography, what they liked and didn't like about the film, what they learned, if anything, and anything else they wanted to tell us.

Another data collection procedure in the field was to interview people who had seen the film. Based on both sets of information, they produced a questionnaire including forced-choice and open-ended items answered by 668 people who had seen the film in the recent past. Pauline Bart and her co-researchers explained the questionnaire and the way the responses were analyzed:

Each of the 42 items on the questionnaire was taken directly from the answers. The statements were about equally divided between pro-and anti-pornography attitudes. The subjects were asked to indicate degree of agreement with each statement, ranging from "strongly agree" to "strongly disagree." There was no zero point. Standard demographic questions were included, as well as a question asking respondents if they were feminist or pro-feminist. . . . We also included a blank space on the questionnaire, which they were told they could use to say anything they wanted. . . . The answers to these 42 pre-coded questions were cross-tabulated by gender and by type of feminism or pro-feminism with gender controlled. . . . The written comments were analysed in two ways. First, Freeman examined all the comments and constructed a typology. In order to have a more rigorous qualitative analysis, a second classification was then constructed, independently of the Freeman classification, which could account for each response.[10]

Thus this project conducted in-the-field interviews in order to develop a questionnaire, and produced an integrated analysis of quantitative and qualitative data concerning people's reactions to a specific film that deals with pornography. Unfortunately, in mainstream research projects open-ended interview data are sometimes collected to supplement surveys, but then are not analyzed.[11]

Commitment to Thoroughness

Feminist researchers combine many methods so as to cast their net as widely as possible in the search for understanding critical issues in women's lives. The multimethod approach increases the likelihood that these researchers will understand what they are studying, and that they will be able to persuade others of the veracity of their findings. Multiple methods work to enhance understanding both by adding layers of information and by using one type of data to validate or refine another.

Psychologist Phyllis Chesler's study about women and madness is an example of a feminist research project that turned to multiple methods because of her commitment to examine thoroughly a phenomenon that was poorly understood. In the introduction to her book, she explains that her material begins with the presentation of

the lives and "psychiatric" histories of four women, based on autobiographical, biographical, and "case history" material. These, and modern women in general, are viewed in terms of what growing up female in the family means. . . . Chapter One describes how female reproductive biology, patriarchal culture, and the modern parent-daughter relationship have so combined as to insure such characteristically female behaviors—and ideals—as self-sacrifice, masochism, reproductive narcissism, compassionate "maternality," dependency, sexual timidity and unhappiness, father-worship—and the overwhelming dislike and devaluation of women.

After this discussion of case studies, she analyzes "both the mental asylum and private therapy as recapitulations or mirrors of the female experience in the family" and then reviews traditional and contemporary clinical theories and practices.

Although Phyllis Chesler is a clinical psychologist, she also deals with such sociological materials as "our nation's mental illness' statistics from 1950 to 1969." In the largest section of the book, she presents her clinical materials. These include the "patient 'careers' of sixty women whom [she] interviewed about their experiences in psychiatric hospitals and private or clinic outpatient therapy—experiences which took place from 1945 to 1971 in America and England." In her concluding comment, she explains that she speaks in "many voices . . . as a psychological researcher, theoretician, and clinician—and as a literary and philosophical person, a lover of poetry and myths." [12]

In my view, Phyllis Chesler's last comment indicates that the use of multiple methods reflects the multifaceted identity of many feminist researchers. We are multifaceted because we are working during a feminist renaissance that transcends disciplinary boundaries and challenges many of our capacities at once. Our multifacetedness makes single-method research seem flat and inadequate to explore and express the complexities of women's lives.

As did Phyllis Chesler, Carolyn Sachs combined historical and contemporary materials in her study of women farmers. In addition to utilizing archival documents from the seventeenth century to the present, she analyzed changing conditions of production and the modification of ideologies concerning the sexual division of labor. To supplement these materials, she conducted in-depth interviews with 21 female farmers so that the women could speak for themselves and suggest ways of eliminating the subordination under which they suffered. Her multiple method research seemed to be motivated by a desire to connect women of the past and present. Similarly sociologist Ruth Wallace combined analysis of documents from Catholic institutions with interviews of Catholic women recently appointed as church administrators in her study of women in the Church hierarchy,[13] and Leila Rupp (historian) and Verta Taylor (sociologist) combined archival analysis and interviews to study the U.S. women's movement in the recent past.[14]

Judith Herman and Lisa Hirschman's illuminating study of incest also used a multiplicity of methods. As feminist clinicians, they were alarmed by the number of women they treated who were incest victims. The lack of available literature on the topic of father–daughter incest inspired them to write their book. They felt driven to be as thorough as possible because of the horrific quality of the phenomenon they investigated and the responsibility they felt to incest survivors. They also believed that they would best be able to fill the vacuum of knowledge on incest by drawing on all the methods available to them. The use of multiple sources of data, I contend, reflects the passion they brought to the study.

At the outset they explain that they divided their book into three parts, each containing different kinds of materials:

> survey data, clinical material, anthropological literature, popular literature, and pornography. For our scholarly sources we naturally relied on libraries; but for much of the popular literature we relied on the help of friends, acquaintances, and strangers who clipped newspaper or magazine articles and called our attention to publications that we would not ordinarily have seen.

Following this overview of relevant materials, they include "a clinical study of [their] own, based upon interviews with patients in therapy or their therapists.

Forty incest victims and twenty women whose father had been seductive but not overtly incestuous participated in our research.''

Feminist theory (in this case, linking concepts of male supremacy and female oppression) enabled them to make sense of these multiple sources of information. But they were not interested in confining their research to analysis and theory building. They were also interested in action. Thus, one part of their book deals with

> the social responses to discovered incest, including crisis intervention, family treatment, and prosecution. It also deals with the possibilities of healing and prevention. Our discussion is based upon interviews with professionals in the mental health system, child protective services, and law enforcement, and upon site visits to programs that have developed innovative approaches to the problems.[15]

In other words, they rounded out their study of the literature and actual clinical cases with an investigation of the social context of incest and a suggestion for preventive action.

Sociologist Lenore Weitzman's study of ''the social, economic, and legal consequences of California's no-fault divorce law'' required a set of methods for each of these three consequences. As she explained in her appendix on research methods:

> The research involved four types of data: systematic random samples of court records; interviews with members of the matrimonial bar; interviews with superior court judges and commissioners who hear family law cases; and, perhaps most important, interviews with recently divorced men and women . . . .
>
> In all of the interviews that we conducted, each respondent (i.e., each judge, lawyer, divorced man and woman) was presented with a series of hypothetical divorce cases (in addition to about one hundred pages of questions). Four of these cases are discussed throughout this book: one involves a young couple with pre-school children, another concerns an older corporate executive and his wife after a twenty-seven-year marriage, the third focuses on a middle-aged nurse who supported her doctor husband through medical school, and the fourth deals with noncompliance with a child support award.

Seeking to avoid U.S. ethnocentrism, she reports that she

> had the opportunity to conduct a similar set of interviews in England and to explore the responses of English judges and attorneys to the same four hypothetical cases. Their reactions serve to highlight the unique features of the California legal perspective.[16]

The records of divorce cases her research team examined were drawn from samples before and after the implementation of the no-fault law and in different counties. All told, the multiplicity of her methods and the skillful manner in which her data were analyzed enabled her to demonstrate the extremely harmful and inequitable effects of the no-fault divorce law on women.

Integration of the Personal and the Social

Kathleen Barry's study of prostitution and the traffic in women, phenomena she labeled ''female sexual slavery,'' required multiple methods because the activities are clandestine and multifaceted.[17] Her very disturbing book begins with a harrowing ethnographic description of a particular form of prostitution in Paris that she was able to observe. Other methods she used include gathering archival material, analyzing documents, sitting in on court trials, and using investigative reporting techniques to identify individuals involved in the traffic. Even after locating women who had escaped from or left prostitution, she found it difficult to interview them because they were convinced she would not believe them. To increase their trust in her, Kathleen Barry conducted lengthy open-ended interviews that enabled the women to speak freely and at length. By encouraging them to describe their experiences accurately, she increased their self-confidence while avoiding exaggerations in their stories.

Although she relied on interviewing for its particular assets, Kathleen Barry was careful not to analyze prostitution as the "personal problem" of the particular woman. Rather, she was interested in the conditions that had enslaved these particular women as prostitutes, and that could have had that influence on any woman. In other words, her multiple methods helped her link the case of the individual woman with a broader complex of social and economic issues. Multiple methods are used by many feminist researchers because of our recognition that the conditions of our lives are always simultaneously the product of personal and structural factors.

The Long Duration of Research Projects

Another rationale feminist researchers offer for using multiple methods is the long time period needed to complete an in-depth study. In that duration, we may learn new ways of doing research or may discover that the circumstances of the people we are studying have changed.

An example can be found in Cynthia Fuchs Epstein's research on women in the law. She writes:

> This analysis of the changing role of women in the legal profession is based on fifteen years of research using a number of different "methods." It is hard to isolate method from general experience when one has spent so much attention on a research subject for a long period of time. . . . I changed methods in the course of those years, partly because it seemed appropriate to my goals and to the changing situation of lawyers. I was also exposed to different styles of work in sociology, work that did not replace earlier perspectives that had formed my sociological vision but that, I felt, added a richness and depth.[18]

Breaking down the barrier between her life and her work, Cynthia Epstein describes research as a fluid, flexible process that takes on different methods in a responsive way.

Betsy Ettore's study of "the London lesbian ghetto" demonstrates how different methods became available to her as the people she was studying began to trust her. Spending a lot of time doing a project communicates seriousness and commitment to the people one is studying:

During the beginning of my research I was able to meet with various lesbians and talk about their particular groups and the purposes of their organizations. Because I was a newcomer to the London lesbian scene, one woman who remained an important contact throughout the research volunteered to take me to a weekly meeting of a lesbian group and to introduce me to its organizer. My initiation into this lesbian group occurred in December 1974. This contact with a local lesbian group and its organizer proved to be important. It was at these weekly meetings that I soon became familiar with the London lesbian ghetto. I went along regularly to these meetings for a period of three years during the course of my research. It was through this particular lesbian organization, "Sappho," that I was able to distribute half of my questionnaires. I became known as a "resident sociologist" and many women were willing to talk to me about my work.

Thus in the first phase of her research, Betsy Ettore relied on participant observation, which in turn provided the foundation for preliminary survey research. She then shared her work with community members, a process many mainstream researchers consider very risky because community members generally do not agree with the researcher's view. On the other hand, Betsy Ettore describes this "sharing" as follows:

The wealth of information which I gathered at these weekly meetings was invaluable. I was able to establish relationships of trust with many of the lesbians with whom I came in contact. Gradually, most members came to know me as a sociologist and as a confidant with whom one could discuss one's life. In order to build up relationships of mutual trust and understanding, I would periodically distribute my written work. Usually, my work was read with enthusiasm and often I was provided with pages of criticism, which proved useful in sharpening my own analysis of the lesbian ghetto.

She also demonstrated her commitment to the women by her active involvement in the community. The number of settings that she observed and in which she took an active role was sizable:

Along with these regular meetings I went regularly to bars, clubs and discos which were either all-lesbian or mixed gay (gay men and lesbians). Also, I attended various women's groups. The women's groups usually had a lesbian caucus which formed a working section of the organization. The groups, organizations or conferences of which I was a member numbered about fourteen.

The trust she developed with the core group made it easier for her to do participant observation in related groups.

From June 1975 until June 1976 I collected the major bulk of my research data. Since I had already become a trusted member of the lesbian community, my contact with other lesbians expanded into social contexts outside of my initial weekly meetings. Frequently, I was invited to lunches, dinners, parties, social gatherings. Also during this time I went to gay bars, gay clubs, lesbian bars, lesbian clubs, discos, etc. regularly. My amount of contact with the lesbian ghetto grew as my research progressed. A "promotion process" through the lesbian ghetto gave me acceptability in the ghetto, as well as validity in terms of my research role. It seemed to me that my analysis was becoming clearer and crystallized on a conceptual level.

After her extensive participant observation, Betsy Ettore was ready to draw on another method—survey research. As she writes:

> At this particular time, I wanted to test out my research concepts and in early 1976 I distributed 700 questionnaires. In February 1976 I attended a national Lesbian Conference. . . . I distributed 400 questionnaires at this time; 101 were returned to me by post. A month later (March) I distributed 300 questionnaires to lesbian magazine subscribers who were affiliated either directly (actually attended some of the meetings) or marginally (knew about the meetings) with my Tuesday evening group, which had the same name as the lesbian magazine; 100 were returned to me.

To complete the range of methods, she did two types of interviewing from March 1976 until December 1976:

> Interviews usually took place in people's home, my flat, place of employment, or at college. They lasted from between 30 minutes to two and a half hours. The average time was 45 minutes. I preceded my taped interviews with a discussion of what I was doing, the guaranteed confidence of the information and a general rundown of why I thought it was important for a sociological discussion of lesbianism to be developed. My formal interviews (20) were taped and followed a definite interview schedule. However, I often asked other lead questions which followed along with the main questions of the interview. My untaped interviews (40) usually centered around one or two lead questions, i.e., What is lesbianism? Why do you think you are a lesbian?

In sum, Betsy Ettore's data analysis techniques combined ethnographic data analysis with quantitative devices that motivated her to develop a "computer programme, Lestudy, in order to facilitate this analysis." [19]

Elissa Melamed's study of women's reactions to their aging [20] also shows how different methods were useful at different stages of her research. In the methodological introduction she writes that her book *Mirror, Mirror* was sparked by an awakening consciousness that her identity had been tied to "pleasing and attracting others (particularly men) and relying on [her] youth and looks to do this." Having turned forty, she began to question who she was apart from that "charming but static young person." Her quest was for understanding and for methods with which to understand.

> I hungered for a perspective broader than my own personal history, for comrades in struggle, and for role models: women who had made peace with aging. What better way to get what I needed than to research the subject? I thought. My early explorations were tentative. I simply began talking to women, asking them how they felt about aging. These first investigations confused me. Most of the women I talked to deprecated the youth game and minimized the amount of time, money, and effort they spent playing it. It seemed as if everyone but the woman I happened to be talking to was buying the Oil of Olay and Loving Care. And then I realized that possibly other women felt as I had: ambivalent about aging, but afraid or ashamed to say so.

Her initial research method—talking to women—was ineffective. To solve the puzzle she turned to self-disclosure:

I decided to confess to my interviewees that I had been having mixed feelings about aging myself that were hard to admit. The response to my candor was interesting. Immediately no one was neutral. Concern over aging was passionately denied (sincerely? defensively?) or it prompted outpourings of acknowledgment, confusion, resentment, and fear. . . . For me, this work of self-confrontation and sharing was profoundly healing. I realized that I had created my own personal consciousness-raising process. Communicating it to others and making it a mutual exchange seemed like the natural next step.

This phase of her quest might be called "creating a focus group."

One morning in 1978, sitting at home in the New Mexico sunshine, I decided to take that step—to create a consciousness-raising group for women over forty, a place where we could let all our age hangups show and, we hoped, re-envision the second half of life. . . . Confessing to our youth hangups. . . . And so we talked. . . . However, new obstacles appeared as our work continued. We became aware that the root causes of our problems were only partially in ourselves. No matter how ready we were to move forward in our lives, there wasn't that far to go. There simply were not enough well-paying jobs, interesting roles, or available partners for older women. In such an unsupportive environment, how could we grow to our full stature? As I began to probe this question, others presented themselves.

Elissa Melamed continued her quest by reaching out for a cross-cultural perspective:

I had begun my investigations in Santa Fe, a city of three cultures—Spanish, Indian, and "Anglo"—and had seen that aging was affected by culture. I wondered how women in other countries, not immersed in the youth culture of America, were dealing with aging. An opportunity to work in Paris gave me the chance to travel through Europe and continue my interviewing. This turned out to be easy. Since I was not attempting to do a formal study, I simply "followed my nose," letting it lead me toward a deeper understanding of women's lives. . . . I developed a questionnaire which I felt free to modify as the need arose; it is included in the appendix. . . . I talked to academics, actresses, farm wives, prostitutes, jet-setters, housecleaners, lesbians, nuns, and others; I talked to over two hundred women in seven countries. . . . If I had ever thought that this was solely an American problem, that idea was quickly dispelled. . . . It goes with urban living and the breakdown of traditional life styles more than with nationality. But it was nevertheless especially virulent among Americans. Even college-age women were affected (my youngest informant was twenty-one and my oldest, ninety-four).

She then went on to include people who had studied the issue, and to include men.

As the book took shape in my mind, I also felt the need to talk to various experts such as physicians, psychologists, and anthropologists. And I also questioned my male friends about their relation to aging.

Finally, she wrote what so many feminist researchers write, as they focus on their population or social problem of interest:

The writing of this book had taken on a new urgency for me. . . . I wanted us to create a context for making the public contribution that is as much our responsibility as it is our right. . . . Older women are currently our most underutilized natural resource—a resource we can no longer continue to neglect.[21]

In sum, Elissa Melamed's methods began with self-examination, and then moved to interviewing, self-disclosure, action research (forming a consciousness-raising group), cross-cultural interviewing, and, finally, formulating a feminist agenda for social change.

Responsiveness to the People Studied

Some feminist researchers use a wide variety of methods because all of their respondents are important to them as individuals, and yet they cannot be studied uniformly. Researchers need multiple methods if they respect individual differences. An example of this set of circumstances can be found in a study by sociologist Athena Theodore, about academic women in protest. Athena Theodore allowed the people she studied to give her information in ways they considered most suitable for them. She collected standardized information only on "age, marital status, academic degree, field, rank or position, tenure status, and number of years employed at the time of their initial protest, or at the termination of employment, if a complaint or suit was instituted after leaving the campus."

The primary material for her study was responses from approximately three-fourths (365) of the women in the final sample to an unstructured questionnaire. Imbedded in the questionnaire were items "suggesting a number of topical areas to help them recall experiences."

> The "topical reminders" in the unstructured questionnaire asked for an account of the full case, the internal grievance procedures used, encounters with government agencies and courts, interpersonal relationships relative to the case, women's studies and feminist research participation, experiences as graduate students, impact of the protest on lives and careers, and changes on campus relative to the protest actions. The amount of documentation was voluminous. Letters and memoranda, reports of various kinds, newspapers and newsletter accounts, government and court briefs and determinations were only a few of these. Some women sent entire files, their own taped biographies, and even scrapbooks containing the history of their cases.

This research project also drew on contextual information, specifically "documentation . . . from other individuals and women's organizations having information about women with pending cases. . . . some of the women's campus colleagues, other academic friends, and spouses." No stone seems to have been unturned in her quest for information:

> Copies of documents from government agencies were solicited under the Freedom of Information Act. Combined with background data, contextual data, and unstructured questionnaires, forty of the women were also interviewed from periods ranging from 30 minutes to three hours, some on an intermittent basis, during the

progress of their cases; approximately a dozen interviews were taped. Many telephone conversations, initiated by the women themselves occurred.

Her responsiveness to the women and her commitment to integrate all possible forms of data led her to produce a particularly rich feminist study of the experiences of 470 academic women "fighting employment discrimination based on sex."[22]

To conduct her study of the in vitro fertilization experience in Australia, Renate Klein combined questionnaires and interviews. She administered 40, 35-page questionnaires, followed by 25 interviews with women who responded to advertisements she had placed in leading newspapers in Melbourne in December 1986.[23] Although her study was not as large or elaborate as Athena Theodore's, Renate Klein shared Athena Theodore's desire to go beyond the questionnaires to learn what specific women had experienced. This "going beyond" one method in order to learn about experience and its distribution is characteristic of much feminist research.

Attempt to Apply Feminist Principles

In a methodologically rich study of women's studies (WS) programs in the United States, the United Kingdom, and West Germany, Renate Klein combined questionnaires, interviews, and participant observation in a self-conscious attempt to apply principles of feminist research she had culled from relevant writing on this topic. She writes that "despite serious doubts about the validity of having people fill in questionnaires, [she] decided in favour of using a questionnaire as a starting point for later follow-up interviews." As she began distributing the questionnaire, she learned that respondents' willingness to complete it depended on whether they knew her. She then followed up with an interview of 37 of the 48 people who had filled out questionnaires in Britain.

> In addition, [she] conducted spontaneous interviews with 5 US, 12 British, 3 German, 3 Australian and 2 New Zealand WS teachers. . . . The interviews took place in University offices, restaurants, trains, parks, homes/student rooms, airports and even cars.

The following is a description of her conversation-like interview process that included self-disclosure:

> In the cases where the interviewees had completed a questionnaire, we started our conversation on some specific remark they had made, but then attempted to cover the general outline of twenty interview questions which were also the basis for those who had not previously filled in the questionnaire. . . . I was very pleased when the interviews turned out to be "conversations": two-way passages of exchanging information that not only benefitted the nature of the discussion by at times bringing up unexpected and exciting topics/insights/questions for both interviewee and interviewer, but also gave me the possibility of sharing some of my experiences/knowledge of WS with the women interviewed and thus relieved my sense of "exploiting them as research objects."

An additional data collecting procedure was participant observation on numerous campuses in England, the United States, Germany, Switzerland, and Australia. Just as some of her interviews had been serendipitous, so too was some of her participant observation:

> In the UK I got some of my most significant insights into the dynamics of Women's Studies—and areas of discrepancies between its theories and its practices— from conversations I had with the MA students on our weekly train rides from London to Canterbury and back.[24]

As is clear from these excerpts, and as she explicitly acknowledges, Renate Klein also utilized experiential analysis[25] and cross-cultural analysis.

Another example of applying feminist principles is discussed at length by Janice Radway in her study, *Reading the Romance: Women, Patriarchy and Popular Culture.* This project combined content analysis, observation, and interviewing methods to collect data concerning Harlequin Romance novels and the women who read them. She began her study with a critique of the standard methods of mass-culture studies that seek to recover "the meaning contained within a singular . . . literary text" and presume that readers imbibe that meaning in a uniform way.

> [S]ince I have abandoned the particular theoretical assumptions that would have justified the presentation of my own reading as a legitimate rendering of the meaning of the genre for those who usually read it, it was necessary to formulate another method for discovering the significance of the romantic narrative.

Instead of this perspective, she adopted a stance called New Criticism that assumes readers construct the meaning of a text in relation to their own contexts. In accordance with its framework, she "developed the method . . . which depends heavily on questionnaire responses and on intensive interviews." Since she viewed readers as actively involved in constructing meaning, her method required that she study the readers, not just the texts they read. Nor could she presume that the texts compensate for problems in the readers' lives. Rather, she had to learn what the women's actual practices and readings consisted of. In her words:

> We are forced . . . by the nature of meaning itself as the construct of a reader always already situated within an interpretive context, to conduct empirical research into the identities of real readers, into the nature of the assumption they bring to the texts, and into the character of the interpretations they produce.

This methodological necessity led her to interviewing and ethnography:

> [My study] is grounded in an ethnographic examination of an actual community of romance readers who buy nearly all of their books from a single salesclerk named Dorothy Evans who has earned herself a local reputation as an "expert" on romantic fiction.
>
> My knowledge of Dot and her readers is based on roughly sixty hours of interviews conducted in June 1980 and February 1981. I have talked extensively with Dot about romances, reading and her advising activities as well as observed her interactions with her customers at the bookstore. I have also conducted both group and individual interviews with sixteen of her regular customers and admin-

istered a lengthy questionnaire to forty-two of her women, most of whom are married, middle-class mothers.

Janice Radway's notion of context extended beyond Dot and the readers, and entered into the economic matrix in which Romance novels are produced and marketed:

> [R]omantic novels do not appear miraculously in Dot's hands or in those of her readers. They are, rather the end products of a much-mediated, highly complex, material and social process that involves writers, literary agents, publishing officials, and editors, as well as hundreds of other people who participate in the manufacture, distribution, and selling of books. *Reading the Romance* begins, then, with an investigation of this process and with a consideration of the possibility that recent changes in its organization and structure may well have contributed substantially to increasing romance sales.

The assumption that readers could speak for themselves and had something to say led her to use a particular set of methods. These data-gathering techniques complemented her content analyses of the novels, a procedure she did not discard for the sake of the New Criticism. Respecting the women's views of their reading, Janice Radway also reports on her own interpretation shaped by her feminist consciousness. As she put it:

> I have attempted to offer an explanation of my informants' self-understanding that accounts also for motives and desires very likely felt by them but not admitted to consciousness precisely because they accept patriarchy as given, the natural organization of sex and gender.[26]

Her inclusion of the text, the talk, and the theory allowed her to show how the taken-for-granted assumptions of patriarchal society are part of the women's thought patterns and inform the way they interact.

The Quest Image

Feminist researchers who use multiple methods conjure up for me the traditional [male] image of the "quest for truth." Feminists embarking on important research projects are like people setting out on important journeys. As the journey continues, they draw on different methods or tools.[27] In their study of women academics, Nadya Aisenberg and Mona Harrington found that some researchers and scholars had actually internalized a self-image of being on a quest.[28]

Multimethod feminist research tends to be written in a way that reveals "the process of discovery." Initial discoveries energize the scholar to continue on her quest. When they fill her with excitement, she feels that she is on a passionate search. For example, Elinor Langer writes that in her study of Josephine Herbst, she acted "as if I were a traveler who had somehow gotten detached from my party, and Josephine Herbst were the rescuer sent out to bring me home."

Being a researcher–traveler means having a self and a body. It means abandoning the voice of "disembodied objectivity" and locating oneself in time and space. As Elinor Langer wrote, "I am writing these words at a geographical place, at a moment in time, at a point in my own history so far removed from the time I first [formulated the study].''[29] It also means acknowledging that the self changes during the journey.

Because of this experienced quest, many feminist researchers present their findings in a ''process format.'' This format, in turn, is linked to their rejection of the discourse of positivism and objectivity. Psychologists Stephanie Riger and Margaret Gordon have written on this topic and suggest some alternatives to current practice:

> We perpetuate the myth that social research is free of bias by the use of the traditional scientific format for writing up studies. The introduction section of papers always discusses previous research, and rarely mentions a personal experience or observation of the researcher that stimulated the research. . . . The use of scientific protocol in report writing seems to be a ritual: if what we do looks like science, then it must be science. And the omission of the mention of human beings (except as subjects) implies that the research is untouched by human hands, and therefore unbiased. Recently some journals have made acceptable use of the first person singular ''I'' to refer to the researcher, instead of translation of action into the passive voice. . . . In its own quiet way, this is change with revolutionary potential for social science, since it acknowledges that the research was done by a human being, with human limitations. Another small step with far-reaching implications would be to write the methods section of reports as a description of how the research was actually done, instead of reconstructing the logic of our techniques.[30]

A reflexive attitude[31] toward the entire research process from ''problem formulation'' to ''write-up'' gives rise to psychological questions (why did I do this study?) and contextual issues (what were the interpersonal or structural effects of doing this project?). Stephanie Riger and Margaret Gordon provide an example:

> On our project on rape, two secretaries burst into tears while typing papers; in the course of trying to calm them, we learned for the first time that they had been rape victims. Publicity about our project in local newspapers stimulated telephone calls from rape victims who wanted to help us in our research, or who wanted our help. It is critical that researchers be responsible for the consequences of their research; yet many do not have the skills or inclination to be counselors. Supporting women's counseling centers, and referring victims to such services may be one solution to this problem.[32]

Feminist researchers who write about research in a ''journey'' format, as a process of discovery of which the product is a part, demystify discoveries. As projects proceed, new experiences are interwoven and new voices heard. The work process of the research becomes an integral component of the issues studied. *The process becomes part of the product.* This approach is humble since ''findings'' are housed in the project's specific features, rather than claimed as disembodied truth.

Some writers begin the research report before the putative start of the project. They share with readers the childhood experiences that provide the context for undertaking the study in the first place. Sara Ruddick writes:

Temperamentally I am a pluralist. From grade school, I welcomed the idea that there were many perspectives and hence many truths. In my childhood, it was Nazis, white supremacists, and later McCarthyites who claimed to speak from a privileged standpoint. Not surprisingly, when I studied philosophy I was drawn to traditions that rejected the ambition, pervasive among philosophers, of ordering ways of knowing from the last to the most adequate. . . . In feminism too I have applauded those who reject the large picture for multiple perspectives.[33]

The person may describe how she came to write the book, why she chose the title, and even defects in the analysis of the study. Liz Stanley and Sue Wise's *Breaking Out,*[34] Robin Lakoff and Rose Lynn Sherr's *Face Value,* and Chung Yuen Kay's *At the Palace*[35] are vivid examples of studies where analysis of the author's background or experience augments more conventional research methods. In these books and others, the typical separation of the process of research from the product of research is eradicated.

Concluding Thoughts

When feminist researchers use multiple methods, the possible permutations and combinations are large. The particular combination of methods depends on the particular quest on which the researcher is embarked. Some of these quests are to link past and present; others to achieve heights of rigor, to integrate individual and social explanations of phenomena, and to test hypotheses generated in the field, as I have shown.

The use of multiple methods requires a multiskilled feminist researcher or a researcher who is able to coordinate a team of individuals with a variety of skills. It requires time and resources. Many people are obviously willing to make the investment it takes to do this type of feminist research. Some cannot.

There are compensations for the difficulties of acquiring multiple skills or making far-ranging commitments. One can be confident that a range of methods allows a range of individuals or circumstances to be understood in a responsive way. Important issues concerning women's lives can be understood in complex and thorough fashion. Researchers can then communicate this understanding to the public in a convincing manner. Multimethod research creates the opportunity to put texts or people in contexts, thus providing a richer and far more accurate interpretation.

A review of multimethod feminist research examples shows that there are many reasons feminists adopt this approach. It is also striking to me, having seen how varied these research approaches are, that feminist research is driven by its subject matter, rather than by its methods. By this I mean that feminist research will use any method available and any cluster of methods needed to answer the questions it sets for itself.

12

Original Feminist Research Methods[1]

> As some women become culture makers and as we communicate with our own students in a new idiom, we must *create new tools of thinking* and establish new norms for feminist research and action.[2]

> My methodological and material routes often have had to be *ad hoc*.[3]

This chapter discusses feminist research that claims to use "original" methods. By underscoring originality here, I do not mean to imply that work discussed in other chapters is unoriginal. There probably is very little on earth that is entirely new. "New" ideas typically are not the property of a single individual but are discovered by many people simultaneously.[4] Social factors, such as the academic culture of competition, inflate the appearance of originality. Inadequate study of the history of feminist scholarship compounds the appearance of originality by hiding our predecessors' work. Sheila Webster's concern about this matter in the field of folklore studies applies generally:

> The recent upsurge in writing by and about women should not blind us to the long line of female folklorists who have been at work since the beginnings of the discipline. . . . the blame for lack of recognition of their work lies not with these foremothers but rather with later historians and teachers of the subject.[5]

If we lack feminist mentors it is difficult to know intimately the experience of other feminist researchers and to see how our work is similar to theirs. Being unaware of developments in other disciplines abets ignorance of yet additional forerunners of our "innovations."

In the early 1960s the choice to study females rather than males seemed strikingly original to those who were doing it. From a more informed historical perspective, it would have been clear that feminist researchers had been studying women all along, and that this work had been "invisibilized" in the disciplinary canons.[6] In the 1980s feminist scholars wrote that "until recently women have played only a minor role as theorists in the social sciences" and that "women have been missing even as research subjects at the formative stages of our psychological theories."[7] Now that we have reached the 1990s, feminist researchers are less likely to claim that their study is innovative simply by virtue of a focus on women. Hopefully we are still aware of feminist research done in the 1960s,

1970s, and 1980s, but Dale Spender is skeptical about the longevity of this awareness:

> While we are prepared to put much energy into reclaiming women from the distant past, our record is not so good when it comes to preserving our more recent heritage. In fact, we have sometimes been careless about the way we have discarded that very heritage. . . . One cannot be a feminist and be unaware of the fate of feminist books. Again and again they have been published over the centuries; and again and again they have been "lost."[8]

Even if we remember that women of the "distant past" and of "our more recent heritage" did study women, we might wrongly consider *other* components of our research projects innovative. While writing *On Becoming a Social Scientist*,[9] for example, I believed mistakenly that I had invented "experiential analysis,"[10] a research approach that rejects the role of the "unembodied scientist" and adopts the role of human knower complete with feelings and ambivalence. I believed it was original to write in the first person singular and to describe the process, not simply the product, of discovery. At the same time, however, other sociologists such as Susan Krieger were working in the same way:

> I spent a year alternately picking up and putting down my interview notes before I learned that, in order to progress, I had to confront the ambivalence of my personal feelings toward the community in which I had lived and done my research. The process of exploring my own experience led me ultimately to see that feelings similar to my own were important in the accounts of the women I had interviewed and enabled me to use those feelings to guide my larger analysis.[11]

The more I developed my ideas about "experiential analysis," the more I realized that it was actually an "original" idea shared by many working independently. I subsequently learned that women in other disciplines had continuously reinvented this approach. An example from anthropology is Ruth Leah Bunzel (1898–1990) who studied the Zuni Indians of the southwestern United States. Her mentor, Franz Boas, advised studying women's pottery making, but she found they "talked . . . in a nonspecific way about their craft." To further her study,

> she became skilled at fashioning the vessels herself, and at one point she could walk about with a pot on her head, and climb a ladder balancing a pot with her hand. *The Pueblo Potter,* the result of her Zuni fieldwork, reflects Bunzel's identification with the thoughts of the women as they performed their craft.[12]

Thus my use of the term "original" does not signify a method never considered or used prior to the instance discussed here. Rather, it reflects the researcher's effort to create a new approach that met her feminist criteria.

Forms of Feminist Research Originality

Feminist research has been innovative in its choice to study particular *groups* of women formerly ignored by social science (e.g., upper-class women,[13] farm women,[14] Japanese-American domestics),[15] particular *behaviors* (e.g., feeding one's family,[16] adult adoption of orthodox religion,[17] improving one's community[18]), and new *forms of data* (e.g., "women's subjective social experience" or "subjective self").

Sociologist Meredith Gould noted that "a feminist perspective is . . . distinguished from other developments in critical sociology in that the definition of 'data' has . . . been subject to scrutiny," requiring a reassessment of "the distinction between theory and method, as well as what is meant by 'data' to begin with."[19] The search for data from everyday life has led some feminists to seek ways of studying conversation such as U.S. psychologist Nancy Henley's work on mundane activities such as interrupting. Her unobtrusively taped conversations of same-sex and mixed-sex pairs revealed that "96% of the interruptions and 100% of the overlaps in conversation were made by male speakers."[20] Bettina Aptheker also discusses the search for a methodology based on everyday life:

> [The] dailiness of women's lives structures a different way of knowing and a different way of thinking. The process that comes from this way of knowing has to be at the center of a women's politics, and it has to be at the center of a women's scholarship. . . . The point is to integrate ideas about love and healing, about balance and connection, about beauty and growing, into our everyday ways of being. We have to believe in the value of our own experiences and in the value of our ways of knowing, our ways of doing things. We have to wrap ourselves in these ways of knowing, to enact daily ceremonies of life.[21]

"New forms of data" also means texts of women and girls who were "not important figures," and physical objects that reveal the social construction of gender. Thus, feminist sociologists have examined such cultural objects as Girl Scout manuals to study gender socialization,[22] and children's art work to study gender ideology.[23] Meredith Gould considers locating innovative data essential: "Doing sociology as a feminist requires recognizing the gendered construction of social reality. . . . virtually all data are transformed by attending to the social construction of sex."[24]

The desire to recover the lives of people who left few public records (e.g., poor immigrant women) has led to the use of short stories and excerpts from novels for social research purposes.[25] Elizabeth Hampsten, a professor of English at the University of North Dakota, explains the significance of "private writing" (e.g., "letters to friends and relations, jottings in a copybook") for understanding a particular class of women that has systematically been ignored. She describes her persistent search for overlooked material concerning women in the U.S. Great Plains in the mid-nineteenth century through the early twentieth century:

> My reading falls in the fifty-year period from 1860 to 1910, most examples dating from 1880–1900. Although these years coincide with major settlement of the Northern Plains, I have not particularly sought out descriptions of that experience; in fact many writings reflect quite other ways of living.[26]

Elizabeth Hampsten's "experienced originality" consisted of doing what she calls "the reverse," i.e., using private material to illustrate something "not important."[27]

Other forms of new data were discussed in the chapter on content analysis, reflecting feminists' long tradition of text analysis.[28] In the current period, the sexism imbedded in medical textbooks,[29] cookbooks,[30] pornography,[31] and advertising has been studied extensively. Feminists have also examined the gendered nature of scientific texts. My own work in this area includes the study of metaphors, examples, and other "trivia" in sociological writing. Such research transforms "trivia" into "data" that reveal the actual "sociology" of the authors.[32]

Feminist research has also been original in its choice of *samples* of women to study. For example Mary Belenky, Blythe Clinchy, Nancy Goldberger, and Jill Tarule's research on women's intellectual development drew on clients of family agencies (which they call "the invisible college") as well as women enrolled in formal academic settings.[33] In addition, feminist research can be innovative in the way the *report itself is written*. Two examples are the work of Kathleen Mac-Pherson, a professor of nursing who studied herself studying her menopause collective,[34] and sociologist Susan Krieger, who strove to write a perspective-free book about a lesbian community. Several authors are original in the way they incorporate the research team into the project. An example is Margaret Gordon, Stephanie Riger, and Andrew Gordon's inclusion of their typists' reactions to the data as part of the research findings.[35] Some feminist writing and research are original in attributing *authorship* to a whole group, such as the Boston Women's Health Book Collective,[36] the Nebraska Sociological Feminist Collective,[37] the Combahee River Collective,[38] the Boston Lesbian Psychologies Collective,[39] and the Hunter College Women's Studies Collective.[40] *Hull-House Maps and Papers,* authored by "The Residents of Hull-House," is a notable forerunner.[41]

Much feminist research is original in *reaching beyond a single discipline*[42] and integrating material not usually discussed in academic writing. An example is Stephanie Demetrakopoulos' study of female wisdom.

> [My] methodology . . . reflects my life and my studies. . . . Due to multiple marriages and many children and stepchildren, I have been all my life steeped in different family situations and questioned the meaning of family for myself and other women. I have also been steeped in literature, art, psychology, philosophy and theology and I bring these disparate disciplines to bear throughout this book. . . . This book, then, is interdisciplinary. I hope the richness I've tried to bring to it can give women insight into what it means to exist within the body of woman.[43]

Many feminist researchers and writers have *invented words* such as herstory,[44] mythography, gynopia,[45] phallism and phallist,[46] motherwork,[47] ltmdt,[48] animal queendom,[49] gynagogy,[50] foresisters, womyn, wimmin,[51] maialogical,[52] and Ms.[53] Robin Morgan explains that instead of "demography," she labeled a section of her Statistical Prefaces in *Sisterhood Is Global* as " 'Gynography,' [her] term for sexual-politics topics . . . and [she labels] the last two sections . . .'Herstory' and 'Mythography.' "[54] Harriet Martineau developed the shocking analogy between women and slaves,[55] and Charlotte Perkins Gilman wrote of woman as horse and cow.[56] Some feminists have used new *metaphors* (e.g., organism rather than mechanism)[57] for the entire research process. Canadian social psychologist Elaine Melamed redefined research itself as "recreation" or "play." She wrote about research as a process rather than a product, about research as experience rather than work, and about research as lived rather than as done:

> Once having clarified the relationship between learning and research, I needed to conduct research in the same way that I learned. If playful learning was something I valued, then this should also be incorporated into the dissertation process. The idea of choosing one method, like adopting one style of learning, was becoming unthinkable; remaining open to experience was one of the keys to playful learning. . . . I was looking for an approach, not a method, which would enable me to develop a rigorous yet playful style. To be true to the open metaphor, it was necessary to let the phenomena lead me, and to remain open to the experience of coming to know. This is not always easy, especially in the world of academe, where we are advised to play the game according to traditional rules.[58]

Some feminists have been innovative by *alterating capitalization, grammar, or phrases*. Examples are bell hooks' conversion of the object—"the feminist movement"—into the process—"feminist movement"—and Stephanie Demetrakopoulos' verb "to sacralize." She explains that she could "use 'to make sacred' instead, but I simply need the verb without the noun because I think the verbal expression of women's spirituality is in a state of process, of beginnings, at this time."[59] Mary Daly has gone the farthest of all in this regard. In *Gyn/Ecology* she invented an entire vocabulary linking the discovery of new forms of data with new ways of naming.[60] She also recovered or rescued older words such as "witch" and "crone." In *Beyond God the Father* she makes the argument that Method is a tyrannical "false god" and that "the tyranny of methodolatry hinders new discoveries":

> it prevents us from raising questions never asked before and from being illuminated by ideas that do not fit into preestablished boxes and forms. The worshippers of Method have an effective way of handling data that does not fit into the Respectable Categories of Questions and Answers. They simply classify it as nondata, thereby rendering it invisible. It should be noted that the god Method is in fact a subordinate deity, serving Higher Powers. These are social and cultural institutions whose survival depends upon the classification of disruptive and disturbing information as nondata. Under patriarchy, Method has wiped out women's questions so totally that even women have not been able to hear and formulate our own questions to meet our own experiences. Women have been unable even to experience our own experience. This book is an effort to begin asking nonquestions and to start discovering, reporting, and analyzing nondata. It is therefore an exercise in Methodicide, a form of deicide.

Methodicide goes hand in hand with the "liberation of language." It requires seizing the power to *name* and to wrench words from their semantic fields. She writes that new words emerge when women really listen to ourselves and each other supportively. All words we hear will not be "new." Rather they will be renewed by a "semantic context that arises from qualitatively new experience."[61]

Mary Daly's point is reminiscent of what Lynn Davidman and I discovered while working on this book. Even when feminist researchers rely on traditional methods of data collection, the very asking of feminist questions and the attempt to create new knowledge in which women's experience is central can create subtle shifts. Similarly, when Mary Daly uses old words in new contexts, she shifts their meaning. These forms of originality suggest that feminism invites researchers to see, write, act, know, and speak in many new ways.

The Creation of New Methods

The rest of this chapter focuses on feminist researchers who create new qualitative or quantitative methods (or use old methods in new ways) because the knowledge they seek *requires* it. Dutch researchers Rosasharn van der Burg and Nelleke Schoemaker provide an example of quantitative research concerning work:

> The concept of labor chances (LC) must be studied: it is a complex variable and similar to the socio-economical status (SES). Once its components are known, empirical enquiries can be made in order to measure relative labor chances . . . for different groups. We will refer to the labor chances of a group as a variable of the labor chances score (LCS). Research reveals that much material is available on the background setback of women in the labor market. However, no method is known to us for the purpose of measuring LCS. This omission inspired us to construct the LCS-measuring methods as described below.[62]

Feminist psychologist Sandra Lipsitz Bem created a new scale to measure what she had experienced as true, that people can be both masculine and feminine, i.e., androgynous. Called the Bem Sex-Role Inventory, this paper-and-pencil instrument distinguishes among masculine, feminine, and androgynous individuals but treats masculinity and femininity as two orthogonal (rather than continuous) dimensions, and presents both as positive rather than the conventional format of masculinity as positive and femininity as its absence.[63]

U.S. sociologist Kathleen Barry needed multiple innovations in her qualitative study of "female sexual slavery" because research literature was nonexistent and traditional methods were not feasible:

> One cannot, for example, find a sample population of sexual slaves, survey them, and then generalize from the results. Nor is participant observation a possibility. And interviewing those held in slavery is impossible. I began to look for the women who have escaped. My approach was to find any evidence of sexual slavery wherever I could, and try to fill out fragmentary facts from interviewing people with a particular case. . . . As I received information about each case of sexual slavery, I would confirm the story by contacting people close to the case— lawyers, reporters, police, district attorneys, anti-slavery organizations, and the victims themselves whenever possible.

Her next challenge was to find ways of interviewing those women she had located:

> Interviewing these women [who had either escaped or left prostitution] presented a special problem as their life experiences had taught them that few if any people are willing to believe their victimization. Indeed, society has been unwilling to even name it as a form of victimization. As a result I conducted long open-ended interviews which provided an opportunity to sort out possible contradictions or

exaggerations. . . . As a further check, I used here only portions of the interviews when I could be satisfied with their report or that I could verify against other evidence.

Her third challenge was to understand the relation between the individual story and the larger social system:

> After days of tracking down people, getting interviews, observing trials, and filling out the details of a particular case, I would consistently find that the extreme incident that I was studying was in fact part of a pervasive practice usually existing clandestinely over many years. Not only did my investigations confirm a particular incident, but that incident in turn revealed larger practices. . . . As a result . . . I came in contact with several organizations whose titles alone suggest the seriousness of the problem. . . . My discovery of these organizations and activities was further evidence of the broad scale of the practice.

Her final challenge was to understand, as Judith Herman and Lisa Hirschman had tried for incest, societal reaction to the abomination of enslaving women for prostitution:

> Once I was convinced of the pervasiveness of the problem, the immediate question facing me was why and how female sexual slavery has remained invisible. . . . For example, most research on prostitution looks at female motivation rather than the objective conditions which bring many women into prostitution, shifting the causal assumptions from those who traffic in women to the psychological states of the women themselves. . . . [T]o sociologists they are deviants, to psychologists they are sadomasochists. Their life and experiences are construed as normal for them while they are supposedly different from the rest of us.
>
> It is in this kind of contradiction that feminists have learned to look for larger truths about female experience. It is in female sexual slavery that I have found conditions which affect all women. Because of these problems it was necessary for me to develop a perspective for analyzing both the documentation of female sexual slavery and the attitudes that define it as normal, which would reveal self-interest on the part of those who label it. . . . As I studied the attitudes that accept female enslavement, I realized that a powerful ideology stems from it and permeates the social order. I have named that ideology cultural sadism.[64]

Consciousness-Raising

Feminist legal scholar Catharine MacKinnon argued that consciousness-raising is the unique feminist method[65] because it embodies principles such as enabling women to discuss and understand their experiences from their own viewpoints. Like other feminist "innovations," consciousness-raising has its roots in women's history. In the United States women formed study clubs in the post-Civil War era so that middle-aged, middle-class women could "enlarge their mental horizons." Originally devoted to educational goals, the clubs turned "from the realm of abstract thought to the arena of practical action."[66] Some women mentioned in earlier chapters, such as Ida B. Wells, led study clubs and used them to develop group solidarity and political activism.

Consciousness-raising now refers to meetings by small groups of women over an extended period of time for the purpose of discussing personal experiences without professional leadership. In these meetings, women attempt to articulate a political analysis that will facilitate change.[67] Feminists typically do not define consciousness-raising as a research method but rather as a political, therapeutic, or educational activity. Its product is usually not a publication but a new way of thinking, relating, naming, or acting.[68] Thus, although Catharine MacKinnon considers consciousness-raising the unique feminist method, I found no examples of its research use other than a few cases that deviate from its typical meaning.

Such an example is psychologist Mary Gergen who chose a consciousness-raising model because she had "specifically . . . feminist criteria in mind." She invited seven female friends, aged 41–48, to participate in "a discussion group about the lives of women between 40–60":

> My goal was to present to a group of peers the notion that menopause marked a new era in a woman's life, when she could become freer, more self-actualized and satisfied with life than in preceding years. I expressed to them the view that the medical model of menopause (that middle-age was a time of loss and decline) was not the most advantageous social construction for us. I joined the group as a member, and invited the other group members to share in the development of the research and its outcomes.

Mary Gergen added conventional data collection techniques such as pre- and post-session questionnaires, measures of opinions about menopause and self-image, and a semantic differential rating test of 20 paired adjectives. The group held additional meetings and at one of these they tape-recorded a 1½-hour discussion:

> As the discussion facilitator, I introduced topics at various times. The first hour was devoted to the exploration of beliefs and feelings about the traditional meaning of menopause. In the last half hour, I introduced the notion of a new social construction of menopause. . . . The participants dealt with this issue during the last portion of the session.[69]

While violating the idea of leaderlessness, and having an imposed theme, Mary Gergen's group did consist of friends who discussed an issue that affected their lives and could be reinterpreted in broader terms. Her "original" research format overlaps with consciousness-raising in some ways, not others. Ann Bristow and Jody Esper also attempted to use consciousness-raising as a model for their rape research. Their format consisted of continuous dialogues between researchers and participants, among researchers, and between researchers and society.[70]

Creating Group Diaries

U.S. psychologist Terry Kramer argued that diaries combined with consciousness-raising is a feminist research method that uncovers the dynamics of women's lives.

> Numerous studies have utilized the small group and consciousness-raising group . . . for information gathering, yet few have utilized the methodology as a complement to diary research. The individual . . . benefits from . . . interaction

with others who are also involved in diary writing. . . . By sharing information, defining common problems, and arriving at solutions, the woman is able to verify her own feelings and experiences. . . . [D]iary research can provide psychology with new knowledge of what it means to be a woman. . . . As a feminist methodology, diary research will . . . enable women to define themselves on an individual and collective basis. The interaction of these two objectives can only lead to future social changes in the way women are perceived and the way in which they perceive themselves.[71]

I located two instances of what might be called a group diary, or might be labelled "write-in" to parallel "speak-out." This "group diary" was carried out by female graduate students in a department of sociology. A computer-based anonymous group diary allowed them to express themselves without fear of reprisal, while also providing a forum for the women to communicate with each other and organize for change. The text was open only to the diary contributors but others were aware of its existence. The document they produced begins with this question:

> Who is writing this?: The Graduate Women's Forum agreed last fall to develop a document which described incidents of sexism within the department. Women participating in its writing include virtually all the graduate women currently doing course work.
>
> Working anonymously and individually, women began the report by entering on the computer our descriptions and comments about being women students in the department. In some cases, a woman would write about the experience of another woman who found it impossible to write of it herself; sometimes passages were written together by two women. The process of writing, reading, responding, and rewriting was simultaneously an individual and a collective task, both a spontaneous and a reflective effort. The report grew quickly away from its original, circumscribed goal of citing individual sexist incidents. It became a collaborative work generated by the unexpressed breadth of our experience and analysis of sexism in the department, and by the unexpected synergy of writing with each other.[72]

The women viewed the computer-based group diary as a strategy for furthering a feminist agenda within the department. They undertook this writing project to challenge the dominant epistemology, research methods, and politics within sociology.

A related research method is a feminist group interview. Unlike a diary, the group interview has a leader, includes face-to-face interaction, and is time-limited. Although not derived from the methodology of focus groups—an established method in market research and a new method for sociological research[73]—feminist group interviews are similar to them in several ways. Focus groups are small groups (usually under 12 people) established by researchers for a one-time discussion of a topic. The researcher leads the discussion by asking a few questions and listens to the way the participants discuss the topic. The discussion is tape-recorded and the transcript is then analyzed.

Sociologists use focus groups to ascertain public opinion about foreign policy and other contemporary issues. Focus groups are generally not composed of "experts'' on these issues but rather attempt to tap the opinions of the general public. Using a group interview, U.S. psychologist Joan Callahan studied attitudes concerning mobility among working class women who had become psychologists. Her nine-person group interview was similar to a focus group in that the women came together for a one-time discussion of the issues. However, the women were ''experts'' in the sense that they themselves were working class women who had become psychologists. Her choice of a group interview format stemmed from Ann Oakley's ideas[74] about interviewing women and from her

> belief that the women's participation and the flow of ideas and information would be enhanced by being able to listen to each other's experience and to interact with each other. . . . a group interview format facilitates women building on each other's ideas and augments the identification of patterns through their shared experience. Because of [her] own intimate involvement with these issues, [she] coled the group interview with a colleague of [hers], Nancy Keyes, who does not come from the working class.[75]

In Germany, Frigga Haug developed a method she calls memory-work in which a group of women wrote stories about memories of different aspects of their bodies. They read these stories to each other, discussed them, and wrote analyses that drew on social theory. At the same time, they compared each other's experiences and developed complex ideas about how girls are socialized to be sexual beings alienated from their bodies.[76]

Drama

British feminist Vivienne Griffiths devised original methods to study ''how girls make sense of their experience of adolescence and what the distinctive features of this experience might be.'' Her interest was substantive and methodological, wanting to see

> how drama can be used in feminist research. . . . What started off as a seemingly straightforward enterprise raised many questions about the nature of feminist research, whether there can or should be a feminist methodology, and what might constitute a feminist approach to research, whatever methods are used. This made me reassess how important the perspective I brought to the drama was in making it feminist.

The subject matter was ''how the girls' attitude to their gender affected their present actions, including their patterns of resistance to authority and their future aspirations.'' The method was dramatic role-play:

> My research project was carried out in two mixed-sex comprehensive schools in the North of England, where I worked with . . . 51 girls aged 13–14 from different class and ethnic backgrounds (6 West Indian, 11 Asian, 34 white/Anglo-Saxon/Christian?). . . . With each group of girls, I worked in 1½ hour sessions over several weeks, taking a particular theme each week such as parent–daughter relationships, what they liked or disliked about being a girl, and their plans or hopes for the future. Many other topics were raised and developed by the girls themselves, and these I considered equally important. The way I used drama in

each session usually followed these stages: (1) a short introductory scene enacted by myself; (2) a group discussion of the scene and the issues raised by it, leading to a consideration of the general theme; (3) improvisations by the girls, working in small groups, around the areas raised in the discussion; (4) looking at some of the scenes and further discussion. For future reference, I tape-recorded my own scene, the discussion and the girls' final improvisations, and made notes of the small group work. I also made general notes about how each session went afterwards. I tried to make the introductory scenes as open-ended as possible, and at all stages to follow-up and include ideas raised by the girls. Discussions were an integral part of the process. Working in this way, I was always an active participant myself.[77]

Her article analyzes four reasons for considering drama to be a qualitative feminist method: it requires collaboration (collective story-building), it enables people to find their voice (drama is both a verbal and a nonverbal medium), it is concrete (rather than abstract), and it is context-dependent. But also, because she is a feminist.

Another example is the work of Honor Ford Smith, a Jamaican woman who helped form a drama collective with black, primarily working-class women.[78] The plays performed by the group, named Sistren, were based on stories the women told about their lives. A resulting book, *Lionheart Gal,* was originally intended to describe the work of the theater group but ended up documenting the process by which the stories were written, and presenting the stories themselves.

The stories here are told by the women of the Sistren Theatre Collective which was founded in 1977. The working-class women who make up most of the group were all drawn from the emergency employment programme . . . a special "make work" project of the democratic socialist government of 1972–1980 led by Michael Manley. Approximately 14,000 people were employed by the government to give temporary relief to the problems of unemployment. Of these about 10,000 were women. Although the work was low paid and temporary—a common feature of women's work—the fact remains that working together to earn a wage offered a space within which the women could begin to organize around their own concerns. This situation offered the women a chance to recognise that they wanted to explore their situation as women further and that they wanted to do it in a way which they would enjoy.

In 1977 I [i.e., Honor Ford Smith] was invited to direct a play for a Workers' Week concert. Thirteen women from the special employment programme came to our first meeting. I asked them what they wanted to do a play about. They said, "We want to do plays about how we suffer as women. We want to do plays about how men treat us bad." "How do you suffer as women?" I asked, and we began the long process of exchange of women's lived experience which has always characterised our work.

Sistren began, thirteen Black women and one Jamaica-white woman (apparently white woman with a partially Black ancestry), to create artifacts on women's lives or, as we put it then, "analyse and comment on the role of women in Jamaica society through theatre, to organise ourselves into a self-reliant co-operative enterprise, and to take drama to working-class communities." Since then, Sistren has become an organisation which administers a professional theatre group, a popular education project using drama as its main tool, a research project, a screen-printing project and a quarterly magazine. What we did not realise when we started was that we were drawing on a legacy of feminism in the Caribbean to begin our work as a collective.

The process for producing the book was the same as producing theater, i.e., the group "took in testimony and shaped it into a final product." They also used drawings, group interviews, and group discussions:

> "Ava's Diary," for example, began from a detailed statement she had written about her experience of domestic violence to give to the police. . . . The fact that we have worked together for many years and are ourselves an organisation meant that the interviews could go quite deep. We could often help each other to recall incidents and to sort out details, to pick out falsifications and to encourage openness. . . . After the final draft of each piece was finished each person was given hers to read. Then, in a long meeting together, we decided on the final modifications. The first draft of the whole thing was presented to the collective and read over. In long meetings we decided on the title of the collection from those proposed, how the authorship credits would go and how money from the book would be used in the collective. In addition, we decided to maintain anonymity so far as the identity of each person was concerned to protect her family and the individuals in the stories.[79]

Another feminist experiment blurring boundaries between social science and drama is the work of sociologist Marianne (Tracy) Paget. After publishing an analysis of a doctor–patient conversation in which the (male) doctor did not relate to the (female) patient's cancer,[80] she decided her article would be even more effective if viewed as theater. Tracy Paget then arranged to have the article performed.[81] In the performance, the roles of author, doctor, patient, cancer, and "concepts" became clarified. In a series of ironic, tragic events, Tracy Paget learned at that very time that she, herself, had developed cancer of the same sort as the patient in the article and play, and that her life was threatened by the same acts of miscommunication. Shortly before her death she completed the manuscript aptly titled "Life Mirrors Work Mirrors Text Mirrors Life" blurring the boundaries between life, social science, theater, and now, sadly, death.

> Strangely too, had I not thought so long about the cancer experience of the patient I examined in "On the Work of Talk," had I not watched the staging of a play in which the terror of cancer was so exquisitely expressed in the whispering of the cast, I would not have been able to describe my own circumstances so plainly. . . . Now I write about my life and my work, and my work and my life, and my writing distracts me from the immediacy of my death. My work still excites me. There is so much more to do and say.[82]

The woman Tracy Paget studied might have said the same. Vivienne Griffiths, Honor Ford Smith, and Tracy Paget clearly used the power inherent in drama to transform players and audience.

Genealogy and Network Tracing

Several feminist researchers developed genealogy[83] to trace women's relationships. Liz Stanley writes that she created this method to understand two puzzles about the African feminist, Olive Schreiner—why she was famous during her lifetime and forgotten shortly thereafter, and why she was considered to be a very sociable woman but was described after her death as unable to sustain relationships. The key is a damaging biography written by Olive Schreiner's husband, Samuel Cronwright Schreiner. To create a fresh understanding, Liz Stanley collected information about Olive Schreiner's friendships with women and constructed diagrams illustrating the friendship webs. These grids display the kinds of networks in which Olive Schreiner was embedded and help explain the type of person she was. They also show how her husband's biography was distorted and served, unwittingly or not, to diminish his wife's later literary standing. Liz Stanley's extraordinarily detailed friendship diagrams shatter the inaccurate image of Olive Schreiner and unveil her previously hidden relationships with women.[84]

Philosopher Janice Raymond uses the term "Genealogy" for the women's history method she developed in *A Passion for Friends*:

> In charting a genealogy of female friendship, it is necessary to trace the lines of contact between various groups of female friends to show that we have a common ancestry. One way to do this is to seek resemblance in diversity. A genealogical method, while demonstrating the differences between and among those who are related, establishes lines of likeness between and among groups of women in different periods of history and in disparate cultures who are apparently dissimilar. . . . [T]he intent of a genealogical tracing . . . challenges a cultural or historical relativism whose effect is to divide women from their Selves and each other. . . . An important tool of genealogy in this book is looking into the background of hetero-theory, hetero-explanations of woman-identified phenomena, and the "disciplines" of hetero-relations. . . . Looking into the background of hetero-explanations and the disciplines of hetero-relations creates a counter-memory. Counter-memory is able to glimpse that which arises in opposition to the prevailing memories of a subject or event.

She explains that doing feminist history in this genealogical way uncovers phenomena that otherwise would have been hidden:

> For example, the history, biology, and psychology of hetero-relations tell us that woman has always been "naturally" attracted to man. If this is true, counter-memory questions why hetero-relations for women have to be enforced by the myriad prohibitions against Gyn-affection, ranging from the brutalities of clitoridectomy, woman-battering, and sexual slavery to so-called soft-core pornography, which keep women "in line" with one man in particular or with men in general. . . . My method of genealogy is not concerned with defining relations of causation, the exact positioning of each clue or fragment vis-a-vis another, overall laws of symmetry between different groups of female friends, or even key periodization points. What I want to establish is a way of tracing genealogy rather than an exhaustive account of the genealogy of female friendship.

Thus, it is not only the specific topic—female friendship—but the new method—genealogy—that she is eager to share.[85]

The "genealogical" approach to the history of women and female friendships is difficult to execute but worth the effort. It inspired my attempt to create a new reading of Manya Wilbushewitz Shohat, about whom I had previously conducted biographical research.[86] In this new version I periodize her life into segments characterized by the most significant female friendship she had at the time.[87] What emerged for me was a new way of understanding her development and the role women played in each other's achievements.[88] Clearly, other researchers can adopt feminists' innovations to deal with specific problems in their own research. In other words, original feminist methods are transferable.

The Nonauthoritative Research Voice or Multiple-Person Stream-of-Consciousness Narrative

In the appendix to *The Mirror Dance*,[89] Susan Krieger explains how fiction can become a model of social science, even though it deviates from standard social science practice. Feminist foremothers who used fiction to communicate sociology are Harriet Martineau,[90] Charlotte Perkins Gilman[91] (who also wrote science fiction),[92] Mari Sandoz,[93] and Zora Neale Hurston,[94] among others, although their definition of fiction was literal and Susan Krieger's seems to be more figurative. Her definition refers to the methodological innovation of writing in a way that belies a perspective,

> an approach in which the details or evidence . . . would tell my story for me, . . . by "showing" rather than "telling". . . . I decided on a form I later came to call a multiple person stream of consciousness narrative. . . . In constructing this composite story, I considered myself to be very much a social scientist in that I was committed to developing an explanation and to being systematic in moving from my data to my interpretation. I deliberately devised and followed rules for doing this. . . . I would allow myself no analytic or theoretical commentary in the body of my text. My evidence, faithfully interpreted, would have to do this work for me. My second rule . . . was that my account should not be partial to any one person or point of view. . . . Rather it would have a primary commitment to making plain a pattern of detail in which everything was important. . . .
>
> My account was written so . . . that the reader could then draw her or his own interpretive conclusions. . . . While I did not explicitly tell my readers what to think, I did implicitly assert my own explanation as one possible alternative by structuring the situation I described at its most basic level: deciding what to admit as evidence, setting up linkages, manipulating detail, piecing together the story . . . as it seemed to me to make sense, or to be explicable.[95]

Susan Krieger wanted the radical removal of her authority as author to shock her reader into recognizing the passivity-inducing style of conventional social science writing.

> *The Mirror Dance* is clearly an experiment, both in women's language and in social science method. It is composed of an interplay of voices that echo, again and again, themes of self and community, sameness and difference, merger and separation, loss and change. Speaking in the colloquial style of the [lesbian] community, these voices provide their own narration. . . . The reader may find that, at times, the voices of these women merge with one another and become indistinguishable; individuals with different names speak as if they were one, reflecting

the extent to which the community is a community of likeness. At other times, the same persons stand out from others as separate and different, and are therefore more easily identifiable. In this way, the text illustrates its own thesis: that clarity about identity occurs through push-and-pull processes as individuals join and draw back; respond to loss and confusion; feel, on the one hand, dependence on community, and on the other, apartness from it.[96]

Deliberately working toward a perspective-free voice, she forces readers to recognize that what is conventionally called an objective social science stance is actually a particular view from a particular standpoint. Her intention was "to show more of what is 'really' going on," rather than to present an analysis limited by whatever theoretical model is in vogue at the time. She created a method that stayed close to the data and silenced her distinct voice: "I added very little of my own wording to my text beyond crediting paraphrased passages to different speakers and identifying when speakers changed. I . . . became almost absent as a narrator." This book takes a radical approach to the feminist ideal of letting women speak for themselves. "It consist[s] solely of the voices of the community with minimal transition between them and no generally integrative narrative voice." She also deliberately avoided the modifications that make for a smooth style, wanting her book to convey the disjointed feel of multiple voices and a contradictory social setting.[97]

At one point I tried to imitate Susan Krieger's method while writing *Feminist Methods in Social Research*. But, as Susan Krieger acknowledges for her book, prepublication readers considered the format cumbersome and confusing. I then reverted to transitions, analysis, and integration, introducing a perspective of my own. I would be disappointed if that decision, however, encouraged readers to rely on my interpretation. I prefer that people read the excerpts and develop their own analysis. Susan Krieger's daring, jarring, approach continues to appeal to me although I did not implement it here.

Other feminist scholars such as Jane Marcus have also experimented with this method. Using the label "direct subjectivity" to describe one end of the "curve of discourse," she believes that the more subjective the voice (i.e., the less mediated by an interpreter), the greater the potential that the material will dissolve differences between the reader and the speaker. When the differences between women are dissolved, they are better able to challenge the dominant ideology. In her words: "The ideology of patriarchy is most effectively undercut for the woman reader by the most unmediated of the voices of female experience." Jane Marcus considers the unmediated voice of women, particularly women mental patients, to be "the testimony of the victim." Such testimony is

the most violent displacer of claims to order and civilization. The less the victim speaks, the less the value of her text for subversion of an oppressive social regime. Our curve of discourse on female [madness] begins in the most subjective mode, autobiography, and moves on to fiction (or poetry); the case study, which retains strong traces of the woman's voice, is next, followed by the historical narrative of women and institutions and the literary-critical analysis of text [about madness]. The clinical psychoanalytical study is the most distancing of all, claiming the most "objectivity." Crucial to these distinctions is the authority of the narrator of each story, from victim to expert.[98]

Susan Krieger and Jane Marcus did feminist experiments with direct subjectivity and dissolving the role of the author. In their view the more "objective" the author, the more distorted the product. This innovation sets most mainstream definitions of social research on their heads.

Conversation

"Conversation" or "dialogue" is another feminist methodological invention that experiments with the nonauthorial voice by using multiple voices. An introduction to an article in two voices explains that the authors, art historians Arlene Raven and Ruth Iskin, used this format to convey open-endedness. They wrote in conversation form

> to define this new [lesbian] sensibility, search out its historical roots, and develop a theoretical understanding of its meaning and impact. The conversation is meant not as any conclusive analysis or statement but rather as a starting point in opening up insight, in developing perspective on the significance of lesbian sensibility as a metaphor for all our lives.[99]

Michal M. McCall and Judith Wittner utilized a modified "conversation" format to convey a nonauthorial voice in oral history. Their unusual article consists of components labeled Headlines, News, and Imaginary Dialogues: "From time to time we will interrupt the news with human interest stories from our own life history research."[100] In their article, no train of thought is presented in its entirety or given its complete context. Instead the authors construct a collage of "thinking fragments" that form a kaleidoscopic whole that feminist political theorist and psychoanalyst Jane Flax[101] describes as characteristic of the postmodern world. They begin an argument and then interrupt it, as people do in conversation.

Similarly, sociologist Rhoda Linton needed to invent a format to convey the originality of an experience she underwent. The result was a type of "conversation in print":

> On November 15th and 16th, 1981, 3500 women gathered in Washington, D.C., to express their fear, their rage, their sorrow, and their hope to the warlords of the Pentagon. In a two-day ritual, intricately woven into a symbolic whole, these women poured themselves into their message. . . . What [she] experienced . . . was an event so powerfully different in its approach to mass political action that she found herself seized by its inventiveness, compelled to try to conceptualize and articulate precisely what it was that made this demonstration "so different" in its approach and its impact on her.
>
> On a rainy day in late March 1982, Rhoda [Linton] sat with Michele Whitham to relate her experiences of the Women's Pentagon Action and to undertake an analysis of its unique "demonstration-ology." Rhoda chose Michele as her collaborator in this effort because of their eight year friendship, their mutual commitment to social justice and the women's movement, and Michele's professional

experience as a Freirian educator and writer on the subject of women's empowerment. What follows, then, is a conversation between two women, friends, sisters, comrades. It is an interaction—not a formal interview—organized around one woman's account and interpretation of the events of the Women's Pentagon Action, another's spontaneous response and analysis.[102]

The article then proceeds with the two women trying to do a "demonstration-ology" using a conversation format.

Philosopher Jane Martin invents a conversation to present ideas concerning the education of women. The six speakers are Plato, Jean-Jacques Rousseau, Mary Wollstonecraft, Catharine Beecher, Charlotte Perkins Gilman, and herself, all of whom lived at different times:

> We need to listen to what Wollstonecraft had to say to Rousseau, and what he had to say to Plato, and what Plato might have said to Wollstonecraft so that we do not repeat their mistakes. We need to know how Beecher's views, for all their divergence from Wollstonecraft's, contribute to the development of the latter's position, as well as how Gilman's views illuminate both Plato's and Rousseau's, and how Rousseau's views, in turn, constitute a check on hers. . . . I use the image of a conversation over time and space rather than that of a debate. The term debate suggests that a single question is being argued and there are two clear-cut positions. . . . A good conversation is neither a fight nor a contest. Circular in form, cooperative in manner, and constructive in intent, it is an interchange of ideas by those who see themselves not as adversaries but as human beings come together to talk and listen and learn from one another. . . . This is the phenomenon I have tried to capture.[103]

Jane Martin's intention is similar to artist Judy Chicago's "dinner party" in which historical figures sat and talked with each other and with those who came to look. In this vein, Mary Jo Deegan supplanted the oppositional "comments" and "rejoinders" format typical of professional journals with a "conversation" department.[104]

Finally, Kim Chernin and Renate Stendhal's book about female friendship and theory is a conversation that consists not of "she said," then "she said," but rather of "letter writing, storytelling, surprise visits, journal entries—even . . . everyday activities like flirting in cafes and changing shoes." In the foreword Shana Penn writes:

> The book's experimental form is provocative and puzzling, like a lover. . . . Chernin and Stendhal have invented a contemporary feminist dialogue recreating Plato's classic discourse between Socrates and Phaedrus on eros and beauty. In *Sex and Other Sacred Games,* too, characters talk and cruise one another. It is impossible to read about this cleverly crafted courtship without also being lured into its erotic labyrinth—and thus entangled and sometimes lost. One is always lost when traversing new territory; being lost is where the new story begins.[105]

Many feminist scholars experiment with conversation as a means of gathering and displaying data and ideas.[106] The conversation format nicely illustrates how knowledge is socially constructed, tentative, and emergent. A conversation is different from an interview with its division of labor between the party who asks

questions, and the other who answers. Reading conversations makes me very sensitive to the way single-authored writing [and published interviews] smooth out
controversy and silence voices. Conversations are harder to read because the reader
has to take part, and work out the differences; in single-voiced writing, readers
can simply sit back and "listen" to the voice of authority.

Using Intuition or Writing Associatively

In the preface of *Woman and Nature: The Roaring Inside Her,* Susan Griffin
describes the methods she used and why these methods made her study "unconventional":

> I found that I could best discover my insights about the logic of civilized man by
> going underneath logic, that is by writing associatively, and thus enlisting my
> intuition, or uncivilized self. Thus my prose in this book is like poetry, and like
> poetry always begins with feeling. One of the loudest complaints which this book
> makes about patriarchal thought (or the thought of civilized man) is that it claims
> to be objective, and separated from emotion, and so it is appropriate that the style
> of this book does not make that separation.

To avoid separating thought and emotion, she wrote her book in two voices: patriarchal thought is a detached, disembodied voice that "rarely uses a personal
pronoun, never speaks as 'I' or 'we', and almost always implies that it has found
absolute truth, or at least has the authority to do so." The feminine voice, using
both emotion and cognition, "began as [her] voice but was quickly joined by the
voices of other women, and voices from nature . . . . is an embodied voice, and
an impassioned one." So instead of a conversation between two or more people
as in Jane Marcus' work, Susan Griffin creates a conversation between two or
more parts of the self.

The preface explains the process of working on this remarkable book, different
parts of which evolved into different "physical spaces" that "began to be real for
me; passing over into work on 'Her Vision' I would feel as if I had entered a free
zone, and breathe a sigh of relief." [107] Making the same point about feminist
scholarship as Barbara DuBois in "Passionate Scholarship," [108] Susan Griffin argues that not separating emotion from cognition, or self from work, is a feminist
alternative to patriarchal thought.

In a style that might be called "feminist synthesis," the writer immerses herself in a deep nonchronological, nontopical intuitive process that differs from a
systematic review or analysis of the relevant literature. Feminist synthesis requires
passivity alternating with integration. U.S. theorist Dorothy Dinnerstein writes
about this method when describing her book *The Mermaid and the Minotaur*:

> It is a distillation from an inner reservoir in which personal experience has flowed
> together with varied streams of formal thought: social-philosophical, social-scientific,
> literary, and psychoanalytic streams, and even some streams from the experimen-
> tal study of perception and cognition, at which I have spent a good part of my
> working life. What it is then, is not a scholarly book: It makes no effort to survey
> the relevant literature. Not only would that task be (for me) unmanageably huge,

it would also be against my principles. I believe in reading unsystematically and taking notes erratically. Any effort to form a rational policy about what to take in, out of the inhuman flood of printed human utterance that pours over us daily, feels to me like a self-deluded exercise in pseudomastery. . . . [My] method is to appeal to the reader's own experience: if the result feels in any way enlightening, the argument is validated insofar as it can be.[109]

Intuition and a nonsystematic approach to reading are cognitive/emotional processes that feel like feminist innovations to those who engage in them because they defy mainstream definitions of how one should do scholarly work or science.[110] On another level, it is a feminist reworking of stream-of-consciousness blending dreams, reading, and thought. Rae Carlson wrote about this in an article that contributed significantly to altering feminist psychologists' methods: "To correct the impoverishment and imbalance in current conceptions of personality, we will need to develop our intuitive and empirical knowledge of femininity in both the agenda of psychological research and in our modes of inquiry."[111]

Identification

Forming a "deep identification" that breathes life into that which is studied and into the woman doing the study is another way in which some feminist researchers try to break out of conventional scientific strictures. The feminist scholar does not hide this identification from the reader. Instead, she discloses herself, sharing her story and inviting the reader to identify with her. Furthermore, the author frequently imbeds her process of identification in a larger personal story of "becoming" and of writing. An example is Elinor Langer's biography of Josephine Herbst, which describes her feelings about Josephine Herbst in detail. It is almost impossible for her to find words intimate enough to describe the experience of first reading Herbst's work:

For sheer absorption, for identification, I felt as I had at no other time in my life except when I read *The Golden Notebook.* . . . . A mysterious kinship linked me with this female stranger as if not only our blood but the cells of our marrow were somehow matched.[112]

Studying Manya Wilbushewitz Shohat, I had a similar sense of exhilaration. Other feminists, however, did not allow me to romanticize or misconstrue Manya just because I identified with her. They showed me that identification is useful, not "sacred."[113]

Many feminists have worked with identification as they retrieve pioneers of feminist thought and practice. In their anthology on women and symbolic interaction, for example, Mary Jo Deegan and Michael R. Hill reprint parts of Jessie Taft's doctoral dissertation, completed in 1915,[114] because they identify with her efforts and recognize the relevance of her work to our times. In her effort to retrieve Harriet Martineau for contemporary feminism,[115] Gayle Graham Yates discussed her identification explicitly:

As an English-language feminist intellectual, I think I would recognize her as my forebear and the ancestor of my culture more readily than I would identify with my illiterate Irish American great-grandmother who came to American in 1850 to escape the potato famine—or Emma Goldman, the Russian-American anarchist feminist whom I would like a great deal, and whose radical twentieth-century ideas I enjoy exploring. But Goldman and our great-grandmothers have had minimal influence on what most American and English women think, and what we socially assume even outside the range of our conscious deliberations, whereas Martineau spelled out a century ahead of us these thoughts and deliberations.

She explains her identification with Harriet Martineau in the following passage:

> Martineau's kind of radicalism rattled the whole Anglo-American cognitive universe as well as the political one. Unlike the radicalism of the Emma Goldmans, it set in place the cognitive assumptions the majority of us, whether socialist, radical, or liberal feminist, operate under today, whether fully consciously or vaguely from within our culture's orientation to the world. These assumptions are the belief in order, the belief that change will bring about betterment, the belief that knowledge is power, the belief that the individual will do good if she or he is taught the good, and, above all, the substitution of a science of society for a theological or speculative base, as the first premise for other individual and collective ideas.[116]

Although feminists obviously did not invent the stance of "identifying with" others, the renewed critique of distancing, neutrality, and objectivity[117] has revived identification as a methodological principle. Susan Krieger identified with the lesbian community she studied and appealed to her reader to identify with it as well.[118] Feminists point out that "being objective" has come to mean "making the other into an object" and "not identifying with" the other. Thus, feminists experiment with ways of "identifying with" in order to "know" the other.[119] "Identifying with" can be risky. In some situations it may bring enormous pain as I described in the chapter on interviewing. Barbara Katz Rothman's identification with the women in her study of decision-making after amniocentesis led her to write that her next book was going to be on something safe, such as flower arranging.

> I need a rest. . . . I began the project knowing there would be sad and unpleasant aspects, but not realizing the depth of it, nor how it would shake me. . . . The first questions were the woman's age at the time of her pregnancy, and the age of her baby now. Dead. It said in shaky pencil, "dead." Age of baby—dead. O my god. On no. I tore through it. She had had an amniocentesis, learned of the baby's having Down's Syndrome, and then aborted, and I had sent this idiotic, dreadful, heartless list of questions: Describe fetal movement in the last three months of pregnancy; what month had she started wearing maternity clothes, stupid, stupid questions.
>
> I dumped the box of letters requesting interviews out of my desk, searched through, and found her letter to me. No, no way I could have known from that letter. She had asked for an interview form to discuss her experience with amniocentesis. No hint of what was to come. She had aborted under pressure; she had been rushed into a decision—the doctor who told her the results over the phone said she had to decide right then, in that very phone call, so that they could schedule her abortion. She was unsure, still, if it was the right or wrong thing to do.[120]

The value of identifying lies in the enhanced understanding one can develop and assistance one can give. The drawback is the pain that comes from identifying with people who are suffering. We may gradually turn away to protect our equanimity and continue our work.

Other feminist social researchers, such as Judith DiIorio who studied "van clubs," have reported strenuously avoiding identification with nonfeminist women. Nevertheless, when doing ethnography in nonfeminist settings, they frequently are forced into traditional sex roles and find themselves identifying with the plight of such women in the settings.[121]

Feminists have also advocated "identification" in the natural sciences such as zoology and genetics. For example, neurophysiologist Ruth Bleier writes the following about Sarah Hrdy and Donna Haraway, two historians of science who

> agree that the entrance of large numbers of women into field primatology and their individual and collective feminist consciousness were responsible for upsetting long-held beliefs and assumptions (for Hrdy, paradigms; for Haraway, narratives and myths of origin). Women primatologists, Hrdy recounts, using herself as an example, identified with the female primates they were observing and with their problems, at the same time (in the 1970s) that they began to be aware of and to articulate problems that women confront in their world. Consequently, they began to formulate questions that had never been asked before concerning the behaviors and coping mechanisms of female primates. These new questions and the observations and interpretations made possible by them transformed a body of beliefs that had been central to primatology.[122]

In her biography of Nobel Prize winning geneticist, Barbara McClintock, Evelyn Fox Keller calls this way of relating "having a feeling for the organism."[123] Mary Belenky and her colleagues call it "connected knowing"[124] and Sara Ruddick calls it "maternal thinking."[125] In my view these are all forms of deep identification in which emotion, cognition, and relating are blended.

Studying Unplanned Personal Experience

Feminist researchers have been innovative in the study of their personal experiences. The impulse, as described in research reports, does not stem from opportunism or exhibitionism but rather from the desire to eradicate the distinction between the researcher and the researched. Psychologist Nancy Datan explains what she calls a "natural ethnography" of the postmastectomy experience as follows:

> It is a central tenet of feminism that women's invisible, private wounds often reflect social and political injustices. It is a commitment central to feminism to share burdens. And it is an axiom of feminism that the personal is political. It is in that spirit that I ask you to come with me in imagination where I hope nobody will ever go in fact, to a hospital bed on the morning after a mastectomy. . . . Breast cancer currently affects one of every eleven women and is expected to affect one out of ten in the near future. Of those, some will inevitably be feminists. I am one of them.[126]

Her study begins with quantitative and qualitative content analyses of the *Reach to Recovery* literature given her in bed.

Some feminist researchers start with their own experience, analyze it, and do not collect other data.[127] Others start with their experience, are troubled by it, and then collect other data to compare with their experience. Yet others intend to study other people's experience, but in the process recognize that they are part of the group studied and use this identification to deepen the study. Barbara Macdonald and Cynthia Rich exemplify the first type.[128] They studied the processes of homophobia and lesbian aging by examining their own experiences and not collecting other data. Sociologist Marianne (Tracy) Paget studied the process of confronting death as she struggled with her own terminal illness.[129] She did not collect information about other people's dying.

Feminist sociologist and psychoanalyst Jennifer Hunt exemplifies the second type. She studied her fieldwork dreams and then the dreams of other fieldworkers.[130] Similarly, I studied my miscarriage experience and then the miscarriage experiences of other women.[131] Liz Stanley and Sue Wise studied obscene phone calls received from men attempting to intimidate them.[132] Theirs is a compelling example of the disappearing distinction between "researcher" and "researched." Their nonlinear article discusses how they presented their findings to colleagues, and how those responses, in turn, became research data. They explain how their research aims to contribute to feminist theory while also "naming the oppressor." British psychologist Wendy Hollway also used her own experience, was troubled by it, and then studied the experience of others.

> I evolved a method and theory which was adequate to the psychological research I wanted to conduct about gender identity, research which was inspired by my own and others' experiences during times of change. . . . At what point can I say that I started doing research, as opposed to something which many other women were doing at the time? I was reading widely any feminist literature: history, social anthropology, political economy, language and psychoanalysis; anything on sexuality, homosexuality and sexual identity, and any social theory which seemed to address the problem of the relation between individual and social. I was also living the problem and—again like many women—keeping a journal. . . . I want this book to provide an example of an alternative theory of subjectivity and an alternative method for psychology. In my theory, this is bound to include a different relation of the researcher to participants, but it also involves a different relation of the researcher to knowledge.[133]

Florence Rush's research on child sexual molestation exemplifies the surprise of finding one is part of the group studied:

> During my many years as a social worker I observed that the pattern of the sexual abuse of children consisted of a male adult and a female child. The victims who came to my attention were primarily socially and economically deprived, but as others from advantaged backgrounds came to my attention I realized that the problem cut across all areas of society. Indeed, I painfully remembered that I, despite the amenities of a middle-class upbringing, had also been sexually abused as a child.[134]

Feminist psychologist Michelle Fine used her personal experience as a volunteer rape counsellor—a role she did not take for research purposes—to reevaluate the assumptions inherent in social psychology. The power of this "non-research project" to yield valuable insights forced her to reevaluate what occurs in formal research, particularly what is lost when we use informed consent procedures. She did not intend to do this study, but felt compelled to do so by the contradictions she encountered between "being a psychologist" and "being helpful." Studying unplanned personal experiences, just as engaging in identification, can have difficult consequences for the feminist researchers.

Structured Conceptualization

U.S. sociologist Rhoda Linton's "structured conceptualization"[135] is a type of concept mapping described in her paper "In Search of Feminist Research Methodology." She developed this method in order to be able to define the meaning of feminism "embodied in practice."[136] To do this, she systematically recorded, analyzed, and synthesized[137] information from feminists and put it in the form of a map. First, she asked feminists to generate as many ideas as possible. Next, she grouped similar ideas. And finally she used computerized statistical procedures to produce a map displaying all the ideas in relation to each other as well as in clusters named by participants. The purpose of this method was "to help feminists understand how they think," an important goal given feminists' diverse and conflicting beliefs and activities:

> The map is a picture of the thinking of the group which can reveal not only what we know we think, but also thinking of which we may not be aware, particularly that thinking which shifts when trying to incorporate diversity. Through inspection of the relationship of the clusters, using distance and direction, the map can reveal *how* we think, or on what underlying bases we organize our thinking.[138]

The "map" is a mirror that reflects women's thinking.

Photography or the Talking-Pictures Technique

Margaret Hagood, the U.S. sociologist discussed in previous chapters, was a pioneer in the use of photography for social research purposes.[139] After having studied southern U.S. tenant farming families using statistical and in-depth interview techniques, she returned to study them with a camera. With fellow sociologist Harriet Herring, and Marion Dost and Dorothea Lange, two photographers from the staff of the Farm Security Administration, "she compiled a detailed photographic record of the patterns of agriculture and farm life in the southeast. This study formed the basis for an exhibit at the University of North Carolina in 1940 and, but for the disruption of World War II, would doubtless have been made into a book."[140]

Photographs are also an integral part of contemporary feminist research.[141] Although Ximena Bunster and her colleagues Elsa Chaney, Carmen Pimente, Gabriela Vilalabos, Hilda Mercado, and Ellan Young do not state explicitly that their method of "talking pictures" was motivated by feminist concerns, they do write that they wanted to engage Peruvian proletarian working women in activities that are typically feminist. These were to "formulate their conventional, explicit and conscious rules of behavior as workers, mothers, and members of unions; to state their values, objectives in life, and aspirations . . . [to reveal] an inner world of feelings, values and significance." Ximena Bunster and her colleagues rejected interviewing as "not the best way of understanding the subjectivity of informants who may have difficulty with language." For an alternative they turned to, and then modified, the work of Margaret Mead who experimented with photography as a research method. They called their approach "talking-pictures technique," an interdisciplinary, collaborative procedure that used photographs to "promote empathy between the interviewer and interviewee and provide a fluid and fruitful context for understanding and data gathering."

To begin, a photographer and an anthropologist took Polaroid photographs of four groups of women: street vendors, market women with fixed stalls, domestic servants or maids, and factory workers. These photographs were given to the women as gifts in exchange for their continued cooperation in an investigation of "working mothers in the city to commemorate International Women's Year." Twenty-five women in the four occupational groups "allowed the photographer and the anthropologist to follow them around during daily, weekly, and monthly work and domestic routines." When the photographs were developed, [the research team] took them to the women and held "elicitation meetings" whose purpose was to choose "the most appropriate pictures to be included in the final photo-interview kit." The "subjects" thus helped define and select "the research instruments." Ximena Bunster and her colleagues asked the "informants to aid us in a tentative arrangement of scenes under researcher-defined categories. For example, which photographs would an informant pick to show the kinds of machines operated by men and by women in a factory?" Through this process, 120 photographs were chosen from the 3000 that had been shot and were pasted in a large album made for the study.

> The format, though bulky, was a versatile interviewing tool. It could be opened on the grass; we talked to many maids while they were taking care of children in parks. It could also be accommodated over crates and piles of vegetables in markets. The pictures were then combined with a structured, but open-ended questionnaire.[142]

Unlike Rorschach and Thematic Apperception Tests that offer informants ambiguous stimuli, or written questionnaires or interview guides that require literacy, the photographs were indigenous to the women who were studied. They selected the photographs and discussed them in ways that enabled the researchers to address the original study questions.

U.S. sociologist Robbie Pfeufer Kahn's review[143] of two books about birth uses photographs to organize her comments. In the review, she "reads" the photographs and projects herself into the various roles—the male physician looking at and holding the birthing woman, the birthing woman, the child being born, the other people in the room—including the role of the reader gazing at the photographs. She writes as a reader of pictures. Marianne Wex has created a book that contains "literally thousands of candid photographs of women and men, in public,

seated, standing and lying down . . . that vividly demonstrates the very systematic differences in women's and men's postures and gestures."[144] In my view, we
have barely scratched the surface of the feminist research potential of photographs. Our preference for the written word is a bias that may keep women sep-
arated from one another because we can hardly see each other. Next, I discuss
another use of technology, in this case the tape recorder.

Speaking Freely into a Tape Recorder or Answering Long, Essay-Type Questionnaires

Cheryl Boudreaux has written a proposal for a sociology doctoral dissertation that
contains, I believe, another innovative methodological twist. Her study is concerned with women's spirituality and combines thematic analysis of the journal
Womanspirit with questionnaires and interviews. Because of her unusual subject
matter, she uses a tape recorder so that a respondent can interview herself and
bypass writing:

> I will also do interviews with women who see themselves as involved in the
> women's spirituality movement and/or identify themselves as spiritual women.
> Some of these interviews will be done by phone and/or by tape recorder. I will
> send them a tape and a list of questions. This will allow them to speak freely
> about their experience with spirituality, and will allow me to interview women
> who are too far away for me to meet in person.[145]

In a related project, Dale Spender and Cheris Kramerae have developed a book,
Knowledge Explosion, based on essays solicited from 40 feminist researchers in
response to a set of 10 questions.[146] Based on the innovative feminist method of
collecting statements from as many people as cared to respond, Shere Hite has
produced three different books about sexuality and love.[147] Some individuals sent
her tapes and others sent written responses to what she calls her "long, essay-type
questionnaires." She defines her method as "scientific" and claims that critics of
her work do not understand the term "scientific." Most feminist researchers who
develop original methods do not argue that these methods meet the norms of
science, as Shere Hite does. Rather, they ignore the debate about science and
strive to find methods that fit their definition of feminism.

Some Final Thoughts

In *On Becoming a Social Scientist,* I argued that every research project should
produce substantive, methodological, and personal understanding. U.S. psychologist Terry Kramer expressed a similar idea of having multiple objectives—involving the participant so "that she is positively affected by the process," and
deriving "new knowledge which will alter the ways in which psychologists and
others perceive women and the effects of oppression on them."[148] Perhaps the
plethora of innovations relates to this desire among feminist social scientists to be
creative in multiple ways.

Not all feminist social research is innovative with regard to method. In fact, some feminist scholars regard methodological innovation as counterproductive because only studies conducted according to "rigorous" scientific procedures will convince the skeptics. For those who do not share this concern, however, feminism typically leads to the study of new topics that require or allow new forms of study. For these people, the feminist spirit is one of breaking free, including breaking free of methodological traditions.

One of the many ways the women's movement has benefitted women is in freeing up our creativity in the realm of research. And one of the ways feminist researchers, in turn, have benefitted the societies in which we live is by the spirit of innovation. Although I have listed several types of "original" research and writing, there is room for many more. As feminists gain greater control of publishing opportunities and academic positions, we will undoubtedly see evidence of more of these.

13

Conclusions

The emphasis on diversity in approaches to knowledge must carry with it *the responsibility for offering modes of integration* of the results of such inquiries.[1]

Psychologist Charlene Depner's opening remark stresses the importance of integration for studies such as this book that focus on "diversity in approaches to knowledge." But can one integrate and still reflect variety and disagreement? Bettina Aptheker's *Tapestries of Life* provides an answer:

The point . . . is not to find the lowest common denominator . . . not so much to unite as to congeal—each element retaining its integrity and value, stuck together for a particular purpose, each of us using our skills to shift and relate, adjust and integrate.[2]

I start with the definition I presented in the first chapter, that feminist methodology is the sum of feminist research methods. This concluding chapter offers a meta-induction, i.e., an inductive definition of feminist methodology that arises from the collection of the previous chapters, just as each chapter offered an inductive analysis of a particular method.

Using this approach, I have identified ten themes as follows:

1. Feminism is a perspective, not a research method.
2. Feminists use a multiplicity of research methods.
3. Feminist research involves an ongoing criticism of nonfeminist scholarship.
4. Feminist research is guided by feminist theory.
5. Feminist research may be transdisciplinary.
6. Feminist research aims to create social change.
7. Feminist research strives to represent human diversity.
8. Feminist research frequently includes the researcher as a person.
9. Feminist research frequently attempts to develop special relations with the people studied (in interactive research).
10. Feminist research frequently defines a special relation with the reader.

Although I focus on these themes, I also discuss exceptions and controversies in this chapter. In this way I hope to illustrate the dialectical process of feminist research whereby former solutions become current problems.[3] These controversies suggest that feminist researchers develop ideas by criticizing the status quo, then criticize the critique, then criticize that critique, or search for a synthesis that will itself be criticized.[4] To write a conflict-free meta-induction would be artificial and inconsistent, just as each chapter contained many dilemmas, contradictions and controversies.

Another writer whose ideas I turned to in preparing this conclusion is Belgian-American classicist and women's studies scholar, Andrée Collard. Her posthumous book, *Rape of the Wild,* offers a definition of the word "ecology" that serves as a metaphor for the relation among the parts of this chapter.

> Ecology is woman-based almost by definition. Eco means house, logos means word, speech, thought. Thus ecology is the language of the house. Defined more formally, ecology is the study of the interconnectedness between all organisms and their surroundings—the house.[5]

In the context of feminist research methodology, "ecology" suggests that feminist research is housed in various contexts. Most feminist researchers acknowledge that they are housed in particular academic disciplines and theories, and in criticism of the disciplines.[6] They are likewise connected to feminist scholarship and to the women's movement, and they live in the house of their body and personal relationships. After reading Andrée Collard's book, I came to see that what I had previously thought was separate items, was actually an ecological system of people, institutions, and ideas, connected to each other in complex ways.

Feminism Is a Perspective, Not a Method

The materials covered in the preceding chapters suggest that feminist researchers do not consider feminism to be a method. Rather they consider it to be a perspective on an existing method in a given field of inquiry or a perspective that can be used to develop an innovative method. The fact that there are multiple definitions of feminism means that there are multiple feminist perspectives on social research methods. One shared radical tenet underlying feminist research is that women's lives are important. Feminist researchers do not cynically "put" women into their scholarship so as to avoid appearing sexist. Rather, for feminist researchers females are worth examining as individuals and as people whose experience is interwoven with other women. In other words, feminists are interested in women as individuals and as a social category.

An exception to the idea of feminism being a perspective rather than a method is in a essay by Susan Leigh Star who writes:

> feminism is, in essence, a *method*—a method of strategic heresy—a method for understanding, from a marginal or boundary-dwelling perspective, one's *own* participation in socially constructed realities, both politically and personally, both socially and cognitively. . . . feminism, viewed methodologically, is an emergent scientific method—one which begins with the death of the subjectivity/objectivity dichotomy and which involves questioning the very bases of socialization and perception.[7]

Although she calls feminism a method, I believe she actually is referring to a perspective. If this is so, her statement helps define an important property of feminist perspectives on research. Her description of "strategic heresy" coincides with Catharine MacKinnon's "rational skepticism of handed-down doctrine,"[8] Marge DeVault's "strategic imprecision,"[9] Elisabeth Schuessler Fiorenza's "hermeneutics of suspicion,"[10] Judith Fetterley's "resistant reading,"[11] Celia Kitzinger's "resisting the discipline,"[12] and my own discussion of "feminist distrust."[13] These terms refer to cognitive/emotional frameworks or *attitudes,* rather than to a set of guidelines for conducting research. Susan Star writes that "heresy is a generic term, meaning that which differs cognitively from the central assumptions of a given society or system." To adopt the perspective of strategic heresy is to engage in deliberate cognitive deviance. To be a heretic is to be purposively different. In her view, feminism is

> historically heretical, challenging the prevailing power structures and assumptions of androcentrism in science and society; feminism is also processually, directionally heretical. . . . "strategic" indicates that this cognitive difference is not simply de facto or arbitrary, but that there is a direction, a strategy, a self-consciousness, which emerges both against the forms of control of the dominant society and from the heretical vision of the possible.[14]

Heresy is a religious concept. It implies that nonfeminist scholarship is a religion with rituals, priests, taboos, and canons.

Criticizing this idea, sociologist Ellen Stone tries to create a different feminist perspective for research, an alternative to distrust, heresy, imprecision, and suspicion. Following a dialectic model, she is working on "feminist belief." In her view, we need to operate with *both* feminist distrust and feminist belief, a more complex perspective:

> We need a different stance in relation to the voices of subordinated cultures—one I call, for the moment, "feminist belief." Feminist belief means putting aside our conditioned responses and allowing ourselves to experience total receptivity to "the other." It means before subjecting previously silenced voices to our critical faculties, we need to take them in to find out how they resonate and what their truth might mean for us.[15]

Several of the projects reviewed in the previous chapters wavered between distrust and belief, an important tension in feminist research methods. Belief is the attitude of the oral historian who wants to "give voice to the voiceless" and the interviewer who believes the interviewee. For example, white U.S. sociologist Kathleen McCourt studied working-class women because they "have been without organized voice and . . . have been absent from the consideration of those who make public and corporate policy."[16] When she found that many of these women were prejudiced against blacks, however, her distrust was invoked. Her book struggles with the tension between the two as she attempts to coordinate material about class, race, and gender.

Feminist social research—whether conducted from a position of distrust, belief, or a tension between them—is research that requires a method supplied by the disciplines (e.g., experimentation, ethnography, survey research, content analysis) or created by the researcher (e.g., drama, genealogy, group diaries). That method is not supplied by feminism itself. The researcher has to learn the disciplinary methods, rules of logic, statistical procedures, procedures for "writing up" research projects, and whatever else is relevant to the field in which she wishes to work. She may learn them only to criticize them, but she has to learn them nonetheless. My chapter on action research referred to Liz Stanley and Sue Wise's analysis of Nancy Kleiber and Linda Light's work. Their analysis is a good example of this point. They write that Kleiber and Light rejected objectivity without rejecting "basic standards" of research; they utilized "very traditional" methods but formulated a new role for "the researched" as recipients and users of feminist research.[17]

[margin handwritten note: Most know the rules before you can claim to be consciously breaking them.]

Feminism supplies the perspective and the disciplines supply the method. The feminist researcher exists at their intersection—feeling like she has a second shift or double burden, or feeling her research will benefit from the tension. Her feminist perspective is continuously elaborated in the light of a changing world and accumulating feminist scholarship. Feminist research, thus, is grounded in two worlds—the world of the discipline, academy, or funder, and the world of feminist scholarship. This two-world position is another reason that feminist researchers have to operate both with distrust and belief, or as discussed in the chapter on surveys, with dual vision.

Feminists Use a Multiplicity of Research Methods

The materials analyzed in this book demonstrate that social research has many feminist voices. Clearly, there is no single "feminist way" to do research. There is little "methodological elitism" or definition of "methodological correctness" in feminist research. Rather there is a lot of individual creativity and variety. There is even creativity about the labels feminist researchers apply to their research projects, a characteristic particularly prominent in interviewing and oral history research.

Feminists demonstrate creativity in the choice of metaphors to characterize research—everything from science to journey to play. Feminist research is amoeba-like; it goes everywhere, in every direction. It reaches into all the disciplines and uses all the methods, sometimes singly and sometimes in combinations. The amoeba is fed by the women's movement. The women's movement, in turn, is fed by women's outrage and hope.

In certain cases, feminist researchers adopt the methods of their discipline without any major modification. They use a discipline for its power, turning its power to feminist ends. In feminist experimental research, for example, although feminist psychologists voiced a great deal of self-criticism, there was little actual modification of experimental design except in terms of the sex of the subjects and the definition of comparison groups. In other instances, feminist researchers found that a method must be modified to meet the demands of feminist research. An example was Vicky Randall's case[18] of using unconventional data about women's political participation in order to undermine the system of male dominance (de-

[margin handwritten note: Use trad. methods for their p[ower].]

scribed in the chapter on cross-cultural research). In other instances, researchers confront major challenges in the work they want to do, and respond by creating what they experience as "original methods" or effective "action research." To develop "original" methods, the feminist researcher needs to free her imagination as she strives to find methods that meet her research questions.

Unfortunately, essays about feminist methodology do not always reflect the multiplicity of feminist research methods, and thus sometimes are at odds with what feminist researchers actually do.[19] Feminist researchers adopt strict conventional methods when they want to utilize "the most rigorous, scientifically sound methodology,"[20] as Diana Russell and Ronnie Steinberg explained. They modify conventional methods when they want to introduce specific feminist elements, such as in the work of Ann Oakley, Meredith Gould, and Sheryl Ruzek. And they create innovative methods if they find conventional methods to be inadequate, as in the work of Jane Addams, Ximena Bunster, Kathleen Barry, Frances Kellor, Patti Lather, Liz Stanley, and others.

Since feminism is a large movement without official leaders,[21] it is not surprising that we lack a single definition of how to do feminist research. In fact, since we value working in all the disciplines and using all the methods, there has been interest in expanding the feminist reach as much as possible, not in narrowing it. We are likely to protest if any particular method receives short shrift in the name of feminism. This demand for openness led U.S. sociologists Nancy Chodorow and Barrie Thorne to protest what they saw as the potentially narrow editorial position of the journal *Gender & Society*. They wrote that they were "troubled by a tendency in feminist sociology . . . to narrow our methods and theories."[22] In response, the editor reaffirmed a pluralist approach.

The emphasis on multiplicity has revived less frequently used social research methods, such as oral history, case studies, and content analysis. Because feminists value inclusiveness more than orthodoxy, we allow room for creativity in all aspects of the research process, including terminology. Even among users of one particular method, there is a variety of approaches, which in turn leads to controversy, as seen in discussions about self-disclosure in interviewing.

This emphasis on inclusiveness in feminist research methods has been productive and has contributed to what Jessie Bernard calls the Female Renaissance or Feminist Enlightenment.[23] Clearly, the empowering impact of the women's movement has led to a massive outpouring of scholarly feminist literature and to the creation of new vehicles for the publication of feminist research. At the same time the United Nations Decade for Women contributed to global consciousness-raising, which fostered responsibility for producing knowledge. Similarly, nineteenth-century U.S. women's protest against discrimination in higher education had an impact on social research. In that case, as we have seen, women initiated the use of interviews, social surveys, and statistics to challenge and invalidate misperceptions about women. The current Feminist Renaissance is rooted in this earlier period.[24]

Multiplicity of methods allows us to study the greatest possible range of subject matters and reach a broad set of goals. Feminist interview and oral history research enable us to hear women's experiences; feminist case studies, cross-cultural research, and ethnography let us understand women in their contexts; feminist surveys allow us to understand variations within and among populations; and feminist experiments make it possible to measure behaviors and attitudes without contextual distractions, to mention only a few.

My finding of methodological multiplicity coincides with several scholars' belief that there have been stages of feminist scholarship.[25] I agree with people such as Gerda Lerner and Cheri Register who write that multiplicity is the hallmark of the current stage, which Cheri Register calls "stage 4." Using literary studies as her example, she writes that in the first stage, we insisted that "there had been great female writers, naming the tokens the critical establishment had already selected." In the second stage, "we looked for pejorative images of women in men's literature and for proof of victimization in women's." In the third stage, "we sought out writers who were socially conscious and angry." And now in the fourth stage, "we tolerate multiple feminist readings of a single work, allowing them all some claim to ideological validity."[26]

Revising Cheri Register's model, I suggest that we are accumulating stages rather than leaving any behind. This is an important distinction, because "stage theories" imply that the present is better than the past, an implication I wish to avoid. Stage theories inadvertently downplay the possibility that people in past generations carried out what people today believe they are inventing. They also create a false homogeneity to describe the work of a given historic period. I found instead that *all* the stages exist simultaneously, and that a woman may go through multiple stages even while working on a single project.

Elaine Hobby wrote about this experience in her work on a book of English women's writings (1649–88):

> When I started this project, in 1979, I "simply" wanted to find out about forgotten women writers, because studying English literature had meant almost solely studying men's writing. I just wanted to know what was there, and wanted to share what I discovered with other women. . . . As the work continued, my perspective shifted. . . . When I began this study, I was working on "forgotten women." By time it was finished, I was concerned with the problem of what happens to subordinate groups living under reactionary regimes, and what happens to radicals when they lose their vision, their sense of purpose.[27]

Just as Elaine Hobby developed different feminist approaches as her project evolved, so too, I found that individual feminist researchers demonstrated different perspectives in various projects. Some people are competent in numerous methods and utilize different feminist perspectives in each project. Valuing multiplicity also underpins the use of multiple methods in a single project.

Multiplicity of perspectives is not a new characteristic of feminist research. Feminists have long done research without consensus.[28] Over time, we have simply exhibited increasing diversity. For this reason, we have fewer guidelines for conducting feminist research than for avoiding sexist methods. My overview of feminist research coincides with a similar statement by anthropologist Marilyn Strathern:

> Much feminist discourse is constructed in a plural way. Arguments are juxtaposed, many voices solicited, in the way that feminists speak about their own

scholarship. There are no central texts, no definitive techniques; the deliberate transdisciplinary enterprise plays with context. Perspectives from different disciplines are held to illumine one another; historical or literary or anthropological insights are juxtaposed by writers at once conscious of the different contexts of these disciplines and refusing to take any single context as an organizing frame.[29]

Because of this disdain for "central texts" or "definitive techniques," discussions of feminist research methods usually do not rely on exemplars.[30] More important is the critique from which research arose in the first place. Perhaps this is why we so frequently reprint articles critical of mainstream methods.

Feminist research's multiplicity does not make it idiosyncratic. On the contrary, it is strikingly cumulative. Research projects build on each other in order to obtain increasingly accurate, imaginative, and useful answers to persistent problems. Theories developed in one country are explored in another. Feminists do case histories to investigate exceptions or key events that other feminist researchers have delineated. Thus the pronounced multiplicity of feminist research includes our looking to each other for concepts, research designs, theories, and inspiration.

Feminist research voices are not free-standing. Rather they are rooted in and draw on many mainstream and critical theoretical traditions.[31] For example, anthropologist Gayle Rubin connects feminist research to Marxist theory,[32] Nancy Chodorow develops feminist research from object relations theory,[33] Louise Levesque-Lopman from phenomenology,[34] Zillah Eisenstein from postpositivism,[35] Mary Jo Deegan and Michael R. Hill from symbolic interactionism,[36] Susan Volentine and Stanley Brodsky from "personal construct" theory,[37] Sarah Fenstermaker Berk from the New Home Economics,[38] Laura Olson from economic and gerontological theory,[39] Wendy McKenna and Sarah Kessler from ethnomethodological theory,[40] and so on.

Just as is true with researchers who are not feminist, feminist researchers use theory in three different relations to data: to explain data, to generate theory, and to test theory. Psychologists Abigail Stewart and David Winter, for example, studied the causes of female oppression (they use the term "suppression") by applying "psychological techniques of data analysis . . . to broader fields of inquiry," thereby "answering theoretical controversy."[41] Feminist researchers frequently do case studies to test theory or use ethnographic research methods to generate theory. Feminist political science research deals with theories of citizen participation, and feminist psychology with theories of psychosocial or moral development. Theories that originate in the disciplines constitute one of the ecological systems in which feminist research lives. Feminist researchers cleverly devise ways of combining aspects of mainstream theory in a larger feminist framework. Feminist research, I believe, contributes to the disciplines, draws from the disciplines, and reacts against the disciplines in terms of data, methods, and theory.

I do not want to paint an overly rosy picture, however. The overwhelming multiplicity of feminist research approaches may still silence voices on the margins. Despite the fact that we may be witnessing a Female Renaissance, most women are still "excluded from the production of forms of thought, images and symbols in which their experience and social relations are expressed and ordered."[42] Moreover, the most innovative voices of feminist research are probably hampered by journal and book editors, and by constraints of space, time, money, and work. It is possible that the truly radical voices are driven out of the academy because, as Jo Freeman wrote, "[The academic] world does not look favorably upon serious dissidents from the status quo—especially if such dissidents are brash enough to live their beliefs (as feminism requires)."[43]

Not necessarily accepted methods

While Jo Freeman is undoubtedly correct, it is also true that the tenure system protects some women who are "not looked upon favorably." This feature of university organization protects radical voices if they have passed over the tenure hurdle in the first place. One of the important objectives of U.S. feminist activities of the previous generation was to enable the current generation to jump over that hurdle. The ability of contemporary lesbian and straight, radical and liberal, black and white, old and young feminists to speak, write, and teach is a gift from our foremothers,[44] not simply a reflection of our individual talents or current policies.

But do you have to tow the line first, to get tenure.

Ongoing Criticism of Nonfeminist Scholarship

Despite this multiplicity, feminism is not open to everything. Rather, since feminist researchers are critics, we constantly are on the look-out for what we perceive to be nonfeminist consciousness. "Feminist distrust" prevents us from accepting uncritically the conventions of any academic discipline. Sometimes, when we do not criticize mainstream methods, we explain why this is so, pointing out that in order to create policy changes we must use the most widely accepted definition of scientific method. Thus in the chapter on experiments I found that feminist psychologists criticized the method, but also defended it for its potential to create policies beneficial to women.

The materials in this book demonstrate that over time we have *not* lost interest in uncovering patriarchal bias in social science. With freshness and urgency current students and long-established scholars continue to criticize the influence of patriarchy on social research. Studying women's experience in social context provides feminist researchers with a new perspective on information derived from the study of men, the male world or androcentric research. Sociologist Sharon Mast, for example, reports on "discussions of the methodology appropriate to feminist research . . . in New Zealand journals and professional meetings"[45] in the last five years. Having discovered that the material we once relied on is not sufficiently nourishing, we have turned to feminist scholarship to satisfy our hunger for knowledge.

Around the globe we continue to work on questions raised more than two decades ago concerning the relation between feminism and social research. We continue to write essays about the possible affinity between gender and research methods. We continue to discover ways in which previously gathered information has been distorted by androcentrism. And we continue to identify topics that have been male-centered and need to be rethought in terms of women's experiences.

This rethinking views all social, psychological, and economic phenomena as gendered and embedded in power relations.

There is no reason to expect that this work of "undistorting" will wane, given the vast feminist project to reevaluate and reform knowledge. Rather, the opposite is true: the greater the development of feminist consciousness, the greater the ability to detect problems of sexism. Improvement in communication technology and the steady flow of feminists into research positions increase the scope and volume of feminist research.

I do not wish to give the impression, however, that the continuing critique always leads to neat resolutions. Feminist researchers have also identified problems in conventional frameworks without being able to rectify them. Some examples are the problem of defining a woman's social class independent of her husband's, if she is married,[46] naming relations to children for the purpose of studying lesbian family life, naming women's community activity as a form of political participation although it may be outside conventional political party structures,[47] defining historical periods to reflect women's lives,[48] and developing a concept of career that fits women's work experience. A recent book by Helena Lopata, Cheryl Miller, and Debra Barnewolt illustrates this point. In a study of careers, their finding that the women's definition was sharply at variance with "what even disagreeing sociologists have in mind" led them to use "the concept of career as understood by the women in the sample."[49]

Much feminist research claims to name new topics, to examine the invisible, to study the unstudied, and to ask why it had been ignored. Carolyn Sachs is one of many researchers who expressed concern that "facts are so often overlooked," in her case, facts about women farmers.[50] Similarly, Jean Reith Schroedel "demanded to know where the working-class women were in literature."[51] Since she did not receive a satisfactory answer, she produced an oral history collection. In the same spirit, Ellen Stone and I compiled a reader with the title *Looking at Invisible Women: An Exercise in Feminist Pedagogy*, based on the work of undergraduates who studied "invisible" female sociologists. Working together, we are developing a feminist perspective on the history of sociology[52] that I call the "sociology of the lack of knowledge." This perspective contrasts with the conventional "sociology of knowledge," which studies how knowledge, information, science, and scholarship reflect the social class position or other interests of its producers. A "sociology of the lack of knowledge" examines how and why knowledge is not produced, is obliterated, or is not incorporated into a canon. In my view, feminist researchers have made an enormous contribution to "the sociology of the lack of knowledge." We have demonstrated how certain people are ignored, their words discounted, and their place in history overlooked. We have shown how certain things are not studied and other things are not even named.

Making the invisible visible, bringing the margin to the center, rendering the trivial important, putting the spotlight on women as competent actors, understanding women as subjects in their own right rather than objects for men—all continue to be elements of feminist research. Looking at the world through women's eyes and seeing how the lack of knowledge is constructed are themes running through feminist research. They reflect the fact that feminist research is grounded both in the disciplines and in a critique of them.

Feminist Research Is Guided
by Feminist Theory

Empirical feminist research is guided by feminist theory, and sometimes by critical and mainstream disciplinary theory as mentioned above. For example, Linda Valli's study of women's work and education, as described in the chapter on feminist ethnography,[53] combines disciplinary and feminist theories. She draws on sociological, economic, and psychological literatures concerning stratification, education, and remunerated labor, and on feminist theory about the definition of work, access to work, and the relation between work, gender, and family. Feminist researchers almost always utilize feminist theory to frame questions and interpret their data. Frequently, in feminist research, gender or femaleness is the variable and power/experience/action the relation under investigation.[54] Feminist social research utilizes feminist theory in part because other theoretical traditions ignore or downplay the interaction of gender and power. Some feminist researchers write that data in feminist research projects *must be* explained by feminist theory.

British sociologist Sylvia Walby and U.S. sociologist Rosabeth Kanter find feminist theory essential because mainstream sociology minimizes gender relations in favor of class.[55] Feminist research concerning incest, to take another example, frames questions in terms of the gender and power of offenders and victims. In contrast, mainstream literature frames its questions in terms of sexuality, deviance, or mental illness. At the conclusion of their study of incest, for example, Judith Herman and Lisa Hirschman wrote that "a frankly feminist perspective [male supremacy/female oppression] offers the best explanation of the existing data," because otherwise one cannot understand "why the vast majority of perpetrators (uncles, older brothers, stepfathers, and fathers) are male, and why the majority of victims (nieces, younger sisters, and daughters) are female." Only a feminist analysis can explain

> why the reality of incest was for so long suppressed by supposedly responsible professional investigators, why public discussion of the subject awaited the women's liberation movement, or why the recent apologists for incest have been popular men's magazines and the closely allied, all-male Institute for Sex Research.[56]

Similarly, sociologist Terry Arendell wrote forcefully about the necessity of utilizing feminist theory to understand data concerning divorce because "divorce is a socially structured experience that reflects the gender-based organization of our society, with all its related inequities."[57] Using feminist theory, feminist researchers attempt to demonstrate the reach of the political into areas typically assumed to be personal, in addition to areas always thought of as political. A feminist perspective means being able to see and analyze gender politics and gender conflict.

Openness to Being Transdisciplinary

In 1978 sociologist Judith Long wrote that feminist scholarship was always interdisciplinary.[58] Four years later psychologist Carolyn Sherif argued that when feminist methodology emerged, it would be cross-disciplinary. She predicted we would use the term "feminist methodology" when we "recognize the need for cross-disciplinary inquiry and the coordination of findings from historical, sociocultural, political, economic, sociopsychological, and bio-psychological analyses in the study of specific problems of human experience and action."[59]

Whether feminist research always has been, is currently, or will be cross-disciplinary seems less important than the fact of an affinity between feminist research and cross-disciplinary work. Feminist research thus not only stretches methodological norms, it also reaches across disciplinary boundaries. As a postmodern phenomenon, it blurs genres by blurring disciplines.[60] It draws on ideas in different disciplines or as U.S. sociologist Mary Ann Campbell put it, it "subsumes a discipline,"[61] rather than the other way around. Psychologist Carol Nagy Jacklin is one of many who enthusiastically endorses cross-disciplinary work. She supports "truly interdisciplinary exchange" and real controversy as "a new academic 'voice,' a break from the male-dominated tradition of confrontational debate."[62] Sometimes feminist research considers its only true home to be the inter- or transdisciplinary field of women's studies.

Feminists seem particularly drawn to work on the borders of, and outside, their fields. As "connected knowers," we live in two worlds and find ways of bridging or blending disciplines.[63] Feminists seem not to feel alienated from fields other than the one(s) in which we have been educated. Sociologist Marcia Westkott, for example, studied the writings of a psychoanalyst [Karen Horney] "to develop a social psychology of women,"[64] while Nancy Chodorow used psychoanalytic theory to develop a new conception of early childhood gender identification. Sociologist Sondra Farganis analyzed a work of fiction—Margaret Atwood's *The Handmaid's Tale*[65]—and Kathleen Barry, Mary Jo Deegan, Karen Hansen, Michael R. Hill, Judith Long, and I, among many others, have reached from sociology into feminist biography and history. Liz Stanley even insists that feminism *requires* that we move from sociology into history in order to understand and "act upon our present."[66] Other feminist sociologists have worked in literary criticism, philosophy, and legal studies. The ability to connect different disciplines may also reflect the general sense of connectedness that Carol Gilligan found to be the hallmark of female moral reasoning.[67] As Carolyn Sherif predicted, venturing beyond one's formal discipline has indeed become a hallmark of much feminist research. Being open to a cross-disciplinary framework does not mean, however, that *all* feminist research has been, is, or will be cross-disciplinary.

Given this openness to other disciplines, I find it surprising that few feminist researchers seem to know much about women of the past who have contributed to their own disciplines. In my search for feminist research literature, I found little acknowledgment of the continuity between the work of nineteenth-century feminist social scientists and of the current period. I hope my efforts raise the historical consciousness of feminist researchers concerning their disciplines.

The Effort to Create Social Change

In addition to the connection with theory, much feminist research is connected to social change and social policy questions. In *Good and Mad Women,* for example, Australian historian Jill Matthews proposes "to understand the lives of Australian women in order that we might change our condition of subordination."[68] Even when a feminist conducts so-called basic research she might conclude with suggestions about how readers can use the findings. Explicit policy recommendations are typical in feminist research. For example, sociologist Barbara Reskin concluded a study of the continuing wage gap between women and men by asking "how can we bring about change?" and answering "increasing the costs men pay to maintain the status quo or rewarding men for dividing resources more equitably may reduce their resistance."[69] The international feminist community remains concerned that social research both contribute to the welfare of women and contribute to knowledge. This is the dual vision[70]—or dual responsibility—that many feminist researchers see as part of their multiple responsibilities. It is part of the general burden on women to satisfy multiple constituencies (including themselves) simultaneously.

For many feminists, research is obligated to contribute to social change through consciousness-raising or specific policy recommendations. In a paper delivered at the 1981 meeting of the American Psychological Association, for example, psychologist Gloria Levin urged feminist researchers to anticipate policy shifts and to conduct studies that policy makers could use. She encouraged feminist researchers to forge direct links with policy makers, the media, and policy-relevant organizations.[71] Although lamenting the fact that feminist researchers have not yet adequately done so, she expected they could. The gradual emergence of women's research centers and policy institutes provides structural support for this kind of work.

An example of the way feminist researchers feed their work directly to policy makers occurred at a meeting in spring 1990 organized in Washington, D.C., by the National Women's Political Caucus (NWPC).

> Over a hundred NWPC National Steering Committee members came to town . . . and joined representatives of other women's groups to hear the "experts" as they presented summaries of their analyses, case studies, and future projections. Political analyst Celinda Lake started . . . with an overview of women's particular voting habits. Roberta Spalter-Roth outlined single mothers' wages and also looked at the economic loss suffered by families without a job-guaranteed family leave policy. Rachel Gold presented hot-off-the-press facts about abortion and women's health. NWPC members used these statistics when they visited their Congress members later in the day, including the fact that 75% of the girls under

16 include parents in an abortion decision and that only one pharmaceutical company continues to manufacture birth control products.[72]

On the local level, feminists conduct surveys of local problems in communities and workplaces to rectify social problems.

This connection to social change makes much feminist research practical as well as scholarly. The practical side is evident in books and articles containing suggestions for direct action that could be taken. In the words of U.S. sociologist Margaret Andersen,

> feminist studies in sociology are not intended to construct abstract empirical analyses of gender, nor to develop grand theories that have no relevance to the lives of actual human beings. . . . [rather] their purpose is the transformation of gender relations and the society in which we live.[73]

I believe feminist social research does all of the above—it constructs abstract empirical analysis of gender, it develops grand theory, *and* it attempts to transform gender relations and the societies in which we live. Cases in point are Nancy Chodorow's theoretical work on gender and family relations that concludes with her advocacy of "equal parenting,"[74] Lenore Weitzman's study of "no-fault divorce" that concludes with a discussion of laws that could promote "fair divorce,"[75] and Susan Yeandle's discussion of the relation between women's paid employment and household responsibilities that concludes with a discussion of theoretical and policy implications.[76] So too, political scientist Jane Mansbridge ends her theoretical and empirical analysis of the failure of the ERA campaign with a recommendation that the campaign not be revived,[77] and Kristin Luker ends her discussion of the pro-life and pro-choice movements with strategic recommendations for the pro-choice movement.[78]

Feminist Research Strives to Recognize Diversity

Feminism acknowledges the paradox that women are all alike in some ways and dissimilar in others. Females include people (and animals) whose ages range from birth to death and who live in all geographic areas. Our economic situation ranges from poor to wealthy. Our sexual orientations range from celibate, to homosexual, bisexual, heterosexual, or any combination of these at various times in our lives. Our reproductive status varies and we believe in the whole gamut of religions or do not believe at all. Some of us are prisoners, others are jailers, lawyers, judges, jurors, and victims. Some of us are sick, disabled, healthy, or dying. We have the full range of political persuasions or no political consciousness at all. We belong to every race and ethnicity.

Feminists take pride in recognizing women's diversity. For example, psychologist Joanna Rohrbaugh writes that recognition of women's diversity is the single undeniable impact that feminism has had on psychology.[79] Feminists also criticize mainstream research in all the disciplines for its blindness to women's diversity. For example, Irish historian Hasia R. Diner writes:

That immigrant women have not been studied is not because the material was not there. That poor, working-class women have not been studied is not because they were "inarticulate." It may be more accurate to say that historians, with their own biases of gender, class, and culture, have been basically deaf to the voices of such women and have assumed that they could not be studied.[80]

Diversity has become a new criterion for feminist research excellence. Susan Geiger, for example, wrote that oral histories can fulfill their potential only if they "reach out to study the greatest possible diversity among women."[81] Arlene Kaplan Daniels, discussed in the chapter on cross-cultural research, wrote that feminists too often

> write about the problems of white women in America (sic) as though they were generic to womankind. Maybe they are, sometimes, but we need the consciousness of examining issues, always and everywhere, with an eye to how widely they apply.[82]

Survey researchers Graham Staines, Carol Tavris, and Toby Epstein Jayaratne wrote that "diversity of women, of many occupations and philosophies" is necessary for even a preliminary empirical look at the Queen Bee syndrome,"[83] the phenomenon they were studying.

In Jill Matthews' view, we also have to recognize the diversity within the individual woman:

> Women are both different among themselves, and different from men, and such diversity must be accommodated in any women's history. . . . Beyond acknowledgment of diversity among the groups of women, there is the need to acknowledge the diversity of each individual woman. There are neither heroines nor villains who are exclusively that.[84]

In feminist hands, affirmative action to alter social institutions has become affirmative action to alter research projects. For example the study by Mary Belenky and her colleagues of women's cognitive styles, included women from nine different academic institutions and "invisible colleges" and from three different family agencies, one of which was in an extremely isolated, impoverished rural area. As they put it, "Bringing together people of such diverse ages, circumstances and outlooks departs from common practice in psychological research."[85] Historian Gerda Lerner, to give another example, "sought . . . documentary selections as representative as the available sources would permit, reflecting variations as to age, economic class, race, religion, and ethnicity."[86] The feminist research goal seems to have changed from Gerda Lerner's earlier "reflecting variations" (of race, class, age, etc.) to the current goal of "showing intersections" (of race, class, age, etc.) An example of the latter is Jacklyn Cock's case study that examines the intersection of race, gender, and class through the specific relationship of the white "madam" and black "maid" in South Africa.[87] Another example is the oral history project that alternated life stories of white Southern female employers and their black female domestics.[88]

In the words of psychologists such as Naomi Weisstein[89] and Sue Cox,[90] feminists first showed psychology that it knew nothing about women; now it can show psychology and other disciplines that they have "similarly been biased from the point of view of white, middle-class, and heterosexual values." They can do this, however, only if feminist psychologists study race, class, and sexual preference in addition to gender. In Margaret Andersen's words: "Because feminist analysis seeks to understand the commonalities and the differences in women's experiences, sound feminist scholarship must entail an understanding of race, class, and heterosexual relations."[91] Having tackled the problem of sexist bias, feminist researchers strive to address racism and heterosexism in their research.[92]

Feminists affirm the belief that diversified samples or case studies improve research quality by allowing more precise conceptualization. For example, in her dissertation concerning eating problems, white U.S. sociologist Becky Thompson argues that the conventional linking of eating problems to white, young, single, heterosexual, middle-class women may reflect the fact that other groups have not been studied. Thus her dissertation examines the meaning of eating problems among blacks, Latinas, and whites, of different ages, some of whom are lesbian and others of whom are heterosexual. Information from this range of women enables her to better understand the etiology of eating problems in terms of specific characteristics and women's lives generally.[93] According to methodologists Lynn Cannon, Elizabeth Higginbotham, and Marianne Leung, however, this type of understanding is lacking in much feminist research because studies based on a small group of volunteers are likely to exclude women different from the researcher.[94]

Because of the significance of the new research criterion of diversity, feminist researchers who are unable to demonstrate diversity in their sample or materials are likely to be criticized. For example, a review of a study of 24 white, 35 black, 4 Hispanic, and 1 Native American street hustlers labeled the results "important but speculative" because of the limited number of Hispanic women.[95] Similarly, the black Jamaican Sistren collective criticized "white feminists of the 1960s and 1970s. . . . who spoke about women's oppression when what they meant was their own experience of it. . . . [and] who spoke about women's history when they really meant European women's history."[96]

Even before the criticism is voiced, feminists are likely to apologize for not including diverse populations. For example, U.S. historian Catherine Clinton writes that she was

> unable to fill in many of the gaps [she] found in the general literature on American women [particularly] . . . on native American women, black women, and other women of color. . . . For those who are dedicated to making women visible in American history, the failure to include these forgotten women seems even more discouraging.[97]

There are many instances of feminist researchers castigating themselves in this way.[98] White, middle-class, heterosexual philosopher Linda LeMoncheck criticized herself for choosing a topic (sex objectification) that may not be considered a pressing feminist issue for "members of other races, classes, or sexual orientations" and for "probably failing to identify some of its features" that are unique to these groups of women.[99] Ann Bristow and Jody Esper criticize themselves for heterosexism, as pointed out by a lesbian rape survivor. We had constructed questions on changing patterns of heterosexual dating following a rape. A lesbian participant stated that she could only answer the questions if we changed the referent to women. Ironically, these questions had been constructed by a lesbian researcher.[100]

Similarly, Elaine Hobby notes that in her "next project" she will attempt to include black women's writings and will tackle her own homophobia.[101]

Producing research that is inadequately diversified with regard to race, age, ethnicity, and sexual preference has become a sign of methodological weakness and moral failure, an impermissible reflection of a lack of effort and unwitting prejudice. A norm has developed that when a researcher does not live up to the standard, she atones with an apology in the publication itself. Lesbian British researcher Celia Kitzinger criticizes her own study of the social construction of lesbianism for its lack of diversity. Even though she had 120 interviewees, she used a snowball technique that began with her friends. This procedure did not lead her to many women different from herself despite the fact that she "expected to find considerable diversity among them." She was able to interview only four black women, 20 self-defined "working-class" women, and two Jewish lesbians. Moreover,

the politically conscious black lesbians . . . refused to be interviewed by a white woman, and radical working-class women declined to cooperate with the work of a hierarchical academic system from whose benefits they are systematically excluded. My own obvious whiteness and middle-classness (and self-definition as non-Jewish) severely limited the extent to which I could be perceived as an "insider" by some women. . . . [T]heir absence is an important loss: the various different identity constructions of white middle-class gentile women are not invalidated or made untrue by my inability to tap the constructions of politically engaged black, working-class, or Jewish lesbians, but they are revealed as a limited and partial selection of the many different visions of the world and of themselves that lesbians as a whole have constructed.

Her discussion raises the dilemma that "lack of diversity" reflects societal distrust rather than the researcher's failings.

In this particular study, many such lesbians chose to align themselves with non-lesbian people and to exclude themselves from my research. While, as a middle-class white, I acknowledge and respect the political imperatives that guided this choice, as a woman and a lesbian I deeply regret the resultant loss to my understanding and description of the full richness of lesbians' experience, identities and ideologies. . . . There are also relatively few very young and very old lesbians in this study . . . [M]y failure to reach many younger and older women should be seen as indicative of the ageism . . . that prevents these women from identifying themselves as lesbians. . . . Some other women refused to be interviewed, including some secretive, closeted lesbians who feared disclosure, and some radical lesbians by whom I, like a black interviewer in another study, was perceived as "selling my people down the river for a few pieces of silver" . . .; many radical feminist lesbians were unconvinced as to the political utility of my decision to pursue an academic career.[102]

While stressing the importance of studying only those people who volunteer, she recognizes that volunteers are themselves a self-selecting group, adding to the white, middle-class bias already inherent in her sample.

In general, feminists have found it difficult to gain access to diversified samples. U.S. sociologist Laurel Richardson is one of many white sociologists who attempts to generate a diversified sample of women and discovers that she has a diversified sample of white women.[103] White U.S. anthropologist Emily Martin wrote:

> The women represented in this book are self-selected rather than randomly sampled. We found women who were willing to participate by explaining the project to them in small groups (exercise classes, school classrooms, childbirth education classes, senior citizen programs, churches, community organizations, health clinics) and asking for volunteers. In this way and by pursuing other women suggested by the volunteers, we built up the numbers. . . . Overall, 43% were working class and 57% middle class. Of all these, 28% were members of Baltimore's (and the nation's) largest ethnic minority, black Americans. . . . By and large, we tried to match interviewer and interviewee. . . . My affiliation with Johns Hopkins University was usually an advantage. . . . Not always, though. One black woman declined to be interviewed because she did not like studies that Johns Hopkins' medical school had done in the poor populations surrounding the university in the inner city, and one administrator in a predominantly black high school located near Johns Hopkins Hospital refused me access to the students, saying, ''We do not want to get involved in any study. This high school has been interviewed and interviewed and interviewed.''[104]

Another white woman, British literary scholar Elaine Hobby, criticized her own book for being ''a white woman's book.'' She acknowledges that the ''prominence and anger of Black people'' taught her that saying she ''would have written about race had there been Black writers,'' was not a valid excuse. In poignant words, she explains that she has learned about the parallelism between sexism and racism:

> Just as feminists are becoming tired of explaining to men that studies of writing or history must include an exploration of the problem of gender, whether the people studied are male or female, Black people (I believe) are weary of trying to make white people think through the implications of race in the work that we do. I cannot pretend that I know yet how this change in my consciousness will affect my future work.[105]

U.S. psychologists Rosalind Barnett and Grace Baruch apologized that ''the greater part'' of their material deals with white, middle-class women, but they explained that as white middle-class women themselves, they were ''not well-equipped to address the situation of black women, who so often play the role of economic provider and whose lives are shaped by many forces that diverge greatly from those influencing whites.''[106]

Alison Jaggar and Paula Rothenberg wrote in the Introduction to the second edition of *Feminist Frameworks* that they added a section entitled ''Feminism and Women of Color'' after debating how best to include the voices of black women

who have "contributed to feminist discourse." Their decision to include a separate section stems from their view of the "separation between the white feminist
movement on the one hand and feminists of color on the other." Putting their
argument very powerfully, Alison Jaggar and Paula Rothenberg write that feminist
frameworks that do not take account of the experience of women of color, are not
only incomplete; they are racially biased.[107] As Sara Karon mentioned in the quotation from her work in the chapter on cross-cultural research, black feminists who
write black history tend to ignore black lesbian history. They thus contribute to
the problem of lesbian erasure just as white heterosexual feminists do.[108]

Thus, feminist researchers face possible accusations of racism despite the intention of avoiding racism, or of homophobia without an awareness of being homophobic. When not vigilant about diversity and successful in its implementation
as part of a research plan, feminist research may be racist, homophobic, ageist,
and ethnocentric.[109] Given this possibility, feminist researchers may feel paralyzed
by anticipatory condemnation. Marilyn Frye's comment that follows is an example
of a feminist philosopher struggling with this problem:

> To readers who might be able to overlook the ways in which my thought is
> limited by race- and class-bound imagination: I have to ask you to take absolutely
> seriously both the warning and the invitation implicit in my occasional reminders
> that there exists a vast variety of women and women's lives which I know just
> enough about to point to but which I cannot speak from or for. To readers who
> could never overlook these limitations because of the insult to what you know: I
> not only invite your criticism but also ask that you use your own creativity and
> insight to make the best of mine, to carry out the translations and codification
> which will make this work as useful to you as it can be.[110]

It is important to recognize that feminist researchers may be stigmatized by mainstream society for studying stigmatized groups,[111] and may be further stigmatized
by feminist researchers for studying homogeneous groups.

Despite the overwhelming endorsement of methodological diversity as a means
to combat racism and homophobia, I have also noticed a few arguments *against*
such an approach. As noted above, Celia Kitzinger and Emily Martin recognize
that some women rightfully refuse to participate in a research project, and their
autonomy to act in their own self-interest should be validated. In light of that
consideration, a researcher's search "for diversity" could actually be a form of
colonialism, manipulation, or exploitation. Black feminists such as bell hooks, for
example, ask why white women should study black women in the first place. She
notices with irony that "white women are given grant money to do research on
black women but I can find no instances where black women have received funds
to research white women's history." She also wonders out loud if "scholars are
motivated by a sincere interest in the history of black women or are merely responding to an available market." [112]

Lynn Davidman implies that the *inattentiveness* of white, middle-class feminist scholars to certain populations has been one impetus for these groups to engage
in scholarship of their own. She writes that "blacks . . . and members of other
minority groups are developing new forms of scholarship, predicated upon the

assumption that the picture of them presented by mainstream writers is necessarily different from their own self-presentation as expressed in their own voices."[113]

Notwithstanding bell hooks' skepticism, the motivation of white women to study black women, as expressed in writing, seems to stem from a sincere appreciation of the difficulties of living with sexism and racism in society. As white U.S. sociologist Cynthia Fuchs Epstein wrote:

> The experiences of the three black lawyers who had been in my original sample led me to do a study of black professional women in 1972. . . . [I then wrote an article about the] problems black women professionals faced because of their double negative status, as well as the special treatment accorded to them as a result of their situation. . . .[114]

Clearly, homophobic, ableist,[115] classist, and ageist assumptions continue to be blindspots in much feminist research. At the same time, feminist sensitivity to issues of diversity has raised many questions. How much of the diversified world of women should be included in a particular research project? When is a group actually diverse? Do members of different subgroups speak only for themselves? Do Western feminists have a right to criticize or must they accept culturally rooted practices in other cultures that seem detrimental to women, as discussed in the chapter on cross-cultural research? A quotation from Charlene Depner summarizes some of these dilemmas: "A feminist research standard of maximum diversity is perhaps logically and practically impossible while desirable as an ideal type".[116]

The Involvement of the Researcher as a Person

The previous chapters have shown that feminist researchers generally consider personal experiences to be a valuable asset for feminist research. To the extent that this is *not* the case in mainstream research, utilizing the researcher's personal experience is a distinguishing feature of feminist research. Personal experience typically is irrelevant in mainstream research, or is thought to contaminate a project's objectivity. In feminist research, by contrast, it is relevant and repairs the project's pseudo-objectivity. Whereas feminist researchers frequently present their research in their own voice, researchers publishing in mainstream journals typically are forbidden to use the first person singular voice.

Many feminist researchers describe how their projects stem from, and are part of, their own lives, as we saw earlier, for example, in Sara Ruddick's discussion of the continuity between her current research and her childhood concerns. In addition to describing the personal origins of a research question, the feminist researcher is likely to describe the actual research process as a lived experience, and she is likely to reflect on what she learned in the process. I believe in the value of this approach and thus I have written in the first person singular, have discussed the origins of my interest in the book's topic, and have mentioned aspects of my experience while working on this book.

Feminists have produced accounts of their experiences as alienated or "orgasmic"[117] researchers in order to correct false images of passionless objectivity.[118] They frequently integrate personal accounts into the report of the project itself, including, in particular, reports of the pain they suffered doing research on women's traumatic experiences. In some cases, feminists reintroduce passion, with its possible enthusiasm, anger, and nastiness, its first-person voice, and its identification with the research "subject." This is the voice of people such as Susan Griffin, whose work I discussed briefly in the chapter on original research methods. She explained that she wrote "associatively and went underneath logic."[119] Passion is a disruption of conventional research etiquette. It requires courage to violate the norms of dispassionate research. Political scientist Jean Bethke Elshtain, for example, wrote about starting her book many times, each time trying to work up greater courage "to be more provocative and less abstracted from the wellsprings of my own thought and action."[120] Feminist research then reads as partly informal, engagingly personal, and even confessional.

While some feminist social researchers have written full autobiographies[121] or have written full reports about their experiences as researchers of women,[122] more commonly the researcher adds a preface or postscript that contains an explanation of her relation to the subject matter at hand. She may also explicitly study a phenomenon that concerns her in her "personal" life.[123] By doing this, she merges the "public" and "private." Joyce Leland is one of many feminists who includes a discussion of her motives as part of her research text. She writes that her motive for studying the masculinity of gay men stems from her being the mother of one such young man as well as the mother of a straight son. She identifies with both of her sons and is angered by homophobia. As a sociologist she is trying to convert her anger into research that might show that gay men are ordinary members of society.[124] Writing such as this is not a confession of "bias" as it would undoubtedly be labeled in a positivist framework. Rather it is an explanation of "the researcher's standpoint" in a feminist framework.

The connection between the research project and the researcher's self frequently takes the form of "starting with one's own experience," particularly when the study concerns a disturbing experience. "Starting from one's own experience" is a way the researcher assures herself that she is "starting from the standpoint of women." Canadian sociologist Dorothy E. Smith, a major advocate of doing sociology from the standpoint of women, begins with her experience when doing research. She writes:

> The work of inquiry in which I am engaged proceeds by taking this experience of mine, this experience of other women . . . and asking how it is organized, how it is determined, what the social relations are which generate it.[125]

She explicitly rejects the idea that inquiry begins with the concerns of her discipline. It must, instead, begin with her experience.

Feminist researchers use the strategy of "starting from one's own experience" for many purposes. It defines our research questions, leads us to sources of useful data, gains the trust of others in doing the research, and enables us to partially test our findings. Feminist researchers frequently start with an issue that bothers them personally and then use everything they can get hold of to study it. In feminist research, then, the "problem" is frequently a blend of an intellectual question and a personal trouble.

Many feminist researchers draw on personal experience to *do* their research. One example of many discussed in this book is Janet Kahn and Patricia Gozemba's study of a lesbian bar, described in the chapter on interviewing. Sometimes the personal experience is simply a recollection that helps her understand an interviewee's response. For example, Marjorie DeVault wrote that while interviewing women about food they prepare for their families, she heard an oddly contradictory phrase but did not know what to make of it. Upon later reflection, she remembered a time in her own life when she thought she could save her marriage by making better salads. With this memory available to her, she began to find this kind of thinking expressed by other people she interviewed.[126] She included this story in her report.

Personal experience can be the very starting point of a study, the material from which the researcher develops questions, and the source for finding people to study. Athena Theodore poignantly acknowledges this in her study discussed in the chapter on multiple methods. As part of her background, Athena Theodore had the experience of fighting to retain her job as a tenured associate professor in a women's college. In the process, she writes that her consciousness was raised because she had never before considered that what was happening to her stemmed from being a woman. Shaken by this insight, she began to discuss her experiences with other academic women and gradually shaped her research project: "documenting in some systematic fashion the experiences of all academic women who were fighting discrimination, using the tools and methods of my discipline."[127]

As we have seen, feminist authors and researchers frequently begin their writing with the "personal connection" they have to the research topic. Adrienne Rich drew on her connection to motherhood,[128] I discussed my experience of miscarriage,[129] Ruth Harriet Jacobs discussed her own aging,[130] Susan Borg and Judith Lasker discussed their connection to failed pregnancy,[131] Judith Arcana discussed her experience as a daughter, Marcia Millman used her experience to understand being overweight,[132] and Lillian Rubin used her experience to study what it means to be a working-class woman, to name only a few.[133] Suzanne Arms explained that her book about childbirth in the United States "is a statement that grew out of my need to understand and explain my own birth experience."[134]

All of these feminists found that their troubling or puzzling experience became a "need to know." Being an insider of the experience enabled them to understand what [some] women have to "say in a way that no 'outsider' could."[135] Researchers who adopt this view draw on a new "epistemology of insiderness" that sees life and work as intertwined. Because of the widespread acceptance of the personal starting point for feminist research, some people have come to almost *expect* a link between the personal experience of the researcher and the research project in which she is engaged.

Transferred to the international level, feminist researchers argue that studies of women in a particular country should be done by women of that country. For these people, an author is an authority insofar as she is also the subject about which she speaks. These researchers adopt the view that even an empathic outsider cannot know women the way women know themselves, a view linked to a more general critique of the concept of objectivity.[136] Del Martin and Phillis Lyon, for example, write that it is impossible to be definitive or objective about lesbians.[137] But, it is possible to be knowledgeable. In their case, they argue that their expertise is the fact that they are lesbians, have lived together as lovers for 19 years, helped found the Daughters of Bilitis in 1955, have been deeply involved in the homophile movement, and have talked to, counseled, and been friends with thousands of lesbians.[138]

"Starting from one's own experience" is an idea that developed in reaction to androcentric social science. While useful in resisting the distortion of androcentrism, the position of "starting from one's own experience" has its limitations, particularly in the sense that it can lay the groundwork for solipsism or projection. Most feminists doing cross-cultural research do not advocate the position because "starting from one's experience" could easily verge into ethnocentrism.

Feminists have typically not converted the "epistemology of insiderness" into the principle that women should study *only* their own experience. As women we are entitled and able to study anything. Nor must we have a personal experience of something in order to study it. But as we study women's experiences we think we do not share, we sometimes find that we actually do share it in some way. Susan Brownmiller has written eloquently on this topic concerning her discovery that rape affects all women. She had initially thought that neither she nor the women's movement had anything to do with women who had been raped. As she wrote: "I wrote this book because I am a woman who changed her mind about rape."[139]

"Starting from one's own experience" violates the conventional expectation that a researcher be detached, objective, and "value neutral." In 1971 British sociologist Ann Oakley had already written that these approaches were themselves not "value neutral" but rather were "often simply a cover for patriarchy."[140] Other feminist scholars challenge the concept of objectivity, concurring instead with biologist Ruth Hubbard, that what passes for "objective" is actually the position of privileged white males. She writes that the only way to actually achieve what "the mythology of science asserts" (i.e., that science is conducted objectively) is to have a truly diversified set of women and men doing science from all sorts of different cultural and social backgrounds "with very different ideologies and interests." Were this to be the case, the personal bias that each person brings would cancel out the bias of another person. But Ruth Hubbard writes that most of the bias runs in a single direction, "predominantly university trained white males from privileged social backgrounds," thus revealing "more about the investigator than about the subject being researched."[141] Similary, philosopher Linda LeMoncheck writes that as

> a white, middle-class, educated, heterosexual woman and feminist, it would be naive to profess any kind of so-called objectivity to the analysis below; indeed, I do not think such a perspective exists, since as inquiring subject one must assume a perspective from which to launch the inquiry.[142]

Nevertheless, some feminist researchers consider "value-free" research to be desirable. They claim that being a member of the group one studies creates more problems than opportunities. U.S. sociologist Cynthia Fuchs Epstein, for example, wrote that social scientists have the power to influence public opinion and therefore must be very careful about the biases they bring to research concerning sex and gender differences. She feels that as members of society, feminist researchers are themselves "contaminated by or invested in a sexual division of the social order," yet they are still able to do research in an objective way.[143]

While some feminist researchers strive for "objectivity" and others believe that "objectivity" is itself the biased stance of privileged white males, still others experience the tension between the two stances. In the introduction to her interview-based study of 500 lesbians in England, for example, sociologist Elizabeth Ettore wrote about the conflict "between the social scientific notion of 'objectivity' which demands detachment, distance, and removal from what I was studying in order to be value-free, and the subjective experience of being a woman and a lesbian, which I am." She writes that the reader jumps back and forth as she thinks of the "researcher as both insider and outsider in the lesbian experience." The reader thinks of the researcher's bias in terms of what the researcher emphasizes, seeing her "more as a woman than as a lesbian sociologist, a sociologist of lesbianism," or however else the reader sees her.[144] Regardless of the reader's view, Elizabeth Ettore, for one, believes that as a researcher she can blend these views and offer facts.

Many feminist scholars find themselves trying to work out the tension between objectivity and subjectivity. Examples are Jessie Bernard and Bev James in the chapter on interviewing, Irene Dabrowski and Karen McCarthy Brown in the chapter on ethnography, and Anne Pugh in the chapter on survey research.[145] In this same vein, U.S. psychologist Virginia O'Leary writes that her book *Toward Understanding Women* is a "personal" book because her perspective as a feminist social psychologist and as a woman has guided her understanding and interpretation of psychological literature. Recognizing that she has a perspective does not mean that she then abandons what she considers to be objectivity. On the contrary, she believes that she can "present material objectively while guided by an explicit perspective."[146]

While valuing the researcher's personal experience, feminist researchers are careful to differentiate their "own experience" from the experience of "other women." Virginia O'Leary, mentioned above, specifically writes that she does "not regard [her] 'female experience' as normative," and she cautions the reader against interpreting her occasional personal illustrations in the book as normative material. U.S. historian Sara Evans studied the roots of the women's movement precisely because she wanted to test what she learned *against* information derived from her own involvement. She tried hard to avoid using her experience as a substitute for information about other people, and she deliberately sought challenges to her assumptions.[147] She stressed the importance of *having experiences* related to her research, *while also being reflexive* about the nature of the relation between experience and research.[148]

Despite these examples and others, psychologist Michelle Fine argues that "the experiences of women researchers as we investigate the lives of women . . . [are a] forbidden pool of data." She says that we collaborate in keeping the pool hidden out of fear that we will be accused of "biased scholarship" or "overidentification" with respondents. She and many others such as Stephanie Riger and Margaret Gordon, discussed in the chapter on multiple methods, think that giving voice to our own experiences is absolutely necessary because otherwise we perpetuate the "historic silencing of women researchers' active and often passionate reactions to our own research." [149]

These feminist researchers have expanded the notion that personal experience is an asset. They make it a *necessity* or a *source of legitimacy*. German sociologist, Maria Mies, for one, wrote that "feminist women must deliberately . . . integrate their repressed, unconscious female subjectivity, i.e. their own experience of oppression and discrimination into the research process." [150] Here we have another example of a feminist methodologist converting a property of *some* feminist researchers into a mandate for *all*.

I conclude from this section that the connection between the researcher's experience and the research project remains a matter of contention among feminist researchers. I, for one, feel most satisfied by a stance that acknowledges the researcher's position right up front, and that does not think of objectivity and subjectivity as warring with each other, but rather as serving each other. I have feminist distrust for research reports that include no statement about the researcher's experience. Reading such reports, I feel that the researcher is hiding from me or does not know how important personal experience is. Such reports seem woefully incomplete and even dishonest.

The Involvement of the People Being Studied

In those projects that involve interaction with people, feminist researchers frequently express a sense of connection to the actual people studied (as distinct from the subject matter being studied). In other forms of research, such as content analysis and experiments, interaction between "subjects" and "researcher" is not part of the data collection process and is thus irrelevant. In this section I will discuss the special properties of that interaction as feminists describe it.

In general, feminist observational or interview-based studies include a strong connection between the "researcher" and "subject" that develops during the course of the study and lasts beyond it, sometimes only in memory, sometimes in actuality. In these studies, the relationship leaves the realm of research and enters the personal lives of the individuals involved. This blurring of the distinction between formal and personal relations, just as the removal of the distinction in the previous section between the research project and the researcher's life, is a characteristic of much, though not all, feminist research. For example, Diane Bell, a white Australian anthropologist, writes about the aboriginal women she studied as her "friends and teachers." Writing in a way that demystifies research, she calls her book "a personal account of four years of [her] life." [151] A research report or book is, thus, a personal narrative and the people in the book are her friends.

These friends sometimes used her house as a refuge from their husbands' violence. On other occasions, the women she studied met her parents, or joined her on a vacation. As with women's friendships more generally, the women gave her insight into her own life.[152]

Another blurring of the distinction between the "subject's" role as subject and as human being is evident in the fact that many feminist researchers give direct assistance to the women they study, as in Christine Webb's study of women recovering from hysterectomies discussed in the chapter on interviewing. Taking this idea one step further, Audrey Bronstein considers good personal relations to be a *prerequisite* for studying women. In her Latin American study described in the chapter on feminist interview research, she states that she studied only those women with whom she already had a bond. Similarly, she wanted readers to share this bond by reading her book. She stressed that she wanted to "learn from," not just "learn about" the women she studied.

The action research examples, in particular, demonstrate the involvement of researchers in the lives of the people with whom they study. The paradigmatic example is the work of Jane Addams, who moved into an immigrant neighborhood in Chicago and subsequently did research with residents of her settlement house about the politics and social conditions of Chicago. A smaller scale contemporary example is Francesca Cancian's participatory research with the secretaries and graduate students in her department, designed to investigate problems and create social or individual change.

In some instances, the feminist researcher identifies with women at the conclusion of the project even though she regarded them with antipathy or ambivalence at the outset.[153] This compassion may develop even while the researcher is strongly identified with a competing group.[154] Lydia O'Donnell's work, as discussed in the chapter on interview research, illustrates how feminist researchers develop connections with the people they study and how those connections inform the researcher's changing sense of self.[155] She began her project looking for "constraints" and "obstacles" women face as mothers. Over the course of the study, meeting mothers and becoming a mother, she claims that she had to rethink her biases. Gradually she shifted her focus to an examination of the positive dimensions of mothering and ultimately dedicated her book to the women who taught her that she should continue to change, primarily by "slowing down and enjoying her early years of mothering." Feminist researchers such as Lydia O'Donnell learn to empathize with a broad range of women and to see them as rational actors in their contexts.

Just as in the topics discussed earlier in this chapter, there is dissensus around the issue of the feminist researcher's relation with the people she studies. Whereas Audrey Bronstein believed it was particularly appropriate to study women she already knew, Liz Kelly[156] and Mary K. Zimmerman[157] believed the opposite to be the case, as I discussed in the chapter on feminist interview research. These researchers did not study women they knew, out of respect for the women's privacy. Studying women they knew would complicate the relationships. Having relationships with the women would similarly complicate the research.

To the extent that part of the ideology of feminism is to transform the competitive and exploitative relations among women into bonds of solidarity and mutuality, we expect assistance and reciprocated understanding to be part of the research/subject relation.[158] In addition, to the extent that a goal of feminist scholarship is to reinterpret or redefine phenomena previously defined from a masculinist perspective, the only way to have access to a new definition is to truly understand the women by way of rapport. Their interpretation of motherhood, rape, incest, sexual harassment, and other phenomena requires an openness that is thought to come only with rapport.

The requirement that feminists establish rapport stems from the ideology that women experience relationships through an ethic of care,[159] and that feminists, in particular, are supposed to be able to establish intimate relations with women because of our political awareness. Put even stronger, feminists are supposed to feel toward other women as if they are their sisters, the presumption being that sisters have profound positive relations and shared interests.[160] For example, anthropologist Marjorie Shostak, in her work discussed in the chapter on oral history, wrote that she explicitly did not use objective (i.e., random or representative) considerations when selecting informants for her study of the !Kung but rather used the criterion of "rapport." After interviewing two men, she felt she could not achieve the "same degree of intimacy with them as she could with women." Intimate relations became her methodological criterion.

> The women I chose were those with whom I felt I could establish good rapport, and who represented a wide range in !Kung conditions of life. . . . In all cases, the women were talking specifically to me, as a person and as a woman.[161]

Marjorie Shostak specifically refers to Nisa as her "distant sister."

By achieving rapport, the feminist researcher reassures herself that she is treating the interviewee in a nonexploitative manner. Rapport thus validates the scholar as a feminist, as a researcher, and as a human being. It symbolizes her sisterhood, her interviewing skill, and her ethical standing. Commenting on Marjorie Shostak's work, Mary Louise Pratt highlighted the importance of "current Western conceptions of female solidarity and intimacy" that produced "cross-cultural harmony." Using words that seem to be describing romantic love, Mary Louise Pratt writes that Marjorie Shostak "and Nisa are bound together in ways that perhaps transcend culture."[162] Taking such descriptions to heart, the "rapport demands" internalized by a feminist researcher, particularly a novice feminist researcher, can be overwhelming. Rapport becomes the normative, not the special, condition.

When feminist expectations of rapport between the researcher and the woman she is studying combine with expectations of ethnic solidarity, "rapport demands" are extreme. Sociologist Denise Connors, whose work I discussed in the chapter on feminist interview research,

> decided to work with women of Irish descent and from working class backgrounds because I believed that given my own Irish ancestry and working class roots, I would be able to readily establish rapport with them.[163]

Expecting to achieve "rapport," a concept that remains undefined, it is possible that the researcher will block out other emotions and reactions to the people she is studying. She might even romanticize the women or see them in stereotypic ways, because of her focus on "achieving rapport." And if she does not "achieve rapport," she may forego the study altogether. In my view it would be unfortunate if we were to introduce self-imposed limits to our research possibilities because of the notion of rapport.

There are also structural barriers to rapport that feminist researchers would do well to recognize. First, there are class differences. Feminist researchers try to overcome these by techniques that minimize educational differences. This is the way I would interpret Ann Oakley's comment that she chose simple questions to enable "some rapport to be established between interviewer and respondent." [164] There are also ideological differences. To her dismay, as I discussed in the chapter on interviewing, British social psychologist Susan Condor discovered that despite her use of an open-ended questionnaire, she could not sympathize with "traditional women who support the existing roles of men and women." Despite her aim of reaching "an understanding of women in their own terms," she uncovered the "possibility that regarding individuals and social events from the perspective of feminism as a world-view may itself encourage the very tendency to objectify our 'subjects' which feminism opposes so forcefully." [165]

The feminist demand for rapport may have led us to put on blinders compelling us to see gender as the most salient characteristic of a woman, even when the woman sees it otherwise. In this regard, U.S. sociologist Beth Hess has written about the difficulty feminists had in understanding the Portuguese-American women of New Bedford, Massachusetts who defended men of their ethnic group who raped a woman not of their group. Feminists outside New Bedford identified with the rape victim and had trouble identifying with, or achieving rapport with, the rapists' female defenders. [166]

Sociologist Janet Billson Mancini, whose work I discussed in the chapter on cross-cultural research, struggled with this problem as well. She noted that when working in the immigrant community in Canada, her status as a woman was less important than her status as an ethnic minority member. The community made it difficult for her to achieve rapport because of its belief that "if you are a feminist then you cannot be equally concerned with issues affecting minority groups." [167] Her research became part of what Roxana Ng has described: an "ongoing endeavour to arrive at an understanding of the situation of immigrant women which does not negate their experience as women and as ethnic minority at the same time." [168]

The theme of the feminist researcher's involvement in the lives of the people she studies is full of ambiguity and controversy. There seems to be a continuum of feminist positions on this topic ranging from those whose projects demand that there be *no* involvement to those whose projects allow for deep, mutually satisfying reciprocal relationships. When we discuss feminist research, it behooves us to remember the entire continuum, and to not focus only on the position of deep, lasting involvement. Many "subjects" simply do not have the time or inclination to incorporate a researcher, even a feminist researcher, into their lives. The women most likely to desire a long-lasting relation with the researcher are those who already know her, those who discover they have many shared interests with the researcher, and those who are isolated and have few friends with whom to share their feelings and ideas.

It seems dangerous to require rapport in all feminist research. I prefer, instead, to think of research projects, researchers, and "research subjects" as varied, each deserving to be analyzed as to the most beneficial relation that could be developed. "Achieving rapport" should not become a burdensome, and sometimes inappropriate, form of "emotion work"[169] feminist researchers must do if they engage in research involving interaction with people. Rather, feminists who do research with people should consider rapport to be a fortunate outcome of some projects rather than a precondition of all research relationships. In general, rapport between any two people develops only with time and a sense of shared interests. To try to "achieve" rapport without these prerequisites is an arduous endeavor prone to failure.

I also believe that we can develop nonexploitative relations with the people involved in our research projects, without attempting to achieve "rapport" or "intimacy" with them. Relations of respect, shared information, openness, and clarity of communication seem like reasonable substitute goals. And there are times when feminist researchers will study people for whom they have little respect. In my view, this, too, can be done without diminishing a feminist researcher's self-esteem. Charlene Depner put this whole problem well when she wrote:

> A disturbing phenomenon has emerged which I label "superwoman meets the academy." This is a model of feminist research which demands that each researcher unflaggingly avoid all pitfalls of conventional psychological research. The feminist researcher must collect endless detailed data, engage in a dialogue with her/his subjects and see that the research process benefits them personally (otherwise, the subject is regarded as exploited).[170]

"Superman" is not a product of female culture. I see no reason to have "superwomen" as feminist research role models.

The Involvement of the Reader

A characteristic of feminist research seems to be a desire on the part of the researcher to address the reader directly and to forge a connection through her between the reader and the people studied. The innovative work with drama is one step in this direction, as discussed in the chapter on original methods. In a very blatant way, it brings the audience in for direct observation of the material the researcher wants to present. Many feminist researchers who interview include quotations from the interviews in the research product in order to give the reader a sense of these people. When the interviewees "speak for themselves" or "use their own voice," the reader is better able to understand.

In Jill Matthews' book *Good and Mad Women*, discussed in the chapter on content analysis, the web of connection between the researcher and reader is particularly strong. Jill Matthews reveals herself doing the research and builds a connection with her readers as we try to understand her struggle to identify with the women she studies. She includes herself and her reader in the pronoun "our" when she writes about "our identification with a woman named Vera."[171]

Susan Yeandle's work, discussed in the chapter on interviewing, is another example of a project in which the author addresses the reader directly in the hope of sharing an "awareness of the women" with whom the researcher spoke.[172] Nancy Seifer's work discussed in the chapter on oral history is an effort to have the middle-class female reader understand the working-class women who narrated their stories of political action.[173] Feminist researchers such as Pat Taylor[174] and Fran Buss, discussed in the chapter on oral history, reveal their background to the reader out of a sense of responsibility. Fran Buss wrote: "Because of the influence I had, it is important that readers have some knowledge of my background, beliefs, and interests."[175] The obligation is met through self-disclosure. And if the reader agrees with the writer's analysis, then the writer is confirmed. Similarly, in the chapter on original methods, I quote Dorothy Dinnerstein as saying, "[My] method is to appeal to the reader's own experience: if the result feels in any way enlightening, the argument is validated insofar as it can be."[176]

The feminist researcher sometimes addresses the reader to engage her in the work of data analysis. In the chapter on content analysis, for example, Laurel Graham writes that "through deconstruction, readers can find in each text the information to construct oppositional readings."[177] Susan Krieger's work, discussed in the chapter on original feminist methods, contains a fully developed discussion of this topic. As I described in the chapter on original methods, she

> invites the reader to join, to take part, to overhear the gossip of women in one particular subcommunity in a midwestern town, to come to know the members of this community, to share their insights and their confusions. The challenge is to adopt these women temporarily as a peer group, to muddle through their difficulties with them, and to confront one's own responses to those difficulties as they appear when articulated through the book's interplay of many voices.[178]

Some feminist researchers address the reader in the hope of helping her to liberate herself from partriarchy. Jane Marcus believes that inclusion of direct quotes is the best route toward this goal. In her words, "The ideology of patriarchy is most effectively undercut for the woman reader by the most unmediated of the voices of female experience."[179] And Katherine Pope, whose work I discussed in the chapter on content analysis, wrote that "the explicit statement that accompanies the imagery helps the reader to understand her own behavior and that of others. The reader sees herself as not alone in her experiences."[180]

Developing a connection with the reader is probably a goal of all writers, feminist or not. Perhaps unlike mainstream writers, however, there is among feminist researchers a broad range of ways in which the reader is engaged.

Final Thoughts

Feminists are creatively stretching the boundaries of what constitutes research. We are versatile, many of us having engaged in numerous methods mentioned in this book. And, most important, we are not uniform. Some of us choose to use a personal voice, but formats are being developed for those who choose not to do so. Some of us see feminist research as self-reflexive, collaborative, attuned to process, oriented to social change, and designed to be *for* women rather than only *of* women. Some of us are concerned with racism and heterosexism (very few with ageism), some express feminist distrust, some begin with their own experience, some incorporate a critique of androcentrism, and some are concerned primarily with the empowerment of women.

I find myself convinced as I end this study that we are in a period of Feminist Culture Building, or Feminist Renaissance, and that we will be self-correcting. I end this book with a quote with which sociologist Sarah Berk opened her book:

> I owe a continuing debt of gratitude to those . . . I know only through their own writings, who have (over the last decade) patiently taught me what it is—what it must be—to practice feminist scholarship. . . . Thus, whatever is of value in this work owes a great deal to the experience, knowledge, and past trials of other women.[181]

NOTES

Chapter 1   Introduction

1. This chapter benefited from a review by Maurice Stein.

2. Roslyn Wallach Bologh, "Feminist Social Theorizing and Moral Reasoning: On Difference and Dialectic," in American Sociological Association, *Sociological Theory, 1984* (San Francisco: Jossey-Bass, 1984), pp. 373–393, p. 388. [emphases added]

3. I mention the nationalities of feminist researchers to illustrate the extent to which feminist research is global.

4. Bernice Lott, *Becoming a Woman: The Socialization of Gender* (Springfield, IL: Charles C Thomas, 1981), p. 9.

5. University of Wisconsin, Madison, Women's Studies, *Research Center Newsletter,* Spring 1984, p. 6.

6. Liz Stanley, " 'The Research Process' in the Social Sciences and Its Part in Producing Discrimination against Women in Higher Education," British Society for Research in Higher Education, Monograph on Gender Biases, Spring/Summer, 1982.

7. Naomi Black, *Social Feminism* (Ithaca, NY: Cornell University Press, 1989), p. 75.

8. Marjorie L. DeVault, "Talking and Listening from Women's Standpoint: Feminist Strategies for Interviewing and Analysis," *Social Problems,* 1990, 37(1): 701–721.

9. Carolyn Greenstein Burke, "Report from Paris: Women's Writing and the Women's Movement," *Signs: Journal of Women in Culture and Society,* 1978, 3(4): 843–855, p. 855.

10. Sue Wilkinson, "Sighting Possibilities: Diversity and Commonality in Feminist Research," in Sue Wilkinson (ed.), *Feminist Social Psychology: Developing Theory and Practice* (Philadelphia, PA: Open University Press, 1986), pp. 7–24.

11. Patricia Cayo Sexton, *The New Nightingales: Hospital Workers, Unions, New Women's Issues* (New York: Enquiry Press, 1982), p. 4.

12. Whereas some might argue that "pluralism" or "plurality" is a cop-out, I consider pluralism a positive attitude reflecting mutual understanding, respect, and desire for inclusiveness. It is the rational response to diversity when the threat of oppression or annihilation is low. In the debate concerning research methods, pluralism is appropriate so long as power differences among researchers are not great.

13. Mary Belenky, Blythe Clinchy, Nancy Goldberger, and Jill Tarule, *Women's Ways of Knowing* (New York: Basic Books, 1986).

14. Naomi Weisstein, *Kinder, Kuche, and Kirche as Scientific Law: Psychology Constructs the Female* (Boston: New England Free Press, 1969); Rae Carlson, "Understanding Women: Implications for Personality Theory and Research," *Journal of Social Issues,* 1972, 28(2): 17–32; Ann Oakley, "The Invisible Woman: Sexism in Sociology," in Ann Oakley (ed.), *The Sociology of Housework* (New York: Pantheon, 1974); Marcia Millman and Rosabeth Kanter (eds.), *Another Voice: Feminist Perspectives on Social Life and Social Science* (Garden City, NY: Doubleday, Anchor Books, 1975); Helen Weinreich, "What Future for the Female Subject? Some Implications of the Women's Movement for Psychological Research," *Human Relations,* 1977, 30(6): 535–543; Paula Johnson, "Doing Psychological Research," in Irene H. Frieze, Jacquelynn Parsons, Paula Johnson, Diane Ru-

ble, and Gail Zellman (eds.), *Women and Sex Roles: A Social Psychological Perspective* (New York: Norton, 1978), pp. 11–27; Jacqueline Voss and Linda Gannon, "Sexism in the Theory and Practice of Clinical Psychology," *Professional Psychology*, 1978, 9(4): 623–632; Bonnie Thornton Dill, "The Dialectics of Black Womanhood," *Signs: Journal of Women in Culture and Society*, 1979, 4(3): 543–555; Marcia Westkott, "Feminist Criticism of the Social Sciences," *Harvard Educational Review*, 1979, 49(4): 422–430; Carolyn Sherif, "Bias in Psychology," in Julia Sherman and Evelyn Beck (eds.), *The Prism of Sex: Essays in the Sociology of Knowledge* (Madison, WI: University of Wisconsin Press, 1979), pp. 93–134; Committee on the Status of Women in Sociology, "Sexist Biases in Sociological Research: Problems and Issues," *Footnotes*, January 1980; Laurie Wardell, Dair L. Gillespie, and Ann Leffler, "Science and Violence against Wives," unpublished paper, 27 April 1981, Department of Sociology, University of Utah, Salt Lake City, Utah; Patricia Campbell, "The Impact of Societal Biases on Research Methods," research reported at the Sixth Annual Conference on Research on Women and Education, February 1981; Margaret Andersen, *Thinking about Women: Sociological and Feminist Perspectives* (New York: Macmillan, 1983); Margrit Eichler and Jeanne Lapointe, *On the Treatment of the Sexes in Research* (Ottawa, Canada: Social Sciences and Humanities Research Council of Canada, 1985); Sharon Begley, "Liberation in the Lab," *Newsweek*, December 2, 1985.

15. Francine D. Blau, "On the Role of Values in Feminist Scholarship," *Signs: Journal of Women in Culture and Society*, 1981, 3(3): 538–540; Michele Wittig, "On Feminism, the Psychology of Women, and General Psychology," paper presented at the 89th Annual Meeting of the American Psychological Association, Los Angeles, 1981; Thelma McCormack, "Good Theory or Just Theory? Toward a Feminist Philosophy of Social Science," *Women's Studies International Quarterly*, 1981, 4(1): 1–12; Rhoda Kesler Unger, "Through the Looking Glass: No Wonderland Yet!" Presidential Address to Division 35, American Psychological Association, 89th Annual Meeting, Los Angeles, 1981; Sandra Harding and Merrill B. Hintikka (eds.), *Discovering Reality: Feminist Perspectives on Epistemology, Metaphysics, Methodology and Philosophy of Science* (Dordrecht: D. Reidel, 1983); Joan Huber, "Do Two Sexes Require Two Research Methodologies?," talk given as part of the Gender and Epistemology series, Radcliffe College, February 23, 1989.

16. See Shulamit Reinharz, "Feminist Research Methodology Groups: Origins, Forms and Functions," in Louise Tilly and Vivian Petraka (eds.), *Feminist Visions and Re-Visions* (Ann Arbor, MI: University of Michigan, 1984), pp. 197–228.

17. This is Renate Klein's term.

18. Shulamit Reinharz, Marti Bombyk, and Janet Wright, "Methodological Issues in Feminist Research: A Bibliography of Literature in Women's Studies, Sociology and Psychology," *Women's Studies International Forum*, 1983, 6(4): 437–454.

19. Peta Tancred-Sheriff (ed.), *Feminist Research: Prospect and Retrospect; Recherche Feministe: Bilan et Perspectives d'Avenir* (Montreal: McGill-Queen's University Press, 1988), p. ix. This book intersperses French and English passages.

20. Shulamit Reinharz, "Feminist Research Principles," in Dale Spender and Cheris Kramerae (eds.), *Knowledge Explosion: Disciplines and Debates* (New York: Pergamon, 1991).

21. "Gynopia" is a word I invented to mean the inability to perceive women; see Shulamit Reinharz, "Feminist Distrust: Problems of Content and Context in Sociological Research," in David Berg and Ken Smith (eds.), *The Self in Social Inquiry: Researching Methods* (Beverly Hills, CA: Sage, 1985, 1988), pp. 153–172. See also Shulamit Reinharz, "Patriarchal Pontifications," *Transaction/SOCIETY*, 1986, 23(6): 23–39. For a discussion of misogynist research see Kate Millett, *Sexual Politics* (New York: Ballantine, 1969).

22. Marjorie L. DeVault, review of Barbara Richardson and Jeana Wirtenberg (eds.), *Sex Role Research: Measuring Social Change* (New York: Praeger, 1983), in *Contemporary Sociology*, 1985, *14*(4): 481–482.

23. Mary O'Brien, *The Politics of Reproduction* (Boston: Routledge & Kegan Paul, 1981), p. 24.

24. Shulamit Reinharz, "Experiential Analysis: A Contribution to Feminist Research Methodology," in Gloria Bowles and Renate Duelli Klein (eds.), *Theories of Women's Studies* (Boston: Routledge & Kegan Paul, 1983), pp. 162–191.

25. Sandra Harding, *The Science Question in Feminism* (Ithaca, NY: Cornell University Press, 1986).

26. See Meredith Gould and Rochelle Kern-Daniels, "Toward a Sociological Theory of Gender and Sex," *The American Sociologist*, 1977, *12*(4): 182–189; Marcia Texler Segal and Catherine White Berheide, "Towards a Women's Perspective in Sociology: Directions and Prospects," in Scott McNall (ed.), *Theoretical Perspectives in Sociology* (New York: St. Martin's Press, 1979); Margrit Eichler, "And the Work Never Ends: Contributions of Feminist Approaches to Canadian Anglophone Sociology," *Canadian Review of Sociology and Anthropology*, 1985, *22*(5): 619–644; Dale Spender (ed.), *Men's Studies Modified: The Impact of Feminism on the Academic Disciplines* (New York: Pergamon, 1981); Ellen DuBois, Gail Kelly, Elizabeth Kennedy, Carolyn Korsmeyer, and Lillian Robinson, *Feminist Scholarship: Kindling in the Groves of Academe* (Chicago: University of Illinois Press, 1985); Kathryn Ward and Linda Grant, "The Feminist Critique and a Decade of Research in Sociology Journals," *Sociological Quarterly*, 1985, *26*(2): 139–157; and Dorothy E. Smith, *The Everyday World as Problematic: A Feminist Sociology* (Boston: Northeastern University Press, 1987).

27. Evelyn Reed, *Sexism and Science* (New York: Pathfinder Press, 1978); Sarah Hoagland, "Naming, Describing, Explaining: Deception and Science," paper delivered at the panel, "Feminism and the Philosophy of Science," Annual Meeting of the American Association for the Advancement of Science, January 6, 1979, Houston, Texas; Ruth Bleier (ed.), *Science and Gender: A Critique of Biology and Its Theories on Women* (New York: Pergamon, 1984); Michelle Wittig, "Metatheoretical Dilemmas in the Psychology of Gender," *The American Psychologist* 1985, *40*(7): 800–811; Ruth Bleier (ed.), *Feminist Approaches to Science* (New York: Pergamon, 1986); Mary Gergen, "Towards a Feminist Metatheory and Methodology," paper presented at the Annual Meeting of the American Psychological Association, August 1986; Mary Gergen (ed.), *Feminist Thought and the Structure of Knowledge* (New York: New York University Press, 1988); Louise Levesque-Lopman, *Claiming Reality: Phenomenology and Women's Experience* (Totowa, NJ: Rowman and Littlefield, 1988).

28. See Jeanne M. Paradise, "In Search of a Research Paradigm for a Human-World Science," unpublished manuscript, Boston University, School of Education, 1983; Kathleen MacPherson, "Feminist Methods: A New Paradigm for Nursing Research," *Advances in Nursing Science*, 1983, *5*(2): 17–25; Joyce McCarl Nielsen (ed.), *Feminist Research Methods: Readings in the Social Sciences* (Boulder, CO: Westview Press, 1989); and Sondra Farganis, "Social Theory and Feminist Theory: The Need for Dialogue," *Sociological Inquiry*, 1986, *56*(1): 50–68.

29. If "everything" is part of the dominant culture, then feminist research is impossible and anything short of total revolution is a form of self-deception. As Jeanne Gross put it: "The dominant ideology of the culture is re-duplicated in the feminist movement through cultural imperialism." See her "Feminist Ethics from a Marxist Perspective," *Radical Religion*, 1977, *3*(2): 52–56; quoted in bell hooks, *Feminist Theory: From Margin to Center* (Boston: South End Press, 1984), pp. 26–27. See also Ruth Bleier, *Science and Gen-*

der: A Critique of Biology and Its Theories on Women* (New York: Pergamon, 1984), p. 205, citing Elizabeth Fee, "A Feminist Critique of Scientific Objectivity," *Science for the People,* 1982, *14*(5–8): 30–33 and Donna Haraway, "Animal Sociology and a Natural Economy of the Body Politic, Part 1: A Political Physiology of Dominance," *Signs: Journal of Women in Culture and Society,* 1978, *4*(1): 21–36; Audre Lorde, "The Master's Tools Will Never Dismantle the Master's House," in Cherrie Moraga and Gloria Anzaldua (eds.), *This Bridge Called My Back* (Watertown, MA: Persephone, 1981).

   30. Mathilde de Jong, "Feminist Research Methodology," unpublished, undated manuscript, University College, Cardiff, Wales; Carol Nagy Jacklin, "Feminist Research and the Scientific Method," unpublished, undated manuscript, Stanford University; Pauline Bart, "Sexism and Social Science: From the Gilded Cage to the Iron Cage, or, The Perils of Pauline," *Journal of Marriage and the Family,* 1971, *33*(4): 734–745; Carol Ehrlich, *The Conditions of Feminist Research* (Baltimore, MD: Research Group One, Report No. 21, February 1976), pp. 1–19; Evelyn Fox Keller, "Gender and Science," *Psychoanalysis and Contemporary Thought,* 1978, *1*(3): 409–433; Julia Sherman and Evelyn Beck (eds.), *The Prism of Sex* (Madison, WI: University of Wisconsin Press, 1979); Pauline Bart, "Psychotherapy, Sexism and Social Control: A Review of *Woman and Madness,*" *Society,* 1974, *11*(2): 95–98; Dee Graham and Edna Rawlings, "Feminist Research Methodology: Comparisons, Guidelines and Ethics," paper presented at the Annual Meeting of the American Psychological Association, August 1980; Evelyn Fox Keller, "Feminist Critique of Science: A Forward or Backward Move?," *Fundamenta Scientiae,* 1980, *1:* 341–349; Meredith Gould, "The New Sociology," *Signs: Journal of Women in Culture and Society,* 1980, *5*(3): 459–467; Jill Leverone, "Is There a Feminist Research Methodology?," *Newsletter of the Association for Women in Psychology,* November–December 1981, p. 5; Evelyn Fox Keller, "Feminism and Science," *Signs: Journal of Women in Culture and Society,* 1982, *7*(3): 589–602; Mirra Komarovsky, "Women Then and Now: A Journey of Detachment and Engagement," *Barnard Alumnae Magazine,* Winter 1982, pp. 7–11; Carolyn Sherif, "Should There Be a Feminist Methodology?," *Newsletter of the Association for Women in Psychology,* January–February 1982, pp. 3–4; Michele Hoffnung, "Feminist Research Methodology," *Newsletter of the Association for Women in Psychology,* July–August, 1982, pp. 7–9; Gloria Bowles and Renate Duelli Klein (eds.), *Theories of Women's Studies* (Boston: Routledge & Kegan Paul, 1983); Rhoda Linton, "In Search of Feminist Research Methodology," unpublished manuscript, Cornell University, July 1983; Christine Webb, "Feminist Methodology in Nursing Research," *Journal of Advanced Nursing,* 1984, *9:* 249–256; Evelyn Fox Keller, *Reflections on Gender and Science* (New Haven, CT: Yale University Press, 1984); Judith Stacey and Barrie Thorne, "The Missing Feminist Revolution in Sociology," *Social Problems,* 1985, *32*(4): 301–316; Judith Cook and Mary Margaret Fonow, "Knowledge and Women's Interests: Feminist Methodology in the Field of Sociology," *Sociological Inquiry,* 1986, *56*(1): 2–29; Barbara Wallston, "Feminist Research Methodology from a Psychological Perspective: Science as the Marriage of Agentic and Communal," in Marilyn Safir, Martha Mednick, Dafna Izraeli, and Jessie Bernard (eds.), *Women's Worlds: From the New Scholarship* (New York: Praeger, 1985); Martha Thompson, Helen Nagel-Bamesberger, Audrey Karabinus, Lana Miller, and Angie Rossiter, "What Makes a Feminist Social Science?," *Program Notes,* Women's Studies Program, Northeastern Illinois University, Spring–Summer, 1985, *10*(2); Sandra Harding "Is There a Feminist Method?," in Sandra Harding (ed.), *Feminism and Methodology: Social Science Issues* (Bloomington, IN: Indiana University Press and Open University Press, 1987); Mirra Komarovsky, "The New Feminist Scholarship: Some Precursors and Polemics," *Journal of Marriage and the Family,* 1988, *50:* 585–593.

   31. Margrit Eichler, *The Double Standard: A Feminist Critique of Feminist Social Sci-*

ence (London: Croom Helm, 1980); Liz Stanley, " 'The Research Process' in the Social Sciences and Its Part in Producing Discrimination against Women in Higher Education," British Society for Research in Higher Education, Monograph on Gender Biases, Spring/ Summer, 1982; Margaret Reid, "A Feminist Sociological Imagination? Reading Ann Oakley," *Sociology of Health and Illness*, 1983, *5*(1): 83–94; Judith Stacey, "Can There Be a Feminist Ethnography?," *Women's Studies International Forum*, 1988, *11*(1): 21–27. Excellent books on this topic are Sue Wilkinson (ed.), *Feminist Social Psychology: Developing Theory and Practice* (Philadelphia, PA: Open University Press, 1986); Joyce McCarl Nielsen (ed.), *Feminist Research Methods: Readings in the Social Sciences* (Boulder, CO: Westview Press, 1989); and Mary Margaret Fonow and Judith A. Cook (eds.), *Beyond Methodology: Feminist Scholarship as Lived Experience* (Bloomington, IN: Indiana University Press, 1991).

32. Naomi Gottlieb summarized feminist criticisms of feminist research: "These include the risks of romanticizing feminist culture. . . , including feminist processes in research production. . . ; the tendency to latch onto findings which make intuitive sense, and to have 'nonreplicated positive findings sweep through the literature'. . . ; the phenomenon that once widely heralded feminist conclusions have come under serious criticism, e.g. androgyny and fear of success. . . . [and] a cycle of heyday and decline, as in black scholarship. The challenge is to recognize the tension between truth-seeking and social reform, the place for polemic and commitment, the danger of over-empathy. . . , the fact that women are not homogeneous. . . , and that much work needs to be done to develop viable, empirically tested theories." Naomi Gottlieb, "Dilemmas and Strategies in Research on Women," in Dianne S. Burden and Naomi Gottlieb (eds.), *The Woman Client* (New York: Tavistock, 1987), pp. 61–62.

33. Mary Daly wrote that concern with method was a symptom of partriarchal culture, that she called "methodolatrous." At the same time, she rejected all previous research because it had helped create an oppressive culture.

34. Margaret Mead, "What Women Bring to Research," *Comment*, February 1979, p. 5; Kathleen McGuire Boukydis, "Existential/Phenomenology as a Philosophical Base for a Feminist Psychology," paper presented at the Annual Meeting of the Association for Women in Psychology, Boston, 1981; Marlene Mackie, "Female Sociologists' Productivity, Collegial Relations and Research Style Examined through Journal Publications," *Sociology and Social Research*, 1985, *69*(2): 189–209; and Linda Grant, Kathryn Ward and Xue Rong, "Is There an Association between Gender and Methods in Sociological Research?," *American Sociological Review*, 1987, *52*(6): 856–862.

35. Charlotte G. O'Kelly and Larry Carney, *Women & Men in Society: Cross-Cultural Perspectives on Gender Stratification* (Belmont, CA: Wadsworth, 2nd ed., 1986), p. vii.

36. Margrit Eichler, *Nonsexist Research Methods: A Practical Guide* (Boston, MA: Allen & Unwin, 1987) and "The Relationship between Sexist, Non-Sexist, Woman-Centered and Feminist Research," paper delivered at the Annual Meeting of the American Sociological Association, 1983; Maureen C. McHugh, Randi Daimon Koeski, and Irene Hanson Frieze, "Issues to Consider in Conducting Nonsexist Psychological Research: A Guide for Researchers," *American Psychologist*, 1986, *41*(8): 879–890.

37. See "Research Methods in Psychology: Are They Anti-Feminist?" Panel presented at the Annual Meeting of the National Women's Studies Association, 1980 (panelists include Aldora Lee, "Social Psychology in the Hands of Feminists," Toby Jayaratne, "Survey Research and Feminist Issues," Nancy Kenney, "A Feminist Look at Psychobiological Research," and Robin Post, "Avoiding the Battered Data Syndrome in Domestic Violence Research"); Lynda Glennon, "Synthesism: A Case of Feminist Methodology," in Gareth Morgan (ed.), *Beyond Method: Strategies for Social Research* (Beverly Hills, CA: Sage,

1983); Liz Stanley and Sue Wise, *Breaking Out: Feminist Consciousness and Feminist Research* (London: Routledge & Kegan Paul, 1983); Danielle Storper-Perez and Rahel Wasserfall, "Methodologie de la raison, methodologie de la resonance d'un devenir-femme de la recherche?," *Revue de l'Institut de Sociologie*, 1988, *1–2*: 189–207; and Rhoda Linton, "Feminist Research Methodology: Exploration and Experimentation," in Alison M. Jaggar and Susan Bordo (eds.), *Gender/Body/Knowledge: Feminist Reconstruction of Being and Knowing* (New Brunswick, NJ: Rutgers University Press, 1989).

38. Helen Roberts (ed.), *Doing Feminist Research* (London: Routledge & Kegan Paul, 1981); Barbara DuBois, "Passionate Scholarship: Notes on Values, Knowing and Method in Feminist Social Science," in Gloria Bowles and Renate Duelli Klein (eds.), *Theories of Women's Studies* (Boston: Routledge & Kegan Paul, 1983), pp. 105–116; and Carla Golden, "Psychology, Feminism and Object Relations," paper presented at the Eighth Annual Meeting of the Association for Women in Psychology, Boston, 1981.

39. C. Wright Mills, *The Sociological Imagination* (New York: Oxford University Press, 1959), p. 195. There is irony in mentioning Mills in this regard, since Mills worked as a co-author with his wives (Dorothy James and Ruth Harper), yet it is he who is considered author. See Irving Louis Horowitz, *C. Wright Mills: An American Utopian* (New York: The Free Press, 1983), esp. pp. 71–72, 79.

40. See Judith Rollins, *Between Women: Domestics and their Employers* (Philadelphia, PA: Temple University Press, 1985), p. 17, for a discussion of this approach.

41. The Mud Flower Collective, *God's Fierce Whimsy: Christian Feminism and Theological Education* (New York: The Pilgrim Press, 1985), pp. 14–15.

42. Barbara Macdonald with Cynthia Rich, *Look Me in the Eye: Old Women, Aging and Ageism* (San Francisco; Spinsters, Ink, 1983).

43. Robin Ruth Linden, Darlene Pagano, Diana Russell, and Susan Star (eds.), *Against Sadomasochism: A Radical Feminist Analysis* (San Francisco: Frog in the Well Press, 1982) and Mary Roth Walsh (ed.), *The Psychology of Women: Ongoing Debates* (New Haven, CT: Yale University Press, 1987).

44. Ruth Levitas, "Feminism and Human Nature," in Ian Forbes and Steve Smith (eds.), *Politics and Human Nature* (New York: St. Martin's Press, 1983).

45. Foreword in Arlyn Diamond and Lee Edwards (eds.), *The Authority of Experience: Essays in Feminist Criticism* (Amherst, MA: University of Massachusetts Press, 1977).

46. Inquiries concerning feminist methodology that examine articles and not books reach the conclusion that feminist research does not deviate much from androcentric standards. See Richard T. Walsh, "Where Is the Research Relationship in Feminist Psychology Research?," paper presented at the Annual Meeting of the American Psychological Association, 1987; and M. Brinton Lykes and Abigail Stewart, "Evaluating the Feminist Challenge to Research in Personality and Social Psychology, 1963–1983," *Psychology of Women Quarterly*, 1986, *10*(4): 393–412. Monographs afford feminists greater control than do journal articles. For this reason it was essential to not confine my study to journals. See also Dale Spender, "The Gatekeepers: A Feminist Critique of Academic Publishing," in Helen Roberts (ed.), *Doing Feminist Research* (London: Routledge & Kegan Paul, 1981). For a discussion of the barriers to publishing books see Dale Spender and Lynne Spender (eds.), *Gatekeeping: The Denial, Dismissal and Distortion of Women*, a special issue of *Women's Studies International Forum*, 1983, *6*(5).

47. Pauline Bart and Patricia O'Brien employed this procedure in their study, "Stopping Rape: Effective Avoidance Strategies," *Signs: Journal of Women in Culture and Society*, 1984, *10*(1): 83–101. "During the initial telephone call, we asked them for their own definition of the situation. . . . In this way, the women defined themselves into two

parts of the sample: rape avoiders vs. raped women. A serendipitous finding was that while there was no problem involved in differentiating rape from seduction, there was no hard and fast 'objective' line differentiating rape from rape avoidance'' (p. 85).

48. Rosalind C. Barnett and Grace K. Baruch, *The Competent Woman: Perspectives on Development* (New York: Irvington Publishers, 1978), vii.

49. Barrie Thorne and Nancy Henley (eds.), *Language and Sex: Difference and Dominance* (Rowley, MA: Newbury House, 1975), p. x.

50. My method reiterates Meredith Gould's statement in 1977: "Some of the most exciting work on women is not 'purely' sociological but interdisciplinary and has been published in *Women's Studies International Forum, Feminist Studies, The Insurgent Sociologist, Quest, Signs,* and *Socialist Review.* Feminist sociologists are increasingly willing to spark the sociological imagination with the formulations of feminist anthropologists, economists, historians, philosophers and poets." See her "The New Sociology," *Signs: Journal of Women in Culture and Society,* 1980, 5(3): 459–467.

51. Dale Spender, *For the Record: The Meaning and Making of Feminist Knowledge* (London: Women's Press, 1985), pp. 5–6.

52. Claire Robertson includes a long, interesting description of methodological issues that arose in her study of women in Ghana. See Claire Robertson, *Sharing the Same Bowl: A Socioeconomic History of Women and Class in Accra, Ghana* (Bloomington, IN: Indiana University Press, 1984).

53. Margarita Kay, Anna Voda, Guadalupe Olivas, Frances Rios, and Margaret Imle, "Ethnography of the Menopause-Related Hot Flash," *Maturitas,* 1982, 4: 217–227.

54. Virginia Bernard, "Cotton Mather's 'Most Unhappy Wife': Reflections on the Use of Historical Evidence," *The New England Quarterly,* 1987, 60(3): 341–362 was recommended to me by Karen Hansen, but the author does not call herself a feminist in this marvelous article.

55. Barbara Strudler Wallston, "What are the Questions in Psychology of Women? A Feminist Approach to Research," *Psychology of Women Quarterly,* 1981, 5(4): 597–617.

56. bell hooks, *op. cit.* (note 29), p. 10.

57. bell hooks, *Ibid.,* p. 7. See also Bernice Zamora, who rejects "feminism" as ignoring race. "The Chicana's relation to Chicano men she says is different from that of feminists with their men, owing among other reasons to the loss of Chicano men to white women. She sees a parallel problem for black women." This comment is in footnote 25 of Michael M. J. Fischer, "Ethnicity and the Arts of Memory," in James Clifford and George Marcus (eds.), *Writing Culture: The Poetics and Politics of Ethnography* (Berkeley, CA: University of California Press, 1986), p. 223. Bernice Zamora, *Restless Serpents* (Menlo Park, CA: Disenos Literarios, 1976). Bound with Jose Antonio Burciaga, *Restless Serpents.* See also Gloria Hull, Patricia Bell Scott, and Barbara Smith (eds.), *All the Women Are White, All the Men Are Black, But Some of Us Are Brave: Black Women's Studies* (Old Westbury, CT: The Feminist Press, 1982); Cherrie Moraga, *Loving in the War Years* (Boston: South End Press, 1983).

58. Barbara Smith, "Racism and Women's Studies," *Frontiers,* 1980, 5(1): 48–49, p. 49.

59. Defining feminist research in terms of "feminist outcome," as recommended by Mary Lou Kendrigan, *Political Equality in a Democratic Society: Women in the United States* (Westport, CT: Greenwood Press, 1984), would rely too much on my personal assessment.

60. In some instances an author identified herself as feminist, produced what I consider to be an important piece of research, but gave no information about how she produced it.

For example, Nancy Chodorow integrated psychoanalytic and sociological concepts without specifying how she went about it. See her *Reproduction of Mothering: Psychoanalysis and the Sociology of Gender* (Berkeley, CA: University of California Press, 1978).

61. Dale Spender, *For the Record; The Making and Meaning of Feminist Knowledge* (London: The Women's Press, 1985), p. 3.

62. Some citations listed as unpublished at the time of writing may now be published.

63. For a discussion of an inductive research approach, see Barney Glaser and Anselm Strauss, *The Discovery of Grounded Theory* (Chicago: Aldine, 1967).

64. See Nancy Reeves, *Womankind: Beyond the Stereotypes* (Chicago: Aldine, 1971) and Naomi Gottlieb (ed.), *Alternative Social Services for Women* (New York: Columbia University Press, 1980).

65. Based on in-depth interviews of 40 women faculty at 10 U.S. colleges and universities, Patricia Gumport showed that interdisciplinary scholarship was a hallmark of their research; see Patricia Gumport, "The Social Construction of Knowledge: Individual and Institutional Commitments to Feminist Scholarship," doctoral dissertation, Stanford University, 1987, and "Feminist Scholarship as a Vocation," in Gail Kelly and Sheila Slaughter (eds.), *Women's Higher Education: Comparative Perspective* (Norwell, MA: Kluwer Press, 1991).

66. Carolyn Wood Sherif, "Should There Be a Feminist Methodology?," *Newsletter of the Association for Women in Psychology,* January–February 1982, pp. 3–4, p. 3.

67. Bernice Lott, *op. cit.* (note 4), p. 6.

68. See T. Moi, *Sexual/Textual Politics: Feminist Literary Theory* (New York: Methuen, 1985). I do discuss four examples of feminist deconstruction in Chapter 8.

69. Liz Kelly, *Surviving Sexual Violence* (Minneapolis, MN: University of Minnesota Press, 1988), p. 1.

70. Shulamit Reinharz, "Women as Competent Community Builders: The Other Side of the Coin," in Annette Rickel, Meg Gerrard, and Ira Iscoe (eds.), *Social and Psychological Problems of Women* (New York: McGraw-Hill/Hemisphere, 1984), pp. 19–43.

71. The terms "first- and second-waves" make invisible all the feminist work that occurred in between. See Leila Rupp and Verta Taylor, *Surviving in the Doldrums: The American Women's Rights Movements, 1945 to the 1960s* (Columbus, OH: Ohio State University Press, 1990).

72. See Jessie Bernard, *The Female World from a Global Perspective* (Bloomington, IN: Indiana University Press, 1987) for a discussion of the importance of recognizing differences between women's struggles in the United States as compared with other countries, and for her discussion of the importance of not using the word "American" as an adjective equivalent to United States.

73. See Louise Michele Newman (ed.), *Men's Ideas/Women's Realities* (New York: Pergamon, 1985); Rosalind Rosenberg, *Beyond Separate Spheres: Intellectual Roots of Modern Feminism* (New Haven, CT: Yale University Press, 1982); Barbara Miller Solomon, *In The Company of Education Women: A History of Women and Higher Education in America* (New Haven, CT: Yale University Press, 1985); and Janet Sayers, *Biological Politics* (London: Tavistock, 1982).

74. Dorothy E. Smith, "Women's Perspective as a Radical Critique of Sociology," *Sociological Inquiry,* 1974, *44*(1): 7–13, p. 7.

75. Elizabeth Minnich, "Discussion," *The Scholar and the Feminist IV: Connecting Theory, Practice, and Values,* a conference sponsored by The Barnard College Women's Center, April 1977, p. 53.

76. The underground may consist of women's studies classroom discussions and feminist organization newsletter articles.

77. Jill McCalla Vickers, "Memoirs of an Ontological Exile: The Methodological Rebellions of Feminist Research," in Geraldine Finn and Angela Miles (eds.), *Feminism in Canada* (Montreal: Black Rose Books, 1982), pp. 27–46, p. 32.

78. Jessie Bernard, "My Four Revolutions: An Autobiographical History of the ASA," *American Journal of Sociology,* 1973, *78*(4): 773–791.

79. See Mary Daly, *Gyn/Ecology: The Metaethics of Radical Feminism* (Boston: Beacon Press, 1978).

80. Jeanne Gross, "Feminist Ethics from a Marxist Perspective," *Radical Religion,* 1977, *3*(2): 52–56; quoted in bell hooks, *op. cit.* (note 29), pp. 26–27.

81. bell hooks, *op. cit.* (note 29), p. 12.

82. Cheryl Townsend Gilkes, "The Roles of Church and Community Mothers; Ambivalent American Sexism or Fragmented African Familyhood?," *Journal of Feminist Studies in Religion,* 1986, *2*(1): 41–59, p. 57.

83. Becky Thompson, "Raisins and Smiles for Me and My Sister: A Feminist Theory of Eating Problems, Trauma, and Recovery in Women's Lives," doctoral dissertation, Department of Sociology, Brandeis University, 1990.

84. Mary Jo Deegan, "Transcending a Patriarchal Past: Teaching the History of Women in Sociology," *Teaching Sociology,* 1988, *16*: 141–150.

85. Shulamit Reinharz, "Teaching the History of Women in Sociology: or Dorothy Swaine Thomas, Wasn't She the Woman Married to William I.?," *The American Sociologist,* 1989, *20*(1): 87–94; Shulamit Reinharz and Ellen Stone (eds.), *Looking at Invisible Women* (Washington, D.C.: University Press of America, 1992); Kathleen E. Grady, "Sex Bias in Research Design," *Psychology of Women Quarterly,* 1981, *5*(4): 628–636.

86. Valerie Pichanik, *Harriet Martineau: The Woman and Her Work, 1802–1876* (Ann Arbor, MI: University of Michigan Press, 1980); Gayle Yates (ed.), *Harriet Martineau on Women* (New Brunswick, NJ: Rutgers University Press, 1985).

87. Michael R. Hill (ed.), Harriet Martineau, *How to Observe Morals and Manners* (1836) (New Brunswick, NJ: Transaction Books, 1989).

88. Ida B. Wells, *A Red Record; Tabulated Statistics and Alleged Causes of Lynchings in the United States, 1892–1893–1894* (reprinted, Salem, NH: Ayer Company, 1987), p. 15.

89. See Debra Kaufman and Barbara Richardson, *Achievement and Women: Challenging the Assumptions* (New York: Free Press, 1982), for another example of how contemporary feminist research questions are embedded in an historical context.

90. Celia Eckhardt, "Fanny Wright: The Woman Who Made the Myth," paper presented at Conference on "Autobiographies, Biographies and Life Histories of Women: Interdisciplinary Perspectives," University of Minnesota, May 23, 1986, p. 1.

91. Celia Kitzinger, "Resisting the Discipline," in Erica Burman (ed.), *The Practice of Psychology by Feminists* (London: Sage, 1990), pp. 26–27.

92. Judith Lorber, "From the Editor," *Gender & Society,* 1988, *2*(1): 5–8.

93. Joseph Adelson, "Androgyny Advocates Pose a Threat to Scientific Objectivity," *Behavior Today,* 1980, *11*(11): 1–3; and Joseph Adelson and Carolyn Sherif, "Resolved: Division 35 of A.P.A. Is/Is Not a Scholarly Disaster Area," *Behavior Today,* June 2, 1980, p. 3.

94. Nancy Henley, *Body Politics: Power, Sex, and Nonverbal Communication* (Englewood Cliffs, NJ: Prentice-Hall, 1977), p. viii.

95. Mary Daly, *Beyond God the Father* (Boston: Beacon Press, 1973), p. 200, fn. 9.

96. Terry Kandal, *The Woman Question in Classical Sociological Theory* (Miami: Florida International University Press, 1988), p. xiv.

97. Carol Ehrlich considers the following to be excellent feminist research done by

men: Joel Aronoff and William Crano, "A Re-examination of the Cross-Cultural Principles of Task Segregation and Sex Role Differentiation in the Family," *American Sociological Review*, 1975, *40:* 12–20; Howard Ehrlich, "Selected Differences in the Life Chances of Men and Women in the United States" (Baltimore, MD: Research Group One, Report no. 13); and Dean Knudsen, "The Declining Status of Women: Popular Myths and the Failure of Functionalist Thought," *Social Forces*, 1969, *48*(Dec.): 183–193. See also Martin Meissner, "The Reproduction of Women's Domination in Organizational Communication," University of British Columbia (unpublished manuscript). For a defense of men's study of women, see Aileen S. Kraditor's foreword in Ronald Hogeland (ed.), *Women and Woman-hood in America* (Lexington, MA: D. C. Heath, 1973).

98. Del Martin, *Battered Wives* (New York: Simon and Schuster, 1976), p. xviii.

99. Edward Donnerstein, Daniel Linz, and Steven Penrod, *The Question of Pornography: Research Findings and Policy Implications* (New York: Free Press, 1987), p. 196.

100. Richard J. Evans, *The Feminists: Women's Emancipation Movements in Europe, America and Australasia 1840–1920* (New York: Barnes and Noble, 1977), preface.

101. Clive Pearson, "Some Problems in Talking about Men," in Sue Webb and Clive Pearson (eds.), *Looking Back: Some Papers from the BSA 'Gender & Society' Conference*, in Liz Stanley and Sue Scott (eds.), *Studies in Sexual Politics* (University of Manchester, Department of Sociology, 1984), pp. 46–59, p. 48.

102. Michelle Fine, "Contextualizing the Study of Social Injustice," in Michael Saks and Leonard Saxe (eds.), *Advances in Applied Social Psychology* (Hillsdale, NJ: Erlbaum, 1985), pp. 103–126.

103. Shulamit Reinharz, "The Concept of Voice," paper presented at a conference on Human Diversity, Department of Psychology, University of Maryland, October 22–24, 1988.

104. Jean Bethke Elshtain, *Public Man, Private Woman: Women in Social and Political Thought* (Princeton, NJ: Princeton University Press, 1981), p. xii.

105. Shulamit Reinharz, "Finding Her Sociological Voice: The Work of Mirra Komarovsky," *Sociological Inquiry*, 1989, *59*(4): 374–395.

106. Catherine Hodge McCoid, "What's in a Name? Non-sexist Transmission of Last Names," *Midwest Feminist Papers*, 1986, 55–59; Mary Jo Deegan, "A Rose Is Not a Rosa, Is Not a Roseann: The Many Names of Mary Elizabeth Burroughs Roberts Smith Coolidge," in Judith Long (ed.), *The New Sociobiography*, manuscript.

107. See Sara Delamont, *Knowledgeable Women: Structuralism and the Reproduction of Elites* (London: Routledge, 1989), p. 4.

108. See Renate Klein, "How To Do What We Want To Do: Thoughts about Feminist Methodology," in Gloria Bowles and Renate Klein (eds.), *Theories of Women's Studies* (Boston: Routledge & Kegan Paul, 1983), pp. 88–104.

109. Mary Ann Campbell, "Creating Feminist Sociology," *SWS Network*, 1982, *12*(1): 23–24, p. 24. See also Judith Long Laws, "Patriarchy as Paradigm: The Challenge from Feminist Scholarship," paper presented at the Annual Meeting of the American Sociological Association, New York, August 1976.

Chapter 2   Feminist Interview Research

1. This chapter benefited from insightful readings by Marjorie L. DeVault and Ellen Stone.

2. Hilary Graham, "Surveying through Stories," in Colin Bell and Helen Roberts (eds.), *Social Researching: Politics, Problems, Practice* (London: Routledge & Kegan Paul, 1984),

p. 112 [emphasis added]. Semistructured refers to a research approach whereby the researcher plans to ask questions about a given topic but allows the data-gathering conversation itself to determine how the information is obtained.

3. Feminist interview researchers tend to interchange the terms unstructured, intensive, in-depth, and open-ended.

4. Ethnographic studies frequently include interviewing components, and interview studies frequently include ethnographic components. An example of the latter is found in Debra Kaufman's interview-based study of newly orthodox Jewish women: "Loosely structured interviews (what I call structured 'conversations') allowed these women to reveal their own significant issues and concerns. . . . To understand these women's ties to one another, their links to families, community and the theology they embraced, I spent many weeks in each community. Although this is neither an ethnographic nor participant observation study, I borrowed many of the techniques both kinds of researchers use. I attended lectures, Sabbath services, classes, informal afternoon gatherings, Sisterhood meetings, and coffee get-togethers. I changed diapers, walked in parks, celebrated holidays, shared La Leche and Lamaze notes from the days when my own children were that young. I visited wig shops, went to a *mikveh* (ritual bathhouse), sat behind a *mechitzah* (partition between men and women in the synagogue), ate meals in strictly kosher restaurants, to put the experiences these women described into a concrete context." Debra Renee Kaufman, *Rachel's Daughters: Newly Orthodox Jewish Women* (New Brunswick, NJ: Rutgers University Press, 1991), p. 4.

5. Closed-end questions ask respondents to choose among the options presented; open-ended questions ask respondents to provide an answer in their own words.

6. Patricia Cayo Sexton, *The New Nightingales: Hospital Workers, Unions, New Women's Issues* (New York: Enquiry Press, 1982), p. 5.

7. Janice Raymond, *The Transsexual Empire: The Making of the She-Male* (Boston: Beacon Press, 1979), p. 16.

8. For example, see Terry Arendell, *Mothers and Divorce: Legal, Economic, and Social Dilemmas* (Berkeley, CA: University of California Press, 1986); Laurel Richardson, *The New Woman: Contemporary Single Women in Affairs with Married Men* (New York: Free Press, 1985); Laura T. Fishman, *Women at the Wall: A Study of Prisoners' Wives Doing Time on the Outside* (Albany, NY: State University of New York Press, 1990).

9. Barney Glaser and Anselm Strauss, *The Discovery of Grounded Theory: Strategies for Qualitative Research* (Chicago: Aldine, 1967). Oliva Espin used their perspective to analyze open-ended questionnaire data, see her, "Issues of Identity in the Psychology of Latina Lesbians," in Boston Lesbian Psychologies Collective (eds.), *Lesbian Psychologies* (Chicago: University of Illinois, 1987), pp. 35–55.

10. Rae Andre, "Evaluating Homemaker's Quality of Working Life: Establishing Criteria of Quality," paper presented at the Annual Conference of the Association for Women in Psychology, Boston, 1981, pp. 5, 12.

11. See Julius Roth, "Hired Hand Research," *The American Sociologist,* 1966, *1*: 190–196.

12. Diana Scully, "Convicted Rapists' Perceptions of Self and Victim: Role Taking and Emotions," *Gender & Society,* 1988, *2*(2): 200–213, pp. 202–204.

13. See Susan E. Bell, "Becoming a Political Woman: The Reconstruction and Interpretation of Experience through Stories," in Alexandra Dumas Todd and Sue Fisher (eds.), *Gender and Discourse: The Power of Talk* (Norwood, NJ: Ablex, 1988), pp. 97–123; see also Catherine Riessman, *Divorce Talk: Women and Men Make Sense of Personal Relationships* (New Brunswick: Rutgers University Press, 1990).

14. Mary Belenky, Blythe Clinchy, Nancy Goldberger, and Jill Tarule, *Women's Ways*

of Knowing: The Development of Self, Voice and Mind (New York: Basic Books, 1986), p. 11. For a critique of the methodology of this study see Mary Crawford, "Agreeing to Differ: Feminist Epistemologies and Women's Ways of Knowing," in Mary Crawford and Margaret Gentry (eds.), *Gender and Thought: Psychological Perspectives* (New York: Springer-Verlag, 1989), pp. 128–145.

15. Sharon Mast, "Qualitative Sociology in New Zealand," in Shulamit Reinharz and Peter Conrad (eds.), *Qualitative Sociology in International Perspective* (special issue), *Qualitative Sociology,* 1988, *11*(1–2): 99–112, citing Bev James, "Taking Gender into Account: Feminist and Sociological Issues in Social Research," *New Zealand Sociology,* 1986, *1*: 18–33, and Bev James, "Mill Wives: A Study of Gender Relations, Family and Work in a Single-Industry Town," doctoral dissertation, Department of Sociology, Waikato University, Hamilton, 1985.

16. Kathy Charmaz, "Intensive Interviewing," Gerontology Program, Sonoma State University, Rohnert Park, CA, December 1986, unpublished manuscript.

17. See also Fiona Poland, "Coming Up with the Goods: Working with Recall Tapes in an Elderly Peoples' Home," in Feminist Research Seminar (eds.), *Feminist Research Processes,* Liz Stanley and Sue Scott (eds.), *Studies in Sexual Politics,* Department of Sociology, University of Manchester, pp. 48–78.

18. Rosanna Hertz, *More Equal Than Others: Women and Men in Dual-Career Marriages* (Berkeley, CA: University of California Press, 1986), p. 223.

19. Robin Gregg, "Pregnancy in a High-Tech Age: Paradoxes of Choice," doctoral dissertation, Brandeis University, 1991.

20. Shulamit Reinharz, "Phenomenology as a Dynamic Process," *Phenomenology and Pedagogy,* 1983, *1*(1): 77–79.

21. Margarete Sandelowski and Christine Pollock, "Women's Experiences of Infertility," *IMAGE: Journal of Nursing Scholarship,* Winter 1986, *18*(4): 140–144.

22. See the "conclusions" chapter for a discussion of this term.

23. Christine Webb, "Feminist Methodology in Nursing Research," *Journal of Advanced Nursing,* 1984, *9:* 249–256, p. 249. For a discussion of this study, see Denise Connors, "A Continuum of Researcher-Participant Relationships: An Analysis and Critique," *Advances in Nursing Science,* 1988, *10*(4): 32–42.

24. Pauline B. Bart and Patricia O'Brien, "Stopping Rape: Effective Avoidance Strategies," *Signs: Journal of Women in Culture and Society,* 1984, *10*(1): 83–101, p. 84.

25. Lydia O'Donnell, *The Unheralded Majority: Contemporary Women as Mothers* (Lexington, MA: Lexington Books, 1985).

26. Lynn Davidman, *Tradition in a Rootless World: Women Turn to Orthodox Judaism* (Berkeley, CA: University of California Press, 1991); see also her "Gender and Religious Experience," paper presented at the American Sociological Association meetings, Atlanta, 1988.

27. Florence Rush, *Best Kept Secret: Sexual Abuse of Children* (Englewood Cliffs, NJ: Prentice-Hall, 1980).

28. Rosanna Hertz, *op. cit.* (note 18); Kristin Luker, *Abortion and the Politics of Motherhood* (Berkeley, CA: University of California Press, 1984).

29. The fact that the duration of an interview is reported more frequently than any other characteristic suggests an implicit norm stating that lengthy interviews reflect the achievement of rapport and the receipt of detailed information. Because of the increasing demands on women's time, it is possible that long interviews will become more burdensome to interviewees and less common.

30. Patricia Yancey Martin, Sandra Seymour, Myrna Courage, Karolyn Godbey, and

Richard State, "Work-Family Policies: Corporate, Union, Feminist, and Pro-Family Leaders' Views," *Gender & Society*, 1988, 2(3): 385–400.

31. Some non-feminist journals have adopted this practice, e.g., *American Journal of Community Psychology*.

32. Sheila M. Rothman, *Woman's Proper Place: A History of Changing Ideals and Practices, 1870 to the Present* (New York: Basic Books, 1978), p. 53.

33. Helen Campbell, *Prisoners of Poverty: Women Wage-Workers, Their Trades and Their Lives* (New York: Garrett Press, 1970 [1883]; Boston, Little Brown & Co. [1887]).

34. Helen Campbell, *Women Wage-earners* (New York: ARNO Press, 1972 [1893]).

35. See also Harriet Martineau, *Illustrations of Political Economy* (London: Charles Fox, 1832–1834), 25 nos. in 6 vols. Similarly, Helen Campbell's decades-long feminist sociologist friend, Charlotte Perkins Gilman (1860–1935), expressed some of her sociological ideas as fiction. See her "Yellow Wall-Paper," *New England Magazine*, 1892, 5: 647–56, reprinted as *The Yellow Wallpaper* (Old Westbury, NY: The Feminist Press, 1973). For a discussion of Charlotte Gilman as a sociologist, see Mary Jo Deegan (ed.), *Women in Sociology: A Bio-Bibliographic Sourcebook* (Westport, CT: Greenwood Press, 1991).

36. Alice Kessler-Harris, *Out to Work: A History of Wage-Earning Women in the United States* (New York: Oxford University Press, 1982), p. 104.

37. Marilyn Frye discusses men's claim to be oppressed in *The Politics of Reality: Essays in Feminist Theory* (Trumansburg, NY: The Crossing Press, 1983).

38. Helen Campbell, *Prisoners of Poverty Abroad* (Boston: Roberts Brothers, 1890), p. 9.

39. Shulamit Reinharz, "Finding a Sociological Voice: The Work of Mirra Komarovsky," *Sociological Inquiry*, 1989, 59(4): 374–395.

40. Margaret Hagood, *Mothers of the South: Portraiture of the White Tenant Farm Woman* (Chapel Hill: University of North Carolina Press, 1939), pp. 224–228.

41. The same rule may apply to men interviewing men.

42. Dale Spender, *Man Made Language* (London: Routledge & Kegan Paul, 1980).

43. Marjorie L. DeVault, "Women's Talk: Feminist Strategies for Analyzing Research Interviews," *Women and Language*, 1987, 10(2): 33–36; and Marjorie DeVault, "Talking and Listening from Women's Standpoint: Feminist Strategies for Interviewing and Analysis," *Social Problems*, 1990, 37(1): 701–721. See also Catharine MacKinnon, "Feminism, Marxism, Method and the State: An Agenda for Theory," in Elizabeth Abel and Emily K. Abel (eds.), *The Signs Reader* (Chicago: University of Chicago Press, 1983), pp. 227–256.

44. Stephanie Riger, "Ways of Knowing and Community Organizational Research," invited address, Conference on Researching Community Psychology: Integrating Theories and Methodologies, Chicago, September 1988. Reprinted in P. Tolan, C. Keys, F. Chertok, and L. Jason, *Researching Community Psychology: Issues of Theory and Methods* (Washington, D.C.: American Psychological Association, 1990).

45. Sharon Mast, *op. cit.* (note 15).

46. Nadya Aisenberg and Mona Harrington, *Women of Academe: Outsiders in the Sacred Grove* (Amherst, MA: University of Massachusetts Press, 1988), p. x.

47. Susan Yeandle, *Women's Working Lives: Patterns and Strategies* (New York: Tavistock, Publications, 1984), pp. vii, 39, 46, 47.

48. Margaret Gordon and Stephanie Riger, *The Female Fear* (New York: Free Press, 1989), p. xii.

49. Naomi Gerstel, "Divorce, Gender, and Social Integration," *Gender & Society*, 1988, 2(3): 343–367.

50. Catherine Riessman, "When Gender Is Not Enough: Women Interviewing Women," *Gender & Society,* 1987, *2*(1): 172–207.

51. Susan Condor, "Sex Role Beliefs and 'Traditional' Women: Feminist and Intergroup Perspectives," in Sue Wilkinson (ed.), *Feminist Social Psychology* (Philadelphia: Open University Press, 1986), pp. 97–118, pp. 102–103, 110.

52. This phrase comes from Hortense Powdermaker, *Stranger and Friend: The Way of an Anthropologist* (New York: Norton, 1966).

53. Denise Segura, "Chicana and Mexican Immigrant Women at Work: The Impact of Class, Race and Gender on Occupational Mobility," *Gender & Society,* 1989, *3*(1): 37–52, pp. 41–42.

54. Mary K. Zimmerman, *Passage through Abortion: The Personal and Social Reality of Women's Experiences* (New York: Praeger, 1977), p. 210. The idea of distance creating good conditions for trust in research relationships is also discussed in David Gordon, "Getting Close by Staying Distant: Fieldwork with Proselytizing Groups," *Qualitative Sociology,* 1987, *10*(3): 267–287.

55. Sara Evans, *Personal Politics: The Roots of Women's Liberation in the Civil Rights Movement and the New Left* (New York: Vintage Books, 1979), p. x.

56. Michelle Fine, "Coping with Rape: Critical Perspectives on Consciousness," *Imagination, Cognition and Personality,* 1983–1984, *3*(3): 249–267, pp. 260–261.

57. For a discussion of the ethical issues raised by deception in participant observation see Judith Rollins, *Between Women: Domestics and their Employers* (Philadelphia, PA: Temple University Press, 1985), pp. 11–17.

58. Ann Oakley, "Interviewing Women: A Contradiction in Terms," in Helen Roberts (ed.), *Doing Feminist Research* (London: Routledge & Kegan Paul, 1981), pp. 30–61.

59. Ann Oakley, *The Sociology of Housework* (Oxford, England: Basil Blackwell, 1985), p. xi.

60. In *On Becoming a Social Scientist: From Survey Research and Participant Observation to Experiential Analysis* (New Brunswick, NJ: Transaction Books, 1984), I contrast the "rape model of research" with an alternative called "temporary affiliation."

61. Ann Oakley, *op. cit.* (note 59).

62. See Erving Goffman, *The Presentation of Self in Everyday Life* (Garden City, NY: Doubleday Anchor, 1959).

63. Emily Abel, "Collective Protest and the Meritocracy: Faculty Women and Sex Discrimination Lawsuits," *Feminist Studies,* 1981, *7*(3): 505–538; reprinted in Mary Jo Deegan and Michael R. Hill (eds.), *Women and Symbolic Interaction* (Winchester, MA: Allen & Unwin, 1987), pp. 347–378; quotation is from latter, pp. 347, 375.

64. Margaret Andersen, "Corporate Wives: Longing for Liberation or Satisfied with the Status Quo?," *Urban Life,* 1981, *10*(3): 311–327, reprinted in Mary Jo Deegan and Michael R. Hill (eds.), *Women and Symbolic Interaction* (Winchester, MA: Allen & Unwin, Inc., 1987), pp. 179–190, pp. 182, 187, 181.

65. Jessie Bernard, *The Future of Marriage* (New Haven, CT: Yale University Press, 1982), 2nd ed. p. 292.

66. Pauline Bart, "Seizing the Means of Reproduction: An Illegal Feminist Abortion Collective—How and Why It Worked," *Qualitative Sociology,* 1987, *10*(4): 339–357.

67. Audrey Bronstein, *The Triple Struggle: Latin American Peasant Women* (Boston: South End Press, 1982), p. 12.

68. Judy Wajcman, *Women in Control: Dilemmas of a Workers' Cooperative* (New York: St. Martin's Press, 1983), p. xiii.

69. Hilary Graham, *op. cit.* (note 2), p. 120.

70. Carol Smart, "Researching Prostitution: Some Problems for Feminist Research,"

in Nebraska Sociological Feminist Collective, *A Feminist Ethic for Social Science Research* (Lewiston, NY: Edwin Mellen Press, 1988), pp. 37–46.

71. Christine Webb, *op. cit.* (note 23), pp. 252–256.

72. Janice Raymond, *The Transsexual Empire: The Making of the She-Male* (Boston: Beacon Press, 1979), pp. 15–16. This approach to method overlaps with Judith Herman and Lisa Hirschman, *Father-Daughter Incest* (Cambridge, MA: Harvard University Press, 1981), discussed in the "multiple methods" chapter.

73. Elissa Melamed, *Mirror Mirror: The Terror of Not Being Young* (New York: Simon & Schuster, 1983).

74. Ann R. Bristow and Jody A. Esper, "A Feminist Research Ethos," in Nebraska Sociological Feminist Collective (ed.), *A Feminist Ethic for Social Science Research* (Lewiston, NY: The Edwin Mellen Press, 1988), pp. 67–81, pp. 67–68, 71.

75. Marti Bombyk, Mary Bricker-Jenkins, and Marilyn Wedenoja, "Reclaiming Our Profession through Feminist Research: Some Methodological Issues in the Feminist Practice Project," paper presented at the Annual Program Meeting of the Council on Social Work Education, February 1985. In her study of conservative women, Rebecca E. Klatch deliberately did *not* self-disclose so as to avoid alienating her interviewees: "I built trust by adopting a nonargumentative approach in the interviews. While I would push to clarify ideas and beliefs, I did not assert my own opinions, judgments, or values nor did I try to debate ideas. If asked, of course, I would state my own doubts or disagreements, but generally I defined my own role entirely in terms of listening and absorbing the other world view. I believe this approach, more than anything else, bridged the gap between men and the women I interviewed." Rebecca E. Klatch, *Women of the New Right* (Philadelphia: Temple University Press, 1987), p. 17.

76. James Ptacek, "Why Do Men Batter Their Wives?," in Kersti Yllo and Michele Bograd (eds.), *Feminist Perspectives on Wife Abuse* (Newbury Park, CA: Sage, 1988), pp. 133–157, pp. 133–134.

77. Terry Arendell, *Mothers and Divorce: Legal, Economic, and Social Dilemmas* (Berkeley, CA: University of California Press, 1986).

78. Ann R. Bristow and Jody A. Esper, *op. cit.* (note 74), p. 71.

79. Becky Thompson, "Raisins and Smiles for Me and My Sister: A Feminist Theory of Eating Problems, Trauma, and Recovery in Women's Lives," doctoral disssertation, Department of Sociology, Brandeis University, 1990, pp. 24, 27, 30–32.

80. Margaret Gordon and Stephanie Riger, *op. cit.* (note 48), p. xiii.

81. Barbara Katz Rothman, "Reflections: On Hard Work," *Qualitative Sociology,* 1986, 9(1): 48–53, p. 48.

82. Janet Kahn, "Qualitative Methods," unpublished paper, Department of Sociology, Brandeis University, 1990, pp. 10–11.

83. Personal communication. See Renate Klein, *The Exploitation of a Desire: Women's Experiences with In Vitro Fertilisation, an Exploratory Survey* (Geelong, Victoria: Deakin University Press, 1989).

84. Lenore Weitzman, *The Divorce Revolution: The Unexpected Social and Economic Consequences for Women and Children in America* (New York: Free Press, 1985).

85. Denise Connors, " 'I've Always Had Everything I've Wanted, But I Never Wanted Very Much': An Experiential Analysis of Irish-American Working-Class Women in Their Nineties," doctoral dissertation, Department of Sociology, Brandeis University, 1986, p. 47.

86. Claire Louise Reinelt, "Towards a Theory of Feminist Political Practice: A Case Study of the Texas Shelter Movement," unpublished paper, Department of Anthropology, The University of Texas at Austin, 1985, p. 33.

87. Liz Kelly, *Surviving Sexual Violence* (Minneapolis, MN: University of Minnesota Press, 1988), p. 13.

88. Robin Gregg, *op. cit.* (note 19), pp. 1, 5, 6.

89. Sarah Fenstermaker Berk, *The Gender Factory; The Apportionment of Work in American Households* (New York: Plenum Press, 1985), pp. viii, 38.

90. Kathleen Daly, "Rethinking Judicial Paternalism: Gender, Work-Family Relations, and Sentencing," *Gender & Society,* 1989, *3*(1): 9–36.

91. Marianne A. Paget, "The Ontological Anguish of Women Artists," *New England Sociologist,* 1981, *3*(6): 65–79.

92. See Paula Nicolson, "Developing a Feminist Approach to Depression Following Childbirth," in Sue Wilkinson (ed.), *Feminist Social Psychology: Developing Theory and Practice* (Philadelphia: Open University Press, 1986), pp. 135–149, for a study that continuously compares interviews with theory and measures.

93. Michelle Fine, *op. cit.* (note 56), p. 253.

94. Marjorie L. DeVault, *op. cit.* (note 43, *Social Problems*).

95. Liz Kelly, *op. cit.* (note 87), p. vii.

96. Catherine Riessman, *op. cit.* (note 13), pp. 18–19.

97. Lillian Breslow Rubin, *Worlds of Pain: Life in the Working-Class Family* (New York: Basic Books, 1976), pp. 9, 10, 11.

98. Judy Wajcman, *op. cit.* (note 68), pp. xii–xiv.

99. Sarah Berk, *op. cit.* (note 89), pp. 38, 40–41, 44, 48–49. For a discussion of diaries in the study of housework, see also Catherine White Berheide, Sarah F. Berk, and Richard A. Berk, "Household Work in the Suburbs: The Job and Its Participants," *Pacific Sociological Review,* 1976, *19*: 491–518.

100. For example, Patricia Martin, Sandra Seymour, Myrna Courage, Karolyn Godbey, and Richard Tate, "Work-Family Policies: Corporate, Union, Feminist, and Pro-Family Leaders' Views," *Gender & Society,* 1988, *2*(3): 385–400. See also Susan Ostrander, *Women of the Upper Class* (Philadelphia: PA: Temple University Press, 1984).

101. Mary Belenky et al., *op. cit.* (note 14), p. 11.

102. Leslie Bender, "From Gender Difference to Feminist Solidarity: Using Carol Gilligan and an Ethic of Care in Law," *Vermont Law Review,* 1990, *15*(1): 1–30; Helen Buss, "The Different Voice of Canadian Feminist Autobiographers," *Biography,* Spring 1990, *13*(2): 154–167; Bill Puka, "The Liberation of Caring: A Different Voice for Gilligan's 'Different Voice'," *Hypatia,* 1990, *5*(1): 58–82; Lad Tobin, "A Radically Different Voice: Gender and Language in the Trials of Anne Hutchinson," *Early American Literature,* 1990, *25*(3): 253–270; M. Urban Walker, "What does the Different Voice Say?: Gilligan's Women and Moral Philosophy," *The Journal of Value Inquiry,* 1989, *23*(2): 123–128; Susan Juster, " 'In a Different Voice': Male and Female Narratives of Religious Conversion in Post-Revolutionary America," *American Quarterly,* 1989, *41*(1): 34–62; Mary Carolyn Cooper, "Gilligan's Different Voice: A Perspective for Nursing," *Journal of Professional Nursing,* 1989, *5*(1): 10–18; Anne Byrd, "A Qualitative Analysis of the Decision to Remarry Using Gilligan's Ethic of Care," *Journal of Divorce,* 1988, *11*(3/4): 87–97; Pamela Chally, "Theory Derivation in Moral Development," *Nursing & Health Care,* 1990, *11*(6): 302–313; Nancy Stiller and Linda Forrest, "An Extension of Gilligan and Lyons' Investigation of Morality: Gender Differences in College Students," *Journal of College Student Development,* 1990, *31*(1): 54–62; Lawrence Blum, "Gilligan and Kohlberg: Implications for Moral Theory," *Ethics,* 1988, *98*(3): 472–491; and Linda Kerber, C. Greeno, and Eleanor Maccoby, "On 'In a Different Voice': An Interdisciplinary Forum," *Signs: Journal of Women in Culture and Society,* 1986, *11*(2): 304–333.

103. Anne Colby and William Damon, "Listening to a Different Voice: A Review of

Gilligan's *In a Different Voice,"* *Merrill-Palmer Quarterly,* 1983, *29*(4): 473–481. For a discussion and additional references, see Mary Roth Walsh (ed.), *The Psychology of Women: Ongoing Debates* (New Haven, CT: Yale University Press, 1987), pp. 274–277; see also Judith Stacey, "On Resistance, Ambivalence and Feminist Theory: A Response to Carol Gilligan," *Michigan Quarterly Review,* 1990, *29*(4): 537–546.

104. Carol Gilligan, *In a Different Voice: Psychological Theory and Women's Development* (Cambridge, MA: Harvard University Press, 1982), pp. 2, 3, 20–21, 72, 112. See Carol Gilligan, Nona Lyons, and Trudy Hanmer, *Making Connections: The Relational Worlds of Adolescent Girls at Emma Willard School* (Cambridge, MA: Harvard University Press, 1990).

105. This book also relies heavily on literary figures such as Shakespeare, Ibsen, Bergman, Kingston, Woolf, and Joyce to make its points.

106. See Toby Jayaratne, "The Value of Quantitative Methodology for Feminist Research," in Gloria Bowles and Renate Duelli Klein (eds.), *Theories of Women's Studies* (Boston: Routledge & Kegan Paul, 1983), pp. 162–191.

107. Diana E. H. Russell, *Rape in Marriage* (New York: Macmillan, 1982), pp. 28–30, 31–33. I discuss a segment of these quotes in the chapter on feminist survey research.

108. Margaret Gordon and Stephanie Riger, *op. cit.* (note 48).

109. Pauline B. Bart and Patricia H. O'Brien, *Stopping Rape: Successful Survival Strategies* (New York: Pergamon, 1985).

Chapter 3   Feminist Ethnography

1. This chapter benefited greatly from thorough readings by Claire Reinelt and P. J. McGann.

2. Judith DiIorio, "Feminist Fieldwork in a Masculinist Setting: Personal Problems and Methodological Issues," paper presented at the North Central Sociological Association Meetings, Detroit, Michigan, May 6, 1982.

3. See Rosalie Wax, *Doing Fieldwork: Warnings and Advice* (Chicago: University of Chicago Press, 1971) for a thorough description by a woman of the experience of doing fieldwork in various settings.

4. Shulamit Reinharz, "So-called Training in the So-called Alternative Paradigm," in Egon Guba (ed.), *The Paradigm Dialog* (Newbury Park, CA: Sage, 1990).

5. I use the terms qualitative methods, human science inquiry, participant observation, fieldwork, and naturalistic inquiry interchangeably.

6. For a rejection of this criticism, see Joey Sprague and Mary K. Zimmerman, "Quality and Quantity: Reconstructing Feminist Methodology," *The American Sociologist,* 1989, *20*(1): 71–86.

7. See Rhoda K. Unger (ed.), *Representations: Social Constructions of Gender* (Amityville, NY: Baywood Publishing Company, 1989).

8. Dorothy E. Smith uses the term "institutional ethnography" to describe "accounts of institutions from the standpoint of those who perform their daily activities." See the review of her *The Everyday World as Problematic: A Feminist Sociology* (Boston: Northeastern University Press, 1987) by Joey Sprague in *Contemporary Sociology,* 1989, *18*(4): 640–641. See also Dorothy Smith, "Institutional Ethnography: A Feminist Method," *Resources for Feminist Research,* 1986 (May): 6–13.

9. Kristen R. Yount, "Ladies, Flirts, and Tomboys: Strategies for Managing Sexual Harassment in an Underground Coal Mine," *Journal of Contemporary Ethnography,* 1991, *19*(4): 396–422.

10. Judith DiIorio, "Feminism, Gender, and the Ethnographic Study of Sport," *Arena: The Institute for Sport and Social Analysis,* 1989, *13*(1): 49–60.

11. Judith Stacey, "Can there be a Feminist Ethnography?" *Women's Studies International Forum,* 1988, *11*(1): 21–27.

12. A synonym for ethnographic in this context.

13. Virginia O'Leary, *Toward Understanding Women* (Monterey, CA: Brooks/Cole, 1977), p. 202. Cited is J. S. Hyde and B. G. Rosenberg, *Half the Human Experience* (Lexington, MA: Heath, 1976).

14. Bronislaw Malinowski, *Argonauts of the Western Pacific* (New York: Dutton, 1922).

15. Annette B. Weiner, *Women of Value, Men of Renown: New Perspectives in Trobriand Exchange* (Austin, TX: University of Texas Press, 1976), p. 228.

16. When I use the word "women," I refer to women and girls.

17. Kamala Visweswaran suggests, however, that "a feminist anthropology cannot assume the willingness of women to talk, and that one avenue . . . is to investigate when and why women do talk, to assess what strictures are placed on their speech, what avenues of creativity they have appropriated, and what degrees of freedom they possess." See Kamala Visweswaran, "Defining Feminist Ethnography," *Inscriptions: Feminism and the Critique of Colonial Discourse,* 1988, *3/4*: 26–44, p. 37.

18. Harriet Martineau, *Society in America* [1837], edited, abridged, and with an introductory essay by Seymour Martin Lipset (Garden City, NY: Anchor Books, 1962), pp. 50, 53–54, 291. See Michael R. Hill, "The Methodological Framework of Harriet Martineau's Feminist Analyses of American Society," paper presented at the Annual Meeting of the American Studies Association, November 2, 1990, New Orleans for a discussion of the androcentric methodological biases in Alexis de Tocqueville's *Democracy in America* (1835–1840).

19. See Celia Eckhardt, *Fanny Wright: Rebel in America* (Cambridge, MA: Harvard University Press, 1984); and Alice Rossi (ed.), *Feminist Papers: From Adams to de Beauvoir* (Boston: Northeastern University Press, 1973, 1988).

20. Joan Mark, *A Stranger in Her Native Land: Alice Fletcher and the American Indians* (Lincoln, NE: University of Nebraska Press, 1988), pp. 39, 41. Like many anthropologists after her, Alice Fletcher brought artifacts from the field for display in museums. A recent controversy about whether or not Alice Fletcher should have removed certain artifacts from the Omaha people led to their return from the Peabody Museum at Harvard University.

21. Hortense Powdermaker, "Field Work," in David L. Sills (ed.), *International Encyclopedia of the Social Sciences* (New York: Macmillan and Free Press, 1972).

22. Robert S. Lynd and Helen Merrell Lynd, *Middletown: A Study in American Culture* (New York: Harcourt and Brace, 1929).

23. Helen Merrell Lynd, *Possibilities* (Ohio: Ink Well Press, 1983), pp. 35, 38, cited in Ronni Rothman, "Beyond *Middletown:* The Life Work of Helen Merrell Lynd," in Shulamit Reinharz and Ellen Stone (eds.), *Looking at Invisible Women: An Exercise in Feminist Pedagogy* (Washington, D.C.: University Press of America, 1992).

24. A follow-up study was done in 1935. The fieldworkers included Robert Lynd as director, three graduate students at Columbia University where Robert Lynd was employed (Bela Gold, Katharine Hogle, and Mary Frances Holter) and two graduates of Sarah Lawrence College (Hannah Cheney and Edna Albers Strewart) where Helen Lynd was employed. Helen Merrell Lynd apparently was not a member of the 1935 fieldwork team, but did participate in writing the second book, *Middletown in Transition: A Study in Cultural Conflicts* (New York: Harcourt Brace, 1937).

25. Some of these topics are discussed in the chapter on cross-cultural research in this book.

26. Lyn Lofland, "The 'Thereness' of Women: A Selective Review of Urban Sociology," in Marcia Millman and Rosabeth Kanter (eds.), *Another Voice: Feminist Perspectives on Social Life and Social Science* (Garden City, NY: Anchor Press, 1975).

27. Carol Stack, *All Our Kin: Strategies for Survival in a Black Community* (New York: Harper & Row, 1974).

28. Denise Connors, " 'I've Always Had Everything I Wanted, . . . But I Never Wanted Very Much': An Experiential Analysis of Irish-American Working Class Women in their Nineties," doctoral dissertation, Department of Sociology, Brandeis University, 1986.

29. Susan Stall, "Women in a Small Town: An Invisible Power Structure," paper presented at the joint Annual Meeting of the Midcontinent American Studies Association and the North Central American Studies Association, University of Iowa, 1983, p. 12.

30. For a discussion of Georg Simmel's views, see Terry R. Kandal, *The Woman Question in Classical Sociological Theory* (Miami: Florida International University Press, 1988); see also *Georg Simmel: On Women, Sexuality, and Love,* translated and with an introduction by Guy Oakes (New Haven, CT: Yale University Press, 1984).

31. Georg Simmel, *Philosophische Kultur* (Leipzig: Werner Klinkhardt, 1911) discussed in Lewis A. Coser, "Georg Simmel's Neglected Contributions to the Sociology of Women," *Signs: Journal of Women in Culture and Society,* 1977, 2(4): 872–873, cited in Catharine MacKinnon, *Sexual Harassment of Working Women* (New Haven, CT: Yale University Press, 1979), p. 3.

32. See Shulamit Reinharz, "Feminist Distrust: Problems of Content and Context in Sociological Research," in David Berg and Ken Smith (eds.), *The Self in Social Inquiry: Researching Methods* (Beverly Hills, CA: Sage, 1985, 1988), pp. 153–172.

33. Irene Dabrowski, "Developmental Job Patterns of Working-Class Women," *Qualitative Sociology,* 1983, 6(1): 29–50, p. 30.

34. Roberta Goldberg, *Organizing Women Office Workers: Dissatisfaction, Consciousness and Action* (New York: Praeger, 1983), pp. 1–11.

35. Christine Delphy, "Women in Stratification Studies," in Helen Roberts (ed.), *Doing Feminist Research* (Boston: Routledge & Kegan Paul, 1981), pp. 114–128.

36. Judith Stacey, "Sexism by a Subtler Name? Postindustrial Conditions and Postfeminist Consciousness in the Silicon Valley," *Socialist Review,* 1987, *17*: 1–28, pp. 13–14. Also see Judith Stacey, *Brave New Families: Stories of Domestic Upheaval in Late Twentieth Century America* (New York: Basic Books, 1990).

37. Carolyn Ellis, *Fisher Folk: Two Communities on Chesapeake Bay* (Lexington, KY: The University Press of Kentucky, 1986), see pp. 4–5.

38. Marjorie Shostak, *Nisa: The Life and Words of a !Kung Woman* (New York: Vintage Books, 1983).

39. Carol Stack, *All Our Kin: Strategies for Survival in a Black Community* (New York: Harper Torchbook, 1975), p. xi.

40. Irene Dabrowski, *op. cit.* (note 33), p. 50.

41. Faye Ginsburg, *Contested Lives: The Abortion Debate in an American Community* (Berkeley, CA: University of California Press, 1989).

42. See Shulamit Reinharz, *On Becoming a Social Scientist* (New Brunswick, NJ: Transaction Books, 1984) and Shulamit Reinharz, "Experiential Analysis: A Contribution to Feminist Research Methodology," in Gloria Bowles and Renate Duelli Klein (eds.), *Theories of Women's Studies* (Boston: Routledge & Kegan Paul, 1983), pp. 162–191.

43. Nickie Charles and Marion Kerr, *Women, Food and Families* (Manchester: Man-

chester University Press, 1988). See also Marion Kerr, "Sharing in a Common Plight?" *Poverty* (Special Issue on Poverty and Food), 1985, *60*: 22–26. For a discussion of the significance of the latter study see Janet Sayers, *Sexual Contradictions: Psychology, Psychoanalysis, and Feminism* (London: Tavistock, 1986), p. 5.

44. Jessie Bernard, *The Sex Game* (New York: Atheneum, 1972), cited and discussed in Nancy Henley, *Body Politics: Power, Sex, and Nonverbal Communication* (Englewood Cliffs, NJ: Prentice-Hall, 1977), p. 74.

45. William Foote Whyte, *Street Corner Society: The Social Structure of an Italian Slum* (Chicago: University of Chicago Press, 1943/1955).

46. Elliot Liebow, *Tally's Corner: A Study of Negro Streetcorner Men* (Boston: Little, Brown, 1967).

47. Laud Humphreys, *Tearoom Trade: Impersonal Sex in Public Places* (Chicago: Aldine, 1970).

48. See Lois Easterday, Diana Papademas, Laura Schorr, and Catherine Valentine, "The Making of a Female Researcher: Role Problems in Fieldwork," *Urban Life,* 1977, *6*(3): 333–348, reprinted in Robert Burgess (ed.), *Field Research: A Sourcebook and Field Manual* (London: George Allen & Unwin, 1982), pp. 62–67.

49. Others might include Nels Anderson, *The Hobo: The Sociology of the Homeless Man* (Chicago: University of Chicago Press, 1923); Howard Becker, Blanche Geer, Everett Hughes, and Anselm Strauss, *Boys in White: Student Culture in Medical School* (Chicago: University of Chicago Press, 1961) [with one female researcher]; Herbert Gans, *The Levittowners: Ways of Life and Politics in a New Suburban Community* (New York: Pantheon, 1967); Herbert Gans, *The Urban Villagers: Group and Class in the Life of Italian Americans* (New York: Free Press, 1962); David Hayano, *Poker Faces: The Life and Work of Professional Card Players* (Berkeley, CA: University of California Press, 1982); and Jerry Jacobs, *Fun City: An Ethnographic Study of a Retirement Community* (New York: Holt, Rinehart & Winston, 1974).

50. John Van Maanen, *Tales of the Field: On Writing Ethnography* (Chicago: University of Chicago Press, 1988), p. 37, fn. 4.

51. Arlene Kaplan Daniels, "Self-Deception and Self-Discovery in Fieldwork," *Qualitative Sociology,* 1983, *6*(3): 195–214.

52. Joan Neff Gurney, "Not One of the Guys: The Female Researcher in a Male-Dominated Setting," *Qualitative Sociology,* 1985, *8*(1): 42–62, p. 43; literature cited is Virginia Olesen and Elvi Whittaker, "Role-Making in Participant Observation: Processes in the Researcher-Actor Relationship," in Norman K. Denzin (ed.), *Sociological Methods: A Sourcebook* (Chicago: Aldine, 1970), pp. 381–397, and John Lofland, *Analyzing Social Settings: A Guide to Qualitative Observation and Analysis* (Belmont, CA: Wadsworth, 1971).

53. Sheryl Ruzek, *The Women's Health Movement: Feminist Alternatives to Medical Control* (New York: Praeger, 1978), pp. ix–xi.

54. Laurie McDade, "The Interweavings of Theory and Practice: Finding the Threads for a Feminist Ethnography," paper presented at the National Women's Studies Association Conference, Columbus, Ohio, 1983, pp. 14, 15, 18, 19.

55. Cynthia Negrey, review of Ursula Sharma, *Women's Work, Class, and the Urban Household: A Study of Shimla, North India* (New York: Tavistock, 1986), in *Gender & Society,* 1989, *3*(1): 143–145, p. 143.

56. Susan Krieger, *The Mirror Dance: Identity in a Women's Community* (Philadelphia, PA: Temple University Press, 1983); Janet Kahn, "Qualitative Methods," Department of Sociology, Brandeis University, 1990; Elizabeth (Betsy) M. Ettore, *Lesbians, Women*

and Society (London: Routledge & Kegan Paul, 1980); and Boston Lesbian Psychologies Collective (eds.), *Lesbian Psychologies* (Chicago: University of Illinois Press, 1987).

57. Cathleen Burnett and Mona J. E. Danner, "Publishing Field Research: Can We Ignore Gender?," unpublished manuscript, University of Missouri, Kansas City, Missouri.

58. "I was a Playboy Bunny," reprinted in Gloria Steinem, *Outrageous Acts and Everyday Rebellions* (New York: New American Library, 1983).

59. Rosabeth Kanter, *Men and Women of the Corporation* (New York: Basic Books, 1977), pp. xiii, 293–296.

60. David Riesman, "Foreword," in Laura Bohanan, *Return to Laughter* (New York: Anchor Books, 1954/1964), p. xvi. The word "penetrate" is revealing here.

61. Hortense Powdermaker, *op. cit.* (note 21), pp. 419–420.

62. Laura Nader, "From Anguish to Exultation," in Peggy Golde (ed.), *Women in the Field: Anthropological Experiences* (Chicago: Aldine, 1970), pp. 113–114; another example is from Virginia Olesen and Elvi Whittaker, *The Silent Dialogue: A Study in the Social Psychology of Professional Socialization* (San Francisco: Jossey-Bass, 1968), p. 22.

63. Laura Bohanan, *op. cit.* (note 60), p. 205.

64. Barrie Thorne, "Political Activist as Participant Observer: Conflicts of Commitment in a Study of the Draft Resistance Movement of the 1960s," *Symbolic Interaction,* 1978, 2(1): 73–88, reprinted in Robert Emerson (ed.), *Contemporary Field Research* (Boston: Little, Brown, 1983), p. 216.

65. P.J. McGann and Harriett E. Hayes, "One Block off Marginal Street: Capitalism, Homelessness, and Dehumanization on the Streets of Boston," paper presented at the annual meetings of the Society for the Study of Symbolic Interaction, August 1991, Washington, D.C. See also Nancy Howell, *Surviving Fieldwork: A Report of the Advisory Panel on Health and Safety in Fieldwork* (Washington: American Anthropological Association, 1990).

66. Catherine Kohler Riessman, *Divorce Talk: Women and Men Make Sense of Personal Relationships* (New Brunswick, NJ: Rutgers University Press, 1990), p. 225.

67. Dorinne K. Kondo, "Dissolution and Reconstitution of Self: Implications for Anthropological Epistemology," *Cultural Anthropology,* 1986, 1(1): 74–88.

68. Lois Easterday et al, also mention roles of "go-fer" and "mascot." Their explanation of the latter makes it seem like a variation of the theme of sex object. Both exemplify the difficulty women have (note 48) being perceived as researchers.

69. Mary Jo Deegan describes leaving the field permanently when affronted by sexist remarks. See Mary Jo Deegan, *American Ritual Dramas: Social Rules and Cultural Meanings* (New York: Greenwood, 1989). In another instance, a researcher "avoided visiting the morgue when one particular male was there." [Easterday et al., *op. cit.* (note 48), p. 64.]

70. Pamela Fishman. "Interactional Shitwork," *Heresies,* May 1977, 99–101; see also her "Interaction: The Work Women Do," *Social Problems,* 1978, 25(4): 397–406.

71. Joy Browne, "Fieldwork for Fun and Profit," in M. Patricia Golden (ed.), *The Research Experience* (Itasca, IL: F. E. Peacock, 1976), p. 78.

72. Peggy Golde, "Odyssey of Encounter," in her *Women in the Field: Anthropological Experiences* (Chicago: Aldine, 1970), p. 86.

73. Mary Jo Deegan, "Having Fun, Killing Time, Getting a Deal," in *American Ritual Dramas: Social Rules and Cultural Meanings* (New York: Greenwood Press, 1989), pp. 51–75, esp. p. 52.

74. Joan Neff Gurney, "Not One of the Guys: The Female Researcher in a Male-Dominated Setting," *Qualitative Sociology,* 1985, 8(1): 42–62.

75. Margaret Mead, *Growing Up in New Guinea* (1930) (New York: William Morrow, 1975); Margaret Mead, *Coming of Age in Samoa* (1928) (New York: William Morrow, 1961).

76. Judith DiIorio, *op. cit.* (note 2).

77. See Lois Easterday et al., *op. cit.* (note 48), p. 64.

78. Nancy Scheper-Hughes, *Saints, Scholars, and Schizophrenics: Mental Illness in Rural Ireland* (Berkeley, CA: University of California Press, 1979), p. 11.

79. Arlene Kaplan Daniels, "The Low-Caste Stranger in Social Research," in Gideon Sjoberg (ed.), *Ethics, Politics, and Social Research* (Cambridge, MA: Schenkman, 1967), pp. 267, 269, 270, 273.

80. Susan E. Martin, "Sexual Politics in the Workplace: The International World of Policewomen," *Symbolic Interaction,* 1978, *1*(2): 44–60; reprinted in Mary Jo Deegan and Michael R. Hill (eds.), *Women and Symbolic Interaction* (Winchester, MA: Allen & Unwin, 1987), pp. 303–321, quotation is from latter, pp. 304–405. See also Susan E. Martin, *Breaking and Entering: Policewomen On Patrol* (Berkeley, CA: University of California Press, 1980).

81. Nancy Stoller Shaw, *Forced Labor: Maternity Care in the United States* (Elmsford, NY: Pergamon Press, 1974).

82. Pamela Dorn, "Gender and Personhood: Turkish Jewish Proverbs and the Politics of Reputation," *Women's Studies International Forum,* 1986, *9*(3): 295–301, p. 296.

83. Similarly, Jean Briggs was unable to study Eskimo shamans and was compelled to study Eskimo emotional expression. See Jean L. Briggs, *Never in Anger: Portrait of an Eskimo Family* (Cambridge, MA: Harvard University Press, 1970).

84. Her name is Judith-Maria Buechler. Hans Buechler thanks her in an initial footnote for "editorial help in writing this paper and for permitting me to use examples from her own experience." Although it is better to have a woman describe her own experience, this acknowledgement suggests that she read and edited her husband's account, thereby probably accepting it.

85. Hans Buechler, "The Social Position of an Ethnographer in the Field," in Frances Henry and Satish Saberwal (eds.), *Stress and Response in Fieldwork* (New York: Holt, Rinehart & Winston, 1969), pp. 8, 13.

86. The role of sex-partner is rarely described as useful by a female researcher, except in instances where becoming someone's partner in a coupled society was the only way she could retain her membership. See Judith DiIorio, *op. cit.* (note 2).

87. Jean Briggs, *op. cit.* (note 83).

88. Marjorie Shostak, *Nisa: The Life and Words of a !Kung Woman* (New York: Vintage Books, 1983), pp. 20–21.

89. Barbara Myerhoff, *Number Our Days* (New York: Simon and Schuster, 1978), pp. 26–27.

90. Dorinne K. Kondo, "Dissolution and Reconstitution of Self: Implications for Anthropological Epistemology," *Cultural Anthropology,* 1986, *1*(1): 74–88, pp. 77–78.

91. Patricia Remmington, "Women in the Police: Integration or Separation?" *Qualitative Sociology,* 1983, *6*(2): 118–135, p. 122.

92. Laura T. Fishman, *Women at the Wall: A Study of Prisoners' Wives Doing Time on the Outside* (Albany, NY: SUNY Press, 1990).

93. Carol Stack, *All Our Kin: Strategies for Survival in a Black Community* (New York: Harper & Row, 1974).

94. See Jennifer Hunt, "The Development of Rapport through the Negotiation of Gender in Field Work among Police," *Human Organization,* 1984, *43*(4): 283–296.

95. In Nancie Gonzales' autobiographical essay comparing various fieldwork experi-

ences, she explains that among the highland Indians of Guatemala, certain topics were taboo for her as an unmarried woman. Among the Garifuna (Black Caribs), however, she achieved rapport precisely because she was an unmarried woman. Later in the Dominican Republic she was unable to achieve rapport with upper-middle-class women. See Nancie Gonzalez, "The Anthropologist as Female Head of Household," *Feminist Studies,* 1984, *10*(1): 97–114.

96. Ruth Horowitz, *Honor and the American Dream: Culture and Identity in a Chicago Community* (New Brunswick, NJ: Rutgers University Press, 1983), pp. 10–11.

97. Lois Easterday et al., *op. cit.* (note 48), p. 64.

98. Linda Valli, *Becoming Clerical Workers* (Boston: Routledge & Kegan Paul, 1986), pp. 232–233.

99. Sherryl Kleinman, "Fieldworkers' Feelings: What We Feel, Who We Are, How We Analyze," in William B. Shaffir and Robert A. Stebbins (eds.), *Experiencing Fieldwork: An Inside View of Qualitative Research* (Newbury Park, CA: Sage Publications, 1991), pp. 184–195.

100. Lois Easterday et al., *op. cit.* (note 48).

101. See David Gordon, "Getting Close by Staying Distant: Fieldwork with Proselytizing Groups," *Qualitative Sociology,* 1987, *10*(3): 267–287.

102. See S. M. Miller, "The Participant Observer and 'Over-Rapport'," *American Sociological Review,* 1952, *17*: 97–99; Morris Freilich, *Marginal Natives: Anthropologists at Work* (New York: Harper & Row, 1970); Ruth Horowitz, "Remaining an Outsider: Membership as a Threat to Research Rapport," *Urban Life,* 1986, *14*(4): 409–430; Carol Warren and Paul Rasmussen, "Sex and Gender in Field Research," *Urban Life,* 1977, *6*(3): 349–369; and Rosalie Wax, "Gender and Age in Fieldwork and Fieldwork Education: No Good Thing Is Done by Any Man Alone," *Social Problems,* 1979, *26*: 509–522.

103. Arlie Hochschild, *The Unexpected Community: Portrait of an Old-age Subculture* (Berkeley, CA: University of California Press, 1978), p. 142, n. 1.

104. Denise Connors, *op. cit.* (note 28), pp. 45–46.

105. Diane Bell, *Daughters of the Dreaming* (North Sydnev: George Allen & Unwin, 1983), pp. 25–26.

106. Carol Gilligan, *In a Different Voice* (Cambridge, MA: Harvard University Press, 1982); Evelyn Fox Keller, "Science and Gender," *Signs: Journal of Women in Culture and Society,* 1982, *7*(3): 589–602; Nancy Chodorow, *The Reproduction of Mothering: Psychoanalysis and the Sociology of Gender* (Berkeley, CA: University of California Press, 1978).

107. Laud Humphreys, *Tearoom Trade: Impersonal Sex in Public Places* (Chicago: Aldine, 1970).

108. Patricia Adler, *Whealing and Dealing: An Ethnography of an Upper-Level Drug Dealing and Smuggling Community* (New York: Columbia University Press, 1985).

109. See Robert W. Janes, "A Note on Phases of the Community Role of the Participant-Observer," *American Sociological Review,* 1961, *26*: 446–450.

110. Raymond Gold, "Roles in Sociological Field Observations," *Social Forces,* 1958, *36*: 217–223.

111. See Robert Kahn and Floyd Mann, "Developing Research Partnerships," *Journal of Social Issues,* 1952, *8*(3): 4–10; also Rebecca E. Klatch, "The Methodological Problems of Studying a Politically Resistant Community," in Robert G. Burgess (ed.), *Studies in Qualitative Methodology,* 1988, vol. 1, pp. 73–88.

112. Arlie Hochschild, *op. cit.* (note 103).

113. Judy Wajcman, *op. cit.* (note 68). pp. x–xiii.

114. An example of a "complete participant" study is Kathleen MacPherson, "Dilem-

mas of Participant-Observation in a Menopause Collective," in Shulamit Reinharz and Graham Rowles (eds.), *Qualitative Gerontology* (New York: Springer, 1988), pp. 184–196.

115. Sheryl Ruzek, *op. cit.* (note 53), pp. xi–xii.

116. Karen McCarthy Brown, "On Feminist Methodology," *Journal of Feminist Studies in Religion,* 1985, *1*(2): 76–79.

117. See Shulamit Reinharz, "Experiential Analysis: A Contribution to Feminist Research Methodology," in Gloria Bowles and Renate Duelli Klein (eds.), *Theories of Women's Studies* (Boston: Routledge & Kegan Paul, 1983), pp. 162–191.

118. Karen Brown, *op. cit.* (note 116), pp. 78–79.

119. Liz Stanley and Sue Wise, "Feminist Research, Feminist Consciousness and Experiences of Sexism," *Women's Studies International Quarterly,* 1979, *2:* 359–374; see also Liz Stanley and Sue Wise, "Back into 'the Personal': Or Our Attempt to Construct 'Feminist Research,' " in Gloria Bowles and Renate Duelli Klein (eds.), *Theories of Women's Studies* (Boston: Routledge & Kegan Paul, 1983).

120. Noelie Maria Rodriguez, "Transcending Bureaucracy: Feminist Politics at a Shelter for Battered Women," *Gender & Society,* 1988, *2*(2): 214–227.

121. Kathleen Ferraro, "Negotiating Trouble in a Battered Women's Shelter," *Urban Life,* 1983, *12*(3): 287–306; reprinted in Mary Jo Deegan and Michael R. Hill (eds.), *Women and Symbolic Interaction* (Winchester, MA: Allen & Unwin, 1987), pp. 379–394, quotation is from latter, p. 380.

122. Judy Wajcman, *Women in Control: Dilemmas of a Workers Cooperative* (New York: St. Martin's Press, 1983), p. xi.

123. Sheryl Ruzek, *op. cit.* (note 53), pp. xii–xiii.

124. Patricia Baker, "Doing Fieldwork in a Canadian Bank: Issues of Gender and Power," *Resources for Feminist Research/Documentation-sur-la-Recherche Feministe,* 1987, *16*(4): 45–47.

125. For a discussion of these points, see Carol A. B. Warren, *Gender Issues in Field Research, Qualitative Research Methods Series 9,* (Beverly Hills, CA: Sage, 1988).

126. Susan Krieger, *The Mirror Dance: Identity in a Women's Community* (Philadelphia, PA: Temple University Press, 1983). Kamala Visweswaran, *op. cit.* (note 17), includes Paula Gunn Allen, *The Woman Who Owned the Shadows* (New York: Strawberry Press, 1983), and Cherrie Moraga, *Loving in the War Years* (Boston: South End Press, 1983).

127. Marianne Paget, "Performing the Text," *Journal of Contemporary Ethnography,* 1990, *19*(1): 136–155.

128. Marian Sandmaier, review of Carole Joffe, *The Regulation of Sexuality: Experiences of Family Planning Workers* (Pittsburgh, PA: Temple University Press, 1986), in *The New York Times Book Review,* Sunday, February 8, 1987, p. 25.

129. Susan Stall, " 'What about the "Non-feminist?" ': The Possibilities for Women's Movement Coalition Building in Small Town America," paper presented at the 35th Annual Meeting of the Society for the Study of Social Problems, Washington, D.C., August 1985, p. 5; cited article is Sara Evans, "Towards a Useable Past: Feminism as History and Politics," paper presented at the Women Making History: Women's Work, Women's Culture Conference, University of Illinois at Chicago, April 1983.

130. Judith Stacey and Barrie Thorne, "The Missing Feminist Revolution in Sociology," *Social Problems,* 1985, *32*(4): 301–316.

131. Sue Webb, "Gender and Authority in the Workplace," in Sue Webb and Clive Pearson (eds.), *Looking Back: Some Papers from the BSA 'Gender & Society' Conference, Studies in Sexual Politics* (University of Manchester: Department of Sociology, 1984), pp. 83–106.

132. Kathleen McCourt, *Working-Class Women and Grass-Roots Politics* (Bloomington, IN: Indiana University Press, 1977). In the methods section of her book, McCourt refers only to the way she recruited people for interviewing, but she refers generally to her research as "fieldwork" and her chapters display a deep knowledge of the neighborhoods, their organizations, and the women leaders that must have been obtained from much greater involvement than interviewing alone.

133. Arlene Kaplan Daniels, *Invisible Careers: Civic Leaders from the Volunteer World* (Chicago: University of Chicago Press, 1988).

134. Michelle Fine, "Sexuality, Schooling, and Adolescent Females: The Missing Discourse of Desire," *Harvard Educational Review*, 1988, *58*(1): 29–53.

135. Rahel Wasserfall, "Gender Identification in an Israeli Moshav," doctoral dissertation, Hebrew University of Jerusalem, 1987.

136. Eleanor M. Miller, *Street Woman* (Philadelphia, PA: Temple University Press, 1986).

137. Marcia Millman, *Such a Pretty Face: Being Fat in America* (New York: W. W. Norton, 1980).

138. Arlie Russell Hochschild, *The Managed Heart* (Berkeley, CA: University of California Press, 1983).

139. Jeanne Harley Guillemin and Lynda Lytle Homstrom, *Mixed Blessings: Intensive Care for Newborns* (New York: Oxford University Press, 1986).

140. Lynn Davidman, *Tradition in a Rootless World: Women Turn to Orthodox Judaism* (Berkeley, CA: University of California Press, 1991).

141. Laura T. Fishman, *Women at the Wall: A Study of Prisoners' Wives Doing Time on the Outside* (Albany, NY: SUNY Press, 1990).

142. Kathleen Kautzer, "Moving against the Stream: An Organizational Study of the Older Women's League," doctoral dissertation, Brandeis University, 1988.

143. Mary Eaton, *Justice for Women? Family, Court and Social Control* (Philadelphia: Open University Press, 1986). See also Cathleen Burnett, "Participant Observation in a Male Setting: Observing in the Courtroom," paper presented at the Annual Meeting of the National Women's Studies Association, Columbus, Ohio, 1983.

144. For a discussion of the political potential of participant observation, see Y. M. Bodemann, "The Fulfillment of Fieldwork in Marxist Praxis," *Dialectical Anthropology*, 1979, *4*(2): 155–161.

145. For personal statements see Ruth Landes, "A Woman Anthropologist in Brazil," in Peggy Golde, *op. cit.* (note 72), p. 122; see Peter Hare, *A Woman's Quest for Science: Portrait of Anthropologist Elsie Clews Parsons* (Buffalo, NY: Prometheus Books, 1985); Hortense Powermarker, *Stranger and Friend: The Way of an Anthropologist* (New York: Norton, 1966); Alice Walker (ed.), *I Love Myself When I Am Laughing: A Zora Neale Hurston Reader* (Old Westbury, NY: The Feminist Press, 1979). For a psychological analysis of the life histories, Rorschachs, and TATs of scientists, published in 1952, see Ann Roe, "A Psychological Study of Eminent Psychologists and Anthropologists, and a Comparison with Biological and Physical Scientists," *Psychological Monographs*, 1952, *67:* 1–55. In contrast with other scientists, anthropologists appeared extremely rebellious vis-à-vis their parents and valued independence highly. Joan Mark wrote that Alice Fletcher was clearly seeking adventure. See Joan Mark, *A Stranger in Her Native Land: Alice Fletcher and the American Indians* (Lincoln, NB: University of Nebraska Press, 1988), p. 41.

146. Manda Cesara, *Reflections of a Woman Anthropologist: No Hiding Place* (New York: Academic Press, 1982), p. 21.

147. Shulamit Reinharz, *On Becoming a Social Scientist: From Survey Research to Participant Observation and Experiential Analysis* (New Brunswick, NJ: Transaction Books, 1984).

148. Renate Klein, *The Dynamics of Women's Studies: Its International Ideas and Practices in Higher Education*, doctoral dissertation, University of London, Institute of Education, 1986, methods chapter, p. 14.

149. Carol A. B. Warren, *op. cit.* (note 125), p. 65.

150. Judith Stacey, *op. cit.* (note 11).

151. For a discussion of Judith Stacey's article, see Marjorie DeVault, "What Counts as Feminist Ethnography?," paper presented at "Exploring New Frontiers: Qualitative Research Conference," May 13–16, 1990, York University, Toronto.

152. See Hortense Powdermaker, *Stranger and Friend* (New York: Norton, 1966). Some reports by women do not discuss their gender at all, e.g., Frances Henry, "Stress and Strategy in Three Field Situations," in Frances Henry and Satish Saberwal (eds.), *Stress and Response in Fieldwork* (New York: Holt, Rinehart & Winston, 1969); Joan Moore, "Political and Ethical Problems in a Large-Scale Study of a Minority Population," in Gideon Sjoberg (ed.), *Ethics, Politics, and Social Research* (Cambridge, MA: Schenkman, 1967), pp. 225–244. Visweswaran claims that the reason for this is that these books are "geared to shoring up anthropology as a positive science" [*op. cit.* (note 17), p. 32].

153. For a discussion of the range of views see Marilyn Strathern, "An Awkward Relationship: The Case of Feminism and Anthropology," *Signs: Journal of Women in Culture and Society,* 1987, *12*(2): 276–292.

Chapter 4   Feminist Survey Research and Other Statistical Research Formats

1. This chapter benefited from a review by Ronnie Steinberg.

2. Diana E. H. Russell, *Rape in Marriage* (New York: Macmillan, 1982), p. 28. [emphases added]

3. See Margaret Andersen, *Thinking about Women: Sociological and Feminist Perspectives* (New York: Macmillan, 1983), for a discussion of this point from a feminist perspective.

4. Edward Donnerstein, Daniel Linz, and Steven Penrod, *The Question of Pornography: Research Findings and Policy Implications* (New York: Free Press, 1987), p. 145.

5. See the publications of the Institute for Women's Policy Research, 1400 20th Street N.W., Suite 104, Washington, D.C. 20036.

6. Joan Mark, *A Stranger in Her Native Land: Alice Fletcher and the American Indians* (Lincoln, NB: University of Nebraska Press, 1988), pp. 24, 76.

7. See Robert Emerson, *Contemporary Field Research* (Boston: Little, Brown, 1983), p. 6, for a discussion of Charles Booth, *Life and Labour of the People in London* (New York: AMS Press. 1970); Beatrice P. Webb, *My Apprenticeship* (New York: Longmans, Green, 1926); Sidney Webb and Beatrice Potter Webb, *Methods of Social Study* (New York: Longmans, Green, and Co., 1932); and Ann Ardis, "Beatrice Webb's Romance with Ethnography," *Women's Studies,* 1990, *18*(2–3): 233–248.

8. Shulamit Reinharz, "Toward a Model of Female Political Action: The Case of Manya Shohat, Founder of the First Kibbutz," *Women's Studies International Forum,* 1984, *7*(4): 275–287, p. 281.

9. See Mary Jo Deegan (ed.), *Women in Sociology: A Bio-bibliographic Sourcebook* (Westport, CT: Greenwood Press, 1991).

10. See Lela B. Costin, *Two Sisters for Social Justice: A Biography of Grace and Edith Abbott* (Chicago: University of Illinois Press, 1983).

11. Mary Jo Deegan, *op. cit.* (note 9).

12. Rosalind Rosenberg, *Beyond Separate Spheres* (New Haven, CT: Yale University Press, 1982), p. 19.

13. Her most extensive name was Mary Elizabeth Burroughs Roberts Smith Coolidge, see Mary Jo Deegan, "A Rose is not a Rosa is not a Roseann: The Many Names of Mary Elizabeth Burroughs Roberts Smith Coolidge," in Judy Long (ed.), *The New Sociobiography* (manuscript).

14. Mary Jo Deegan, *op. cit.* (note 9), p. 100.

15. Louise Michele Newman (ed.), *Men's Ideas/Women's Realities: Popular Science, 1870–1915* (New York: Pergamon Press, 1985), p. 116.

16. Mary Jo Deegan, *Jane Addams and the Men of the Chicago School, 1892–1918* (New Brunswick, NJ: Transaction Books, 1988), p. 46.

17. Mary Jo Deegan, *Ibid.*

18. Jane Addams, *Twenty Years at Hull-House* (Phillips Publishing Company, 1910). Reprinted by New American Library (New York: 1981).

19. William L. O'Neill, *Feminism in America: A History* (2nd revised edition, New Brunswick, NJ: Transaction Books, 1989), p. 65, quoting Helen L. Sumner, *Equal Suffrage* (New York, 1909; reprint, New York: Arno Press, 1972), pp. 95–96, 148.

20. Blanche Wiesen Cook (ed.), *Crystal Eastman: On Women & Revolution* (New York: Oxford University Press, 1978), pp. 6–7. Her book, *Work Accidents and the Law* (1910, 2nd edition, 1916; reprint, New York: Arno Press, 1970).

21. Mari Sandoz, "The Stranger at the Curb," reissued by Michael R. Hill in *Mid-American Review of Sociology*, 1989, pp. 1–14 in manuscript, pp. 2, 9.

22. Toby Jayaratne, "The Value of Quantitative Methodology for Feminist Research," in Gloria Bowles and Renate Duelli Klein (eds.), *Theories of Women's Studies* (Boston: Routledge & Kegan Paul, 1983), pp. 140–161, 158–159. [emphases added]

23. Betty Friedan, *The Feminine Mystique* (New York: Norton, 1963), p. 215.

24. See Paula England and George Farkas, *Households, Employment and Gender* (New York: Aldine, 1986); Valerie K. Oppenheimer, *The Female Labor Force in the United States*, Population Monograph Series No. 5. Berkeley, CA: Institute of International Studies, University of California, 1970; and Barbara F. Reskin and Heidi I. Hartmann, *Women's Work, Men's Work* (Washington, D.C.: National Academy Press, 1986).

25. Vivian Gornick and Barbara K. Moran (eds.), *Woman in Sexist Society: Studies in Power and Powerless* (New York: Mentor Book, 1971).

26. Edward Gondolf with Ellen R. Fisher, *Battered Women as Survivors: An Alternative to Treating Learned Helplessness* (Lexington, MA: Lexington Books, 1988), p. 5.

27. See "Twenty Major Changes in the Norms Guiding American Life," *Psychology Today*, April 1981, p. 68.

28. See Howard J. Ehrlich, Natalie Sokoloff, Fred Pincus, and Carol Ehrlich, *Women and Men: A Socioeconomic Factbook* (Baltimore, MD: Vacant Lots Press, 1975); Barbara F. Reskin, "Bringing the Men Back In: Sex Differentiation and the Devaluation of Women's Work," *Gender & Society*, March 1988, 2(1): 58–81.

29. Lenore Weitzman, *The Divorce Revolution* (New York: The Free Press, 1985).

30. "President Futter Calls for New Direction for Women's Movement," *Barnard College Reporter*, New York, 1986, p. 1.

31. Elizabeth Almquist, "Black Women and the Pursuit of Equality," in Jo Freeman (ed.), *Women: A Feminist Perspective* (Palo Alto, CA: Mayfield Publishing, 1979), pp. 430–449.

32. Faye Wattleton, "A Special Report on a Recent International Trip to India and Indonesia," *Planned Parenthood*, 1986.

33. For a history of the vaginal orgasm see Daniel Brown, "Female Orgasm and Sex-

ual Inadequacy," reprinted in Edward Brecher and Ruth Brecher (eds.), *Human Sexual Response* (New York: New American Library, 1966), pp. 125–175.

34. Barbara Risman, "Men Who Mother," *Gender & Society*, March 1987, *1*(1): 6–32.

35. Jeanne M. Plas and Barbara Strudler Wallston, "Women Oriented Toward Male Dominated Careers: Is the Reference Group Male or Female?" *Journal of Counseling Psychology*, 1983, *30*(1): 46–54, pp. 47–48.

36. Sue Eisenberg and Patricia Micklow, University of Michigan Law School, "The Assaulted Wife: 'Catch 22' Revisited," 1974, published in *Women's Rights Law Reporter*, 1976.

37. Edith Hoshino Altbach, *Women in America* (Lexington, MA: Heath, 1974), p. 9.

38. Susan Brownmiller, *Against Our Will: Men, Women and Rape* (New York: Bantam Books, 1975). For a critique of this book's failure to challenge the idea that women's consent to engage in sex with a man can be freely given in a patriarchal society see Catharine MacKinnon, *Sexual Harassment of Working Women* (New Haven, CT: Yale University Press, 1979), p. 298.

39. *The New York Times*, Monday, May 29, 1989, p. 28.

40. Susan Brownmiller, *op. cit.* (note 38), pp. xiii, 195.

41. Sandra Baxter and Marjorie Lansing, *Women and Politics: The Visible Majority* (Ann Arbor, MI: The University of Michigan Press, 1983), pp. 9, 10.

42. Karen Oppenheim Mason and Yu-Hsia Lu, "Attitudes Toward Women's Familial Roles: Changes in the United States, 1977–1985," *Gender & Society*, 1988, *2*(1): 39–57, p. 43.

43. Betty Friedan, *op. cit.* (note 23).

44. Graham Staines, Carol Tavris, and Toby Epstein Jayaratne, "The Queen Bee Syndrome," *Psychology Today*, 1974, 55–60.

45. Howard Ehrlich et al., *op. cit.* (note 28).

46. See Pauline B. Bart, "Why Men Rape," in Pauline B. Bart and Patricia H. O'Brien, *Stopping Rape: Successful Survival Strategies* (New York: Pergamon Press, 1985).

47. Gloria Joseph and Jill Lewis, *Common Differences: Conflicts in Black and White Feminist Perspectives* (Boston: South End Press, 1981/1986). $N = 1000$, personal communication, April 2, 1984.

48. *On Campus with Women*, Project on the Status and Education of Women, Association of American Colleges, Washington, D.C., Number 32, Fall 1981, p. 1.

49. Dafna N. Izraeli and Ephraim Tabory, "The Political Context of Feminist Attitudes in Israel," *Gender & Society*, 1988, *2*(4): 463–481, p. 478.

50. Bhavani Sitaraman, "Abortion Situations and Abortion Morality: A Factorial Survey Analysis of Abortion Attitudes," paper presented at the Eastern Sociological Society meetings, Boston, MA, April 1990.

51. Martha E. Thompson, "Breastfeeding in Public," paper presented at the National Women's Studies Association Annual Meetings, Champaign-Urbana, IL, June 1986.

52. Dee Graham and Edna Rawlings, "Feminist Research Methodology: Comparisons, Guidelines and Ethics," paper presented at the Annual Meetings of the American Psychological Association, August 1980, p. 15.

53. For example, Robert Groves and Nancy Fultz found that male interviewers get more optimistic economic attitudes from women than female interviewers obtain. See Robert Groves and Nancy Fultz, "Gender Effects among Telephone Interviewers in a Survey of Economic Attitudes," *Sociological Methods & Research*, 1985, *14*(1): 31–52.

54. Del Martin, *Battered Wives* (New York: Pocket Books, 1976), pp. 20–21.

55. Betty MacMorran Gray, "Economics of Sex Bias: The 'Disuse' of Women," *Nation*, June 14, 1971, 742–744, see note 57.

56. Del Martin, *op. cit.* (note 54).

57. Edith Hoshino Altbach, *Women in America* (Lexington, MA: Heath, 1974), pp. 9, 43.

58. Margaret Anderson, *Thinking about Women: Sociological and Feminist Perspectives* (New York: Macmillan, 1983), pp. 132–133.

59. Ann Oakley and Robin Oakley, "Sexism in Official Statistics," in John Irvine, Ian Miles, and Jeff Evans (eds.), *Demystifying Social Statistics* (London: Pluto, 1979/1981), pp. 172–189.

60. *Older Women: Research Issues and Data Sources*, April 8–10, 1984, background document for invitational conference, March 1984, Institute of Gerontology, the University of Michigan, p. 1.

61. A. Regula Herzog, Karen C. Holden, and Mildred M. Seltzer (eds.), *Health & Economic Status of Older Women* (Amityville, NY: Baywood, 1989).

62. Lisa D. Brush, "Violent Acts and Injurious Outcomes in Married Couples: Methodological Issues in the National Survey of Families and Households," *Gender & Society*, 1990, *4*(1): 56–67, p. 65.

63. Nancy Weiner, "Tradition and Change: Conflict in the Life of Moroccan Women," honors thesis, Department of Anthropology, Brandeis University, 1989.

64. Barbara Rogers, *The Domestication of Women: Discrimination in Developing Societies* (New York: St. Martin's Press, 1980). As quoted in Nancy Weiner, *Ibid.*, p. 46.

65. In the report, the authors do not identify themselves or their purposes as feminist, yet I include their material since their methodological comments are a useful overview of the assets and limitations of surveys on issues of interest to many feminists.

66. Sidney Verba, with Joseph DiNunzio and Christina Spaulding, "Unwanted Attention: Report on a Sexual Harassment Survey," report to the faculty council of the Faculty of Arts and Sciences, Harvard University, September 1983, pp. 2, 3.

67. See Shulamit Reinharz, *On Becoming a Social Scientist* (New Brunswick, NJ: Transaction Books, 1984), chapter 2.

68. *Capitol: Woman*. A Newletter of the House Committee on Constitutional Revision and Women's Rights. April 1982, volume 6, no. 1, p. 2.

69. Nijole Benokraitis and Joe Feagan, *Modern Sexism* (Englewood Cliffs, NJ: Prentice Hall, 1986), pp. 2–3.

70. Ronnie J. Steinberg, "Dilemmas of Advocacy Research: Experiences with Comparable Worth," paper prepared for Plenary Panel: Social Science Research and Law Reform, Law and Society Association, June 12, 1987, pp. 14–20.

71. Anne Pugh, "My Statistics and Feminism—a True Story," in Liz Stanley and Sue Scott (eds.), *Feminist Research Processes* (Manchester: University of Manchester, 1987), pp. 79, 82, 87.

72. The word "feminine" means "female" in this context.

73. Charlene Depner, "Toward the Further Development of Feminist Psychology," paper presented at the 8th Annual National Meeting of the Association for Women in Psychology, Boston, March 1981, p. 7.

74. Roberta Spalter-Roth and Heidi Hartmann, *Unnecessary Losses: Costs to Americans of the Lack of Family and Medical Leave* (Washington, D.C.: Institute for Women's Policy Research, 1989).

75. See Judith Cook and Mary Margaret Fonow, "Knowledge and Women's Interests: Issues of Epistemology and Methodology in Feminist Sociological Research," *Sociological Inquiry*, 1986, *56*(1): 2–29.

76. Roberta M. Spalter-Roth and Heidi I. Hartmann, "Science and Politics: The 'Dual Vision' of Feminist Policy Research, the Example of Family and Medical Leave," Institute for Women's Policy Research, Washington, D.C. 1987, 1988, pp. 1, 6, 32.

Chapter 5 Feminist Experimental Research

1. This chapter benefited greatly from readings by Loraine Obler and Arnold Kahn.

2. Rhoda Kesler Unger, "Sex as Social Reality: Field and Laboratory Research," *Psychology of Women Quarterly*, 1981, 5(4): 645–653. [emphasis added]

3. Marcia Texler Segal, "Feminism and the Self-Conscious Sociologist: An Essay on the Sociology of Knowledge," paper presented for the Sociology Departmental Seminar, University of Malawi, November 1984, p. 22.

4. Michelle Fine and Susan Merle Gordon, "Feminist Transformations of/Despite Psychology," In M. Crawford and M. Gentry (eds.), *Gender and Thought: Psychological Pespectives* (New York: Springer-Verlag, 1989), pp. 146–174.

5. For a full discussion of this work, its citation patterns, replication, and current criticism by Sandra Bem herself, see Mary Roth Walsh (ed.), *The Psychology of Women: Ongoing Debates* (New Haven, CT: Yale University Press, 1987), pp. 203–245.

6. Gayle L. Ormiston and Raphael Sassower, *Narrative Experiments: The Discursive Authority of Science and Technology* (Minneapolis: University of Minnesota Press, 1989).

7. Phillip Bonacich and John Light, "Laboratory Experimentation in Sociology," in Ralph Turner, James Coleman, and Renée Fox (eds.), *Annual Review of Sociology*, 1978, 4: 145–170. The journal *Social Psychology Quarterly*, formerly *Sociometry*, reports sociological laboratory experiments. One stream of such work concerns individual behavior in small groups. For an early, classic review see Gardner Lindzey (ed.), *Handbook of Social Psychology* (Cambridge, MA: Addison-Wesley, 1954), 2 vols.

8. One excellent overview is Beverly Walker's "Psychology and Feminism—If You Can't Beat Them, Join Them," in Dale Spender (ed.), *Men's Studies Modified: The Impact of Feminism on the Academic Disciplines* (New York: Pergamon, 1981), pp. 111–124. See also Kathleen E. Grady, "Sex Bias in Research Design," *Psychology of Women Quarterly*, 1981, 5(4): 628–636.

9. See for example, Earl Babbie, *The Practice of Social Research* (Belmont, CA: Wadsworth, 1983), 3rd ed., chapter 8; Kenneth D. Bailey, *Methods of Social Research* (New York: Free Press, 1982), 2nd ed., chapter 9.

10. See Carolyn Wood Sherif, "Bias in Psychology," in Julia Sherman and Evelyn Torton Beck (eds.), *The Prism of Sex: Essays in the Sociology of Knowledge* (Madison, WI: University of Wisconsin Press, 1979), pp. 93–134.

11. See Laurel Furumoto, "The New History of Psychology," paper presented as part of the G. Stanley Hall Lecture Series at the meeting of the American Psychological Association in Atlanta, August 1988; Agnes O'Connell and Nancy Felipe Russo (eds.), special issue of *Psychology of Women Quarterly*, 1980, "Eminent Women in Psychology," Agnes O'Connell and Nancy Felipe Russo (eds.), *Women in Psychology: A Bio-bibliographic Sourcebook* (Westport, CT: Greenwood, 1990); and Agnes O'Connell and Nancy Felipe Russo (eds.), *Models of Achievement: Reflections of Eminent Women in Psychology* (New York: Columbia University Press, 1983).

12. See Elizabeth Scarborough and Laurel Furumoto, *Untold Lives: The First Generation of American Women Psychologists* (New York: Columbia University, 1987); see also Mary Roth Walsh, *op. cit.* (note 5), pp. 1–5.

13. See Carolyn Wood Sherif, *op. cit.* (note 10).

14. See Laurel Furumoto, "Mary Whiton Calkins (1863–1930)," *Psychology of Women Quarterly,* 1980, *5*(1): 55–68.

15. Rosalind Rosenberg, *Beyond Separate Spheres: Intellectual Roots of Modern Feminism* (New Haven, CT: Yale University Press, 1982), p. 72.

16. Jill Gladys Morawski, "The Measurement of Masculinity and Femininity: Engendering Categorical Realities," *Journal of Personality,* 1985, *53*(2): 196–223.

17. Rosalind Rosenberg, *op. cit.* (note 15), p. 95.

18. See Emily Martin, *The Woman in the Body: A Cultural Analysis of Reproduction* (Boston: Beacon Press, 1987), p. 116.

19. Wendy Kaminer describes the case of Helen Hamilton Gardener who in the 1890s had studied the human brain in order to dispel ideas that women's brains possessed less intelligence than men's because they were smaller on average. When she died, Helen Hamilton Gardener bequeathed her brain to researchers at Cornell, who found that her "gray matter" exceeded that of the best brains in their collection. See Wendy Kaminer, *The Fearful Freedom: Women's Flight from Equality* (Reading, MA: Addison-Wesley, 1990), pp. xii–xiv. See also Stephanie Shields, "The Variability Hypothesis: The History of a Biological Model of Sex Difference in Intelligence," *Signs: Journal of Women in Culture and Society,* 1982, *7:* 769–797.

20. For example, feminist sociologist Kersti Yllo studied wife abuse using in-depth interviews with abused women and secondary analyses of survey data on family violence. A respected feminist publication declined to publish the survey-based material stating that her methodology was "inherently patriarchal" and could contribute no feminist insights. See Kersti Yllo, "Political and Methodological Debates in Wife Abuse Research," working paper for the National Council on Family Relations Theory and Methodology Workshop, Detroit, 1986; Kersti Yllo and M. Bograd (eds.), *Feminist Perspectives on Wife Abuse* (Newbury Park, CA: Sage, 1986); and Letitia Anne Peplau and Eva Conrad, "Beyond Nonsexist Research: The Perils of Feminist Methods in Psychology," *Psychology of Women Quarterly,* 1989, *13*(4): 379–400.

21. Ellen Fitzpatrick, *Endless Crusade: Women Social Scientists and Progressive Reform* (New York: Oxford University Press, 1990), pp. 62–65. See Mary Jo Deegan's entry on Frances A. Kellor in Mary Jo Deegan (ed.), *Women in Sociology: A Bio-bibliographic Sourcebook* (Greenwood, CT: Greenwood Press, 1991).

22. Naomi Weisstein, "Kinde, Kuche, Kirche as Scientific Law: Psychology Constructs the Female," in Robin Morgan (ed.), *Sisterhood is Powerful* (New York: Vintage, 1970), pp. 205–215.

23. Rae Carlson, "Understanding Women: Implications for Personality Theory and Research, *Journal of Social Issues,* 1972, *28*(2): 17–32.

24. Beverly Walker, *op. cit.* (note 8), p. 112.

25. See Jeanette Silveira, "The Effect of Sexism on Thought: How Male Bias Hurts Psychology and Some Hopes for a Woman's Psychology," in Jean Ramage Leppaluoto (ed.), *Women on the Movement: A Feminist Perspective* (Pittsburgh: KNOW, 1973); Paula Heiser, "Feminist Issues in Menstrual Research," paper presented at the National Conference for the Association for Women in Psychology, 1981. The five-stage model is taken from Irene H. Frieze, Jacquelynne E. Parsons, Paula Johnson, Diane Ruble, and Gail Zellman (eds.), *Women and Sex Roles: A Social Psychological Perspective* (New York: Norton, 1978). An eleven-stage model is offered in Margrit Eichler, *Nonsexist Research Methods: A Practical Guide* (Boston: Allen & Unwin, 1987). A set of 10 ubiquitous flaws is offered by Carol Jacklin, "Methodological Issues in the Study of Sex-Related Differences," *Developmental Review,* 1981, *1:* 266–273.

26. Although some feminists do not use the word "subjects," I am using it to convey

the standard steps in experimental research. Several psychological journals, e.g., *American Journal of Community Psychology,* have substituted "research participant" for "subject."

27. Barbara Strudler Wallston, "What Are the Questions in Psychology of Women? A Feminist Approach to Research," *Psychology of Women Quarterly,* 1981, *5*(4): 597–617.

28. Susan Gordon, "What's New in Endocrinology? Target: Sex Hormones," in Myra Fooden, Susan Gordon, and Betty Hughley (eds.), *Genes & Gender IV* (Staten Island, NY: Gordian Press, 1983), pp. 39–48, pp. 39, 48.

29. See Andrée Collard, *Rape of the Wild: Man's Violence against Animals and the Earth* (Bloomington, IN: Indiana University Press, 1989).

30. Donna Spring, "Medical Science without Cruelty to Animals," *Women of Power,* 1978, *11*: 58–61.

31. A counter argument, defending animal research and arguing against alternatives, is Gordon Gallup, Jr. and Susan Suarez, "Alternatives to the Use of Animals in Psychology Research," *American Psychologist,* 1985, *40*(10): 1104–1111.

32. Martin E. P. Seligman and Steven F. Maier, "Failure to Escape Traumatic Shock," *Journal of Experimental Psychology,* 1967, *74*(1): 1–9.

33. Lenore E. Walker, *The Battered Woman* (New York: Harper & Row, 1979), p. 46.

34. For a contrasting theory, and an alternative interpretation of Lenore Walker's research, see Edward Gondolf with Ellen Fisher, *Battered Women as Survivors: An Alternative to Treating Learned Helplessness* (Lexington, MA: Lexington Books, 1988).

35. Lenore Walker, *op. cit.* (note 33), p. 47.

36. See Earl Carlson and Rae Carlson, "Male and Female Subjects in Personality Research," *Journal of Abnormal and Social Psychology,* 1960, *61*(3): 482–483; see also Brinton Lykes and Abigail Stewart, "Evaluating the Feminist Challenge to Research in Personality and Social Psychology, 1963–1983," *Psychology of Women Quarterly,* 1986, *10*(4): 393–421.

37. Michelle Fine and Susan Gordon, *op. cit.* (note 4).

38. Rhoda Kesler Unger, "Through the Looking Glass: No Wonderland Yet! (The Reciprocal Relationship between Methodology and Models of Reality)," *Psychology of Women Quarterly,* 1983, *8*(1): 9–32.

39. The word "stranger" means that the "subjects" do not know one another.

40. Those tested do not trust one another, do not have long lasting relations, and have no connection to one another.

41. I added the internal footnotes to prevent misunderstanding of the meaning of particular phrases in this quotation.

42. See Robert Rosenthal, *Experimenter Effects in Behavioral Research* (New York: Appleton-Century-Crofts, 1967).

43. Janice Moulton, George Robinson, and Cherin Elias, "Sex Bias in Language Use," *The American Psychologist,* 1978, *33*(11): 1032–1036.

44. Reesa M. Vaughter, "Psychology," *Signs: Journal of Women in Culture and Society,* 1976, *2*(1): 120–146, p. 144. [emphases added]

45. Alice Eagly, "Sex Differences in Influenceability," *Psychological Bulletin,* 1978, *85*(1): 86–116, p. 86.

46. Elliot G. Mishler, "Meaning in Context: Is There Any Other Kind?," *Harvard Educational Review,* 1979, *49*(1): 1–19.

47. Mary Brown Parlee, "Psychology and Women," *Signs: Journal of Women in Culture and Society,* 1979, *5*(1): 121–133, p. 123. Alice Eagley offers a rejoinder to this point in her chapter in Janet S. Hyde and Marcia C. Linn, *The Psychology of Women: Advances through Meta-Analysis* (Baltimore: Johns Hopkins University Press, 1986), p. 171.

48. Susan Condor, "Sex Role Beliefs and 'Traditional' Women: Feminist and Intergroup Perspectives," in Sue Wilkinson (ed.), *Feminist Social Psychology: Developing Theory and Practice* (Philadelphia, PA: Open University Press, 1986), pp. 97–118, pp. 101–102.

49. Mary Brown Parlee, "Appropriate Control Groups in Feminist Research," *Psychology of Women Quarterly,* 1981, 5(4): 637–644.

50. Laurie Wardell, Dair Gillespie, and Ann Leffler, "Science and Violence against Wives," Department of Sociology, University of Utah, 1981.

51. Paula Johnson, "Doing Psychological Research," in Frieze et al., *op. cit.* (note 25), pp. 11–27.

52. See Brinton Lykes and Abigail Stewart, *op. cit.* (note 36).

53. "This is the method (Garfinkel, 1967) by which members decide meanings and assemble a body of knowledge on the basis of documentary evidence. In Garfinkel's demonstration with a 'rigged' question and answer format, he showed how, in searching for patterns, members make sense of incomplete, inappropriate, and contradictory material, and how they hear such answers as answers to their questions." This footnote is in the original article. See Harold Garfinkel, *Studies in Ethnomethodology* (Englewood Cliffs, NJ: Prentice-Hall, 1967).

54. Wendy McKenna and Sarah Kessler, *Gender: An Ethnomethodological Approach* (New York: Wiley, 1978; Chicago: University of Chicago, 1985), pp. 142, 145–146.

55. Ninety-six figures were shown to 10 different adults.

56. The researchers use the term "participants" rather than "subjects" here.

57. Wendy McKenna and Sarah Kessler, *op. cit.* (note 54), p. 149. Sigmund Freud is one of many psychologists who found the penis "conspicuous and apparently impossible to ignore." Perhaps this is why his "entire account of women's psychic development depended on his arbitrary definition of them as human beings without penises." Barbara J. Harris, "History and the Psychology of Women," in Miriam Lewin (ed.), *In the Shadow of the Past: Psychology Portrays the Sexes* (New York: Columbia, 1984), pp. 1–25, p. 6. In his view, women's passivity, narcissism, masochism, undeveloped conscience, and inferior intellect result from penis deprivation.

58. Mary Glenn Wiley and Dale E. Woolley, "Interruptions among Equals: Power Plays that Fail," *Gender & Society,* 1988, 2(1): 90–102, p. 92.

59. Joseph W. Schneider and Sally L. Hacker, "Sex Role Imagery and Use of the Generic 'Man' in Introductory Texts: A Case in the Sociology of Sociology," *The American Sociologist,* 1973, 8(1): 12–18; Janet Shibley Hyde, "Children's Understanding of Sexist Language," and Sharlene Hesse-Biber, "The Linguistic Validity of Polling Language: Generic Terms that Aren't," papers presented as part of a symposium, "Sexism in Language: Psychological and Sociological Research," American Psychological Association, August 1982, Washington, D.C. For a discussion of all of this literature, see Nancy M. Henley, "This New Species that Seeks a New Language: On Sexism in Language and Language Change," in Joyce Penfield (ed.), *Women & Language in Transition* (Albany, NY: SUNY, 1987), pp. 3–27.

60. Carol Gerwin, "The Attractive Blonde was Found Dead: Linguistic Sexism in U.S. Newspapers," honors thesis, Department of Sociology, Brandeis University, 1990.

61. Joyce McCarl Nielsen and Jeana Abromeit, "Paradigm Shifts and Feminist Phase Theory in Women Studies Curriculum Transformation Projects," paper presented at the 84th Annual Meeting of the American Sociological Association, San Francisco, California, August 1989, p. 5. In attempting to publish this paper, the authors have received a reaction from journal editors similar to that of Kersti Yllo, see note 20.

62. Philip Goldberg, "Are Women Prejudiced against Women?" *Transaction/SOCI-*

ETY, 1968, *5:* 28–30. Goldberg's article is discussed in Sandra L. Bem and Daryl J. Bem, "Case Study of a Nonconscious Ideology: Training the Woman to Know Her Place," in Daryl Bem, *Beliefs, Attitudes, and Human Affairs* (Belmont, CA: Brooks/Cole, 1970), pp. 89–99. They repeated it with male subjects in their classrooms and found the same prejudice. See also Laurel Richardson and Verta Taylor, *Feminist Frontiers: Rethinking Sex, Gender and Society* (New York: Random House, 1983).

63. From Kate Millett, *Sexual Politics* (New York: Ballantine Books, 1969), pp. 36, 77.

64. Kenneth J. Gruber and Jacquelyn Gaebelein, "Sex Differences in Learning Comprehension," *Sex Roles,* 1979, *5*(4): 519–535.

65. Abigail Drexler, "Men and Their Coursework," Department of Sociology, Brandeis University, 1990.

66. Presumably both men and women were chairpersons.

67. L. S. Fidell, "Empirical Verification of Sex Discrimination in Hiring Practices in Psychology," *American Psychologist,* 1970, *25*(12): 1094–1097; as discussed in Dorothy E. Smith, "An Analysis of Ideological Structures and How Women Are Excluded: Considerations for Academic Women," *Canadian Review of Sociology and Anthropology,* 1975, *12*(4): 353–369, p. 363.

68. Robert Blauner and David Wellman, "Toward the Decolonization of Social Research," in Joyce A. Ladner (ed.), *The Death of White Sociology* (New York: Vintage, 1973), pp. 310–330, p. 318. See also Mary Roth Walsh, "Psychology," in Cheris Kramarae and Dale Spender (eds.), *The Knowledge Explosion* (New York: Pergamon, 1991), for a discussion of other cases.

69. Matina Horner, "Sex Differences in Achievement Motivation and Performance in Competitive and Noncompetitive Situations," doctoral dissertation, University of Michigan, 1968; see also Judith Bardwick, Elizabeth Douvan, Matina Horner, and David Gutmann, *Feminine Personality and Conflict* (Belmont, CA: Brooks/Cole, 1970); and Matina Horner, "Achievement-Related Conflicts in Women," *Journal of Social Issues,* 1972, *28*(2): 157–175.

70. Susan Volentine and Stanley Brodsky, "Personal Construct Theory and Stimulus Sex and Subject Sex Differences," in Rhoda K. Unger (ed.), *Representations: Social Constructions of Gender* (Amityville, NY: Baywood Publishing Company, 1989), pp. 112–125.

71. See also David W. Tresemer, *Fear of Success* (New York: Plenum, 1977); John Condry and Sharon Dyer, "Fear of Success: Attribution of Cause to the Victim," *Journal of Social Issues,* 1976, *32*(3): 63–83; and Nancy Henley, "Psychology and Gender," *Signs: Journal of Women in Culture and Society,* 1985, *11*(1): 101–119.

72. Sheila Rothman, *Woman's Proper Place* (New York: Basic Books, 1978), pp. 238–239.

73. See, for example, Edward Donnerstein, Daniel Linz, and Steven Penrod, *The Question of Pornography: Research Findings and Policy Implications* (New York: Free Press, 1987). Sheila Rothman, *Ibid.,* suggests that the 1954 Brown Supreme Court issue spurred research on blacks, which in turn spurred research on sex, such as the synthesis of sex difference research, compiled by Eleanor Maccoby and Carol Jacklin, *The Psychology of Sex Differences* (Stanford: Stanford University Press, 1974).

74. Nancy Henley, *Body Politics: Power, Sex, and Nonverbal Communication* (Englewood Cliffs, NJ: Prentice-Hall, 1977).

75. Inge Broverman, Donald Broverman, Frank Clarkson, Paul Rosenkrantz, and Susan Vogel, "Sex-role Stereotypes and Clinical Judgments of Mental Health," *Journal of Counseling and Clinical Psychology,* 1970, *34*(1): 1–7.

76. Dafna Izraeli, "Sex Effects or Structural Effects? An Empirical Test of Kanter's Theory of Proportions," *Social Forces*, 1983, *62*: 153–165; E. Spangler, M. A. Gordon, and R. M. Pipkin, "Token Women: An Empirical Test of Kanter's Hypothesis," *American Journal of Sociology*, 1978, *84*: 160–170.

77. Michelle Fine and Susan Gordon, *op. cit.* (note 4), p. 23.

78. Letitia Peplau and Eva Conrad, *op. cit.* (note 20).

79. Annette M. Brodsky, "Sex, Race & Class Issues in Psychotherapy Research," paper presented at the American Psychological Association, 1982, pp. 30–32.

80. Letitia Peplau and Eva Conrad, *op. cit.* (note 20), p. 388.

81. Edward Donnerstein, Daniel Linz, and Steven Penrod, *op. cit.* (note 73), p. 157.

82. Catharine A. MacKinnon, "Pornography, Civil Rights, and Speech," *Harvard Civil Rights & Civil Liberties Review*, 1985, *2*: 1.

83. Pauline B. Bart, review of Neil Malamuth and Edward Donnerstein (eds.), *Pornography and Sexual Aggression* (Orlando, FL: Academic Press, 1984). Her review in is *Contemporary Sociology*, 1986, *15*(4): 572–573, p. 573.

84. Eleanor Maccoby, "Woman's Intellect," in Seymour Farber and Roger H. L. Wilson (eds.), *Man and Civilization: The Potential of Woman* (New York: McGraw-Hill, 1963).

Chapter 6 Feminist Cross-Cultural Research

1. Patricia Bell Scott, "Debunking Sapphire: Toward a Non-Racist and Non-Sexist Social Science," *Journal of Sociology and Social Welfare*, 1977, *4*(6): 864–871.

2. Carol MacCormack, "Anthropology: A Discipline with a Legacy," in Dale Spender (ed.), *Men's Studies Modified: The Impact of Feminism on the Disciplines* (New York: Pergamon, 1981), p. 100.

3. Linda Mitteness, "Anthropological Thinking about Age: Grown up at Last?" *Reviews in Anthropology*, 1985, *12*(3): 232–240, pp. 235–236. See also Elizabeth Colson, "The Reordering of Experience: Anthropological Involvement with Time," *Journal of Anthropological Research*, 1984, *40*: 1–13; Gilbert Herdt, *Guardians of the Flutes: Idioms of Masculinity* (New York: McGraw-Hill, 1980); Gilbert Herdt, *Rituals of Manhood: Male Initiation in Papua New Guinea* (Berkeley: University of California Press, 1982); Margaret Mead, *Male and Female: A Study of the Sexes in a Changing World* (New York: Morrow, 1949); Margaret Mead, *Sex and Temperament in Three Primitive Societies* (New York: Morrow, 1963); Esther Newton, *Mother Camp: Female Impersonators in America* (Chicago: University of Chicago Press, 1979); and Michelle Z. Rosaldo and Louise Lamphere (eds.), *Women, Culture and Society* (Stanford: Stanford University Press, 1974).

4. Robin Morgan, (ed.), *Sisterhood Is Global: The International Women's Movement Anthology* (New York: Anchor/Doubleday, 1984), pp. xii–xiv.

5. Helen Campbell, "Both Sides of the Sea," in *Prisoners of Poverty Abroad* (Boston: Roberts Brothers, 1890), pp. 7, 14–15.

6. Alva Myrdal and Viola Klein, *Women's Two Roles: Home and Work* (London: Routledge & Kegan Paul, 1956); see also Sissela Bok, *Alva Myrdal: A Daughter's Memoir* (Reading, MA: Addison-Wesley, 1991), and Allan C. Carlson, *Swedish Experiment in Family Politics: The Myrdals and the Interwar Population Crisis* (New Brunswick, NJ: Transaction Books, 1990).

7. Ann Pescatello, *Power and Pawn: The Female in Iberian Families, Societies, and Cultures* (Westport, CT: Greenwood Press, 1976), pp. xiii–xiv.

8. Janet Mancini Billson, "The Progressive Verification Method: Toward a Feminist

Methodology for Studying Women Cross-Culturally," *Women's Studies International Forum,* 1991, *14*(3): 201–208.

9. Diane Bell, *Daughters of the Dreaming* (Melbourne, Australia: McPhee Gribble, 1983), p. 246.

10. Robin Morgan, *op. cit.* (note 4).

11. Robin Morgan, *Ibid.,* p. xiii.

12. Sylvia Marcos, "Curing and Cosmology: The Challenge of Popular Medicine," *Development: Seeds of Change,* 1987, *1*: 20–25.

13. Lisa Leghorn and Katherine Parker, *Woman's Worth: Sexual Economics and the World of Women* (Boston: Routledge & Kegan Paul, 1981), pp. 4, 6.

14. The author uses this term to refer to women who were born in a country other than the one in which they lived and who are married to native men.

15. Anne Imamura, "The Loss That Has No Name: Social Womanhood of Foreign Wives," *Gender & Society,* 1988, *2*(3): 291–307, pp. 293–294.

16. See Marilyn Strathern, "An Awkward Relationship: The Case of Feminism and Anthropology," *Signs: Journal of Women in Culture and Society,* 1987, *12*(2): 276–292, p. 287.

17. See Nancy Scheper-Hughes, "Introduction: The Problem of Bias in Androcentric and Feminist Anthropology," *Women's Studies,* 1983, *10:* 115.

18. Deanne Bonnar, "When the Bough Breaks: A Feminist Analysis of Income Maintenance Strategies for Female-based Households," doctoral dissertation, Heller School, Brandeis University, 1985, p. 25.

19. John Court, "Sex and Violence: A Ripple Effect," in Neil M. Malamuth and Edward Donnerstein (eds.), *Pornography and Sexual Aggression* (Orlando, FL: Academic Press, 1984), pp. 143–172.

20. Peggy Reeves Sanday, *Female Power and Male Dominance: On the Origins of Sexual Inequality* (New York: Cambridge University Press, 1981).

21. Sherry B. Ortner, "Is Female to Male as Nature Is to Culture?," in M. Z. Rosaldo and L. Lamphere (eds.), *Woman, Culture, and Society* (Stanford: Standford University Press, 1974), pp. 67–88.

22. George P. Murdock and Douglas R. White. "Standard Cross-cultural Sample," *Ethnology,* 1969, *8*: 329–369.

23. Peggy Sanday, *op. cit.* (note 20), pp. xv–xvi, 232.

24. Vicky Randall, *Women and Politics: An International Perspective* (Chicago: The University of Chicago Press, 1982, 1987), p. 49.

25. See also Eva Etzioni-Halevy and Ann Illy, "Women in Parliament: Israel in a Comparative Perspective," paper delivered at the International Interdisciplinary Congress on Women, Haifa, Israel, December 1981.

26. Marian Sawer and Marian Simms, *A Woman's Place: Women and Politics in Australia* (Boston: George Allen & Unwin, 1984).

27. Rae Lesser Blumberg, "A General Theory of Gender Stratification," in American Sociological Association, *Sociological Theory 1984* (San Francisco: Jossey-Bass, 1984), pp. 23–101, pp. 86–87.

28. Carmen Diana Deere and Magdalena Leon de Leal, "Peasant Production, Proletarianization, and the Sexual Division of Labor in the Andes," *Signs: Journal of Women in Culture and Society,* 1981, *7*(2): 338–360, p. 340. See also their edited volume, *Rural Women and State Policy: Feminist Perspectives on Latin American Agricultural Development* (Boulder, CO: Westview Press, 1987).

29. Vandana Shiva, *Staying Alive: Women, Ecology and Development* (London: Zed Books, 1988), p. 223.

30. Shulamit Reinharz, "Controlling Women's Lives: A Cross-Cultural Interpretation of Miscarriage Accounts," in Dorothy Wertz (ed.), *Research in the Sociology of Health Care,* volume 7 (Greenwich, CT: JAI Press, 1988), pp. 2–37.

31. Marcia Texler Segal and Catherine White Berheide, "Towards a Women's Perspective in Sociology: Directions and Prospects," in Scott McNall (ed.), *Theoretical Perspectives in Sociology* (New York: St. Martin's Press, 1979), pp. 69–82.

32. *The World & I* Magazine, 1987, *2*(6): 82–83.

33. bell hooks, *Feminist Theory: From Margin to Center* (Boston: South End Press, 1984), p. 56.

34. Elise Boulding, *Women in the Twentieth Century World* (New York: Wiley, 1977), pp. 9–10.

35. Arlene Kaplan Daniels uses the word "we" to refer to members of Sociologists for Women in Society, a U.S. organization of feminist sociologists.

36. Ms. Manners, *SWS Network,* October 1987, *5*(1): 18–19 (Arlene K. Daniels).

37. Elly Bulkin, "Racism and Writing," *Sinister Wisdom, 7*: 3–22.

38. Sara Karon, "The Politics of Naming: Lesbian Erasure in a Feminist Context," in Shulamit Reinharz and Ellen Stone (eds.), *Looking at Invisible Women: An Exercise in Feminist Pedagogy* (Washington, D.C.: University Press of America, 1992).

39. Marilyn Frye, "Assignment: NWSA—Bloomington—1980: Speak on 'Lesbian Perspectives on Women's Studies,' " *Sinister Wisdom,* 1980, *14*: 3–7.

40. Sarah Lucia Hoagland, *Lesbian Ethics: Toward New Value* (Palo Alto: Institute of Lesbian Studies, 1988).

41. The terms "Western" and "non-Western" are Aihwa Ong's.

42. Aihwa Ong, "Colonialism and Modernity: Feminist Representations of Women in Non-Western Societies," *Inscriptions,* Special Issue: *Feminism and the Critique of Colonial Discourse,* 1988, *3/4,* pp. 78–93, pp. 80, 82.

43. See B. Awe, "Reflections on the Conference on Women and Development, I," *Signs: Journal of Women in Culture and Society,* 1977, *3*(1): 314–316; L. Casal, "Reflections on the Conference on Women and Development, II," *Signs: Journal of Women in Culture and Society,* 1977, *3*(1): 317–319.

44. Sistren with Honor Ford Smith, "Introduction," in *Lionheart Gal: Life Stories of Jamaican Women* (London: The Women's Press, 1986), p. xxiv.

45. Lila Abu-Lughod, *Veiled Sentiments: Honor and Poetry in a Bedouin Society* (Berkeley, CA: University of California Press, 1986), p. 11.

46. Claire Reinelt, "Feminist Ways of Knowing," unpublished paper, Department of Sociology, Brandeis University, 1989, p. 6.

47. Fatima Mernissi, *Beyond the Veil: Male-Female Dynamics in Modern Muslim Society* (Bloomington, IN: Indiana University Press, 1987), p. 167.

48. Claire Reinelt, *op. cit.* (note 46).

49. Marla N. Powers, *Oglala Women: Myth, Ritual and Reality* (Chicago: University of Chicago Press, 1986), pp. 6–7.

50. Rae Andre, "Multi-cultural Research: Developing a Participative Methodology for Cross-Cultural Psychology," paper presented at the Annual Convention of the International Council of Psychologists, Princeton, New Jersey, 1979.

51. Chandra Talpade Mohanty, "Under Western Eyes: Feminist Scholarship and Colonial Discourses," *Boundary 2,* 1984/1985, *12*(3), *13*(1): 333–358.

52. Andrea Dworkin, "Gynocide: Chinese Footbinding," in Andrea Dworkin (ed.), *Women Hating* (New York: E. P. Dutton, 1974).

53. Sistren with Honor Ford Smith, *op. cit.* (note 44), p. xiii. The classic work in this field is Ester Boserup, *Women's Role in Economic Development* (London: George Allen &

Unwin, 1970). For a discussion see Lourdes Beneria and Gita Sen, "Accumulation, Reproduction, and Women's Role in Economic Development: Boserup Revisited," *Signs: Journal of Women in Culture and Society,* 1981, 7(2): 279–298.

54. Chandra Mohanty, *op. cit.* (note 51), pp. 336–337. See for example, Janet W. Salaff, *Working Daughters of Hong Kong: Filial Piety or Power in the Family?* (New York: Cambridge University Press, 1981).

55. Kathleen Barry, *Female Sexual Slavery* (New York: Avon Books, 1979), pp. 163–164.

56. Betsy Hartmann, *Reproductive Rights and Wrongs: The Global Politics of Population Control & Contraceptive Choice* (New York: Harper & Row, 1987), pp. xii–xiii.

57. See Charlotte Bunch, "UN World Conference in Nairobi: A View from the West," in Charlotte Bunch (ed.), *Passionate Politics: Feminist Theory in Action* (New York: St. Martin's Press, 1987), pp. 321–327.

58. See Arvonne S. Fraser, *The U.N. Decade for Women: Documents and Dialogue* (Boulder, CO: Westview Press, 1987) for an analysis of these events from a feminist perspective. See Georgina Ashworth (ed.), *The UN Decade for Women: An International Evaluation,* Special Issue of *Women's Studies International Forum,* 1985, 8(2).

59. See Charlotte Bunch, *op. cit.* (note 57).

60. Marilyn Safir, Martha Mednick, Dafna Izraeli, and Jessie Bernard (eds.), *Women's Worlds: From the New Scholarship* (New York: Praeger, 1985).

61. For a discussion of the implications of this network, see Gena Corea, *The Mother Machine: Reproductive Technologies from Artificial Insemination to Artificial Wombs* (New York: Harper & Row, 1985).

62. Jane Jacquette (ed.), *The Women's Movement in Latin America: Feminism and the Transition to Democracy* (Boston: Unwin Hyman, 1989), p. 1.

63. *Newsletter,* Section on Sex and Gender, American Sociological Association, Fall 1989, p. 1. [emphasis added]

64. Rayna Reiter (ed.), *Toward an Anthropology of Women* (New York: Monthly Review Press, 1975) p. 16.

Chapter 7   Feminist Oral History

1. R. Ruth Linden and Margaret Fearey gave me helpful reviews of this chapter.

2. Sherna Gluck, "What's So Special about Women? Women's Oral History," *Frontiers,* 1979, 2(2): 3–11, p. 5.

3. See Sheila Rowbotham and Jean McCrindle, *Dutiful Daughters: Women Talk about Their Lives* (Austin, TX: University of Texas Press, 1977). This book contains married women's oral testimonies on sexuality.

4. Sherna Gluck, *op. cit.* (note 2).

5. See Shulamit Reinharz, "The Sociological Value of Biographies of Female Scientists," paper presented at the Annual Meetings of the History of Science Society, Cincinnati, Ohio, December 28, 1988.

6. Elisabeth Griffith, *In Her Own Right: The Life of Elizabeth Cady Stanton* (New York: Oxford University Press, 1984), p. xix.

7. Judith Schachter Modell, *Ruth Benedict: Patterns of a Life* (Philadelphia: University of Pennsylvania Press, 1983), p. 104.

8. Margaret M. Caffrey, *Ruth Benedict: Stranger in This Land* (Austin, TX: University of Texas Press, 1989), pp. 78–79.

9. Margaret Caffrey, *Ibid.,* p. 89.

10. Jill Matthews, *Good and Mad Women: The Historical Construction of Femininity in 20th Century Australia* (Sydney: George Allen & Unwin, 1984), p. 18.

11. Shulamit Reinharz, "Toward a Model of Female Political Action: The Case of Manya Shohat, Founder of the First Kibbutz," *Women's Studies International Forum,* 1984, 7(4): 275–287. See also Shulamit Reinharz, "Finding a Sociological Voice: The Work of Mirra Komarovsky," *Sociological Inquiry,* 1989, 59(4): 374–394.

12. See Marjorie Shostak, *Nisa: The Life and Words of a !Kung Woman* (Cambridge, MA: Harvard University Press, 1981; New York: Vintage, 1983).

13. See Nancy Seifer, *Nobody Speaks for Me!: Self-Portraits of American Working Class Women* (New York: Touchstone, 1976). See *The Oral History Review,* journal of the Oral History Association.

14. See M. Brinton Lykes, "Discrimination and Coping in the Lives of Black Women: Analyses of Oral History Data," *Journal of Social Issues,* 1983, 39(3): 79–100.

15. See Stephanie Dowrick and Sibyl Grundberg (eds.), *Why Children?* (New York: Harcourt Brace Jovanovich, 1980).

16. See Diana E. H. Russell, *Lives of Courage: Women for a New South Africa* (New York: Basic Books, 1989).

17. Review by Clara Sue Kidwell of Gretchen M. Bataille and Kathleen Mullen Sands, *American Indian Women: Telling Their Lives* (Lincoln, NB: University of Nebraska Press, 1984), in *Women's Studies International Forum,* 1985, 8(5): 533–538, p. 533.

18. Cheryl Gilkes, "Going up for the Oppressed: The Career Mobility of Black Women Community Workers," *Journal of Social Issues,* 1983, 39(3): 115–139.

19. Cheryl Gilkes' study is discussed in Michelle Fine, "Contextualizing the Study of Social Injustice," in Michael Saks and Leonard Saxe (eds.), *Advances in Applied Social Psychology* (Hillsdale, NJ: Erlbaum, 1985), pp. 103–128.

20. Brinton Lykes, *op. cit.* (note 14), p. 82.

21. The Murray Research Center at Radcliffe College contains qualitative data available for secondary analysis. See Shulamit Reinharz, "Empty Explanations for Empty Wombs: An Illustration of a Secondary Analysis of Qualitative Data," in Michael Schratz (ed.), *Qualitative Voices in Educational Research* (London: Falmer Press, 1992).

22. Susan Tucker, *Telling Memories among Southern Women: Domestic Workers and Their Employers in the Segregated South* (Baton Rouge, LA: Louisiana State University Press, 1988).

23. Kathryn Anderson, Susan Armitage, Dana Jack, and Judith Wittmer, "Beginning Where We Are: Feminist Methodology in Oral History," *Oral History Review,* 1987, 57: 103–127, p. 104.

24. The tapes are of Sissela Bok (on Alva Myrdal), Rose Coser, Mary Jo Deegan (on Jane Addams), Ellen Fitzpatrick, Laurel Furumoto (on Mary Calkins), Deborah Gordon, Helen Hughes, Joan Mark (on Alice Fletcher), Judi Marshall, Alice Rossi, Dorothy E. Smith, Mary Terrell (on Florence Nightingale), Mary Roth Walsh, and Doris Wilkinson.

25. Mary E. Gilfus, "Life Histories of Women in Prison," paper presented at the Third National Family Violence Research Conference, University of New Hampshire, Durham, NH, July 6–9, 1987.

26. Faye Ginsburg, "From Dissonance to Harmony: The Symbolic Function of Abortion in Activists' Life Stories," paper presented at conference on "Autobiographies, Biographies and Life Histories of Women: Interdisciplinary Perspectives," University of Minnesota, May 23, 1986, pp. 4–5; see also Faye Ginsburg, "Dissonance to Harmony: The Symbolic Function of Abortion in Activitists' Life Stories," in Personal Narratives Group (eds.), *Interpreting Women's Lives: Feminist Theory and Personal Narratives* (Bloomington, IN: Indiana University Press, 1989), pp. 59–84.

27. Faye Ginsburg, *Ibid.*, fn. 4.

28. R. Ruth Linden, " 'The Story of Our Lives Becomes Our Lives': Post-Positivism and the Life History Method," unpublished manuscript, Brandeis University, 1988; R. Ruth Linden, *Making Stories, Making Selves: Writing Sociology After the Holocaust* (Columbus: The Ohio State University Press, forthcoming).

29. See Dale Spender (ed.), *Personal Chronicles: Women's Autobiographical Writings,* Special issue of *Women's Studies International Forum,* 1987, *10*(1).

30. Marcia Wright, "Since 'Women in Peril': Reconsiderations of Biography, Autobiography and Life Stories of Some African Women with Special Reference to Marriage," paper presented at conference on "Autobiographies, Biographies and Life Histories of Women: Interdisciplinary Perspectives," University of Minnesota, May 23, 1986, pp. 3–4, 6.

31. Amy Blythe Millstone, *Biographical Research in Women's Studies: Subjects, Issues, Problems* (Columbia, S.C.: University of South Carolina, forthcoming); Shulamit Reinharz, "Pain, Joy and Dilemmas in Feminist Biography" in Judith Long (ed.), *The New Sociobiography,* manuscript.

32. Mary Gilfus, *op. cit.* (note 25), p. 4.

33. See C. Wright Mills, *The Sociological Imagination* (New York: Grove Press, 1959); Sue Middleton, "On Being a Feminist Educationist Doing Research on Being a Feminist Educationist: Life History Analysis as Consciousness Raising," *New Zealand Cultural Studies Working Group Journal,* 1984, *8*: 29–37.

34. See Jean Reith Schroeder, *Alone in a Crowd: Women in the Trades Tell Their Stories* (Philadelphia: Temple University Press, 1986); see also Suzanne Gail, "The Housewife," in Ronald Fraser, *Work: Twenty Personal Accounts* (Harmondsworth: Penguin, 1968).

35. See M. Brigid O'Farrell and Lydia Kleiner, "Anna Sullivan: Trade Union Organizer," *Frontiers,* 1979, *2*(2): 24–29.

36. Carolyn Sachs, *The Invisible Farmers: Women in Agricultural Production* (Totowa, NJ: Rowman & Allanheld, 1983), p. xii.

37. For a critical discussion of this method see Elizabeth Hardwick's "The Teller and the Tape," *New York Review of Books,* May 30, 1985, pp. 3–4.

38. This definition is based on the work of M. Brinton Lykes, "Discrimination and Coping in the Lives of Black Women: Analyses of Oral History Data," *Journal of Social Issues,* 1983, *39*(3): 79–100; see M. Brinton Lykes, "Perspective on Self and Community among Guatemalan Indian Women: An Oral History Project," unpublished manuscript; see also E. Burgos-Debray (ed.), *I, 'Rigoberta Menchu: An Indian woman in Guatemala* (trans. by A. Wright), (Longon: Verso Ed., 1984).

39. Examples of discussion of methods used in oral history are Elizabeth Dixon and James Mink, *Oral History at Arrowhead: Proceedings of the First National Colloquium on Oral History* (Los Angeles: The Oral History Association, 1969); Edward D. Ives, *The Tape-Recorded Interview: A Manual for Fieldworkers in Folklore and Oral History* (Knoxville, TN: University of Tennessee, 1980); Thad Sitton, George Mehaffy, and O. L. Davis, Jr. *Oral History: A Guide for Teachers (and Others)* (Austin, TX: University of Texas Press, 1983).

40. "Rebecca Courser: Profile of a Service Award Winner," *The News Messenger,* July 25, 1990, p. 12.

41. One article reviewing these projects included "The Twentieth Century Trade Union Woman: Vehicle for Social Change"; Southern Oral History Program at the University of North Carolina at Chapel Hill; the Feminist History Research Project at Topanga, California; the Ohio Labor History Project; the Pennsylvania State University Oral History Program; Southern Labor Archives at Georgia State University; the Black Woman Oral History

Project of the Schlesinger Library at Radcliffe College; the Oregon Jewish Oral History and Archives Project; and the California Historical Society Oral History Project.

42. Marcia Wright, *op. cit.* (note 30), pp. 19–20; see also, Marcia Wright, "Personal Narratives, Dynasties, and Women's Campaigns: Two Examples from Africa," in Personal Narratives Group (ed.), *Interpreting Women's Lives: Feminist Theory and Personal Narratives* (Bloomington, IN: Indiana University Press, 1989), pp. 155–171.

43. Daniel Bertaux (ed.), *Biography and Society: The Life History Approach in the Social Sciences* (Beverly Hills, CA: Sage, 1981).

44. An example is Fran Leeper Buss, *Dignity: Lower Income Women Tell of Their Lives and Struggles* (Ann Arbor, MI: University of Michigan Press, 1985).

45. Some examples are W. I. Thomas and Florian Znaniecki, *The Polish Peasant in Europe and America* (2nd ed., New York, 1927), II, 1931–2244; Clifford R. Shaw, *The Jack-Roller: A Delinquent Boy's Own Story* (Chicago: University of Chicago Press, 1930), reprinted in 1966; Daniel Bertaux (ed.), *Biography and Society: The Life History Approach in the Social Sciences* (Beverly Hills, CA: Sage Publications, 1981); Studs Terkel, *Division Street: America* (New York: Pantheon, 1967); Studs Terkel, *Hard Times: An Oral History of the Great Depression* (New York: Pantheon, 1970); Studs Terkel, *Working: People Talk about What They Do All Day and How They Feel about It* (New York: Pantheon, 1974); Ronald Blythe, *Akenfield: Portrait of an English Village* (New York: Dell, 1973); Trevor Lummis, "The Occupational Community of East Anglican Fishermen: an Historical Dimension through Oral Evidence," *British Journal of Sociology*, 1977, *28*(1): 51–74; and Theda Perdue, *Nations Remembered: An Oral History of the Five Civilized Tribes, 1865–1907* (Westport, CT: Greenwood Press, 1980).

46. Sara Evans, *Personal Politics: The Roots of Women's Liberation in the Civil Rights Movement and the New Left* (New York: Vintage, 1979), p. xi.

47. Michal McCall and Judith Wittner, "The Good News about Life History," in Howard S. Becker and Michal M. McCall (eds.) *Symbolic Interaction and Cultural Studies* (Chicago: University of Chicago Press, 1990), pp. 46–89.

48. Susan Bell, "Becoming a Political Woman: The Reconstruction and Interpretation of Experience through Stories," in Alexandra Dundas Todd and Sue Fisher (eds.), *Gender and Discourse: The Power of Talk* (Norwood, NJ: Ablex, 1988).

49. Elizabeth Higginbotham, "Oral History Refutes Stereotypes," *The Newsletter*, Center for Research on Women, Memphis State University, Fall, 1986, *5*(1): 3. This review concludes with the following list of oral histories of Southern women: Shirley Abbott, *Womenfolk: Growing up Down South* (New Haven, CT: Tichnor and Fields, 1983); Maxine Alexander, *Speaking for Ourselves: Women of the South* (New York: Pantheon, 1984); Hollinger F. Bernard (ed.), *Outside the Magic Circle: The Autobiography of Virginia Foster Durr* (University, Alabama: University of Alabama Press, 1985); JoElla Powell Exley (ed.), *Texas Tears and Texas Sunshine: Voices of Frontier Women* (University Station, TX: Texas A&M Press, 1985); Mamie Garvin Fields and Karen Fields, *Lemon Swamp and Other Places: A Carolina Memoir* (New York: The Free Press, 1985); Chris Mayfield, *Growing up Southern* (New York: Pantheon, 1981); Mab Segrest, *My Mama's Dead Squirrel: Lesbian Essays on Southern Culture* (Ithaca, NY: Firebrand Books, 1985); Emily Wilson, *Hope and Dignity: Older Black Women of the South* (Philadelphia: Temple University Press, 1983); Ruth Winegarten (ed.), *I Am Annie Mae: The Personal Story of a Black Texas Woman* (Austin: Rosegarden Press, 1983); and Thordis Simonsen (ed.), *You May Plow Here: The Narrative of Sara Brooks* (New York: Norton, 1986).

50. Judy Long, "Telling Women's Lives: The New Sociobiography," paper presented at the Annual Meetings of the American Sociological Association, August 1987, Chicago, Illinois, p. 5.

51. Liz McMillen, "Woman Who Won Tenure Fight Gets Cool Reception at Harvard," *The Chronicle of Higher Education,* 1986, *33*(5): 1, 16.

52. Mary Jo Deegan, *Jane Addams and the Men of the Chicago School: 1892–1918* (New Brunswick, NJ: Transaction Books, 1988), pp. 1–2.

53. Sara Evans, *op. cit.* (note 46), p. xi.

54. Mary Jo Maynes, "The Proletarian Muse: How French and German Working-class Men and Women became Autobiographers," paper presented at Conference on "Autobiographies, Biographies and Life Histories of Women: Interdisciplinary Perspectives," University of Minnesota, May 23, 1986, p. 1; see also her "Gender and Narrative Form in French and German Working-Class Autobiographies," in Personal Narratives Group (ed.), *op. cit.* (note 26), pp. 103–117.

55. Susan N. G. Geiger, "Women's Life Histories: Method and Content," *Signs: Journal of Women in Culture and Society,* 1986, *11*(2): 334–351.

56. Margaret Randall, *Sandino's Daughters: Testimonies of Nicaraguan Women in Struggle* (Toronto, Canada: New Star Books, 1981), p. vii.

57. Lynda Yanz, "Preface," to Margaret Randall, *Ibid.,* pp. i–ii.

58. Elizabeth Roberts, *A Woman's Place: An Oral History of Working-Class Women 1890–1940* (Oxford: Basil Blackwell, 1984), pp. 1–2.

59. Sydelle Kramer and Jenny Masur (eds.), *Jewish Grandmothers* (Boston: Beacon Press, 1976), p. xi.

60. Jewell Babb and Pat Ellis Taylor, *Border Healing Woman: The Story of Jewell Babb as Told to Pat Ellis Taylor* (Austin, TX: The University of Texas Press, 1981), p. xvi.

61. Evelyn Nakano Glenn, *Issei, Nisei, War Bride: Three Generations of Japanese American Women in Domestic Service* (Philadelphia, PA: Temple University Press, 1986), p. ix.

62. Jean Bethke Elshtain, *Public Man, Private Woman: Women in Social and Political Thought* (Princeton, NJ: Princeton University Press, 1981), p. xii.

63. Daphne Patai, "Ethical Problems of Personal Narratives or, Who Should Eat the Last Piece of Cake?" paper presented at Conference on "Autobiographies, Biographies and Life Histories of Women: Interdisciplinary Perspectives," University of Minnesota, May 23, 1986, p. 7.

64. Marjorie Shostak, *op. cit.* (note 12).

65. Barbara Myerhoff, *Number Our Days* (New York: E. P. Dutton, 1978).

66. Marjorie Shostak, "What the Wind Won't Take Away: Methodological and Ethical Considerations of the Oral History of a Hunting-Gathering Woman," paper presented at Conference on "Autobiographies, Biographies and Life Histories of Women: Interdisciplinary Perspectives," University of Minnesota, May 23, 1986, p. 16; see also Marjorie Shostak, " 'What the Wind Won't Take Away': The Genesis of *Nisa—The Life and Words of a !Kung Woman,*" in Personal Narratives Group (ed.), *op. cit.* (note 26), pp. 228–240.

67. Diana Russell, *op. cit.* (note 16), p. xi.

68. Jeff Collmann, " 'I'm Proper Number One Fighter, Me': Aborigines, Gender, and Bureaucracy in Central Australia," *Gender & Society,* 1988, *2*(1): 9–23. See also Sally Morgan, *My Place* (New York: Arcade, 1980) and Ruby Langford, *Don't Take My Love to Town* (New York: Penguin, 1988).

69. Nancy Seifer, *op. cit.* (note 13), p. 25.

70. See Rosemary Novitz, "Feminism," in Paul Spoonely, David Pearson, and Ian Shirley (eds.), *New Zealand: Sociological Perspectives* (Palmerston North: The Dunmore Press, 1982), pp. 293–323.

71. See Cherrie Moraga and G. Anzaldua (eds.), *This Bridge Called My Back* (Watertown, MA: Persephone Press, 1981); Evelyn Torton Beck (ed.), *Nice Jewish Girls: A Lesbian Anthology* (Watertown, MA: Persephone Press, 1982).

72. Patricia Cayo Sexton, *The New Nightingales: Hospital Workers, Unions, New Women's Issues* (New York: Enquiry Press, 1982), p. 4.

73. Elizabeth Hampsten, "Let Them Speak for Themselves: Experiments in Editing and Biography," paper presented at the Conference on "Autobiographies, Biographies and Life Histories of Women: Interdisciplinary Perspectives," University of Minnesota, May 23, 1986; see her "Considering More Than a Single Reader," in Personal Narratives Group (ed.), *op. cit.* (note 26), pp. 129–138.

74. Elizabeth Hampsten, *Ibid.*, p. 7.

75. Fran Buss, *op. cit.* (note 44), pp. 15–16.

76. Diana Russell, *op. cit.* (note 16).

77. Julia Swindells, "Liberating the Subject? Autobiography and 'Women's History': A Reading of *The Diaries of Hannah Cullwick*," paper presented at Conference on "Autobiographies, Biographies and Life Histories of Women: Interdisciplinary Perspectives," University of Minnesota, May 23, 1986, p. 1; reprinted in Personal Narratives Group (ed.), *op. cit.* (note 26), pp. 24–38.

78. Julia Swindells, *Ibid.*, p. 18.

79. Katherine Goodman, "Poetry and Truth in Autobiography," paper presented at Conference on "Autobiographies, Biographies and Life Histories of Women: Interdisciplinary Perspectives," University of Minnesota, May 23, 1986; see also Katherine R. Goodman, "Poetry and Truth: Elisa von der Recke's Sentimental Autobiography," in Personal Narratives Group (ed.), *op. cit.* (note 26), 118–128.

80. Marjorie Shostak, *op. cit.* (note 12), p. 4.

81. Jewell Babb and Pat Taylor, *op. cit.* (note 60), p. xvi. Mamie Garvin Fields and Karen Fields, *Lemon Swamp and Other Places: A Carolina Memoir* (New York: The Free Press, 1985) is similar in form.

82. Jewell Babb and Pat Taylor, *op. cit.* (note 60).

83. Ruth Harriet Jacobs, *Life After Youth: Female, 40, What Next?* (Boston: Beacon Press, 1979).

84. Lee Zevy with Sahli A. Cavallaro, "Invisibility, Fantasy, and Intimacy: Princess Charming Is Not a Prince," in Boston Lesbian Psychologies Collective (eds.), *Lesbian Psychologies* (Chicago: University of Illinois Press, 1987), pp. 83–94, p. 83.

85. Kathryn Anderson et al., *op. cit.* (note 23).

86. See Denise Connors, " 'I've Always Had Everything I've Wanted, But I Never Wanted Very Much': An Experiential Analysis of Irish-American Working Class Women in the Nineties," doctoral dissertation, Department of Sociology, Brandeis University, 1986.

87. Kathryn Anderson et al., *op. cit.* (note 23), p. 118.

88. Michal McCall and Judith Wittner, *op. cit.* (note 47), p. 8.

89. Ann Oakley, "Interviewing Women: A Contradiction in Terms," in Helen Roberts (ed.), *Doing Feminist Research* (London: Routledge & Kegan Paul, 1981), pp. 30–61.

90. Fran Buss, *op. cit.* (note 44), p. 17.

91. See my chapter on feminist action research.

92. Patricia Sexton, *The New Nightingales* (New York: Enquiry Press, 1982), pp. 1–6.

93. Fran Buss, *op. cit.* (note 44), p. 14.

94. Marcia Wright, *op. cit.* (note 30), p. 7.

95. Stephanie Dowrick and Sibyl Grundberg (eds.), *op. cit.* (note 15), p. 8; see also

Sara Ruddick and Pamela Daniels, (eds.) *Working It Out: 23 Women Writers, Artists, Scientists, and Scholars Talk about Their Lives and Work* (New York: Pantheon Books, 1977), esp. pp. xi, xxx.

96. Fran Buss, *op. cit.* (note 44).

97. Kathryn Anderson et al., *op. cit.* (note 23), pp. 126–127.

Chapter 8 Feminist Content Analysis

1. This chapter benefited from readings by Karen V. Hansen and Andrea Walsh.

2. Harriet Martineau, *How to Observe Morals and Manners,* 1838; Michael R. Hill (ed.), (New Brunswick, NJ: Transaction Books, 1988), p. 73.

3. Rose Weitz, *Sex Roles* (New York: Oxford University Press, 1977), p. 194.

4. Harriet Martineau, *op. cit.* (note 2), pp. 73–74.

5. Eugene Webb, Donald T. Campbell, Richard D. Schwartz, and Lee Sechrest, *Unobtrusive Measures: Nonreactive Research in the Social Sciences* (Chicago: Rand McNally, 1966).

6. Andrea Walsh, personal communication.

7. Gaye Tuchman, *Edging Women Out: Victorian Novelists, Publishers, and Social Change* (New Haven: Yale, 1989).

8. Kay Richards Broschart discusses Ida Bell Wells-Barnett as a sociologist in ''In Search of our Mothers' Gardens: The Process and Consequences of Discovering Our Foremothers,'' paper presented at the ASA/SWS Annual Meeting, New York, 1986. See Ida Wells, *Southern Horrors, Lynch Law in All Its Phases* (1892); *The Reason Why the Colored American Is Not in the World's Columbian Exposition* (1893); *A Red Record: Tabulated Statistics and Alleged Causes of Lynchings in the United States* (1895); *Mob Rule in New Orleans* (1900). Alfreda Duster (ed.), *Crusade for Justice: The Autobiography of Ida B. Wells* (Chicago: University of Chicago Press, 1970).

9. Paula Giddings, *When and Where I Enter: The Impact of Black Women on Race and Sex in America* (New York: Morrow, 1984), pp. 28–31; Mildred I. Thompson, *Ida B. Wells-Barnett: An Exploratory Study of an American Black Woman, 1893–1930* (New York: Carlson, 1990).

10. Molly Haskell, *From Reverence to Rape: The Treatment of Women in the Movies* (Baltimore, MD: Penguin, 1973); Joan Mellon, *Women and Sexuality in the New Film* (New York: Dell, 1973); Horace Newcomb, *TV: The Most Popular Art* (New York: Anchor Books, 1974); Rose Goldsen, *The Show and Tell Machine* (New York: Dell, 1974); Gaye Tuchman, Arlene Kaplan Daniels, and James Benet (eds.), *Hearth and Home: Images of Women in the Mass Media* (New York: Oxford University Press, 1978).

11. Lenore Weitzman, Deborah Eifler, Elizabeth Hokada, and Catherine Ross, ''Sex Role Socialization in Picture Books for Pre-School Children,'' *American Journal of Sociology,* 1972, 77(6): 1125–1150. Lenore Weitzman, in *Sex Role Socialization* (Palo Alto, CA: Mayfield, 1979), pp. 7–11, discusses this and related material. Ravenna Helson, ''E. Nesbit's Forty-First Year: Her Life, Times, and Symbolizations of Personality Growth,'' in Rhoda K. Unger (ed.), *Representations: Social Constructions of Gender* (Amityville, NY: Baywood, 1989), pp. 29–44, offers a feminist analysis of a year in the life of a writer of children's books.

12. Jennifer Waelti-Walters, ''On Princesses: Fairy Tales, Sex Roles and Loss of Self,'' *International Journal of Women's Studies,* 1979, 2(2): 180–188.

13. Dolores Hayden, *Redesigning the American Dream: The Future of Housing, Work and Family Life* (New York: Norton, 1984).

14. Elly Bulkin, "Racism and Writing: Some Implications for White Lesbian Critics," *Sinister Wisdom, 7:* 3–22.

15. Joy B. Reeves and Nydia Boyette, "What Does Children's Art Work Tell Us About Gender?," *Qualitative Sociology,* 1983, *6*(4): 322–333.

16. Kennedy Fraser, *The Fashionable Mind: Reflections on Fashion, 1970–1982* (Boston: David R. Godine, 1985).

17. Mary Jo Deegan and Michael R. Hill, "The Presentation of the City in Fat-Letter Postcards," in Mary Jo Deegan (ed.), *American Ritual Dramas: Social Rules and Cultural Meanings* (New York: Greenwood Press, 1989).

18. Carol Auster, "Manuals for Socialization: Examples from Girl Scout Handbooks 1913–1984," in Meredith Gould (ed.), *Innovative Sources and Uses of Qualitative Data,* Special Issue of *Qualitative Sociology,* 1985, *8*(4): 359–367.

19. Charlotte O'Kelly, "Gender Role Stereotypes in Fine Art: A Content Analysis of Art History Books," *Qualitative Sociology,* 1983, *6*(2): 136–148.

20. Gill Seidel (ed.), *The Nature of the Right: A Feminist Analysis of Order Patterns* (Philadelphia: John Benjamins, 1988).

21. Jill Matthews, *Good and Mad Women: The Historical Construction of Femininity in Twentieth Century Australia* (Sydney, Australia: George Allen & Unwin, 1984).

22. Margrit Eichler used the following approach in her study of sexism in research: "My method was simple: I went into a library and picked up whatever recent issue of journals from different disciplines was lying on top in the journal pigeon holes. I assumed that it would make little difference which journal or issue I picked, and that I would find at least one example of sexism in every single one." See Margrit Eichler, *Nonsexist Research Methods: A Practical Guide* (Boston: Allen & Unwin, 1987), p. 10.

23. Elaine J. Hall, "One Week for Women? The Structure of Inclusion of Gender Issues in Introductory Textbooks," *Teaching Sociology,* 1988, *16*(4): 431–432.

24. Marianne A. Ferber, "Citations and Networking," *Gender & Society,* 1988, *2*(1): 82–89.

25. Joan T. Pennell, "Ideology at a Canadian Shelter for Battered Women: A Reconstruction," *Women's Studies International Forum,* 1987, *10*(2): 113–123.

26. See Karen V. Hansen, "Feminist Conceptions of Public and Private: A Critical Analysis," *Berkeley Journal of Sociology,* 1987, *32*: 105–128.

27. Karen Keller, "Freudian Tradition versus Feminism in Science Fiction," in T. Nygren and Mary Jo Deegan (eds.), *Wimmin in the Mass Media* (Lincoln, NB: University of Nebraska, 1980), pp. 41–52.

28. Annette Kuhn, *Women's Pictures: Feminism and Cinema* (London: Routledge & Kegan Paul, 1982); Kathi Maio, *Feminist in the Dark: Reviewing the Movies* (Freedom, CA: The Crossing Press, 1988).

29. Nancy Grant-Colson, "Women in Sitcoms: 'I Love Lucy'," in T. Nygren and Mary Jo Deegan (eds.), *Wimmin in the Mass Media,* (Lincoln, NB: University of Nebraska, 1981) pp. 21–30; Barbara Hollands Peevers, "Androgyny on the TV Screen? An Analysis of Sex-Roles Portrayal," *Sex Roles,* 1979, *5*(6): 797–809; Joseph Dominick, "The Portrayal of Women in Prime Time, 1953–1977," *Sex Roles,* 1979, *5*(4): 405–411.

30. C. Adams and R. Laurikietis (eds.), *The Gender Trap, A Closer Look at Sex Roles 3: Messages and Images* (London: Virago, 1980); Micaela di Leonardo, "The Female World of Cards and Holidays: Women, Families and the Work of Kinship," *Signs: Journal of Women in Culture and Society,* 1987, *12*(3): 440–453.

31. Sheila M. Krueger, "Images of Women in Rock Music: Analysis of B-52's and Black Rose," and Jane Pemberton, "Examining the Top Ten or Why Those Songs Make the Charts," both in T. Nygren and Mary Jo Deegan (eds.), *Wimmin in the Mass Media* (Lincoln, NB: University of Nebraska, 1981).

32. Judith A. McGaw, "Women and the History of American Technology," *Signs: Journal of Women in Culture and Society,* 1982, *7*(4): 798–828.

33. H. L. Rheingold and K. V. Cook, "The Contents of Boys' and Girls' Rooms as an Index of Parent's Behavior," *Child Development,* 1975, *46*(2): 459–463.

34. Susan Groag Bell, "Medieval Women Book Owners: Arbiters of Lay Piety and Ambassadors of Culture," *Signs: Journal of Women in Culture and Society,* 1982, *7*(4): 742–768.

35. See Cynthia Neggrey's film review of "Still Killing Us Softly," *SWS Network News,* October 1988, *6*(1): 21.

36. Nancy Chodorow and Susan Contratto, "The Fantasy of the Perfect Mother," in Barrie Thorne, with Marilyn Yalom (eds.), *Rethinking the Family: Some Feminist Questions* (New York: Longman, 1982); Susan Contratto, "Mother: Social Sculptor and Trustee of the Faith," in Miriam Lewin (ed.), *In the Shadow of the Past: Psychology Portrays the Sexes* (New York: Columbia University Press, 1984). Nancy Chodorow and Susan Contratto discuss, among others, Judith Arcana, *Our Mothers' Daughters* (Berkeley, CA: Shameless Hussy Press, 1979); Phyllis Chesler, *With Child: A Diary of Motherhood* (New York: Berkley Publications, 1981); Dorothy Dinnerstein, *The Mermaid and the Minotaur: Sexual Arrangements and Human Malaise* (New York: Harper & Row, 1976); Jane Flax, "The Conflict between Nurturance and Autonomy in Mother–Daughter Relationships and Within Feminism," *Feminist Studies,* 1978, *4*(2): 171–189; Nancy Friday, *My Mother/ Myself* (New York: Dell, 1981); Jane Lazarre, *The Mother Knot* (Boston: Beacon, 1986); Adrienne Rich, *Of Women Born* (New York: Norton, 1976); and Alicc Rossi, "Sexuality, Maternalism and the New Feminism," in J. Zubin and J. Money (eds.), *Critical Issues in Contemporary Sexual Behavior* (Baltimore: Johns Hopkins Press, 1972).

37. Judith DiIorio, "Toward a Phenomenological Feminism: A Critique of Gender Role Research," paper presented at the National Women's Studies Association Annual Meetings, 1980, Bloomington, Indiana.

38. Emile Durkheim, *Suicide: A Study in Sociology,* tr. by John Spaulding and George Simpson, ed. by George Simpson (New York: Free Press, 1951).

39. Emile Durkheim, *Rules of Sociological Method* (1895), tr. by Sarah A. Solovay and John Mueller, ed. by George Catlin (New York: Free Press, 1966). This work was accepted as an innovation 60 years after similar methodological statements by Harriet Martineau.

40. Candace West and Bonita Iritani, "Gender Politics in Mate Selection: The Male Older Norm," paper presented at the 80th Annual Meeting of the American Sociological Association, August 1985, Washington, D.C.

41. See Nancy Cott, "Eighteenth Century Family and Social Life Revealed in Massachusetts Divorce Records," in Nancy Cott and Elizabeth Pleck (eds.), *A Heritage of Her Own* (New York: Simon and Schuster, 1979).

42. She also did participant observation of pro-life and pro-choice group meetings but did not formally include this material in her book.

43. Kristin Luker, *Abortion and the Politics of Motherhood* (Berkeley, CA: University of California Press, 1984), pp. 247–249.

44. See Lynn Chancer, "Abortion without Apology," in Marlene Gerber Fried (ed.), *From Abortion to Reproductive Freedom: Transforming a Movement* (Boston: South End

Press, 1990), pp. 113–119 for a discussion of the dilemma of incurring an antifeminist bias when using "pro-life" terminology.

45. See Vivian Petraka and Louise Tilly (eds.), *Feminist Re-Visions: What Has Been and Might Be* (Ann Arbor, MI: University of Michigan, Women's Studies Program, 1983).

46. See also Jonathan Culler, "Reading as a Woman," in Jonathan Culler (ed.), *On Deconstruction* (Ithaca, NY: Cornell University Press, 1982), pp. 43–64.

47. Laurel Graham, "A Year in the Life of Dr. Lillian Moller Gilbreth: Four Representations of the Struggle of a Woman Scientist," paper presented at the Gregory Stone Symposium, January, 1990, St. Petersburg Beach, Florida, pp. 3, 4.

48. Marilyn French, *The Women's Room* (New York: Jove Publications, 1977).

49. Linda Blum, "Feminism and the Mass Media: A Case Study of *The Women's Room* as Novel and Television Film," *Berkeley Journal of Sociology*, 1982, 27: 1–24, reprinted in Mary Jo Deegan and Michael R. Hill (eds.), *Women and Symbolic Interaction* (Winchester, MA: Allen & Unwin, 1987), pp. 395–417, p. 396.

50. Joanne Martin, "Deconstructing Organizational Taboos: The Suppression of Gender Conflict in Organizations," *Organization Science*, 1990, *1*(4): 339–359, p. 339.

51. Cynthia Fuchs Epstein, "Symbolic Segregation: Similarities and Differences in the Language and Non-Verbal Communication of Women and Men," *Sociological Forum*, 1986, *1*(1): 27–45 is a review of feminist research on nonverbal communication and linguistics.

52. Celia Kitzinger, *The Social Construction of Lesbianism* (Beverly Hills, CA: Sage, 1987).

53. Celia Kitzinger, "The Rhetoric of Pseudoscience," in Ian Parker and John Shotter (eds.), *Deconstructing Social Psychology* (London: Sage, 1990), p. 27.

54. Barbara Gray, "A Poststructuralist Critique of *Collaborating*," unpublished manuscript available from the author, Pennsylvania State University, University Park, PA 16802. See Barbara Gray, *Collaborating: Finding Common Ground for Multiparty Problems* (San Francisco: Jossey-Bass, 1989).

55. See Daphne Patai, "Beyond Defensiveness: Feminist Research Strategies," *Women's Studies International Forum*, 1983, *6*(2): 177–189. See also Celia Kitzinger, "The Constructing of Lesbian Identities," doctoral dissertation, University of Reading, U.K., 1984, esp. pp. 25–26; and Celia Kitzinger, *op. cit.* (note 52).

56. Betty Friedan, *The Feminine Mystique* (New York: Dell, 1963), p. 38; see also H. H. Franzwa, "Female Roles in Women's Magazine Fiction," in Rhoda K. Unger and Florence L. Denmark (eds.), *Woman: Dependent or Independent Variable* (New York: Psychological Dimensions, 1975), pp. 42–53.

57. Francesca Cancian and Steven Gordon, "Changing Emotion Norms in Marriage: Love and Anger in U.S. Women's Magazines Since 1900," *Gender & Society*, 1988, *2*(3): 308–342, pp. 312–313, 324–325.

58. Wendy Simonds, "Confessions of Loss: Maternal Grief in *True Story*, 1920–1985," *Gender & Society*, 1988, *2*(2): 149–171.

59. Barbara Ehrenreich and Deirdre English, *For Her Own Good: 150 Years of the Experts' Advice to Women* (Garden City, NY: Anchor Press, 1978).

60. See Bonnie J. Fox, "Selling the Mechanized Household: 70 Years of Ads in *Ladies Home Journal*," *Gender & Society*, 1990, *4*(1): 25–40.

61. Catherine Itzin, "Media Images of Women: The Social Construction of Ageism and Sexism," in Sue Wilkinson (ed.), *Feminist Social Psychology* (Philadelphia: Open University Press, 1986), pp. 119–134.

62. Marjorie Rosen, *Popcorn Venus: Women, Movies and the American Dream* (New

York: Avon Books, 1973); Julia Lesage, "Feminist Film Criticism: Theory and Practice," *Women and Film,* 1974, *1*(5–6): 12–18; Molly Haskell, *From Reverence to Rape: The Treatment of Women in the Movies* (Baltimore: Penguin Books, 1974); Claire Johnston, "Women's Cinema as Counter-Cinema," in Bill Nichols (ed.), *Movies and Methods: An Anthology* (Berkeley, CA: University of California Press, 1976); K. Kay and G. Peary (eds.), *Woman and the Cinema: A Critical Anthology* (New York: E. P. Dutton, 1977); Editorial, "Feminism and Film: Critical Approaches," *Camera Obscura,* 1978, *1*: 3–10; B. Ruby Rich, "In the Name of Feminist Film Criticism," *Heresies #9,* 1980, *3*(1): 74–81; Andrea S. Walsh, *Women's Film and Female Experience, 1940–1950* (New York: Praeger, 1984); and Ella Taylor, *Prime Time Families: Television Culture in Postwar America* (Berkeley, CA: University of California Press, 1989).

63. Denise Farran, "A Photograph of Marilyn Monroe," in Feminist Research Seminar (ed.), *Feminist Research Processes,* Sociology Department, University of Manchester, 1987, pp. 1–22, 19.

64. Erving Goffman, *Frame Analysis* (New York: Harper, 1974); Erving Goffman, "The Arrangement between the Sexes," *Theory & Society,* 1977, *4*(3): 301–331; Erving Goffman, "Gender Display, Picture Frames, Gender Commercials," in *Gender Advertisements, Studies in Anthropology of Visual Communication,* 1976, *3*(2): 69–95.

65. Mary Jo Deegan, "A Feminist Frame Analysis of 'Star Trek'," *Free Inquiry in Creative Sociology,* 1983, *11*(2): 182–188.

66. Cambridge Documentary Films, 1987. See also Lucy Komisar, "The Image of Woman in Advertising," and Marjorie U'Ren, "The Image of Woman in Textbooks," in Vivian Gornick and Barbara Moran (eds.), *Woman in Sexist Society: Studies in Power and Powerlessness* (New York: New American Library, 1971).

67. Dolores Hayden, *Redesigning the American Dream: The Future of Housing, Work, and Family Life* (New York: W. W. Norton, 1984), pp. 217–219.

68. See Susan Moller Okin, *Women in Western Political Thought* (Princeton, NJ: Princeton University Press, 1979).

69. Louise Michele Newman (ed.), *Men's Ideas/Women's Realities: Popular Science, 1870–1915* (New York: Pergamon, 1985).

70. See Elisabeth Schussler Fiorenza, *Bread Not Stone: The Challenge of Feminist Biblical Interpretation* (Boston: Beacon Press, 1985); Phyllis Trible, discussed in Gerda Lerner, *The Creation of Patriarchy* (New York: Oxford University Press, 1986), p. 184; Shulamit Reinharz, "The 'Nature' of Judaism: From Adam to Noah," unpublished manuscript, 1989.

71. Elizabeth Cady Stanton, *The Original Feminist Attack on the Bible* (The Woman's Bible) (New York: Arno Press, 1974). See also Letty Russell (ed.), *Feminist Interpretation of the Bible* (Philadelphia: Westminster, 1985).

72. Elisabeth Griffith, *In her Own Right: The Life of Elizabeth Cady Stanton* (New York: Oxford University Press, 1984), pp. 211, 212, 213.

73. J. Cheryl Exum, " 'Mother in Israel': A Familiar Figure Reconsidered," in Letty M. Russell (ed.), *Feminist Interpretation of the Bible* (Philadelphia: The Westminister Press, 1985), p. 74.

74. Carol Meyers, *Discovering Eve: Ancient Israelite Women in Context* (New York: Oxford University Press, 1988), p. 11.

75. Jennifer Pierce, "Gender, Paralegals, and the Tyranny of Niceness," paper presented at the Gregory Stone Symposium, January 1990, St. Petersburg Beach, Florida.

76. See Shulamit Reinharz, "Patriarchal Pontifications," *Transaction/SOCIETY,* 1986, *23*(6): 23–29.

77. Jean Bethke Elshtain, *Public Man, Private Woman: Women in Social and Political Thought* (Princeton, NJ: Princeton University Press, 1981), p. xii.

78. See for example, Arlyn Diamond and Lee R. Edwards (eds.), *The Authority of Experience: Essays in Feminist Criticism* (Amherst, MA: University of Massachusetts Press, 1977).

79. Kate Millett, *Sexual Politics* (New York: Ballantine, 1969).

80. Katherine V. Pope, "The Divided Lives of Women in Literature," in Rhoda K. Unger (ed.), *Representations: Social Constructions of Gender* (Amityville, NY: Baywood, 1989), pp. 21–28.

81. Margaret Wetherell, "Linguistic Repertoires and Literary Criticism: New Directions for a Social Psychology of Gender," in Sue Wilkinson (ed.), *Feminist Social Psychology: Developing Theory and Practice* (Philadelphia: Open University Press, 1987), pp. 77–95, pp. 92–93.

82. An example is a study of all the words in platforms of the Republican and Democratic parties since the formation of those parties. See Robert Weber, "Computer-Aided Content Analysis: A Short Primer," in Peter Conrad and Shulamit Reinharz (eds.), *Computers and Qualitative Data: Qualitative Sociology*, 1984, *7*(1–2): 126–147.

83. Paula J. Caplan and Ian Hall-McCorquodale, "Mother-Blaming in Major Clinical Journals," *American Journal of Orthopsychiatry*, 1985, *55*(3): 345–353.

84. Diana Scully and Pauline Bart, "A Funny Thing Happened on the Way to the Orifice: Women in Gynecology Textbooks," *American Journal of Sociology*, 1971, *78*(4): 1045–1050; see also Sarah Stage, *Female Complaints: Lydia Pinkham and the Business of Women's Medicine* (New York: W. W. Norton, 1979); and Pauline Bart, "Social Structure and Vocabularies of Discomfort: What Happened to Female Hysteria?," *Journal of Health and Social Behavior*, 1968, *9*(3): 188–193.

85. See Cancian and Gordon, *op. cit.* (note 57).

86. See for example, Kathryn Ward and Linda Grant, "The Feminist Critique and a Decade of Published Research in Sociology Journals," *Sociological Quarterly*, 1985, *26*: 139–157; Marlene Mackie, "Female Sociologists' Productivity, Collegial Relations, and Research Style Examined through Journal Publications," *Sociology and Social Research*, 1985, *69*: 189–209; Linda Grant, Kathryn Ward, and Xue Lan Rong, "Is there an Association between Methods and Gender in Published Sociological Research?," *American Sociological Review*, 1987, *52*(6): 856–864; Xue Lan Rong, Linda Grant, and Kathryn Ward, "Productivity of Women Scholars and Gender Researchers: Is Funding a Factor?," *The American Sociologist*, 1989, *20*(1): 95–100.

87. See Margaret L. Signorella, Maria E. Vegega, and Margaret E. Mitchell, "Subject Selection and Analyses for Sex-Related Differences: 1968–1970 and 1955–1977." Available from Margaret Mitchell, Pennsylvania State University, Institute for Policy Research and Evaluation.

88. M. Brinton Lykes and Abigail J. Stewart, "Evaluating the Feminist Challenge to Research in Personality and Social Psychology: 1963–1983," *Psychology of Women Quarterly*, 1986, *10*(4): 393–412.

89. Historical research concerning recent periods may be supplemented by interviews or questionnaires, which are not unobtrusive measures.

90. See Claude Levi-Strauss, *The Raw and the Cooked* (New York: Harper, 1969).

91. Gerda Lerner, *The Creation of Patriarchy* (New York: Oxford University Press, 1986), p. 226.

92. Frank Stricker, "Cookbooks and Lawbooks: The Hidden History of Career Women in Twentieth Century America," in Nancy Cott and Elizabeth Pleck (eds.), *A Heritage of*

Her Own: Toward a New Social History of American Women (New York: Simon and Schuster, 1979).

93. See Nancy F. Cott and Elizabeth Pleck, *ibid;* Carl Degler, *At Odds: Women and the Family in America from the Revolution to the Present* (New York: Oxford University Press, 1980).

94. See, for example, Jane Lewis, *Women in England, 1870–1950: Sexual Divisions and Social Change* (Bloomington, IN: Indiana University Press, 1984).

95. Elizabeth Hampsten, *Read This Only to Yourself: The Private Writings of Midwestern Women, 1880–1910* (Bloomington, IN: Indiana University Press, 1982), p. vii.

96. Judith C. Brown, *Immodest Acts: The Life of a Lesbian Nun in Renaissance Italy* (New York: Oxford University Press, 1986).

97. See Marlene Springer and Haskell Springer (eds.), *Plains Woman: The Diary of Martha Fransworth, 1882–1922* (Bloomington, IN: Indiana University Press, 1986); Claudia Bushman, *A Good Poor Man's Wife: Being a Chronicle of Harriet Hanson Robinson and Her Family in Nineteenth-Century New England* (Hanover, NH: University Press of New England, 1981).

98. Elizabeth Minnich, "Discussion," *The Feminist and the Scholar IV: Connecting Theory, Practice, and Values,* a Conference Sponsored by The Barnard College Women's Center, April 23, 1977, pp. 51–55, 54.

99. For example, in *The Ties that Bound: Peasant Families in Medieval England* (New York: Oxford University Press, 1986), Barbara Hanawalt shows that historians' reliance on manorial court rolls as census documents is improper since "the rolls are biased against females, children under twelve and against poorer elements who made fewer court appearances." (pp. 94–95).

100. Elizabeth Hampsten, *op. cit.* (note 95), p. viii.

101. Nancy Cott, *The Bonds of Womanhood: 'Woman's Sphere' in New England, 1780–1835* (New Haven, CT: Yale University Press, 1977), pp. 2–3, 9–10, 13–15, 17.

102. Jane Lewis, "Women, Lost and Found: The Impact of Feminism on History," in Dale Spender (ed.), *Men's Studies Modified: The Impact of Feminism on the Academic Disciplines* (New York: Pergamon Press, 1981), p. 57. The examples she offers are Linda Gordon, *Woman's Body, Woman's Right* (Middlesex: Penguin, 1977); Gerda Lerner, "New Approaches to the Study of Women in American History," *Journal of Social History 3* (Fall) 1960: 5–14; Carroll Smith Rosenberg, "The New Woman and the New History," *Feminist Studies, 3* (Fall) 1975: 185–198; Natalie Zemon-Davis, "Women's History in Transition: The European Case," *Feminist Studies* 3 (Spring-Summer), 1976: 83–103.

103. Marina Warner, *Joan of Arc: The Image of Female Heroism.* (New York: Vintage, 1981), p. 6.

104. See Shulamit Reinharz and Ellen Stone (eds.), *Looking at Invisible Women: An Exercise in Feminist Pedagogy* (Washington, D.C.: University Press of America, 1992).

105. Gerda Lerner, *op. cit.* (note 91), p. 225.

106. Elaine Showalter, *A Literature of Their Own: British Women Novelists from Bronte to Lessing* (Princeton: Princeton University Press, 1977), pp. 8–9.

107. Joan T. Pennell, *op. cit.* (note 25).

108. Judith Sabronsky, *From Rationality to Liberation* (Westport, CT: Greenwood Press, 1979).

109. Lynda Glennon, *Women and Dualism: A Sociology of Knowledge Analysis* (New York: Longman, 1979), p. 5.

110. Shulamit Reinharz, "Feminist Distrust: Content and Context in Sociological Work," in David Berg and Ken Smith (eds.), *The Self in Social Inquiry: Researching Methods* (Beverly Hills, CA: Sage, 1985, 1988), pp. 153–172.

111. Sherri Broder, "Child Care or Child Neglect? Baby Farming in Late-Nineteenth-Century Philadelphia," *Gender & Society,* 1988, *2*(2): 128–148.

112. Liz Stanley (ed.), *The Diaries of Hannah Cullwick, Victorian Maidservant* (New Brunswick, NJ: Rutgers University Press, 1984), pp. 24, 25.

113. Deborah Bernstein, *The Struggle for Equality: Urban Women Workers in Prestate Israeli Society* (New York: Praeger, 1987), p. ix. [emphasis added]

114. Renate Klein, personal communication.

115. Pauline Bart used the same logic in her "Depression in Middle-Aged Women," in Vivian Gornick and Barbara Moran (eds.), *Woman in Sexist Society* (New York: New American Library, 1972).

116. Jill Matthews, *op. cit.* (note 21).

117. A study of *Woman, Woman's Own,* and *Woman's Weekly* is contained in Marilyn Ferguson, *Forever Feminine, Women's Magazines and the Cult of Femininity* (London: Heinemann, 1983).

118. Mary Louise Ho, "Patriarchal Ideology and Agony Columns," in Sue Webb and Clive Pearson (eds.), *Looking Back: Some Papers from the BSA 'Gender and Society' Conference* (Manchester, UK: University of Manchester, Department of Sociology, 1984), pp. 1–13.

119. In another study, I examined in-depth one account published in a popular book about miscarriage, see Shulamit Reinharz, "The Social Psychology of a Miscarriage: An Application of Symbolic Interactionist Theory and Method," in Mary Jo Deegan and Michael R. Hill (eds.), *Women and Symbolic Interaction* (Winchester, MA: Allen & Unwin, 1987), pp. 229–250.

120. Shulamit Reinharz, "Controlling Women's Lives: A Cross-cultural Interpretation of Miscarriage Accounts," in Dorothy Wertz (ed.), *Research in the Sociology of Health Care,* volume 7 (Greenwich, CT: JAI Press, 1988), pp. 2–37.

121. Sara Karon, "The Politics of Naming: Lesbian Erasure in a Feminist Context," in Shulamit Reinharz and Ellen Stone, *op. cit.* (note 104).

122. Shulamit Reinharz, "What's Missing in Miscarriage?" *Journal of Community Psychology,* 1988, *16*(1): 84–103.

123. Cynthia Epstein, *Woman's Place* (Berkeley: University of California Press, 1970), p. 30.

124. J. E. O'Brien, "Violence in Divorce-prone Families," *Journal of Marriage and the Family,* 1971, *33*(4): 692–698; and R. J. Gelles, "Violence in the Family: A Review of Research in the Seventies," *Journal of Marriage and the Family,* 1980, *42*(4): 873–885.

125. Rhoda Unger, *op. cit.* (note 11), p. 322.

126. Nancy Datan, "Androgyny and the Life Cycle: The Bacchae of Euripides," in Rhoda K. Unger, *Ibid.,* pp. 273–281, p. 274, 275.

127. Jane Haggis, "The Feminist Research Process—Defining a Topic," in Feminist Research Seminar (eds.), *Feminist Research Processes, Studies in Sexual Politics* (Manchester, UK: University of Manchester, Department of Sociology, 1987), pp. 23–37.

128. Angela V. John, *By the Sweat of Their Brow; Women Workers at Victorian Coal Mines* (London: Croom Helm, 1980), p. 11.

Chapter 9   Feminist Case Studies

1. Berenice Carroll (ed.), *Liberating Women's History: Theoretical and Critical Essays* (Chicago: University of Illinois Press, 1976), p. xii.

2. For a critique see Dianne Hunter, "Hysteria, Psychoanalysis, and Feminism: The Case of Anna O," *Feminist Studies,* 1983, *9*(3): 464–488.

3. See the journal, *Case Analysis,* 1978–1985.

4. Jean Baker Miller, *Toward a New Psychology of Women* (Boston: Beacon Press, 1976).

5. George A. Theordorson and Achilles G. Theordorson, *A Modern Dictionary of Sociology* (New York: Thomas Y. Crowell, 1969).

6. Sometimes a researcher develops several case studies in depth and then compares them. An example is Elisabeth J. Cross, "Women in Rural Production and Reproduction in the Soviet Union, China, Cuba and Tanzania: Case Studies," which was published in tandem with another article, "Women in Rural Production and Reproduction in the Soviet Union, China, Cuba, and Tanzania: Socialist Development Experiences," in *Signs: Journal of Women in Culture and Society,* 1981, *7*(2): 361–399.

7. For a case study of the significance of events of the 1920s for solidifying the American literary canon that is being energetically challenged today, see Paul Lauter, "Race and Gender in the Shaping of the American Literary Canon: A Case Study from the Twenties," *Feminist Studies,* 1983, *9*(3): 435–463.

8. For a case study explaining the change in relations between black women and feminism, for example, see Diane K. Lewis, "A Response to Inequality: Black Women, Racism, and Sexism," *Signs: Journal of Women in Culture and Society,* 1977, *3*(2): 339–361.

9. Rebecca Shuster, "Sexuality as a Continuum: The Bisexual Identity," in Boston Lesbian Psychologies Collective (eds.), *Lesbian Psychologies* (Chicago: University of Illinois Press, 1987), pp. 56–71, pp. 56, 57.

10. Jane Mansbridge, *Why We Lost the ERA* (Chicago: University of Chicago Press, 1986), pp. x–xi.

11. Jacklyn Cock, "Trapped Workers: Constraints and Contradictions Experienced by Black Women in Contemporary South Africa," *Women's Studies International Forum,* 1987, *10*(2): 133–140, p. 133.

12. Eva Gamarnikow, "Sexual Division of Labour: The Case of Nursing," in Annette Kuhn and AnnMarie Wolpe (eds.), *Feminism and Materialism: Women and Modes of Production* (London: Routledge & Kegan Paul, 1978), pp. 96–123, pp. 97, 121. See also Kate Young, "Modes of Appropriation and the Sexual Division of Labour: A Case Study from Oaxaca, Mexico," in Annette Kuhn and AnnMarie Wolpe, *Ibid.,* pp. 124–154.

13. See Howard S. Becker, "Social Observation and Social Case Studies," in David Sills (ed.), *International Encyclopedia of the Social Sciences,* volume 14 (New York: Crowell Collier and Macmillan, 1968), pp. 232–238, reprinted in *Sociological Work: Method and Substance* (New Brunswick, NJ: Transaction Books, 1977), chapter 5; see also Robert K. Yin, *Case Study Research: Design and Methods* (Beverly Hills, CA: Sage, 1984).

14. For example, Elliot Liebow, *Tally's Corner: A Study of Negro Streetcorner Men* (Boston: Little, Brown, 1967).

15. Kai Erikson, *Everything in Its Path* (New York: Simon and Schuster, 1976); Adeline Levine, *Love Canal: Science, Politics and People* (Lexington, MA: Heath Books, 1982).

16. Alfred Stanton and Morris Schwartz, *The Mental Hospital* (New York: Basic Books, 1954).

17. Herbert Gans, *The Urban Villagers* (New York: Free Press, 1962); William Foote Whyte, *Street Corner Society: The Social Structure of an Italian Slum* (Chicago: University of Chicago Press, 1943).

18. See Mary Jo Deegan, *Jane Addams and the Men of the Chicago School* (New Brunswick, NJ: Transaction Books, 1988).

19. See Michael R. Hill, "Mary Abby van Kleeck," in Mary Jo Deegan (ed.), *Women in Sociology: A Bio-Bibliographic Sourcebook* (Greenwood, CT: Greenwood Press, 1991).

20. Examples can be found in Naomi Gottlieb (ed.), *Alternative Social Services for Women* (New York: Columbia University Press, 1980). See also Shulamit Reinharz, "Women as Competent Community Builders: The Other Side of the Coin," in Annette Rickel, Meg Gerrard, and Ira Iscoe (eds.), *Social and Psychological Problems of Women* (New York: Hemisphere, 1984).

21. Joyce Mancini Billson, "The Progressive Verification Method: Toward a Feminist Methodology for Studying Women," *Women's Studies International Forum*, 1991, *14*(3): 201–208. This topic is discussed at length in chapter 6.

22. Cathy Rakowski, "Women in Steel: The Case of Ciudad Guayana, Venezuela," *Qualitative Sociology*, 1987, *10*(1): 3–28, p. 3.

23. Jessie Bernard, *The Female World* (New York: Free Press, 1981), pp. 318–319, discussing Kathleen McCourt, *Working-class Women and Grass-roots Politics* (Bloomington, IN: Indiana University Press, 1977).

24. Howard S. Becker, "Social Observation and Case Studies," reprinted in Howard S. Becker, *Sociological Work: Method and Substance* (New Brunswick, NJ: Transaction Books, 1977), p. 84, citing the work of David War and Gene Kassebaum, *Women's Prison: Sex and Social Structure* (Chicago: Aldine, 1965) and Rose Giallombardo, *Society of Women* (New York: Wiley, 1966).

25. See Kathryn Pyne Parsons, "Moral Revolution," in Julia Sherman and Evelyn Beck (eds.), *Prism of Sex: Essays in the Sociology of Knowledge* (Madison, WI: University of Wisconsin Press, 1979), pp. 204–211; Pauline B. Bart, "Seizing the Means of Reproduction: An Illegal Feminist Abortion Collective—How and Why It Worked," *Qualitative Sociology*, 1987, *10*(4): 339–357; and " 'Jane,' Just Call 'Jane,' " in Marlene Gerber Fried (ed.), *From Abortion to Reproductive Freedom: Transforming a Movement* (Boston: South End Press, 1990), pp. 93–100.

26. Melinda Bart Schlesinger and Pauline B. Bart, "Collective Work and Self-Identity: Working in a Feminist Illegal Abortion Collective," in Frank Lindenfeld and Joyce Rothschild-Whitt (eds.), *Workplace Democracy and Social Change* (Boston: Porter Sargent Publishers Inc., 1982), pp. 139–153, p. 142.

27. Paige Cousineau, "The Support Function and Social Change—A Feminist Case History," *Women's Studies International Forum*, 1985, *8*(2): 137–144. See also T. A. Caplan, "The Adaptation of a Traditional Structure for Non-Traditional Aims: A Case Study," *Research on the Psychology of Woman*, 1980, *9*(2): 11–12.

28. See Shulamit Reinharz, "Feminist Distrust: Problems of Content and Context in Sociological Work," in David Berg and Ken Smith (eds.), *The Self in Social Inquiry: Researching Methods* (Beverly Hills, CA: Sage, 1985, 1988), pp. 153–172.

29. See for example, Marla N. Powers, *Oglala Women: Myth, Ritual, and Reality* (Chicago: University of Chicago Press, 1986), pp. 1–19.

30. See Shulamit Reinharz, "Patriarchial Pontification," *Transaction/SOCIETY*, 1986, *23*(6): 23–29.

31. Lynn Lofland, "The 'Thereness' of Women: A Selective Review of Urban Sociology," in Marcia Millman and Rosabeth Kanter (eds.), *Another Voice: Feminist Perspectives on Social Life and Social Science* (Garden City, NY: Anchor Books, 1975).

32. A notable exception is Herbert Gans' study of Levittown, New Jersey, as discussed in Sheila Rothman, *Woman's Proper Place* (New York: Basic Books, 1978), pp. 224–226.

33. For example, Virginia Olesen and Elvi Whittaker, *The Silent Dialogue: A Study in the Social Psychology of Professional Socialization* (San Francisco: Jossey-Bass, 1968), a study of nurses; or Nicole Hahn Rafter, "Hard Times: Custodial Prisons for Women and

the Example of the NY State Prison for Women at Auburn, 1893–1933,'' in Nicole Hahn Rafter and Elizabeth A. Stanko (eds.), *Judge, Lawyer, Victim, Thief: Women, Gender Roles, and Criminal Justice* (Boston: Northeastern University Press, 1982), pp. 237–260; Kristin Luker, *Abortion and the Politics of Motherhood* (Berkeley, CA: University of California Press, 1984).

34. Ellen Fitzpatrick, *Endless Crusade: Women Social Scientists and Progressive Reform* (New York: Oxford University Press, 1990), p. 215.

35. Ellen Cassedy and Karen Nussbaum, *9 to 5: The Working Woman's Guide to Office Survival* (New York: Penguin, 1983), p. 15.

36. Mary Roth Walsh, *Doctors Wanted: No Women Need Apply* (New Haven, CT: Yale University Press, 1977), pp. x–xi.

37. Annette B. Weiner, *Women of Value, Men of Renown: New Perspectives in Trobriand Exchange* (Austin, TX: University of Texas Press, 1976), p. 11. It should also be noted that a major factor contributing to the ignoring of women's activities in anthropological case studies conducted by men is the cultural imperative or personal interest of the indigenous women to avoid contact with men.

38. See for example, Clifford Shaw, *The Jack-Roller: A Delinquent Boy's Own Story* (Chicago: University of Chicago Press, 1930/1966).

39. See, for example, Marjorie Shostak, *Nisa: The Life and Words of a !Kung Woman* (New York: Vintage Books, 1983) [originally published in 1981 by Harvard University Press].

40. See, for example, Elinor Langer, *Josephine Herbst* (Boston: Little, Brown, 1983); and Carol Asher, Louise deSalvo, and Sara Ruddick (eds.), *Between Women: Biographers, Novelists, Critics, Teachers and Artists Write about Their Work on Women* (Boston: Beacon Press, 1984).

41. Ann Jones, *Women Who Kill* (New York: Holt, Rinehart & Winston, 1980), pp. xv–xvi.

42. Cynthia K. Gillespie, *Justifiable Homicide: Battered Women, Self-Defense, and the Law* (Columbus, OH: Ohio University Press, 1990).

43. Catharine MacKinnon, *Sexual Harassment of Working Women* (New Haven, CT: Yale University Press, 1979), pp. xii–xiii.

44. Nawal El Saadawi, *Woman at Point Zero* (London: Zed Books, 1983).

45. Janice Raymond, ''Mary Daly: A Decade of Academic Harassment and Feminist Survival,'' in Mary Spencer, Monika Kehoe, and Karen Speece (eds.), *Handbook for Women Scholars: Strategies for Success* (San Francisco: Center for Women Scholars, Americas Behavioral Research Corporation, 1982), pp. 81–88.

46. Judith Stacey and Susan Elizabeth Gerard, ''We Are Not Doormats: The Influence of Feminism on Contemporary Evangelicals in the United States,'' paper presented at the 84th Annual Meeting of the American Sociological Association, August 1989, San Francisco, California.

47. Kathleen Kautzer, ''Moving against the Stream: An Organizational Study of the Older Women's League,'' unpublished doctoral dissertation, Heller School, Brandeis University, 1988, pp. 8, 13.

48. Naomi Black, *Social Feminism* (Ithaca, NY: Cornell University Press, 1989), pp. 4–5.

49. Delores Rainey, Theresa Goings, Denise Martin, Florence Dumont, Bertha Franklin, Roslyn David, and Rosalie Johnson, ''Weaving New Hopes,'' in Rochelle Lefkowitz and Ann Withorn (eds.), *For Crying Out Loud: Women and Poverty in the United States* (New York: The Pilgrim Press, 1986), pp. 265–272.

50. Susan Hertz, ''The Politics of the Welfare Mothers Movements: A Case Study,'' *Signs: Journal of Women in Culture and Society,* 1977, 2(3): 531–553.

51. Ellen Cassedy and Karen Nussbaum, *9 to 5: The Working Woman's Guide to Office Survival* (New York: Penguin Books, 1983).

52. Robin Morgan (ed.), *Sisterhood Is Global: The International Women's Movement Anthology* (New York: Anchor, Doubleday, 1984).

53. Jo Freeman, "The Tyranny of Structurelessness," in A. Koedt, E. Levine, and A. Rapone (eds.), *Radical Feminism* (New York: Quadrangle, 1973).

54. Mary Jo Deegan, "Multiple Minority Groups: A Case Study of Physically Disabled Women," in Mary Jo Deegan and Nancy Brooks (eds.), *Women and Disability: The Double Handicap* (New Brunswick, NJ: Transaction Books, 1985), pp. 37–55, p. 37, 38.

55. Mary Jo Deegan and Nancy A. Brooks (eds.), *op. cit.* (note 54), p. xi.

56. Kathleen M. Weston and Lisa B. Rofel, "Sexuality, Class and Conflict in a Lesbian Workplace," *Signs: Journal of Women in Culture and Society,* 1984, 9(4): 623–646, reprinted in Mary Jo Deegan and Michael R. Hill (eds.), *Women and Symbolic Interaction* (Winchester, MA: Allen & Unwin, 1987), pp. 419–440, pp. 419–420.

57. See for example, Amy Blumenthal, Martha Thompson, and Grace Young, "Chicago Women's Uprising, 1981–1983," paper presented at the Midwest Sociological Society Meetings, Des Moines, Iowa, March 1986 (available from Martha Thompson, Department of Sociology, Northeastern Illinois University); Mary Frances Berry, *Why ERA Failed: Politics, Women's Rights and the Amending Process of the Constitution* (Bloomington, IN: Indiana University Press, 1986); Joan Hoff-Wilson (ed.), *Rights of Passage: The Past and Future of the ERA* (Bloomington, IN: Indiana University Press, 1986); and *Women's Pentagon Action Statement* (New York: Women's Pentagon Action, 1980).

58. See, for example, Gloria Steinem, *Outrageous Acts and Everyday Rebellions* (New York: Holt, Rinehart & Winston, 1983); Closing Session, *Congress Monthly,* February/March, 1985, 52(2): 54.

59. Betty Friedan, *It Changed My Life* (New York: Random House, 1963–76), p. 92.

60. Erin Pizzey, *Scream Quietly or the Neighbours Will Hear* (Harmondsworth, England: Penguin, 1974).

61. Patricia Searles and Ronald Berger, "The Feminist Self-Defense Movement: A Case Study," *Gender & Society,* March 1987, *1*(1): 61–84, p. 69.

62. Jo Freeman, "The Women's Liberation Movement: Its Origins, Organizations, Activities and Ideas," in Jo Freeman (ed.), *Women: A Feminist Perspective* (Palo Alto, CA: Mayfield, 1979), pp. 557–574.

63. Sections of this dissertation are reprinted in Mary Jo Deegan and Michael R. Hill, *op. cit.* (note 56).

64. Naomi Black, *op. cit.* (note 48).

65. For example, Marjorie Mayo (ed.), *Women in the Community* (London: Routledge & Kegan Paul, 1977) describes the creation and struggles of the working women's charter campaign, an abortion campaign, day care establishment, child-minders' association, housing struggles, and self-help groups in England.

66. Judy Wajcman, *Women in Control: Dilemmas of a Workers Co-operative* (New York: St. Martin's Press, 1983).

Chapter 10   Feminist Action Research

1. This chapter benefited from a reading by P. J. McGann.

2. Carla Golden, "Psychology, Feminism, and Object Relations Theory," paper prepared for preconference training seminar, Eighth Annual National Conference on Feminist Psychology, Boston, March 1981, p. 1.

3. Rayna Reiter (ed.), *Toward an Anthropology of Women* (New York: Monthly Review Press, 1975), p. 19.

4. Cynthia Fuchs Epstein, *Woman's Place: Options and Limits in Professional Careers* (Berkeley, CA: University of California Press, 1970), p. 4.

5. Rhoda Kesler Unger, "Some Neglected Issues in the Creation of a Sex-Related Reality," paper presented at the symposium, "The Future of the Psychology of Women: Separation, Integration, Elimination?" Annual Meeting of the American Psychological Association, 1982, p. 10.

6. Sandra Harding, *The Science Question in Feminism* (Ithaca, NY: Cornell University Press, 1986), pp. 241–242.

7. Del Martin, *Battered Wives* (New York: Simon and Schuster, Pocket Books, 1976).

8. Robin Ruth Linden, Darlene R. Pagano, Diana E. H. Russell, and Susan Leigh Star (eds.), *Against Sadomasochism: A Radical Feminist Analysis* (East Palo Alto, CA: Frog in the Well Press, 1982).

9. Margaret Sanger, *My Fight for Birth Control* (New York: Farrar & Rinehart, 1931) and *Margaret Sanger: An Autobiography* (New York: Dover Publications, 1938).

10. Kathleen Barry, *Female Sexual Slavery* (New York: Avon, 1979).

11. Roger Jeffery, Patricia Jeffery, and Andrew Lyon, "Female Infanticide and Amniocentesis," *Social Science and Medicine,* 1984, *19*(11): 1207–1212.

12. Gena Corea, *The Mother Machine: Reproductive Technologies from Artificial Insemination to Artificial Wombs* (New York: Harper & Row, 1986).

13. Pauline B. Part and Patricia H. O'Brien, *Stopping Rape: Successful Survival Strategies* (New York: Pergamon, 1985).

14. Patti Lather, "Feminist Perspectives on Empowering Research Methodologies," *Women's Studies International Forum,* 1988, *11*(6): 569–581.

15. Rosalind Rosenberg, *Beyond Separate Spheres: Intellectual Roots of Modern Feminism* (New Haven, CT: Yale University Press, 1982), pp. 43–48.

16. Crystal Eastman, "Work-Accidents and Employers' Liability," *The Survey,* September 3, 1910, reprinted in Blanche Wiesen Cook (ed.), *Crystal Eastman: On Women & Revolution* (New York: Oxford University Press, 1978), pp. 269–280.

17. Mary Jo Deegan, *Jane Addams and the Men of the Chicago School, 1892–1918* (New Brunswick, NJ: Transaction Books, 1988), p. 71.

18. Ellen Fitzpatrick, *Endless Crusade: Women Social Scientists and Progressive Reform* (New York: Oxford University Press, 1990).

19. Mary Brown Parlee, "Psychology and Women," *Signs: Journal of Women in Culture and Society,* 1979, *5*(1): 121–133.

20. Kathleen Barry, Charlotte Bunch, and Shirley Castley (eds.), *International Feminism: Networking Against Female Sexual Slavery* (New York: The International Women's Tribune Centre, Inc., 1984), p. 11.

21. Feminist science fiction is attractive to many people in sketching a feminist utopia. Two examples are Charlotte Perkins Gilman's *Herland* [1915] (New York: Pantheon, 1979) and Sally Miller Gearhart, *The Wanderground* (Watertown, MA: Persephone Press, 1979).

22. Roslyn Wallach Bologh, "Gender, Repression and Liberation: An Alternative Feminist Theory, Method and Politics," paper presented at Annual Meeting of the American Sociological Association, Washington, D.C., 1985.

23. Ann Bristow and Jody Esper, "A Feminist Research Ethos," in Nebraska Sociological Feminist Collective (eds.), *A Feminist Ethic for Social Science Research* (Lewiston, NY: The Edwin Mellen Press, 1988), pp. 80, 81.

24. See, for example, Ruth Moulton, "Anxiety and the New Feminism," in Irwin Lutash and Louis Schlesinger (eds.), *Handbook on Stress and Anxiety* (San Francisco, CA: Jossey-Bass, 1980), pp. 267–284; Annette Brodsky, "A Decade of Feminist Influence on

Psychotherapy," *Psychology of Women Quarterly*, 1980, *4*(3): 331–344; and Annette Brodsky and Rachel Hare-Mustin (eds.), *Women and Psychotherapy: An Assessment of Research and Practice* (New York: Guilford Press, 1980).

25. For a discussion of the meaning of empowerment for women, see Susan Barrett, "Making 'Empowerment' Useful," paper presented at Association for Women in Psychology meeting, Boston, March 1981.

26. For a discussion of one attempt to do this, see Laurel Richardson, "Disseminating Research to Popular Audiences: The Book Tour," *Qualitative Sociology*, 1987, *10*(2): 164–176.

27. Joseph Schneider and Sally Hacker, "Sex Role Imagery and Use of the Generic 'Man' in Introductory Texts: A Case in the Sociology of Sociology," *The American Sociologist*, 1973, *8*(1): 12–18, p. 17.

28. Cynthia Chertos, "In Praise of Useable Research," in Christine Bose and Glenna Spitze (eds.), *Ingredients for Women's Employment Policy* (Albany: State University of New York Press, 1987), p. 261.

29. Christine Bose and Glenna Spitze, "Introduction" in Christine Bose and Glenna Spitze, *Ibid.*, p. xii.

30. Roberta J. Apfel and Susan Fisher, *To Do No Harm: DES and the Dilemmas of Modern Medicine* (New Haven, CT: Yale University Press, 1984), p. 129.

31. Linda Wastila, "Perceptions of RU 486: Views of Pro-Choice and Feminist Activists," unpublished paper, Department of Sociology, Brandeis University, 1990.

32. Jane Mansbridge, *Why We Lost the ERA* (Chicago: University of Chicago Press, 1986), p. ix.

33. "First International Feminist Think Tank Formed," *Ms.*, March 1985, p. 46. [emphasis in original]

34. Barbara Smail, Judith Shyte, and Alison Kelly, "Girls into Science and Technology: The First Two Years," *SSR*, 1982, *64:* 620–630, p. 620.

35. Maria Mies, "Towards a Methodology for Feminist Research," in Edith Altbach, Jeanette Clausen, Dagmar Schultz, and Naomi Stephan (eds.), *German Feminism: Readings in Politics and Literature* (Albany: State University of New York Press, 1984), pp. 357–366. For a discussion of Maria Mies' work see Renate Duelli Klein, "How To Do What We Want To Do: Thoughts about Feminist Methodology," in Gloria Bowles and Renate Duelli Klein (eds.), *Theories of Women's Studies* (Boston: Routledge & Kegan Paul, 1983).

36. A related activity is Pauline Bart's study of attitudes toward pornography based on questionnaire and interview responses of people exiting from a showing of an antipornography documentary, *Not a Love Story*. See Pauline Bart, Linda Freeman, and Peter Kimball, "The Different Worlds of Women and Men: Attitudes toward Pornography and Responses to *Not a Love Story*—a Film about Pornography," *Women's Studies International Forum*, 1985, *8*(4): 307–322.

37. Discussed in Patti Lather, *op. cit.* (note 14), p. 572.

38. Jalna Hanmer and Sheila Saunders, *Well-Founded Fear: A Community Study of Violence to Women* (London: Hutchinson, 1984).

39. Patti Lather, *op. cit.* (note 14), p. 572.

40. Budd Hall, "Participatory Research: An Approach for Change," *Convergence, an International Journal of Adult Education*, 1975, *8*(2): 24–32. See Budd Hall, "Notes on the Development of the Concept of Participatory Research in an International Context," *International Journal of University Adult Education*, 1978, *17*(1): 6–12.

41. This change in relation with "subjects" is called "temporary affiliation" in my book, *On Becoming a Social Scientist: From Survey Research and Participant Observation to Experiential Analysis* (New Brunswick, NJ: Transaction Books, 1984); see also Ann

Oakley, "Interviewing Women: A Contradiction in Terms," in Helen Roberts (ed.), *Doing Feminist Research* (Boston: Routledge & Kegan Paul, 1981), pp. 30–61.

42. See also Barbara Du Bois, "Passionate Scholarship: Notes on Values, Knowing and Method in Feminist Social Science," in Gloria Bowles and Renate Duelli Klein, *op. cit.* (note 35), pp. 105–116.

43. Brinton Lykes, "Dialogue with Guatemalan Indian Women: Critical Perspectives on Constructing Collaborative Research," in Rhoda K. Unger (ed.), *Representations: Social Constructions of Gender* (Amityville, NY: Baywood, 1989), pp. 167–185.

44. See also Shulamit Reinharz, "Experiential Analysis: A Contribution to Feminist Research," in Gloria Bowles and Renate Duelli Klein, *op. cit.* (note 35), pp. 162–191.

45. Francesca Cancian, "Participatory Research and Working Women: Democratizing the Production of Knowledge," paper presented at the Annual Meeting of the American Sociological Association, August 1989, San Francisco.

46. Barbara Strudler Wallston, "What Are the Questions in Psychology of Women? A Feminist Approach to Research," *Psychology of Women Quarterly*, 1981, 5(4): 597–617, p. 609, citing Reesa Vaughter, "Review Essay: Psychology," *Signs: Journal of Women in Culture and Society*, 1976, 2(1): 120–146.

47. Marcia Texler Segal, "Feminism and the Self-Conscious Sociologist: An Essay on the Sociology of Knowledge," unpublished paper prepared for the Sociology Departmental Seminar, University of Malawi, November 1984, p. 23. Cited is Laurel Richardson, presentation at Annual Meeting of the National Women's Studies Association, Columbus, Ohio, June 1983. [emphases added]

48. Marcia Texler Segal, *Ibid.*, pp. 22–23.

49. Patti Lather, *op. cit.* (note 14), pp. 573–575.

50. Patti Lather, "Empowering Research Methodologies," paper prepared for American Educational Researchers' Association, Chicago, 1985, pp. 17–19, 23–24; discussing Mary Kay Thompson Tetreault, "Feminist Phase Theory: An Experience-derived Evaluation Model," *Journal of Higher Education*, 1985, 56(4): 363–384.

51. Nancy Kleiber and Linda Light, *Caring for Ourselves* (Vancouver, BC: University of British Columbia, 1978).

52. From Liz Stanley and Sue Wise, *Breaking Out* (Boston: Routledge & Kegan Paul, 1983), pp. 19–20.

53. An example is Billie Wright Dziech and Linda Weiner, *The Lecherous Professor: Sexual Harassment on Campus* (Boston: Beacon, 1984).

54. Catharine MacKinnon, *Sexual Harassment of Working Women: A Case of Sex Discrimination* (New Haven, CT: Yale University Press), p. 26, citing Working Women United Institute, "Speak-out on Sexual Harassment," Ithaca, NY, May 4, 1975. See also Claire Safran, *Redbook Magazine* (November 1976), p. 149. Commenting on the *Redbook* survey, MacKinnon writes: "Scholars who look down upon such popular journalistic forays into policy research (especially by 'women's magazines') should ask themselves why *Redbook* noticed sexual harassment before they did." [*Ibid.*, p. 248, fn 1.]

55. Julie Campbell, Irma Levine, and Jane Page, "Women in Midstream," in Naomi Gottlieb (ed.), *Alternative Social Services for Women* (New York: Columbia University Press, 1980), pp. 310–312.

56. In a play on the term "speak-out," Patricia Cayo Sexton used the term "sing-out" for the section of her book in which three women (a nursing assistant, a lab technician, and a registered nurse) talk about their work as hospital employees. Patricia Cayo Sexton, *The New Nightingales: Hospital Workers, Unions, New Women's Issues* (New York: Enquiry Press, 1982).

57. Carol Mowbray, Susan Lanir, and Marilyn Hulce (eds.), *Women and Mental Health: New Directions for Change* (New York: The Haworth Press, 1984).

58. Carol T. Mowbray, "A Key Informant Approach to Assessing Women's Mental Health Problems and Treatment Needs," Innovations Division, Michigan Department of Mental Health, October 1980. See also Women's Task Force, Michigan Department of Mental Health, *For Better or for Worse? Women and the Mental Health System* (Michigan Department of Mental Health, 1982).

59. See also Teresa Bernardez, "United States," in Torill Stokland, Maillica Vajra-thon, and Davidson Nicol (eds.), *Creative Women in Changing Societies: A Quest for Alternatives* (Dobbs Ferry, NY: Transnational Publishers, Inc., n.d., pp. 76–79.

60. Diana E. H. Russell and Nicole Van de Ven (eds.), *Proceedings of the International Tribunal of Crimes against Women* (Millbrae, CA: Les Femmes, 1976).

61. For a description of a speak-out by women who had lost their academic jobs, see Janice Raymond, "Mary Daly: A Decade of Academic Harassment and Feminist Survival," in Mary Spencer, Monika Kehoe, and Karen Speece, (eds.), *Handbook for Women Scholars: Strategies for Success* (San Francisco: Center for Women Scholars, Americas Behavioral Research Corporation, 1982), pp. 81–88.

62. See N. Connell and C. Wilson (eds.), *Rape: The First Sourcebook for Women by NY Radical Feminists* (New York: Plume/NAL, 1974).

63. Susan Brownmiller, *Against Our Will: Men, Women and Rape* (New York: Bantam Books, 1975), p. 455.

64. *Growing Numbers, Growing Force: Report from the White House Mini-Conference on Older Women* (Oakland, CA: Older Women's League Educational Fund, 1980), p. 5.

65. "Caregivers Support: Midlife and Older Women," occasional paper, Bunker Hill Community College, Boston.

66. Linda Kamens, "Evaluating Evaluation Research from a Feminist Perspective," paper presented at the Annual Meeting of the Association for Women in Psychology, Boston, March 1981.

67. Pauline Bart and Patricia O'Brien, *Stopping Rape: Successful Survival Strategies* (New York: Pergamon, 1985), pp. 2–3. Building on the work of Pauline Bart and Patricia O'Brien, psychologist Sarah Ullman investigated the effectiveness of different responses at various points in a rape scenario. See Sarah E. Ullman, "A Social Psychological Analysis of Women's Resistance Strategies to Rape," doctoral dissertation, Brandeis University, 1990.

68. See Erin Pizzey, *Scream Quietly or the Neighbors Will Hear* (Short Hills, NJ: Ridley Enslow Publishers, 1974).

69. Linda Valli, *Becoming Clerical Workers* (Boston: Routledge & Kegan Paul, 1986), p. 186.

70. Available from Project on the Status and Education of Women, 1818 R Street., NW, Washington, D.C. 20009.

71. Pamela Roby, "Union Stewards and Women's Employment Conditions," in Christine Bose and Glenna Spitze, *op. cit.* (note 28), p. 153.

72. Lenore Weitzman, *The Divorce Revolution: The Unexpected Social and Economic Consequences for Women and Children in America* (New York: Free Press, 1985).

73. Susan Estrich, *Real Rape* (Cambridge, MA: Harvard University Press, 1987).

74. See Sandra Tangri and Georgia Strasburg, "Can Research on Women Be More Effective in Shaping Policy?," *Psychology of Women Quarterly*, 1979, *3*(4): 321–343.

75. Lenore Weitzman, *op. cit.* (note 72), p. xiv.

76. Linda Kamens, *op. cit.* (note 66), p. 2.

77. Joan Poliner Shapiro and Beth Reed, "Consideration of Ethical Issues in the Assessment of Feminist Projects: A Case Study Using Illuminative Evaluation," in The Nebraska Sociological Feminist Collective (eds.), *A Feminist Ethic for Social Science Research* (Lewiston, NY: The Edwin Mellen Press, 1988), pp. 100–118.

78. Christine Bose and Glenna Spitze, *op. cit.* (note 28), pp. xii–xiii.

79. Mary Louise Ho, "Patriarchal Ideology and Agony Columns," in Sue Webb and Clive Pearson (eds.), *Looking Back: Some Papers from the BSA 'Gender & Society' Conference, Studies in Sexual Politics,* no. 1 (Manchester, UK: Department of Sociology, 1984), pp. 1–13, pp. 12–13.

80. Kathy E. Ferguson, *The Feminist Case Against Bureaucracy* (Philadelphia, PA: Temple University Press, 1984), p. x.

81. The Boston Women's Health Book Collective, *The New Our Bodies, Ourselves* (New York: Simon & Schuster, 1984), pp. xi, xvii.

82. See also Michelle Koetke, "Women's Work," *The Boston Herald Sunday Magazine,* December 8, 1985.

83. Nawal El Saadawi, *The Hidden Face of Eve: Women in the Arab World* (Boston: Beacon Press, 1980), pp. 2–3.

84. Alice S. Rossi, *Feminists in Politics: A Panel Analysis of the First National Women's Conference* (New York: Academic Press, 1982), pp. xxi–xxiv.

85. Lea Shamgar-Handelman, *Israeli War Widows: Beyond the Glory of Heroism* (South Hadley, MA: Bergin & Garvey, 1986), p. xiii.

86. Shulamit Reinharz, *op. cit.* (note 41).

87. Del Martin, *op. cit.* (note 7), xv–xvii.

88. Billie Wright Dziech and Linda Weiner, *op. cit.* (note 53), pp. 6–7.

89. Judith Fetterley, *The Resisting Reader: A Feminist Approach to American Fiction* (Bloomington, IN: Indiana University Press, 1978), p. viii.

90. Lydia O'Donnell, *The Unheralded Majority: Contemporary Women as Mothers* (Lexington, MA: Lexington Books, 1985), p. 5.

Chapter 11   Feminist Multiple Methods Research

1. This chapter benefited from a reading by Ellen Stone.

2. Renate Klein, "The Dynamics of Women's Studies: Its International Ideas and Practices in Higher Education," doctoral dissertation, Institute of Education, University of London, 1986, p. 16.

3. See Kevin Eckert, "Ethnographic Research on Aging," in Shulamit Reinharz and Graham Rowles (eds.), *Qualitative Gerontology* (New York: Springer Publishing, 1988), pp. 241–255.

4. Agnes Riedmann, "Margaret Loyd Jarman Hagood," in Mary Jo Deegan (ed.), *Women in Sociology: A Bio-bibliographic Sourcebook* (Westport, CT: Greenwood Press, 1990). All of the material for my discussion of Margaret Hagood is based on Agnes Riedmann's article.

5. Margaret Hagood, *Mothers of the South: Portraiture of the White Tenant Farm Woman* (Chapel Hill, NC: University of North Carolina Press, 1939), p. 226. This study is also discussed in chapter 2, on interview research perspectives.

6. Margaret Hagood, *Statistics for Sociologists* (New York: Reynal and Hitchcock, 1941).

7. Shulamit Reinharz, "Finding a Sociological Voice: The Work of Mirra Komarovsky," *Sociological Inquiry,* 1989, *59*(4): 374–394.

8. Mirra Komarovsky, *Women in College: Shaping New Feminine Identities* (New York: Basic Books, 1985), pp. 7–11.

9. Bernice Lott, Mary Ellen Reilly, and Dale R. Howard, "Sexual Assault and Harassment: A Campus Community Case Study," *Signs: Journal of Women in Culture and Society,* 1982, *8*(2): 296–319.

10. Pauline Bart, Linda Freeman, and Peter Kimball, "The Different Worlds of Women and Men: Attitudes toward Pornography and Responses to *Not a Love Story*—a Film about Pornography," *Women's Studies International Forum,* 1985, *8*(4): 307–322, p. 309.

11. See Shulamit Reinharz, *On Becoming a Social Scientist: From Survey Research and Participant Observation to Experiential Analysis* (New Brunswick, NJ: Transaction Books, 1984), chapter 2.

12. Phyllis Chesler, *Women & Madness* (New York: Avon, 1972), pp. xxi–xxiii.

13. Ruth Wallace, "Catholic Women and the Creation of a New Social Reality," *Gender & Society,* 1988 2(1): 24–38.

14. Leila J. Rupp and Verta Taylor, *Survival in the Doldrums: The American Women's Rights Movement, 1945 to the 1960s* (Columbus, OH: Ohio State University Press, 1990).

15. Judith Herman with Lisa Hirschman, *Father–Daughter Incest* (Cambridge, MA: Harvard University Press, 1981), p. viii.

16. Lenore J. Weitzman, *The Divorce Revolution: The Unexpected Social and Economic Consequences for Women and Children in America* (New York: Free Press, 1985), pp. 403–404.

17. Kathleen Barry, *Female Sexual Slavery* (Englewood Cliffs, NJ: Prentice-Hall, 1979). The methods in this book are discussed in chapter 12, on original research methods.

18. Cynthia Fuchs Epstein, "Appendix: Methodology," in *Women in Law* (New York: Basic Books, 1981), p. 387.

19. Elizabeth (Betsy) M. Ettore, *Lesbians, Women and Society* (London: Routledge & Kegan Paul, 1980), pp. 10–13.

20. Another part of this book is discussed in chapter 2, on feminist interview research.

21. Elissa Melamed, *Mirror, Mirror. The Terror of Not Being Young* (New York: Simon & Schuster, 1983), pp. 13–17.

22. Athena Theodore, *The Campus Troublemakers: Academic Women in Protest* (Houston, TX: Cap and Gown Press, 1986), p. 266.

23. Renate Klein, "When Medicalization Equals Experimentation and Creates Illness: The Impact of the New Reproductive Technologies on Women," paper presented at the Forum International Sur les Nouvelles Technologies de la Reproduction Humaine organisé par le Conseil du Statut de la Femme, Université Concordia, Montreal, Canada, published in *Conference Proceedings,* 1988, fn 1. See also Renate Klein, "Pain, Infertility and Women's Experiences with IVF," paper presented at the Meeting of the Australian Federation of University Women, Lyceum Club, Melbourne, April 1987, and Renate Klein, "Where Choice Amounts to Coercion: The Experiences of Women on IVF Programmes," paper presented at the Third Interdisciplinary Congress on Women, Dublin, Ireland, July 1987.

24. Renate Klein, "The Dynamics of Women's Studies: Its International Ideas and Practices in Higher Education," doctoral dissertation, Institute of Education, University of London, 1986, Methods chapter, p. 14.

25. Shulamit Reinharz, "Experiential Analysis: A Contribution to Feminist Research Methodology," in Gloria Bowles and Renate Duelli Klein (eds.), *Theories of Women's Studies* (Boston: Routledge & Kegan Paul, 1983), pp. 162–191.

26. Janice Radway, *Reading the Romance: Women, Patriarchy and Popular Literature* (Chapel Hill, NC: University of North Carolina Press, 1984), pp. 5–7, 9–12.

27. For a discussion of the journey of feminists, see Mary Daly, *Gyn/Ecology: The Metaethics of Radical Feminism* (Boston: Beacon Press, 1978) and of feminist researchers, see Jill McCalla Vickers, "Memoirs of an Ontological Exile: The Methodological Rebellions of Feminist Research," in Geraldine Finn and Angela Miles (eds.), *Feminism in Canada* (Montreal: Black Rose Books, 1982).

28. Nadya Aisenberg and Mona Harrington discuss this idea by drawing on terms developed by Carolyn Heilbrun in her *Writing a Woman's Life* (New York: Ballantine Books, 1988). See Nadya Aisenberg and Mona Harrington, *Women of Academe: Outsiders in the Sacred Grove* (Amherst, MA: University of Massachusetts Press, 1988), p. 6. The authors do not cite Carolyn Heilbrun, but do cite Rachel Blau DuPlessis in *Writing Beyond the Ending: Narrative Strategies of Twentieth-Century Women Writers* (Bloomington: Indiana University Press, 1985), Blanche Gelfant in *Women Writing in America: Voices in Collage* (Hanover, NH: University Press of New England, 1985), and Carol P. Christ, *Diving Deep and Surfacing: Women Writers on Spiritual Quest* (Boston: Beacon Press, 1980).

29. Elinor Langer, *Josephine Herbst* (Boston: Little, Brown, 1983), pp. 4, 12.

30. Stephanie Riger and Margaret Gordon, "Dilemmas in the Practice of Feminist Research," paper presented at the meeting of the American Psychological Association, Los Angeles, August 1981, pp. 5–6.

31. See Alvin Gouldner, *The Coming Crisis of Western Sociology* (New York: Avon, 1970); see also Shulamit Reinharz, "An Assessment of Alvin Gouldner's *The Coming Crisis of Western Sociology*," paper presented at the Eastern Sociological Society Meetings, Boston, March 1990.

32. Stephanie Riger and Margaret Gordon, *op. cit.* (note 30), pp. 3–4.

33. Sara Ruddick, *Maternal Thinking: Toward a Politics of Peace* (New York: Ballantine Books, 1989), pp. 127–128.

34. Liz Stanley and Sue Wise, *Breaking Out: Feminist Consciousness and Feminist Research* (London: Routledge & Kegan Paul, 1983).

35. Chung Yuen Kay, *At the Palace: Worth, Ethnicity & Gender in a Chinese Restaurant,* in Liz Stanley and Sue Scott (eds.), *Studies in Sexual Politics* (Manchester, UK: Department of Sociology, University of Manchester, 1985), pp. 1–83.

Chapter 12   Original Feminist Research Methods

1. This chapter benefited from a review by Michael R. Hill.

2. Jill McCalla Vickers, "Memoirs of an Ontological Exile: The Methodological Rebellions of Feminist Research," in Geraldine Finn and Angela Miles (eds.), *Feminism in Canada* (Montreal: Black Rose Books, 1982), pp. 27–46.

3. Ann Pescatello, *Power and Pawn: The Female in Iberian Families, Societies, and Cultures* (Westport, CT: Greenwood Press, 1976), p. xv.

4. See Robert K. Merton, "Singletons and Multiples in Scientific Discovery: A Chapter in the Sociology of Science," *Proceedings of the American Philosophical Society,* 1961, *105:* 470–486; Robert K. Merton, *On the Shoulders of Giants* (New York: Free Press, 1965); Robert K. Merton, *Social Theory and Social Structure* (New York: Free Press, 1968).

5. Sheila K. Webster, *Women and Foklore,* special issue, *Women's Studies International Forum,* 1986, *9*(3): 219–301, p. 222.

6. See Shulamit Reinharz, "A Contextualized, Chronological Chart of Primarily U.S. Women's Contributions to Social Theory," in Shulamit Reinharz, and Ellen Stone (eds.), *Looking at Invisible Women: An Exercise in Feminist Pedagogy* (Washington, D.C.: University of America Press, 1992); see Alice Rossi, *The Feminist Papers* (Boston: Northeastern University Press, 1988 [first published in 1973]).

7. Mary Belenky, Blythe Clinchy, Nancy Goldberger, and Jill Tarule, *Women's Ways of Knowing: The Development of Self, Voice and Method* (New York: Basic Books, 1986), p. 6.

8. Dale Spender, *For the Record: The Making and Meaning of Feminist Knowledge* (London: The Women's Press, 1985), p. 2.

9. Shulamit Reinharz, *On Becoming a Social Scientist: From Survey Research and Participant Observation to Experiential Analysis* (San Francisco: Jossey-Bass, 1979).

10. See also Shulamit Reinharz, "Experiential Analysis: A Contribution to Feminist Research Methodology, in Gloria Bowles and Renate Duelli Klein (eds.), *Theories of Women's Studies* (Boston: Routledge & Kegan Paul, 1983), pp. 162–191.

11. Susan Krieger, *The Mirror Dance: Identity in a Women's Community* (Philadelphia, PA: Temple University Press, 1983).

12. Catharine McClellan, "Ruth Lea Bunzel," in Ute Gacs, Asiha Khan, Jerrie McIntyre, and Ruth Weinberg (eds.), *Women Anthropologists: A Biographical Dictionary* (New York: Greenwood Press, 1988), p. 31.

13. See Susan Ostrander, *Women of the Upper Class* (Philadelphia, PA: Temple University Press, 1984); and Arlene Kaplan Daniels, *Invisible Careers: Women Civic Leaders from the Volunteer World* (Chicago: University of Chicago Press, 1988).

14. Susan Stall, " 'What about the Non-feminist?': The Possibilities for Women's Movement Coalition Building in Small-Town America," paper presented at the 35th Annual Meeting of the Society for the Study of Social Problems, Washington, D.C., August 1985.

15. Evelyn Glenn, *Issei, Nisei, War Bride: Three Generations of Japanese American Women in Domestic Service* (Philadelphia, PA: Temple University Press, 1986).

16. Marjorie L. DeVault, "Doing Housework: Feeding and Family Life," in Naomi Gerstel and Harriet E. Gross (eds.), *Families and Work: Toward Reconceptualization* (Philadelphia, PA: Temple University Press, 1987).

17. Lynn Davidman, *Tradition in a Rootless World: Women Turn to Orthodox Judaism* (Berkeley, CA: University of California Press, 1991); Debra Renee Kaufman, *Rachel's Daughters: Newly Orthodox Jewish Women* (New Brunswick, NJ: Rutgers University Press, 1991).

18. Shulamit Reinharz, "Women's Collective Community Competence: The Other Side of the Coin," in Annette Rickel, Meg Gerrard, and Ira Iscoe (eds.), *Social and Psychological Problems of Women* (New York: Hemisphere, 1984), pp. 19–43.

19. Meredith Gould, "Innovative Sources and Uses of Qualitative Data," in Meredith Gould (ed.), *Innovative Sources and Uses of Qualitative Data,* A Special Issue of *Qualitative Sociology,* 1985, *8*(4): 303–308, pp. 304, 305.

20. Nancy M. Henley, *Body Politics: Power, Sex, and Nonverbal Communication* (Englewood Cliffs, NJ: Prentice Hall, 1977), p. 74. See also Dale Zimmerman and Candace West, "Sex Roles, Interruptions and Silences in Conversation," in Barrie Thorne and Nancy M. Henley (eds.), *Language and Sex: Difference and Dominance* (Rowley, MA: Newbury House Publishers, 1975); and Mary Brown Parlee, "Conversational Politics," *Psychology Today,* May 1979, *12*(12): 48–56.

21. Bettina Aptheker, *Tapestries of Life: Women's Work, Women's Consciousness, and the Meaning of Daily Experience* (Amherst, MA: University of Massachusetts Press, 1989), pp. 253–254.

22. Carol Auster, "Manuals for Socialization: Examples from Girl Scout Handbooks 1913–1984," *Qualitative Sociology,* 1985, *8*(4): 359–367.

23. Joy Reeves and Nydia Boyette, "What Does Children's Artwork Tell Us about Gender?" *Qualitative Sociology,* 1983, *6*(4): 322–333.

24. Meredith Gould, *op. cit.* (note 19).

25. Maxine Schwartz Seller, *Immigrant Women* (Philadelphia, PA: Temple University Press, 1981), p. 12.

26. Elizabeth Hampsten, *Read This Only to Yourself: The Private Writings of Midwestern Women, 1880–1910* (Bloomington, IN: Indiana University Press, 1982), pp. vi–viii.

27. See also Penelope Franklin (ed.), *Private Pages: Diaries of American Women: 1830–1970s* (New York: Ballantine, 1986).

28. For a discussion see Elaine Showalter, "Literary Criticism," *Signs: Journal of Women in Culture and Society,* 1975, *1*(2): 435–460.

29. Diana Scully and Pauline B. Bart, "A Funny Thing Happened on the Way to the Orifice: Women in Gynecology Textbooks," *American Journal of Sociology,* 1973, *78*(4): 1045–1050.

30. Anne Murcott, "Women's Place: Cookbooks' Images of Technique and Technology in the British Kitchen," *Women's Studies International Forum,* 1983, *6*(1): 33–40.

31. Andrea Dworkin, *Pornography: Men Possessing Women* (New York: Perigee, 1981); see also Mary Jo Deegan and Michael C. Stein, "Pornography as a Strip and a Frame," *Sociological Symposium,* 1977, *20*: 27–44.

32. Shulamit Reinharz, "Feminist Distrust: Problems of Context and Content in Sociological Work," in David Berg and Ken Smith (eds.), *The Self in Social Inquiry: Researching Methods* (Beverly Hills, CA: Sage, 1985, 1988), pp. 153–172.

33. Mary Belenky et al., *op. cit.* (note 7), pp. 12–13.

34. Kathleen MacPherson, "Feminist Praxis in the Making: The Menopause Collective," doctoral dissertation, Brandeis University, 1986; see also Jill Matthews, *Good and Mad Women: The Historical Construction of Femininity in Twentieth Century Australia* (Sidney: George Allen & Unwin Australia, 1984).

35. Margaret T. Gordon, Stephanie Riger, and Andrew C. Gordon, "Victimology, Academia, and Academics: A Study in (Primarily Negative) Sanctions," Center for Urban Affairs, Northwestern University, Evanston, IL, 1981.

36. The Boston Women's Health Book Collective, *Our Bodies, OurSelves: A Book by and for Women* (New York: Simon and Schuster, 1971, 1973, 1976); The Boston Women's Health Book Collective, *The New Our Bodies, OurSelves* (New York: Simon and Schuster, 1984).

37. The Nebraska Feminist Collective, "A Feminist Ethic for Social Science Research," *Women's Studies International Forum,* 1983, *6*(5): 535–543; and Nebraska Sociological Feminist Collective, *A Feminist Ethic for Social Science Research* (Lewiston/ Queenston: The Edwin Mellen Press, 1988).

38. Combahee River Collective, "Why Did They Die? A Document of Black Feminism," *Radical America,* 1979, *13*(6): 41–50.

39. The Boston Lesbian Psychologies Collective, *Lesbian Psychologies* (Urbana, IL: University of Illinois Press, 1987).

40. Hunter College Women's Studies Collective, *Women's Realities, Women's Choices* (New York: Oxford University Press, 1983).

41. These are discussed in Jane Addams, *Twenty Years at Hull-House* (1910) (New York: New American Library, 1981).

42. Thomas S. Kuhn, in *The Structure of Scientific Revolutions* (Chicago: University of Chicago Press, 1970), argues that it is precisely those who transcend the shackles of disciplines who create revolutionary insights.

43. Stephanie Demetrakopoulos, *Listening to Our Bodies: The Rebirth of Feminine Wisdom* (Boston: Beacon Press, 1983), p. xi.

44. See Ylanda T. Moses and Lillian H. Jones, "Doing the Job: Ethnic and Women's Studies in a Polytechnic University," *Women's Studies International Forum*, 1986, 9(2): 145–150.

45. Shulamit Reinharz, *op. cit.* (note 32); see also Daphne Patai, "Beyond Defensiveness: Feminist Research Strategies," *Women's Studies International Quarterly*, 1983, 6(2): 177–189.

46. Marilyn Frye, "The Problem that Has No Name," in Marilyn Frye (ed.), *The Politics of Reality: Essays in Feminist Theory* (Trumansburg, NY: The Crossing Press, 1983).

47. See Marjorie L. DeVault, "Talking and Listening from Women's Standpoint: Feminist Strategies for Interviewing and Analysis," *Social Problems*, 1990, 37(1): 701–721.

48. See Shulamit Reinharz, "Patriarchal Pontifications," *Transaction/SOCIETY*, 1986, 23(6): 23–39.

49. Andrée Collard, *Rape of the Wild* (Bloomington, IN: Indiana University Press, 1989), p. 39; Patti Lather, *Getting Smart: Feminist Research and Pedagogy with/in the Postmodern* (New York: Routledge, Chapman and Hall, 1991), p. xvi.

50. Renate Klein, "The Dynamics of the Women's Studies Classroom: A Review Essay of the Teaching Practice of Women's Studies in Higher Education," *Women's Studies International Forum*, 1987, 10(2): 187–206.

51. See an explanation for this term in Nebraska Sociological Feminist Collective (ed.), *op. cit.* (note 37), pp. xiv–xvi.

52. Roberta Pfeufer Kahn, *The Language of Birth: Female Generativity in Western Tradition* (Chicago: University of Illinois, in press).

53. See Gloria Steinem, "Words and Change," in *Outrageous Acts and Everyday Rebellions* (New York: New American Library, 1983), pp. 149–160.

54. Robin Morgan (ed.), *Sisterhood Is Global: The International Women's Movement Anthology* (Garden City, NY: Anchor Books, 1984), pp. xx–xxi.

55. See Gayle Graham Yates (ed.), *Harriet Martineau on Women* (New Brunswick, NJ: Rutgers University Press, 1985).

56. Charlotte Perkins Gilman, *Women & Economics* (1898) (New York: Harper Torchbook, 1966).

57. Jeanne M. Paradise, "In Search of a Research Paradigm for a Human-World Science," unpublished manuscript, Boston University, School of Education.

58. Elaine Melamed, "Play and Playfulness in Women's Learning and Development," doctoral dissertation, Department of Education, University of Toronto, 1985, pp. 3, 5.

59. Stephanie Demetrakopoulos, *op. cit.* (note 43), pp. ix–x.

60. Mary Daly, *Gyn/Ecology: The Metaethics of Radical Feminism* (Boston: Beacon Press, 1978).

61. Mary Daly, *Beyond God the Father: Toward a Philosophy of Women's Liberation* (Boston: Beacon Press, 1973), pp. 11–12.

62. Rosaharn van der Burg and Nelleke Schoemaker, "Scoring Women on Their Labor Chances," *Women's Studies International Forum*, 1985, 8(4): 273–278, p. 273.

63. See Sandra Lipsitz Bem, "Probing the Promise of Androgyny," in Mary Roth

Walsh (ed.), *The Psychology of Women: Ongoing Debates* (New Haven, CT: Yale University Press, 1987), pp. 206–225.

64. Kathleen Barry, *Female Sexual Slavery* (New York: Avon, 1979), pp. 6–9.

65. Catharine MacKinnon, "Feminism, Marxism, Method, and the State: An Agenda for Theory," in Elizabeth Abel and Emily K. Abel (eds.), *The Signs Reader* (Chicago: University of Chicago Press, 1983), pp. 227–256. See also Samuel A. Culbert, "Consciousness-Raising: A Five Stage Model for Social and Organizational Change," in Cary L. Cooper (ed.), *Theories of Group Process* (New York: Wiley, 1975).

66. Theodora Penny Martin, *The Sound of Our Own Voices: Women's Study Clubs, 1860–1910* (Boston: Beacon Press, 1987), pp. 1, 4.

67. Charlene Eldridge Wheeler and Peggy L. Chinn, *Peace & Power: A Handbook of Feminist Process* (Buffalo, NY: Margaretdaughters, 1984). Unfortunately, consciousness-raising is frequently ridiculed, even by feminists, because of its alleged disregard of macrosociological and economic phenomena in favor of feelings. See, for example, Betty MacMorran Gray, "Economics of Sex Bias: The 'Disuses of Women'," *The Nation*, June 14, 1971, pp. 742–744.

68. See Diane Kravetz, "Consciousness-Raising in the 1970s," *Psychology of Women Quarterly*, 1978, *3*(2): 168–186.

69. Mary Gergen, "Towards a Feminist Metatheory and Methodology," paper presented at the Annual Meeting of the American Psychological Association, Washington, D.C., August 1986, p. 3. See Mary M. Gergen (ed.), *Feminist Thought and the Structure of Knowledge* (New York: New York University Press, 1988). See also Judith Posner, "It's All in Your Head: Feminist and Medical Models of Menopause (Strange Bedfellows)," *Sex Roles*, 1979, *5*(2): 179–190.

70. Ann R. Bristow and Jody A. Esper, "A Feminist Research Ethos," in Nebraska Sociological Feminist Collective (ed.), *A Feminist Ethic for Social Science Research* (Lewiston, NY: The Edwin Mellen Press, 1988), pp. 67–81.

71. Terry Kramer, "The Diary as a Feminist Research Method," *Newsletter of the Association for Women in Psychology*, Winter 1983, pp. 3–4.

72. Memo, from Graduate Women's Forum, to All Faculty and Graduate Students, unpublished manuscript, Department of Sociology, Boston College, May 6, 1987.

73. See David L. Morgan and Margaret T. Spanish, "Focus Groups: A New Tool for Qualitative Research," *Qualitative Sociology*, 1984, *7*(3): 253–270.

74. Ann Oakley, "Interviewing Women: A Contradiction in Terms," in Helen Roberts (ed.), *Doing Feminist Research* (London: Routledge & Kegan Paul, 1981), pp. 30–61.

75. Joan Thompson Callahan, "Upward Mobility from the Inside: A Phenomenological Study of Female Psychologists from Working-class Backgrounds," doctoral dissertation, Massachusetts School of Professional Psychology, 1983, p. 38.

76. Frigga Haug and Others, *Female Sexualization: A Collective Work of Memory* (translated from the German by Erica Carter) (London: Verso, 1983).

77. Vivienne Griffiths, "Feminist Research and the Use of Drama," *Women's Studies International Forum*, 1984, *7*(6): 511–519, pp. 511, 513–514.

78. See Honor Ford Smith, "Sistren: Exploring Women's Problems through Drama," *Jamaica Journal*, 1986, *19*(1).

79. Sistren, with Honor Ford-Smith, *Lionheart Gal: Life Stories of Jamaican Women* (London: The Women's Press, 1986), pp. xxii, xxvii–xxx.

80. Marianne A. Paget, "On the Work of Talk: Studies in Misunderstandings," in Sue Fisher and Alexander Dundas Todd (eds.), *The Social Organization of Doctor-Patient Communication* (Washington, D.C.: Center for Applied Linguistics, 1983), pp. 55–74.

81. Marianne A. Paget, "Performing the Text," *Journal of Contemporary Ethnography*, 1990, *19*(1): 136–155.

82. Marianne A. Paget, "Life Mirrors Work Mirrors Text Mirrors Life," *Social Problems*, 1990, *37*(2): 137–151.

83. Kathy Ferguson, "Interpretation and Genealogy in Feminism," *Signs: Journal of Women in Culture and Society*, 1991, *16*(2): 322–339.

84. Liz Stanley, *Feminism and Friendship: Two Essays on Olive Schreiner*, in *Studies in Sexual Politics* (Manchester, UK: University of Manchester, Department of Sociology, 1985).

85. Janice Raymond, *A Passion for Friends: Toward a Philosophy of Female Affection* (Boston: Beacon Press, 1986), pp. 3–27. Kathy E. Ferguson uses the term "genealogy" to contrast with "interpretation," both of which are fluid, active "strategies of argument" or "ways of comprehending the world." See Kathy E. Ferguson, "Interpretation and Genealogy in Feminism," *Signs: Journal of Women in Culture and Society*, 1991, *16*(2): 322–339.

86. Shulamit Reinharz, "Toward a Model of Female Political Action: The Case of Manya Shohat, Founder of the First Kibbutz," *Women's Studies International Forum*, 1984, *7*(4): 275–287.

87. See also Ann J. Lane, *To 'Herland' and Beyond: The Life and Work of Charlotte Perkins Gilman* (New York: Pantheon, 1990).

88. Shulamit Reinharz, "Manya Shohat and Her Friends," unpublished manuscript.

89. Susan Krieger, *op. cit.* (note 11).

90. Harriet Martineau, *Deerbrook*, 3 vols. (London: Edward Moxon, 1839); and Harriet Martineau, *Illustrations of Political Economy, The Moral of Many Fables*, 25 vols. (London: Charles Fox, 1832–34).

91. Charlotte Perkins Gilman, *The Yellow Wallpaper* (New York: The Feminist Press, 1973).

92. Charlotte Perkins Gilman, *Herland* (New York: Pantheon, 1979).

93. Mari Sandoz, *Capital City* (Boston: Little, Brown, 1939).

94. See Zora Neale Hurston, *Their Eyes Were Watching God* (New York: J. B. Lippincott, 1937); *Dust Tracks on a Road* (New York: J. B. Lippincott, 1970); and *I Love Myself When I Am Laughing: A Zora Neale Hurston Reader* (New York: The Feminist Press, 1979).

95. Susan Krieger, *op. cit.* (note 11), pp. 186–190.

96. Susan Krieger, *op. cit.* (note 11), p. xvii. See also Susan Krieger, "Beyond 'Subjectivity': The Use of the Self in Social Science," in Meredith Gould (ed.), *Innovative Sources and Uses of Qualitative Data*, A Special Issue of *Qualitative Sociology*, 1985, *8*(4): 309–324.

97. Susan Krieger, *op. cit.* (note 11), pp. 191, 194.

98. Jane Marcus, "Of Madness and Method," *Women's Review of Books*, 1986, *3*(11): 3.

99. Arlene Raven and Ruth Iskin, "Through the Peephole: Toward a Lesbian Sensibility in Art," *Chrysalis*, 1977, *4*: 19–31, p. 20.

100. Michal McCall and Judith Wittner, "The Good News about Life History," in Howard Becker and Michal McCall (eds.), *Symbolic Interaction and Cultural Studies* (Chicago: University of Chicago Press, 1990), pp. 46–89.

101. Jane Flax, *Thinking Fragments: Psychoanalysis, Feminism and Postmodernism in the Contemporary West* (Berkeley, CA: University of California Press, 1989); see Patti Lather, *op. cit.* (note 49).

102. Rhoda Linton and Michele Whitham, "With Mourning, Rage, Empowerment and Deviance: The 1981 Women's Pentagon Action," in Diana Russell (ed.), *Exposing Nuclear Phallacies* (New York: Pergamon, 1989).

103. Jane Roland Martin, *Reclaiming a Conversation: The Ideal of the Educated Woman* (New Haven, CT: Yale University Press, 1985), pp. 9–10.

104. See Mary Jo Deegan, "Sociology and Conviviality: A Conversation with Ellenhorn on Convivial Sociology," *Humanity and Society*, 1989, *13*(1): 85–88.

105. Shana Penn, "Foreword," in Kim Chernin and Renate Stendhal (eds.), *Sex and Other Sacred Games* (New York: Fawcett Columbine, 1990).

106. See Deborah Gordon (ed), *Feminism and the Critique of Colonial Discourse*, a special issue of *Inscriptions*, 1988, 3/4, which contains several "panel discussions"; see also Karen Sims and Rose Mason, with Darlene R. Pagano, "Racism and Sadomasochism, a Conversation with Two Black Lesbians," in Robin Ruth Linden, Darlene Pagano, Diana Russell, and Susan Leigh Star (eds.), *Against Sadomasochism: A Radical Feminist Analysis* (East Palo Alto, CA: Frog in the Well Press, 1982), pp. 99–105.

107. Susan Griffin, *Woman and Nature: The Roaring Inside Her* (New York: Harper & Row, 1978), pp. xv–xvi.

108. Barbara DuBois, "Passionate Scholarship: Notes on Values, Knowing and Method in Feminist Social Science," in Gloria Bowles and Renate Duelli Klein (eds.), *Theories of Women's Studies* (Boston: Routledge & Kegan Paul, 1983), pp. 105–116.

109. Dorothy Dinnerstein, *The Mermaid and the Minotaur: Sexual Arrangements and Human Malaise* (New York: Harper & Row, 1976), pp. viii–ix.

110. See Ruth Bleier (ed.), *Feminist Approaches to Science* (New York: Pergamon, 1986).

111. Rae Carlson, "Understanding Women: Implications for Personality Theory and Research," *Journal of Social Issues*, 1972, 28(2): 17–32.

112. Elinor Langer, *Josephine Herbst* (Boston: Little, Brown, 1983), pp. 3, 5.

113. Shulamit Reinharz, *op. cit.* (note 86).

114. Jessie Taft, "The Woman Movement and Social Consciousness," in Mary Jo Deegan and Michael R. Hill (eds.), *Women and Symbolic Interaction* (Winchester, MA: Allen & Unwin, 1987), pp. 19–50.

115. See also Harriet Martineau, *Society in America* [1837], edited, abridged, and with an introductory essay by Seymour Martin Lipset (Garden City, NY: Anchor Books, 1962), and Harriet Martineau, *How to Observe Morals and Manners,* with an introduction and analytical index by Michael R. Hill (New Brunswick, NJ: Transaction Books, 1988), originally published in 1838.

116. Gayle Graham Yates (ed.), *Harriet Martineau on Women,* (New Brunswick, NJ: Rutgers University Press, 1985), p. 6.

117. See Evelyn Fox Keller, "Feminism and Science," *Signs: Journal of Women in Culture and Society,* 1982, 7: 589–602; and Nancy Chodorow, *The Reproduction of Mothering: Psychoanalysis and the Sociology of Gender* (Berkeley, CA: University of California Press, 1978).

118. Susan Krieger, *op. cit.* (note 11).

119. See Ann Oakley, "Interviewing Women: A Contradiction in Terms," in Helen Roberts, *Doing Feminist Research* (London: Routledge & Kegan Paul, 1981).

120. Barbara Katz Rothman, "Reflections: On Hard Work," *Qualitative Sociology,* 1986, 9(1): 48–53. Unfortunately, Barbara Katz Rothman may find there is little refuge in the world of flower arrangement. Mary Abby Van Kleeck discovered abuses in the artificial flowermaking industry, and many of the people in contemporary florist shops doing arrang-

ing are poorly paid women. See her *Artificial Flower Makers* (New York: Russell Sage Foundation, 1913).

121. Judith DiIorio, "Feminist Fieldwork in a Masculinist Setting: Personal Problems and Methodological Issues," paper presented at the North Central Sociological Association Meetings, Detroit, Michigan, May 6, 1982. See also Judith DiIorio, "Sex, Glorious Sex: The Social Construction of Masculine Sexuality in a Youth Group," in Laurel Richardson and Verta Taylor (eds.), *Feminist Frontiers II: Rethinking Sex, Gender and Society* (New York: Random House, 2nd ed., 1989) and Judith DiIorio, "Being and Becoming Coupled: The Emergence of Female Subordination in Heterosexual Relationships," in Barbara J. Risman and Pepper Schwartz (eds.), *Gender in Intimate Relationships* (Belmont, CA: Wadsworth Press, 1989).

122. Ruth Bleier, *op. cit.* (note 110), pp. 13–14.

123. Evelyn Fox Keller, *A Feeling for the Organism: The Life and Work of Barbara McClintock* (San Francisco: W. H. Freeman, 1983).

124. Mary Belenky et al., *op. cit.* (note 7).

125. Sara Ruddick, *Maternal Thinking: Towards a Politics of Peace* (Boston: Beacon Press, 1989).

126. Nancy Datan, "Illness and Imagery: Feminist Cognition, Socialization, and Gender Identity," in Mary Crawford and Margaret Genry (eds.), *Gender and Thought: Psychological Perspectives* (New York: Springer-Verlag, 1989), pp. 175–188, p. 175.

127. See Pauline Bart, "How I Lost My False Consciousness and Found Women's Liberation" (mimeo); Jessie Bernard, "My Four Revolutions: An Autobiographical History of the American Sociological Association," *American Journal of Sociology*, 1973, 78(4): 773–791; Helen MacGill Hughes, "Maid of All Work or Departmental Sister-in-Law? The Faculty Wife Employed on Campus," *American Journal of Sociology*, 1973, 78(4): 767–772; Helen MacGill Hughes, "On Becoming a Sociologist," Address to the Third Undergraduate Research Conference in Sociology, Providence College, April 8, 1978 (mimeo); Gerda Lerner, "Introduction," *A Majority Finds its Past: Placing Women in History* (New York: Oxford University Press, 1979), pp. xiii–xxxii; Shulamit Reinharz, "Feminist Research Methodology Groups: Origins, Forms and Functions," in Vivian Petraka and Louise Tilly (eds.), *Feminist Re-Visions: What Has Been and Might Be* (Women's Studies Program, University of Michigan, 1983), pp. 197–228; and Carolyn Sherif, "Bias in Psychology," in Julia Sherman and Evelyn Torton Beck (eds.), *The Prism of Sex* (Madison, WI: University of Wisconsin Press, 1979), pp. 93–134.

128. Barbara Macdonald and Cynthia Rich, *Look Me in the Eye: Old Women, Aging and Ageism* (San Francisco: Spinsters Ink, 1983).

129. See Marianne A. Paget, *op. cit.* (note 82).

130. Jennifer C. Hunt, *Psychoanalytic Aspects of Fieldwork*, Sage University Paper Series on Qualitative Research Methods, Vol. 18 (Newbury Park, CA: Sage, 1989).

131. Shulamit Reinharz, "What's Missing in Miscarriage?," *Journal of Community Psychology*, 1988, 16(1): 84–103. See also Shulamit Reinharz, "The Social Psychology of a Miscarriage: An Application of Symbolic Interactionist Theory and Method," in Mary Jo Deegan and Michael R. Hill (eds.), *Women and Symbolic Interaction* (Winchester, MA: Allen & Unwin, 1987), pp. 229–250; "Controlling Women's Lives: A Cross-Cultural Interpretation of Women's Miscarriage Accounts," in Dorothy Wertz (ed.), *Research in the Sociology of Health Care* (Greenwich, CT: JAI Press, 1988), 2–37; and "Empty Explanations for Empty Wombs: An Illustration of Secondary Analysis of Qualitative Data," in Michael Schratz (ed.), *Qualitative Voices in Educational Research* (London: Falmer Press, 1992). Monika Leuzinger and Bigna Rambert resisted prenatal diagnosis when they

were pregnant, even though they were over the age of 35. They then examined their experience, interviewed 10 pregnant women over the age of 35, and had discussions with "other feminists" to study the "motives which cause a woman to say yes or no to prenatal diagnosis." See their " 'I Can Feel It—My Baby is Healthy': Women's Experiences with Prenatal Diagnosis in Switzerland," *Reproductive and Genetic Engineering: Journal of International Feminist Analysis,* 1988, *1*(3): 239–249.

132. Liz Stanley and Sue Wise, "Feminist Research, Feminist Consciousness and Experiences of Sexism," *Women's Studies International Quarterly,* 1979, *2*(3): 359–374; see also Liz Stanley and Sue Wise, " 'Back into the Personal': Or Our Attempt to Construct 'Feminist Research,' " in Gloria Bowles and Renate Duelli Klein (eds.), *Theories of Women's Studies* (Boston: Routledge & Kegan Paul, 1983), pp. 192–209.

133. Wendy Hollway, *Subjectivity and Method in Psychology: Gender, Meaning and Science* (Newbury Park, CA: Sage, 1989), pp. 1, 9, 23.

134. See Florence Rush, *The Best Kept Secret: Sexual Abuse of Children* (Englewood Cliffs, NJ: Prentice-Hall, 1980).

135. A related work is Celia Kitzinger, *The Social Construction of Lesbianism* (Beverly Hills, CA: Sage, 1987).

136. Rhoda Linton, "Conceptualizing Feminism: Clarifying Social Science Concepts," *Evaluation and Program Planning,* 1989, *12*: 25–29, p. 25.

137. See also Rhoda Linton, "Feminist Research Methodology: Exploration and Experimentation," in Alison Jaggar and Susan Bordo (eds.), *Gender/Body/Knowledge: Feminist Reconsiderations of Being and Knowing* (New Brunswick, NJ: Rutgers University Press, 1989).

138. Rhoda Linton, "Conceptualizing Feminism: A Structured Method," doctoral dissertation, Cornell University, 1985, abstract, pp. 9–10.

139. About 10 housing studies by Edith Abott and Sophonisba Breckinridge of Hull-House or their students appeared in *The American Journal of Sociology.* These studies used photographs extensively. In addition, Jane Addams used lithographs in *Twenty Years at Hull-House,* uniting "art" and "sociology."

140. Agnes Riedmann, "Margaret Loyd Jarman Hagood," in Mary Jo Deegan (ed.), *Women Sociologists: A Bio-bibliographical Sourcebook* (Greenwood, CT: Greenwood Press, 1990), p. 158.

141. See also Batya Weinbaum, *Pictures of Patriarchy* (Boston: South End Press, 1983), with its creative coda using snapshots of television, movies, family, work, and life-styles that constitute examples of patriarchy.

142. Ximena Bunster, "Talking Pictures: Field Method and Visual Mode," *Signs: Journal of Women in Culture and Society,* 1977, *2*(1): 278–293.

143. Roberta Pfeufer Kahn, "Taking Charge of Birth," *Women's Review of Books,* 1984, *2*(3): 5–7.

144. Marianne Wex, *Let's Take Back our Space: "Female" and "Male" Body Language as a Result of Patriarchal Structures* (West Germany: Frauenliteraturverlag Hermine Pees, 1979). Cited in Marilyn Frye, *The Politics of Reality: Essays in Feminist Theory* (Trumansburg, NY: The Crossing Press, 1983), p. 15. Marianne Wex's remarkable book illuminates the relation between age, gender, and body position.

145. Cheryl A. Boudreaux, "The Nature of the Women's Spirituality Movement and Its Relationship to the Formation of a Feminist World View," proposal for doctoral dissertation, Department of Sociology, Brandeis University, 1986, pp. 10–11.

146. Cheris Kramarae and Dale Spender (eds.), *The Knowledge Explosion* (New York: Pergamon Press, 1991).

147. Shere Hite, *The Hite Report: A Nationwide Study on Female Sexuality* (New York:

Macmillan, 1976); Shere Hite, *The Hite Report on Male Sexuality* (New York: Alfred A. Knopf, 1981); Shere Hite, *Women and Love: A Cultural Revolution in Progress* (New York: Alfred A. Knopf, 1987).

148. Terry Kramer, *op. cit.* (note 71), p. 3.

Chapter 13 Conclusions

1. Charlene Depner, "Toward the Further Development of Feminist Psychology," paper presented at the 8th Annual Meeting of the Association for Women in Psychology, Boston, March 1981, p. 10. [emphases added].

2. Bettina Aptheker, *Tapestries of Life: Women's Work, Women's Consciousness, and the Meaning of Daily Experience* (Amherst, MA: University of Massachusetts Press, 1989), p. 251.

3. Jennifer Ring, "Toward a Feminist Epistemology," *American Journal of Political Science,* 1987, *31*(4): 753–772.

4. Louise Lamphere, "Feminism and Anthropology: The Struggle to Reshape Our Thinking about Gender," in Christie Farnham (ed.), *The Impact of Feminist Research in the Academy* (Bloomington, IN: Indiana University Press, 1987), pp. 1–11.

5. Andrée Collard, *Rape of the Wild* (Bloomington, IN: Indiana University Press, 1989), p. 137.

6. Judi Marshall, "Re-visioning Career Concepts: A Feminist Invitation," in M. B. Arthur, D. T. Hall, and B. S. Lawrence (eds.), *Handbook of Career Theory* (Cambridge: Cambridge University Press, 1989), pp. 275–291.

7. Susan Leigh Star, "Strategic Heresy as Scientific Method: Feminism and the Psychology of Consciousness," paper presented to the American Association for the Advancement of Science, Houston, Texas, January 6, 1979, p. 3.

8. Gerda Lerner, "Placing Women in History: A 1975 Perspective," in Berenice Carroll (ed.), *Liberating Women's History* (Chicago: University of Illinois Press, 1976), pp. 357–367; quote is from pp. 365–366.

9. Marjorie L. DeVault, "Talking and Listening to Women's Standpoint: Feminist Strategies for Interviewing and Analysis," *Social Problems,* 1990, *37*(1): 701–721.

10. Elizabeth Schuessler Fiorenza, *Bread Not Stone: The Challenge of Feminist Biblical Interpretation* (Boston: Beacon Press, 1984).

11. Judith Fetterley, *The Resisting Reader: A Feminist Approach to American Fiction* (Bloomington, IN: Indiana University Press, 1978).

12. Celia Kitzinger, "Resisting the Discipline," in Erica Burman (ed.), *Feminists and Psychological Practice* (London: Sage, 1990).

13. Shulamit Reinharz, "Feminist Distrust: Problems of Context and Content in Sociological Work," in David Berg and Ken Smith (eds.), *The Self in Social Inquiry: Researching Methods* (Beverly Hills, CA: Sage, 1985, 1988), pp. 153–172.

14. Susan Star, *op. cit.* (note 7), pp. 3–4.

15. Ellen Stone, "Claiming the Third Story: The Challenge to White Feminists of Black Feminist Theory," unpublished manuscript, Brandeis University, 1990.

16. Kathleen McCourt, *Working-Class Women and Grass-Roots Politics* (Bloomington, IN: Indiana University Press, 1977), p. 3.

17. Liz Stanley and Sue Wise, *Breaking Out* (Boston: Routledge & Kegan Paul, 1983), pp. 19–20.

18. Vicky Randall, *Women and Politics: An International Perspective* (Chicago: The University of Chicago Press, 1982, 1987).

19. Sharon B. Berlin, "Dichotomous and Complex Thinking," *Social Service Review*, 1990, *64*(1): 46–59.

20. Diana Russell, *Rape in Marriage* (New York: Macmillan, 1982), p. 28.

21. Some women have been leaders *of* specific feminist organizations without being leaders *over* the mass movement known as the women's movement. See Marcia Cohen, *The Sisterhood: The Inside Story of the Women's Movement and the Leaders Who Made it Happen* (New York: Fawcett Columbine, 1988).

22. *SWS Network News*, p. 3.

23. See Jessie Bernard, *The Female World from a Global Perspective* (Bloomington, IN: Indiana University Press, 1987).

24. Mary Jo Deegan, "The Golden Era of Women Sociologists: 1892–1918," unpublished manuscript, University of Nebraska-Lincoln, 1985.

25. See Mary Kay Thompson Tetreault, "Feminist Phase Theory," *Journal of Higher Education*, 1985, *56:* 363–384: Marilyn R. Schuster and Susan R. Van Dyne (eds.), *Women's Place in the Academy: Transforming the Liberal Arts Curriculum* (Totowa, NJ: Rowman and Allanheld, 1985); and Gerda Lerner, "Priorities and Challenges in Women's History Research," *American Historical Association Newsletter*, 1988, *26*(4): 17–20.

26. Cheri Register, "Literary Criticism," *Signs: Journal of Women in Culture and Society*, 1980, *6*(2): 268–282, pp. 281–282.

27. Elaine Hobby, *Virtue of Necessity: English Women's Writing, 1649–88* (Ann Arbor, MI: University of Michigan Press, 1988), p. 204.

28. Shulamit Reinharz, "Sources of Diversity in Feminist Psychology," paper presented as part of a panel organized by Arnold Kahn and Paula Jean, *The Future of the Psychology of Women: Separation, Integration or Elimination?*, American Psychological Association, 1982.

29. Marilyn Strathern, "Out of Context: The Persuasive Fictions of Anthropology," *Current Anthropology*, 1987, *28*(3): 251–281.

30. An exception is Joyce Nielsen (ed.), *Feminist Research Methods: Exemplary Readings in the Social Sciences* (Boulder, CO: Westview Press, 1990).

31. Alvin Gouldner, *The Coming Crisis of Western Sociology* (New York: Avon, 1970); Joyce Ladner (ed.), *The Death of White Sociology* (New York: Vintage, 1973); and Maria Mies, "Towards a Methodology for Feminist Research," in Edith Altbach, Jeanette Clausen, Dagmar Schultz, and Naomi Stephan (eds.), *German Feminism: Readings in Politics and Literature* (Albany, NY: State University of New York Press, 1984), pp. 357–366.

32. Gayle Rubin, "The Traffic in Women," in Allison Jaggar and Paula Struhl (eds.), *Feminist Frameworks* (New York: McGraw-Hill, 1978), pp. 154–167, p. 157. See also Sylvia Walby, *Patriarchy at Work* (Minneapolis, MN: University of Minnesota Press, 1986); and Mariarosa Dalla Costa, *The Power of Women and the Subversion of the Community* (Bristol, UK: Falling Wall Press, 1972).

33. Nancy Chodorow, *The Reproduction of Mothering: Psychoanalysis and the Sociology of Gender* (Berkeley, CA: University of California Press, 1978).

34. Louise Levesque-Lopman, "Women's Subjective Experience: Phenomenological Sociology as Method of Inquiry," paper presented at the 57th Annual Meeting of the Eastern Sociological Society, Boston, May 1–3, 1987; *Claiming Reality: Phenomenology and Women's Experience* (Totowa, NJ: Rowman & Littlefield, 1988).

35. Zillah Eisenstein, "Comment," on Sarah H. Matthews, "Rethinking Sociology from a Feminist Perspective," *The American Sociologist*, 1982, *17*(1): 36; Thomas Kuhn, *The Structure of Scientific Revolutions* (Chicago: University of Chicago Press, 1962).

36. Mary Jo Deegan and Michael R. Hill (eds.), *Women and Symbolic Interaction* (Winchester, MA: Allen & Unwin, 1987).

37. Susan Volentine and Stanley Brodsky, "Personal Construct Theory and Stimulus

Sex and Subject Sex Differences," in Rhoda K. Unger (ed.), *Representations: Social Constructions of Gender* (Amityville, NY: Baywood, 1989), pp. 112–125.

38. Sarah Fenstermaker Berk, *The Gender Factory: The Apportionment of Work in American Households* (New York: Plenum, 1985).

39. Laura Katz Olson, *The Political Economy of Aging: The State, Private Power and Social Welfare* (New York: Columbia University Press, 1982); Shulamit Reinharz, "Friends or Foes? Feminist and Gerontological Theory," *Women's Studies International Forum,* 1986, *9*(5/6): 503–514, reprinted in Renate D. Klein and Deborah Lynn Steinberg (eds.), *Radical Voices* (New York: Pergamon, 1989), pp. 222–242.

40. Wendy McKenna and Sarah Kessler, *Gender: An Ethnomethodological Approach* (New York: Wiley, 1978; Chicago: University of Chicago, 1985).

41. Abigail Stewart and David Winter, "The Nature and Causes of Female Suppression," *Signs: Journal of Women in Culture and Society,* 1977, *2*(3): 531–553.

42. Dorothy E. Smith, "An Analysis of Ideological Structures and How Women Are Excluded: Considerations for Academic Women," *Canadian Review of Sociology and Anthropology,* 1975, *12*(4): 353–369.

43. Jo Freeman, "The Feminist Scholar," *Quest,* 1980, pp. 26–36, pp. 26–28.

44. Andrée Collard, *op. cit.* (note 5).

45. Sharon Mast, "Qualitative Sociology in New Zealand," in Shulamit Reinharz and Peter Conrad (eds.), *Qualitative Sociology in International Perspective,* Special Issue of *Qualitative Sociology,* 1988, *11*(1–2): 99–112, p. 105.

46. Lillian B. Rubin, *Women of a Certain Age: The Midlife Search for Self* (New York: Harper & Row, 1979), pp. 215–218.

47. Shulamit Reinharz, "Women's Collective Community Competence," in Annette Rickel, Meg Gerrard, and Ira Iscoe (eds.), *Social and Psychological Problems of Women* (New York: Hemisphere, 1984); Guida West and Rhoda Blumberg (eds.), *Women and Social Protest* (New York: Oxford University Press, 1990).

48. Bonnie S. Anderson and Judith P. Zinsser, *A History of Their Own: Women in Europe from Prehistory to the Present* (New York: Harper & Row, 1988), vol. 2.

49. Helena Lopata, Cheryl Miller, and Debra Barnewolt, *City Women in America: Work, Jobs, Occupations, Careers* (New York: Praeger, 1986), p. 15.

50. Carolyn Sachs, *The Invisible Farmers: Women in Agricultural Production* (Totowa, NJ: Rowman & Allanheld, 1983).

51. Jean Reith Schroedel, *Alone in a Crowd: Women in the Trades Tell Their Stories* (Philadelphia: Temple University Press, 1985), p. x.

52. Shulamit Reinharz, "A Partial, Chronological, Contextualized Chart of Mostly U.S. Women's Sociological Work," in Shulamit Reinharz and Ellen Stone (eds.), *Looking at Invisible Women: An Exercise in Feminist Pedagogy* (Washington, D.C.: University Press of America, 1992).

53. Linda Valli, *Becoming Clerical Workers* (Boston: Routledge & Kegan Paul, 1986).

54. Jessica Benjamin, *Psychoanalysis, Feminism and the Problem of Domination* (New York: Pantheon, 1989). For a critique of the emphasis on gender, see Sarah Matthews, "Rethinking Sociology through a Feminist Perspective," *The American Sociologist,* 1982, *17*(1): 29–35.

55. Sylvia Walby, *op. cit.* (note 32), p. 6; Rosabeth Kanter, *Men and Women of the Corporation* (New York: Basic Books, 1977).

56. Judith Herman with Lisa Hirschman, *Father–Daughter Incest* (Cambridge, MA: Harvard University Press, 1981).

57. Terry Arendell, *Mothers and Divorce* (Berkeley, CA: University of California Press, 1986), p. 157.

58. Judy Long Laws, "Feminism and Patriarchy: Competing Ways of Doing Social

Science,'' paper presented at the Annual Meeting of the American Sociological Association, San Francisco, 1978.

59. Carolyn Sherif, ''Should There Be a Feminist Methodology?'' *Newsletter of the Association for Women in Psychology*, January–February 1982, pp. 3–4, p. 4.

60. Laurel Richardson, ''The Collective Story: Postmodernism and the Writing of Sociology,'' *Sociological Focus*, 1988, *21*(3): 199–208; Clifford Geertz, ''Blurred Genres,'' *American Scholar*, 1980, *49*: 165–179.

61. Mary Ann Campbell, ''Creating Feminist Sociology,'' *SWS Network*, January 1982, *12*(1): 23–24, p. 23.

62. Carol Nagy Jacklin, ''Editor's Note,'' *Signs: Journal of Women in Culture and Society*, 1986, *11*(2): 304.

63. Mary Belenky, Blythe Clinchy, Nancy Goldberger, and Jill Tarule, *Women's Ways of Knowing: The Development of Self, Voice and Mind* (New York: Basic Books, 1986).

64. Marcia Westkott, *The Feminist Legacy of Karen Horney* (New Haven, CT: Yale University Press, 1986), p. 5.

65. Sondra Farganis, ''The Social Construction of Gender: The Turn to Fiction,'' in Rhoda K. Unger (ed.), *Representations: Social Constructions of Gender* (Amityville, NY: Baywood, 1989).

66. Liz Stanley, *The Diaries of Hannah Cullwick* (New Brunswick, NJ: Rutgers University Press, 1984), pp. 24–25.

67. Carol Gilligan, *In a Different Voice* (Cambridge, MA: Harvard University Press, 1982).

68. Jill Matthews, *Good and Mad Women: The Historical Construction of Femininity in Twentieth-Century Australia* (Sydney: George Allen and Unwin, 1984), p. 29.

69. Barbara Reskin, ''Bringing the Men Back In: Sex Differentiation and the Devaluation of Women's Work,'' *Gender & Society*, 1988, *2*(1): 58–81.

70. Roberta M. Spalter-Roth and Heidi I. Hartmann, ''Science and Politics: The 'Dual Vision' of Feminist Policy Research, the Example of Family and Medical Leave,'' Institute for Women's Policy Research, 1987, 1988.

71. Gloria Levin, ''Making Feminist Research Policy Relevant,'' paper presented at the Annual Meeting of the American Psychological Association, Los Angeles, August 1981.

72. Pat Reuss, ''Women and Public Policy: Effective Leadership for the 1990s,'' *Women's Political Times*, 1990, *15*(1): 1.

73. Margaret Andersen, *Thinking about Women: Sociological and Feminist Perspectives* (New York: Macmillan, 1983), pp. viii–ix.

74. See ''Afterword,'' in Nancy Chodorow, *op. cit.* (note 33).

75. Lenore Weitzman, *The Divorce Revolution* (New York: Free Press, 1985).

76. Susan Yeandle, *Women's Working Lives: Patterns and Strategies* (New York: Tavistock, 1985).

77. Jane Mansbridge, *Why We Lost the ERA* (Chicago: University of Chicago Press, 1986).

78. Kristin Luker, *Abortion and the Politics of Motherhood* (Berkeley, CA: University of California Press, 1984).

79. Joanna Bunker Rohrbaugh, *Women: Psychology's Puzzle* (New York: Basic Books, 1979), p. 467.

80. Hasia R. Diner, *Erin's Daughters in America: Irish Immigrant Women in the Nineteenth Century* (Baltimore: The Johns Hopkins University Press, 1983), p. 160.

81. Susan N. G. Geiger, ''Women's Life Histories: Method and Content,'' *Signs: Journal of Women in Culture and Society*, 1986, *11*(2): 334–351.

82. Ms. Manners, *SWS Network*, October 1987, vol. 5, no. 1, pp. 18–19 (Arlene K. Daniels).

83. Graham Staines, Carol Tavris, and Toby Epstein Jayaratne, "The Queen Bee Syndrome," *Psychology Today,* 1974, *7*(8): 55–65.

84. Jill Matthews, *op. cit.* (note 68), p. 17.

85. Mary Belenky et al., *op. cit.* (note 63), pp. 12–13.

86. Gerda Lerner, *The Female Experience: An American Documentary* (Indianapolis: Bobbs-Merrill, 1977), p. xxii.

87. Jacklyn Cock, "Trapped Workers: Constraints and Contradictions Experienced by Black Women in Contemporary South Africa," *Women's Studies International Forum,* 1987, *10*(2): 133–140, p. 133.

88. Susan Tucker, *Telling Memories among Southern Women: Domestic Workers and Their Employers in the Segregated South* (Baton Rouge, LA: Louisiana State University Press, 1988).

89. Naomi Weisstein, *Kinder, Kuche, and Kirche as Scientific Law: Psychology Constructs the Female* (Boston: New England Free Press, 1969).

90. Sue Cox, *Female Psychology: The Emerging Self* (Chicago: Science Research Associates, 1976).

91. Margaret Andersen, *op. cit.* (note 73), p. ix.

92. Patricia Bell Scott, "Debunking Sapphire: Toward a Non-Racist and Non-Sexist Social Science," *Journal of Sociology and Social Welfare,* 1977, *4*(6): 864–871; see Elly Bulkin, "Racism and Writing: Some Implications for White Lesbian Critics," *Sinister Wisdom,* 1980, *7*: 3–22.

93. Becky Thompson, "Raisins and Smiles for Me and My Sister: A Feminist Theory of Eating Problems, Trauma, and Recovery in Women's Lives," doctoral disseration, Brandeis University, 1990.

94. Lynn Weber Cannon, Elizabeth Higginbotham, and Marianne L. A. Leung, "Race and Class Bias in Qualitative Research on Women," *Gender & Society,* 1988, *2*(4): 449–463; Bonnie Thornton, "Race, Class and Gender: Prospects for an All-Inclusive Sisterhood," *Feminist Studies,* 1983, *9*(1): 131–150.

95. Margaret Andersen, review of *Street Woman,* by Eleanor Miller, in *Gender & Society,* March 1988, *2*(1): 118–119, p. 118.

96. Sistren with Honor Ford Smith, "Introduction," in *Lionheart Gal: Life Stories of Jamaican Women* (London: The Women's Press, 1986), p. xxiv.

97. Catherine Clinton, *The Other Civil War: American Women in the Nineteenth Century* (New York: Hill and Wang, 1984), pp. vii–viii.

98. Diana E. H. Russell, *op. cit.* (note 20).

99. Linda LeMoncheck, *Dehumanizing Women: Treating Persons as Sex Objects* (Totowa, NJ: Rowman & Allanheld, 1985), p. xi.

100. Ann R. Bristow and Jody A. Esper, "A Feminist Research Ethos," in Nebraska Sociological Feminist Collective (ed.), *A Feminist Ethic for Social Science Research* (Lewiston, NY: The Edwin Mellen Press, 1988), pp. 67–81, p. 73.

101. Elaine Hobby, *op. cit.* (note 27), p. 205.

102. Celia Kitzinger, *The Social Construction of Lesbianism* (Beverly Hills, CA: Sage, 1987), pp. 87–89.

103. Laurel Richardson, "Sexual Freedom and Sexual Constraint: The Paradox for Single Women in Liaisons with Married Men," *Gender & Society,* 1988, *2*(3): 368–384, pp. 370–372.

104. Emily Martin, *The Woman in the Body: A Cultural Analysis of Reproduction* (Boston: Beacon Press, 1987), pp. 8, 9, 11.

105. Elaine Hobby, *op. cit.* (note 27), p. 205.

106. Rosalind Barnett and Grace Baruch, *The Competent Woman* (New York: Irvington Publishers, 1978), p. vi.

107. Alison Jaggar and Paula Rothenberg (eds.), *Feminist Frameworks: Alternative Theoretical Accounts of the Relations between Women and Men* (New York: McGraw Hill, 1984), pp. xii–xiv.

108. Sara Karon, "The Politics of Naming: Lesbian Erasure in a Feminist Context," in Shulamit Reinharz and Ellen Stone (eds.), *op. cit.* (note 52).

109. Laurie Wardell, Dair L. Gillespie, and Ann Leffler, "Science and Violence against Wives," unpublished paper, Department of Sociology, University of Utah, 1981.

110. Marilyn Frye, *The Politics of Reality: Essays in Feminist Theory* (Trumansburg, NY: The Crossing Press, 1983), pp. ix–x.

111. Carol Warren, "Fieldwork in the Gay World: Issues in Phenomenological Research," *Journal of Social Issues,* 1977, *33*(4): 93–107.

112. bell hooks, *Ain't I a Woman?: Black Women and Feminism* (Boston: South End Press, 1981), p. 10.

113. Lynn Davidman, "Sex and the Modern Jewish Woman: An Overview," in Joan Brewer (ed.), *Sex and the Modern Jewish Woman: An Annotated Bibliography* (Fresh Meadows, NY: Biblio Press, 1986), p. 2.

114. Cynthia Fuchs Epstein, *Women in Law* (New York: Basic Books, 1981), p. 389; see also "Positive Effects of the Multiple Negative: Explaining the Success of Black Professional Women," *American Journal of Sociology,* 1973, *78*(4): 912–935.

115. Barbara Macdonald with Cynthia Rich, *Look Me in the Eye: Old Women, Aging and Ageism* (San Francisco: Spinsters Ink, 1983).

116. Charlene Depner, *op. cit.* (note 1).

117. See Vivian Gornick, "By Science Possessed," *Voice,* April 1–7, 1981, review of June Goodfield, *An Imagined World: A Story of Scientific Discovery* (New York: Harper & Row).

118. See Shulamit Reinharz, *op. cit.* (note 47); Leanna Standish, "Women, Work, and the Scientific Enterprise," unpublished manuscript, Smith College, 1981.

119. Susan Griffin, *Woman and Nature: The Roaring Inside Her* (New York: Harper & Row, 1978).

120. Jean Bethke Elshtain, *Public Man, Private Woman: Women in Social and Political Thought* (Princeton, NJ: Princeton University Press, 1981), p. xii.

121. Pauline B. Bart, "How I Lost My False Consciousness and Found Women's Liberation," unpublished manuscript; Jessie Bernard, "My Four Revolutions: An Autobiographical History of the ASA," *American Journal of Sociology,* 1973, *78*(4): 773–791; Helen MacGill Hughes, "Maid of All Work or Departmental Sister-in-Law? The Faculty Wife Employed on Campus," *American Journal of Sociology,* 1973, *78*(4): 767–772; Helena Znaniecki Lopata, "A Life Record of an Immigrant," *Transaction/SOCIETY,* 1975, *13*(1): 64–74; Helen MacGill Hughes, "Wasp/Woman/Sociologist," *Transaction/SOCIETY,* 1977, *14*(5): 69–80; Gerda Lerner, "Autobiographical Notes, By Way of an Introduction," *A Majority Finds Its Past* (New York: Oxford University Press, 1980); Ann Oakley, *Taking It Like a Woman* (New York: Random House, 1984); Cherrie Moraga and Gloria Anzaldua (eds.), *This Bridge Called My Back: Writing by Radical Women of Color* (Watertown, MA: Persephone Press, 1981); Sylvia Ann Hewlett, *Lesser Life: The Myth of Women's Lives in America* (New York: Morrow, 1986); and Matilda White Riley (ed.), *Sociological Lives* (Beverly Hills, CA: Sage, 1988).

122. See Michelle Fine, Chair, Symposium on "Women's Voices in the Research Relationship: Feminist Alternatives to 'Objectivity'," American Psychological Association, Toronto, August 1984.

123. Thelma McCormack, "The Professional Ethic and the Spirit of Sexism," *International Journal of Women's Studies,* 1981, *4*(5): 132–140.

124. Joyce Leyland, "On the Conflicts of Doing Feminist Research into Masculinity," in Feminist Research Seminar (eds.), *Feminist Research Processes,* Liz Stanley and Sue Scott (eds.), *Studies in Sexual Politics* (Manchester, UK: Department of Sociology, University of Manchester, 1987), pp. 38–47, p. 43.

125. Dorothy E. Smith, "A Sociology for Women," in Julia Sherman and Evelyn Torton Beck (eds.), *The Prism of Sex: Essays in the Sociology of Knowledge* (Madison, WI: University of Wisconsin Press, 1979), p. 135.

126. Marjorie L. DeVault, *op. cit.* (note 9).

127. Athena Theodore, *The Campus Troublemakers: Academic Women in Protest* (Houston, TX: Cap and Gown Press, 1986), pp. xiii–xiv; see also Nadya Aisenberg and Mona Harrington, *Women of Academe* (Amherst, MA: University of Massachusetts Press, 1988).

128. Adrienne Rich, *Of Woman Born: Motherhood as Experience and Institution* (New York: W. W. Norton, 1976).

129. Shulamit Reinharz, "The Social Psychology of a Miscarriage: An Application of Symbolic Interactionist Theory and Method," in Mary Jo Deegan and Michael R. Hill (eds.), *Women and Symbolic Interaction* (Winchester, MA: Allen & Unwin, 1987), pp. 229–250; Shulamit Reinharz, "What's Missing in Miscarriage?," *Journal of Community Psychology,* 1988, *16*(1): 84–103; Shulamit Reinharz, "Controlling Women's Lives: A Cross-Cultural Interpretation of Miscarriage Accounts," in Dorothy Wertz (ed.), *Research in the Sociology of Health Care* (Greenwich, CT: JAI Press, 1988), vol. 7, pp. 2–37.

130. Ruth Jacobs, *Life after Youth: Female, Forty—What Next?* (Boston: Beacon Press, 1979).

131. Susan Borg and Judith Lasker, *When Pregnancy Fails: Families Coping with Miscarriage, Stillbirth, and Infant Death* (Boston: Beacon Press, 1981).

132. Marcia Millman, *Such a Pretty Face: Being Fat in America* (New York: W. W. Norton, 1980).

133. Lillian Breslow Rubin, *Worlds of Pain: Life in the Working-Class Family* (New York: Basic Books, 1976).

134. Suzanne Arms, *Immaculate Deception: A New Look at Women and Childbirth* (New York: Bantam Books, 1975), pp. xiv–xv.

135. Sara Evans, *Personal Politics: The Roots of Women's Liberation in the Civil Rights Movement and the New Left* (New York: Alfred A. Knopf, 1979), p. x.

136. Susan Bordo, "The Cartesian Masculinization of Thought," *Signs: Journal of Women in Culture and Society,* 1986, *11*(3): 439–455. See also Shulamit Reinharz, *op. cit.* (note 47).

137. Del Martin and Phillis Lyon, *Lesbian/Woman* (San Francisco: Glide Publications, 1972), pp. 8–9.

138. Del Martin and Phillis Lyon, *Ibid.*

139. Susan Brownmiller, *Against Our Will: Men, Women and Rape* (New York: Bantam, 1975), pp. xi–xiii.

140. Ann Oakley, *The Sociology of Housework* (Oxford: Martin Robertson, 1974; reprinted in 1985, Oxford: Basil Blackwell), p. 237, n. 5.

141. Ruth Hubbard, "Have Only Men Evolved?," in Ruth Hubbard, Mary Sue Henifin, and Barbara Fried (eds.), *Women Look at Biology Looking at Women* (Boston: Schenkman, 1979), pp. 8–35, p. 31.

142. Linda LeMoncheck, *op. cit.* (note 99), p. x.

143. Cynthia Fuchs Epstein, "Symbolic Segregation: Similarities and Differences in the Language and Non-Verbal Communication of Women and Men," *Sociological Forum,* 1986, *1*(1): 27–49, p. 45.

144. Elizabeth M. Ettore, *Lesbians, Women, and Society* (Boston: Routledge & Kegan Paul, 1980), p. 13.

145. Anne Pugh, "My Statistics and Feminism—a True Story," in Liz Stanley and Sue Scott (eds.), *Feminist Research Processes*, University of Manchester, 1987, pp. 79–87.

146. Virginia E. O'Leary, *Toward Understanding Women* (Belmont, CA: Brooks/Cole, 1977), p. vii.

147. Sara Evans, *op cit.* (note 135), p. x.

148. See also Barbara Gray, "The Pathways of My Research: A Journey of Personal Engagement and Change," *Journal of Applied Behavioral Science,* 1989, *25*(4): 383–398.

149. Michelle Fine, "Women's Voices in the Research Relationship: Feminist Alternatives to 'Objectivity'," paper presented at the Annual Meeting of the American Psychological Association meetings, Toronto, Canada, August 1984, pp. 1–3.

150. Marie Mies, *op. cit.* (note 31), p. 358.

151. Diane Bell, *Daughters of the Dreaming* (Sydney, Australia: George Allen & Unwin, 1983), p. 1.

152. *Ibid.,* p. 25.

153. Barbara Myerhoff, *Number our Days* (New York: Simon and Schuster, 1978).

154. Kristin Luker, *op. cit.* (note 78).

155. Lydia O'Donnell, *The Unheralded Majority: Contemporary Women as Mothers* (Lexington, MA: Lexington Books, D. C. Heath, 1985).

156. Liz Kelly, *Surviving Sexual Violence* (Minneapolis, MN: University of Minnesota Press, 1988), p. 13.

157. Mary K. Zimmerman, *Passage through Abortion: The Personal and Social Reality of Women's Experiences* (New York: Praeger, 1977).

158. Joan Roberts locates the subject–object distinction, and the research posture it generates, in the patriarchal paradigm. See her *Beyond Intellectual Sexism: A New Woman, A New Reality* (New York: D. McKay Co., 1976).

159. Carol Gilligan, *op. cit.* (note 67).

160. See Toni A. H. McNaron (ed.), *The Sister Bond: A Feminist View of a Timeless Connection* (New York: Pergamon, 1985).

161. Marjorie Shostak, *Nisa: The Life and Words of a !Kung Woman* (New York: Vintage Books, 1983), pp. 20–21.

162. Mary Louise Pratt, "Fieldwork in Common Places," in James Clifford and George Marcus (eds.), *Writing Culture: The Poetics and Politics of Ethnography* (Berkeley, CA: University of California Press, 1986), pp. 27–50, p. 45.

163. Denise Donnell Connors, " 'I've Always Had Everything I've Wanted . . . But I Never Wanted Very Much': An Experiential Analysis of Irish-American Working-Class Women in Their Nineties," doctoral dissertation, Brandeis University, 1986, p. 5.

164. Ann Oakley, *op. cit.* (note 140).

165. Susan Condor, "Sex Role Beliefs and 'Traditional' Women: Feminist and Intergroup Perspectives," in Sue Wilkinson (ed.), *Feminist Social Psychology* (Philadelphia: Open University Press, 1986), pp. 97–118, pp. 102–103, 110.

166. Beth B. Hess, "Beyond Dichotomy: Drawing Distinctions and Embracing Differences," *Sociological Forum,* 1990, *5*(1): 75–94.

167. Janet Mancini Billson, "The Progressive Verification Method: Toward a Feminist Methodology for Studying Women Cross-Culturally," *Women's Studies International Forum,* 1991, *14*(3): 201–208.

168. Roxana Ng, "Sex, Ethnicity or Class?: Some Methodological Considerations," in Sue Webb and Clive Pearson (eds.), *Looking Back: Some Papers from the BSA 'Gender*

& *Society' Conference,* in Liz Stanley and Sue Scott (eds.), *Studies in Sexual Politics* (Manchester, UK: Department of Sociology, University of Manchester, 1984), p. 14.

169. Arlie Russell Hochschild, *The Managed Heart: Commercialization of Human Feeling* (Berkeley, CA: University of California Press, 1983).

170. Charlene Depner, *op. cit.* (note 1), p. 15.

171. Jill Matthews, *op. cit.* (note 68), p. 4. [emphasis added]

172. Susan Yeandle, *Women's Working Lives: Patterns and Strategies* (New York: Tavistock, 1984).

173. Nancy Seifer, *Nobody Speaks for Me!: Self-Portraits of American Working Class Women* (New York: Touchstone, 1976).

174. Jewell Babb and Pat Ellis Taylor, *Border Healing Woman: The Story of Jewell Babb as told to Pat Ellis Taylor* (Austin, TX: The University of Texas Press, 1981).

175. Fran Leeper Buss, *Dignity: Lower Income Women Tell of Their Lives and Struggles* (Ann Arbor, MI: The University of Michigan Press, 1985).

176. Dorothy Dinnerstein, *The Mermaid and the Minotaur: Sexual Arrangements and Human Malaise* (New York: Harper & Row, 1976), pp. viii–ix.

177. Laurel Graham, "A Year in the Life of Dr. Lillian Moller Gilbreth: Four Representations of the Struggle of a Woman Scientist," paper presented at the Gregory Stone Symposium, January 25–28, 1990, St. Petersburg Beach, Florida.

178. Susan Krieger, *The Mirror Dance: Identity in a Women's Community* (Philadelphia, PA: Temple University Press, 1983).

179. Jane Marcus, "Of Madness and Method," *Women's Review of Books,* 1986, 3(11): 3.

180. Katherine V. Pope, "The Divided Lives of Women in Literature," in Rhoda K. Unger (ed.), *Representations: Social Constructions of Gender* (Amityville, NY: Baywood, 1989), pp. 21–28.

181. Sarah Fenstermaker Berk, *The Gender Factory: The Apportionment of Work in American Households* (New York: Plenum Press, 1985), p. viii.

BIBLIOGRAPHY

Abbott, Shirley. *Womenfolk: Growing Up Down South*. New Haven, Conn.: Tichnor & Fields, 1983.

Abel, Emily. "Collective Protest and the Meritocracy: Faculty Women and Sex Discrimination Lawsuits." *Feminist Studies* 7 (1981):505–538.

Abu-Lughod, Lila. *Veiled Sentiments: Honor and Poetry in a Bedouin Society*. Berkeley: University of California Press, 1986.

Adams, C. and Laurikietis, R., eds. *The Gender Trap, A Closer Look at Sex Roles 3: Messages and Images*. London: Virago, 1980.

Addams, Jane. *Twenty Years at Hull-House*. 1910. New York: New American Library, 1981.

Adelson, Joseph. "Androgyny Advocates Pose a Threat to Scientific Objectivity." *Behavior Today*, March 24, 1980, pp. 1–3.

——— and Sherif, Carolyn. "Resolved: Division 35 of A.P.A. is/is not a Scholarly Disaster Area." *Behavior Today*, June 2, 1980, p. 3.

Adler, Patricia. *Wheeling and Dealing: An Ethnography of an Upper-Level Drug Dealing and Smuggling Community*. New York: Columbia University Press, 1985.

Aisenberg, Nadya and Harrington, Mona. *Women of Academe: Outsiders in the Sacred Grove*. Amherst, Mass.: University of Massachusetts Press, 1988.

Albrecht, Lisa and Brewer, Rose M., eds. *Bridges of Power: Women's Multicultural Alliances*. Philadelphia: New Society, 1990.

Alexander, Maxine. *Speaking for Ourselves: Women of the South*. New York: Pantheon, 1984.

Allen, Paula Gunn. *The Woman Who Owned the Shadows*. New York: Strawberry Press, 1983.

Almquist, Elizabeth. "Black Women and the Pursuit of Equality." In *Women: A Feminist Perspective*, edited by Jo Freeman. Palo Alto, Calif.: Mayfield Publishing, 1979.

Altbach, Edith Hoshino. *Women in America*. Lexington, Mass.: Heath, 1974.

Andersen, Margaret. "Corporate Wives: Longing for Liberation or Satisfied with the Status Quo?" *Urban Life* 10 (1981):311–327.

———. Review of *Street Woman*, by Eleanor Miller. In *Gender & Society* 2 (1988):118–119.

———. *Thinking about Women: Sociological and Feminist Perspectives*. New York: Macmillan, 1983.

Anderson, Bonnie S. and Zinsser, Judith P. *A History of Their Own: Women in Europe from Prehistory to the Present*. Vol. 2. New York: Harper & Row, 1988.

Anderson, Kathryn; Armitage, Susan; Jack, Dana; and Wittmer, Judith. "Beginning Where We Are: Feminist Methodology in Oral History." *Oral History Review* 57 (1987): 103–127.

Anderson, Nels. *The Hobo*. Chicago: University of Chicago Press, 1923.

Andre, Rae. "Evaluating Homemaker's Quality of Working Life: Establishing Criteria of Quality." Paper presented at the Annual Conference of the Association for Women in Psychology, 1981.

———. "Multi-cultural Research: Developing a Participative Methodology for Cross-Cultural

Psychology." Paper presented at the Annual Convention of the International Council of Psychologists, 1979.

Apfel, Roberta J. and Fisher, Susan. *To Do No Harm: DES and the Dilemmas of Modern Medicine*. New Haven, Conn.: Yale University Press, 1984.

Aptheker, Bettina. *Tapestries of Life: Women's Work, Women's Consciousness, and the Meaning of Daily Experience*. Amherst, Mass.: University of Massachusetts Press, 1989.

Aracana, Judith. *Our Mothers' Daughters*. Berkeley, Calif.: Shameless Hussy Press, 1979.

Ardis, Ann L. "Beatrice Webb's Romance with Ethnography." *Women's Studies* 18 (1990): 233–248.

Arendell, Terry. *Mothers and Divorce: Legal, Economic, and Social Dilemmas*. Berkeley: University of California Press, 1986.

Arms, Suzanne. *Immaculate Deception: A New Look at Women and Childbirth*. New York: Bantam Books, 1975.

Aronoff, Joel and Crano, William. "A Re-examination of the Cross-cultural Principles of Task Segregation and Sex Role Differentiation in the Family." *American Sociological Review* 40 (1975):12–20.

Asher, Carol; deSalvo, Louise; and Ruddick, Sara, eds. *Between Women: Biographers, Novelists, Critics, Teachers and Artists Write about Their Work on Women*. Boston: Beacon Press, 1984.

Ashworth, Georgina, ed. *The UN Decade for Women: An International Evaluation*, Special Issue of *Women's Studies International Forum* 8 (1985).

Auster, Carol. "Manuals for Socialization: Examples from Girl Scout Handbooks 1913– 1984." In *Innovative Sources and Uses of Qualitative Data*, edited by Meredith Gould. Special Issue of *Qualitative Sociology* 8 (1985):359–367.

Awe, B. "Reflections on the Conference on Women and Development, I." *Signs: Journal of Women in Culture and Society* 3 (1977):314–316.

Babb, Jewell and Taylor, Pat Ellis. *Border Healing Woman: The Story of Jewell Babb as Told to Pat Ellis Taylor*. Austin, Tex.: University of Texas Press, 1981.

Babbie, Earl. *The Practice of Social Research*. 3rd ed. Belmont, Calif.: Wadsworth, 1983.

Bailey, Kenneth D. *Methods of Social Research*. 2d ed. New York: Free Press, 1982.

Baker, Patricia. "Doing Fieldwork in a Canadian Bank: Issues of Gender and Power." *Resources for Feminist Research/Documentation-sur-la-Recherche Feministe* 16 (1987):45–47.

Bannister, Robert C. *Jessie Bernard: The Making of a Feminist*. New Brunswick, N.J.: Rutgers University Press, 1991.

Bardwick, Judith; Douvan, Elizabeth; Horner, Matina; and Gutmann, David. *Feminine Personality and Conflict*. Belmont, Calif.: Brooks/Cole, 1970.

Barnett, Rosalind C. and Baruch, Grace K. *The Competent Woman: Perspectives on Development*. New York: Irvington, 1978.

Barrett, Susan. "Making 'Empowerment' Useful." Paper presented at the Annual Meeting of the Association for Women in Psychology, 1981.

Barry, Kathleen. *Female Sexual Slavery*. New York: Avon Books, 1979.

———; Bunch, Charlotte; and Castley, Shirley, eds. *International Feminism: Networking Against Female Sexual Slavery*. New York: The International Women's Tribune Centre, 1984.

Bart, Pauline B. "Depression in Middle-Aged Women." In *Woman in Sexist Society*, edited by Vivian Gornick and Barbara Moran. New York: New American Library, 1972.

————. "How I Lost My False Consciousness and Found Women's Liberation." Mimeographed. Undated.

————. "Psychotherapy, Sexism and Social Control: A Review of *Women and Madness.*" *Society* 11 (1974):95–98.

————. Review of Neil Malamuth and Edward Donnerstein, eds. *Pornography and Sexual Aggression.* Orlando, Fla.: Academic Press, 1984. In *Contemporary Sociology* 15 (1986):572–573.

————. "Seizing the Means of Reproduction: An Illegal Feminist Abortion Collective—How and Why it Worked." *Qualitative Sociology* 10 (1987):339–357.

————. "Sexism and Social Science: From the Gilded Cage to the Iron Cage, or, The Perils of Pauline." *Journal of Marriage and the Family* 33 (1971):734–745.

————. "Social Structure and Vocabularies of Discomfort: What Happened to Female Hysteria?" *Journal of Health and Social Behavior* 9 (1968):188–193.

————; Freeman, Linda; and Kimball, Peter. "The Different Worlds of Women and Men: Attitudes toward Pornography and Responses to *Not a Love Story*—A Film about Pornography." *Women's Studies International Forum* 8 (1985):307–322.

———— and O'Brien, Patricia. "Stopping Rape: Effective Avoidance Strategies." *Signs: Journal of Women in Culture and Society* 10 (1984):83–101.

———— and O'Brien, Patricia. *Stopping Rape: Successful Survival Strategies.* New York: Pergamon, 1985.

Baxter, Sandra and Lansing, Marjorie. *Women and Politics: The Visible Majority.* Ann Arbor, Mich.: University of Michigan Press, 1983.

Becker, Howard. "Social Observation and Social Case Studies." In *International Encyclopedia of the Social Sciences,* edited by David Sills. New York: Crowell Collier and Macmillan, 1968.

————; Geer, Blanche; Hughes, Everett; and Strauss, Anselm. *Boys in White.* Chicago: The University of Chicago Press, 1961.

Begley, Sharon. "Liberation in the Lab." *Newsweek,* Dec. 2, 1985.

Belenky, Mary; Clinchy, Blythe; Goldberger, Nancy; and Tarule, Jill. *Women's Ways of Knowing: The Development of Self, Voice and Mind.* New York: Basic Books, 1986.

Bell, Diane. *Daughters of the Dreaming.* North Sydney: George Allen & Unwin, 1983.

Bell, Susan E. "Becoming a Political Woman: The Reconstruction and Interpretation of Experience through Stories." In *Gender and Discourse: The Power of Talk,* edited by Alexandra Dumas Todd and Sue Fisher. Norwood, N.J.: Ablex, 1988.

Bell, Susan Groag. "Medieval Women Book Owners: Arbiters of Lay Piety and Ambassadors of Culture." *Signs: Journal of Women in Culture and Society* 7 (1982):742–768.

Bem, Sandra. "Probing the Promise of Androgyny." In *The Psychology of Women: Ongoing Debates,* edited by Mary Roth Walsh. New Haven, Conn.: Yale University Press, 1987.

———— and Bem, Daryl. "Case Study of a Nonconscious Ideology: Training the Woman to Know Her Place," in Daryl Bem, *Beliefs, Attitudes, and Human Affairs.* Belmont, Calif.: Brooks/Cole, 170.

Bender, Leslie. "From Gender Difference to Feminist Solidarity: Using Carol Gilligan and an Ethic of Care in Law." *Vermont Law Review* 15 (1990):1–30.

Beneria, Lourdes and Sen, Gita. "Accumulation, Reproduction, and Women's Role in Economic Development: Boserup Revisited." *Signs: Journal of Women in Culture and Society* 7 (1981):279–298.

Benjamin, Jessica. *Psychoanalysis, Feminism and the Problem of Domination.* New York: Pantheon, 1989.

Benokraitis, Nijole and Feagan, Joe. *Modern Sexism.* Englewood Cliffs, N.J.: Prentice Hall, 1986.

Berheide, Catherine White; Berk, Sarah F.; and Berk, Richard A. "Household Work in the Suburbs: The Job and Its Participants." *Pacific Sociological Review* 19 (1976):491–518.

Berk, Sarah Fenstermaker. *The Gender Factory: The Apportionment of Work in American Households.* New York: Plenum Press, 1985.

Berlin, Sharon B. "Dichotomous and Complex Thinking." *Social Service Review* 64 (1990):46–59.

Bernard, Hollinger F., ed. *Outside the Magic Circle: The Autobiography of Virginia Foster Durr.* University, Ala.: University of Alabama Press, 1985.

Bernard, Jessie. *The Female World.* New York: Free Press, 1981.

———. *The Female World from a Global Perspective.* Bloomington, Ind.: Indiana University Press, 1987.

———. *The Future of Marriage.* 2d ed. New Haven, Conn.: Yale University Press, 1982.

———. "My Four Revolutions: An Autobiographical History of the ASA." *American Journal of Sociology* 78 (1973):773–791.

———. "Reviewing the Impact of Women's Studies on Sociology." In *The Impact of Feminist Research in the Academy,* edited by Christie Farnham. Bloomington, Ind.: Indiana University Press, 1987.

———. *The Sex Game.* New York: Atheneum, 1972.

Bernard, Virginia. "Cotton Mather's 'Most Unhappy Wife': Reflections on the Use of Historical Evidence." *The New England Quarterly* 60 (1987):341–362.

Bernardez, Teresa. "United States." In *Creative Women in Changing Societies: A Quest for Alternatives,* edited by Torill Stockland, Mallica Vajrathon, and Davidson Nicol. Dobbs Ferry, New York: Transnational Publishers, Inc., 1982.

Bernstein, Deborah. *The Struggle for Equality: Urban Women Workers in Prestate Israeli Society.* New York: Praeger, 1987.

Berry, Mary Frances. *Why ERA Failed: Politics, Women's Rights and the Amending Process of the Constitution.* Bloomington, Ind.: Indiana University Press, 1986.

Bertaux, D., ed. *Biography and Society: The Life History Approach in the Social Sciences.* Beverly Hills, Calif.: Sage, 1981.

Billson, Janet Mancini. "The Progressive Verification Method: Toward a Feminist Methodology for Studying Women Cross-Culturally." *Women's Studies International Forum* 14 (1991):201–208.

Black, Naomi. *Social Feminism.* Ithaca, New York: Cornell University Press, 1989.

Blau, Francine D. "On the Role of Values in Feminist Scholarship." *Signs: Journal of Women in Culture and Society* 3 (1981):538–540.

Blauner, Robert and Wellman, David. "Toward the Decolonization of Social Research." In *The Death of White Sociology,* edited by Joyce A. Ladner. New York: Vintage, 1973.

Bleier, Ruth, ed. *Science and Gender: A Critique of Biology and its Theories on Women.* New York: Pergamon, 1984.

———, ed. *Feminist Approaches to Science.* New York: Pergamon, 1986.

Blum, Lawrence. "Gilligan and Kohlberg: Implications for Moral Theory." *Ethics* 98 (1988):472–491.

Blum, Linda. "Feminism and the Mass Media: A Case Study of *The Women's Room* as Novel and Television Film." *Berkeley Journal of Sociology* 27 (1982):1–24.

Blumberg, Rae Lesser. "A General Theory of Gender Stratification." In *Sociological Theory 1984,* edited by American Sociological Association. San Francisco: Jossey-Bass, 1984.

Blumenthal, Amy; Thompson, Martha; and Young, Grace. "Chicago Women's Uprising, 1981–1983." Paper presented at the Midwest Sociological Society Meetings, 1986.

Blythe, Ronald. *Akenfield: Portrait of an English Village. New York:* Dell, 1973.

Bodemann, Y. M. "The Fulfillment of Fieldwork in Marxist Praxis." *Dialectical Anthropology* 4 (1979):155–161.

Bologh, Roslyn Wallach. "Feminist Social Theorizing and Moral Reasoning: On Difference and Dialectic." In *Sociological Theory, 1984,* edited by the American Sociological Association. San Francisco: Jossey-Bass, 1984.

————. "Gender, Repression and Liberation: An Alternative Feminist Theory, Method and Politics." Paper presented at the Annual Meeting of the American Sociological Association, 1985.

Bombyk, Marti; Bricker-Jenkins, Mary; and Wedenoja, Marilyn. "Reclaiming Our Profession through Feminist Research: Some Methodological Issues in the Feminist Practice Project." Paper presented at the Annual Program Meeting of the Council on Social Work Education, 1985.

Bonacich, P. and Light, J. "Laboratory Experimentation in Sociology." In *Annual Review of Sociology,* edited by Ralph Turner et al. 4 (1978):145–170.

Bonnar, Deanne. "When the Bough Breaks: A Feminist Analysis of Income Maintenance Strategies for Female-Based Households." Ph.D. dissertation, Brandeis University, 1985.

Booth, Charles. *Life and Labour of the People in London.* New York: AMS Press, 1970.

Bordo, Susan. "The Cartesian Masculinization of Thought." *Signs: Journal of Women in Culture and Society* 11 (1986):439–455.

Borg, Susan and Lasker, Judith. *When Pregnancy Fails: Families Coping with Miscarriage, Stillbirth, and Infant Death.* Boston: Beacon Press, 1981.

Boserup, Ester. *Women's Role in Economic Development.* London: George Allen & Unwin, 1970.

The Boston Women's Health Book Collective. *Our Bodies, OurSelves: A Book by and for Women.* New York: Simon & Schuster, 1971, 1973, 1976.

————. The New *Our Bodies, OurSelves.* New York: Simon & Schuster, 1984.

Boston Lesbian Psychologies Collective, eds. *Lesbian Psychologies.* Chicago: University of Illinois Press, 1987.

Boukydis, Kathleen McGuire. "Existential/Phenomenology as a Philosophical Base for a Feminist Psychology." Paper presented at the Annual Meeting of the Association for Women in Psychology, 1981.

Boulding, Elise. *Women in the Twentieth Century World.* New York: Wiley, 1977.

Bowles, Gloria and Duelli Klein, Renate, eds. *Theories of Women's Studies.* Boston: Routledge & Kegan Paul, 1983.

Briggs, Jean L. *Never in Anger: Portrait of an Eskimo Family.* Cambridge: Harvard University Press, 1970.

Bristow, Ann R. and Esper, Jody A. "A Feminist Research Ethos." In *A Feminist Ethic for Social Science Research,* edited by The Nebraska Sociological Feminist Collective. Lewiston, N.Y.: The Edwin Mellen Press, 1988.

Broder, Sherri. "Child Care or Child Neglect? Baby Farming in Late-nineteenth-century Philadelphia." *Gender & Society* 2 (1988):128–148.

Brodsky, Annette. "A Decade of Feminist Influence on Psychotherapy." *Psychology of Women Quarterly* 4 (1980):331–344.

——. "Sex, Race & Class Issues in Psychotherapy Research." Paper presented at the American Psychological Association, 1982.

—— and Hare-Mustin, Rachel, eds. *Women and Psychotherapy: An Assessment of Research and Practice.* New York: Guilford Press, 1980.

Bronstein, Audrey. *The Triple Struggle: Latin American Peasant Women.* Boston: South End Press, 1982.

Broschart, Kay Richards. "In Search of Our Mothers' Gardens: The Process and Consequences of Discovering Our Foremothers." Paper presented at the Annual Meeting of the American Sociological Association and Sociologists for Women in Society, 1986.

Broverman, Inge; Broverman, Donald; Clarkson, Frank; Rosenkrantz, Paul; and Vogel, Susan. "Sex-role Stereotypes and Clinical Judgments of Mental Health." *Journal of Counseling and Clinical Psychology* 34 (1970):1–7.

Brown, Daniel. "Female Orgasm and Sexual Inadequacy." Reprinted in *Human Sexual Response,* edited by Edward Brecher and Ruth Brecher. New York: New American Library, 1966.

Brown, Judith C. *Immodest Acts: The Life of a Lesbian Nun in Renaissance Italy.* New York: Oxford University Press, 1986.

Brown, Karen McCarthy. "On Feminist Methodology." *Journal of Feminist Studies in Religion* 1 (1985):76–79.

Browne, Joy. "Fieldwork for Fun and Profit." In *The Research Experience,* edited by M. Patricia Golden. Itasca, Ill.: F. E. Peacock, 1976.

Brownmiller, Susan. *Against Our Will: Men, Women and Rape.* New York: Bantam Books, 1975.

Brush, Lisa D. "Violent Acts and Injurious Outcomes in Married Couples: Methodological Issues in the National Survey of Families and Households." *Gender & Society* 4 (1990):56–67.

Buechler, Hans. "The Social Position of an Ethnographer in the Field." In *Stress and Response in Fieldwork,* edited by Frances Henry and Satish Saberwal. New York: Holt, Rinehart and Winston, 1969.

Bulkin, Elly. "Racism and Writing: Some Implications for White Lesbian Critics." *Sinister Wisdom* 7 (1980):3–22.

Bunch, Charlotte. "UN World Conference in Nairobi: A View from the West." In *Passionate Politics: Feminist Theory in Action,* edited by Charlotte Bunch. New York: St. Martin's Press, 1987.

Bunster, Ximena. "Talking Pictures: Field Method and Visual Mode." *Signs: Journal of Women in Culture and Society* 2 (1977):278–293.

Burgess, Robert, ed. *Field Research: A Sourcebook and Field Manual.* London: George Allen & Unwin, 1982.

Burgos-Debray, E., ed. *I, 'Rigoberta Menchu': An Indian Woman in Guatemala.* Translated by A. Wright. London: Verso, 1984.

Burke, Carolyn Greenstein. "Report from Paris: Women's Writing and the Women's Movement." *Signs: Journal of Women in Culture and Society* 3 (1978):843–855.

Burnett, Cathleen. "Participant Observation in a Male Setting: Observing in the Courtroom." Paper presented at the Annual Meeting of the National Women's Studies Association, 1983.

—— and Danner, Mona J. E. "Publishing Field Research: Can We Ignore Gender?" Mimeographed. University of Missouri, Kansas City. Undated.

Bushman, Claudia. *A Good Poor Man's Wife: Being a Chronicle of Harriet Hanson Robinson and Her Family in Nineteenth-Century New England.* Hanover, N.H.: University Press of New England, 1981.

Buss, Fran Leeper. *Dignity: Lower Income Women Tell of Their Lives and Struggles.* Ann Arbor, Mich.: University of Michigan Press, 1985.

Buss, Helen. "The Different Voice of Canadian Feminist Autobiographers." *Biography* 13 (1990):154–167.

Byrd, Anne. "A Qualitative Analysis of the Decision to Remarry Using Gilligan's Ethic of Care." *Journal of Divorce* 11 (1988):87–97.

Caffrey, Margaret M. *Ruth Benedict: Stranger in This Land.* Austin, Tex.: University of Texas Press, 1989.

Callahan, Joan Thompson. "Upward Mobility from the Inside: A Phenomenological Study of Female Psychologists from Working-Class Backgrounds." Ph.D. dissertation, Massachusetts School of Professional Psychology, 1983.

Campbell, Helen. "Both Sides of the Sea." In *Prisoners of Poverty Abroad.* Boston: Roberts Brothers, 1890.

———. *Darkness and Daylight.* Hartford, Conn.: 1892.

———. *Prisoners of Poverty: Women Wage-Workers, Their Trades and Their Lives.* 1883. New York: Garrett Press, 1970.

Campbell, Julie; Levine, Irma; and Page, Jane. "Women in Midstream." In *Alternative Social Services for Women,* edited by Naomi Gottlieb. New York: Columbia University Press, 1980.

Campbell, Mary Ann. "Creating Feminist Sociology," *SWS Network* 12 (1982):23–24.

Campbell, Patricia. "The Impact of Societal Biases on Research Methods." Paper presented at the Sixth Annual Conference on Research on Women and Education, February 1981.

Cancian, Francesca. "Participatory Research and Working Women: Democratizing the Production of Knowledge." Paper presented at the Annual Meeting of the American Sociological Association, 1989.

——— and Gordon, Steven. "Changing Emotion Norms in Marriage: Love and Anger in U.S. Women's Magazines Since 1900." *Gender & Society* 2 (1988):308–342.

Cannon, Lynn Weber; Higginbotham, Elizabeth; and Leung, Marianne L. A. "Race and Class Bias in Qualitative Research on Women." *Gender & Society* 2 (1988):449–463.

Capitol: Woman. A Newsletter of the House Committee on Constitutional Revision and Women's Rights 6 (1982).

Caplan, Paula J. and Hall-McCorquodale, Ian. "Mother-Blaming in Major Clinical Journals." *American Journal of Orthopsychiatry* 55 (1985):345–353.

Caplan, T. A. "The Adaptation of a Traditional Structure for Non-Traditional Aims: A Case Study." *Research on the Psychology of Woman* 9 (1980):11–12.

Carlson, Earl and Carlson, Rae. "Male and Female Subjects in Personality Research." *Journal of Abnormal and Social Psychology* 61 (1960):482–483.

Carlson, Rae. "Understanding Women: Implications for Personality Theory and Research." *Journal of Social Issues* 28 (1972):17–32.

Carroll, Berenice, ed. *Liberating Women's History: Theoretical and Critical Essays.* Chicago: University of Illinois Press, 1976.

Casal, L. "Reflections on the Conference on Women and Development, II." *Signs: Journal of Women in Culture and Society* 3 (1977):317–319.

Cassedy, Ellen and Nussbaum, Karen. *9 to 5: The Working Woman's Guide to Office Survival.* New York: Penguin, 1983.

Cesara, Manda. *Reflections of a Woman Anthropologist: No Hiding Place*. New York: Academic Press, 1982.

Chally, Pamela. "Theory Derivation in Moral Development." *Nursing & Health Care* 11 (1990):302–313.

Chancer, Lynn. "Abortion without Apology." In *From Abortion to Reproductive Freedom: Transforming a Movement,* edited by Marlene Gerber Fried. Boston: South End Press, 1990.

Charles, Nickie and Kerr, Marion. *Women, Food and Families*. Manchester and New York: Manchester University Press, 1988.

Charmaz, Kathy. "Intensive Interviewing." Mimeographed. Rohnert Park, Calif.: Gerontology Program, Sonoma State University, 1986.

Chertos, Cynthia. "In Praise of Useable Research." In *Ingredients for Women's Employment Policy,* edited by Christine Bose and Glenna Spitze. Albany: State University of N.Y. Press, 1987.

Chesler, Phyllis. *With Child: A Diary of Motherhood*. New York: Crowell, 1979.

———. *Women & Madness*. New York: Avon, 1972.

Chodorow, Nancy. *The Reproduction of Mothering: Psychoanalysis and the Sociology of Gender*. Berkeley, Calif.: University of California Press, 1978.

——— and Contratto, Susan. "The Fantasy of the Perfect Mother." In *Rethinking the Family: Some Feminist Questions,* edited by Barrie Thorne, with Marilyn Yalom. New York: Longman, 1982.

Christ, Carol P. *Diving Deep and Surfacing: Women Writers on Spiritual Quest*. Boston: Beacon Press, 1980.

Clinton, Catherine. *The Other Civil War: American Women in the Nineteenth Century*. New York: Hill and Wang, 1984.

Cock, Jacklyn. "Trapped Workers: Constraints and Contradictions Experienced by Black Women in Contemporary South Africa." *Women's Studies International Forum* 10 (1987):133–140.

Cohen, Marcia. *The Sisterhood: The Inside Story of the Women's Movement and the Leaders Who Made it Happen*. New York: Fawcett Columbine, 1988.

Colby, Anne and Damon, William. "Listening to a Different Voice: A Review of Gilligan's *In a Different Voice*." *Merrill-Palmer Quarterly* 29 (1983):473–481.

Collard, Andrée. *Rape of the Wild: Man's Violence against Animals and the Earth*. Bloomington, Ind.: Indiana University Press, 1989.

Collins, Patricia Hill. "Learning from the Outsider Within." In *Beyond Methodology: Feminist Scholarship as Lived Research,* edited by Mary Margaret Fonow and Judith A. Cook. Bloomington, Ind.: Indiana University Press, 1991.

Collmann, Jeff. " 'I'm Proper Number One Fighter, Me': Aborigines, Gender, and Bureaucracy in Central Australia." *Gender & Society* 2 (1988):9–23.

Colson, Elizabeth. "The Reordering of Experience: Anthropological Involvement with Time." *Journal of Anthropological Research* 40 (1984):1–13.

Combahee River Collective. "Why did they Die? A Document of Black Feminism." *Radical America* 13 (1979):41–50.

Committee on the Status of Women in Sociology. "Sexist Biases in Sociological Research: Problems and Issues." *Footnotes* (January 1980).

Condor, Susan. "Sex Role Beliefs and 'Traditional' Women: Feminist and Intergroup Perspectives." In *Feminist Social Psychology,* edited by Sue Wilkinson. Philadelphia: Open University Press, 1986.

Condry, John and Dyer, Sharon. "Fear of Success: Attribution of Cause to the Victim." *Journal of Social Issues* 32 (1976):63–83.

Connell, N. and Wilson, C., eds. *Rape: The First Sourcebook for Women by NY Radical Feminists.* New York: Plume, 1974.

Connors, Denise Donnell. "A Continuum of Researcher–Participant Relationships: An Analysis and Critique." *Advances in Nursing Science* 10 (1988):32–42.

———. " 'I've Always had Everything I've Wanted, but I Never Wanted Very Much': An Experiential Analysis of Irish-American Working Class Women in their Nineties." Ph.D. dissertation, Brandeis University, 1986.

Contratto, Susan. "Mother: Social Sculptor and Trustee of the Faith." In *In the Shadow of the Past: Psychology Portrays the Sexes,* edited by Miriam Lewin. New York: Columbia University Press, 1984.

Cook, Blanche Wiesen, ed. *Crystal Eastman: On Women & Revolution.* New York: Oxford University Press, 1978.

Cook, Judith and Fonow, Mary Margaret. "Knowledge and Women's Interests: Feminist Methodology in the Field of Sociology." *Sociological Inquiry* 56 (1986):2–29.

Cooper, Mary Carolyn. "Gilligan's Different Voice: A Perspective for Nursing." *Journal of Professional Nursing* 5 (1989):10–18.

Corea, Gena. *The Mother Machine: Reproductive Technologies from Artificial Insemination to Artificial Wombs.* New York: Harper & Row, 1985.

Coser, Lewis A. "Georg Simmel's Neglected Contributions to the Sociology of Women." *Signs: Journal of Women in Culture and Society* 2 (1977):872–873.

Costa, Mariarosa Della. *Women and the Subversion of the Community.* San Leandro, Calif.: Bristol, 1972.

Costin, Lela B. *Two Sisters for Social Justice: A Biography of Grace and Edith Abbott.* Chicago: University of Illinois Press, 1983.

Cott, Nancy F. *The Bonds of Womanhood: 'Woman's Sphere' in New England, 1780–1835.* New Haven, Conn.: Yale University Press, 1977.

———. "Eighteenth Century Family and Social Life Revealed in Massachusetts Divorce Records." In *A Heritage of Her Own,* edited by Nancy Cott and Elizabeth Pleck. New York: Simon & Schuster, 1979.

"Rebecca Courser: Profile of a Service Award Winner." *The News Messenger,* July 25, 1990.

Court, John. "Sex and Violence: A Ripple Effect." In *Pornography and Sexual Aggression,* edited by Neil M. Malamuth and Edward Donnerstein. Orlando, Fla.: Academic Press, 1984.

Cousineau, Paige. "The Support Function and Social Change—A Feminist Case History." *Women's Studies International Forum* 8 (1985):137–144.

Cox, Sue. *Female Psychology: The Emerging Self.* Chicago: Science Research Associates, 1976.

Crawford, Mary. "Agreeing to Differ: Feminist Epistemologies and Women's Ways of Knowing." In *Gender and Thought: Psychological Perspectives,* edited by Mary Crawford and Margaret Gentry. New York: Springer-Verlag, 1989.

Cross, Elisabeth J. "Women in Rural Production and Reproduction in the Soviet Union, China, Cuba and Tanzania: Case Studies" and "Women in Rural Production and Reproduction in the Soviet Union, China, Cuba, and Tanzania: Socialist Development Experiences." *Signs: Journal of Women in Culture and Society* 7 (1981):361–399.

Culbert, Samuel A. "Consciousness-raising: A Five Stage Model for Social and Organization Change." In *Theories of Group Processes,* edited by Cary L. Cooper. New York: John Wiley, 1975.

Culler, Jonathan. "Reading as a Woman." In *On Deconstruction,* edited by Jonathan Culler. Ithaca, N.Y.: Cornell University Press, 1982.

Dabrowski, Irene. "Developmental Job Patterns of Working-Class Women." *Qualitative Sociology* 6 (1983):29–50.

Daly, Kathleen. "Rethinking Judicial Paternalism: Gender, Work-Family Relations and Sentencing." *Gender & Society* 3 (1989):9–36.

Daly, Mary. *Beyond God the Father: Toward a Philosophy of Women's Liberation.* Boston: Beacon Press, 1973.

———. *Gyn/Ecology: The Metaethics of Radical Feminism.* Boston: Beacon Press, 1978.

Daniels, Arlene Kaplan. *Invisible Careers: Civic Leaders From the Volunteer World.* Chicago: The University of Chicago Press, 1988.

———. [Ms. Manners]. *SWS Network* 5 (1987):18–19.

———. "The Low-Caste Stranger in Social Research." In *Ethics, Politics, and Social Research,* edited by Gideon Sjoberg. Cambridge, Mass.: Schenkman, 1967.

———. "Self-Deception and Self-Discovery in Fieldwork." *Qualitative Sociology* 6 (1983):195–214.

Datan, Nancy. "Androgyny and the Life Cycle: The Bacchae of Euripides." In *Representations: Social Constructions of Gender,* edited by Rhoda K. Unger. Amityville, N.Y.: Baywood, 1989.

———. "Illness and Imagery: Feminist Cognition, Socialization, and Gender Identity." In *Gender and Thought: Psychological Perspectives,* edited by Mary Crawford and Margaret Gentry. New York: Springer-Verlag, 1989.

Davidman, Lynn. "Gender and Religious Experience." Paper presented at the Annual Meeting of the American Sociological Association, August 1988.

———. "Sex and the Modern Jewish Woman: An Overview." In *Sex and the Modern Jewish Woman: An Annotated Bibliography,* edited by Joan Brewer. Fresh Meadows, N.Y.: Biblio Press, 1986.

———. *Tradition in a Rootless World: Women Turn to Orthodox Judaism.* Berkeley: University of California Press, 1991.

de Jong, Mathilde. "Feminist Research Methodology." Mimeographed. University College, Cardiff, Wales. Undated.

Deegan, Mary Jo. "A Feminist Frame Analysis of 'Star Trek'." *Free Inquiry in Creative Sociology* 11 (1983):182–188.

———. "Having Fun, Killing Time, Getting a Deal." In *American Ritual Dreams: Social Rules and Cultural Meanings,* edited by Mary Jo Deegan. Westport, Conn.: Greenwood Press, 1989.

———. *Jane Addams and the Men of the Chicago School, 1892–1918.* New Brunswick, N.J.: Transaction Books, 1988.

———. "Frances A. Kellor." In *Women in Sociology: A Bio–bibliographic Sourcebook,* edited by Mary Jo Deegan. Westport, Conn.: Greenwood Press, 1991.

——— "Multiple Minority Groups: A Case Study of Physically Disabled Women." In *Women and Disability: The Double Handicap,* edited by Mary Jo Deegan and Nancy Brooks. New Brunswick, N.J.: Transaction Books, 1985.

———. "A Rose is not a Rosa, is not a Roseann: The Many Names of Mary Elizabeth Burroughs Roberts Smith Coolidge." In *The New Sociobiography,* edited by Judy Long. Manuscript.

———. "Sociology and Conviviality: A Conversation with Ellenhorn on Convivial Sociology." *Humanity and Society* 13 (1989):85–88.

———. "Transcending a Patriarchal Past: Teaching the History of Women in Sociology." *Teaching Sociology* 16 (1988):141–150.

———, ed. *Women in Sociology: A Bio-Bibliographic Sourcebook.* Westport, Conn.: Greenwood Press, 1991.

——— and Hill, Michael R. "The Presentation of the City in Fat-Letter Postcards." In *American Ritual Dramas: Social Rules and Cultural Meanings,* edited by Mary Jo Deegan. Westport, Conn.: Greenwood Press, 1989.

——— and Hill, Michael R., eds. *Women and Symbolic Interaction.* Winchester, Mass.: Allen & Unwin, 1987.

——— and Stein, Michael C. "Pornography as a Strip and a Frame." *Sociological Symposium* 20 (1977):27–44.

Deere, Carmen Diana and de Leal, Magdalena Leon. *Rural Women and State Policy: Feminist Perspectives on Latin American Agricultural Development.* Boulder, Colo.: Westview Press, 1987.

———. "Peasant Production, Proletarianization, and the Sexual Division of Labor in the Andes." *Signs: Journal of Women in Culture and Society* 7 (1981):338–360.

Degler, Carl. *At Odds: Women and the Family in America From the Revolution to the Present.* New York: Oxford University Press, 1980.

Delamont, Sara. *Knowledgeable Women: Structuralism and the Reproduction of Elites.* London and New York: Routledge, 1989.

Delphy, Christine. "Women in Stratification Studies." In *Doing Feminist Research,* edited by Helen Roberts. Boston: Routledge & Kegan Paul, 1981.

Demetrakopoulos, Stephanie. *Listening to our Bodies: The Rebirth of Feminine Wisdom.* Boston: Beacon Press, 1983.

Depner, Charlene. "Toward the Further Development of Feminist Psychology." Paper presented at the Annual Meeting of the Association for Women in Psychology, 1981.

DeVault, Marjorie L. "Doing Housework: Feeding and Family Life." In *Families and Work: Toward Reconceptualization,* edited by Naomi Gerstel and Harriet E. Gross. Philadelphia: Temple University Press, 1987.

———. Review of Barbara Richardson and Jeana Wirtenberg, eds. *Sex Role Research: Measuring Social Change.* New York: Praeger, 1983. In *Contemporary Sociology* 14 (1985):481–482.

———. "Talking and Listening from Women's Standpoint: Feminist Strategies for Analyzing Interview Data." Paper presented at the Annual Meeting of the Society for the Study of Symbolic Interaction, August 1986.

———. "Talking and Listening from Women's Standpoint: Feminist Strategies for Interviewing and Analysis." *Social Problems* 37 (1990):701–721.

———. "What Counts as Feminist Ethnography?" Paper presented at Exploring New Frontiers: Qualitative Research Conference, York University, Toronto, 1990.

———. "Women's Talk: Feminist Strategies for Analyzing Research Interviews." *Women and Language* 10 (1987):33–36.

Diamond, Arlyn and Edwards, Lee, eds. *The Authority of Experience: Essays in Feminist Criticism.* Amherst, Mass: University of Massachusetts Press, 1977.

DiIorio, Judith. "Being and Becoming Coupled: The Emergence of Female Subordination in Heterosexual Relationships." In *Gender in Intimate Relationships,* edited by Barbara J. Risman and Pepper Schwartz. Belmont, Calif.: Wadsworth Press, 1989.

———. "Feminism, Gender, and the Ethnographic Study of Sport." *Arena: The Institute for Sport and Social Analysis* 13 (1989):49–60.

———. "Feminist Fieldwork in a Masculinist Setting: Personal Problems and Methodological Issues." Paper presented at the North Central Sociological Association Meetings, 1982.

———. "Sex, Glorious Sex: The Social Construction of Masculine Sexuality in a Youth Group." In *Feminist Frontiers II: Rethinking Sex, Gender and Society,* edited by Laurel Richardson and Verta Taylor. 2d ed., New York: Random House, 1989.

————. "Toward a Phenomenological Feminism: A Critique of Gender Role Research." Paper presented at the Annual Meeting of the National Women's Studies Association, 1980.

Dill, Bonnie Thornton. "The Dialectics of Black Womanhood." *Signs: Journal of Women in Culture and Society* 4 (1979):543–555.

Diner, Hasia R. *Erin's Daughters in America: Irish Immigrant Women in the Nineteenth Century.* Baltimore: Johns Hopkins University Press, 1983.

Dinnerstein, Dorothy. *The Mermaid and the Minotaur: Sexual Arrangements and Human Malaise.* New York: Harper & Row, 1976.

Dixon, Elizabeth and Mink, James. *Oral History at Arrowhead: Proceedings of the First National Colloquium on Oral History.* Los Angeles: The Oral History Association, 1969.

Dominick, Joseph. "The Portrayal of Women in Prime Time, 1953–1977." *Sex Roles* 5 (1979):405–411.

Donnerstein, Edward; Linz, Daniel; and Penrod, Steven. *The Question of Pornography: Research Findings and Policy Implications.* New York: Free Press, 1987.

Dorn, Pamela. "Gender and Personhood: Turkish Jewish Proverbs and the Politics of Reputation." *Women's Studies International Forum* 9 (1986):295–301.

Dowrick, Stephanie and Grundberg, Sibyl, eds. *Why Children?* New York: Harcourt Brace Jovanovich, 1980.

Drexler, Abigail. "Men and Their Coursework." Mimeographed. Brandeis University, Department of Sociology, 1990.

DuBois, Barbara. "Passionate Scholarship: Notes on Values, Knowing and Method in Feminist Social Science." In *Theories of Women's Studies,* edited by Gloria Bowles and Renate Duelli Klein. Boston: Routledge & Kegan Paul, 1983.

DuBois, Ellen; Kelly, Gail; Kennedy, Elizabeth; Korsmeyer, Carolyn; and Robinson, Lillian. *Feminist Scholarship: Kindling in the Groves of Academe.* Chicago: University of Illinois Press, 1985.

Duffy, A. "Feminist Methodology in Sociology: Unresolved Issues of Context, Content and Power." Paper presented at the Annual Meeting of the American Sociological Association, 1991.

DuPlessis, Rachel Blau. *Writing Beyond the Ending: Narrative Strategies of Twentieth-Century Women Writers.* Bloomington, Ind.: Indiana University Press, 1985.

Durkheim, Emile. *Rules of Sociological Method.* 1895. Translated by Sarah A. Solovay and John Mueller. Edited by George Catlin. New York: Free Press, 1966.

————. *Suicide: A Study in Sociology.* Translated by John Spaulding and George Simpson. Edited by George Simpson. New York: Free Press, 1951.

Duster, Alfreda, ed. *Crusade for Justice: The Autobiography of Ida B. Wells.* Chicago: The University of Chicago Press, 1970.

Dworkin, Andrea. "Gynocide: Chinese Footbinding." In *Women Hating,* edited by Andrea Dworkin. New York: E. P. Dutton, 1974.

————. *Pornography: Men Possessing Women.* New York: Perigee, 1981.

Dziech, Billie Wright and Weiner, Linda. *The Leacherous Professor: Sexual Harassment on Campus.* Boston: Beacon, 1984.

Eagly, Alice. "Sex Differences in Influenceability." *Psychological Bulletin* 85 (1978):86–116.

Easterday, Louis; Papademas, Diana; Schorr, Laura; and Valentine, Catherine. "The Making of a Female Researcher: Role Problems in Fieldwork." *Urban Life* 6 (1977):333–348.

Eastman, Crystal. *Work Accidents and the Law.* 1910. New York: Arno Press, 1970.

————. "Work-Accidents and Employers' Liability." Reprinted in *Crystal Eastman: On*

Women & Revolution, edited by Blanche Wiesen Cook. New York: Oxford University Press, 1978.

Eaton, Mary. *Justice for Women? Family, Court and Social Control.* Philadelphia: Open University Press, 1986.

Eckert, Kevin. "Ethnographic Research on Aging." In *Qualitative Gerontology,* edited by Shulamit Reinharz and Graham Rowles. New York: Springer, 1988.

Eckhardt, Celia. "Fanny Wright: The Woman Who Made the Myth." Paper presented at Conference on "Autobiographies, Biographies and Life Histories of Women: Interdisciplinary Perspectives." University of Minnesota, May 23, 1986.

———— *Fanny Wright: Rebel in America.* Cambridge: Harvard University Press, 1984.

Editorial, "Feminism and Film: Critical Approaches." *Camera Obscura* 1 (1978):3–10.

Ehrenreich, Barbara and English, Deirdre. *For Her Own Good: 150 Years of the Experts' Advice to Women.* Garden City, N.Y.: Anchor Press, 1978.

Ehrlich, Carol. *The Conditions of Feminist Research.* Baltimore: Research Group One, Report No. 21, February 1976.

Ehrlich, Howard. *Selected Differences in the Life Chances of Men and Women in the United States.* Baltimore: Research Group One, Report No. 13, 1975.

————; Sokoloff, Natalie; Pincus, Fred; and Ehrlich, Carol. *Women and Men: A Socio-economic Factbook.* Baltimore: Vacant Lots Press, 1975.

Eichler, Margrit. "And the Work Never Ends: Contributions of Feminist Approaches to Canadian Anglophone Sociology." *Canadian Review of Sociology and Anthropology* 22 (1985):619–644.

————. *The Double Standard: A Feminist Critique of Feminist Social Science.* London: Croom Helm, 1980.

————. *Nonsexist Research Methods: A Practical Guide.* Boston: Allen & Unwin, 1987.

————. "Power, Dependency, Love and the Sexual Division of Labour: A Critique of the Decision-making Approach to Family Power and an Alternative Approach. With an Appendix on Washing My Dirty Linen in Public." *Women's Studies International Quarterly* 4 (1981):201–219.

————. "The Relationship between Sexist, Non-Sexist, Woman-Centered and Feminist Research." Paper presented at the Annual Meeting of the American Sociological Association, 1983.

————. "The Relationship between Sexist, Nonsexist, Woman-Centered, and Feminist Research." In *Gender and Society: Creating a Canadian Woman's Sociology,* edited by Arlene Tigar McLaren. Toronto: Copp Clark Pitman, 1988.

———— and Lapointe, Jeanne. *On the Treatment of the Sexes in Research.* Ottawa, Canada: Social Sciences and Humanities Research Council of Canada, 1985.

Eisenberg, Sue and Micklow, Patricia. "The Assaulted Wife: 'Catch 22' Revisited." 1974. *Women's Rights Law Reporter,* 1976.

Eisenstein, Zillah. Comment on Matthews, Sarah H. "Rethinking Sociology from a Feminist Perspective." *The American Sociologist* 17 (1982):36.

El Saadawi, Nawal. *Woman at Point Zero.* London: Zed Books, 1983.

Ellis, Carolyn. *Fisher Folk: Two Communities on Chesapeake Bay.* Lexington, Ky.: The University Press of Kentucky, 1986.

Elshtain, Jean Bethke. *Public Man, Private Woman: Women in Social and Political Thought.* Princeton: N.J.: Princeton University Press, 1981.

Emerson, Robert, ed. *Contemporary Field Research: A Collection of Readings.* Boston: Little, Brown, 1983.

England, Paula and Farkas, George. *Households, Employment and Gender: A Social, Economic and Demographic View.* New York: Aldine, 1986.

Epstein, Cynthia Fuchs. "Positive Effects of the Multiple Negative: Explaining the Success of Black Professional Women." *American Journal of Sociology* 78 (1973):913–918.

―――. "Symbolic Segregation: Similarities and Differences in the Language and Non-Verbal Communication of Women and Men." *Sociological Forum* 1 (1986):27–45.

―――. *Women in Law.* New York: Basic Books, 1981.

―――. *Woman's Place: Options and Limits in Professional Careers.* Berkeley: University of California Press 1970.

Erikson, Kai. *Everything in Its Path: Destruction of Community in the Buffalo Creek Flood.* New York: Simon & Schuster, 1976.

Espin, Oliva. "Issues of Identity in the Psychology of Latina Lesbians." In *Lesbian Psychologies,* edited by the Boston Lesbian Psychologies Collective. Chicago: University of Illinois Press, 1987.

Estrich, Susan. *Real Rape.* Cambridge: Harvard University Press, 1987.

Ettore, Elizabeth M. *Lesbians, Women and Society.* London: Routledge & Kegan Paul, 1980.

Etzioni-Halevy, Eva and Illy, Ann. "Women in Parliament: Israel in a Comparative Perspective." Paper presented at the International Interdisciplinary Congress on Women, Haifa, Israel, 1981.

Evans, Richard J. *The Feminists: Women's Emancipation Movements in Europe, America and Australasia 1840–1920.* New York: Barnes and Noble, 1977.

Evans, Sara. *Personal Politics: The Roots of Women's Liberation in the Civil Rights Movement and the New Left.* New York: Alfred A. Knopf, 1979.

―――. "Towards a Useable Past: Feminism as History and Politics." Paper presented at the Women Making History: Women's Work, Women's Culture Conference. University of Illinois at Chicago, 1983.

Exley, JoElla Powell, ed. *Texas Tears and Texas Sunshine: Voices of Frontier Women.* University Station, Tex.: Texas A & M Press, 1985.

Exum, J. Cheryl. " 'Mother in Israel': A Familiar Figure Reconsidered." In *Feminist Interpretation of the Bible,* edited by Letty M. Russell. Philadelphia: Westminster, 1985.

Farganis, Sondra. "The Social Construction of Gender: The Turn to Fiction." In *Representations: Social Constructions of Gender,* edited by Rhoda K. Unger. Amityville, N.Y.: Baywood, 1989.

―――. "Social Theory and Feminist Theory: The Need for Dialogue." *Sociological Inquiry* 56 (1986):50–68.

Farran, Denise. "A Photograph of Marilyn Monroe." In *Feminist Research Processes,* edited by Feminist Research Seminar. University of Manchester, Department of Sociology, 1987.

Fee, Elizabeth. "A Feminist Critique of Scientific Objectivity." *Science for the People* 14 (1982):30–33.

Ferber, Marianne A. "Citations and Networking." *Gender & Society* 2 (1988):82–89.

Ferguson, Kathy E. *The Feminist Case Against Bureaucracy.* Philadelphia: Temple University Press, 1984.

―――. "Interpretation and Genealogy in Feminism." *Signs: Journal of Women in Culture and Society* 16 (1991):322–339.

Ferguson, Marilyn. *Forever Feminine, Women's Magazines and the Cult of Femininity.* London: Heinemann, 1983.

Ferraro, Kathleen. "Negotiating Trouble in a Battered Women's Shelter." *Urban Life* 12 (1983):287–306.

Fetterley, Judith. *The Resisting Reader: A Feminist Approach to American Fiction.* Bloomington, Ind.: Indiana University Press, 1978.

Fidell, L. S. "Empirical Verification of Sex Discrimination in Hiring Practices in Psychology." *American Pychologist* 25 (1970):1094–1097.

Fields, Mamie Garvin and Fields, Karen. *Lemon Swamp and Other Places: A Carolina Memoir.* New York: Free Press, 1985.

Fine, Michelle. "Contextualizing the Study of Social Injustice." In *Advances in Applied Social Psychology,* edited by Michael Saks and Leonard Saxe. Hillsdale, N.J.: Lawrence Erlbaum, 1985.

———. "Coping with Rape: Critical Perspectives on Consciousness." *Imagination, Cognition and Personality* 3 (1983–1984):249–267.

———. "Sexuality, Schooling, and Adolescent Females: The Missing Discourse of Desire." *Harvard Educational Review* 58 (1988):29–53.

———. "Women's Voices in the Research Relationship: Feminist Alternatives to 'Objectivity.' " Symposium presented at the Annual Meeting of the American Psychological Association, 1984.

——— and Gordon, Susan Merle. "Feminist Transformations of/Despite Psychology." In *Gender and Thought: Psychological Perspectives,* edited by Mary Crawford and Margaret Gentry. New York: Springer-Verlag, 1989.

Fiorenza, Elisabeth Schussler. *Bread Not Stone: The Challenge of Feminist Biblical Interpretation.* Boston: Beacon Press, 1985.

Fischer, Michael M. J. "Ethnicity and the Arts of Memory." In *Writing Culture: The Poetics and Politics of Ethnography,* edited by James Clifford and George Marcus. Berkeley: University of California Press, 1986.

Fishman, Laura T. *Women at the Wall: A Study of Prisoners' Wives Doing Time on the Outside.* Albany, N.Y.: State University of New York Press, 1990.

Fishman, Pamela. "Interaction: The Work Women Do." *Social Problems* 25 (1978):397–406.

———. "Interactional Shitwork." *Heresies* (May 1977):99–101.

Fitzpatrick, Ellen. *Endless Crusade: Women Social Scientists and Progressive Reform.* New York: Oxford University Press, 1990.

Flax, Jane. "The Conflict between Nurturance and Autonomy in Mother-Daughter Relationships and within Feminism." *Feminist Studies* 4 (1978):171–189.

———. *Thinking Fragments: Psychoanalysis, Feminism and Postmodernism in the Contemporary West.* Berkeley: University of California Press, 1989.

Ford Smith, Honor. "Sistren: Exploring Women's Problems through Drama." *Jamaica Journal* 19 (1986).

Fox, Bonnie J. "Selling the Mechanized Household: 70 Years of Ads in *Ladies' Home Journal.*" *Gender & Society* 4 (1990):25–40.

Franklin, Penelope, ed. *Private Pages: Diaries of American Women: 1830–1970s.* New York: Ballantine, 1986.

Franzwa, H. H. "Female Roles in Women's Magazine Fiction." In *Woman: Dependent or Independent Variable,* edited by Rhoda K. Unger and Florence Denmark. New York: Psychological Dimensions, 1975.

Fraser, Arvonne S. *The U.N. Decade for Women: Documents and Dialogue.* Boulder, Colo.: Westview Press, 1987.

Fraser, Kennedy. *The Fashionable Mind: Reflections on Fashion, 1970–1982.* Boston: David R. Godine, 1985.

Freeman, Jo. *The Politics of Women's Liberation.* New York: McKay, 1975.

———. "The Tyranny of Structurelessness." In *Radical Feminism,* edited by A. Koedt, E. Levine, and A. Rapone. New York: Quadrangle, 1973.

———. "The Women's Liberation Movement: Its Origins, Organizations, Activities and Ideas." In *Women: A Feminist Perspective,* edited by Jo Freeman. Palo Alto, Calif.: Mayfield, 1979.

Freilich, Morris. *Marginal Natives: Anthropologists at Work.* New York: Harper & Row, 1970.

French, Marilyn. *The Women's Room.* New York: Jove Publications, 1977.

Friday, Nancy. *My Mother/Myself: A Daughter's Search for Identity.* New York: Dell, 1977.

Friedan, Betty. *The Feminine Mystique.* New York: Norton, 1963.

———. *It Changed My Life.* New York: Random House, 1976.

Frieze, Irene H.; Parsons, Jacquelynne E.; Johnson, Paula; Ruble, Diane; and Zellman, Gail, eds. *Women and Sex Roles: A Social Psychological Perspective.* New York: Norton, 1978.

Frye, Marilyn. "Assignment: NWSA—Bloomington—1980: Speak on 'Lesbian Perspectives on Women's Studies.' " *Sinister Wisdom* 14 (1980):3–7.

———. *The Politics of Reality: Essays in Feminist Theory.* Trumansburg, N.Y.: The Crossing Press, 1983.

Furumoto, Laurel. "Mary Whiton Calkins (1863–1930)." *Psychology of Women Quarterly* 5 (1980):55–68.

———. "The New History of Psychology." Paper presented at the Annual Meeting of the American Psychological Association, 1988.

Gail, Suzanne. "The Housewife." In *Work: Twenty Personal Accounts,* edited by Ronald Fraser. Harmondsworth: Penguin, 1968.

Gallup, Gordon Jr. and Suarez, Susan. "Alternatives to the Use of Animals in Psychology Research." *American Psychologist* 40 (1985):1104–1111.

Gamarnikow, Eva. "Sexual Division of Labour: The Case of Nursing." In *Feminism and Materialism: Women and Modes of Production,* edited by Annette Kuhn and AnnMarie Wolpe. London: Routledge & Kegan Paul, 1978.

Gans, Herbert. *The Levittowners.* New York: Pantheon, 1967.

———. *The Urban Villagers.* New York: Free Press, 1962.

Garfinkel, Harold. *Studies in Ethnomethodology.* Englewood Cliffs, N.J.: Prentice-Hall, 1967.

Gearhart, Sally Miller. *The Wanderground.* Watertown, Mass.: Persephone Press, 1979.

Geertz, Clifford. "Blurred Genres." *American Scholar* 49 (1980):165–179.

Geiger, Susan N. G. "Women's Life Histories: Method and Content." *Signs: Journal of Women in Culture and Society* 11 (1986):334–351.

Gelfant, Blanche. *Women Writing in America: Voices in Collage.* Hanover, N.H.: University Press of New England, 1985.

Gelles, R. J. "Violence in the Family: A Review of Research in the Seventies." *Journal of Marriage and the Family* 42 (1980):873–885.

Gergen, Mary. "Towards a Feminist Metatheory and Methodology." Paper presented at the Annual Meeting of the American Psychological Association, 1986.

———, ed. *Feminist Thought and the Structure of Knowledge.* New York: New York University Press, 1988.

Gerstel, Naomi. "Divorce, Gender, and Social Integration." *Gender & Society* 2 (1988):343–367.

Gerwin, Carol. "The Attractive Blonde was Found Dead: Linguistic Sexism in U.S. Newspapers." Honors Thesis, Department of Sociology, Brandeis University, 1990.

Giallombardo, Rose. *Society of Women.* New York: Wiley, 1966.

Giddings, Paula. *When and Where I Enter: The Impact of Black Women on Race and Sex in America.* New York: Morrow, 1984.

Giele, Janet Zollinger. *Women: Roles and Status in Eight Countries.* New York: Wiley, 1977.

———. *Women and the Future: Changing Sex Roles in America.* New York: Free Press, 1978.

Gilfus, Mary E. "Life Histories of Women in Prison." Paper presented at the Third National Family Violence Research Conference, University of New Hampshire, Durham, N.H., 1987.

Gilkes, Cheryl Townsend. "Going up for the Oppressed: The Career Mobility of Black Women Community Workers." *Journal of Social Issues* 39 (1983):115–139.

———. "The Roles of Church and Community Mothers: Ambivalent American Sexism or Fragmented African Familyhood?" *Journal of Feminist Studies in Religion* 2 (1986):41–59.

Gillespie, Cynthia K. *Justifiable Homicide: Battered Women, Self-Defense, and the Law.* Columbus: Ohio University Press, 1990.

Gilligan, Carol. *In a Different Voice: Psychological Theory and Women's Development.* Cambridge: Harvard University Press, 1982.

———; Lyons, Nona; and Hanmer, Trudy. *Making Connections: The Relational Worlds of Adolescent Girls at Emma Willard School.* Cambridge: Harvard University Press, 1990.

Gilman, Charlotte Perkins. *Herland.* 1915. Reprint. New York: Pantheon, 1979.

———. *Women & Economics.* 1898. Reprint. New York: Harper Torchbook, 1966.

———. "Yellow Wall-Paper." *New England Magazine* 5 (1892):647–656. Reprinted as *The Yellow Wallpaper.* Old Westbury, N.Y.: The Feminist Press, 1973.

Ginsburg, Faye. *Contested Lives: The Abortion Debate in an American Community.* Berkeley: University of California Press, 1989.

———. "Dissonance to Harmony: The Symbolic Function of Abortion in Activists' Life Stories." In *Interpreting Women's Lives: Feminist Theory and Personal Narratives,* edited by Personal Narratives Group. Bloomington, Ind.: Indiana University Press, 1989.

Glaser, Barney and Strauss, Anselm. *The Discovery of Grounded Theory.* Chicago: Aldine, 1967.

Glenn, Evelyn Nakano. *Issei, Nisei, War Bride: Three Generations of Japanese American Women in Domestic Service.* Philadelphia: Temple University Press, 1986.

Glennon, Lynda. "Synthesism: A Case of Feminist Methodology." In *Beyond Method: Strategies for Social Research,* edited by Gareth Morgan. Beverly Hills, Calif.: Sage, 1983.

———. *Women and Dualism: A Sociology of Knowledge Analysis.* New York: Longman, 1979.

Gluck, Sherna. "What's So Special about Women? Women's Oral History," *Frontiers* 2 (1979):3–11.

Goffman, Erving. "The Arrangement between the Sexes." *Theory & Society* 4 (1977):301–331.

———. *Frame Analysis.* New York: Harper, 1974.

———. "Gender Display, Picture Frames, Gender Commercials." *Gender Advertisements, Studies in Anthropology of Visual Communication* 3 (1976):69–95.

———. *The Presentation of Self in Everyday Life.* Garden City, N.Y.: Doubleday Anchor, 1959.

Gold, Raymond. "Roles in Sociological Field Observations." *Social Forces* 36 (1958):217–223.

Goldberg, Philip. "Are Women Prejudiced against Women?" *Transaction/SOCIETY* 5 (1968):28–30.

Goldberg, Roberta. *Organizing Women Office Workers: Dissatisfaction, Consciousness and Action.* New York: Praeger, 1983.

Golde, Peggy. "Odyssey of Encounter." In *Women in the Field: Anthropological Experiences,* edited by Peggy Golde. Chicago: Aldine, 1970.

Golden, Carla. "Psychology, Feminism and Object Relations." Paper presented at the Annual Meeting of the Association for Women in Psychology, 1981.

Goldsen, Rose. *The Show and Tell Machine.* New York: Dell, 1974.

Gondolf, Edward with Fisher, Ellen R. *Battered Women as Survivors: An Alternative to Treating Learned Helplessness.* Lexington, Mass.: Lexington Books, 1988.

Gonzalez, Nancie. "The Anthropologist as Female Head of Household." *Feminist Studies* 10 (1984):97–114.

Goodman, Katherine R. "Poetry and Truth in Autobiography." Paper presented at the Conference on "Autobiographies, Biographies and Life Histories of Women: Interdisciplinary Perspectives." University of Minnesota, 1986.

———. "Poetry and Truth: Elisa von der Recke's Sentimental Autobiography." In *Interpreting Women's Lives: Feminist Theory and Personal Narratives,* edited by Personal Narratives Group. Bloomington, Ind.: Indiana University Press, 1989.

Gordon, David. "Getting Close by Staying Distant: Fieldwork with Proselytizing Groups." *Qualitative Sociology* 10 (1987):267–287.

Gordon, Deborah, ed. *Feminism and the Critique of Colonial Discourse.* Special Issue of *Inscriptions* 3/4 (1988).

Gordon, Linda. *Woman's Body, Woman's Right.* Middlesex: Penquin, 1977.

Gordon, Margaret T. and Riger, Stephanie. *The Female Fear: The Social Cost of Rape.* New York: Free Press, 1989.

———; Riger, Stephanie; and Gordon, Andrew C. "Victimology, Academia, and Academics: A Study in (Primarily Negative) Sanctions." Mimeographed. Center for Urban Affairs, Northwestern University, Evanston, Ill., 1981.

Gordon, Susan. "What's New in Endocrinology? Target: Sex Hormones." In *Genes & Gender IV,* edited by Myra Fooden, Susan Gordon, and Betty Hughley. Staten Island, N.Y.: Gordian Press, 1983.

Gornick, Vivian. "By Science Possessed." *Voice* April 1–7, 1981. Review of June Goodfield. *An Imagined World: A Story of Scientific Discovery.* New York: Harper & Row, 1981.

——— and Moran, Barbara K., eds. *Woman in Sexist Society: Studies in Power and Powerlessness.* New York: New American Library, 1971.

Gottlieb, Naomi. "Dilemmas and Strategies in Research on Women." In *The Woman Client,* edited by Dianne S. Burden and Noami Gottlieb. New York: Tavistock, 1987.

———, ed. *Alternative Social Services for Women.* New York: Columbia University Press, 1980.

Gould, Meredith. "Innovative Sources and Uses of Qualitative Data." In *Innovative Sources and Uses of Qualitative Data,* edited by Meredith Gould. Special Issue of *Qualitative Sociology* 8 (1985):303–308.

———. "The New Sociology." *Signs: Journal of Women in Culture and Society* 5 (1980):459–467.

Gouldner, Alvin. *The Coming Crisis of Western Sociology.* New York: Avon, 1970.

Graduate Women's Forum, Department of Sociology, Boston College. "Memo to All Faculty and Graduate Students." Mimeographed. May 6, 1987.

Grady, Kathleen E. "Sex Bias in Research Design." *Psychology of Women Quarterly* 5 (1981):628–636.

Graham, Dee and Rawlings, Edna. "Feminist Research Methodology: Comparisons, Guidelines and Ethics." Paper presented at the Annual Meeting of the American Psychological Association, 1980.

Graham, Hilary. "Surveying through Stories." In *Social Researching: Politics, Problems, Practice,* edited by Colin Bell and Helen Roberts. London: Routledge & Keagan Paul, 1984.

Graham, Laurel. "A Year in the Life of Dr. Lillian Moller Gilbreth: Four Representations of the Struggle of a Woman Scientist." Paper presented at the Gregory Stone Symposium, 1990.

Grant, Linda; Ward, Kathryn; and Rong, Xue. "Is There an Association between Gender and Methods in Sociological Research?" *American Sociological Review* 52 (1987):856–862.

Grant-Colson, Nancy. "Women in Sitcoms: 'I Love Lucy'." In *Wimmin in the Mass Media,* edited by T. Nygren and Mary Jo Deegan. Lincoln, Nebr.: University of Nebraska, 1980.

Gray, Barbara. *Collaborating: Finding Common Ground for Multiparty Problems.* San Francisco: Jossey-Bass, 1989.

———. "The Pathways of My Research: A Journey of Personal Engagement and Change." *Journal of Applied Behavioral Science* 25 (1989):383–398.

———. "A Poststructuralist Critique of *Collaborating.*" Mimeographed. Pennsylvania State University, 1990.

Gray, Betty MacMorran. "Economics of Sex Bias: The 'Disuse' of Women." *Nation,* June 14, 1971, pp. 742–747.

Gregg, Robin. "Pregnancy in a High-Tech Age: Paradoxes of Choice." Ph.D. dissertation, Brandeis University, 1991.

Griffin, Susan. *Woman and Nature: The Roaring Inside Her.* New York: Harper & Row, 1978.

Griffith, Elisabeth. *In her Own Right: The Life of Elizabeth Cady Stanton.* New York: Oxford University Press, 1984.

Griffiths, Vivienne. "Feminist Research and the Use of Drama." *Women's Studies International Forum* 7 (1984):511–519.

Gross, Jeanne. "Feminist Ethics from a Marxist Perspective." *Radical Religion* 3 (1977):52–56.

Groves, Robert and Fultz, Nancy. "Gender Effects Among Telephone Interviewers in a Survey of Economic Attitudes." *Sociological Methods & Research* 14 (1985):31–52.

Growing Numbers, Growing Force: Report from the White House Mini-Conference on Older Women. Oakland, Calif: Older Women's League Educational Fund, 1980.

Gruber, Kenneth J. and Gaebelein, Jacquelyn. "Sex Differences in Learning Comprehension." *Sex Roles* 5 (1979):519–535.

Guillemin, Jeanne Harley and Homstrom, Lynda Lytle. *Mixed Blessings: Intensive Care for Newborns.* New York: Oxford University Press, 1986.

Gumport, Patricia. "The Social Construction of Knowledge: Individual and Institutional Commitments to Feminist Scholarship." Ph.D. dissertation, Stanford University, 1987.

———. "Feminist Scholarship as a Vocation." In *Women's Higher Education in Comparative Perspective,* edited by Gail Kelly and Sheila Slaughter. Dordrecht and London: Kluwer Academic Publishers, 1991.

Gurney, Joan Neff. "Not One of the Guys: The Female Researcher in a Male-Dominated Setting." *Qualitative Sociology* 8 (1985):42–62.

Haggis, Jane. "The Feminist Research Process—Defining a Topic." In *Feminist Research Processes,* edited by Feminist Research Seminar. In *Studies in Sexual Politics,* edited by Liz Stanley and Sue Scott. Manchester, Eng.: Department of Sociology, University of Manchester, 1987.

Hagood, Margaret. *Mothers of the South: Portraiture of the White Tenant Farm Woman.* Chapel Hill, N.C.: University of North Carolina Press, 1939. Reissued by W. W. Norton, 1977.

———. *Statistics for Sociologists.* New York: Reynal & Hitchcock, 1941.

Hall, Budd. "Notes on the Development of the Concept of Participatory Research in an International Context." *International Journal of University Adult Education* 17 (1978):6–12.

———. "Participatory Research: An Approach for Change." *Convergence, an International Journal of Adult Education* 8 (1975):24–32.

Hall, Elaine J. "One Week for Women? The Structure of Inclusion of Gender Issues in Introductory Textbooks." *Teaching Sociology* 16 (1988):431–432.

Hampsten, Elizabeth. "Let Them Speak for Themselves: Experiments in Editing and Biography." Paper presented at the Conference on "Autobiographies, Biographies and Life Histories of Women: Interdisciplinary Perspectives." University of Minnesota, 1986.

———. "Considering More Than a Single Reader." In *Interpreting Women's Lives: Feminist Theory and Personal Narratives,* edited by Personal Narratives Group. Bloomington, Ind.: Indiana University Press, 1989.

———. *Read this Only to Yourself: The Private Writings of Midwestern Women, 1800–1910.* Bloomington, Ind.: Indiana University Press, 1982.

Hanawalt, Barbara A. *The Ties that Bound: Peasant Families in Medieval England.* New York: Oxford University Press, 1986.

Hanmer, Jalna and Saunders, Sheila. *Well-founded Fear: A Community Study of Violence to Women.* London: Hutchinson, 1984.

Hansen, Karen V. "Feminist Conceptions of Public and Private: A Critical Analysis." *Berkeley Journal of Sociology* 32 (1987):105–128.

Haraway, Donna. "Animal Sociology and a Natural Economy of the Body Politic, Part 1: A Political Physiology of Dominance." *Signs: Journal of Women in Culture and Society* 4 (1978):21–36.

Harding, Sandra. "Is There a Feminist Method?" In *Feminism and Methodology: Social Science Issues,* edited by Sandra Harding. Bloomington, Ind.: Indiana University Press and Open University Press, 1987.

———. *The Science Question in Feminism.* Ithaca, N.Y.: Cornell University Press, 1986.

——— and Hintikka, Merrill B., eds. *Discovering Reality: Feminist Perspectives on Epistemology, Metaphysics, Methodology and Philosophy of Science.* Dordrecht: D. Reidel, 1983.

Hardwick, Elizabeth. "The Teller and the Tape." *New York Review of Books,* May 30, 1985, pp. 3–4.

Hare, Peter. *A Woman's Quest for Science: Portrait of Anthropologist Elsie Clews Parsons.* Buffalo, N.Y.: Prometheus Books, 1985.

Harris, Barbara J. "History and the Psychology of Women." In *In the Shadow of the Past: Psychology Portrays the Sexes,* edited by Miriam Lewin. New York: Columbia University Press, 1984.

Hartmann, Betsy. *Reproductive Rights and Wrongs: The Global Politics of Population Control & Contraceptive Choice.* New York: Harper & Row, 1987.

Haskell, Molly. *From Reverence to Rape: The Treatment of Women in the Movies.* rev. ed. Baltimore: Penguin, 1973.

Haug, Frigga. *Female Sexualization: A Collective Work of Memory.* Translated by Erica Carter. London: Verso, 1983.

Hayano, David. *Poker Faces: The Life and Work of Professional Card Players.* Berkeley: University of California Press, 1982.

Hayden, Dolores. *Redesigning the American Dream: The Future of Housing, Work and Family Life.* New York: Norton, 1984.

Heilbrun, Carolyn. *Writing a Woman's Life.* New York: Ballantine, 1988.

Heiser, Paula. "Feminist Issues in Menstrual Research." Paper presented at the Annual Meeting of the Association for Women in Psychology, 1981.

Helson, Ravenna. "E. Nesbit's Forty-First Year: Her Life, Times, and Symbolizations of Personality Growth." In *Representations: Social Constructions of Gender,* edited by Rhoda K. Unger. Amityville, N.Y.: Baywood, 1989.

Henley, Nancy M. *Body Politics: Power, Sex, and Nonverbal Communication.* Englewood Cliffs, N.J.: Prentice-Hall, 1977.

———. "This New Species that Seeks a New Language: On Sexism in Language and Language Change." In *Women & Language in Transition,* edited by Joyce Penfield. Albany, N.Y.: State University of New York Press, 1987.

———. "Psychology and Gender." *Signs: Journal of Women in Culture and Society* 11 (1985):101–119.

Henry, Frances. "Stress and Strategy in Three Field Situations." In *Stress and Response in Fieldwork,* edited by Frances Henry and Satish Saberwal. New York: Holt, Rinehart and Winston, 1969.

Herdt, Gilbert. *Guardians of the Flutes: Idioms of Masculinity.* New York: McGraw-Hill, 1980.

———. *Rituals of Manhood: Male Initiation in Papua New Guinea.* Berkeley: University of California Press, 1982.

Herman, Judith, with Hirschman, Lisa. *Father-Daughter Incest.* Cambridge: Harvard University Press, 1981.

Hertz, Rosanna. *More Equal than Others: Women and Men in Dual-Career Marriages.* Berkeley: University of California Press, 1986.

Hertz, Susan. "The Politics of the Welfare Mothers Movements: A Case Study." *Signs: Journal of Women in Culture and Society* 2 (1977):531–553.

Hess, Beth B. "Beyond Dichotomy: Drawing Distinctions and Embracing Differences." *Sociological Forum* 5 (1990):75–94.

Hesse-Biber, Sharlene. "The Linguistic Validity of Polling Language: Generic Terms that Aren't." Paper presented in the Symposium, "Sexism in Language: Psychological and Sociological Research." Annual Meeting of the American Psychological Association, 1982.

Hewlett, Sylvia Ann. *Lesser Life: The Myth of Women's Lives in America.* New York: Morrow, 1986.

Higginbotham, Elizabeth. "Oral History Refutes Stereotypes." *The Newsletter* (Center for Research on Women, Memphis State University) 5 (1986):3.

Hill, Michael R. "Mary Abby van Kleeck." In *Women in Sociology: A Bio-Bibliographic Sourcebook,* edited by Mary Jo Deegan. Westport, Conn.: Greenwood Press, 1991.

———. "The Methodological Framework of Harriet Martineau's Feminist Analyses of American Society." Paper presented at the Annual Meeting of the American Studies Association, 1990.

Hite, Shere. *The Hite Report: A Nationwide Study on Female Sexuality.* New York: Macmillan, 1976.

———. *The Hite Report on Male Sexuality.* New York: Knopf, 1981.

———. *Women and Love: A Cultural Revolution in Progress.* New York: Knopf, 1987.

Ho, Mary Louise. "Patriarchal Ideology and Agony Columns." In *Looking Back: Some Papers from the BSA 'Gender and Society' Conference,* edited by Sue Webb and Clive Pearson. In *Studies in Sexual Politics,* edited by Liz Stanley and Sue Scott. Manchester, Eng.: Department of Sociology, University of Manchester, 1984.

Hoagland, Sarah Lucia. *Lesbian Ethics: Toward New Value.* Palo Alto, Calif.: Institute of Lesbian Studies, 1988.

———. "Naming, Describing, Explaining: Deception and Science." Paper presented in the panel, "Feminism and the Philosophy of Science." Annual meeting of the American Association for the Advancement of Science, 1979.

Hobby, Elaine. *Virtue of Necessity: English Women's Writing, 1649–88.* Ann Arbor, Mich.: University of Michigan Press, 1988.

Hochschild, Arlie Russell. *The Managed Heart: Commercialization of Human Feeling.* Berkeley: University of California Press, 1983.

———. *The Unexpected Community: Portrait of an Old Age Subculture.* Berkeley: University of California Press, 1978.

Hoff-Wilson, Joan, ed. *Rights of Passage: The Past and Future of the ERA.* Bloomington, Ind.: Indiana University Press, 1986.

Hoffnung, Michele. "Feminist Research Methodology." *Newsletter of the Association for Women in Psychology* (July–August, 1982):7–9.

Hollway, Wendy. *Subjectivity and Method in Psychology: Gender, Meaning and Science.* Newbury Park, Calif.: Sage, 1989.

hooks, bell. *Ain't I a Woman?: Black Women and Feminism.* Boston: South End Press, 1981.

———. *Feminist Theory: From Margin to Center.* Boston: South End Press, 1984.

Horner, Matina. "Achievement-related Conflicts in Women." *Journal of Social Issues* 28 (1972):157–175.

———. "Sex Differences in Achievement Motivation and Performance in Competitive and Noncompetitive Situations." Ph.D. dissertation, University of Michigan, 1968.

Horowitz, Irving Louis. *C. Wright Mills: An American Utopian.* New York: Free Press, 1983.

Horowitz, Ruth. *Honor and the American Dream: Culture and Identity in a Chicano Community.* New Brunswick, N.J.: Rutgers University Press, 1983.

———. "Remaining an Outsider: Membership as a Threat to Research Rapport." *Urban Life* 14 (1986):409–430.

Hubbard, Ruth. "Have only Men Evolved?" In *Women Look at Biology Looking at Women,* edited by Ruth Hubbard, Mary Sue Henifin, and Barbara Fried. Boston: Schenkman, 1979.

Huber, Joan. "Do Two Sexes Require Two Research Methodologies?" Gender and Epistemology series, Radcliffe College, 1989.

Hughes, Helen MacGill. "Maid of All Work or Departmental Sister-in-Law? The Faculty Wife Employed on Campus." *American Journal of Sociology* 78 (1973):767–772.

———. "On Becoming a Sociologist." Address to the Third Undergraduate Research Conference in Sociology. Providence College, 1978.

———. "Wasp/Woman/Sociologist." Transaction/SOCIETY 14 (1977):69–80.

Hull, Gloria; Scott, Patricia Bell; and Smith, Barbara, eds. *All the Women Are White, All the Men Are Black, But Some of Us Are Brave: Black Women's Studies.* Old Westbury, N.Y.: The Feminist Press, 1982.

Humphreys, Laud. *Tearoom Trade: Impersonal Sex in Public Places.* Chicago: Aldine, 1970.

Hunt, Jennifer C. "The Development of Rapport through the Negotiation of Gender in Field Work among Police." *Human Organization* 43 (1984):283–296.

———. *Psychoanalytic Aspects of Fieldwork.* Sage University Paper Series on Qualitative Research Methods, Vol. 18. Newbury Park, Calif.: Sage, 1989.

Hunter, Dianne. "Hysteria, Psychoanalysis, and Feminism: The Case of Anna O." *Feminist Studies* 9 (1983):464–488.

Hunter College Women's Studies Collective. *Women's Realities, Women's Choices.* New York: Oxford University Press, 1983.

Hurston, Zora Neale. *Their Eyes Were Watching God.* New York: Lippincott, 1937.

———. *Dust Tracks on a Road.* New York: Lippincott, 1970.

———. *I Love Myself when I am Laughing: A Zora Neale Hurston Reader.* New York: The Feminist Press, 1979.

Hyde, Janet Shibley. "Children's Understanding of Sexist Language." Paper presented in the Symposium, "Sexism in Language: and Psychological Sociological Research." Annual Meeting of the American Psychological Association, 1982.

——— and Linn, Marcia C. *The Psychology of Women: Advances through Meta-Analysis.* Baltimore: Johns Hopkins University Press, 1986.

——— and Rosenberg, B. G. *Half the Human Experience: The Psychology of Women.* 2d ed. Lexington, Mass.: Heath, 1976.

Imamura, Anne. "The Loss that has No Name: Social Womanhood of Foreign Wives." *Gender & Society* 2 (1988):291–307.

Itzin, Catherine. "Media Images of Women: The Social Construction of Ageism and Sexism." In *Feminist Social Psychology,* edited by Sue Wilkinson. Philadelphia: Open University Press, 1986.

Ives, Edward D. *The Tape-recorded Interview: A Manual for Fieldworkers in Folklore and Oral History.* Knoxville, Tenn.: University of Tennessee, 1980.

Izraeli, Dafna. "Sex Effects or Structural Effects? An Empirical Test of Kanter's Theory of Proportions." *Social Forces* 62 (1983):153–165.

——— and Tabory, Ephraim. "The Political Context of Feminist Attitudes in Israel." *Gender & Society* 2 (1988):463–481.

Jacklin, Carol Nagy. "Editor's Note." *Signs: Journal of Women in Culture and Society* 11 (1986):304.

———. "Feminist Research and the Scientific Method." Mimeographed. Stanford University (undated).

———. "Methodological Issues in the Study of Sex-related Differences." *Developmental Review* 1 (1981):266–273.

Jacobs, Jerry. *Fun City: An Ethnographic Study of a Retirement Community.* New York: Holt, Rinehart and Winston, 1974.

Jacobs, Ruth Harriet. *Life After Youth: Female, 40, What Next?* Boston: Beacon, 1979.

Jacquette, Jane, ed. *The Women's Movement in Latin America: Feminism and the Transition to Democracy.* Boston: Unwin Hyman, 1989.

Jaggar, Alison and Rothenberg, Paula, eds. *Feminist Frameworks: Alternative Theoretical Accounts of the Relations between Women and Men.* New York: McGraw-Hill, 1984.

James, Bev. "Mill Wives: A Study of Gender Relations, Family and Work in a Single-industry Town." Ph.D. dissertation, Waikato University, Hamilton, New Zealand, 1985.

———. "Taking Gender into Account: Feminist and Sociological Issues in Social Research." *New Zealand Sociology* 1 (1986):18–33.

"Jane." "Just Call 'Jane'." In *From Abortion to Reproductive Freedom: Transforming a Movement,* edited by Marlene Gerber Fried. Boston: South End Press, 1990.

Janes, Robert W. "A Note on Phases of the Community Role of the Participant Observer." *American Sociological Review* 26 (1961):446–450.

Jayaratne, Toby Epstein. "The Value of Quantitative Methodology for Feminist Research." In *Theories of Women's Studies,* edited by Gloria Bowles and Renate Duelli Klein. Boston: Routledge & Kegan Paul, 1983.

Jeffery, Roger; Jeffery, Patricia; and Lyon, Andrew. "Female Infanticide and Amniocentesis." *Social Science and Medicine* 19 (1984):1207–1212.

John, Angela V. *By the Sweat of Their Brow: Women Workers at Victorian Coal Mines.* London: Croom Helm, 1980.

Johnson, Paula. "Doing Psychological Research." In *Women and Sex Roles: A Social Psychological Perspective,* edited by Irene H. Frieze, Jacquelynn Parsons, Paula Johnson, Diane Ruble, and Gail Zellman, New York: Norton, 1978.

Johnston, Claire. "Women's Cinema as Counter-Cinema." In *Movies and Methods: An Anthology,* edited by Bill Nicholas. Berkeley: University of California Press, 1976.

Jones, Ann. *Women Who Kill.* New York: Holt, Rinehart and Winston, 1980.

Joseph, Gloria and Lewis, Jill. *Common Differences: Conflicts in Black and White Feminist Perspectives.* Boston: South End Press, 1986.

Juster, Susan. " 'In a Different Voice': Male and Female Narratives of Religious Conversion in Post-Revolutionary America." *American Quarterly* 41 (1989):34–62.

Kahn, Janet. "Qualitative Methods." Mimeographed. Brandeis University, Sociology Department, 1990.

Kahn, Robert and Mann, Floyd. "Developing Research Partnerships." *Journal of Social Issues* 8 (1952):4–10.

Kahn, Roberta Pfeufer. *The Language of Birth: Female Generativity in Western Tradition.* Chicago: University of Illinois Press, forthcoming.

———. "Taking Charge of Birth." *Women's Review of Books* 2 (1984):6.

Kamens, Linda. "Evaluating Evaluation Research from a Feminist Perspective." Paper presented at the Annual Meeting of the Association for Women in Psychology, 1981.

Kaminer, Wendy. *The Fearful Freedom: Women's Flight from Equality.* Reading, Mass.: Addison-Wesley, 1990.

Kandal, Terry. *The Woman Question in Classical Sociological Theory.* Miami: Florida International University Press, 1988.

Kanter, Rosabeth. *Men and Women of the Corporation.* New York: Basic, 1977.

Karon, Sara. "The Politics of Naming: Lesbian Erasure in a Feminist Context." In *Looking at Invisible Women: An Exercise in Feminist Pedagogy,* edited by Shulamit Reinharz and Ellen Stone. Washington, D.C.: University Press of America, forthcoming.

Kaufman, Debra Renee. *Rachel's Daughters: Newly Orthodox Jewish Women.* New Brunswick, N.J.: Rutgers University Press, 1991.

——— and Richardson, Barbara. *Achievement and Women: Challenging the Assumptions.* New York: Free Press, 1982.

Kautzer, Kathleen. "Moving against the Stream: An Organizational Study of the Older Women's League." Ph.D. dissertation, Brandeis University, 1988.

Kay, Chung Yuen. *At the Palace: Work, Ethnicity & Gender in a Chinese Restaurant.* In *Studies in Sexual Politics,* edited by Liz Stanley and Sue Scott. Manchester, Eng.: Department of Sociology, University of Manchester, 1985.

Kay, K. and Peary, G., eds. *Woman and the Cinema: A Critical Anthology.* New York: E. P. Dutton, 1977.

Kay, Margarita; Voda, Anna; Olivas, Guadalupe; Rios, Frances; and Imle, Margaret. "Ethnography of the Menopause-related Hot Flash." *Maturitas* 4 (1982):217–227.

Keller, Evelyn Fox. *A Feeling for the Organism: The Life and Work of Barbara McClintock.* San Francisco: Freeman, 1983.

———. "Gender and Science." *Psychoanalysis and Contemporary Thought* 1 (1978):409–433.

———. "Feminism and Science." *Signs: Journal of Women in Culture and Society* 7 (1982):589–602.

———. "Feminist Critique of Science: A Forward or Backward Move?" *Fundamenta Scientiae* 1 (1980):341–349.

———. *Reflections on Gender and Science.* New Haven, Conn.: Yale University Press, 1984.

———. "Women in Science: A Social Analysis," *Harvard Magazine* 77 (1974):14–19.

Keller, Karen. "Freudian Tradition versus Feminism in Science Fiction." In *Wimmin in the Mass Media,* edited by T. Nygren and Mary Jo Deegan. Lincoln, Nebr.: University of Nebraska, 1980.

Kelly, Liz. *Surviving Sexual Violence.* Minneapolis: University of Minnesota Press, 1988.

Kendrigan, Mary Lou, ed. *Gender Differences: Their Impact on Public Policy.* Westport, Conn.: Greenwood Press, 1991.

———. *Political Equality in a Democratic Society: Women in the United States.* Westport, Conn.: Greenwood, 1984.

Kerber, Linda; Greeno, C.; Maccoby, Eleanor, et al. "On *In a Different Voice:* An Interdisciplinary Forum." *Signs: Journal of Women in Culture and Society* 11 (1986):304–333.

Kerr, Marion. "Sharing in a Common Plight?" *Poverty (Special Issue on Poverty and Food)* 60 (1985):22–26.

Kessler-Harris, Alice. *Out to Work: A History of Wage-Earning Women in the United States.* New York: Oxford University Press, 1982.

Kidwell, Clara Sue. Review of *American Indian Women: Telling their Lives,* edited by Gretchen M. Bataille and Kathleen Mullen Sands. Lincoln, Nebr.: University of Nebraska Press, 1984. In *Women's Studies International Forum* 8 (1985):533–538.

Kitzinger, Celia. "The Constructing of Lesbian Identities." Ph.D. dissertation, University of Reading, United Kingdom, 1984.

———. "Resisting the Discipline." In *The Practice of Psychology by Feminists,* edited by Erica Burman. London: Sage, 1990.

———. "The Rhetoric of Pseudoscience." In *Deconstructing Social Psychology,* edited by I. Parker and J. Shotter. Sage: London, forthcoming.

———. *The Social Construction of Lesbianism.* Beverly Hills, Calif.: Sage, 1987.

Klatch, Rebecca E. *Women of the New Right.* Philadelphia: Temple University Press, 1987.

Klein, Renate. "The Dynamics of Women's Studies: Its International Ideas and Practices in Higher Education." Ph.D. dissertation, University of London, Institute of Education, 1986.

———. "The Dynamics of the Women's Studies Classroom: A Review Essay of the Teaching Practice of Women's Studies in Higher Education." *Women's Studies International Forum* 10 (1987):187–206.

———. *The Exploitation of a Desire: Women's Experiences with In Vitro Fertilisation, an Exploratory Survey.* Geelong, Victoria: Deakin University Press, 1989.

———. "How to Do What We Want to Do: Thoughts about Feminist Methodology." In *Theories of Women's Studies,* edited by Gloria Bowles and Renate Duelli Klein. Boston: Routledge & Kegan Paul, 1983.

————. "Pain, Infertility and Women's Experiences with IVF." Paper presented at the Meeting of the Australian Federation of University Women. Melbourne, April 1987.

————. "When Medicalisation Equals Experimentation and Creates Illness: The Impact of the New Reproductive Technologies on Women." Paper presented at the Forum International Sur les Nouvelles Technologies de la Reproduction Humaine organisé par le Conseil du Statut de la Femme, Université Concordia, Montreal, Canada, 1988.

————. "Where Choice Amounts to Coercion: The Experiences of Women on IVF Programmes." Paper presented at the Third Interdisciplinary Congress on Women. Dublin, Ireland, July 1987.

Kleinman, Sherryl. "Fieldworkers' Feelings: What We Feel, Who We Are, How We Analyze." In *Experiencing Fieldwork: An Inside View of Qualitative Research,* edited by William Shaffir and Robert Stebbins. Newbury Park, Calif.: Sage, 1991.

Knudsen, Dean. "The Declining Status of Women: Popular Myths and the Failure of Functionalist Thought." *Social Forces* 48 (1969):183–193.

Komarovsky, Mirra. "The New Feminist Scholarship: Some Precursors and Polemics." *Journal of Marriage and the Family* 50 (1988):585–593.

————. *Women in College: Shaping New Feminine Identities.* New York: Basic Books, 1985.

————. "Women Then and Now: A Journey of Detachment and Engagement." *Barnard Alumnae Magazine* (Winter 1982):7–11.

Komisar, Lucy. "The Image of Woman in Advertising." In *Woman in Sexist Society: Studies in Power and Powerlessness,* edited by Vivian Gornick and Barbara Moran. New York: New American Library, 1971.

Kondo, Dorinne K. "Dissolution and Reconstruction of Self: Implications for Anthropological Epistemology." *Cultural Anthropology* 1 (1986):74–88.

Kraditor, Aileen S. Foreword to *Women and Womanhood in America,* Ronald Hogeland, ed. Lexington, Mass.: D.C. Heath, 1973.

Kramarae, Cheris and Spender, Dale, eds. *The Knowledge Explosion: Generations of Feminist Scholarship.* New York: Teachers College Press, 1992.

Kramer, Sydelle and Masur, Jenny, eds. *Jewish Grandmothers.* Boston: Beacon Press, 1976.

Kramer, Terry. "The Diary as a Feminist Research Method." *Newsletter of the Association for Women in Psychology* (Winter 1983):3–4.

Kravetz, Diane. "Consciousness-raising in the 1970s." *Psychology of Women Quarterly* 3 (1978):168–186.

Krieger, Susan. "Beyond 'Subjectivity': The Use of the Self in Social Science." In *Innovative Sources and Uses of Qualitative Data,* edited by Meredith Gould. Special Issue of *Qualitative Sociology* 8 (1985):309–324.

————. *The Mirror Dance: Identity in a Women's Community.* Philadelphia: Temple University Press, 1983.

Krueger, Sheila M. "Images of Women in Rock Music: Analysis of B-52's and Black Rose." In *Wimmin in the Media,* edited by T. Nygren and Mary Jo Deegan. Lincoln, Nebr.: University of Nebraska, 1980.

Kuhn, Annette. *Women's Pictures: Feminism and Cinema.* London: Routledge & Kegan Paul, 1982.

Kuhn, Thomas S. *The Structure of Scientific Revolutions.* Chicago: The University of Chicago Press, 1970.

Ladner, Joyce, ed. *The Death of White Sociology.* New York: Vintage, 1973.

Lamphere, Louise. "Feminism and Anthropology: The Struggle to Reshape Our Thinking about Gender." In *The Impact of Feminist Research in the Academy,* edited by Christie Farnham. Bloomington, Ind.: Indiana University Press, 1987.

Landes, Ruth. "A Woman Anthropologist in Brazil." In *Women in the Field: Anthropological Experiences,* edited by Peggy Golde. Chicago: Aldine, 1970.

Lane, Ann J. *To 'Herland' and Beyond: The Life and Work of Charlotte Perkins Gilman.* New York: Pantheon, 1990.

Langer, Elinor. *Josephine Herbst.* Boston: Little, Brown, 1983.

Langford, Ruby. *Don't Take My Love to Town.* London: Penguin, 1988.

Lather, Patti. "Feminist Perspectives on Empowering Research Methologies." *Women's Studies International Forum* 11 (1988):569–581.

Lauter, Paul. "Race and Gender in the Shaping of the American Literary Canon: A Case Study from the Twenties." *Feminist Studies* 9 (1983):435–463.

Laws, Judith Long. "Feminism and Patriarchy: Competing Ways of Doing Social Science." Paper presented at the Annual Meeting of the American Sociological Association, 1978.

———. "Patriarchy as Paradigm: The Challenge from Feminist Scholarship." Paper presented at the Annual Meeting of the American Sociological Association, 1976.

Lazarre, Jane. *The Mother Knot.* Boston: Beacon, 1986.

Leghorn, Lisa and Parker, Katherine. *Woman's Worth: Sexual Economics and the World of Women.* Boston: Routledge & Kegan Paul, 1981.

LeMoncheck, Linda. *Dehumanizing Women: Treating Persons as Sex Objects.* Totowa, N.J.: Rowman & Allanheld, 1985.

Leonardo, Micaela di. "The Female World of Cards and Holidays: Women, Families and the Work of Kinship." *Signs: Journal of Women in Culture and Society* 12 (1987):440–453.

Lerner, Gerda. "Autobiographical Notes, by way of an Introduction." *A Majority Finds Its Past: Placing Women in History.* New York: Oxford University Press, 1980.

———. *The Creation of Patriarchy.* New York: Oxford University Press, 1986.

———. *The Female Experience: An American Documentary.* Indianapolis: Bobbs-Merrill, 1977.

———. "New Approaches to the Study of Women in American History." *Journal of Social History* 3 (1960):5–14.

———. "Placing Women in History: A 1975 Perspective." In *Liberating Women's History,* edited by Berenice Carroll. Chicago: University of Illinois Press, 1976.

———. "Priorities and Challenges in Women's History Research." *American Historical Association Newsletter* 26 (1988):17–20.

Lesage, Julia. "Feminist Film Criticism: Theory and Practice." *Women and Film* 1 (1974):12–18.

Leuzinger, Monika and Rambert, Bigna. " 'I Can Feel It—My Baby is Healthy': Women's Experiences with Prenatal Diagnosis in Switzerland." *Reproductive and Genetic Engineering: Journal of International Feminist Analysis* 1 (1988):239–249.

Leverone, Jill. "Is There a Feminist Research Methodology?" *Newsletter of the Association for Women in Psychology* (November–December 1981):5.

Levesque-Lopman, Louise. *Claiming Reality: Phenomenology and Women's Experience.* Totowa, N.J.: Rowman & Littlefield, 1988.

———. "Women's Subjective Experience: Phenomenological Sociology as Method of Inquiry." Paper presented at the Annual Meeting of the Eastern Sociological Society, 1987.

Lévi-Strauss, Claude. *The Raw and the Cooked.* New York: Harper, 1969.

Levin, Gloria. "Making Feminist Research Policy Relevant." Paper presented at the Annual Meeting of the American Psychological Association, 1981.

Levine, Adeline. *Love Canal: Science, Politics and People.* Lexington, Mass.: Heath, 1982.

Levitas, Ruth. "Feminism and Human Nature." In *Politics and Human Nature,* edited by
Ian Forbes and Steve Smith. New York: St. Martin's Press, 1983.

Lewis, Diane K. "A Response to Inequality: Black Women, Racism, and Sexism." *Signs:
Journal of Women in Culture and Society* 3 (1977):339–361.

Lewis, Jane. *Women in England, 1870–1950: Sexual Divisions and Social Change.*
Bloomington, Ind.: Indiana University Press, 1984.

————. "Women, Lost and Found: The Impact of Feminism on History." In *Men's Studies Modified: The Impact of Feminism on the Academic Disciplines,* edited by Dale
Spender. New York: Pergamon, 1981.

Leyland, Joyce. "On the Conflicts of Doing Feminist Research into Masculinity." In *Fem-
inist Research Processes,* edited by Feminist Research Seminar. In *Studies in Sexual
Politics,* edited by Liz Stanley and Sue Scott. Manchester, Eng.: Department of
Sociology, University of Manchester, 1987.

Liebow, Elliot. *Tally's Corner: A Study of Negro Streetcorner Men.* Boston: Little, Brown,
1967.

Linden, R. Ruth. " 'The Story of Our Lives becomes our Lives': Post-Positivism and the
Life History Method." Mimeographed. Department of Sociology, Brandeis University, 1988.

————; Pagano, Darlene; Russell, Diana E. H.; and Star, Susan L., eds. *Against Sadomasochism: A Radical Feminist Analysis.* San Francisco: Frog in the Well Press,
1982.

Lindzey, Gardner, ed. *Handbook of Social Psychology.* 2 vols. Cambridge, Mass.: Addison-Wesley, 1954.

Linton, Rhoda. "Conceptualizing Feminism: A Structured Method." Ph.D. dissertation,
Cornell University, 1985.

————. "Conceptualizing Feminism: Clarifying Social Science Concepts." *Evaluation and
Program Planning* 12 (1989):25–29.

————. "Feminist Research Methodology: Exploration and Experimentation." In *Gender/
Body/Knowledge: Feminist Reconstructions of Being and Knowing,* edited by Alison
Jaggar and Susan Bordo. New Brunswick, N.J.: Rutgers University Press, 1989.

———— and Whitham, Michele. "With Mourning, Rage, Empowerment and Deviance: The
1981 Women's Pentagon Action." In *Exposing Nuclear Phallacies,* edited by Diana
E. H. Russell. New York: Pergamon, 1989.

Lofland, John. *Analyzing Social Settings: A Guide to Qualitative Observation and Analysis.* Belmont, Calif.: Wadsworth, 1971.

Lofland, Lyn. "The 'Thereness' of Women: A Selective Review of Urban Sociology." In
Another Voice: Feminist Perspectives on Social Life and Social Science, edited by
Marcia Millman and Rosabeth Kanter. Garden City, N.Y.: Anchor Press, 1975.

Long, Judy. "Telling Women's Lives: The New Sociobiography." Paper presented at the
Annual Meeting of the American Sociological Association, 1987.

————. *Telling Women's Lives.* Manuscript.

Lopata, Helena Znaniecki. "A Life Record of an Immigrant." *Transaction/SOCIETY* 12
(1975):64–74.

————; Miller, Cheryl; and Barnewolt, Debra. *City Women in America: Work, Jobs, Occupations, Careers.* New York: Praeger, 1986.

Lorber, Judith. "From the Editor." *Gender & Society* 2 (1988):5–8.

Lorde, Audre. "The Master's Tools will Never Dismantle the Master's House." In *This Bridge Called My Back,* edited by Cherrie Moraga and Gloria Anzaldua. Watertown, Mass.: Persephone, 1981.

Lott, Bernice. *Becoming a Woman: The Socialization of Gender.* Springfield, Ill.: Charles C Thomas, 1981.

———; Reilly, Mary Ellen; and Howard, Dale R. "Sexual Assault and Harassment: A Campus Community Case Study." *Signs: Journal of Women in Culture and Society* 8 (1982):296–319.

Luker, Kristin. *Abortion and the Politics of Motherhood.* Berkeley: University of California Press, 1984.

Lummis, Trevor. "The Occupational Community of East Anglican Fishermen: An Historical Dimension through Oral Evidence." *British Journal of Sociology* 28 (1977):51–74.

Lykes, M. Brinton. "Dialogue with Guatemalan Indian Women: Critical Perspectives on Constructing Collaborative Research." In *Representations: Social Constructions of Gender,* edited by Rhoda K. Unger. Amityville, N.Y.: Baywood, 1989.

———. "Discrimination and Coping in the Lives of Black Women: Analyses of Oral History Data." *Journal of Social Issues* 39 (1983):79–100.

———. "Perspective on Self and Community among Guatemalan Indian Women: An Oral History Project." Mimeographed. Boston College.

——— and Stewart, Abigail. "Evaluating the Feminist Challenge to Research in Personality and Social Psychology, 1963–1983." *Psychology of Women Quarterly* 10 (1986):393–412.

Lynd, Helen Merrell. *Possibilities.* Youngstown, Ohio: Ink Well Press, 1983.

Lynd, Robert S. and Lynd, Helen Merrell. *Middletown: A Study in American Culture.* New York: Harcourt and Brace, 1929.

———. *Middletown in Transition: A Study in Cultural Conflicts.* New York: Harcourt Brace, 1937.

Maccoby, Eleanor E. "Woman's Intellect." In *Man and Civilization: The Potential of Woman,* edited by Seymour Farber and Roger H. L. Wilson. New York: McGraw-Hill, 1963.

——— and Jacklin, Carol N. *The Psychology of Sex Differences.* Stanford, Calif.: Stanford University Press, 1974.

MacCormack, Carol. "Anthropology: A Discipline with a Legacy." In *Men's Studies Modified: The Impact of Feminism on the Disciplines,* edited by Dale Spender. New York: Pergamon, 1981.

Macdonald, Barbara with Rich, Cynthia. *Look Me in the Eye: Old Women, Aging and Ageism.* San Francisco: Spinsters, Ink, 1983.

Mackie, Marlene. "Female Sociologists' Productivity, Collegial Relations and Research Style Examined through Journal Publications." *Sociology and Social Research* 69 (1985):189–209.

MacKinnon, Catharine. "Feminism, Marxism, Method and the State: An Agenda for Theory." In *The Signs Reader,* edited by Elizabeth Abel and Emily K. Abel. Chicago: The University of Chicago Press, 1983.

———. "Pornography, Civil Rights, and Speech." *Harvard Civil Rights & Civil Liberties Review* 2 (1985):1.

———. *Sexual Harassment of Working Women.* New Haven, Conn.: Yale University Press, 1979.

MacPherson, Kathleen. "Dilemmas of Participant-Observation in a Menopause Collective.'' In *Qualitative Gerontology,* edited by Shulamit Reinharz and Graham Rowles. New York: Springer, 1988.

———. ''Feminist Methods: A New Paradigm for Nursing Research.'' *Advances in Nursing Science* 5 (1983):17–25.

———. ''Feminist Praxis in the Making: The Menopause Collective.'' Ph.D. dissertation, Brandeis University, 1986.

Malinowski, Bronislaw. *Argonauts of the Western Pacific.* New York: Dutton, 1922.

Mansbridge, Jane. *Why We Lost the ERA.* Chicago: The University of Chicago Press, 1986.

Marcos, Sylvia. ''Curing and Cosmology: The Challenge of Popular Medicine.'' *Development: Seeds of Change* 1 (1987):20–25.

Marcus, Jane. ''Of Madness and Method.'' *Women's Review of Books* 3 (1986):3.

Mark, Joan. *A Stranger in Her Native Land: Alice Fletcher and the American Indians.* Lincoln, Nebr.: University of Nebraska Press, 1988.

Marshall, Judi. ''Re-visioning Career Concepts: A Feminist Invitation.'' In *Handbook of Career Theory,* edited by M. B. Arthur, D. T. Hall, and B. S. Lawrence. Cambridge: Cambridge University Press, 1989.

Martin, Del. *Battered Wives.* New York: Simon & Schuster, 1976.

——— and Lyon, Phillis. *Lesbian/Woman.* San Francisco: Glide Publications, 1972.

Martin, Emily. *The Woman in the Body: A Cultural Analysis of Reproduction.* Boston: Beacon Press, 1987.

Martin, Jane Roland. *Reclaiming a Conversation: The Ideal of the Educated Woman.* New Haven, Conn.: Yale University Press, 1985.

Martin, Joanne. ''Deconstructing Organizational Taboos: The Suppression of Gender Conflict in Organizations.'' *Organization Science* 1 (1990):339–359.

Martin, Patricia Yancey; Seymour, Sandra; Courage, Myrna; Godbey, Karolyn; and State, Richard. ''Work-family Policies: Corporate, Union, Feminist, and Pro-family Leaders' Views.'' *Gender & Society* 2 (1988):385–400.

Martin, Susan Ehrlich. *Breaking and Entering: Policewomen on Patrol.* Berkeley: University of California Press, 1980.

———. ''Sexual Politics in the Workplace: The Interactional World of Policewomen.'' *Symbolic Interaction* 1 (1978):44–60.

Martin, Theodora Penny. *The Sound of Our Own Voices: Women's Study Clubs, 1860–1910.* Boston: Beacon Press, 1987.

Martineau, Harriet. *Deerbrook.* 3 vols. London: Moxon, 1839.

———. *How to Observe Morals and Manners* (1836). Edited by Michael R. Hill. New Brunswick, N.J.: Transaction Books, 1989.

———. *Illustrations of Political Economy, The Moral of Many Fables.* 6 vols. London: Charles Fox, 1832–1834.

———. *Society in America.* 1837. Edited by Seymour Martin Lipset. Garden City, New York: Anchor Books, 1962.

Mason, Karen Oppenheim and Lu, Yu-Hsia. ''Attitudes Toward Women's Familial Roles: Changes in the United States, 1977–1985.'' *Gender & Society* 2 (1988): 39–57.

Mast, Sharon. ''Qualitative Sociology in New Zealand.'' In *Qualitative Sociology in International Perspective,* edited by Shulamit Reinharz and Peter Conrad. Special Issue, *Qualitative Sociology* 11 (1988):99–112.

Matthews, Jill. *Good and Mad Women: The Historical Construction of Femininity in 20th Century Australia.* Sydney: George Allen & Unwin, 1984.

Matthews, Sarah H. ''Rethinking Sociology through a Feminist Perspective.'' *The American Sociologist* 17 (1982):29–35.

Mayfield, Chris. *Growing Up Southern.* New York: Pantheon, 1981.

Mayo, Marjorie, ed. *Women in the Community*. London: Routledge & Kegan Paul, 1977.

Maynes, Mary Jo. "The Proletarian Muse: How French and German Working-Class Men and Women Became Autobiographers." Paper presented at Conference on "Autobiographies, Biographies and Life Histories of Women: Interdisciplinary Perspectives." University of Minnesota, 1986.

———. "Gender and Narrative Form in French and German Working-Class Autobiographies." In *Interpreting Women's Lives: Feminist Theory and Personal Narratives,* edited by Personal Narratives Group. Bloomington, Ind.: Indiana University Press, 1989.

McCall, Michal and Wittner, Judith. "The Good News about Life History." In *Symbolic Interaction and Cultural Studies,* edited by Howard Becker and Michal McCall. Chicago: The University of Chicago Press, 1990.

McClellan, Catharine. "Ruth Lea Bunzel." In *Women Anthropologists: A Biographical Dictionary,* edited by Ute Gacs, Asiha Khan, Jerrie McIntyre, and Ruth Weinberg. Westport, Conn.: Greenwood, 1988.

McCoid, Catherine Hodge. "What's in a Name? Non-sexist Transmission of Last Names." *Midwest Feminist Papers* (1986):55–59.

McCormack, Thelma. "Good Theory or Just Theory? Toward Feminist Philosophy of Social Science." *Women's Studies International Quarterly* 4 (1981):1–12.

———. "Feminism, Women's Studies and the New Academic Freedom." In *Women and Education: A Canadian Perspective,* edited by Jane Gaskell and Arlene McLaren. Calgary: Detselig, 1987.

———. "The Professional Ethic and the Spirit of Sexism" *International Journal of Women's Studies* 4 (1981):132–140.

McCourt, Kathleen. *Working-Class Women and Grass-Roots Politics*. Bloomington, Ind.: Indiana University Press, 1977.

McDade, Laurie. "The Interweavings of Theory and Practice: Finding the Threads for a Feminist Ethnography." Paper presented at the National Women's Studies Association Conference, 1983.

McGann, P. J. and Hayes, Harriett E. "One Block Off Marginal Street: Capitalism, Homelessness, and Dehumanization on the Streets of Boston." Paper presented at the Annual Meeting of the Society for the Study of Symbolic Interaction, 1991.

McGaw, Judith A. "Women and the History of American Technology." *Signs: Journal of Women in Culture and Society* 7 (1982):798–828.

McHugh, Maureen C., Koeski, Randi Daimon; and Frieze, Irene Hanson. "Issues to Consider in Conducting Nonsexist Psychological Research: A Guide for Researchers." *American Psychologist* 41 (1986):879–890.

McKenna, Wendy and Kessler, Sarah. *Gender: An Ethnomethodological Approach*. 1978. 2d ed. Chicago: The University of Chicago Press, 1985.

McMillen, Liz. "Woman Who Won Tenure Fight Gets Cool Reception at Harvard." *The Chronicle of Higher Education* 33 (1986):1, 16.

McNaron, Toni A. H., ed. *The Sister Bond: A Feminist View of a Timeless Connection*. New York: Pergamon, 1985.

Mead, Margaret. *Coming of Age in Samoa*. 1928. New York: William Morrow, 1961.

———. *Growing Up in New Guinea*. 1930. New York: William Morrow, 1975.

———. *Male and Female: A Study of the Sexes in a Changing World*. New York: Morrow, 1949.

———. *Sex and Temperament in Three Primitive Societies*. New York: Morrow, 1963.

———. "What Women Bring to Research." *Comment* (February 1979):5.

Meissner, Martin. "The Reproduction of Women's Domination in Organizational Communication." Mimeographed. University of British Columbia. Undated.

Melamed, Elaine. "Play and Playfulness in Women's Learning and Development." Ph.D. dissertation, University of Toronto, 1985.

Melamed, Elissa. *Mirror Mirror: The Terror of Not Being Young.* New York: Simon & Schuster, 1983.

Mellon, Joan. *Women and Sexuality in the New Film.* New York: Dell, 1973.

Mernissi, Fatima. *Beyond the Veil: Male-Female Dynamics in Modern Muslim Society.* Bloomington, Ind.: Indiana University Press, 1987.

Merton, Robert K. *On the Shoulders of Giants.* New York: Free Press, 1965.

———. "Singletons and Multiples in Scientific Discovery: A Chapter in the Sociology of Science." *Proceedings of the American Philosophical Society* 105 (1961):470–486.

———. *Social Theory and Social Structure.* New York: Free Press, 1968.

Meyers, Carol. *Discovering Eve: Ancient Israelite Women in Context.* New York: Oxford University Press, 1988.

Middleton, Sue. "On Being a Feminist Educationist Doing Research on Being a Feminist Educationist: Life History Analysis as Consciousness Raising." *New Zealand Cultural Studies Working Group Journal* 8 (1984):29–37.

Mies, Maria. "Towards a Methodology for Feminist Research." In *Theories of Women's Studies,* edited by Gloria Bowles and Renate Duelli Klein. Boston: Routledge & Kegan Paul, 1983.

———. "Towards a Methodology for Feminist Research." In *German Feminism: Readings in Politics and Literature,* edited by Edith Altbach, Jeanette Clausen, Dagmar Schultz, and Naomi Stephan. Albany, N.Y.: State University of N.Y. Press, 1984.

Miller, Eleanor M. *Street Woman.* Philadelphia: Temple University Press, 1986.

Miller, Jean Baker. *Toward a New Psychology of Women.* Boston: Beacon Press, 1976.

Miller, S. M. "The Participant Observer and 'Over-Rapport'." *American Sociological Review* 17 (1952):97–99.

Millett, Kate. *Sexual Politics.* New York: Ballatine, 1969.

Millman, Marcia. *Such a Pretty Face: Being Fat in America.* New York: W. W. Norton, 1980.

——— and Kanter, Rosabeth, eds. *Another Voice: Feminist Perspectives on Social Life and Social Science.* Garden City, New York: Doubleday, Anchor Books, 1975.

Mills, C. Wright. *The Sociological Imagination.* New York: Oxford University Press, 1959.

Minnich, Elizabeth. "Discussion." In *The Scholar and the Feminist IV: Connecting Theory, Practice, and Values.* Conference sponsored by The Barnard College Women's Center, 1977.

Mishler, Elliot G. "Meaning in Context: Is There Any Other Kind?" *Harvard Educational Review* 49 (1979):1–19.

Mitteness, Linda. "Anthropological Thinking about Age: Grown Up at Last?" *Reviews in Anthropology* 12 (1985):232–240.

Modell, Judith Schachter. *Ruth Benedict: Patterns of a Life.* Philadelphia: University of Pennsylvania Press, 1983.

Mohanty, Chandra Talpade. "Under Western Eyes: Feminist Scholarship and Colonial Discourses." *Boundary 2* 12/13 (1984/1985):333–358.

Moi, T. *Sexual/textual Politics: Feminist Literary Theory* New York: Methuen, 1985.

Moore, Joan. "Political and Ethical Problems in a Large-Scale Study of a Minority Population." In *Ethics, Politics, and Social Research,* edited by Gideon Sjoberg. Cambridge, Mass.: Schenkman, 1967.

Moraga, Cherrie. *Loving in the War Years.* Boston: South End Press, 1983.

——— and Anzaldua, Gloria, eds. *This Bridge Called My Back: Writing by Radical Women of Color.* Watertown, Mass.: Persephone Press, 1981.

Morawski, J. G. "The Measurement of Masculinity and Femininity: Engendering Categorical Realities." *Journal of Personality* 53 (1985):196–223.

Morgan, David and Spanish, Margaret. "Focus Groups: A New Tool for Qualitative Research." *Qualitative Sociology* 7 (1984):253–270.

Morgan, Robin, ed. *Sisterhood is Global: The International Women's Movement Anthology.* New York: Anchor, Doubleday, 1984.

Morgan, Sally. *My Place.* New York: Arcade, 1980.

Moses, Ylanda T. and Jones, Lillian H. "Doing the Job: Ethnic and Women's Studies in a Polytechnic University." *Women's Studies International Forum* 9 (1986):145–150.

Moulton, Janice; Robinson, George; and Elias, Cherin. "Sex Bias in Language Use." *The American Psychologist* 33 (1978):1032–1036.

Moulton, Ruth. "Anxiety and the New Feminism." In *Handbook on Stress and Anxiety,* edited by Irwin Lutash and Louis Schlesinger. San Francisco: Jossey-Bass, 1980.

Mowbray, Carol; Lanir, Susan; and Hulce, Marilyn, eds. *Women and Mental Health: New Directions for Change.* New York: The Haworth Press, 1984.

Mud Flower Collective, The. *God's Fierce Whimsy: Christian Feminism and Theological Education.* New York: The Pilgrim Press, 1985.

Murcott, Anne. "Women's Place: Cookbooks' Images of Technique and Technology in the British Kitchen." *Women's Studies International Forum* 6 (1983):33–40.

Murdock, George P. and White, Douglas R. "Standard Cross-cultural Sample." *Ethnology* 8 (1969):329–369.

Myerhoff, Barbara. *Number Our Days.* New York: Simon & Schuster, 1978.

Myrdal, Alva and Klein, Viola. *Women's Two Roles: Home and Work.* London: Routledge & Kegan Paul, 1956.

Nader, Laura. "From Anguish to Exultation." In *Women in the Field: Anthropological Experiences,* edited by Peggy Golde. Chicago: Aldine, 1970.

Nebraska Feminist Collective. "A Feminist Ethic for Social Science Research." *Women's Studies International Forum* 6 (1983):535–543.

Nebraska Sociological Feminist Collective. *A Feminist Ethic for Social Science Research.* Lewiston, N.Y. and Queenston, Ontario: The Edwin Mellen Press, 1988.

Neggrey, Cynthia. Film review of "Still Killing us Softly." *SWS Network News* 6 (1988):21.

———. Review of Ursula Sharma, *Women's Work, Class, and the Urban Household: A Study of Shimla, North India.* New York: Tavistock, 1986. In *Gender & Society* 3 (1989):143–145.

Newcomb, Horace. *TV: The Most Popular Art.* New York: Anchor Books, 1974.

Newman, Louise Michele, ed. *Men's Ideas/Women's Realities: Popular Science, 1870–1915.* New York: Pergamon, 1985.

Newton, Esther. *Mother Camp: Female Impersonators in America.* Chicago: The University of Chicago Press, 1979.

Ng, Roxana. "Sex, Ethnicity or Class?: Some Methodological Considerations." In *Looking Back: Some Papers from the BSA 'Gender & Society' Conference,* edited by Sue Webb & Clive Pearson. In *Studies in Sexual Politics,* edited by Liz Stanley and Sue Scott. Manchester, Eng.: Department of Sociology, University of Manchester, 1984.

Nicolson, Paula. "Developing a Feminist Approach to Depression Following Childbirth." In *Feminist Social Psychology: Developing Theory and Practice,* edited by Sue Wilkinson. Philadelphia: Open University Press, 1986.

Nielsen, Joyce McCarl, ed. *Feminist Research Methods: Readings in the Social Sciences.* Boulder, Colo.: Westview Press, 1989.

——— and Abromeit, Jeana. "Paradigm Shifts and Feminist Phase Theory in Women

Studies Curriculum Transformation Projects.'' Paper presented at the Annual Meeting of the American Sociological Association, 1989.

Novitz, Rosemary. "Feminism." In *New Zealand: Sociological Perspectives*, edited by Paul Spoonely, David Pearson, and Ian Shirley. Palmerston North, New Zealand: The Dunmore Press, 1982.

Oakley, Ann. "Interviewing Women: A Contradiction in Terms." In *Doing Feminist Research*, edited by Helen Roberts. London: Routledge & Kegan Paul, 1981.

―――. "The Invisible Woman: Sexism in Sociology." In *The Sociology of Housework*, edited by Ann Oakley. New York: Pantheon, 1974.

―――. *The Sociology of Housework*. 1974. Oxford: Basil Blackwell, 1985.

―――. *Taking it Like a Woman*. New York: Random House, 1984.

――― and Oakley, Robin. "Sexism in Official Statistics." In *Demystifying Social Statistics*, edited by John Irvine, Ian Miles, and Jeff Evans. London: Pluto, 1981.

O'Brien, J. E. "Violence in Divorce-prone Families." *Journal of Marriage and the Family* 33 (1971):692–698.

O'Brien, Mary. *The Politics of Reproduction*. Boston: Routledge & Kegan Paul, 1981.

O'Connell, Agnes N. and Russo, Nancy Felipe, eds. "Eminent Women in Psychology." Special Issue, *Psychology of Women Quarterly* 5 (1980).

―――, eds. *Models of Achievement: Reflections of Eminent Women in Psychology*. New York: Columbia University Press, 1983.

O'Donnell, Katherine. " 'A Class Act'." Paper presented at the Annual Meeting of the American Sociological Association, 1991.

O'Donnell, Lydia. *The Unheralded Majority: Contemporary Women as Mothers*. Lexington, Mass.: Lexington Books, 1985.

O'Farrell, M. Brigid and Kleiner, Lydia. "Anna Sullivan: Trade Union Organizer." *Frontiers* 2 (1979):24–29.

O'Kelly, Charlotte. "Gender Role Stereotypes in Fine Art: A Content Analysis of Art History Books." *Qualitative Sociology* 6 (1983):136–148.

――― and Carney, Larry. *Women & Men in Society: Cross-Cultural Perspectives on Gender Stratification*. 2d ed. Belmont, Calif.: Wadsworth Publishing Company, 1986.

Okin, Susan Moller. *Women in Western Political Thought*. Princeton, N.J.: Princeton University Press, 1979.

Older Women: Research Issues and Data Sources, April 8–10, 1984, Institute of Gerontology, University of Michigan, 1984.

O'Leary, Virginia. *Toward Understanding Women*. Belmont, Calif.: Brooks/Cole, 1977.

Olesen, Virginia and Whittaker, Elvi. *The Silent Dialogue: A Study in the Social Psychology of Professional Socialization*. San Francisco: Jossey-Bass, 1968.

―――. "Role-making in Participant Observation: Processes in the Researcher-actor Relationship." In *Sociological Methods: A Sourcebook*, edited by Norman K. Denzin. Chicago: Aldine, 1970.

Olson, Laura Katz. *The Political Economy of Aging: The State, Private Power and Social Welfare*. New York: Columbia University Press, 1982.

O'Neill, William L. *Feminism in America: A History*. 2d rev. ed. New Brunswick, N.J.: Transaction Books, 1989.

Ong, Aihwa. "Colonialism and Modernity: Feminist Re-presentations of Women in Non-Western Societies." *Inscriptions*, Special Issue: *Feminism and the Critique of Colonial Discourse* 3/4 (1988):78–93.

Oppenheimer, Valerie K. *The Female Labor Force in the United States*. Population Monograph Series, no. 5. Berkeley: Institute of International Studies, University of California, 1970.

The Oral History Review, journal of the Oral History Association.

Ormiston, Gayle L. and Sassower, Raphael. *Narrative Experiments: The Discursive Authority of Science and Technology.* Minneapolis: University of Minnesota Press, 1989.

Ortner, Sherry B. "Is Female to Male as Nature is to Culture?" In *Woman, Culture, and Society,* edited by Michelle Z. Rosaldo and Louise Lamphere. Stanford: Stanford University Press, 1974.

Ostrander, Susan. *Women of the Upper Class.* Philadelphia: Temple University Press, 1984.

Paget, Marianne A. "Life Mirrors Work Mirrors Text Mirrors Life." *Social Problems* 37 (1990):137–150.

———. "The Ontological Anguish of Women Artists." *New England Sociologist* 3 (1981):65–79.

———. "On the Work of Talk: Studies in Misunderstandings." In *The Social Organization of Doctor-Patient Communication,* edited by Sue Fisher and Alexander Dundas Todd. Washington, D.C.: Center for Applied Linguistics, 1983.

———. "Performing the Text." *Journal of Contemporary Ethnography* 19 (1990):136–155.

Paradise, Jeanne M. "In Search of a Research Paradigm for a Human-World Science." Mimeographed. Boston University, School of Education, 1983.

Parlee, Mary Brown. "Appropriate Control Groups in Feminist Research." *Psychology of Women Quarterly* 5 (1981):637–644.

———. "Conversational Politics." *Psychology Today* 12 (1979):48–56.

———. "Psychology and Women." *Signs: Journal of Women in Culture and Society* 5 (1979):121–133.

Parsons, Kathryn Pyne. "Moral Revolution." In *The Prism of Sex: Essays in the Sociology of Knowledge,* edited by Julia Sherman and Evelyn Beck. Madison, Wis.: University of Wisconsin Press, 1979.

Patai, Daphne. "Beyond Defensiveness: Feminist Research Strategies." *Women's Studies International Forum* 6 (1983):177–189.

———. "Ethical Problems of Personal Narratives or, Who Should Eat the Last Piece of Cake?" Paper presented at Conference on "Autobiographies, Biographies and Life Histories of Women: Interdisciplinary Perspectives." University of Minnesota, 1986.

Pearson, Clive. "Some Problems in Talking about Men." In *Looking Back: Some Papers from the BSA 'Gender & Society' Conference,* edited by Sue Webb and Clive Pearson. In *Studies in Sexual Politics,* edited by Liz Stanley and Sue Scott. Manchester, Eng.: Department of Sociology, University of Manchester, 1984.

Peevers, Barbara Hollands. "Androgyny on the TV Screen? An Analysis of Sex-Roles Portrayal." *Sex Roles* 5 (1979):797–809.

Pemberton, Jane. "Examining the Top Ten or Why Those Songs Make the Charts." In *Wimmin in the Media,* edited by T. Nygren and Mary Jo Deegan. Lincoln, Nebr.: University of Nebraska, 1980.

Penn, Shana. Foreword to *Sex and Other Sacred Games,* by Kim Chernin and Renate Stendhal. New York: Fawcett Columbine, 1990.

Pennell, Joan T. "Ideology at a Canadian Shelter for Battered Women: A Reconstruction." *Women's Studies International Forum* 10 (1987):113–123.

Peplau, Letitia Anne and Conrad, Eva. "Beyond Nonsexist Research: The Perils of Feminist Methods in Psychology." *Psychology of Women Quarterly* 13 (1989):379–400.

Perdue, Theda. *Nations Remembered: An Oral History of the Five Civilized Tribes, 1865–1907.* Westport, Conn.: Greenwood, 1980.

Pescatello, Ann. *Power and Pawn: The Female in Iberian Families, Societies, and Cultures.* Westport, Conn.: Greenwood, 1976.

Petraka, Vivian and Tilly, Louise, eds. *Feminist Re-Visions: What Has Been and Might Be.* Ann Arbor, Mich.: University of Michigan, Women's Studies Program, 1983.

Pichanik, Valerie. *Harriet Martineau: The Woman and Her Work, 1802–1876.* Ann Arbor, Mich.: University of Michigan Press, 1980.

Pierce, Jennifer. "Tyranny of Niceness." Paper presented at the Gregory Stone Symposium, 1990.

Pizzey, Erin. *Scream Quietly or the Neighbours Will Hear.* Harmondsworth, Eng.: Penguin, 1974.

Plas, Jeanne M. and Wallston, Barbara Strudler. "Women Oriented toward Male-Dominated Careers: Is the Reference Group Male or Female?" *Journal of Counseling Psychology* 30 (1983):46–54.

Poland, Fiona. "Coming Up with the Goods: Working with Recall Tapes in an Elderly Peoples' Home." In *Feminist Research Processes,* edited by Feminist Research Seminar. In *Studies in Sexual Politics* series, edited by Liz Stanley and Sue Scott. Manchester, Eng.: Department of Sociology, University of Manchester, 1987.

Pope, Katherine V. "The Divided Lives of Women in Literature." In *Representations: Social Constructions of Gender,* edited by Rhoda K. Unger. Amityville, N.Y.: Baywood, 1989.

Posner, Judith. "It's All in Your Head: Feminist and Medical Models of Menopause (Strange Bedfellows). *Sex Roles* 5 (1979):179–190.

Powdermaker, Hortense. "Field Work." In *International Encyclopedia of the Social Sciences,* edited by David L. Sills. New York: Macmillan & Free Press, 1972.

———. *Stranger and Friend: The Way of an Anthropologist.* New York: Norton, 1966.

Powers, Marla N. *Oglala Women: Myth, Ritual and Reality.* Chicago: The University of Chicago Press, 1986.

Pratt, Mary Louise. "Fieldwork in Common Places." In *Writing Culture: The Poetics and Politics of Ethnography,* edited by James Clifford and George Marcus. Berkeley: University of California Press, 1986.

"President Futter Calls for New Direction for Women's Movement." *Barnard College Reporter.* New York: Barnard College, 1986.

Project on the Status and Education of Women. *On Campus with Women.* Association of American Colleges, Washington, D.C.

Ptacek, James. "Why Do Men Batter their Wives?" In *Feminist Perspectives on Wife Abuse,* edited by Kersti Yllo and Michele Bograd. Newbury Park, Calif.: Sage, 1988.

Pugh, Anne. "My Statistics and Feminism—a True Story." In *Feminist Research Processes,* edited by Feminist Research Seminar. In *Studies in Sexual Politics,* edited by Liz Stanley and Sue Scott. Manchester, Eng.: Department of Sociology, University of Manchester, 1987.

Puka, Bill. "The Liberation of Caring: A Different Voice for Gilligan's 'Different Voice'." *Hypatia* 5 (1990):58–82.

Radway, Janice. *Reading the Romance: Women, Patriarchy and Popular Literature.* Chapel Hill, N.C.: University of North Carolina Press, 1984.

Rafter, Nicole Hahn. "Hard Times: Custodial Prisons for Women and the Example of the New York State Prison for Women at Auburn, 1893–1933." In *Judge, Lawyer, Victim, Thief: Women, Gender Roles, and Criminal Justice,* edited by Nicole Hahn Rafter and Elizabeth A. Stanko. Boston: Northeastern University Press, 1982.

Rainey, Delores: Goings, Theresa; Martin, Denise; Dumont, Florence; Franklin, Bertha; David, Roslyn; and Johnson, Rosalie. "Weaving New Hopes." In *For Crying Out Loud: Women and Poverty in the United States,* edited by Rochelle Lefkowitz and Ann Withorn. New York: Pilgrim, 1986.

Rakowski, Cathy. "Women in Steel: The Case of Ciudad Guayana, Venezuela." *Qualitative Sociology* 10 (1987):3–28.

Randall, Margaret. *Sandino's Daughters: Testimonies of Nicaraguan Women in Struggle.* Toronto: New Star Books, 1981.

Randall, Vicky. *Women and Politics: An International Perspective.* 1982. Chicago: The University of Chicago Press, 1987.

Raven, Arlene and Iskin, Ruth. "Through the Peephole: Toward a Lesbian Sensibility in Art." *Chrysalis* 4 (1977):19–31.

Raymond, Janice. "Mary Daly: A Decade of Academic Harassment and Feminist Survival." In *Handbook for Women Scholars: Strategies for Success,* edited by Mary Spencer, Monika Kehoe, and Karen Speece. San Francisco: Center for Women Scholars, Americas Behavioral Research Corporation, 1982.

―――. *A Passion for Friends: Toward a Philosophy of Female Affection.* Boston: Beacon Press, 1986.

―――. *The Transsexual Empire: The Making of the She-Male.* Boston: Boston Press, 1979.

Reed, Evelyn. *Sexism and Science.* New York: Pathfinder, 1978.

Reeves, Joy B. and Boyette, Nydia. "What Does Children's Art Work Tell Us about Gender?" *Qualitative Sociology* 6 (1983):322–333.

Reeves, Nancy. *Womankind: Beyond the Stereotypes.* Chicago: Aldine, 1971.

Register, Cheri. "Literary Criticism." *Signs: Journal of Women in Culture and Society* 6 (1980):268–282.

Reid, Margaret. "A Feminist Sociological Imagination? Reading Ann Oakley." *Sociology of Health and Illness* 5 (1983):83–94.

Reinelt, Claire Louise. "Feminist Ways of Knowing." Mimeographed. Department of Sociology, Brandeis University, October 1989.

―――. "Towards a Theory of Feminist Political Practice: A Case Study of the Texas Shelter Movement." M.A. thesis, The University of Texas at Austin, 1985.

Reinharz, Shulamit. "An Assessment of Alvin Gouldner's *The Coming Crisis of Western Sociology.*" Paper presented at the Annual Meeting of the Eastern Sociological Society, 1990.

―――. "The Concept of Voice." Paper presented at the Conference on Human Diversity, 22–24 October 1988, Department of Psychology, University of Maryland, Mimeographed.

―――. "A Partial, Chronological, Contextualized Chart of Primarily U.S. Women's Contributions to Sociology." In *Looking at Invisible Women: An Exercise in Feminist Pedagogy,* edited by Shulamit Reinharz and Ellen Stone. Washington, D.C.: University of America Press, forthcoming.

―――. "Controlling Women's Lives: A Cross-Cultural Interpretation of Miscarriage Accounts." In *Research in the Sociology of Health Care,* edited by Dorothy Wertz. 7 (1988):2–37. Greenwich, Conn.: JAI Press.

―――. "Empty Explanations for Empty Wombs: An Illustration of a Secondary Analysis of Qualitative Data." In *Qualitative Voices in Educational Research,* edited by Michael Schratz. London: Falmer Press, forthcoming.

―――. "Experiential Analysis. A Contribution to Feminist Research Methodology." In *Theories of Women's Studies,* edited by Gloria Bowles and Renate Duelli Klein. Boston: Routledge & Kegan Paul, 1983.

————. "Feminist Distrust: Problems of Content and Context in Sociological Research." In *The Self in Social Inquiry,* edited by David Berg and Ken Smith. Beverly Hills, Calif.: Sage, 1985/1988.

————. "Feminist Research Methodology Groups: Origins, Forms and Functions." In *Feminist Visions and Re-Visions,* edited by Louise Tilly and Vivian Petraka. Ann Arbor, Mich.: University of Michigan, Women's Studies Program, 1984.

————. "Feminist Research Principles." In *Knowledge Explosion: Generations of Feminist Scholarship,* edited by Cheris Kramarae and Dale Spender. New York: Teachers College Press, 1992.

————. "Finding her Sociological Voice: The Work of Mirra Komarovsky." *Sociological Inquiry* 59 (1989):374–395.

————. "Friends or Foes? Feminist and Gerontological Theory." *Women's Studies International Forum* 9 (1986):503–514.

————. "The 'Nature' of Judaism." Mimeographed. Brandeis University, 1989.

————. *On Becoming a Social Scientist: From Survey Research and Participant Observation to Experiential Analysis.* San Francisco: Jossey-Bass, 1979; New Brunswick, N.J.: Transaction Books, 1984.

————. "Pain, Joy and Dilemmas in Feminist Biography." In *The New Sociobiography,* edited by Judy Long. Manuscript.

————. "Patriarchal Pontifications." *Transaction/SOCIETY* 23 (1986):23–29.

————. "Phenomenology as a Dynamic Process." *Phenomenology and Pedagogy* 1 (1983):77–79.

————. "So-called Training in the So-called Alternative Paradigm." In *The Paradigm Dialog,* edited by Egon Guba. Newbury Park, Calif.: Sage, 1990.

————. "The Social Psychology of a Miscarriage: An Application of Symbolic Interactionist Theory and Method." In *Women and Symbolic Interaction,* edited by Mary Jo Deegan and Michael R. Hill. Winchester, Mass.: Allen & Unwin, 1987.

————. "The Sociological Value of Biographies of Female Scientists." Paper presented at the Annual Meeting of the History of Science Society, 1988.

————. "Sources of Diversity in Feminist Psychology." Paper presented at the Annual Meeting of the American Psychological Association, 1982.

————. "Teaching the History of Women in Sociology: Or Dorothy Swaine Thomas, Wasn't She the Woman Married to William I.?." *The American Sociologist* 20 (1989):87–94.

————. "Toward a Model of Female Political Action: The Case of Manya Shohat, Founder of the First Kibbutz." *Women's Studies International Forum* 7 (1984):275–287.

————. "What's Missing in Miscarriage?" *Journal of Community Psychology* 16 (1988):84–103.

————. "Women as Competent Community Builders: The Other Side of the Coin." In *Social and Psychological Problems of Women,* edited by Annette Rickel, Meg Gerrard, and Ira Iscoe. New York: McGraw-Hill/Hemisphere, 1984.

————; Bombyk, Marti; and Wright, Janet. "Methodological Issues in Feminist Research: A Bibliography of Literature in Women's Studies, Sociology and Psychology." *Women's Studies International Forum* 6 (1983):437–454.

———— and Stone, Ellen, eds. *Looking at Invisible Women: An Exercise in Feminist Pedagogy.* Washington, D.C.: University Press of America, forthcoming.

Reiter, Rayna, ed. *Toward an Anthropology of Women.* New York: Monthly Review Press, 1975.

Remmington, Patricia "Women in the Police: Integration or Separation?" *Qualitative Sociology* 6 (1983):118–135.

"Research Methods in Psychology: Are they Anti-Feminist?" Lee Aldora. 'Social Psychology in the Hands of Feminists.'' Jayaratne, Toby, "Survey Research and Feminist Issues." Kenney, Nancy. "A Feminist Look at Psychobiological Research." Post, Robin. "Avoiding the Battered Data Syndrome in Domestic Violence Research." Panel presented at the Annual Meeting of the National Women's Studies Association, 1980.

Reskin, Barbara F. "Bringing the Men Back In: Sex Differentiation and the Devaluation of Women's Work." *Gender & Society* 2 (1988):58–81.

———— and Hartmann, Heidi I. *Women's Work, Men's Work.* Washington, D.C.: National Academy Press, 1986.

Reuss, Pat. "Women and Public Policy: Effective Leadership for the 1990s." *Women's Political Times* 15 (1990):1.

Rheingold, H. L. and Cook, K. V. "The Contents of Boys' and Girls' Rooms as an Index of Parent's Behavior." *Child Development* 46 (1975):459–463.

Ribbens, Jane. "Interviewing—An 'Unnatural Situation'?" *Women's Studies International Forum* 12 (1989):579–592.

Rich, Adrienne. *Of Women Born: Motherhood as Experience and Institution.* New York: Norton, 1976.

Rich, B. Ruby. "In the Name of Feminist Film Criticism." *Heresies #9* 3 (1980):74–81.

Richardson, Laurel. "The Collective Story: Postmodernism and the Writing of Sociology." *Sociological Focus* 21 (1988):199–208.

————. "Disseminating Research to Popular Audiences: The Book Tour." *Qualitative Sociology* 10 (1987):164–176.

————. *The New Woman: Contemporary Single Women in Affairs with Married Men.* New York: Free Press, 1985.

————. "Sexual Freedom and Sexual Constraint: The Paradox for Single Women in Liaisons with Married Men." *Gender & Society* 2 (1988):368–384.

———— and Taylor, Verta. *Feminist Frontiers: Rethinking Sex, Gender and Society.* New York: Random House, 1983.

Riedmann, Agnes. "Margaret Jarman Hagood." In *Women in Sociology: A Bio-bibliographic Sourcebook,* edited by Mary Jo Deegan. Westport, Conn.: Greenwood, 1990.

Riesman, David. Foreword to *Return to Laughter,* by Laura Bohanan. 1954. New York: Anchor Books, rev. ed., 1964.

Riessman, Catherine. *Divorce Talk: Women and Men Make Sense of Personal Relationships.* New Brunswick, N.J.: Rutgers University Press, 1990.

————. "When Gender is Not Enough: Women Interviewing Women." *Gender & Society* 2 (1987):172–207.

Riger, Stephanie. "Ways of Knowing and Community Organizational Research." Conference on Researching Community Psychology: Integrating Theories and Methodologies, 1988.

———— and Gordon, Margaret. "Dilemmas in the Practice of Feminist Research." Paper presented at the Annual Meeting of the American Psychological Association, 1981.

Riley, Matilda White, ed. *Sociological Lives.* Beverly Hills, Calif.: Sage, 1988.

Ring, Jennifer. "Toward a Feminist Epistemology." *American Journal of Political Science* 31 (1987):753–772.

Risman, Barbara. "Men Who Mother." *Gender & Society* 1 (1987):6–32.

Roberts, Elizabeth. *A Woman's Place: An Oral History of Working-Class Women 1890–1940.* Oxford: Basil Blackwell, 1984.

Roberts, Helen, ed. *Doing Feminist Research.* London: Routledge & Kegan Paul, 1981.

Roberts, Joan. *Beyond Intellectual Sexism: A New Woman, A New Reality.* New York: McKay, 1976.

Robertson, Claire. *Sharing the Same Bowl: A Socioeconomic History of Women and Class in Accra, Ghana*. Bloomington, Ind.: Indiana University Press, 1984.

Roby, Pamela. "Union Stewards and Women's Employment Conditions." In *Ingredients for Women's Employment Policy*, edited by Christine Bose and Glenna Spitze. Albany: State University of N.Y. Press, 1987.

Rodriguez, Noelie Maria. "Transcending Bureaucracy: Feminist Politics at a Shelter for Battered Women." *Gender & Society* 2 (1988):214–227.

Roe, Ann. "A Psychological Study of Eminent Psychologists and Anthropologists, and a Comparison with Biological and Physical Scientists." *Psychological Monographs* 67 (1952):1–55.

Rogers, Barbara. *The Domestication of Women: Discrimination in Developing Societies*. New York: St. Martin's Press, 1980.

Rohrbaugh, Joanna Bunker. *Women: Psychology's Puzzle*. New York: Basic Books, 1979.

Rollins, Judith. *Between Women: Domestics and their Employers*. Philadelphia: Temple University Press, 1985.

Rong, Xue Lan; Grant, Linda; and Ward, Kathryn. "Productivity of Women Scholars and Gender Researchers: Is Funding a Factor?" *The American Sociologist* 20 (1989):95–100.

Rosaldo, Michelle Z. and Lamphere, Louise, eds. *Women, Culture and Society*. Stanford: Stanford University Press, 1974.

Rosen, Marjorie. *Popcorn Venus: Women, Movies and the American Dream*. New York: Avon Books, 1973.

Rosenberg, Rosalind. *Beyond Separate Spheres: Intellectual Roots of Modern Feminism*. New Haven, Conn.: Yale University Press, 1982.

Rosenthal, Robert. *Experimenter Effects in Behavioral Research*. New York: Appleton-Century-Crofts, 1967.

Rossi, Alice S. *Feminists in Politics: A Panel Analysis of the First National Women's Conference*. New York: Academic Press, 1982.

———, ed. *Feminist Papers: From Adams to de Beauvoir*. 2d rev. ed. Boston: Northeastern University Press, 1988.

———. "Maternalism, Sexuality and the New Feminism." In *Critical Issues in Contemporary Sexual Behavior*, edited by J. Zubin and J. Money. Baltimore: Johns Hopkins University Press, 1972.

Roth, Julius. "Hired Hand Research." *The American Sociologist* 1 (1966):190–196.

Rothman, Barbara Katz. "Reflections: On Hard Work." *Qualitative Sociology* 9 (1986):48–53.

Rothman, Ronni. "Beyond *Middletown:* The Life Work of Helen Merrell Lynd." In *Looking at Invisible Women: An Exercise in Feminist Pedagogy*, edited by Shulamit Reinharz and Ellen Stone. Washington, D.C.: University Press of America, forthcoming.

Rothman, Sheila M. *Woman's Proper Place: A History of Changing Ideals and Practices, 1870 to the Present*. New York: Basic Books, 1978.

Rowbotham, Sheila and McCrindle, Jean. *Dutiful Daughters: Women Talk about their Lives*. Austin, Tex.: University of Texas Press, 1977.

Rubin, Gayle. "The Traffic in Women." In *Feminist Frameworks*, edited by Alison Jaggar and Paula Struhl. New York: McGraw-Hill, 1978.

Rubin, Lillian Breslow. *Women of a Certain Age: The Midlife Search for Self*. New York: Harper & Row, 1979.

———. *Worlds of Pain: Life in the Working-Class Family*. New York: Basic Books, 1976.

Ruddick, Sara. *Maternal Thinking: Toward a Politics of Peace*. New York: Ballantine, 1989.

———— and Daniels, Pamela. *Working it Out: 23 Women Writers, Artists, Scientists, and Scholars Talk about their Lives and Work*. New York: Pantheon, 1977.

Rupp, Leila and Taylor, Verta. *Surviving in the Doldrums: The American Women's Rights Movements, 1945 to the 1960s*. Columbus: Ohio State University Press, 1990.

Rush, Florence. *Best Kept Secret: Sexual Abuse of Children*. Englewood Cliffs, N.J.: Prentice-Hall, 1980.

Russell, Diana E. H. *Rape in Marriage*. New York: Macmillan, 1982.

———— *Lives of Courage: Women for a New South Africa*. New York: Basic Books, 1989.

———— and Van de Ven, Nicole, eds. *Proceedings of the International Tribunal of Crimes against Women*. Millbrae, Calif.: Les Femmes, 1976.

Russell, Letty, ed. *Feminist Interpretation of the Bible*. Philadelphia: Westminster, 1985.

Ruzek, Sheryl. *The Women's Health Movement: Feminist Alternatives to Medical Control*. New York: Praeger, 1978.

Sabronsky, Judith. *From Rationality to Liberation*. Westport, Conn.: Greenwood, 1979.

Sachs, Carolyn. *The Invisible Farmers: Women in Agricultural Production*. Totowa, N.J.: Rowman & Allanheld, 1983.

Safir, Marilyn; Mednick, Martha; Izraeli, Dafna; and Bernard, Jessie, eds. *Women's Worlds: From the New Scholarship*. New York: Praeger, 1985.

Salaff, Janet W. *Working Daughters of Hong Kong: Filial Piety or Power in the Family?* New York: Cambridge University Press, 1981.

Sanday, Peggy Reeves. *Female Power and Male Dominance: On the Origins of Sexual Inequality*. New York: Cambridge University Press, 1981.

Sandelowski, Margarete and Pollock, Christine. "Women's Experiences of Infertility." *IMAGE: Journal of Nursing Scholarship* 18 (1986):140–144.

Sandmaier, Marian. Review of *The Regulation of Sexuality: Experiences of Family Planning Workers*, by Carole Joffe. Philadelphia: Temple University Press, 1986. In *The New York Times Book Review*. February 8, 1987, p. 25.

Sandoz, Mari. "The Stranger at the Curb." Reissued by Michael R. Hill. *Mid-American Review of Sociology*, 1989.

————. *Capital City*. Boston: Little, Brown, 1939.

Sanger, Margaret. *My Fight for Birth Control*. New York: Farrar & Rinehart, 1931.

————. *Margaret Sanger: An Autobiography*. 1938. New York: Dover, 1971.

Sawer, Marian and Simms, Marian. *A Woman's Place: Women and Politics in Australia*. Boston: George Allen & Unwin, 1984.

Sayers, Janet. *Biological Politics*. London: Tavistock, 1982.

————. *Sexual Contradictions: Psychology, Psychoanalysis, and Feminism*. London: Tavistock, 1986.

Scarborough, Elizabeth and Furumoto, Laurel. *Untold Lives: The First Generation of American Women Psychologists*. New York: Columbia University Press, 1987.

Scheper-Hughes, Nancy. "Introduction: The Problem of Bias in Androcentric and Feminist Anthropology." *Women's Studies* 10 (1983):115.

————. *Saints, Scholars, and Schizophrenics: Mental Illness in Rural Ireland*. Berkeley: University of California Press, 1979.

Schlesinger, Melinda Bart and Bart, Pauline B. "Collective Work and Self-Identity: Working in a Feminist Illegal Abortion Collective." In *Workplace Democracy and Social Change*, edited by Frank Lindenfeld and Joyce Rothschild-Whitt. Boston: Porter Sargent, 1982.

Schneider, Joseph and Hacker, Sally. "Sex Role Imagery and Use of the Generic 'Man' in Introductory Texts: A Case in the Sociology of Sociology." *The American Sociologist* 8 (1973):12–18.

Schroeder, Jean Reith. *Alone in a Crowd: Women in the Trades Tell Their Stories.* Philadelphia: Temple University Press, 1986.

Schuster, Marilyn R. and Van Dyne, Susan R., eds. *Women's Place in the Academy: Transforming the Liberal Arts Curriculum.* Totowa, N.J.: Rowman & Allanheld, 1985.

Scott, Patricia Bell. "Debunking Sapphire: Toward a Non-Racist and Non-Sexist Social Science." *Journal of Sociology and Social Welfare* 4 (1977):864–871.

Scully, Diana. "Convicted Rapists' Perceptions of Self and Victim: Role Taking and Emotions." *Gender & Society* 2 (1988):200–213.

———— and Bart, Pauline. "A Funny Thing Happened on the Way to the Orifice: Women in Gynecology Textbooks." *American Journal of Sociology* 78 (1971):1045–1050.

Searles, Patricia and Berger, Ronald. "The Feminist Self-Defense Movement: A Case Study." *Gender & Society* 1 (1987):61–84.

Section on Sex and Gender, American Sociological Association, *Newsletter,* Fall 1989.

Segal, Marcia Texler. "Feminism and the Self-Conscious Sociologist: An Essay on the Sociology of Knowledge." Mimeographed. Paper presented for the Sociology Departmental Seminar, University of Malawi, Africa 1984.

———— and Berheide, Catherine White. "Towards a Women's Perspective in Sociology: Directions and Prospects." In *Theoretical Perspectives in Sociology,* edited by Scott McNall. New York: St. Martin's Press, 1979.

Segrest, Mab. *My Mama's Dead Squirrel: Lesbian Essays on Southern Culture.* Ithaca, N.Y.: Firebrand Books, 1985.

Segura, Denise. "Chicana and Mexican Immigrant Women at Work: The Impact of Class, Race and Gender on Occupational Mobility." *Gender & Society* 3 (1989):37–52.

Seidel, Gill, ed. *The Nature of the Right: A Feminist Analysis of Order Patterns.* Philadelphia: John Benjamins, 1988.

Seifer, Nancy. *Nobody Speaks for Me: Self-Portraits of American Working Class Women.* New York: Touchstone, 1976.

Seligman, Martin and Maier, Steven. "Failure to Escape Traumatic Shock." *Journal of Experimental Psychology* 74 (1967):1–9.

Seller, Maxine Schwartz. *Immigrant Women.* Philadelphia: Temple University Press, 1981.

Sexton, Patricia Cayo. *The New Nightingales: Hospital Workers, Unions, New Women's Issues.* New York: Enquiry Press, 1982.

Shamgar-Handelman, Lea. *Israeli War Widows: Beyond the Glory of Heroism.* South Hadley, Mass.: Bergin & Garvey, 1986.

Shapiro, Joan Poliner and Reed, Beth. "Consideration of Ethical Issues in the Assessment of Feminist Projects: A Case Study Using Illuminative Evaluation." In *A Feminist Ethic for Social Science Research,* edited by the Nebraska Sociological Feminist Collective. Lewiston, N.Y. and Queenston, Ontario: The Edwin Mellen Press, 1988.

Shaw, Clifford R. *The Jack-Roller: A Delinquent Boy's Own Story.* 1930. Chicago: The University of Chicago Press, 1966.

Shaw, Nancy Stoller. *Forced Labor: Maternity Care in the United States.* Elmsford, N.Y.: Pergamon, 1974.

Sherif, Carolyn. "Bias in Psychology." In *The Prism of Sex: Essays in the Sociology of Knowledge,* edited by Julia Sherman and Evelyn Beck. Madison, Wis.: University of Wisconsin Press, 1979.

————. "Should There be a Feminist Methodology?" *Newsletter of the Association for Women in Psychology* (January–February 1982):3–4.

Sherman, Julia and Beck, Evelyn, eds. *The Prism of Sex: Essays in the Sociology of Knowledge.* Madison, Wis.: University of Wisconsin Press, 1979.

Shields, Stephanie. "The Variability Hypothesis: The History of a Biological Model of Sex Difference in Intelligence." *Signs: Journal of Women in Culture and Society* 7 (1982):769–797.

Shiva, Vandana. *Staying Alive: Women, Ecology and Development.* London: Zed Books, 1988.

Shostak, Marjorie. 1981. *Nisa: The Life and Words of a !Kung Woman.* New York: Vintage Books, 1983.

———. "What the Wind Won't Take Away: Methodological and Ethical Considerations of the Oral History of a Hunting-Gathering Woman." Paper presented at Conference on "Autobiographies, Biographies and Life Histories of Women: Interdisciplinary Perspectives." University of Minnesota, 1986.

———. " 'What the Wind Won't Take Away': The Genesis of *Nisa—The Life and Words of a !Kung Woman.*" In *Interpreting Women's Lives: Feminist Theory and Personal Narratives,* edited by Personal Narratives Group. Bloomington, Ind.: Indiana University Press, 1989.

Showalter, Elaine. "Literary Criticism." *Signs: Journal of Women in Culture and Society* 1 (1975):435–460.

———. *A Literature of their Own: British Women Novelists from Bronte to Lessing.* Princeton, N.J.: Princeton University Press, 1977.

Shuster, Rebecca. "Sexuality as a Continuum: The Bisexual Identity." In *Lesbian Psychologies,* edited by Boston Lesbian Psychologies Collective. Chicago: University of Illinois Press, 1987.

Silveira, Jeanette. "The Effect of Sexism on Thought: How Male Bias Hurts Psychology and Some Hopes for a Woman's Psychology." In *Women on the Movement: A Feminist Perspective,* edited by Jean Ramage Leppaluoto. Pittsburgh: KNOW, 1973.

Simmel, Georg. *Georg Simmel: On Women, Sexuality, and Love.* Translated and with an Introduction by Guy Oakes. New Haven, Conn.: Yale University Press, 1984.

———. *Philosophische Kultur.* Leipzig: Warner Klinkhardt, 1911.

Simonds, Wendy. "Confessions of Loss: Maternal Grief in *True Story,* 1920–1985." *Gender & Society* 2 (1988):149–171.

Simonsen, Thordis, ed. *You May Plow Here: The Narrative of Sara Brooks.* New York: Norton, 1986.

Sims, Karen and Mason, Rose with Pagano, Darlene R. "Racism and Sadomasochism, a Conversation with Two Black Lesbians." In *Against Sadomasochism: A Radical Feminist Analysis,* edited by Robin R. Linden, Darlene Pagano, Diana Russell, and Susan Leigh Star. East Palo Alto, Calif.: Frog in the Well Press, 1982.

Sistern, with Smith, Honor Ford. *Lionheart Gal: Life Stories of Jamaican Women.* London: The Women's Press, 1986.

Sitaraman, Bhavani. "Abortion Situations and Abortion Morality: A Factorial Survey Analysis of Abortion Attitudes." Paper presented at the Annual Meeting of the Eastern Sociological Society, 1990.

Sitton, Thad; Mehaffy, George; and Davis, O. L., Jr. *Oral History: A Guide for Teachers (and Others).* Austin, Tex.: University of Texas Press, 1983.

Smail, Barbara; Whyte, Judith; and Kelly, Alison. "Girls into Science and Technology: The First Two Years." *SSR* 64 (1982):620–630.

Smart, Carol. "Researching Prostitution: Some Problems for Feminist Research." In *A Feminist Ethic for Social Science Research,* edited by Nebraska Sociological Feminist Collective. Lewiston, N.Y.: The Edwin Mellen Press, 1988.

———. *Women, Crime and Criminology: A Feminist Critique.* London: Routledge & Kegan Paul, 1976.

Smith, Barbara. "Racism and Women's Studies." *Frontiers* 5 (1980):48–49.

Smith, Dorothy E. "An Analysis of Ideological Structures and How Women Are Excluded: Considerations for Academic Women." *Canadian Review of Sociology and Anthropology* 12 (1975):353–369.

———. *The Everyday World as Problematic: A Feminist Sociology.* Boston: Northeastern University Press, 1987.

———. "Institutional Ethnography: A Feminist Method." *Resources for Feminist Research/Documentation-sur-la-Recherche Feministe* 15 (1986):6–13.

———. "A Sociology for Women." In *The Prism of Sex: Essays in the Sociology of Knowledge,* edited by Julia Sherman and Evelyn Torton Beck. Madison, Wis.: University of Wisconsin Press, 1979.

———. "Women's Perspective as a Radical Critique of Sociology." *Sociological Inquiry* 44 (1974):7–13.

Smith-Rosenberg, Carroll. "The New Woman and the New History." *Feminist Studies* 3 (1975):185–198.

Solomon, Barbara Miller. *In the Company of Educated Women: A History of Women and Higher Education in America.* New Haven, Conn.: Yale University Press, 1985.

Spalter-Roth, Roberta M. and Hartmann, Heidi I. "Science and Politics: The 'Dual Vision' of Feminist Policy Research, the Example of Family and Medical Leave." Washington, D.C.: Institute for Women's Policy Research, 1987, 1988.

———. *Unnecessary Losses: Costs to Americans of the Lack of Family and Medical Leave.* Washington, D.C.: Institute for Women's Policy Research, 1989.

Spangler, E.; Gordon, M. A.; and Pipkin, R. M. "Token Women: An Empirical Test of Kanter's Hypothesis." *American Journal of Sociology* 84 (1978):160–170.

Spender, Dale. *For the Record: The Meaning and Making of Feminist Knowledge.* London: Women's Press, 1985.

———. "The Gatekeepers: A Feminist Critique of Academic Publishing." In *Doing Feminist Research,* edited by Helen Roberts. London: Routledge & Kegan Paul, 1981.

———. *Man Made Language.* London: Routledge & Kegan Paul, 1980.

———, ed. *Men's Studies Modified: The Impact of Feminism on the Academic Disciplines.* New York: Pergamon, 1981.

———, ed. *Personal Chronicles: Women's Autobiographical Writings.* Special Issue of *Women's Studies International Forum* 10 (1987).

——— and Spender, Lynne. eds. *Gatekeeping: The Denial, Dismissal and Distortion of Women.* Special Issue of *Women's Studies International Forum* 6 (1983).

Sprague, Joey. Review of Dorothy E. Smith, *The Everyday World as Problematic: A Feminist Sociology.* In *Contemporary Sociology* 18 (1989):640–641.

——— and Zimmerman, Mary K. "Quality and Quantity: Reconstructing Feminist Methodology." *The American Sociologist* 20 (1989):71–86.

Spring, Donna. "Medical Science without Cruelty to Animals." *Women of Power* 11 (1978):58–61.

Springer, Marlene and Springer, Haskell, eds. *Plains Woman: The Diary of Martha Farnsworth, 1882–1922.* Bloomington, Ind.: Indiana University Press, 1986.

Stacey, Judith. *Brave New Families: Stories of Domestic Upheaval in Late Twentieth Century America.* New York: Basic Books, 1990.

———. "Can There Be a Feminist Ethnography?" *Women's Studies International Forum* 11 (1988):21–27.

———. "On Resistance, Ambivalence and Feminist Theory: A Response to Carol Gilligan." *Michigan Quarterly Review* 29 (1990):537–546.

―――. "Sexism by a Subtler Name? Postindustrial Conditions and Postfeminist Consciousness in the Silicon Valley." *Socialist Review* 17 (1987):1–28.

――― and Gerard, Susan Elizabeth. "We Are Not Doormats: The Influence of Feminism on Contemporary Evangelicals in the United States." Paper presented at the Annual meeting of the American Sociological Association, 1989.

――― and Thorne, Barrie. "The Missing Feminist Revolution in Sociology." *Social Problems* 32 (1985):301–316.

Stack, Carol. *All Our Kin: Strategies for Survival in a Black Community.* New York: Harper & Row, 1974.

Stage, Sarah. *Female Complaints: Lydia Pinkham and the Business of Women's Medicine.* New York: W. W. Norton, 1979.

Staines, Graham; Tavris, Carol; and Jayaratne, Toby Epstein. "The Queen Bee Syndrome." *Psychology Today* 8 (1974):55–60.

Stall, Susan. " 'What about the Non-feminist?': The Possibilities for Women's Movement Coalition Building in Small Town America." Paper presented at the Annual Meeting of the Society for the Study of Social Problems, 1985.

―――. "Women in a Small Town: An Invisible Power Structure." Paper presented at the Joint Annual Meeting of the Midcontinent American Studies Association and the North Central American Studies Association, 1983.

Standish, Leanna. "Women, Work, and the Scientific Enterprise." Mimeographed. Smith College, Fall 1981.

Stanley, Liz, ed. *The Diaries of Hannah Cullwick, Victorian Maidservant.* New Brunswick, N.J.: Rutgers University Press, 1984.

―――. *Feminism and Friendship: Two Essays on Olive Schreiner.* In *Studies in Sexual Politics,* edited by Liz Stanley and Sue Scott. Manchester, Eng.: Department of Sociology, University of Manchester, 1984.

―――. " 'The Research Process' in the Social Sciences and its Part in Producing Discrimination against Women in Higher Education." *British Society for Research in Higher Education, Monograph on Gender Biases,* 1982.

――― and Wise, Sue. "Back into 'the Personal': Or Our Attempt to Construct 'Feminist Research.' " In *Theories of Women's Studies,* edited by Gloria Bowles and Renate Duelli Klein. Boston: Routledge & Kegan Paul, 1983.

―――. *Breaking Out: Feminist Consciousness and Feminist Research.* London: Routledge & Kegan Paul, 1983.

―――. "Feminist Research, Feminist Consciousness and Experiences of Sexism." *Women's Studies International Quarterly* 2 (1979):359–374.

Stanton, Alfred and Schwartz, Morris. *The Mental Hospital.* New York: Basic Books, 1954.

Stanton, Elizabeth Cady. *The Original Feminist Attack on the Bible (The Woman's Bible).* New York: Arno Press, 1974.

Star, Susan Leigh. "Strategic Heresy as Scientific Method: Feminism and the Psychology of Consciousness." Paper presented to the American Association for the Advancement of Science, 1979.

Steinberg, Ronnie J. "Dilemmas of Advocacy Research: Experiences with Comparable Worth." Paper prepared for Plenary Panel: Social Science Research and Law Reform, Law and Society Association, 1987.

Steinem, Gloria. "I was a Playboy Bunny." In *Outrageous Acts and Everyday Rebellions,* edited by Gloria Steinem. New York: New American Library, 1983.

―――. *Outrageous Acts and Everyday Rebellions.* New York: New American Library, 1983.

Stewart, Abigail and Winter, David. "The Nature and Causes of Female Suppression." *Signs: Journal of Women in Culture and Society* 2 (1977):531–553.

Stiller, Nancy and Forrest, Linda. "An Extension of Gilligan and Lyons' Investigation of Morality: Gender Differences in College Students." *Journal of College Student Development* 31 (1990):54–62.

Stone, Ellen. "Claiming the Third Story: The Challenge to White Feminists of Black Feminist Theory." Mimeographed. Brandeis University, 1990.

Storper-Perez, Danielle and Wasserfall, Rahel. "Methodologie de la Raison, Methodologie de la Resonance d'un Devenir-Femme de la Recherche?" *Revue de l'Institut de Sociologie* 1–2 (1988):189–207.

Strathern, Marilyn. "An Awkward Relationship: The Case of Feminism and Anthropology." *Signs: Journal of Women in Culture and Society* 12 (1987):288–292.

———. "Out of Context: The Persuasive Fictions of Anthropology." *Current Anthropology* 28 (1987):251–281.

Stricker, Frank. "Cookbooks and Lawbooks: The Hidden History of Career Women in Twentieth Century America." In *A Heritage of Her Own: Toward a New Social History of American Women,* edited by Nancy Cott and Elizabeth Pleck. New York: Simon & Schuster, 1979.

Sumner, Helen Laura [Woodbury]. *Equal Suffrage.* 1909. New York: Arno Press, 1972.

Swindells, Julia. "Liberating the Subject? Autobiography and Women's History': A Reading of *The Diaries of Hannah Cullwick.*" In *Interpreting Women's Lives: Feminist Theory and Personal Narratives,* edited by Personal Narratives Group. Bloomington, Ind.: Indiana University Press, 1989.

Taft, Jessie. "The Woman Movement and Social Consciousness." In *Women and Symbolic Interaction,* edited by Mary Jo Deegan and Michael R. Hill. Winchester, Mass.: Allen & Unwin, 1987.

Tancred-Sheriff, Peta, ed. *Feminist Research: Prospect and Retrospect; Recherche Feministe: Bilan et Perspectives d'Avenir.* Montreal: McGill-Queen's University Press, 1988.

Tangri, Sandra and Strasburg, Georgia. "Can Research on Women Be More Effective in Shaping Policy?" *Psychology of Women Quarterly* 3 (1979):321–343.

Taylor, Ella. *Prime Time Families: Television Culture in Postwar America.* Berkeley: University of California Press, 1989.

Terkel, Studs. *Division Street: America.* New York: Pantheon, 1967.

———. *Hard Times: An Oral History of the Great Depression.* New York: Pantheon, 1970.

———. *Working: People Talk about What they Do All Day and How they Feel about It.* New York: Pantheon, 1974.

Tetreault, Mary Kay. "Feminist Phase Theory: An Experience-Derived Evaluation Model." *Journal of Higher Education* 56 (1985):363–384.

Theodore, Athena. *The Campus Troublemakers: Academic Women in Protest.* Houston, Tex.: Cap and Gown Press, 1986.

Theodorson, George A. and Theodorson, Achilles G. *A Modern Dictionary of Sociology.* New York: Thomas Y. Crowell, 1969.

Thomas, William I. and Znaniecki, Florian. *The Polish Peasant in Europe and America.* 2d ed. New York: Alfred Knopf, 1927.

Thompson, Becky. "Raisins and Smiles for Me and My Sister: A Feminist Theory of Eating Problems, Trauma, and Recovery in Women's Lives." Ph.D. dissertation, Brandeis University, 1990.

Thompson, Martha E. "Breastfeeding in Public." Paper presented at the Annual Meetings of the National Women's Studies Association, 1986.

——— et al. "What Makes a Feminist Social Science?" *Program Notes*. Women's Studies Program, Northeastern Illinois University 10 (1985).

Thompson, Mildred I. *Ida B. Wells-Barnett: An Exploratory Study of an American Black Woman, 1893–1930*. New York: Carlson, 1990.

Thorne, Barrie. "Political Activist as Participant Observer: Conflicts of Commitment in a Study of the Draft Resistance Movement of the 1960s." *Symbolic Interaction* 2 (1978):73–88.

——— and Henley, Nancy, eds. *Language and Sex: Difference and Dominance*. Rowley, Mass.: Newbury House, 1975.

Thornton, Bonnie. "Race, Class and Gender: Prospects for an All-Inclusive Sisterhood." *Feminist Studies* 9 (1983):131–150.

Tobin, Lad. "A Radically Different Voice: Gender and Language in the Trials of Anne Hutchinson." *Early American Literature* 25 (1990):253–270.

"Toward a Feminist Theory of Motherhood." Special Issue of *Feminist Studies*. 4 (1978):1–199.

Tresemer, David W. *Fear of Success*. New York: Plenum, 1977.

Tuchman, Gaye. *Edging Women Out: Victorian Novelists, Publishers, and Social Change*. New Haven: Yale University Press, 1989.

———; Daniels, Arlene Kaplan; and Benet, James, eds. *Hearth and Home: Images of Women in the Mass Media*. New York: Oxford University Press, 1978.

Tucker, Susan. *Telling Memories among Southern Women: Domestic Workers and their Employers in the Segregated South*. Baton Rouge, La.: Louisiana State University Press, 1988.

"Twenty Major Changes in the Norms Guiding American Life." *Psychology Today* 15 (1981):68.

Unger, Rhoda Kesler, ed. *Representations: Social Constructions of Gender*. Amityville, N.Y.: Baywood, 1989.

———. "Sex as Social Reality: Field and Laboratory Research." *Psychology of Women Quarterly* 5 (1981):645–653.

———. "Some Neglected Issues in the Creation of a Sex-related Reality." Paper presented at the Annual Meeting of the American Psychological Association, 1982.

———. "Through the Looking Glass: No Wonderland Yet! (The Reciprocal Relationship between Methodology and Models of Reality)." *Psychology of Women Quarterly* 8 (1983):9–32.

University of Wisconsin, Madison, Women's Studies, *Research Center Newsletter*, Spring 1984.

U'Ren, Marjorie. "The Image of Woman in Textbooks." In *Woman in Sexist Society: Studies in Power and Powerlessness*, edited by Vivian Gornick and Barbara Moran. New York: New American Library, 1971.

Valli, Linda. *Becoming Clerical Workers*. Boston: Routledge & Kegan Paul, 1986.

van der Burg, Rosaharn and Schoemaker, Nelleke. "Scoring Women on their Labor Chances." *Women's Studies International Forum* 8 (1985):273–278.

Van Kleeck, Mary Abby. *Artificial Flower Makers*. New York: Russell Sage Foundation, 1913.

Van Maanen, John. *Tales of the Field: On Writing Ethnography*. Chicago: The University of Chicago Press, 1988.

Vaughter, Reesa M. "Psychology." *Signs: Journal of Women in Culture and Society* 2 (1976):120–146.

Verba, Sidney with DiNunzio, Joseph and Spaulding, Christina. "Unwanted Attention:

Report on a Sexual Harassment Survey.'' Report to the Faculty Council of the Faculty of Arts and Sciences, Harvard University, 1983.

Vickers, Jill McCalla. ''Memoirs of an Ontological Exile: The Methodological Rebellions of Feminist Research.'' In *Feminism in Canada*, edited by Geraldine Finn and Angela Miles. Montreal: Black Rose Books, 1982.

Visweswaran, Kamala. ''Defining Feminist Ethnography.'' *Inscriptions: Feminism and the Critique of Colonial Discourse* 3/4 (1988):26–44.

Volentine, Susan and Brodsky, Stanley. ''Personal Construct Theory and Stimulus Sex and Subject Sex Differences.'' In *Representations: Social Constructions of Gender*, edited by Rhoda K. Unger. Amityville, N.Y.: Baywood, 1989.

Voss, Jacqueline and Gannon, Linda. ''Sexism in the Theory and Practice of Clinical Psychology.'' *Professional Psychology?* 9 (1978):623–632.

Waelti-Walters, Jennifer. ''On Princesses: Fairy Tales, Sex Roles and Loss of Self.'' *International Journal of Women's Studies* 2 (1979):180–188.

Wajcman, Judy. *Women in Control: Dilemmas of a Workers' Co-operative*. New York: St. Martin's Press, 1983.

Walby, Sylvia. *Patriarchy at Work*. Minneapolis: University of Minnesota Press, 1986.

Walker, Alice, ed. *I Love Myself when I Am Laughing: A Zora Neale Hurston Reader*. Old Westbury, N.Y.: The Feminist Press, 1979.

Walker, Beverly. ''Psychology and Feminism—if You Can't Beat Them, Join Them.'' In *Men's Studies Modified: The Impact of Feminism on the Academic Disciplines*, edited by Dale Spender. New York: Pergamon, 1981.

Walker, Leonore E. *The Battered Woman*. New York: Harper & Row, 1979.

Walker, M. Urban. ''What Does the Different Voice Say?: Gilligan's Women and Moral Philosophy.'' *The Journal of Value Inquiry* 23 (1989):123–128.

Wallace, Ruth. ''Catholic Women and the Creation of a New Social Reality.'' *Gender & Society* 2 (1988):24–38.

Wallston, Barbara Strudler. ''Feminist Research Methodology from a Psychological Perspective: Science as the Marriage of Agentic and Communal.'' In *Women's Worlds: From the New Scholarship*, edited by Marilyn Safir, Martha Mednick, Dafna N. Izraeli, and Jessie Bernard. New York: Praeger, 1985.

———. ''What are the Questions in Psychology of Women? A Feminist Approach to Research.'' *Psychology of Women Quaerterly* 5 (1981):597–617.

Walsh, Andrea S. *Women's Film and Female Experience, 1940–1950*. New York: Praeger, 1984.

Walsh, Mary Roth. *Doctors Wanted: No Women Need Apply*. New Haven, Conn.: Yale University Press, 1977.

———. ''Psychology.'' In *The Knowledge Explosion*, edited by Cheris Kramarae and Dale Spender. New York: Teachers College Press, 1992.

———, ed. *The Psychology of Women: Ongoing Debates*. New Haven, Conn.: Yale University Press, 1987.

Walsh, Richard T. ''Where is the Research Relationship in Feminist Psychology Research?'' Paper presented at the Annual Meeting of the American Psychological Association, 1987.

War, David and Kassebaum, Gene. *Women's Prison: Sex and Social Structure*. Chicago: Aldine, 1965.

Ward, Kathryn and Grant, Linda. ''The Feminist Critique and a Decade of Research in Sociology Journals.'' *Sociological Quarterly* 26 (1985):139–157.

Wardell, Laurie; Gillespie, Dair L.; and Leffler, Ann. ''Science and Violence against Wives.'' Mimeographed. Department of Sociology, University of Utah, 1981.

Warner, Marina. *Joan of Arc: The Image of Female Heroism*. New York: Vintage, 1981.

Warren, Carol A. B. "Fieldwork in the Gay World: Issues in Phenomenological Research." *Journal of Social Issues* 33 (1977):93–107.

———. *Gender Issues in Field Research.* Beverly Hills, Calif.: Sage, 1988.

——— and Rasmussen, Paul. "Sex and Gender in Field Research." *Urban Life* 6 (1977):349–369.

Wasserfall, Rahel. "Gender Identification in an Israeli Moshav." Ph.D. dissertation, Hebrew University of Jerusalem, 1987.

Wastila, Linda. "Perceptions of RU 486: Views of Pro-Choice and Feminist Activists." Mimeographed. Brandeis University, 1990.

Wattleton, Faye. "A Special Report on a Recent International Trip to India and Indonesia." *Planned Parenthood,* 1986.

Wax, Rosalie. *Doing Fieldwork: Warnings and Advice.* Chicago: The University of Chicago Press, 1971.

———. "Gender and Age in Fieldwork and Fieldwork Education: No Good Thing is Done by Any Man Alone." *Social Problems* 26 (1979):509–522.

Webb, Beatrice P. *My Apprenticeship.* 1926. London: Cambridge University Press, 1979.

Webb, Christine. "Feminist Methodology in Nursing Research." *Journal of Advanced Nursing* 9 (1984):249–256.

Webb, Eugene; Campbell, Donald T.; Schwartz, Richard D.; and Sechrest, Lee. *Unobtrusive Measures: Nonreactive Research in the Social Sciences.* Chicago: Rand McNally, 1966.

Webb, Sidney and Webb, Beatrice Potter. *Methods of Social Study.* New York: Longmans, Green, 1932.

Webb, Sue. "Gender and Authority in the Workplace." In *Looking Back: Some Papers from the BSA 'Gender & Society' Conference,* edited by Sue Webb and Clive Pearson. In *Studies in Sexual Politics,* edited by Liz Stanley and Sue Scott. Manchester, Eng.: Department of Sociology, University of Manchester, 1984.

Weber, Robert. "Computer-aided Content Analysis: A Short Primer." In *Computers and Qualitative Data,* edited by Peter Conrad and Shulamit Reinharz. Special Issue of *Qualitative Sociology* 7 (1984):126–147.

Webster, Sheila K. *Women and Folklore.* Special Issue, *Women's Studies International Forum* 9 (1986):219–301.

Weinbaum, Batya. *Pictures of Patriarchy.* Boston: South End Press, 1983.

Weiner, Annette B. *Women of Value, Men of Renown: New Perspectives in Trobriand Exchange.* Austin, Tex.: University of Texas Press, 1976.

Weiner, Nancy. "Tradition and Change: Conflict in the Life of Moroccan Women." Honors Thesis, Department of Anthropology, Brandeis University, 1989.

Weinreich, Helen. "What Future for the Female Subject? Some Implications of the Women's Movement for Psychological Research." *Human Relations* 30 (1977):535–543.

Weisstein, Naomi. *Kinder, Kuche, and Kirche as Scientific Law: Psychology Constructs the Female.* Boston: New England Free Press, 1969.

———. "Kinder, Kuche, Kirche as Scientific Law: Psychology Constructs the Female." In *Sisterhood is Powerful,* edited by Robin Morgan. New York: Vintage, 1970.

Weitz, Rose. *Sex Roles.* New York: Oxford University Press, 1977.

Weitzman, Lenore. *The Divorce Revolution: The Unexpected Social and Economic, Consequences for Women and Children in America.* New York: Free Press, 1985.

———. *Sex Role Socialization.* Palo Alto, Calif.: Mayfield, 1979.

———; Eifler, Deborah; Hokada, Elizabeth; and Ross, Catherine. "Sex Role Socialization in Picture Books for Pre-School Children." *American Journal of Sociology* 77 (1972):1125–1150.

Wells, Ida B. *A Red Record: Tabulated Statistics and Alleged Causes of Lynchings in the United States, 1892–1893–1894.* Contains *Southern Horrors, Lynch Law in All Its Phases* (1892); *The Reason Why the Colored American Is Not in the World's Columbian Exposition* (1893); *Mob Rule in New Orleans* (1900). Reprint. Salem, N.H.: Ayer Company, 1987.

West, Candace and Iritani, Bonita. "Gender Politics in Mate Selection: The Male Older Norm." Paper presented at the Annual Meeting of the American Sociological Association, 1985.

Westkott, Marcia. "Feminist Criticism of the Social Sciences." *Harvard Educational Review* 49 (1979):422–430.

———. *The Feminist Legacy of Karen Horney.* New Haven, Conn.: Yale University Press, 1986.

Weston, Kathleen M. and Rofel, Lisa B. "Sexuality, Class and Conflict in a Lesbian Workplace." *Signs: Journal of Women in Culture and Society* 9 (1984):623–646.

Wetherell, Margaret. "Linguistic Repertoires and Literary Criticism: New Directions for a Social Psychology of Gender." In *Feminist Social Psychology: Developing Theory and Practice,* edited by Sue Wilkinson. Philadelphia: Open University Press, 1986.

Wex, Marianne. *Let's Take Back Our Space: "Female" and "Male" Body Language as a Result of Patriarchal Structures.* Translated by Johanna Albert. West Berlin: Frauenliteraturverlag Hermine Fees, 1979.

Wheeler, Charlene and Chinn, Peggy. *Peace & Power: A Handbook of Feminist Process.* Buffalo, N.Y.: Margaretdaughters, 1984.

Whyte, William Foote. *Street Corner Society: The Social Structure of an Italian Slum.* rev. ed. Chicago: The University of Chicago Press, 1955.

Wiley, Mary Glenn and Woolley, Dale E. "Interruptions among Equals: Power Plays that Fail." *Gender & Society* 2 (1988):90–102.

Wilkinson, Sue, ed. *Feminist Social Psychology: Developing Theory and Practice.* Philadelphia: Open University Press, 1986.

———. "Sighting Possibilities: Diversity and Commonality in Feminist Research." In *Feminist Social Psychology: Developing Theory and Practice,* edited by Sue Wilkinson. Philadelphia: Open University Press, 1986.

Wilson, Emily Herring. *Hope and Dignity: Older Black Women of the South.* Philadelphia: Temple University Press, 1983.

Winegarten, Ruth, ed. *I Am Annie Mae: The Personal Story of a Black Texas Woman.* Austin, Tex.: Rosegarden Press, 1983.

Wittig, Michele. "On Feminism, the Psychology of Women, and General Psychology." Paper presented at the Annual Meeting of the American Psychological Association, 1981.

Women's Task Force, Michigan Department of Mental Health. *For Better or for Worse? Women and the Mental Health System.* E. Lansing, Mich.: Michigan Department of Mental Health, 1982.

The World & I Magazine 2 (1987):82–83.

Wright, Marcia. "Personal Narratives, Dynasties, and Women's Campaigns: Two Examples from Africa." In *Interpreting Women's Lives: Feminist Theory and Personal Narratives,* edited by Personal Narratives Group. Bloomington, Ind.: Indiana University Press, 1989.

———. "Since 'Women in Peril': Reconsiderations of Biography, Autobiography and Life Stories of Some African Women with Special Reference to Marriage." Paper presented at Conference on "Autobiographies, Biographies and Life Histories of Women: Interdisciplinary Perspectives." University of Minnesota, 1986.

Yanz, Lynda. Preface to *Sandino's Daughters: Testimonies of Nicaraguan Women in Struggle,* by Margaret Randall. Toronto: New Star Books, 1981.

Yates, Gayle, ed. *Harriet Martineau on Women.* New Brunswick, N.J.: Rutgers University Press, 1985.

Yeandle, Susan. *Women's Working Lives: Patterns and Strategies* New York: Tavistock Publications, 1984.

Yin, Robert K. *Case Study Research: Design and Methods.* Beverly Hills, Calif.: Sage, 1984.

Yllo, Kersti. "Political and Methodological Debates in Wife Abuse Research." Working Paper presented at the National Council on Family Relations Theory and Methodology Workshop, 1986.

———— and Bograd, M., eds. *Feminist Perspectives on Wife Abuse.* Newbury Park, Calif.: Sage, 1986.

Young, Kate. "Modes of Appropriation and the Sexual Division of Labour: A Case Study from Oaxaca, Mexico." In *Feminism and Materialism: Women and Modes of Production,* edited by Annette Kuhn and Ann Marie Wolpe. London: Routledge & Kegan Paul, 1978.

Yount, Kristen R. "Ladies, Flirts, and Tomboys: Strategies for Managing Sexual Harassment in an Underground Coal Mine." *Journal of Contemporary Ethnography* 19 (1991):396–422.

Zamora, Bernice. *Restless Serpents.* Menlo Park, Calif.: Disenos Literarios. Bound with Jose Antonio Burciaga, *Restless Serpents,* 1976.

Zemon-Davis, Natalie. "Women's History in Transition: The European Case." *Feminist Studies* 3 (1976):83–103.

Zevy, Lee with Cavallaro, Sahli A. "Invisibility, Fantasy, and Intimacy: Princess Charming is not a Prince." In *Lesbian Psychologies,* edited by Boston Lesbian Psychologies Collective. Chicago: University of Illinois Press, 1987.

Zimmerman, Dale and West, Candace. "Sex Roles, Interruptions and Silences in Conversation." In *Language and Sex: Difference and Dominance,* edited by Barrie Thorne and Nancy M. Henley. Rowley, Mass.: Newbury House, 1975.

Zimmerman, Mary K. *Passage through Abortion: The Personal and Social Reality of Women's Experiences.* New York: Praeger, 1977.

INDEX